Beethoven's Conversation Books

Beethoven in 1818.
Engraving by C. Fischer (1843), after a portrait by August Kloeber (1818).
Courtesy Ira F. Brilliant Center for Beethoven Studies, San José State University.

Beethoven's Conversation Books

Volume 1: Nos. 1 to 8
(February 1818 to March 1820)

Edited and translated by

Theodore Albrecht

THE BOYDELL PRESS

First published 2018
The Boydell Press, Woodbridge

ISBN 978 1 78327 150 4

The Boydell Press is an imprint of Boydell & Brewer Ltd
PO Box 9, Woodbridge, Suffolk IP12 3DF, UK
and of Boydell & Brewer Inc.
668 Mt Hope Avenue, Rochester, NY 14620–2731, USA
website: www.boydellandbrewer.com

A catalogue record for this book is available
from the British Library

This publication is printed on acid-free paper

Typeset by BBR, Sheffield

Printed and bound in Great Britain by
TJ International Ltd, Padstow, Cornwall

MIX
Paper from
responsible sources
FSC® C013056

This volume is dedicated to
Anton Felix Schindler (1795–1864),
who saved the conversation books from dispersal and destruction,
and served as their first "editor."

Contents

General Introduction to
the English Edition

Ludwig van Beethoven (1770–1827) is recognized the world over as one of the greatest composers of all time and is especially known for his musical triumphs in the face of increasing deafness, beginning around 1798.[1]

In 1801 he confided his early hearing loss to Dr. Franz Wegeler in Bonn and schoolmaster/violinist Carl Amenda in Latvia, friends who had lived in Vienna but were now safely far away.[2] By the summer of 1802 others were starting to perceive lapses in his hearing, and his fear and confusion are reflected in the Heiligenstadt Testament in October of that year.[3] With more good days than bad, Beethoven's hearing slowly became weaker, although it had not yet interfered with his performing in public, even with orchestra on the marathon concert of December 22, 1808.[4]

Between 1812 and 1816 he tried using ear trumpets (made for him by Johann

---

[1] There are many medical accounts of Beethoven's deafness. Possibly the most complete and objective in English is by the Australian physician Peter J. Davies, *Beethoven in Person: His Deafness, Illnesses, and Death* (Westport, Conn.: Greenwood Press, 2001), pp. 42–65 and 217–218.

[2] On June 29, 1801, Beethoven wrote to Franz Gerhard Wegeler: "For the last three years my hearing has become weaker and weaker." Two days later, on July 1, he wrote to Amenda: "My most prized possession, my hearing, has greatly deteriorated. While you were still with me, I already felt the symptoms, but I said nothing about them." Amenda had left Vienna shortly after June 25, 1799. See Emily Anderson, transl. and ed., *The Letters of Beethoven*, 3 vols. (London: Macmillan, 1961), Nos. 51 and 53; and (for Amenda's reply) Theodore Albrecht, transl. and ed., *Letters to Beethoven and Other Correspondence*, 3 vols. (Lincoln: University of Nebraska Press, 1996), No. 31.

[3] Ferdinand Ries noted brief lapses while walking with Beethoven in the rural paths around Heiligenstadt, confirmed in the composer's so-called "Heiligenstadt Testament." See Franz Gerhard Wegeler and Ferdinand Ries, *Beethoven Remembered*, transl. Frederick Noonan (Arlington, Va.: Great Ocean Publishers, 1987), pp. 86–87; and Anderson, Vol. 3, Appendix A, pp. 1351–1354 (the Heiligenstadt Testament, actually close to a fair copy, dated October 6 and 10, 1802).

[4] Alexander Wheelock Thayer, *Thayer's Life of Beethoven*, ed. Elliot Forbes (Princeton: Princeton University Press, 1964/67), pp. 446–449. The breakdown in the performance of the *Choral Fantasy*, Op. 80, the last item on the program, was probably caused by orchestral fatigue at the tricky transition between the nocturnal *Adagio, ma non troppo* in 6/8 and the ensuing *Marcia, assai vivace* in 2/4 (*Gesamtausgabe*, p. 22).

Nepomuk Mälzel and possibly his brother Leonhard, also an inventor) with varying, but largely disappointing, degrees of success.[5] Between December 8, 1813, and February 27, 1814, Beethoven conducted (or attempted to conduct) four benefit concerts with an orchestra of ca. 113 professionals, causing considerable commentary about his exaggerated motions, some of which by now were the inevitable result of his weakened hearing.[6] At the performances, which included the premieres of his Symphonies Nos. 7 and 8, as well as *Wellington's Victory*, Beethoven's motions were probably shadowed, much more accurately, by conductor Michael Umlauf. In the fall of 1814, as the Congress of Vienna assembled, Beethoven composed a cantata, *Der glorreiche Augenblick*, for the occasion. On October 10 the Prague pianist and pedagogue Johann Wenzel Tomaschek visited Beethoven, found sketches for the cantata on the piano, and reported that the composer "was especially hard of hearing this day, so that one had to shout, rather than speak, in order to be understood." Tomaschek returned on November 24, just as the parts for the cantata were being copied: "Beethoven received me very politely, but appeared to be very deaf on this day, for I had to exert myself to the utmost to make myself understood." Even though many of his other comments were caustic, Tomaschek did not report that any portion of their conversation took place in writing.[7]

On November 15, 1815, Beethoven's younger brother Carl died, leaving the composer as the contested guardian of his son Karl (b. September 4, 1806). Beethoven soon placed nephew Karl in a boarding school run by Cajetan Giannatasio del Rio, but paid frequent visits, to the extent that Giannatasio's daughter Franziska (Fanny) developed a crush on the composer and reported their spoken conversations in her diary.[8]

The Beginnings of Written Conversations by 1816

In September, 1816, Peter Joseph Simrock (1792–1868), son of the Bonn publisher Nikolaus Simrock (1751–1832), came to Vienna to reestablish his father's earlier close

---

[5] Davies, pp. 50–52, provides a sufficient survey. On April 8, 1823, Beethoven confided his disappointment in such mechanical devices to a chance acquaintance, Herr Sandra, also going deaf. See Heft 28, Blätter 41v–42v.

[6] For a good survey of accounts of the rehearsals and concerts by Louis Spohr and others, see Thayer-Forbes, pp. 564–567.

[7] Oscar George Sonneck, ed., *Beethoven: Impressions by his Contemporaries* (New York: G. Schirmer, 1926; repr. New York: Dover Publications, 1967), pp. 100 and 102–103.

[8] Ludwig Nohl, ed., *Eine stille Liebe zu Beethoven. Nach dem Tagebuche einer jungen Dame* (Leipzig: Ernst Julius Günther, 1875), *An Unrequited Love: An Episode in the Life of Beethoven (from the Diary of a Young Lady)*, transl. Annie Wood (London: Richard Bentley & Son, 1876).

connections with Beethoven[9] and later told biographer Alexander Wheelock Thayer of his activities. Young Simrock often visited Beethoven at Baden (his summer apartment), at his apartment in the Sailerstätte (inside the City walls), and at the restaurant *Zur goldenen Birne* (Hauptstrasse 42 in the nearby suburb of Landstrasse), where Beethoven often ate midday dinner.[10]

Simrock told Thayer that "he had no difficulty in making Beethoven understand him if he spoke into his left ear; but anything personal or confidential had to be communicated in writing." Thayer continues: on one occasion the composer handed him [Simrock] paper and pencil, remarking that his servant was an eavesdropper, etc. A few days afterwards, when Simrock visited again, Beethoven said: "Now we can talk because I have given my servant 5 Gulden, a kick in the rear, and sent him to the devil!" Everywhere in public, said Simrock, Beethoven complained about Emperor Franz because of the reduction of paper money,[11] but he was known and the police officials let him do what he pleased.[12]

Simrock probably departed Vienna on September 29 or 30, 1816, after having spent approximately a month in the Austrian capital.[13]

From roughly November, 1816, through April, 1817, Beethoven reportedly gave

[9] Peter Joseph Simrock had been born in Bonn on August 18, 1792, and therefore had reached his majority of 24 years only on August 18, 1816. As such, he probably could not have made any legally-binding business agreements before that date. Thus he must have arrived in Vienna sometime in early September, 1816. For young Simrock's dates, see Lothar Niefind and Walther Ottendorff-Simrock, "Simrock," *MGG*, 2nd ed., *Personenteil*, vol. 15, cols. 835–838. While Beethoven still lived in Bonn, Nikolaus Simrock had been second (low) hornist in the Electoral orchestra, and the young composer (whose lower lip, from portraits and the life mask, seems appropriate to a low hornist) seemingly took lessons from him.

[10] Beethoven's City address during this time was on the 3rd floor [4th floor, American] of Count Lamberti's building, Sailerstätte Nos. 1055–1056 [renumbered as 994 in 1821]. Beethoven's surviving letter to Simrock during this period indicates that the visitor was staying at Landstrasser Hauptstrasse No. 40 [renumbered as 50 in 1821], only two buildings north of the *Birne*, No. 42 [renumbered as 52 in 1821], on the east side of the street. See Anderson, Nos. 647, 661, and 662; Brandenburg, No. 977, 979, and 982; Behsel, pp. 30 and 71.

[11] At this point, the English-language editions by Krehbiel (who *may* have seen Thayer's original notes) and Forbes (copying Krehbiel) quote Beethoven concerning Emperor Franz: "Such a rascal ought to be hanged to the first tree." Thayer's original publication and Thayer-Deiters-Riemann omit this sentence and, instead, drop to a footnote, saying (in German), "We shall pass over the very severe expressions imparted by Simrock."

[12] Thayer (1879), III, pp. 402–403; Thayer-Deiters-Riemann, III, p. 566; Thayer-Krehbiel, III, pp. 343–344; and Thayer-Forbes, p. 647; also excerpted in Davies, p. 52.

[13] Unfortunately, Simrock's name does not appear among the selective daily Arrivals and Departures listed in the *Wiener Zeitung* during this period. Simrock later told Ludwig Nohl that he had eaten midday dinner with Beethoven at the *Mehlgrube* on Neuer Markt (in the City) every day for two weeks (Kopitz and Cadenbach, II, p. 915). Added to the locations reported to Thayer, this suggests a month's stay. Fanny Giannatasio del Rio reported in her diary that Beethoven brought Simrock with him for a visit on September 28, and letters to German destinations that Simrock took with him

harmony lessons to Carl Friedrich Hirsch (1801–1881), a grandson of his own teacher Georg Albrechtsberger. In summer 1880 Hirsch told Theodor Frimmel that Beethoven's deafness had advanced to a point where one had to speak to him very loudly. During his lessons Beethoven watched the student's hands closely and was able to detect his mistakes. Frimmel does not report Hirsch's mentioning any written conversations.[14]

On June 19, 1817, Beethoven wrote to his old friend and patron, Countess Anna Marie Erdödy, who seems to have been living in Paucovecz (Paukovec), Croatia, that he had been ill since mid-October, 1816, adding: "Although my health has improved a little, […] my hearing has become worse."[15]

The Beginnings of Conversation Books by 1818

By 1818 Beethoven's deafness had progressed to such an extent that, with increasing frequency, he began to carry blank books with him, so that his friends and acquaintances, especially when in public, could write their sides of conversations without being overheard, while Beethoven himself customarily replied orally.[16] He wrote in them, too, however: shopping lists, errands to run, or books advertised in the local newspapers.[17] He also used them for the conversations and draft memoranda

---

suggest that Simrock departed Vienna on September 29 or 30 (Ludwig Nohl, *Eine stille Liebe*, p. 129; Nohl, *An Unrequited Love*, p. 125; Kopitz and Cadenbach, I, pp. 313–314; Anderson, Nos. 660 and 661; Brandenburg, Nos. 978 and 979).

[14] Theodor von Frimmel, "Carl Friedrich Hirsch," in his *Beethoven-Studien* 2 (Munich: Müller, 1906), pp. 53–69, especially pp. 61–62; Kopitz and Cadenbach, I, pp. 443–454; summarized in Thayer-Forbes, pp. 664–665. Although Frimmel reported Hirsch to be sound of mind and body in 1880, many details in the old man's account are mildly or even wildly inaccurate in light of later research, and Frimmel himself was the first to question them.

[15] Anderson, No. 783; Brandenburg, No. 1132 (with more details concerning Erdödy's whereabouts). Paukovec is 10 miles northeast of Zagreb.

[16] Much of this material appeared in Theodore Albrecht, "Time, Distance, Weather, Daily Routine, and Wordplay as Factors in Interpreting Beethoven's Conversation Books," *Beethoven Journal* 28, No. 2 (Winter, 2013), pp. 64–75.

[17] Heft (booklet) 1, a brief booklet of only 12 pages, filled between ca. February 26 and shortly after March 2, 1818, is almost a chronological anomaly and does not exhibit many of the practices of making entries found in later Hefte. It was seemingly not in Schindler's possession and found its way independently to the Beethoven-Haus, Bonn. Heft 2, a much longer book of 210 pages, was filled between March 17 and after May 15/16, 1819. It is the earliest of the booklets that Schindler deposited in the Royal Library in Berlin in 1846. Here we find some of Beethoven's friends (notably Franz Oliva) making horizontal lines between their conversational entries, and Beethoven himself jotting down specific advertisements from recognizable newspapers. There is another chronological break before Heft 3, 136 pages, filled between November 20 and ca. December 6, 1819. Probably three long or several shorter Hefte are missing between May and November, 1819, but beginning with Heft 3, on November 20, Beethoven's use of conversations books seemingly becomes relatively constant.

pertaining to the protracted negotiations, hearings, and lawsuits surrounding the guardianship of his nephew Karl.[18]

The first surviving conversation book, the relatively impromptu Heft 1, dating from February–March, 1818, demonstrates only the earliest phases of the little formalities that would characterize the conversation books in their more mature phases: the writers placing a horizontal line after their entries as a signal for Beethoven to reply, and so forth.

On Monday, November 16, 1818, Beethoven visited the Giannatasio del Rio family, whom he had not seen in a long time, and stayed for three hours. Daughter Franziska (Fanny), who had earlier been smitten with the composer, noted in her diary, "Since his hearing was especially bad on this day, we wrote everything."[19] The conversational entries for this visit must have been extensive—covering nephew Karl's progress in school, the Giannatasio family's activities, Beethoven's latest works, and general gossip around town—but no conversation book survives.

Thus Beethoven must have had associates write down portions of their conversations on individual pieces of paper by ca. 1816, and if his hearing deteriorated during the winter of 1816–1817, he must have begun using gatherings of leaves to make impromptu conversation books (such as Heft 1) by the winter of 1817–1818. Thereafter, the first surviving *systematic* booklet, Heft 2 (from mid-March to mid-May, 1819), presumably a commercially manufactured blank book, dates from only four months after Beethoven's visit to the Giannatasio family.

Preservation and Loss, 1819–1822

From May 1819 until roughly September 1820 Beethoven apparently set aside the conversation books with major references to Karl's guardianship in one pile, while the others probably went into a trunk or box with most of the rest of the correspondence that he had received over the years. Then, around November 1, 1822, as Beethoven was moving from his summer residence in Baden to an apartment in the suburb of Windmühle, back in Vienna, the trunk or box with the correspondence

[18] Karl-Heinz Köhler, *"... tausendmal leben!": Konversationen mit Herrn van Beethoven* (Leipzig: VEB Deutscher Verlag für Musik, 1978). A good English-language summary of this 200-page book can be found in Köhler's "The Conversation Books: Aspects of a New Picture of Beethoven," in *Beethoven, Performers, and Critics: The International Beethoven Congress, Detroit, 1977*, ed. by Robert Winter and Bruce Carr (Detroit: Wayne State University Press, 1980), pp. 147–161. An even briefer overview of the topic may be found in Nicholas Marston, "Conversation Books," in *The Beethoven Compendium*, ed. Barry Cooper (New York: Thames & Hudson, 1991), pp. 164–167.

[19] Ludwig Nohl, *Eine stille Liebe zu Beethoven*, p. 198, and *An Unrequited Love*, p. 185; Kopitz and Cadenbach, I, p. 331. Fanny's description—that Beethoven's hearing "was especially bad that day"—is remarkably similar to Tomaschek's observations in October and November, 1814, above.

and all but sixteen of his conversation books up to that point probably fell off of the wagon transporting his possessions and was lost.[20] This, rather than any other factor, probably accounts for the gap in the surviving conversation books between 1820 and 1822.

Continuity, 1822–1827

In November 1822 Beethoven simply continued his practice of using blank conversation books on a regular basis, as he needed them. Most often he again squirreled them away in some box or trunk, and this time most of them were *not* lost, though he himself probably lost a few or even gave a few away as souvenirs, as he did to Maurice Schlesinger on September 9, 1825. By the end of the first week in March 1827, his supply of purchased blank booklets may have run out as his health sharply declined, leaving the last three weeks of his life without a systematic record of his conversations.

Posterity and Publication

When Beethoven died on March 26, 1827, his unpaid secretary and future biographer Anton Schindler deemed the nearly 140 surviving conversation books of no particular monetary value to Beethoven's estate, and took them with the intention of using them to document his projected biography of the composer.[21] At first Schindler probably went through them, identifying every author of conversational entries that he could—and in that he has proven to be remarkably accurate, although a few identifications did elude him. He also probably began jotting in reminders to himself about conversations that did take place, and then—getting

---

[20] Johann Chrysostomus Sporschil, "Musikalischer Wegweiser," *Allgemeine Theater-Zeitung* (Vienna) 17, No. 137 (November 15, 1823), p. 548, signed "S … l." Corresponding from Vienna, Sporschil (1800–1863) had recently published the article in the *Stuttgarter Morgenblatt für gebildete Stände*, No. 265 (November 5, 1823). The Viennese publication has been reprinted (among others) in Albert Leitzmann, ed., *Ludwig van Beethoven: Berichte der Zeitgenossen …*, 2 vols. (Leipzig: Insel-Verlag, 1921), I, pp. 264–267. It was cited in Köhler *et al.*, *Beethovens Konversationshefte*, Vol. 4 (1968), p. 372 (endnote 492).

On July 12, 1823, seemingly when writing about the previous summer, Beethoven noted that "an unfortunate accident robbed me of a considerable portion of my papers," independently confirming what Sporschil would report in November. See Anderson, *Letters*, No. 1207; Brandenburg, *Briefwechsel*, No. 1698.

[21] Schindler explained that Stephan von Breuning, Beethoven's executor, had given the conversation books to him as a token payment for his efforts on the composer's behalf, and this seems credible enough.

into dangerous territory—commandeered blank pages and partially filled pages to write or reflect his own opinions or conversations that may or may not have taken place while the composer was alive. Fortunately, once we know that these "falsified" entries exist, we can see that most of them have a tone all their own and can safely regard or disregard them as circumstances warrant.

In 1842 Schindler wrote that he possessed many more than a hundred ("viel über hundert") conversation books.[22] Three years later, in the seldom cited 1845 second edition of his *Biographie*, the publisher wrote of the conversation books: "There are 138 of them in Prof. Schindler's possession."[23]

In 1846 Schindler, who probably lacked a pension from his earlier employers,[24] sold his Beethoven documents—including 137 conversation books—to the *Königliche Bibliothek*, the Prussian Royal Library in Berlin, for what amounted to a pension stipend. This number corresponds almost exactly to the 138 estimated a year before and certainly fits the description of "many more than a hundred" that Schindler had written four years earlier.

A few years later the American Alexander Wheelock Thayer, working on a modern, scientifically based biography of Beethoven, spent months going through the conversation books in Berlin, extracting notes to be used in his work.[25] In the process, in 1854, he also went to Frankfurt, where Schindler now lived, and asked him about the conversation books. Consistent with his earlier reports, Schindler probably told him that there were "viel über hundert" (many more than a hundred) booklets, which Thayer, as proficient as his German was, probably misheard as "vier hundert" (four hundred). Thus began the erroneous perception that there were 400 conversation books present when Beethoven died and that Schindler had destroyed

[22] Anton Schindler, *Beethoven in Paris: Ein Nachtrag zur Biographie Beethoven's* (Münster: Aschendorff, 1842), p. 31.

[23] The original German reads: "Es befinden sich davon 138 im Besitz des Herrn Prof. Schindler." Anton Schindler, *Biographie von Ludwig van Beethoven*, Zweite mit zwei Nachträgen vermehrte Ausgabe (Münster: Aschendorff, 1845), p. 275.

[24] Pensions, when they existed at all, were often based on full decades of employment. Therefore, an employee who had worked for 10 full years would receive a pension equal to 25% of his normal salary; an employee who had worked for 20 full years would receive a pension of 50%, and so on. Schindler had never worked for any theater, either in Vienna, Aachen, or Münster, for the requisite ten years, and so would probably not have been eligible for any pension.

[25] Grant W. Cook, "Alexander Wheelock Thayer: A New Biographical Sketch," *Beethoven Journal* 17, No. 1 (Summer, 2002), pp. 2–11. Thayer spent from October, 1849, to spring, 1851; November, 1854, to February, 1856; September, 1858, to May, 1859; and December, 1859, to February, 1860 (among other periods) working in Berlin.

perhaps two-thirds of them.[26] The answer is plain and simple: Schindler didn't do it! *Nobody* did!

Just as researchers were assembling and editing ever larger compilations of Beethoven's correspondence, so they began to perceive the desirability of having a printed edition of the conversation books. Around the time of World War I, Walther Nohl (b. 1866) began to publish them but was overwhelmed by the amount of editing that they needed as well as by the economics in post-War Germany.[27] In the late 1930s and into the 1940s Georg Schünemann (1884–1945), head of the Music Department at the Prussian State Library, began a much more organized effort with better transcriptions and annotations and published three volumes, a job that took him to July 1823, before World War II and his own death put an end to his project.[28]

In 1943 the conversation books, along with many of the Library's other valuable holdings, were transferred to rural bunkers, but at war's end they came back to Berlin to find that their Unter den Linden home had survived the bombings but was now on the Communist east side of the city.[29] Then, on May 1, 1951, Joachim Krüger, the forty-year-old head of the Music Department of the Deutsche Staatsbibliothek, stole a number of boxes of rare materials—including all of the Konversationshefte—from the Library and took them to the West, claiming that he had saved them from transport to the Soviet Union. The theft caused a worldwide scandal, especially when Krüger established himself as an antiquarian book dealer. In 1956 Karl-Heinz Köhler (1928–1997), Krüger's successor as head of the Music Department in East Berlin, learned that the stolen conversation books were in the Beethoven-Haus, Bonn, and

[26] Even hypothetically filling in the gaps that occur between March, 1819 (when continuous use seems to have begun), and March, 1827, would only bring the total number to ca. 300. For a slightly different estimate, see Theodore Albrecht, "Anton Schindler as Destroyer and Forger of Beethoven's Conversation Books: A Case for Decriminalization," in *Music's Intellectual History*, ed. Zdravko Blažeković and Barbara Dobbs Mackenzie (New York: RILM, 2009), pp. 169–181, specifically 173–174.

[27] In addition to several essays based on various later conversation books, Nohl systematically published booklets (today termed Hefte 2 and 3) covering from March, 1819 to March, 1820. Walther Nohl, ed., *Ludwig van Beethovens Konversationshefte* (Munich: O.C. Rech/Allgemeine Verlagsanstalt, 1923–1924). By 1935, Nohl had transferred the publication rights to the Akademische Verlagsgesellschaft Athenaion in Berlin-Potsdam, which sought subscriptions for the *Konversationshefte*. In a "Beethoven-Sonderheft" of its *Athenaion Blaetter* 4, No. 1 (1935), pp. 2–29, the press published a descriptive essay about the conversation books (pp. 2–6), an essay by Nohl about how he became interested in the conversation books and his experiences in editing them (pp. 6–8), noteworthy quotes from the conversation books, as well as illustrations of Beethoven's own handwriting in them.

[28] Georg Schünemann, ed., *Ludwig van Beethovens Konversationshefte*, 3 vols. (Berlin: Max Hesse, 1941–1943).

[29] Horst Kunze, "Geleitwort," in Köhler *et al.*, *Beethovens Konversationshefte*, Vol. 4, pp. 5–6.

called for their return. Finally, in August 1961, a decade after they were stolen, the conversation books were restored to their rightful owners in East Berlin.[30]

Almost immediately, Köhler organized an editorial team including Grita Herre (in 1963) and Dagmar Beck (added in 1971),[31] to make state-of-the-art diplomatic transcriptions with a more sophisticated scholarly apparatus, and to continue editing the conversation books where Schünemann had left off. But now, increasingly isolated behind the Berlin Wall, they enlisted the aid of their counterparts at Vienna's Austrian National Library and other Viennese institutions to help with the documentation needed for dating, identification, and other annotations, and they published Volume 4 in 1968 and Volume 5 in 1970. At the same time, they began replacing Schünemann's now outdated volumes, starting with a new Volume 1, published in 1972.[32] Then, in 1977, Peter Stadlen (1910–1996), a Viennese-born music critic living in London, created virtually a criminal sensation when he detected that Schindler had falsified many of his (Schindler's) entries in the conversation books and implied that the East Berlin team had been negligent in not making such an obvious discovery.[33] The Berliners, who themselves had begun to suspect this problem as they worked ahead on the project, published a list of these falsified entries already with Volume 7 in 1978 and continued to identify them in subsequent volumes. But their swift forward momentum was broken by this distraction, and Grita Herre finally published Volume 11, taking the 139 surviving booklets[34] through early March 1827, only in 2001.[35]

---

[30] Köhler, *"tausendmal leben,"* pp. 186–188; and especially Martin Hollender, "Joachim Krüger … Bücherdieb …," *Bibliothek* 30, No. 1 (2006), pp. 69–75. While Köhler discreetly declined to name names, the investigative reporter Hollender openly revealed that the conversation books had been in the Beethoven-Haus, Bonn, and that Joseph Schmidt-Görg, then its Director, had denied that the stolen goods were there. The demeanor of that venerable institution has changed remarkably in the ensuing half century.

[31] Köhler, *"tausendmal leben,"* p. 200.

[32] Therefore, the material in the present Volumes 1–3 (Hefte 1–31) is based on the "second wave" of the East Germans' experience, as published in 1972, 1976, and (post-Stadlen) 1983.

[33] For Stadlen's possible motivation, see Albrecht, "Anton Schindler as Destroyer and Forger," pp. 171–172.

[34] In addition to Schindler's 137 conversation books in the Staatsbibliothek zu Berlin—Preussischer Kulturbesitz, two more booklets, Hefte 1 and 95, are in the collection of the Beethoven-Haus Bonn, making a total of 139 that survive reasonably intact.

[35] This standard German-language edition is Karl-Heinz Köhler, Grita Herre, and Dagmar Beck, eds., *Ludwig van Beethovens Konversationshefte,* in collaboration with Ignaz Weinmann, Peter Pötschner, Renate Bormann, Heinz Schöny, and Günther Brosche, 11 volumes to date (Leipzig: VEB Deutscher Verlag für Musik, 1968–2001). The three primary editors were based in Berlin, their numerous collaborators in Vienna. More recently, Heft 95 has seen a separate facsimile publication: *Beethoven im Gespräch: Ein Konversationsheft vom 9. September 1825,* transcription and commentary by Grita Herre, with English translation by Theodore Albrecht (Bonn: Verlag Beethoven-Haus, 2002).

Therefore, when set against more than a half century of war and political division, theft and recovery, ideological and geographical isolation, and attempts to discredit it, the East Berlin edition of *Beethovens Konversationshefte* remains one of the true miracles of modern musicology, and no one can reasonably diminish the accomplishment of its editors!

The Quest for an English Edition of the Konversationshefte

As early as 1977, *Konversationshefte* editor Karl-Heinz Köhler announced that "a translation of this edition into English is being contemplated by a press in the United States."[36] During the 1980s a British team including author-researcher Susan Lund and Dr. Robert Terence (Terry) Llewellyn (1933–2013) began negotiations with Oxford University Press for such an edition. Llewellyn was on the German faculty of Christ's College, Cambridge, with research interests in Beethoven and Goethe.[37] In 1985, however, Oxford University Press announced, "A complete English translation of the Conversation Books is being prepared by Professor Lewis Lockwood of Harvard University."[38] Nothing came of that project, but Lockwood teamed up with the Trieste-born Dr. Piero Weiss of Peabody Conservatory with the idea of compiling a one-volume English-language anthology of the most significant entries in the conversation books and made selections through Volume 2 of the German edition.

Meanwhile, I had published my three-volume *Letters to Beethoven and Other Correspondence* in 1996 and was researching Beethoven's orchestral colleagues. I had included draft letters from the conversation books in my *Letters* collection so was aware of Lockwood's involvement. By 1998, however, he indicated that he was no longer interested in the project. Sometime later he made his materials available to me,[39] and I tentatively embarked on the present complete edition in

---

[36] Köhler, "The Conversation Books: Aspects of a New Picture of Beethoven," p. 148. Köhler's paper, delivered in Detroit in 1977, may have been revised, with this parenthetical statement added, shortly before its publication in 1980.

[37] Susan Lund (London), personal communication, August 16, 2015. A third participant in the project was to have been Llewellyn's Viennese-born wife Gudrun, who predeceased him. See Geoffrey Ingham, "In Memoriam," *Christ's College Magazine* (2014), pp. 93–94.

[38] The announcement appeared in Martin Cooper, *Beethoven: The Last Decade, 1817–1827*, revised edition (Oxford/New York: Oxford University Press, 1985), p. 470 (at the end of Cooper's bibliography).

[39] Lewis Lockwood, personal communication with files, Cambridge, Mass., January 27, 2004. Lockwood's files consisted of 128 double-spaced typed pages, seemingly generated between ca. 1985 and 1989/1991. The selection of entries seems to have been Lockwood's work, while the translations

English.[40] By 1998, however, it was also obvious that the *Konversationshefte* (which, after all, had begun to appear three decades before) would need a major revision in conjunction with any translation into English.

The Present English Edition of the Conversation Books

The German editors were diligent in establishing a rough chronology for the entries at the beginning of each *Heft* (or booklet) and provided ample endnotes to identify individuals and explain those entries. Even so, the inexperienced user (and especially the English speaker) was likely to view the unadorned diplomatic transcriptions as a virtual stream of consciousness without any immediately perceptible relationship to specific place or time. As a result, many misunderstandings and misinterpretations arose from even these published conversation books—problems that a closer identification of their organization, chronology, and contents might clarify.

Translations

When I began this project, several colleagues warned me that translation would be especially difficult because many of the conversational entries were "in the Viennese dialect." At the time of writing this General Introduction, I have drafted translations and annotations through Heft 79 (more than halfway through the project) and have encountered very few entries in *Wienerisch*, something of a Viennese counterpart to London's Cockney.[41] Instead there are often regional terms used by the normal population: *Kren* (rather than *Meerrettich*) for horseradish, *Semmel* (rather than

---

into facile, colorful, and idiomatic English were Piero Weiss's work. The final entry in the material that I received was from Heft 22, Blatt 61v (February, 1823), from the very end of Vol. 2 of the *Konversationshefte*.

[40] Although the Staatsbibliothek zu Berlin—Preussischer Kulturbesitz had granted me permission to make a translation and edition in 1999, and the Beethoven-Haus, Bonn, did likewise in 2001, I concentrated my work on the period surrounding the premiere of the Ninth Symphony in 1824. Only in 2007, as Boydell & Brewer undertook negotiations to license the published material from Breitkopf und Härtel, did I embark on a systematic translation and edition, starting with Heft 1, Blatt 1, and with strong encouragement from Lewis Lockwood.

[41] To this end, however, there is a vast literature on the subject, including Peter Wehle, *Sprechen Sie Wienerisch?* (Vienna: Ueberreuter, 1981/2003); Hans Eidherr, *Also fåhr ma Euer Gnadn: Wiener Redensart—Wiener Musik*, book with 4 CDs (Vienna: Edition Wien/Pichler, 1996); and Susanne Finsterl-Lindlar, *Lilliput Wienerisch* (Berlin/Munich: Langenscheidt, 2011). For the last-named dictionary of 381 pages, I am grateful to Herr Franz-Josef Schmiedl (Wiener Stadt- und Landesarchiv) and Frau Gertraud Heindl (Archiv, Allgemeines Krankenhaus, Vienna).

Brötchen) for rolls, *Fisolen* for green beans,[42] *Licitation* for an auction, and so on. These examples might be similar to using couch, sofa, or davenport for the same (or similar) piece of furniture in the English language.

German spelling was not yet fully standardized in Beethoven's time, and so B could be phonetically interchangeable with P, and C with G or K, or D with T, and even F with V. Haydn could be spelled Haidn or Heiden. A "tz" sound could be represented as a "z" or a "c." The name Joseph in Beethoven's time would frequently be spelled "Josef" as the century progressed and Germans sought to distance their language from foreign influences.

Compared to many of his contemporaries, Beethoven was a tolerably good writer. His handwriting was an extension of late Baroque style, more akin to Johann Sebastian Bach's than to an early nineteenth-century clerk's. His variable phonetic spelling was more standardized than that of most musicians of his time,[43] and when he copied an advertisement from a newspaper, it was usually remarkably accurate.[44] By comparison, his brother Johann (1776–1848), a trained apothecary and landowner whose entries are frequent in the *Conversation Books*, was a less advanced writer than Ludwig. On an understandably lower level, Beethoven's favorite copyist Wenzel Schlemmer (1758–1823) and his housekeeper-cook Barbara Holzmann (1755–1831) wrote almost exclusively in a phonetic and ungrammatical style, and one must often read their entries aloud to "hear" how they sounded and understand what they meant.

The conversational entries themselves have largely been translated into modern conversational American English, to include contractions that might not otherwise be proper to scholarly English. There has been no attempt at rendering them into "a sort of timeless English," as Emily Anderson characterized her translation of Beethoven's letters.[45]

---

[42] See the menu in "Das himmlische Leben," the fourth movement of Gustav Mahler's Symphony No. 4.

[43] Brandenburg, *Beethoven: Briefwechsel*, I, pp. xxi–xxxiv; and Harald Süss, *Deutsche Schreibschrift* (Augsburg: Augustus Verlag, 1995), pp. 11–13.

[44] Judging from his letters from ca. 1802 to 1805, Beethoven's younger brother Carl (1774–1815) was probably the best writer of the three surviving siblings.

[45] Anderson, *Letters*, Introduction, Vol. 1, p. xix, circularly terming it "an English translation that would stand the test of time."

Dictionaries

My home library includes almost two dozen German dictionaries in varying degrees of depth and focus. For everyday translation I have used a *Cassell's German-English, English-German Dictionary* from the 1970s, but also editions in Gothic lettering as far back as Cassell and Heath in 1909. One of my major criteria for any such dictionary was that the English translations of the German word *Kur* had to include an Elector or some historical Electoral function.

In addition, I have regularly used the two-volume *Muret-Sanders Enzyklopädisches englisch-deutsches und deutsch-englisches Wörterbuch* from 1910, and the four-volume *Muret-Sanders encyclopädisches Wörterbuch der Englischen und Deutschen Sprache* from 1899.

Among specialty dictionaries, *Lang's German-English Dictionary of Terms Used in Medicine* (1924)[46] and the *Illustriertes Landwirtschafts-Lexikon* (1884)[47] have proven helpful, as has, occasionally, the *Österreichisches Wörterbuch* (2006). Various German-language dictionaries by Wahrig, Duden, or Grimm have been potentially helpful, although the 32-volume Grimm (like the Oxford English Dictionary) is a bit excessive for our purposes.

One of translationdom's relics, the *Thieme-Preusser: Neues vollständiges kritisches Wörterbuch der Englischen und Deutschen Sprache* (1859),[48] once widely used, contains some amusing and archaic definitions, but also mistranslations that are misleading or even unintentionally harmful in the area of musical terminology.

For translation of occasional French terms, I have used Cassell's (1960–1980s), the original two-volume Clifton and Grimaux (ca. 1880), and the two-volume Harrap (1940/1961). Other languages have followed similar patterns.

While the translations are overwhelmingly my own work, I have occasionally sought assistance from colleagues, including Dr. Michael Lorenz, Ing. Walther Brauneis, Dr. Helmut Weihsmann, Karl Misar, Dr. Karen Wilde, Josef Bednarik, Thomas Gröger, Dr. Bernhard Paul, Dr. Ernst Kobau, Dr. Rita Steblin, Klaus George Roy, Dr. Irving Godt, Dr. Alan Krueck, and my wife, Dr. Carol Padgham Albrecht. For mistranslations or misinterpretations (and there may be many in these volumes), I alone am responsible.

---

[46] *Lang's*, ed. Milton K. Meyers (Philadelphia: K. Blakiston's Son, 1924), although it (like other dictionaries) does not list or define the term *Schleimschlag*.

[47] *Landwirtschaft*, ed. Guido Krafft (Berlin: Paul Parey, 1884).

[48] *Thieme-Preusser*, ed. H. Breithaupt (Hamburg: Haendcke & Lehmkuhl, 1846/1859). This dictionary was probably used for the century-old English translation of Richard Wagner's *Mein Leben*.

Conclusion

There have been several editions of Beethoven's correspondence in both German and English over the past 150 years, and so a succession of editors and translators has had the opportunity and good fortune to learn from the mistakes of others.[49] The East Berlin edition of Beethoven's *Konversationshefte*, which appeared from 1968 to 2001, was roughly the third edition of the conversation books to be begun but only the first to be completed.

This edition of the *Conversation Books* is likewise only the first in English, and yet it has had the privilege, after the four-decade gestation period of the German edition, to enlarge upon and clarify it. As with my *Letters to Beethoven* (1996), I have tried to do so in an appropriately objective manner[50] and in the interest of scholarly progress, knowing full well that errors in my own translations and annotations will naturally be corrected by scholars in the future.[51] I merely beg my successors' indulgence with the same perspective in mind. Music research is still a cumulative effort, over the years and across national and linguistic boundaries. If I have made these conversation books more useful to scholars, performers, and admirers of Beethoven for even a moment in that continuum, then my efforts will have been richly rewarded.

Theodore Albrecht
Vienna, Austria
Kent, Ohio
August 30, 2015

---

[49] In fact, Emily Anderson was highly critical or dismissive of virtually all of her predecessors, German or English, in compiling and editing collections of Beethoven's letters. See Anderson, *Letters*, Introduction, Vol. 1, pp. xii–xix and *passim*.

[50] When I detect minor inaccuracies in the German edition of the *Konversationshefte*, I usually correct them silently, without further commentary.

[51] Subsequent volumes in the English-language *Conversation Books* will provide an opportunity to correct substantive mistakes made here.

Acknowledgements

A project as massive as this one could not have come even this far—the publication of the first three of a projected twelve volumes—without the assistance of a great number of individuals, both known and unknown to me. For the source materials themselves, I am most grateful to Dr. Helmut Hell, Frau Grita Herre, and Dr. Martina Rebmann (Staatsbibliothek zu Berlin–Preussischer Kulturbesitz) and to Dr. Sieghard Brandenburg, Dr. Bernhard Appel, and Dr. Michael Ladenburger (Beethoven-Haus, Bonn), as well as to Breitkopf und Härtel/VEB Deutscher Verlag für Musik (Wiesbaden and Leipzig), who negotiated with Dr. Bruce Phillips and, most recently and effectively, Dr. Michael Middeke of Boydell & Brewer (Martlesham, Suffolk) to secure the rights for this English translation, adaptation, and new edition.

This project has become one developed in Vienna (and indeed in suburban Josefstadt) as much as in the United States, and in that I am grateful to Dr. Otto Biba, Dr. Ingrid Fuchs, and Frau Ilse Kosz (Library/Archive, Gesellschaft der Musikfreunde), as well as Herr Karl Misar (Handschriften-Sammlung, Wiener Stadt- und Landesbibliothek, Rathaus) and his wife Edith. Herr Misar's gift for imitating and clarifying accents and dialects as used in the conversation books has proven invaluable.

Much of my work has been done in non-musical libraries and archives such as the Wiener Stadt- und Landesarchiv, where Dr. Michaela Laichmann, Dr. Klaralinda Ma-Kircher, Dr. Susanna Pils, Dr. Heinrich Berg, Dr. Brigitte Psarakis, and Dr. Andreas Weigl, as well as their reading-room colleagues, Herr Mehmet Urhan, Herr Franz-Josef Schmiedl, Herr Edmund Knapp, Herr Alfred Prohsmann, Herr Erich Denk, and Frau Sylvia Ablaidinger (among others), have provided continued assistance over the years.

At the Haus-, Hof- und Staatsarchiv, I am grateful to Dr. Joachim Tepperberg, as well as its retired director, Dr. Leopold Auer, and its retired librarian, Dr. Clemens Höslinger. At the world-renowned Musical Instrument Collection of the Kunsthistorisches Museum (whose future and location are currently seriously threatened), its director Dr. Rudolf Hopfner has been especially encouraging of this project, which has, in turn, benefited from his research.

The Österreichisches Theatermuseum is located in the Lobkowitz Palace. Three rooms east of its famed *Eroica*-Saal is the Library where, for over two decades, Herr Othmar Barnert has provided what is possibly the most expert (and the most effortless) reference service in Vienna, including answering questions about various details from across the Atlantic.

Most of Vienna's church records (for baptisms, marriages, and funerals) have now been placed online, but before they were, the following representative churches were particularly generous with access to these *Matriken*: Stephansdom, archivist Dr. Reinhard H. Gruber; Augustinerkirche, Frau Ursula Lechner, but also P. Matthias Schlögl and P. Albin Scheuch (welcoming us non-Catholics, especially on Sundays); Michaelerkirche, Frau Constanze Gröger; Paulaner Kirche, Frau Monika Bauer and Msgr. Franz Wilfinger (who often stopped, pipe in hand, to ask researchers about their projects); St. Joseph ob der Laimgrube, Frau Maria Doberer; and the Karlskirche, with Herr Josef Macháček, P. Milan Kučera, and especially Frau Stella Pfarrhund.

For over a decade the Gesellschaft der Freunde der Wiener Oboe has kindly supported my study of orchestral instrumentalists in Beethoven's time with a grant, and has encouraged the edition of the *Conversation Books* as an extension of it, especially in connection with the Ninth Symphony. Josef Bednarik, Bernarda Bobro, Thomas Gröger, Dr. Bernhard Paul, Dr. Ernst Kobau, and Dr. Rudolf Führer deserve special recognition in this connection.

Likewise, the Wiener Beethoven-Gesellschaft has always been encouraging through Ing. Walther and Frau Vera Brauneis, Frau Rosemarie and Prof. Martin Bjelik. I am especially grateful for the tour of Beethoven's apartment in the Laimgrubengasse that Ing. Brauneis and Frau Bjelik provided my wife Carol and me. On the American side, Dr. William R. Meredith, Patricia Stroh, and Dr. William George of the American Beethoven Society and the Ira. F. Brilliant Center for Beethoven Studies at San Jose State University in California have been friends and supporters since the 1980s.

At the University of Vienna, Dr. Gerhard Kubik and Dr. Regine Allgayer-Kaufmann (ethnomusicology) have been supportive, as has Dr. Michael Lorenz (musicology), who probably knows more about archival work in Vienna than anyone and is always generous in offering many details as he discovers them. Dr. Rita Steblin and the professional bass tubist Mag. Gerhard Zechmeister are also active archival researchers and helpful, as well. The violinist and conductor Dr. Eduard Melkus and artist Frau Marlis Melkus deserve special thanks for their encouragement and generosity.

Living accommodations and meals were important to Beethoven, and Carol and

I have learned firsthand the Viennese concept of a *Stammlokal* from Frau Elisabeth Schmid (Pension Columbia), Frau Grazyna Gierlichs and Frau Maria Ribar (Pension Lehrerhaus), Frau Sushma Sood (Oliva Verde), Frau Ernestine Rathgeber and Rudi (*Zur goldenen Schale* [Josephstadt No. 96] and *Berg'l Wirt*), and, for the past decade, Mag. Werner Kremser, Frau Dika Masić, Frau Leila Masić, and Frau Ana Mostić (*Weinhaus Sittl, Zum goldenen Pelikan* [Neulerchenfeld No. 1]). The *Pelikan* was first mentioned in documents by ca. 1740, and it is possible that Beethoven and Franz Oliva walked by it (or even stopped in for a glass of wine) on an excursion to or from the more distant Gallizinberg.

Several colleagues at Kent State University (some no longer living) have been encouraging and helpful over the years: Dr. F. Joseph Smith (musicology), Dr. Kazadi wa Mukuna (ethnomusicology), Mary Sue Hyatt (director), Raymond DiMattia (flute), David DeBolt (bassoon), Harry Herforth (trumpet), Ma Si-Hon (violin), Dr. Moshe Amitay (violoncello), Lois Ozanich and Dr. Robert Palmieri (piano), Dr. John Lee and Dr. Ralph Lorenz (directors), Scott Curfman (bands), Jack Scott (music librarian), and especially former orchestra director John Ferritto, with whom I happily shared an office for nine years.

In Vienna, these are well-matched by our engaging and perceptive colleagues Prof. Eugenie Russo (piano, Akademie der Musik, Wiener Neustadt) and her husband Dr. Helmut Weihsmann (architecture historian).

Several scholars around the world have read and commented upon my rough drafts as they have emerged over the years: Dr. Barry Cooper (University of Manchester), Susan Lund (London), Dr. Susan Kagan (Hunter College), Dr. Bathia Churgin (Bar-Ilan University), and especially this project's most enthusiastic and encouraging supporter, Dr. Lewis Lockwood (Harvard University).

But the final and most appreciative word must be reserved for my wife, Dr. Carol Padgham Albrecht, who has walked every one of Beethoven's Viennese miles with me.

Reader's Guide

Beethoven's Vienna

BEETHOVEN'S DAILY ROUTINE

Except for unusual circumstances (clearly presented in the German edition), the entries in most of Beethoven's conversation books start at the beginning of a Heft and continue to its end. Internally, the entries essentially reflect the composer's daily routine, even though it changed periodically, depending upon whether he employed a cook at home or ate his meals at a restaurant, whether he lived in Vienna or in a summer apartment in the country, and so on.

In the third edition of his biography,[1] Anton Schindler described Beethoven's routine, as he knew it from roughly November 1822 through May 1824. Moreover, the young journalist Johann Chrysostom Sporschil became acquainted with Beethoven in late 1822 or early 1823, and in November 1823 published essentially a feature story about Beethoven that corroborates many of Schindler's observations.[2] From these, and random comments like Franz Oliva's that Beethoven got up at 5 o'clock in the morning,[3] we can reach a composite daily routine that would, of course, vary from time to time and place to place:

---

[1] Anton Felix Schindler, *Biographie von Ludwig van Beethoven*, third edition, 2 vols. (Münster: Aschendorff, 1860), Vol. 2, p. 192, translated as *Beethoven As I Knew Him*, ed. Donald W. MacArdle, trans. Constance S. Jolly (Chapel Hill: University of North Carolina Press, 1966; repr. Mineola, N.Y.: Dover, 1996), pp. 385–386.

[2] Sporschil, "Musikalischer Wegweiser," p. 548.

[3] Heft 7, Blatt 66r (February 11, 1820), in Köhler *et al.*, *Konversationshefte*, Vol. 1, p. 259. Oliva (1786–1848) was a bank official and friend of Beethoven's, who helped the composer in financial and practical affairs until he moved to Russia in late December, 1820. For a chart comparing Schindler's, Sporschil's, and Oliva's accounts, see Albrecht, "Time, Distance, Weather, Daily Routine," p. 65.

Early morning   Beethoven rose early and, while fresh, worked as long as he
(ca. 5 a.m.)   could (composing and/or writing letters) without distrac-
                     tions, often jotting lists of errands and shopping items along
                     the way.

ca. 12 noon   He might wash and leave his apartment about noon and run
                     a few errands before dinner.

ca. 2 p.m.   He ate his midday dinner at 2 p.m. or so (often with
                     friends).[4] If he ate at his apartment, he might invite friends
                     to arrive about 1:30 p.m.

ca. 3:30 p.m.   After dinner, more errands and shopping.

ca. 5 p.m.   A late afternoon visit to a coffee house to drink coffee,
                     perhaps smoke a pipe, read current newspapers, and make
                     notes of advertisements that interested him.

until ca. 7 p.m.   Perhaps a late errand or a meeting.

Evening   Perhaps a light supper, possibly some reading, and then to
                     bed by 10 o'clock.

In getting around Vienna, except for special occasions such as major performances of his own works, Beethoven *walked* virtually everywhere, and so distance and time must also be factored into his daily routine and other activities.

DIRECTIONS OF THE COMPASS

Directions in Vienna can be difficult. As any map of Europe will show, the Danube River generally flows from west to east across Austria, with the left bank on the north side and the right bank on the south side. A dozen miles upstream from Vienna, however, the Danube turns to the southeast and when it reaches the City, its Channel (*Canal*) decidedly flows from northwest to southeast, with the Inner

---

[4] On May 6, 1803, Ferdinand Ries in Vienna reported to Nikolaus Simrock in Bonn that he received three lessons a week from Beethoven from 1 to 2:30 p.m., suggesting that the composer ate dinner after that on those days, consistent enough with Schindler's observation that Beethoven ate at 2 or 3 o'clock, and a few instances in the conversation books (1820–1824) where Beethoven met someone for dinner at 1:30 p.m. It suggests a routine consistent with Viennese practice at the time, but without rigidity. See Albrecht, *Letters to Beethoven*, No. 58.

City on the right bank to the southwest and suburban Leopoldstadt on the left bank to the northeast. A century ago Bertha Koch had problems of directionality in her volume of photographs of surviving Beethoven residences and attempted to solve them by designating views as northeast and southwest, but also as north, south, east, and west.[5]

This edition of the *Conversation Books* adopts a more Vienna-specific orientation and views the Danube as more of a north-to-south axis when it reaches the City, with the sun rising over the Leopoldstadt to the east and setting in the vicinity of the Gallizinberg or the Schmelz in the west (please see the maps on pp. xxxviii–xxxix). Suburban Rossau is therefore north, and suburban Landstrasse south, with the Burgtor looking west. All of these directions still remain approximate (and even open to individual interpretation), depending upon the season of the year, but once the Danube has passed Vienna, it can safely turn again toward Pressburg (Bratislava) to the east.

HOUSE NUMBERS

Vienna enjoyed three separate *Haus* (house or general building) numberings during Beethoven's lifetime there. These are often called *Konskriptions-Nummern*, whereby every building in the walled City and every building in each of the suburbs had its own individual number in addition to its street location. When Beethoven arrived in 1792 he found a numbering system that had been in effect since 1770. In the ensuing years new buildings would have been built, or two smaller old buildings might have been torn down to make room for a single larger building. Thus a new numbering was needed by 1795.

This numbering of 1795 was in effect in 1818 when the conversation books began, and remained so until still another renumbering, generally called the "renumbering of 1821," although several parts of the City had received their new numbers by late 1820. In the walled City and most suburbs, the renumbering of 1821 remained in effect until 1862, although several of the growing suburbs (most notably Landstrasse, Wieden, Mariahilf, and Gumpendorf) needed another renumbering by 1830.

In this edition of the *Conversation Books*, buildings mentioned in or associated with entries before 1821 (i.e., in Hefte 1–16) are also identified by their future numbers in the renumbering of 1821 supplied in brackets, for instance: City, Seilergasse No. 1154 [renumbered as 1088 in 1821]. This is done so as to avoid confusion of

---

[5] Bertha Koch, *Beethovenstätten in Wien und Umgebungen, mit 124 Abbildungen* (Berlin: Schuster & Loeffler, 1912), for instance pp. 9, 18, 20, 22–23, 27–29, 33–35, 38, 40–41, 53–54, 65–66, 72, 81, 83–84, 90, 94, and 96.

numberings and in an effort to make the renumbering of 1821 the consistent identification of houses throughout the conversational entries.

The best contemporary source for comparing house numbers is Anton Behsel, *Verzeichniss aller in … Wien mit ihren Vorstädten befindlichen Häuser*, dating from 1829. This guide, arranged by the 1821 house numbers, also provides the 1795 and 1770 numberings; the name of the building's owner in 1829; its house sign, if any (e.g., Golden Dragon or St. Florian); the street or square where the building was located; the administrative unit handling its affairs (usually the *Magistrat*, but also possibly an ecclesiastical division such as the Cathedral Chapter); its Police district; and its parish.

Behsel's *Verzeichniss* is located in several libraries in Vienna and is now available online, but the copy used for this edition of the *Conversation Books* is located in the Wiener Stadt- und Landesarchiv, and is also latterly supplied with the house numberings of 1830 (as applicable).[6]

MAPS

One of the most helpful attributes of Sieghard Brandenburg's *Beethoven: Briefwechsel* (1996) was the inclusion, as a Supplement to Volume 3, of a separate folder containing two full-sized maps of Vienna and its suburbs: one published by J.V. Degen in 1809, the other published by Artaria in 1824. The Degen map includes the house numberings used from 1795 to 1821, the Artaria map those initiated in 1820–1821. The most accurate modern maps of the Inner City and selected suburbs are found as folded supplements to the historical/topographical studies by Robert Messner, dating from 1962 to 1998.

Virtually all of the addresses mentioned in this edition of the *Conversation Books* have been verified (usually without further source citation) in Behsel's *Verzeichniss* and the Degen and Artaria maps, often supplemented by Messner. The reader may wish to consult them as well for the additional perspectives that they may offer.

---

[6] Some readers will be disappointed that I have not also added today's street numberings for these locations, but that seemed a separate activity and could have created potential confusion. Readers can readily find these later parallels in the guides to the buildings of the Inner City (1996–1998), as well as the Leopoldstadt (1962), Landstrasse (1978), Wieden (1975), Josefstadt (1972), and Alsergrund (1970) by Robert Messner, all cited in the Bibliography.

CURRENCY VALUES

The lowest practical value in Austrian coinage and currency in Beethoven's time was the *kreuzer* (sometimes spelled *kreutzer*).[7] Other values included:

1 groschen	=	ca. 3 kreuzer
1 gulden	=	60 kreuzer
1 gulden	=	1 florin, abbreviated as fl., but still pronounced "gulden"
1 fl.	=	60 kreuzer (kr.)
1 ducat (#)	=	ca. 4½ gulden (or 4½ florins)
10 gulden	=	ca. £1 (British)

After Austria officially went bankrupt as a result of inflation during the Napoleonic Wars, the government initiated a *Finanz-Patent* on February 20, 1811, and ultimately a number of reforms in currency values, with figures given in *Conventions-Münze* (C.M., convention coinage) and in local paper currency, *Wiener Währung* (W.W., Viennese currency).[8] Under this system, in effect during the entire period covered by the conversation books,

1 fl. C.M.	=	2½ fl. W.W.

Beethoven never forgave Emperor Franz for allowing the devaluation of paper money, and said so, loudly, in public in 1816.[9] Shortly thereafter he began using conversation books.

Guide to the Conversational Entries

GERMAN TERMS

The English-language reader who uses this edition of the *Conversation Books* must still learn two German terms, most often used for locating conversational entries within the texts:

---

[7] Some writers used upper case while others used lower case for currency values (e.g., Kreuzer *versus* kreuzer or Ducats *versus* ducats). In the service of sanity in these and similar situations, I have not attempted any standardized form for this edition.

[8] A concise view of the whole subject appears in Barry Cooper, "Economics," *Beethoven Compendium*, ed. Cooper (London/New York: Thames and Hudson, 1991), pp. 68–70.

[9] As reported by Peter Joseph Simrock, visiting from Bonn in September, 1816. Thayer (1879), III, pp. 402–403; Thayer-Deiters-Riemann, III, p. 566; Thayer-Krehbiel, III, pp. 343–344; and Thayer-Forbes, p. 647.

| *Heft*: | a booklet, the individual *Konversationsheft* (conversation book); its plural is *Hefte*. |
| *Blatt*: | a sheet, page, double-sided page (front: *recto*; back: *verso*; abbreviated r and v); its plural is *Blätter*. |

In addition, a few other German terms may occasionally be helpful:

Stadt:	City, generally meaning the walled City of Vienna.
Haus:	house or building.
Stiege:	stairway.
Wohnpartei:	apartment.

CONVERSATIONAL ENTRY FORMATS

In this English edition of the *Conversation Books*, the names of the writers of conversational entries appear in CAPITAL LETTERS in normal typeface, followed (to the extent that they can be determined) by **place, day of the week, date, and time of day** in bold face and brackets. Sometimes this designation will include other elements—religious holidays, for instance—where these might affect Beethoven's environment.[10]

In many cases the method of determining a date and time for conversational entries will be found in an explanatory footnote, although in general it will be assumed that Beethoven loosely followed a daily routine, as described above.

The entries themselves are presented in a paragraph format, with a new paragraph for every apparent change in conversational topic. This largely clarifies the problem of a cluttered stream-of-consciousness format found in diplomatic transcriptions. Even so, the reader should be aware that, given the ambiguous nature of some entries, this system is susceptible to error.

As noted elsewhere, when Beethoven's conversational partners place a horizontal line at the ends of their entries for him to reply, this line is represented by // in the present paragraph format. Where there is no horizontal line in the original, but a pause of some sort seems apparent in context, that pause is represented as [//]. In early conversation books, where the horizontal line had not yet become a standard division in conversation, pauses in the entries are already designated editorially as [//]. A Blatt number in brackets pertains to the material following the designation;

---

[10] Beethoven very seldom attended church services, and his acquaintances often had to remind him that a certain day in the future was a religious holiday. Therefore, he was still affected by closed businesses, school visitation days, etc. Even so, his lawyer Johann Baptist Bach often held office hours on Sunday mornings, the same time frame when Matthäus Andreas Stein might come to his apartment to regulate his piano.

therefore, [Blatt 33v] indicates that the following material appears on the verso of Blatt 33.

External movements during conversations—for instance, the **arrival** or **departure** of correspondents, the **continuation of conversations** that might be unclear, or the **ending of long conversations**—are given in **bold print** and brackets, in order to clarify what is happening in Beethoven's immediate environment.

The result is very much like the script of a play, with character designations, dialogue, and stage directions. With this almost three-dimensional quality, it might bring Beethoven's world to life to an unprecedented degree.

SCHINDLER'S FALSIFIED ENTRIES

When excerpted entries from Beethoven's conversation books began appearing in Schindler's *Biographie* (especially the third edition of 1860) and then Thayer's *Leben* (1866–1911), musicologists thought that they had discovered the mother lode, from compositional processes (*Zwei Principe*) to nicknames for compositions (*Tempest* Sonata). They embellished these terms, titles, and slogans into seminal articles and books that helped to build major careers and influential positions within the field.[11] Then in 1977 Peter Stadlen demonstrated that many of Schindler's conversation book entries were *fingierte*, falsified, forged, fictitious—in any case entered into the conversation books (often at improper places, reflecting improbable subject contexts or chronology) long after Beethoven's death.

Scholars who had set their hopes on Schindler's slogans now felt betrayed by their unlikable hero and turned on him with a vengeance, virtually vying with each other to assassinate him, using the most vitriolic names and epithets. Gradually, however, it began to emerge that at least some of Schindler's falsified entries, if viewed in a reasonable and adjusted context, might contain a grain of historically useful truth.[12]

When I began translating and editing Beethoven's *Conversation Books*, several respected scholars in the field (still under Stadlen's spell) advised me to omit Schindler's falsified entries altogether. Ultimately we agreed that the entries had a certain function in the surviving documents and that I would retain them, generally with the sufficiently visible designations: [falsified entries begin→] and

---

[11] See, for instance, Arnold Schmitz, *Beethovens Zwei Principe; ihre Bedeutung für Themen- und Satzbau* (Berlin: F. Dümmler, 1923).

[12] See, for instance, Theodore Albrecht, "Beethoven and Shakespeare's *Tempest*: New Light on an Old Allusion," *Beethoven Forum* 1 (1992), pp. 81–92; his "Anton Grams: Beethoven's Double Bassist," *Bass World* 26 (October, 2002), pp. 19–23; and especially his "Anton Schindler as Destroyer and Forger … Decriminalization," pp. 177–181.

[←falsified entries end].[13] Posterity may be glad that the "falsified" entries remain, as there is still a great deal to be learned from them about both Schindler and Beethoven.

EXTRA CONVERSATION BOOK BLÄTTER

Many individual Blätter were ripped out of Beethoven's conversation books while he was alive. In fact, he probably did so himself: he might send his housekeeper, his nephew Karl, or an acquaintance on an errand and jot the address on a blank conversation book page before tearing it out and giving it to the person. At least one of the individual Blätter preserved at the Beethoven-Haus, Bonn, served this function.[14] If there were entries already on the other side of the sheet that was removed, that might have been immaterial to Beethoven at the moment. The German editors often indicated where a sheet may have been removed from a conversation book, and I have designated several more, often in bold print in between entries. Dozens of such sheets survive in libraries and private collections worldwide.[15] Frau Grita Herre will include them in a Volume 12 of her Berlin edition, and so this English edition of the *Conversation Books* will not duplicate or "scoop" that project in any way.

FOOTNOTES

In the German edition, a diplomatic transcription with annotations and explanatory endnotes, footnotes were used to note technical variants or visual anomalies within the transcribed texts: the mistaken upper- or lower-case beginning of a German word; other mistakes in starting or spelling a German word; reinforced words or letters in them (sometimes covering a penciled word in ink), corrected on the spot; and routine flourishes or other doodles. These notes have generally been omitted as not pertinent to an English-language edition.

Occasionally, in the early years, young nephew Karl drew profile heads and other cartoons into the conversation books; these are noted in German footnotes and largely retained in the present edition. Karl also used the pages for calligraphic and spelling practice, footnoted in the German edition; these are selectively retained here. The German footnotes also indicate editorially how the authorship of an entry has been authenticated; these are largely retained in the present edition

---

[13] Very brief falsified entries, possibly only a word or two, might have a commensurately brief designation of the fact.

[14] My gratitude to Dr. Michael Ladenburger for making these materials available to me when I visited the Beethoven-Haus in September, 2014.

[15] Some of these are available as illustrations on the internet.

as one of the English-language footnotes and generally designated KH (meaning Konversationshefte).

Explanatory notes (which had appeared almost exclusively as endnotes in the German edition) generally appear as footnotes at the bottom of the appropriate page in the English language edition. Notes simply translated from the German edition (*Konversationshefte*) with virtually no change are "signed" at the end of the note as KH. Notes from the German edition that have been significantly updated, corrected, or otherwise changed in the English edition are noted as KH/TA. Footnotes that are new to the present edition are designated TA.[16]

STANDARD FOOTNOTE SOURCES

As consistent with scholarly practice, sources are not cited for material that is available in multiple sources. The German edition cited articles in the encyclopedia *MGG* (*Die Musik in Geschichte und Gegenwart*) without providing the names of the authors of individual articles. This edition provides the names of those authors and abbreviated titles of their articles in the footnotes, but (in the name of economy) cites only *MGG* (under M) in the Bibliography. English-language users will know to consult *The New Grove Dictionary of Music and Musicians* for parallel articles, and so these will not be given here. For the most part, this edition will eschew citing the second editions of *MGG* and *New Grove* as editorially and often factually problematical. Similarly, this edition retains references to Frimmel's *Beethoven-Handbuch*[17] but largely avoids the most recent Beethoven encyclopedias and compendia in German. For relatively recent biographical articles concerning Beethoven's contemporaries, however, Peter Clive's *Beethoven and His World* (2001) provides a convenient, if not exhaustive, source in English.[18]

Oddly enough, there are materials collected by Alexander Wheelock Thayer and available in the German editions of his biography that have never been included or translated in full in its English-language editions. The names of the members of the Bonn orchestra in the 1780s or Stumpff's account of visiting Beethoven in September 1824—and its direct application to interpreting the conversation book entries—are just two of many such instances. Therefore the German edition's

---

[16] If I have inadvertently misattributed the authorship of any footnote among the 4,800 in these first three volumes, I apologize.

[17] An abridged English translation of the Frimmel *Handbuch* (1926), along with a few items translated from Wurzbach, appeared as *Beethoven Encyclopedia*, ed. Paul Nettl (New York: Philosophical Library, 1956).

[18] Clive's articles are often based on the first edition of *MGG*, but also include more unusual sources.

references to Thayer-Deiters-Riemann have been retained, usually paired with references to corresponding passages in the English-language Thayer-Forbes.

Fortunately, modern editions of Beethoven's correspondence by Anderson, Albrecht, and Brandenburg largely supersede their predecessors and are cited almost exclusively here.[19]

COMMON ABBREVIATIONS

Whenever possible this edition prefers full words, rather than any system of cryptic initials or acronyms, no matter how standardized. Thus the source of a death or estate record is given as "Wiener Stadt- und Landesarchiv" rather than "WStLA." Fully written out surnames such as Anderson, Behsel, Brandenburg, Clive, Thayer, Wurzbach, and so forth are probably recognizable, but in any case will send the less experienced reader to the appropriate item in the Bibliography, as will the abbreviation *MGG*. The few abbreviations used are mostly common sense. There may be a few inconsistencies through these many volumes, but the intention should still be relatively clear.

CROSS-REFERENCING AND INDEXES

The amount of detail in the *Conversation Books* is enormous and almost impossible to control without an index as voluminous as the volumes themselves. A cumulative index for the entire set of *Conversation Books* is almost unthinkable. Therefore, during the translating and editing processes, cross-references from one subject to another, sometimes across Hefte and volumes, were made using Heft and Blatt numbers to identify the location of the reference. After the pagination was applied, an Index of Persons, an Index of Beethoven's Compositions, and a General Index could be made, with page numbers used to designate the location of a reference.

MISCELLANEOUS EDITORIAL MATTERS

Names are generally given in their original languages. The Austrian emperor during this period was Franz rather than Francis; his military younger brother was Archduke Carl (or occasionally Karl), rather than Charles. Most cities like Vienna and Munich, however, are given in their English forms, but Wagner's *Meistersinger* still sang in Nürnberg (with an Umlaut and only two syllables).

---

[19] Even so, *New Beethoven Letters*, transl. and ed. Donald W. MacArdle and Ludwig Misch (Norman: University of Oklahoma Press, 1957), remains valuable for its extensive and lively commentaries and explanations.

The capitalized word City generally refers to within the walled city alone. When used from a distant location, it can refer to metropolitan Vienna as a whole.

Because the translator/editor is an American, spellings and editorial practice will follow American style. One of the few exceptions is that the editor prefers the monosyllabic "bar" rather than "measure" when referring to locations in a piece of music.

This edition transliterates the German ess-zet (ß) as "ss" or rarely "sz" (so as to avoid the novice's temptation to render it as "B"), but retains the vowels with Umlauts, as having some counterpart in English orthography.

Translations may vary: titles such as *Wellingtons Sieg* and *Wellington's Victory*, for instance, are used interchangeably.

When referring to a building, *Stock* generally designates the *Oberstock*, the number of the floor *above* the ground level. Therefore, the 1st *Stock* or floor in Viennese terminology would be called the 2nd floor in America. In an effort to achieve accuracy and clarity (but not pedantry), this edition will identify the floor in Viennese terms, with the American designation in brackets: "3rd floor [4th floor, American]."

In this edition of the *Conversation Books* the abbreviations p. (page) and pp. (pages) are used more extensively than usual, in the interest of clarity and completeness. This is true in other instances, as well, including library sigla.

Editorial Conventions

In most cases, the following symbols or editorial directions are based, for relative consistency, on the common-sense practice followed by the German edition:

//	Signifies a pause in the conversation where Beethoven's conversational partner drew a horizontal line as a signal for Beethoven to reply. This practice took some time to be standardized, and always remained open to variations. Few conversationalists wrote a line under the final entry on a page, for instance. Conversationalists new to Beethoven's circle (or merely passing through) often did not follow the practice. Sometimes Beethoven himself used the horizontal line to divide advertisements copied from newspapers, items to buy, or errands to run.
[//]	Signifies a place in a conversation where a pause seems to have occurred, but the conversationalist did not insert a horizontal line for Beethoven to reply. This editorially supplied "line" is very common throughout the early conversation books.

[Blatt ___]   Indicates that the text that follows was taken from a particular Blatt in the manuscript, as indicated in the German edition. Thus, a bracketed [Blatt 35r] indicates that the following text came from Blatt 35r. Retaining these locations is especially helpful in locating editorial cross-references.

[written vertically→] [←written vertically]
Indicates that part (or all) of the designated text was written vertically (or at least diagonally) as opposed to the customary horizontal entries.

[falsified entries begin→] [←falsified entries end]
Points out Schindler's falsified entries at the point where they are found in the manuscript. Brief falsified entries have commensurately brief designations.

<crossed out>   Indicates a text that has been crossed out in the manuscript, and generally follows the German editors' attempts to read or reconstruct it.

[illegible word] Signifies what it says. This and similar phrases in editorial brackets occur frequently throughout the conversation books.

Directionality in Vienna (True and Perceived)

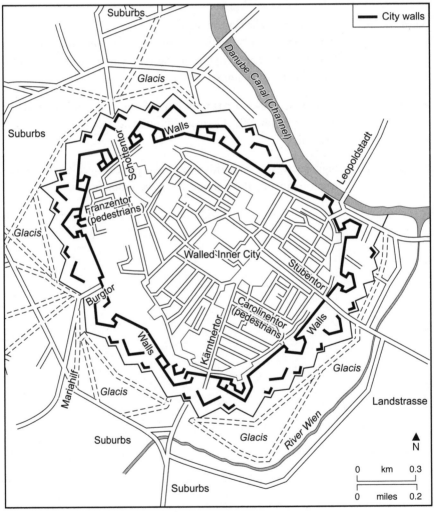

True, with the Danube flowing from West to East at 45 degrees

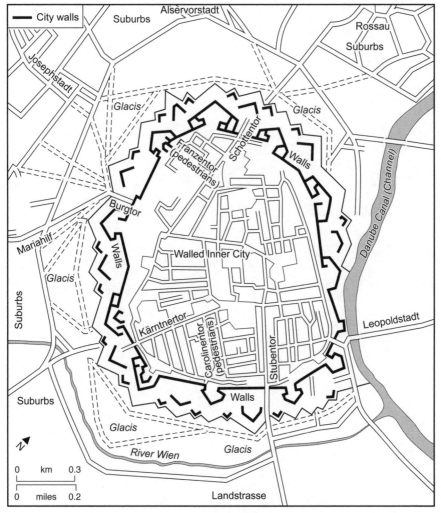

Perceived, with the Danube essentially flowing from North to South

Heft 1

(ca. February 26, 1818 – after March 2, 1818)[1]

[Inside front cover]

BEETHOVEN [presumably away from his apartment in suburban Landstrasse;[2] possibly in a nearby restaurant, the *Goldene Birne*;[3] ca. Thursday, February 26, 1818]:

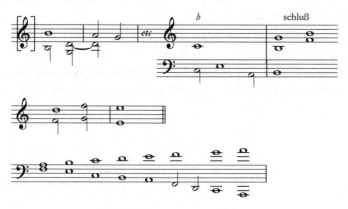

See <19 black> bottles with Karl in the [illegible word].[4]

---

[1] Much of this Heft is smudged and illegible, or nearly so. It largely lacks the formalities in format (horizontal lines between entries, represented by "//" in this English-language edition, for instance) that would become fairly standard among Beethoven's regular acquaintances later on. Even so, in the interest of coherence (as much as can be inferred), this Heft is edited in a manner consistent with the remainder of the booklets in this volume.—TA

[2] From October 1817 to October 1819 Beethoven lived at Landstrasse No. 268, at the sign of the *Grüner Kranz* [renumbered as 299 in 1821] today's Landstrasser Hauptstrasse 26. See Klein, p. 107; Behsel, p. 78.—TA

[3] When Beethoven lived in this area, his *Stammlokal*, his favorite place to eat and drink, was the *Goldene Birne* (Golden Pear) on the east side of Landstrasser Hauptstrasse, No. 42 [renumbered as 52 in 1821 and 63 in 1830], diagonally across the street from his residence at that time; see Behsel, p. 71.—TA

[4] Karl van Beethoven (1806–1858), son of Beethoven's brother Caspar Anton Carl and his wife Johanna, *née* Reiss (1786–1868). After his brother's death (November 15, 1815), Beethoven engaged in a legal suit, lasting for years, for guardianship of his nephew Karl. From 1816 to 1818 nephew Karl

[Blatt 1r]

16 bottles in the kitchen. //

UNKNOWN "A" [at an unknown location, possibly the same as above; ca. Thursday, February 26]: Fricart. Lives in the *Rebhendel* [Partridge], 3rd floor [4th floor, American], door at the right.[6] //

NEPHEW KARL [in a restaurant; probably early afternoon of Friday, February 27, 1818]: I went [illegible word/s] today. //
   But this doesn't follow that I too should eat sausages the way that you do. For if one person gets into the habit of doing one thing, won't another person also do something another way [?] // The casing without sausage is also good, but with sausage, it is better than the meat alone. [//]

[Blatt 1v]

NEPHEW KARL [continuing, but covered by Czerny's subsequent entries]: ... say ... because, in general, a person is accustomed to [eating] sausages with the ....

attended Cajetan Giannatasio del Rio's Institute, from March 1819 that of Johann Kudlich, and on June 22, 1819, he came to Joseph Blöchlinger, where he received a fine education until August 1823, after which he entered the University. Karl's subsequent attendance at the Polytechnic Institute, where he was to prepare himself for a profession in business, was terminated by his attempted suicide in summer 1826. Thereafter, he devoted himself to a military career, which he ended in 1832, subsequently living as a *Privatmann* (i.e., from his own resources). From April 1820, the co-guardian was Court Councillor Karl Peters, tutor to the Lobkowitz family. See Schmidt-Görg, pp. 66–67; Weise, pp. 44–45.
   In 1817 Giannatasio had bought a house at Landstrasse No. 379 [renumbered as 426 in 1821], facing the Glacis and at the site of today's Reisnerstrasse 3, where he conducted his school. See Klein, pp. 91–92 and 107.—KH/TA
   [5] My thanks to Dr. Michael Ladenburger, who determined this reading (pedal–release–pedal) during my visit to the Beethoven-Haus, Bonn, September 9, 2014.—TA
   [6] Joseph Frikard, mine owner, b. 1759, lived in the walled City, in the *Rebhühnel*, Goldschmiedgasse No. 632 [renumbered as 593 in 1821], just north of St. Stephan's Cathedral. With his wife Anna (b. 1780), he had two children, Felix (b. 1809) and Karl (b. 1816). See Conscriptions-Bogen, Stadt No. 593 (Wiener Stadt- und Landesarchiv). N.B. Here and elsewhere, birthdates derived from the Conscriptions-Bögen may be approximate, subject to verification in other documents.—KH/TA

JOSEPH CZERNY:[7] Treitschke[8] will visit you here[9] today. [//] No. 10 is the Spanish Prince Don Francesco.[10]

The director of the orchestra ... [four faint lines]

UNKNOWN "B" [at Beethoven's apartment or possibly a nearby restaurant or coffee house; presumably Friday, February 27]: I am fine, but I was afraid for you, since you said on Sunday [February 22] that you were not well, and I had not seen you since then. [Blatt 2r]

I have the [illegible word] by Büsching;[11] [it] is the most comprehensible. On the whole, it has much grandiosity, but in the individual characters, the a[rt] of language, which is probably more than [illegible word] is, finally also [illegible words]. [//]

---

[7] Joseph Czerny (1785–1831), born in Horzin, Bohemia, piano teacher and composer. According to Carl Czerny, to whom he was not related, he took over the piano instruction of Beethoven's nephew Karl. His best-known student was Leopoldine Blahetka (1809–1887). In 1824 he became a partner in the firm of Cappi & Co. (Cappi & Czerny from 1826, and Czerny [alone], 1828–1832). He lived with his wife Theresia (b. 1790) and their children Caroline (b. ca. 1814), Joseph (b. ca. 1815), and August (b. ca. 1818)—a fourth child Christina was born ca. 1829—and his mother Ludmilla (b. 1756) on the Schottenbastei No. 134 [renumbered as 127 in 1821], with house shield: *Kögel* or *Goldener Kegel* (Golden Bowling Pin). On December 22, 1831, he died of tuberculosis at his apartment in the Trattnerhof on the Graben, No. 618. See Conscriptions-Bogen, Stadt, Haus 127, Wohnpartei 10; and Totenbeschauprotokoll, 1831, C, fol. 6r (both in Wiener Stadt- und Landesarchiv); Böckh, *Wiens lebende Schriftsteller*, p. 365; Frimmel, *Handbuch*, I, p. 102; Schilling, vol. 2, p. 346; Weinmann, *Beiträge*, p. ix; Behsel, p. 5; Clive, p. 82.—KH/TA

[8] Georg Friedrich Treitschke (here spelled "Treitske"), 1776–1842, poet, actor, and theater manager, came to Vienna in 1800. Probably as early as 1811, as vice director of the Theater an der Wien, he met Beethoven and, now associated with the Kärntnertor Theater, re-worked the libretto of *Fidelio* for him in 1814. See Frimmel, *Handbuch*, II, pp. 332–334; Clive, pp. 371–372; Gräffer-Czikann, V, p. 410; Thayer-Deiters-Riemann, II, pp. 438–439, and III, pp. 410–412; summarized in Thayer-Forbes, p. 571.—KH/TA

[9] The indication "here" seems to suggest that Czerny has met Beethoven at a restaurant or coffee house, rather than at his apartment.—TA

[10] The Spanish *infante*, Don Francisco de Paula (1794–1865) spent February and March 1818 in Vienna, as part of a long tour of ten European cities, ordered by his elder brother King Ferdinand VII (r. 1814–1833) to delay Francisco's return to Spain after an embarrassing love affair with his servant's mistress. On February 12, 1818, Francisco, along with several other personalities, was named an honorary member of the *Wiener Akademie der bildenden Künste*. In March Ferdinand finally ordered the chastised Francisco home to Spain. See *Hof- und Staats-Schematismus*, 1819, I, p. 27; *Wanderer*, No. 42 (February 21, 1818), pp. 81–82; *Wiener Zeitung*, No. 38 (February 17, 1820), p. 149.

The significance of "No. 10" is not clear. Stadt, No. 10 was the k.k. Brunnstube, just west of the Staatskanzlei. No. 10 was also the number of Joseph Czerny's apartment (see above). The *Wiener Zeitung* (as surveyed from January 1 to the end of February 1820) does not list when the *infante* arrived or where he stayed. Kanne's *Wiener Allgemeine musikalische Zeitung* does not mention him.—KH/TA

[11] Johann Gustav Gottlieb Büsching (1783–1829), a scholar specializing in antiquity. He devoted himself especially to research on German literature of the Middle Ages, and belonged among the earliest exponents of German philology and history of literature. From 1816 to 1819 he edited the *Wöchentliche Nachrichten für Freunde der Geschichte*. See *Allgemeine Deutsche Biographie*, vol. 3, pp. 645–646.—KH

Yesterday [Thursday, February 26], I saw *Don Gutierre*.[12] I liked it very much. [//]
By Schreyvogel, after Calderon.[13] [//]

Trattnerhof.[14] // [Blatt 2v] Stein[15] was recently at my place for the entire evening. He promised me my new instrument within 3 weeks. He is happy about your English [piano].[16] [//]

The metronomes that are sold in the Jägerzeile[17] cost 20 fl. C.M. [//]

I shall tell Praitschopf[18] that he should visit you one of these days. Probably

---

[12] *Don Gutiere*, tragedy in 5 acts by Carl August West (pseudonym of Joseph Schreyvogel), after the grim drama *El médico de su honra* (1635) by Pedro Calderón de la Barca (1600–1681), was first performed in the Burgtheater on January 18, 1818. Further performances took place on January 19, 24, 27, and 31, February 5 and 26, and March 3 and 30, 1818. See *Sammler*, No. 11 (January 24, 1818), pp. 43–45, and following issues; *Wiener Zeitung*, No. 10 (January 22, 1818), pp. 79–80; *Enciclopedia dello spettacolo*, vol. 2; col. 1502.—KH/TA

[13] Joseph Schreyvogel (1768–1832), author (pseudonyms: Thomas and Carl August West, also West Brothers) was, from 1802 to 1804 and from 1814, Court Theater Secretary and Dramaturg of the two united Court Theaters. The original playwright had been the Spanish Pedro Calderón de la Barca (1600–1681). See Wurzbach, vol. 31, pp. 292–294; Clive, p. 325.—KH

[14] The Trattnerhof, No. 659 [renumbered as 618 in 1821] on the Graben, built in 1773–1776 by Peter Mollner, upon commission from the Court Book Printer Johann Thomas (Edler) von Trattner, numbered among the largest apartment rental buildings in the city.

Beethoven may have asked the unknown writer where he lived, with this reply.—KH/TA

[15] From 1794, Matthäus Andreas Stein (1776–1842), son of the famed Augsburg piano maker Andreas Stein, carried on a piano-making business in Vienna in conjunction with his sister Nannette, but, in 1802 became independent. Later, his son Karl Andreas (1797–1863) also entered the business. See Frimmel, *Handbuch*, II, p. 253; *MGG*, vol. 12, cols. 1230–1232; Clive, p. 351.—KH/TA

[16] The piano that Beethoven received from the English firm of Broadwood as a gift in 1818. The instrument had probably been sent from London in the last week of December 1817 and was the subject of considerable discussion and correspondence about this time. It would not actually arrive in Vienna until after May 19, 1818, when Beethoven moved to summer quarters in Mödling, and would be forwarded to him there. See Beethoven's entry in his *Tagebuch*, dated Mödling, May 19, 1818, and a report on the Broadwood piano, "Ehrende Auszeichnung," which appeared in Schickh's *Wiener Zeitschrift für Kunst, Literatur, Theater und Mode* 4, No. 10 (January 23, 1819), pp. 78–79, describing its tone in detail and indicating that it had been delivered to Beethoven in Mödling. As will be seen in later Hefte, Matthäus Andreas Stein was the technician whom Beethoven called most often to work on the Broadwood. See Brandenburg, *Briefwechsel*, IV, pp. 170–171, 191.—KH/TA

[17] Jägerzeile (today's Praterstrasse), a stretch of road leading through the suburbs Leopoldstadt and Jägerzeile. In this street, two residences of Leonhard Mälzel can be traced: Leopoldstadt No. 460 [renumbered as 520 in 1821] and No. 17 [renumbered as 20 in 1821 and as 44 in 1827] in the Jägerzeile suburb (on the south side of Praterstrasse). In one document he is called a "musician," in another a "mechanical engineer, born in Regensburg, Bavaria." According to various Conscriptions-Bögen (census sheets), Leonhard Mälzel was born in 1773 or 1776; Frimmel, *Handbuch*, 1783. In any case, he died in 1855. Like his more famous brother Johann Nepomuk, he was a maker of mechanical musical instruments. See Conscriptions-Bogen, Leopoldstadt, Haus 520, Wohnpartei 15; Conscriptions-Bögen, Jägerzeile, Haus 44, Wohnpartei 1 (both in Wiener Stadt- und Landesarchiv); Frimmel, *Handbuch*, I, pp. 378–380; Groner (1922), p. 89; Guetjahr, p. 108.—KH/TA

[18] Franz von Praitschopf, riding master of the Imperial Body Guard, who, as such, presumably participated in Court church ceremonies, lived in the k.k. German Nobles Guard, Rennweg No. 485 (Belvedere Palace) in the suburb of Landstrasse. It was possibly to him that Schindler referred as

he should meet you in the mornings? [//] The question is whether he can do it tomorrow [Saturday, February 28], since there is a Church service at Court. [Blatt 3r] [//] *Obsequies.*[19] [//]

He is irritated about Hauschka.[20] [//]

UNKNOWN "C" **[continuing the previous conversation]**:[21] They drag terribly; in the aria I am following the singer. The Overture to *Coriolan* confused the violoncelli.[22] [//]

UNKNOWN "B" **[resuming]**:[23] I still remember the problem that you had with the timpanist at the rehearsal of *Egmont*.[24]
[end of entries for Friday, February 27.]

the "Captain of the Emperor's Arcieren Body Guard," who ca. 1816, belonged to the circle around Beethoven in the beer tavern "Zum Blumenstock." See Guetjahr, p. 158; *Hof- und Staats-Schematismus*, 1819, I, p. 110; Schindler, 3rd ed. (1860), pt. 1, p. 231; Schindler-MacArdle, p. 204.—KH/TA

[19] Memorial services commemorating the death day of Joseph II were held in the Hofpfarrkirche (Augustiner Kirche) on February 19 and 20, and the death day of Leopold II on February 27 and 28. Memorandum from Trauttmannsdorff, Obersthofmeister, to Count Ferdinand Kuefstein, Hofmusikgraf, February 16, 1818. See Hofmusikkapelle, K. 11 (1818–1820), fol. 13 (Haus-, Hof- und Staatsarchiv, Vienna).—TA

[20] Vincenz Hauschka (1766–1840), a friend of Beethoven's, finance councillor and lived in the Schottengasse No. 111, where the composer would have dinner on St. Stephan's Day (December 26) 1819 (see Heft 5, Blätter 54r–56r). He was one of the founders of the Gesellschaft der Musikfreunde, whose orchestra he occasionally led. From 1813 to 1834 he was a member of the board of directors of the Gesellschaft, and was also active as a violoncellist and virtuoso on the viola di bordone (Baryton). He was among the very few friends with whom Beethoven was on a familiar "du" basis. See Frimmel, *Handbuch*, I, p. 201; *Hof- und Staats-Schematismus*, 1819, I, p. 119; Wurzbach, vol. 8, pp. 78–79; Clive, pp. 153–154.—KH/TA

[21] From context, Unknown "C" seems to be a member of the Gesellschaft der Musikfreunde's orchestra. If he was in a position to "follow" the singers, he may have been among the concertino string players, possibly a violoncellist or contrabassist.—TA

[22] On Sunday, March 1, 1818, Hauschka conducted the second concert of the Gesellschaft der Musikfreunde with the following program: Beethoven, Overture to *Coriolan*, Op. 62; Ferdinando Paër, duet for soprano and tenor from the opera *Sargino*; Bernhard Henrik Crusell, two movements from a clarinet concerto (no soloist listed); Giuseppe Nicolini, quartet from the opera *Traiano in Dacia*; Joseph Eybler, grand Chorus; Karl Ludwig Blum, Overture to the opera *Zoraide*. See Perger, pp. 280 and 286; program files, Gesellschaft der Musikfreunde.—KH/TA

[23] In contrast to Unknown "C," Unknown "B" seems not to have been an orchestra member, but instead a member of the audience, though one who attended rehearsals as well. If he was purchasing a piano from Stein and possibly lived in the Trattnerhof, he was probably financially secure. He was well educated, attended at least two theatrical performances and one concert within the week covered by this conversation book, and was comfortable conversing with individuals of moderately high rank.—TA

[24] Possibly a reference to the Gesellschaft der Musikfreunde's concert of March 10, 1816, which had included the *Egmont* Overture, whose timpani part is not problematical. The same concert, however, had also included the Adagio and Allegro from Beethoven's Violin Concerto. The *Allgemeine musikalische Zeitung*'s correspondent noted that the performance of the Overture "could not have been

[Seemingly no entries on Saturday, February 28, or Sunday, March 1.]

BEETHOVEN **[possibly reading an advertisement posted in a restaurant or coffee house in the Landstrasse; probably early afternoon of Monday, March 2]**: Electro-vibrations machine, for hardness of hearing and total deafness.[25]

[Blatt 3v]

UNKNOWN "B" **[the same, commenting on the above]**: I think that in constructing a sound machine, one must consult not merely a musician, but instead a well-grounded physicist—therefore an acoustician. [//]

    Don't you have a thematic catalogue of your piano compositions? I have many of them, but I would like to get more of them little by little. [//] [Blatt 4r]

    Second to your Overture, the Quartet from Nicolini's *Trajan* was especially edifying for me to hear. Then, the *so-called* Overture by one Herr Blum at the end. Hauschka was also picturesque, looking like a *swimming master*.[26] [//] Everything was unsatisfactory, though. [//] They can make an impression only upon the masses, [Blatt 4v] and concert music, as a rule, means little to them. The more educated among the people are already satiated with mediocrity. The duet from *Sargino* was impossible to hear—so false. [//] So you weren't present at all during your Overture? [//] [Blatt 5r] All the better for you. [//] I'll bet that the director

bettered," but that in the Concerto, "the soloist was unsuccessful." Perhaps the first movement of the Concerto had also been projected and even rehearsed—unlike the *Egmont* Overture, this movement contains one of the most deceptively difficult timpani parts in the entire literature, especially in terms of tuning with the rest of the orchestra, originally written for the Theater an der Wien's sharp-eared Ignaz Manker. See the *AmZ* 18, No. 17 (April 24, 1816), col. 290; plus the Gesellschaft der Musikfreunde program, March 10, 1816, which specifies that only two movements of the Concerto were played.

    Despite the contextual association with the *Coriolan* Overture and the Gesellschaft's concerts, however, this unknown writer did not specify the *overture* to *Egmont*. As premiered at the Burgtheater in 1810, the entire score (with songs, entr'actes, melodrama, and finale) includes an entr'acte featuring an oboe fantasia followed by a march in which the timpani enter explosively on an unexpected beat. The Burgtheater's timpanist at the time was the refined but possibly reticent Anton Eder. Thus, if the *Egmont* association is correct, the unknown writer may also have been hearkening back as far as 1810, as Thayer believed (Thayer-Forbes, p. 485).—TA

    [25] The "Electro-vibrations machine" was located in the Sulfur Fumigation Institute of Carl Joseph Mayer, in the Landstrasse, in the building of the Elisabethiners, No. 283–284 [renumbered as 317 in 1821]. The Elisabethiner Nuns operated a hospital at 315–317 [today's No. 4–4a], on the west side of Landstrasser Hauptstrasse, the block south of the point where it met the Glacis. The hospital remains active today. See also Heft 2, Blatt 47r.—KH/TA

    [26] Seemingly a reference to Hauschka's motions while conducting.—TA

did not heed a single word about what the Overture should portray. [//] Baryton.[27]
[//] Then may he have much to laugh about in all the specialties! [//]

Today [Monday, March 2] I am going to the Theater an der Wien: *Das Gefängnis von Grypsholm*—for Küstner's benefit.[28] [Blatt 5v]

At these concerts [of the Gesellschaft der Musikfreunde], it is a requirement that *everything*, even the worst, be applauded. [//]

I am going to the Theater with him today. [//]

BEETHOVEN: They speak of becoming cheaper?

UNKNOWN "B": In large matters, everything is dropping considerably (though in small ones, [things are] extremely unimportant)—as a result of poor administration.

[Blatt 6r]

BEETHOVEN [**similarly reading an advertisement posted in a restaurant or coffee house in the Landstrasse; possibly a day or so after Monday, March 2**]:
Gewölbe No. 309: 2 apartments, actually one on the 2nd floor [3rd floor, American], and one at ground level.[29]

45

45

23

UNKNOWN "D"?: Joseph Wagner.[30]

---

[27] *Bariton*: probably a reference to the archaic stringed instrument that Hauschka played, rather than to a singer in that range.—TA

[28] *Das Gefängnis in Gripsholm*, romantic drama in acts, after Heinrich Zschokke's tale "Cesarolli, oder die schwarze oder die eiserne Maske," was premiered at the Theater an der Wien on March 2, 1818, and repeated six times during that month. The performance was given for the monetary benefit of the actor and director Joseph Küstner (originally Joseph Reichel). See *Wiener Zeitung*, No. 28 (March 5, 1818), p. 227; Ignaz von Seyfried, "Journal des Theaters an der Wien, 1795–1829" (Handschriften Sammlung, 84958 Jb; Wiener Stadt- und Landesbibliothek).—KH/TA

[29] No such advertisement can be traced in the *Intelligenzblatt*. If these apartments were in the walled City, No. 309 [renumbered as 287 in 1821] was in the Naglergasse, and in 1829 was owned by one Johann Michael Mozart. If, however, the advertisement meant Landstrasse No. 309 [renumbered as 347 in 1821], that address was in the Ungargasse, the summer home of Prince Lobkowitz, three-quarters of the way to the *Linie* [today's *Gürtel*]. See Behsel, pp. 9 and 79.—KH/TA

[30] Among the many people with this name was Joseph Wagner (b. 1791), violinist in the Court Theater, who lived in the suburb of Landstrasse, No. 246 [renumbered as 276 in 1821], in the Krügel- or Kriegelgasse, directly behind the Rochuskirche. At this time, Beethoven was living at Landstrasser Hauptstrasse, No. 268 [renumbered as 299 in 1821], only a few minutes' walk away. See Conscriptions-Bögen, Landstrasse, No. 276, Wohnpartei 4 (Wiener Stadt- und Landesarchiv).—KH

BEETHOVEN [**possibly reading an advertisement posted in a restaurant or coffee house in the Landstrasse; sometime after Monday, March 2**]: Ungargasse No. 35: furniture sale on June 1.[31]

Private tutor,[32] 127 fl. 30 kr. monthly.

Meals	60 fl.		Take the wine only at	30
Salary	25		Meals	" " 45
Wine	42			
	127		Then the monthly is	100 fl.
Yearly:	1524 [fl.]			

[Blatt 6v]

Gray blankets[33]	2
Floor covering	2
Feather quilt	1
White sheet	1
Night shirts	2
Mattress on the floor	1

Wood-saving and air-cleaning ovens, pottery implements, and remedies against smoke, at Andre Durst, Fayence- and Pottery-Implements Maker. Alservorstadt, next to the Josephstadt Glacis, Wickenburg Gasse No. 23.

Wine from Ofen [Buda] in Pest, per barrel, old from 40 to 80 fl.[34]

[Interior of back cover:]

Dorian:

---

[31] An advertisement concerning this matter has not been found. House no. 35 in the suburb of Landstrasse was not in the Ungargasse, but rather in the Hauptstrasse. Houses no. 350–356, however, *were* in the Ungargasse, a block west of Beethoven's residence.—KH/TA

[32] *Hofmeister* in German; Beethoven was evidently contemplating such a teacher for nephew Karl, possibly one to live with them, and may have been setting it up.—TA

[33] *Schazen* in the original, meaning woolen blankets (*Decken*), according to Schünemann.—KH

[34] These two advertisements cannot be traced, but are diverse enough that they must have come from a newspaper. In the *Handlungsgremien* (business directories), Andreas Durst was listed as a "[kitchen] implements maker in the Rossau, No. 14." Perhaps he had a warehouse in the Alservorstadt that cannot be traced. See Redl, 1818, p. 128.—KH/TA

Elec[tro-vibrations machine?]

2 fl. 13 kr. in the bath

E

Bread.
Lentils.[35]

End of Heft I

---

[35] The original *Lenz* probably meant "lentils" (*Linsen*) in this context, rather than "spring."—TA

Heft 2

(March 17, 1819 – after May 15/16, 1819)

N.B. The chronological gaps evident in this Heft suggest strongly that Beethoven was not yet dependent upon the conversation books, even in public, to carry on business and social interactions. As a result, many of the places, dates, and times posited below remain open to question and further interpretation.

[Blatt 1r]

BEETHOVEN [possibly at the *Birne* restaurant in Landstrasser Hauptstrasse, reading the *Wiener Zeitung* and its *Intelligenzblatt*; possibly at midday dinner, ca. 2 p.m. on Wednesday, March 17, 1819]:[1]

---

[1] From October 1817 to October 1819 Beethoven lived in the suburb of Landstrasse, at Landstrasser Hauptstrasse No. 268 [renumbered as 299 in 1821 and 340 in 1830] on the west side of the street, on the 2nd floor [3rd floor, American]. Diagonally across the street, a few feet further out from the walled City, was the *Goldene Birne* (the Golden Pear) at No. 42 [renumbered as 52 in 1821 and 63 in 1830]. In Beethoven's day many Viennese (especially if they had no domestic servants) would customarily eat their meals at one or two favorite restaurants or taverns near their apartments. In the composer's case, while living in the Landstrasser Hauptstrasse, it was the *Birne*. See Behsel, pp. 71 and 78; Klein, pp. 100–102, 163.

If Beethoven ate dinner in early- to midafternoon and then visited a coffee house to read the daily newspapers later, and if the following advertisements date from newspapers of March 17, 1819, then he must have copied them sometime that afternoon, if his later, better-documented pattern of such activities provides any evidence.

Beethoven read the *Wiener Zeitung* (containing news, weather, arrivals/departures, deaths, currency exchange rates, and stock prices, as well as selected advertisements for sheet music and prominent concerts) and its *Intelligenzblatt* (containing business news, plus advertisements for employment; and property rental and purchase, as well as advertisements of many book dealers) virtually every day, and would often jot down excerpts from them. Occasionally he would read the *Beobachter* or some other newspaper, but most often, if he noted a book that is not found in one of these journals, it is likely that he either saw the item in a bookshop window, or stopped inside to browse, and wrote it down upon first-hand examination. For the most part, Beethoven copied these advertisements and other book information with amazing accuracy.—TA

Türk, *Grosse Klavierschule*, 12 fl. 30 kr., at Traeg's.[2]

Donau-Fahrten by J.A. Schultes, Vol. 1, with maps, sewn binding, 6 fl. 30 kr., at Pichler's, Plankengasse 1125; also at Anna [*sic*] Strauss's on Petersplatz.[3]

Inquiry concerning Baron Praun [?][4]

[2] Excerpt from an advertisement in the *Wiener Zeitung*, No. 62 (March 17, 1819), p. 248: "The following new music has arrived at Johann Traeg's, Art Dealer, in the newly built Klosterneuburger Hof, No. 1177, next to Plankengasse: Türk, *grosse Clavierschule*, 12 fl. 30 kr. …." The same advertisement also appeared on March 11, 1819. Beethoven owned a copy of Türk's *Anweisung zum Generalbasspielen* (Halle, 1791) when he died (see Albrecht, *Letters to Beethoven*, No. 483; Inventory No. 6).—KH/TA

[3] Excerpt from an advertisement in the *Intelligenzblatt*, No. 62 (March 17, 1819), p. 521: "New items to be had from Anton Doll the Younger, Book Dealer, Bischofgasse, next to the Lichtensteg, across from the Grosser Federhof: *Donau-Fahrten. Ein Handbuch für Resisende auf der Donau*, by J.A. Schultes, Court Councillor and Professor, First Volume, with Maps, size 8vo. 1819, sewn binding; 6 fl. 30 kr." Although this advertisement appeared several times, the dating of March 17, 1819, can be accepted with certainty here. On this day, Anton Doll's announcement appeared directly under those of the book dealers Anton Pichler and Anton Strauss, a proximity that explains Beethoven's error in copying the entries.—KH

[4] The person mentioned here could be Sigismund Otto, Freiherr von Praun (1811–1830), called "der junge Baron Praun" (the young Baron Praun) in journalistic reports. Already in 1815 he had appeared in Vienna as a violin-playing Wunderkind, and in 1817 became a student of Joseph Mayseder (see Schilling, vol. 5, p. 539; article signed by Baron von Winzingerode). On April 13, 1817, the five-and-a-half-year-old Praun gave a concert, reported in the *Allgemeine musikalische Zeitung* 19, No. 22 (May 28, 1817), col. 381.

Another possibility could be Peter, Freiherr von Braun (b. Vienna, October 18, 1764; d. Vienna, November 15, 1819), Court banker, silk manufacturer, living in the Kohlmarkt, No. 1220. From August 1794 to December 1806 he managed both Viennese Court Theaters (see Frimmel, *Handbuch*, I, pp. 58–59; Wurzbach, vol. 2, p. 123; Clive, pp. 43–45).

In the orthography of the time, B and P were often interchangeable, and it is conceivable that Braun and Praun could designate the same individual, although "brown" as a color and a surname would generally be spelled "braun." When dealing with or discussing theater manager Baron von Braun, Beethoven had occasion to write his name four times in his surviving letters: in a letter to librettist Joseph von Sonnleithner, in February/March 1804 he spelled Braun's name "Baron Braun" (Brandenburg, *Briefwechsel*, No. 177). In a letter to singer Friedrich Sebastian Meyer, shortly before April 10, 1806, Beethoven referred to him as "Baron braun" and "B. braun" (Brandenburg, *Briefwechsel*, No. 247), with his surname in lower-case letters. In a letter to Braun himself, on or shortly before May 5, 1806, Beethoven had no occasion to refer to him in the third person in the salutation or text, but on the exterior address designated in French: "Le Baron de Braun" (Brandenburg, *Briefwechsel*, No. 251). Braun, who had been out of the theatrical scene for years, died on November 15, 1819 (Wurzbach, vol. 2, p. 123). Thus, from 1804 to 1806 Beethoven seems not to have confused the phonetic B with P in spelling Braun's name, and in March, 1819, eight months before Braun's death, there seems little motivation, in context, for Beethoven suddenly to have brought his name up here. By the same token, the child violinist Baron von Praun (who cried onstage during his debut as a performer) seems to have been a current topic in sundry journals and is probably the individual meant in Beethoven's fleeting note among these newspaper advertisements, some of whose sources proved elusive. Possibly one of the unknown sources for the advertisements might also yield the motivation for Beethoven to have noted young Praun's name.—KH/TA [possibly at Traeg's music shop, Plankengasse No. 1177, in the walled City,[5] looking at Türk and Burney; mid-afternoon of Wednesday, March 17:]

Reise Musikalische[:] Österreich, Preussen, Sachsen, Bayern, Hannover, Württemberg, Baden, Kurhessen, u. s. f. noch 31 Bundesstaaten allein in Deutschland.[6] [Blatt 1v]

[possibly at a coffee house in the City, now reading the *Wiener Zeitung*'s *Amtsblatt*; late afternoon of Wednesday, March 17:]

The Bank now gives advance payments only on 500 Gulden in banknotes, under the address, "Loan and Deposit Office of the priv. Austrian National Bank." N.B. But only on state paper.—6½.[7] [Blatt 2r]

[possibly at a coffee house in the City, reading the *Wiener Zeitung*'s *Intelligenzblatt*; late afternoon of Thursday, March 18:]

In Neubau [suburb], Wenger's House, No. 156, 2nd floor [3rd floor, American], at Fr[au] v[on] Rieselbach's.[8]

[possibly walking by Gräffer's book shop on the Franziskaner Platz (on his way home); possibly later in the afternoon of Thursday, March 18:]

---

[5] From the suburban *Birne*, Beethoven would have walked north on Landstrasser Hauptstrasse, through the Stubentor (Stuben Gate), then wending his way through the City streets to Stephansplatz, the Graben, and perhaps Dorotheergasse to the Plankengasse, depending upon where his other errands took him, and then possibly to Traeg's music shop. No. 1177 was renumbered as 1111 in 1821; see Blatt 7v below.—TA

[6] All of the elements in this entry pertain, in one way or another, to Charles Burney's *The Present State of Music in Germany, the Netherlands and United Provinces* (London, 1773); indeed, the element Bundesstaaten (*United Provinces*) provides the crucial link. Burney's *Present State of Music in France and Italy* had already been published in a German translation by Christoph Daniel Ebeling, and was considered as vol. 1 of a series. In 1773 Burney's *Present State of Music in Germany, the Netherlands and United Provinces* was translated into German by Johann Joachim Christoph Bode and published in two volumes (considered as vols. 2 and 3) in Hamburg in 1773, as *Carl Burney's der Musik Doctors Tagebuch seiner Musikalischen Reisen*, with vol. 2 subtitled *Durch Flandern, die Niederlande und am Rhein bis Wien*, and vol. 3, subtitled *Durch Böhmen, Sachsen, Brandenburg, Hamburg und Holland*.

Since the element *United Provinces* in the English title was not included on the title pages of the German volumes, its counterpart, *Bundesstaaten*, must have come from the pages of the books themselves. Therefore, two possible scenarios are possible: (1) a dealer had a copy of the German translation for sale, and Beethoven picked it up and thumbed through it, making note of its contents; or (2) a dealer had a copy of the original English publication for sale, and had a sign or slip with a locally-made German translation of its title and contents, which Beethoven jotted down in random order.

Beethoven owned a copy of Burney's *A General History of Music* (London, 1789) when he died (see Albrecht, *Letters*, No. 483, Inventory No. 42).—TA

[7] Excerpt from a "Kundmachung" (Notice) of the Austrian National Bank in the *Amtsblatt* of the *Wiener Zeitung*, No. 22 (March 17, 1819), p. 63.—KH/TA

[8] This concerns an advertisement in which an official's widow seeks a position as a housekeeper. See *Intelligenzblatt*, No. 63 (March 18, 1819), p. 523. The same advertisement also appeared on March 16 and 20, 1819.—KH

Des Meister Hans Sachs Historien u[nd] gute Schwänke, etc., small 8vo, 1818, sewn binding, 2 fl. 30 kr., at Gräffer's on Franziskanerplatz.[9] [//]

UNKNOWN[10] [**possibly in a public place; ca. Thursday, March 18, or Friday, March 19**]: I now ask you for her [Johanna van Beethoven's] house number. [//]

BEETHOVEN [**presumably replying, in part so as not to be overheard**]: la Ellmaurer.[11]

No. 238 in the Tiefer Graben: Fr[au] Beethoven.[12] [//]

[Blatt 2v]

UNKNOWN [**continuing**]: Smetana wants to try something concerning your hearing.[13]

[Blatt 3r]

UNKNOWN [**continuing**]: 16 fl.

[Blatt 3v] [Empty—no writing.]

[Blatt 4r]

[9] An advertisement with this wording cannot be located. See Kayser, vol. 5, p. 3: *Des Meisters Hans Sachs Historien und gute Schwänke*, ed. Conr[ad] Spät, called Frühauf (W.A. Gerle). 8vo (Pesth, 1818).—KH

[10] The unknown writer is presumably someone having to do with Beethoven's litigation over the guardianship of his nephew Karl.—TA

[11] The word "Ellmaurer" (entered later onto this page) presumably refers to the educational institute of Carl Ellmaurer, founded in 1808 and located in the Josephstadt (although technically in Strozzi Grund), Kaisergasse No. 26 until, at latest, May 1, 1819, when Joseph Blöchlinger moved into this building (the former Palais Strozzi) with his own boarding school (see Blatt, 86v below), which nephew Karl would attend from June 22, 1819, through summer 1823. The address today is Josefstädter Strasse No. 39. See *Intelligenzblatt*, No. 237 (August 25, 1814), p. 351.—KH/TA

[12] Johanna van Beethoven (ca. 1786–1868), daughter of the Viennese upholsterer/draper Anton Reiss, married Beethoven's brother Caspar Anton Carl (1774–1815) on May 25, 1806. In 1818–1819, she lived in the Tiefer Graben, No. 238 [renumbered as 231 in 1821], 2nd floor [3rd floor, American]. In this entry Beethoven spelled the surname phonetically, "Beethowen." See Schmidt-Görg, p. 119; Thayer-Deiters-Riemann, IV, p. 550; Thayer-Forbes, p. 399; Heft 10, Blatt 70r.—KH/TA

[13] Carl von Smetana (1774–1827), surgeon, government physician, operated on Beethoven's nephew Karl at Giannatasio's Institute in 1816, and later also became Beethoven's doctor. See Frimmel, *Handbuch*, II, p. 185; Schmidt, *Nekrolog*, vol. 5, p. 1101; Clive, p. 340.—KH/TA

BERNARD[14] [possibly at a restaurant in the City;[15] possibly at midday dinner, ca. 2 p.m., on Friday, March 19]: The main point is to choose as guardian a man who possesses your complete confidence in both moral and pedagogical matters, and with whom you could always remain on friendly terms concerning this matter. Since Kudlich[16] has a better effect upon Karl than [continues on Blatt 5r→]

[Blatt 4v]

BEETHOVEN: Kudlich 292[17]

---

[14] Joseph Carl Bernard (1786 – March 31, 1850), author and journalist, friend of both Beethoven and Cajetan Giannatasio del Rio, was born in Horatitz near Saaz, Bohemia, and came to Vienna in ca. 1800. After brief activity in the *Hofkriegsrat*, he worked solely as an author. In 1814 he reworked Weissenbach's cantata text *Der glorreiche Augenblick* for Beethoven (see also Heft 3, Blatt 1r), and, in 1818, received the commission to write an oratorio text for him (see Blatt 13r below). In 1818 he was coeditor of the *Wiener Zeitschrift*, and from October 1819, the principal editor of the *Wiener Zeitung*. See Böckh, *Wiens lebende Schriftsteller*, p. 7; extensive entry in Frimmel, *Handbuch*, I, pp. 36–38; Clive, pp. 29–30; Czeike, I, pp. 336–337.

Viennese sources agree that the order of his names should be Joseph Carl, and suggest that he might have called himself Karl. In secondary sources, his birth year ranges from 1775 to 1786. Among contemporary Conscriptions-Bögen (census sheets), those for Stadt, No. 933/9 (taken after 1816) give his birth as 1785 (twice); that for Wieden, No. 784/8 (taken in 1824) as 1786. His marriage record to Magdalena Grassl in Wieden's Paulanerkirche, November 25, 1823 (Trauungs-Register, Tom 5, fol. 137), however, gives his age as thirty-six, suggesting that he was born between November 26, 1786, and November 25, 1787. Combining these sources points to Bernard's likely birth date in late November or December 1786.

If Bernard left Bohemia and wandered through Germany for two years as a young man, as he later tells Beethoven, then an arrival date of 1800 in Vienna may be too early. Moreover, although a Franz Bernard worked as a scribe in the Hofkriegsrat from 1801 (living in Landstrasse Nos. 24 and then 36), there is no record of a Joseph Carl Bernard in the *Hof- und Staats-Schematismen* in 1800, 1801, 1803, 1804, 1805, or 1808.—KH/TA

[15] Unless Bernard and (presumably) Tuscher came out to suburban Landstrasse, the most convenient place for Beethoven to have met them would have been within the walled City.—TA

[16] Johann Baptist Kudlich (1786–1831), director of an educational institution in the Viennese suburb of Landstrasse, Erdberggasse No. 96, which nephew Karl attended for a short time in 1819, after he left Giannatasio's Institute, which faced the Glacis. See Franz Kysselak, *Memorabilien, Wiens Verstorbene 1814–1839*, Bogen 109 (Wiener Stadt- und Landesarchiv); Böckh, *Wiens lebende Schriftsteller*, p. 533; Frimmel, *Handbuch*, I, p. 308; Thayer-Deiters-Riemann, IV, pp. 138–139; Thayer-Forbes, p. 722; Clive, p. 198.

Erdberggasse No. 96 [renumbered as 91 in 1821], was only two buildings north of Antonie Brentano's former residence, No. 98 [renumbered as 93 in 1821]. See Behsel, p. 72, indicating that she still owned No. 93 in 1829.—KH/TA

[17] The significance of the number 292, which Beethoven presumably associated with Kudlich, is not clear. If it refers to a house number current in the suburb of Landstrasse in 1819, the address would have been in the Ungargasse, almost directly behind (and to the west) of where Beethoven was living in Landstrasser Hauptrasse No. 268. If in suburban Erdberg in 1819, the building would have been very remote, on a cross street at the far south end of Antonigasse, facing a dry canal or channel. Therefore, Erdberg No. 292 seems unlikely.

[Blatt 5r]

BERNARD [continuing]: Giannatasio,[18] then I maintain that he be given preference if you cannot find anyone else who would be completely appropriate. [//] Of course it is extremely troublesome for you. [//] [Blatt 5v] If you want to achieve some degree of peace, I believe that it would be good for you to appoint a guardian, as you were willing to do yesterday. If it should work out, however, that the boy can be taken to Sailer[19] in Landshut, it would of course be even better, since you could have all reassurance to that extent, because you would know that he was in the best hands. [//] [Blatt 6r]

Even if you have Tuscher[20] as co-guardian, then nothing in your situation would change by doing so, because all of the cares would always be left to you. [//] Perhaps Tuscher could take over the guardianship simultaneously with Kudlich, which could also be very advantageous. // Anyhow, even if you send [Karl] away, everything will remain as it has been up to now. Until there is a change, he indeed remains at Kudlich's anyhow. [//] [Blatt 6v] As long as you are the guardian and Karl stays

---

Old Frau Kudlich is discussed on Blatt 12v; Conscriptions-Bögen (census sheets) for Landstrasse No. 292 [renumbered as 330 in 1821 and 371 in 1830] do not reveal any listings for her.—TA

[18] Cajetan Giannatasio del Rio (1764–1828), proprietor of an educational institute for sons from the nobility that was located in the suburb Landstrasse, Glacis No. 426. Karl van Beethoven attended this institute from February 2, 1816, to January 24, 1818. See Böckh, *Merkwürdigkeiten* (1823), p. 175; Frimmel, *Handbuch*, II, p. 69; Thayer-Deiters-Riemann, IV, pp. 35 and 91; Thayer-Forbes (summary), pp. 666 and 696; Clive, pp. 128–130.—KH/TA

[19] Johann Michael Sailer (1751–1832), Catholic theologian. After he had taught at the University of Dillingen as professor of practical theology, he went to Landshut in 1800 as professor of moral and pastoral theology, became Rector of that University in 1805, went to Regensburg as Canon in 1821, and became Bishop in 1829. Bernard phonetically spelled his name "Seiler" here.

The conversation here concerns Beethoven's scheme to send his nephew to Landshut for his education, thereby getting one up on his sister-in-law, who sought a subsidized place for her son in the k.k. *Konvikt* in Vienna. On February 22, 1819, Antonie Brentano (living in Frankfurt) had written Sailer, whom she knew personally, a letter on Beethoven's behalf. See *Allgemeine Deutsche Biographie*, vol. 30, pp. 178–180; Frimmel, *Handbuch*, II, p. 94; Thayer-Deiters-Riemann, IV, pp. 139–141, 564; Thayer-Forbes, pp. 723–724; Clive, pp. 301–302; Weise, p. 33; Albrecht, *Letters*, No. 256; Brandenburg, *Briefwechsel*, No. 1289.—KH

[20] Mathias Tuscher (b. Eisenstadt, 1775), Magistrat's Criminal Councillor, lived on the Haarmarkt, No. 682 [renumbered as 641 in 1821]. He belonged to the Board of Representatives of the Gesellschaft der Musikfreunde and was also a practicing member (singing). In 1834 he still lived at Haarmarkt No. 641, Wohnpartei 2, with his wife Susanna (b. 1780); at the same time, Ripelly lived in Wohnpartei 1; see Conscriptions-Bogen, Stadt No. 641; new collation 641/22 (Wiener Stadt- und Landesarchiv). Indeed, almost all of the ca. twenty apartments in No. 641 were occupied by city officials.

After Beethoven was denied the guardianship at the Magistrat's second court hearing, Tuscher was installed as legal guardian. He served in this office from March 26 to July 5, 1819. See Böckh, *Wiens lebende Schriftsteller*, p. 353; *Hof- und Staats-Schematismus*, 1819, I, p. 656; Thayer-Deiters-Riemann, IV, pp. 139–140 and 144; Thayer-Forbes, pp. 722–723 and 726; Clive, pp. 373–374; Behsel, p. 20.—KH/TA

here, you will have to battle not only all the cares that you have had up to now, but also, constantly, his mother and her intrigues. [//]

For the present, just have Karl brought to Kudlich; meanwhile, the matter can be put in order. [//]

[Blatt 6a-recto]

TUSCHER [?][21] **[evidently present during at least part of Bernard's discussion]**: v[on] Rippely[22] [//]

BERNARD **[continuing]**: Perhaps he [Tuscher] would be more easily persuaded to [do] it, if a co-guardian such as Kudlich were also named. [//] Everything need not be finished by tomorrow. If we go to see Ohmayer[23] tomorrow morning, and then to Tuscher and to Kudlich, that way we can already make up our minds about who is perceived as the best. [//] [Blatt 6a-verso] Between 8 and 9 o'clock. [//]

TUSCHER [?][24] **[continuing]**: Before Sunday.[25] [//] Where is he? With his mother? [//] But the mother will always find the means to influence [him]. // Her personality. [//] Few words from her about the boy's spirit. [//] A clergyman? There are [sentence ends] [//] All communication with the mother must be made impossible. [//] [Blatt 7r] I shall take the liberty of visiting you one of these days. [//] As co-guardian? [//] These days I am extraordinarily busy *ex officio*. [//] This matter requires leisurely reflection and counsel. [//] It cannot be settled with just a few words. It requires knowledge of the personalities and the circumstances. [//] But the foundation of the development of Education is homework and personal contact. [//]

---

[21] This entry was made by the same unknown person who wrote on Blatt 105r below. Schünemann suggests that the writer of this group of entries may have been Mathias von Tuscher.—TA

[22] Johann Baptist Ripelly (b. Vienna, 1777/78), Magistrat's Councillor for Civil Law Inquiries, living at the Grosses Waaghaus, Haarmarkt, No. 682 [renumbered as 641 in 1821], Wohnpartei 2 before 1830; possibly renumbered as 1 by 1834. According to a census sheet before 1830, he was born in 1778, and his family included his wife Thekla (b. 1785), sons Johann (b. 1813), Anton (b. 1816), and another Johann (b. 1819), and a daughter, Elisabeth (b. 1815). According to a census sheet of 1834, he was born in 1777; his wife Thekla (b. 1788); his sons Anton (b. 1816), Johann (b. 1819), and Karl (b. 1820). In 1826 he became Vice-Bürgermeister (Vice-Mayor), and retired in 1847. See *Hof- und Staats-Schematismus*, 1819, I, p. 656; Behsel, p. 20; Conscriptions-Bögen, Stadt No. 641; new collation 641/2 and 641/22 (Wiener Stadt- und Landesarchiv); Czeike, IV, p. 680.—KH/TA

[23] Dr. Joseph *Edler* von Ohmayer, Court and Legal Attorney, at the same time Court War Attorney and sworn Notary, member of the Faculty of Jurisprudence, lived at Salzgries No. 192. He functioned as Dr. Bach's substitute at the legal inventory and evaluation of Beethoven's estate. Bernard spelled his name "Omayer" here. See *Hof- und Staats-Schematismus*, 1819, II, pp. 96, 110, 351, 377; Thayer-Deiters-Riemann, II, pp. 201 and 608; Thayer-Forbes, p. 723; Heft 11, Blatt 54r.—KH/TA

[24] Same handwriting as on Blatt 105r below.—KH

[25] Probably Sunday, March 21.—TA

[End of entries presumably on Friday, March 19.]

[Blatt 7v]

BEETHOVEN **[presumably at a coffee house, reading the *Wiener Zeitung*;
probably the late afternoon of Saturday, March 20]:**

2 fl. 30 kr. *Sappho*, on postal-thin paper, at Wallishauser's.[26]

[There seems to be nearly a week's gap here without entries.]

BEETHOVEN **[presumably at a coffee house, reading the day's *Intelligenzblatt*;
probably the late afternoon of Friday, March 26:]**

Nützliche u[nd] Interessante Militair-Skizzen, etc., etc., 2nd Volume, by Johann
von Nucé, sewn binding; 5 fl. at Gerold's.[27]

At Wimmer's, across from the Jägerhorn [Hunter's Horn], [Blatt 8r] J.M. Sailer's
Rede von der Priesterweihung, 8vo, Landshut, 1817; 40 kr.[28]

UNKNOWN: His contrabass had to be given a pass to leave the [Musik-]Verein.[29]

---

[26] Excerpt from an advertisement in the *Wiener Zeitung*, No. 65 (Saturday, March 20, 1819),
p. 260: "Just appeared from Joh[ann] Wallishausser, k.k. privil. Book Dealer and Book Printer,
Neuburgergasse No. 1177: *Sappho* Tragedy in five acts, by Franz Grillparzer. Vienna, 1819. Edition
in 12mo, on postal-thin paper, in boards […] 2 fl. 30 kr. […]." The same advertisement appeared on
March 4, 8, and 12, 1819, but did not appear on Friday, March 26, 1819. *Sappho* had been performed
at the Burgtheater on April 21, 1818 (see Hadamowsky, *1811–1974*, p. 529). It was also performed on
November 15 and December 13, 1819, but the poster did not list the author's name (Theater Zettel,
Bibliothek, Österreichisches Theatermuseum; courtesy of librarian Othmar Barnert).
  Neuburgergasse No. 1177 was renumbered as 1111 in 1821 (Behsel, p. 30), and was also the address
for Traeg's music shop, and the residences of amateur pianist Albin Pfaller and author Ignaz von
Mosel.—TA
[27] Excerpt from an advertisement in the *Intelligenzblatt*, No. 69 (Friday, March 26, 1819), p. 590:
"Just appeared from Carl Gerold's book dealership in Vienna, Stephansplatz, on the left corner of
Goldschmidgasse, No. 666: *Nützliche und interessante Militär-Skizzen für Soldaten und ihre Freunde
im österreichischen Kaiserstaate* (Useful and Interesting Military Sketches for Soldiers and their Friends
in the Austrian Imperial State), by Johann v. Nucé, I.R. Captain, vol. 2, price unbound 4 fl. 45 kr.
W.W., sewn binding, in color boards, as was vol. 1, 5 fl. W.W." The same advertisement appeared
(among others) on April 1, 6, and 19, 1819.—KH/TA
[28] Excerpt from an advertisement in the *Intelligenzblatt*, No. 69 (March 26, 1819), p. 592: "Just
arrived at Franz Wimmer, book dealer, Dorotheergasse, across from the *Goldenes Jägerhorn* (Golden
Hunting Horn): J.M. Sailer, *Rede von der Priesterweihung* (Lectures from Priestly Consecration), size
8vo, Landshut, 1817, 40 kr." The same advertisement appeared on March 12 and April 5, 1819. See
also Beethoven's note about organ playing before the Kyrie of a Mass, possibly the first thoughts
concerning the *Missa solemnis*, Op. 123, on Blatt 10r below.—KH/TA
[29] The Gesellschaft der Musikfreunde owned many instruments; one of the musicians who played
one must have borrowed it without consulting the organization.—TA

BEETHOVEN [presumably at his apartment, Landstrasser Hauptstrasse No. 268; possibly the morning of Tuesday, March 30]:

Paper.
Barber's razor.
Archduke's receipt.[30]
Watch.
Suspenders.
Blotting paper.
    [Blatt 8v]
Shoe-horn for Karl.
Chamber pot.

NEPHEW KARL [possibly at Kudlich's school in the Erdberggasse]:

<1¾ yards for the [dress] coat
⅔>
1¼ yards for the trousers
2¾ yards for the coat

BEETHOVEN: 24 fl. per yard [*Elle*]   68 fl.
                    Maker's payment   18
                                        ———
                                         86

[Blatt 9r]

[presumably at a restaurant or beer house; afternoon of Tuesday, March 30:]
18 kr. per tankard of beer. [Blatt 9v]
[reading the *Wiener Zeitung* of March 30:]
At Schrämbl's, Dorotheergasse [No.] 1182: 2nd printing of *Cours-Tabellen, etc.*, sewn binding, 45 kr.[31]

---

[30] Presumably concerning the pension [i.e., annual allowance] that Beethoven received from the Archduke Rudolph, as well as from Princes Lobkowitz and Kinsky. See Blatt 15r below.—KH

[31] Excerpt from an advertisement in the *Wiener Zeitung*, No. 72 (March 30, 1819), p. 288: "Appeared from Schrämbl's book publishing house, Dorotheergasse No. 1182, *Cours-Tabellen*, in a second, newly revised edition, in which, according to the prevailing rate of exchange, one can quickly know how much an amount in *Conventionsmünze* (C.M.) corresponds to in paper bills (*Wiener Währung*, W.W.) and, conversely, how much an amount in paper bills corresponds to in *Conventionsmünze*; at the same time, one can perceive how high a Bank Note corresponds to certain exchange rates in *Conventionsmünze* ..., sewn binding, 45 kr." The same advertisement appeared on April 14, 1819. In general, 1 fl. C.M. was equal to about 2½ fl. W.W. Beethoven would have found such a table helpful in converting most of the prices noted here to the other currency.—KH/TA

NEPHEW KARL: Count Dunin.[32] Dunin. // Now you will go to eat immediately, if he comes.

[Blatt 10r]

BEETHOVEN [at a restaurant or coffee house; possibly the early afternoon of Friday, April 2]:[33] The organist plays the Kyrie prelude loudly, and then comes down to *piano* [just] before the Kyrie.[34] [//]

Wolfsohn on the Bauernmarkt, No. 619 [*sic*]; k.k. Provincial Factory.[35]

[Blatt 10v]

[walking through the Stephansplatz, examining the following two books at Gerold's book shop:][36]

No. 1: Fr. König, *Die leichteste Art den Kindern das rechnen auf eine angenehme Art bey zubringen* [The Easiest Way to Teach Children Arithmetic in a Pleasant Manner], etc., etc., 2nd improved edition, 2 parts, 8vo, Prague, 4 fl. 30 kr. W.W.[37]

No. 2: H.A. Kerndörffer's *Materialien für den ersten Unterricht in der Declamation, zur Bildung eines guten, richtigen, u[nd] schönen Mündlichen Vortrags,* [Materials for the First Instruction in Declamation, for the Development of Good, Correct, and Pleasant Reciting Skills], 8vo, Leipzig, 1 fl. 18 kr. W.W.[38] [Blatt 11r]

No. 1 and No. 2 may both be had at Gerold's on Stephansplatz.

---

[32] Presumably a member of the Dunin-Borkowski family. The *Hof- und Staats-Schematismus,* 1819, lists three individuals under Borkowski, and none under Dunin. It cannot be determined who is meant here. See Wurzbach, vol. 2, pp. 67–69.—KH/TA

[33] Beethoven may have stopped for coffee or even *beer* at the *Birne,* or he may have waited until he reached the walled City, reading the *Intelligenzblatt* briefly while there. He then seemingly went about his errands, which took him to Gerold's bookshop on the Stephansplatz and possibly to Wolfsohn's on the Bauernmarkt, only a block or two north, and he ultimately stopped at the same or different coffee house late in the afternoon, reading the *Intelligenzblatt* again.—TA

[34] Beethoven may have been thinking about this while walking from his apartment into the walled City. This may be the first musical indication that Beethoven had been commissioned to compose the *Missa solemnis,* Op. 123, for the consecration of Archduke Rudolph as Cardinal-Archbishop of Olmütz. See also the reference to Sailer's book on Blätter 7v–8r, above.—TA

[35] Excerpt from an advertisement in the *Intelligenzblatt,* No. 75 (April 2, 1819), p. 645: "Announcement. The great turnover of my newly invented machines, trusses, and bandages gives me sufficient proof that complete trust would in general be given to me […] I.R. priv. provincial factory, on the Bauernmarkt, No. 629." The same advertisement also appeared on March 27 and April 21, 1819. Concerning Sigmund Wolfsohn (1767–1852), see Heft 6, Blatt 18r: gives the address correctly as No. 629; the factory made surgical instruments.—KH

[36] Beethoven himself says so on Blatt 11r, after the second item.—TA

[37] An advertisement with this wording cannot be traced. See Kayser, vol. 3, pp. 389–391: Franz König, *Die leichteste Art, den Kindern das Rechnen [sic—TA] auf eine angenehme Weise beizubringen, …* 3 parts, 8vo, Prague, 1815/1819.—KH

[38] An advertisement with this wording cannot be traced. See Kayser, vol. 3, p. 330: Heinrich August Kerndörffer, *Materialien für den ersten Unterricht in der Declamation zur Bildung eines guten, richtigen und schönen Vortrags,* 8vo, Leipzig, 1815, 2nd ed., 1820.—KH

[at a restaurant or coffee house, perhaps the *Birne*, reading the *Intelligenzblatt* again; late afternoon of Friday, April 2:]

Vorlesungen über Akustik u[nd] Meteormassen [Lectures on Acoustics and the Meteoric Masses][39] by Dr. Chladny.[40] N.B. It would be good to speak with him.

[Blatt 11v]

COURT OFFICIAL OF ARCHDUKE RUDOLPH [at the Archduke's apart-ments,[41] presumably in the Hofburg; possibly midday or early afternoon of Saturday, April 3]: Yesterday morning at 5 o'clock, His I[mperial] H[ighness] had an attack of his usual illness,[42] and is already somewhat better today. I shall have you informed when you can come, and tomorrow I shall tell His Highness that you were here today. [//]

BEETHOVEN [at a coffee house, reading the current issue of the *Wiener Zeitung*; probably the late afternoon of Saturday, April 3]:

Geistliche Übungen für 3 Tage [Spiritual Lessons for 3 Days], poetry by L.Z. Werner, 8vo, Vienna, 1 fl. 30 kr., at Wallishauser's.[43]

[Blatt 12r]
[seemingly looking at a two-day-old issue of the *Intelligenzblatt*:]

A lady from an upstanding house wishes to find employment as a companion or

---

[39] Excerpt from an advertisement in the *Intelligenzblatt*, No. 75 (April 2, 1819), p. 645: "*Vorlesungen über Akustik und Meteormassen*. With Imperial permission, Dr. Chladni will give a course of 12 to 14 lectures; [...] beginning on April 14, the Wednesday after Easter." The same advertisement appeared on March 27 and 31 and April 7, 9, and 13, as well as in Kanne's *Wiener AmZ* 3, No. 28 (April 7, 1819), p. 227.—KH/TA

[40] Ernst Florens Friedrich Chladni (1756–1827), physicist, discoverer of the *Klangfiguren* (acoustic figures) named for him, as well as inventor of new musical instruments (the *Euphon* and the *Klavizylinder*). In 1802 he published his textbook *Die Akustik* and, in 1817, *Neue Beiträge zur Akustik*. See Fritz Winckel, "Chladni," *MGG*, vol. 2, cols. 1216–1218; Sachs, pp. 133 and 218.—KH

[41] This entry was written in ink (rather than the customary pencil); therefore it must have been written in a reception room or office that had a desk with pen and ink.—KH/TA

[42] Beethoven's patron and pupil, the Archduke Rudolph (1788–1831) suffered from epilepsy. See Kagan; Frimmel, *Handbuch*, II, p. 85.—KH/TA

[43] Excerpt from an advertisement in the *Wiener Zeitung*, No. 74 (Saturday, April 3, 1819), p. 290: "To be had at Joh. Bapt. Wallishausser: *Geistliche Uebungen für drey Tage*, poetry by Fr. Ludw. Zacar. Werner, 8vo, Vienna, 1818, 1 fl. 30 kr." Although this advertisement appeared several times, this entry can only concern the issue cited, since Beethoven's note is in the immediate vicinity of the conversation concerning the concert of April 4, 1819 (Blatt 13v below).

Friedrich Ludwig Zacharias Werner (1768–1823), a priest and convert from Protestantism, whose polemic political sermons were then popular in Vienna (see Heft 4, Blatt 42v). Perhaps Beethoven considered sending this booklet as a "get well" gift for Rudolph, but the composer and his closest associates (excluding Bernard) ultimately considered Werner to be uncomfortably extreme in his reactionary views. See Clive, p. 395.—KH/TA

housekeeper for only room and board, speaks French. Whoever wants to speak with her should leave his address, sealed, with the inscription E. C., at the tobacco shop in the Plankengasse Casino, No. 1163.[44]

BEETHOVEN [possibly at his apartment; possibly mid-to-late morning of Monday, April 5]:[45]

Waterproof cloth[46]
Blotting paper
Lind[47]
K[arl?], about carrying handkerchiefs in his pants—about wash [underwear??].
Fr. K. [—] Wash-line
Obladen [wafer cookies] for K[arl]
Sugar tin

[Blatt 12v]

166 fl. 40 kr. is half of the pension.[48]

$$
\begin{array}{r}
166 \\
27 \\
27 \\
\hline
220
\end{array}
$$

It is to be considered, meanwhile, that the pension will be lost after her death or marriage. //

[44] Advertisement, *Intelligenzblatt*, No. 74 (Thursday, April 1, 1819), p. 633. The same advertisement also appeared on March 27 and 30, 1819. In 1819 No. 1163 was also considered to be in the Spiegelgasse, one door west of Plankengasse (see Behsel, p. 33).—KH/TA

[45] There is no particular dividing line at this point, but (unless he made this list while sitting in the restaurant or coffee house on Saturday, April 3), Beethoven seemed more accustomed to making such lists before leaving his apartment for his day's business affairs. Since he would not be conducting such business on Sunday, April 4, it is more likely that he made this list on Monday morning, April 5.—TA

[46] Original: *Barchet*, Beethoven's spelling of the French participle *bâché* (covered with tarpaulin) or the noun *bâche* (tarpaulin, oilcloth, or waterproof cloth in general). See Clifton *et al.*, *A New French-English and English-French Dictionary*, p. 86. Beethoven also mentions the term, this time in the context of being used as a (possibly external) lining for trousers, in Heft 6, Blatt 29r.—TA

[47] Joseph Lind (1773–1837), in 1820, one of the most respected tailors in Vienna. See Frimmel, *Handbuch*, I, pp. 363–364; also Heft 5, Blatt 62v.—KH

[48] The pension of Karl's mother, Johanna van Beethoven, which would provide financial support for Karl's education. This was the government pension that she received (probably as the result of an application) after the death of Beethoven's brother Carl on November 15, 1815. He had worked in the Treasury since 1800 and therefore would have received a benefit based on ten years of experience, since he had not yet passed the next milestone of twenty years. See Thayer-Deiters-Riemann, IV, p. 550.—KH/TA

NEPHEW KARL [presumably at Kudlich's school in the Erdberggasse; possibly late morning on Monday, April 5]: Old Frau v[on] Kudlich is already here. [//] [Blatt 13r] He already told her that she [Karl's mother Johanna] is not to come here so often. //

OLIVA[49] [at a restaurant or coffee house; probably early afternoon, Monday, April 5]: & Puts on airs.[50]—Is the oratorio [text][51] finished? [//] I cannot imagine how he [Bernard] occupies himself.—His professional work amounts to nothing, & otherwise he doesn't do anything else, and yet he always talks about so much work and so many business matters. //

He gives protection.[52] [//] [Blatt 13v]
[reporting on Clement's concert, Palm Sunday evening, April 4:]
Poor stuff, empty,—without any effect.[53] Your theme was in bad hands. He played 15 to 20 variations with a great deal of monotony, & played a fermata at [the end of]

---

[49] Franz Oliva (b. Vienna, November 24, 1786; d. St. Petersburg, 1848), a friend of Beethoven's since 1809. In early May 1811 he had delivered Beethoven's letter of April 12 to poet Johann Wolfgang von Goethe in Weimar. The art collector Sulpice Boisserée was visiting Goethe, and described Oliva as "a short, thin, black-clothed little man in silken stockings, with a completely hunched back." During his stay there, Oliva also played some of Beethoven's piano compositions for Goethe and his guests.
Oliva's Viennese application for a passport (dated April 11, 1811) indicates that he had a "film [Fell] over the right eye" (probably due to smallpox as a child), but no mention of any spinal deformity.
At the time of these entries (April, 1819), Oliva had been a bookkeeper at the firm of the Offenheimer Brothers (also known as Offenheimer & Herz), Bauernmarkt No. 620 [renumbered as 581 in 1821]. From December 16, 1819, he was in the wholesale/banking house of Mayer & Landauer; and, from July, 1820, with Joseph Biedermann (see Heft 11, inside front cover). In late December, 1820, he accompanied Biedermann on a journey to Russia, and then settled in St. Petersburg as a language teacher, married, and had a daughter. He died during a wide-spread cholera epidemic in 1848.
See Boisserée, vol. 1, pp. 111–113; Conscriptions-Bogen, Stadt, No. 731; Passprotokolle, 1801–1816; 1811, fol. 51, No. 95 (both in Wiener Stadt- und Landesarchiv); Frimmel, Handbuch, I, pp. 465–467; Thayer-Deiters-Riemann, III, pp. 131–132; Clive, pp. 250–252; Heft 11, Blätter 66v–67r; Heft 61, Blatt 11v; Brandenburg, Briefwechsel, Nos. 617 and 654; Behsel, p. 18; Ullrich, pp. 7–29.—KH/TA

[50] This paragraph concerns newspaper editor Joseph Carl Bernard. Through a series of conversation book entries over many months, it becomes obvious that Oliva does not like Bernard.—TA

[51] In 1815 the Gesellschaft der Musikfreunde had commissioned Beethoven to write an oratorio with a libretto by Bernard, Der Sieg des Kreuzes. He showed Beethoven parts of the libretto by early 1820, but finished it only in 1823. Beethoven then rejected it early in 1824.—KH/TA

[52] Possibly a reference to journals including the Aglaja, Schickh's Wiener Zeitschrift, etc., with which Bernard was associated in one way or another.—TA

[53] The conversation in this paragraph concerns an Akademie [concert] that Franz Clement (1780–1842) gave at the Theater an der Wien on April 4, 1819, in which he played a movement from a violin concerto of his own as well as an introduction and variations for violin on a "new theme by Beethoven." See the Allgemeine musikalische Zeitung 21, No. 29 (April 10, 1819), cols. 234–235 (noting that Clement's concert took place in the evening); Kanne's Wiener AmZ 3, No. 27 (April 3, 1819), col. 221.—KH/TA

each one. [//] You can imagine what one had to endure. [//] He has lost a great deal, & seems too old to entertain with his acrobatics on the fiddle. // [Blatt 14r]

Can I be of help to you in some way? // Have you already spoken concerning the journey to Bavaria?[54] [//] But because you are not the guardian? [//] Then later, you can be restrained by the Magistrat and [will] have to bring him back. [//] He cannot be accepted into the higher schools if has not studied in the lower ones in this country. [//] In any case, it would be good to make your precise intentions about this known beforehand. [//] [Blatt 14v] Lilienfeld would therefore be good.[55] //

I may not eat any of these cold dishes.[56] [//]

He [Karl] appears to me an almost innocent sacrifice to extraneous schemes. // He should be completely separated from the influence of his mother, and be treated very *strictly*. [//] [Blatt 15r] Just begin judiciously, however, because this hot-headed woman would create quite a noise here if everything were not in order, and you know how people are inclined to take everything in a bad light here. // You just need the Archduke Ludwig,[57] because the Empress is absent—. You can promise to bring him back in several years, so that [Blatt 15v] he can continue his studies here; then it will appear insignificant, and you will be successful.[58]—and with the petition directly to the Imperial office;—the Archduke Rudolph[59] can deliver it to his brother. // She [Johanna] has too much power over him [Karl]—he may know *absolutely nothing* himself, however, [Blatt 16r] otherwise the matter is half-done without any benefit. // That allows [Karl] to make up for lost time, and in Bavaria, they speak more French in general than they do here. // But away from here— and vain about his person. [//] Women are very fine—and primarily in household matters. // But to look after a young person demands perhaps more than they are able to do .... [Blatt 16v]

---

[54] The plan of sending nephew Karl to Professor Sailer in Landshut. See Blatt 5v above.—KH

[55] Lilienfeld, a town ca. 12 miles south of St. Pölten, and ca. 35 miles southwest of Vienna, with a Cistercian school and monastery. See Raffelsperger, vol. 4, pp. 281–282.—KH/TA

[56] From several such entries, it becomes obvious that Oliva (who was also a hunchback) has a sensitive stomach; he customarily ate his midday meal in a boarding house near the famous *Rother Igel* restaurant in the Tuchlauben, and the two lady proprietors of the boarding house often prepared special meals for him. See Blatt 13r above.—TA

[57] Ludwig, Archduke of Austria (1784–1864), brother of Emperor Franz I, was a member of the State Council and, after 1822, General Director of Artillery. He substituted for the Emperor when he was absent and dealt with a part of State business. In the latter half of May 1819 Beethoven asked Archduke Rudolph to intercede with his brother, Archduke Ludwig, for support in his efforts to send nephew Karl to Landshut for education. See Anderson, No. 946; Brandenburg, *Briefwechsel*, No. 1300; Thayer-Deiters-Riemann, IV, pp. 141–142; Wurzbach, vol. 6, pp. 447–448.—KH/TA

[58] Oliva uses the term "reussieren."—KH

[59] Rudolph (1788–1831) was the youngest brother of Emperor Franz.—KH/TA

He has rapidly worked his way up. He is your fellow countryman. // Tettenborn[60] became very rich from it, and the Hamburgers poor. [//] He was full of debts, and now he is in glittering circumstances. // I find it expensive here. //

With wine and coffee, it comes to 50 fl. per month. [//] [Blatt 17r]

His Excellency, Baron Reichmann;[61] Paumgarten.[62] [Blatt 17v]

[End of conversation, afternoon of Monday, April 5.]

BEETHOVEN **[presumably visiting Karl at Kudlich's school in the Erdberggasse, but writing, so as not to be overheard; possibly Tuesday, April 6]**: Where is he?

NEPHEW KARL **[answering]**: <left> He's left for Klafterbrunn.[63]

BEETHOVEN **[continuing]**: Are these always the usual conditions around you? [//] [Blatt 18r] Are there nothing but students here? Isn't there a private tutor here?

NEPHEW KARL: Mostly Kudlich himself, or the classes are filled by teachers, who supervise for the time that they are present. [Blatt 18v]

[Beethoven leaves Kudlich's school.]

LIND[64] **[presumably at his tailor shop, Hohe Brücke; possibly early afternoon of Wednesday, April 7]**:[65]

---

[60] Baron Friedrich Karl von Tettenborn (1778–1845). An officer, he came to Vienna on February 20, 1819, as Baden's ambassador and remained in this post until his death. In 1824 he left the military service and received extensive estates in Westphalia. During the Napoleonic Wars, Hamburg was occupied by the French. Tettenborn, in Russian service under Czar Alexander, conquered Hamburg on March 18, 1813, but on May 30 had to vacate it again. See *Allgemeine Deutsche Biographie*, vol. 37, pp. 596–598; *Wiener Zeitung*, No. 43 (February 23, 1819), p. 171; Wurzbach, vol. 44, pp. 39–41.—KH

[61] August Reichmann, Baron of Hochkirchen (ca. 1754–1828), Privy Councillor, President of the Lower Austrian Regional Government and of the Academy of the Arts. See *Hof- und Staats-Schematismus*, 1819, I, p. 380; Schmidt, *Nekrolog*, vol. 6, pp. 979–980.—KH

[62] This reference remains unclear. Possibly Baron Johann Baptist von Paumgarten (1770–1849), an officer married to Therese von Beck (b. 1772). See Wurzbach, vol. 21, pp. 372–374. Or possibly Reichsritter Karl von Paumgarten (1796–1877), whose father Sigismund was Court and Legal Advocate, and who was married to a woman from the Sonnleithner family. He himself was in the service of Count von Hoyos. See *Allgemeine deutsche Biographie*, vol. 25, p. 300. Or possibly Ferdinand Ritter von Paumgarten, official in the Emperor's Privy Chamber. See *Hof- und Staats-Schematismus*, 1819, I, p. 194.—KH

[63] Klafterbrunn, a small castle near Lilienfeld, ca. 8 miles south of St. Pölten, in which instruction for boys occasionally took place. See Raffelsperger, vol. 3, p. 923.—KH/TA

[64] Same handwriting as in Heft 5, Blatt 62v. Lind's shop and residence were in the City, on the east side of Hohe Brücke, No. 149 [renumbered as 142 in 1821], at the corner of Renngasse.—KH

[65] Lind's shop at the east end of Renngasse in the City was roughly an hour's walk north of Kudlich's school in suburban Erdberg. It is unlikely that Beethoven, upset as he was with the neglect that he perceived at Kudlich's, would have walked directly to Lind's shop on the same day. It is much more likely that he would have walked into the City the next day, as posited here.—TA

White: 2 fl. 18 kr.

Blue: 2   30

BEETHOVEN [presumably at a restaurant or coffee house, reading the current issue of the *Intelligenzblatt*; afternoon of Wednesday, April 7]:

For Sale: Organ with 3 registers [stops], for 160 fl.; inquire at Alservorstadt, at the end of Höfergasse, No. 178, in the 1st floor [2nd floor, American].[66]

[For sale] on the Stephansplatz, next to the Bishop's Palace: *Gründliches Kochbuch zum tägl[ichen] Gebrauche* [Fundamental Cookbook for Daily Use], etc., etc., [Blatt 19r] 8vo, Vienna, 1 fl.[67]

No. 682,[68] at the Lugeck.[69]

Knife.

Sugar tin.

Pen knife.

Combs.

Snuffing tobacco.

Neckerchiefs.

Obladen [wafer cookies].

[Blatt 19v]

---

[66] *Intelligenzblatt*, No. 79 (April 7, 1819), p. 693 (Advertisements). The same advertisement also appeared on April 9 and 13, 1819. Alservorstadt No. 178 [renumbered as 201 in 1821 was the building just east of the Schwarzspanierhaus, No. 177 [renumbered as 200 in 1821], where Beethoven would die in 1827. No. 178 was a large building that also faced Währinger Strasse (Behsel, p. 201).—KH/TA

[67] Excerpt from an advertisement in the *Intelligenzblatt*, No. 79 (April 7, 1819), p. 698: "To be had in the publisher's shop of Grund's Book Printing Shop, on Stephansplatz, next to the Bishop's Palace: [title as above, plus *for all Kinds of the Situations. Containing a Collection of the Newest Dishes, including Soups, Meat Dishes, Grain and Fasting Dishes, Fish, Cakes, Boiled Dishes, Pickled Foods, and Juices, Creams, Compots, and Frozen Punches*]. 8vo, Vienna, 1 fl."

Leopold Grund had his printing shop in the Landstrasse, Gärtnergasse No. 509, and his book sales shop on the Stephansplatz, No. 919 [renumbered as 868 in 1821], one building south of the Bishop's Palace; see Redl, 1817, p. 224. Then as now, the large building also faced the Wollzeile; even today it includes a book shop facing Stephansplatz. Grund's shop also mentioned on Blatt 21v below.—KH/TA

[68] At No. 682 in the City was the old weighing house, a building that went from the Haarmarkt through to the Rothgässel. Several Magistrat Councillors lived in this building, among them Mathias Tuscher. See Groner, p. 143; *Hof- und Staats-Schematismus*, 1820, I, p. 662.

In Heft 7, Blatt 54v, quoted by Solomon, p. 262 (citing Nohl's *Leben*, rather than the available Köhler edition of the *Konversationshefte*), Janschikh asked Beethoven why he was on the Haarmarkt recently and the composer supposedly answered "Blame it on the flesh." While Janschikh referred to nephew Karl as "Flesh and Blood" (see Heft 6, Blatt 45r), the phrase *Culpam transferre in alium* was actually written, not by Beethoven, but by Janschikh himself.—KH/TA

[69] No. 682 was located on the north side of Haarmarkt, two buildings east of Lugeck (called Lug Eck here). Therefore, given the shopping list that follows, Beethoven probably intended a shopping errand in the building, rather than visiting Tuscher. The sugar tin and *Obladen* (cookies) already appeared on a shopping list on Blatt 12r (possibly Monday, April 5).—TA

OLIVA [at Lind's tailor shop, Hohe Brücke, with Beethoven; no later than Good Friday, April 9, 1819]: The fine ones are too expensive. He wants 3 fl. 30 [kr.] apiece. 1 fl. 45 [kr.] apiece.

BEETHOVEN [replying, so as not to be heard]: Where one used to cost 2 fl.

OLIVA: $\dfrac{2 \cdot 3^{70}}{6}$ C v B[71] 2 fl. 30 [kr.] apiece

BEETHOVEN [column]:	OLIVA [column]:	BEETHOVEN [column]:
1 fl. 45 kr.	10 fl.	2 fl. 30 kr.
1 45		2 30
1 45		2 30
1 45	32	2 30
1 45	6	2 30
1 45	192	2 30
7 fl. 30 kr.[72]	9.	15 fl.

BEETHOVEN [continuing]:
  10 fl. 30 kr.
  15

[Blatt 20r]

OLIVA [more computations]:

  2 fl.   2/5[73]
  6
  ——
  12
  2 fl. 24 kr.
  14 fl. 24 kr.

---

[70] Oliva was indicating that 2 fl. 30 kr. C.M. was equal to 6 fl. W.W. See a similar conversion on Blatt 20r below.—TA

[71] Nephew Karl's initials (Carl van Beethoven), probably to be stitched on all of his clothing purchased at Lind's, to identify them at Kudlich's school.—TA

[72] The German edition reads "1 fl. 30 kr." here. Beethoven would have known that the initial number had to be a "7," and the two numbers are easily confused when transcribing out of context. Beethoven's column to the right represents twice this amount.—TA

[73] As on Blatt 19v above, this figure indicates that 2 fl. C.M. was approximately equal to 5 fl. W.W. Actually, 1fl. C.M. was equal to 2½ fl. W.W., thus the 2 fl. 24 kr. added on after the initial multiplication.—TA

$$
\begin{array}{rl}
9 & 36 \\
1 & 30^{74} \\
 & 16 \\
 & \underline{3} \\
26 & 6 \\
 & \underline{36} \\
26 & 42
\end{array}
$$

[Blatt 20v]

[continuing:] You should get everything by Sunday morning [Easter Sunday, April 11]; he wants to give you a *Gillet*,[75] made *in full*, for 9 fl. This doesn't seem too expensive to me, but I want to try to negotiate. [Blatt 21r] He doesn't want to give you one for 50 fl.—but I believe that he ought to give it to you for 52 fl. The cloth,[76] however, is very beautiful, & you are not being overcharged.[77]

[End of the visit to Lind's tailor shop.]

[Blatt 21v]

BEETHOVEN [**presumably in a coffee house; late afternoon of Saturday, April 10**]: Zeller's *Vortheile zur Kopfrechnung, für Schulen der 2ten Klasse*—8 fl. 36 kr.

Mein Verfahrung bey dem Kopfrechnung, für Schüler der 2ten Klasse—8 fl. 24 kr., [for sale] at Grund's Book Publishing House, on the Stephansplatz, next to the Bishop's Palace.[78]

[Blatt 22r]

BERNARD [**probably at a restaurant, possibly Seelig's *Zur Stadt Triest*,[79] inconsiderately filling up only the *recto* sides of Blätter 22 through 30; possibly**

---

[74] Oliva made changes in his computations. This "1 fl. 30" was originally "2 fl. 30;" "16" was originally "33." The single "3" below them probably represented "30" without a zero in the right-most position. In any case, Oliva's sum, while close, is not an accurate representation of all the variables.—KH/TA

[75] *Gilet* (French), a vest or waistcoat. See Grimm, vol. 4, col. 7502.—KH/TA

[76] *Zeug*: designation for clothing materials in general, and especially thin material. See Grimm, vol. 25, col. 835.—KH

[77] *Überhalten*, Viennese expression.—KH

[78] Excerpt from an advertisement in the *Intelligenzblatt*, No. 82 (April 10, 1819), p. 730. The same advertisement also appeared on May 7, 1819. For details on Grund's shop, see Blätter 18v–19r above.—KH/TA

[79] See the reference to a cuttlefish, possibly calamari (squid), at the very end of this conversation on Blatt 30r below. By November/December, 1819, Bernard and his friends (including Beethoven) often congregated at Heinrich Seelig's wine house, restaurant, and grocery *Zur Stadt Triest*, at the

sometime on Easter Sunday, April 11]: Court Councillor Ohms.[80] // He says: You ought to make a petition to the High Police Direction, in which the motives are stated briefly. Then it ought to be said that one wants to take the boy to [stay with] relatives in Ingolstadt for a year,[81] in order to distance him from the present circumstances. With this petition, we ought to go to Herr Court Councillor Laroche in the Passport Office,[82] or if he is not there, **[continues on Blatt 23r]**

[Blatt 22v][83]

OLIVA **[finding the *verso* page blank after Bernard's conversation; possibly on Easter Monday, April 12]**: The people have their own horses and will generally drive you out inexpensively.[84]

[Blatt 23r]

BERNARD **[continuing directly]**: then to the secretary Kreibich,[85] and say that we have come from the Police Administration. Perhaps the petition will have to go to the Government Administration, but the matter will encounter no difficulty. I believe that Herr von Tuscher [guardian] will agree, and this could facilitate it even more. [//] [Blatt 23v: no writing] [Blatt 24r] Court Councillor Ohms says that it is not necessary to name Professor Sailer, and one simply ought to state that the boy will be taken to [stay with] relatives for one or two years.[86] [//] Concerning this case, the Police Administration will merely be asked whether they have nothing

northwest corner of Plankengasse and Neuer Markt. Seelig occasionally imported oysters, and it is possible that he imported calamari as well.—TA

[80] Anton von Ohms (b. Erfurt, Prussia, ca. 1763; d. Vienna, November 9, 1843) was a *Hofrat* (Court Councillor) in the Imperial Police and Censor's Bureau, and subordinate to Police President Count von Sedlnitzky. See *Hof- und Staats-Schematismus*, 1819, I, p. 267; Schmidt, *Nekrolog*, vol. 21, p. 1260; Totenbeschauprotokoll. 1843, O, fol. 7r, November 9 (Wiener Stadt- und Landesarchiv).—KH/TA

[81] Beethoven had no relatives in Ingolstadt or Landshut. Bernard is therefore advising the composer to lie to the Police. See also Blatt 24r below.—TA

[82] Philipp-Viktor La-Roze, Court Councillor and Administrative Councillor in the High Police Direction and Director at the Passport Conscription Office. See *Hof- und Staats-Schematismus*, 1819, I, pp. 591–592.—KH

[83] From Blatt 22r through Blatt 30r Bernard writes only on the *recto* side of the sheet.—TA

[84] Oliva obviously wrote this entry at a different time than its physical location suggests. While conversing on Blatt 33r below, probably the next day, Oliva probably found an empty page later, in between Bernard's *recto*-only entries.

Beethoven is still living in suburban Landstrasse, but already seems to be contemplating a move to summer lodgings well beyond the *Linie* or away from customary public coach routes. He begins looking for lodgings by Blatt 33, and ultimately spends the summer in relatively remote Mödling.—TA

[85] Joseph Kreibich, Secretary of the princely household of Duke Albrecht of Sachsen-Teschen. He lived in the ducal House, No. 1229. Bernard spells his name "Kreiblich." See *Hof- und Staats-Schematismus*, 1819, I, p. 187.—KH

[86] As on Blatt 22, above, Bernard proposes that Beethoven lie to achieve his purpose.—TA

against it! [//] [Blatt 24v: no writing] [Blatt 25r] If Tuscher agrees, there will be no obstacle. [//] If the Police Administration knows that you have resigned from the guardianship, then they can interfere with the matter. I believe that it ought to be pursued candidly to the end. [//] He will certainly have it done gladly. [Blatt 25v: no writing] [Blatt 26r] If need be, we can speak with him beforehand, ….

BEETHOVEN [writing so as not to be overheard]: Perhaps he is not thinking of the guardianship, or even the guardian, at all.

BERNARD [continuing]: I have no time. [//]

So where have you left Kanne?[87] He wrote an article for Schickh,[88] in which there appears a parable about bugs. Schickh [Blatt 26v: no writing] [Blatt 27r] paid him a hundred Gulden in advance, and now cannot use the essay in the [Zeitung für] die elegante Welt. [//] Aesthetically he has gone to seed in the taverns. [//]

The most clever and most decisive officials are in the Police Office. [//] Court Councillor Ohms is the closest to the Police President. [//] [Blatt 27v: no writing] [Blatt 28r] I believe that the matter is very much exaggerated. [//]

Don't you know who the other surgeon is? [//] That's not necessary. The matter will probably be managed. [//] It is in the Landstrasse. Dr. Mayer,[89] who has combined a sulphur-fumigation institution with vibrations; by these means, he has already healed several [Blatt 28v: no writing] [Blatt 29r] whose hearing suffered, and [in whom] there was no organic defect. Among others, he has healed a woman who was without hearing for 15 years. [//] But you have taken all the treatments that you have done [?]. [//]

The whole thing, though, is always your concern, and T[uscher] is in some way to remove only *pro forma* about the collisions with the mother. [Blatt 29v: no writing]

---

[87] Friedrich August Kanne (1778–1833), writer, composer, and music critic, was born in Delitzsch, Saxony, and (like Schickh, below) entered the service of Prince Joseph Franz Maximilian von Lobkowitz in Vienna in 1808, but was soon active as a free-lance writer. The creative, multi-faceted and gifted man was editor of the *Wiener Allgemeine musikalische Zeitung*, and wrote reports for Bäuerle's *Allgemeine Theater-Zeitung* and Schickh's *Wiener Zeitschrift für Kunst, Literatur, Theater und Mode*, among others. See Frimmel, *Handbuch*, I, pp. 247–248; Clive, pp. 181–182; Ferdinand von Seyfried, pp. 205–207; Wurzbach, vol. 10, pp. 438–440.—KH

[88] Johann Schickh (1770–1835), "municipal dealer in small silk and white fashion wares" and founder of the *Wiener Zeitschrift für Kunst, Literatur, Theater und Mode*, which he directed/edited from 1816 to 1835. The silk business and the newspaper office were in the House "Zu den Grazien" on the Kohlmarkt No. 268. In 1807 Schickh came from Leipzig to Vienna, where (like Kanne, above) he at first entered the service of Prince Joseph Franz Maximilian von Lobkowitz. See Frimmel, *Handbuch*, II, pp. 103–104; Redl, 1818, p. 36; Wurzbach, vol. 29, p. 266; Clive, p. 308.—KH/TA

[89] Dr. Carl Joseph Mayer, Doctor of Medicine and Surgery, practicing physician, lived at Landstrasse No. 317. Concerning the Schwefelräucherungsanstalt (sulphur-fumigation institution), see Blatt 47r below. See also Phillebois, p. 6.—KH

[Blatt 30r] I have already known Leitenberger[90] since my time in Prague; but I don't know whether he was here recently. In terms of its education and knowledge, the family is one of the most prominent.

It is a cuttlefish.[91] [//] [Blatt 30v: no writing]

[End of Bernard's *recto*-side conversation; possibly on Easter Sunday, April 11.]

[Blatt 31r]

OLIVA [at an undetermined location; possibly Easter Monday, April 12]: Someone will make trouble for you later, and what use is it, then, if you have to bring the boy back?[92] It appears as if the mother has found a channel in order to negotiate with Tuscher, then, where possible, you should notify him first if you have the passport. [//] Court Councillor Ohms knows everything exactly; since he thinks [that] it would work, there is nothing more to doubt. [//] [Blatt 31v] What is his name? [Blatt 32r] In these places, life is entirely different than for us. // Merely say very simply: Since conditions make it desirable for you to take your nephew away for a few years, then, most submissively, however, you are requesting a passport for yourself and for him,—otherwise [say] nothing. //

I am so hoarse that I can hardly say a word out loud.[93] [//] [Blatt 32v] It is finally at a point where it does not help. // Where does this doctor live? //

If he, too, makes some trouble, then they are immediately removed if you summon the High Police Office. // I thought that you wanted to take Karl to Landshut, not to Ingolstadt. [//] [Blatt 33r]

On Sunday, though, the fiacres[94] will be more expensive;—we could drive only as far as the *Linie*,[95] & then go further by foot?[96] // Then in no case should you take

---

[90] Franz Leitenberger, manufacturer in Cosmanoss, Bohemia, had a warehouse at Renngasse No. 183 in Vienna, and stocked "all sorts of printed cloth, cottons, and calicos." See Redl, 1820, p. 243.—KH

[91] Original German: *Tintenfisch*; possibly calamari (squid), as served in a restaurant.—TA

[92] Oliva wisely counters Bernard's partially deceitful advice with truthful common sense.—TA

[93] Oliva's hoarseness is also mentioned three weeks later on Blatt 69r.—TA

[94] *Fiacre* (in various spellings), a two-horse rental carriage.—KH

[95] The *Linie* was the outer row of defenses (more embankments than walls), beyond the closest groups of suburbs and roughly a mile distant from the walled City and the Glacis around it. Today's *Gürtel* (a broad street) essentially follows the old *Linie*. Certain forms of transportation operated solely within the *Linie*, while others passed beyond it, with a toll collected at the passageways through the embankments. Typical of urban growth in Europe, by the mid-1700s settlements catering to travelers began to spring up directly outside of the *Linie*'s passageways. See Groner, 1922, pp. 276–277.—TA

[96] If Beethoven was also thinking about seeking summer lodgings in Penzing, he and Oliva might have taken a public coach out to the *Linie* beyond Mariahilf, and then walked the remaining hour or so west to Penzing, rather than hiring a *fiacre* for a half day. See Oliva's complementary entry to this conversation on Blatt 22v above.—TA

the apartment. // There are several nice ones, though, in this pretty area. // Are you coming to see me tomorrow [possibly Tuesday, April 13] midday, at 1 o'clock? [//] [Blatt 33v] Get yourself *one* doctor and the simplest manner of treatment. // Are we coming back on Sunday [April 18]? // and fairly early. Perhaps we can find the fiacre that I had when I came to see you,—which drove [the distance] in an hour. // I always make better deals for others than I do for myself. [//] [Blatt 34r]

We won't live to see the end of this constantly changing situation. // The Emperor can make his money *good* again, but not what he has spoiled in the morals of his subjects thereby. // He has so many creatures around him who are worthless. // I myself believe that if you go there, then you [will] not stand for it. [//] [Blatt 34v] Your old friend. // Bad administration. // I am completely as one with you—it can *not* last *so* long. [//] and Baron von Kutschera![97]—the single confidant and friend! [//] [Blatt 35r]

I have no heart for her, and she has no money for me.[98]

BEETHOVEN [presumably at his apartment, Landstrasser Hauptstrasse; in the morning, before going out, possibly Tuesday, April 13]:
Blotting paper.
1½ Ell [yard] linen.
w/ S-z at 54 and at 57.
Molded candles, 48; Ordinary [dipped?] candles, 42.[99]

[Blatt 35v]

BERNARD: Philosophy: logic, metaphysics, aesthetics, mathematics, history, Classical literature. [//] I can be alone the whole day, without books and writing

---

[97] Baron (Freiherr) Johann von Kutscherá (1766–1832), Lieutenant Field Marshall. After a military career, he had been Adjutant General to the Emperor since 1805. See Franz Kysselak, "Memorabilien, Österreichs, Verstorbene 1814–1839," p. 115 (Tresor, Wiener Stadt- und Landesarchiv); *Hof- und Staats-Schematismus*, 1820, I, p. 295; Wurzbach, vol. 13, p. 294.—KH/TA

[98] Beethoven had evidently suggested a marriage prospect to Oliva, who indicated here that he did not love the woman and that she had no dowry to bring to a marriage. Eventually, Oliva would marry after he moved to St. Petersburg in late 1820.—TA

[99] An advertisement for similar products had appeared in the *Intelligenzblatt*, No. 62 (March 17, 1819), p. 517: "Fine refined burning oil, 57 kr. per pound; ordinary burning oil, 42 kr. per pound; molded Russian candles, 48 kr. per pound." That advertisement, however, was not the source of this entry.—KH/TA

materials, and still occupy myself very well. [//] Clemens [Brentano][100] in Berlin. [//] Christian [Brentano].[101]

[Blatt 36r]

OLIVA [probably at Oliva's apartment in the City; probably 1 p.m. on Tuesday, April 13]:[102] There and back? By what time do you want to be back here? [//]
[probably at a coach stand in the City:]
   13 fl.   12 fl.[103] //
[in Mödling, seeking summer lodgings for Beethoven; mid-afternoon of the same day]: At the vinegar maker's, across from here, one can learn whether apartments are still free. // One must ask .... [//] [Blatt 36v]

Three rooms and kitchen, without furniture, 100 fl. for the summer; all the rooms, with furniture, for 250 fl. over the summer.

The house where you lived has been sold. // You get the small room here with [furniture]. [//] [Blatt 37r] What have you decided? [//] Until now, the first one for 100 fl. also appears to be the best, because, as the woman says, <there is no noise in the garden> no commotion in the garden. //

For 3 fl.—You are generally known here. [Blatt 37v] He probably has no better wine, because the maiden said that the proprietor himself was in the cellar to bring something good for you. [//] Like the chickens. // Do you want coffee? [//] I don't believe so. // Then you may absolutely not live here. [//] [Blatt 38r]

The woman knows 2 rooms next door with kitchen with a view to the outside.[104] // But you must tell me approximately how expensive I can take it;—if I get it, may I take it in any case? [//] But I can say that only later. // We can see what she reckons [that it costs]. [//] [Blatt 38v] For everything she asks 200 fl., and will also have another stove installed for you if it becomes cold. // The other rooms will be

---

[100] Clemens Brentano (1778–1842), poet, representative of the Romantic school. He probably met Beethoven in 1811, either Teplitz or in Vienna. In 1813 Brentano was in Vienna for a second time and attended Beethoven's concert of January 2, 1814. He was back in Berlin in 1816 and, from 1818 to 1824, was in Dülmen (Westphalia), in the circle of Katharina Emmerich. Together with Achim von Arnim (the husband of his sister Bettina Brentano), he edited the collection *Des Knaben Wunderhorn* in 1806/1808. See *Allgemeine deutsche Biographie*, vol. 3, pp. 310–312; Clive, p. 51.—KH/TA

[101] Christian Brentano (1784–1854), brother of Clemens Brentano, after a restless wanderer's life, devoted himself entirely to religious problems and went to Landshut, to be educated by Sailer. In 1819 he lived in Switzerland. See *Allgemeine deutsche Biographie*, vol. 3, pp. 301–302.—KH

[102] On Blatt 33r Oliva had been discussing the costs of getting a *fiacre* on Sunday, but since Easter Sunday and Monday were both religious holidays, and since businesses were evidently open, it is more likely that Beethoven and Oliva delayed their visit to Mödling until Tuesday, April 13. He determined their meeting time to be 1 o'clock.—TA

[103] These are probably the fees for hiring a *fiacre* for the rest of the day; see Blatt 40v below.—TA

[104] As opposed to a view of an inner courtyard.—TA

painted. // Then she will give the room for the maid with it. // She will absolutely not give it for anything less than 190 fl. // These rooms are more expensive; they cost 250 fl. [//] [Blatt 39r] In no case will she give these rooms to someone else. Since people come every day to rent them, she wants to know beforehand which rooms you want. [//] Until the end of this week. // She doesn't want to give the small room along with it. // It all depends upon which apartment you prefer. // [Blatt 39v] She[105] says that the house still belongs to him,—and he would have rented the apartment for 300 fl., about which, however, he would hear further only on next Tuesday [probably April 20]. // If you want, you can take the deposit[106] back immediately. [//] [Blatt 40r]

I believe that we should inquire again very soon, because the landlord would make no reduction [in price] today, but the apartment is nice. // You are near to the bath. //

But it bears absolutely no interest, & costs yearly.

[returning from Mödling to Vienna; ca. 6 p.m. or even later:]

The fiacre pays [the toll] for itself; we can probably have him [the driver] given something, but [Blatt 40v] even now he is asking more than 11 fl.—because you stayed [in Mödling] later than 5 o'clock. Then one can give him something more to smooth the matter out. // You have to give some smaller denominations because the bill is 1 kr.

[End of entries presumably of Tuesday, April 13.]

BEETHOVEN **[possibly at his apartment; possibly late morning of Wednesday, April 14]**:

Shaving mug. [Blatt 41r]

[probably at a coffee house or restaurant; probably the afternoon of Wednesday, April 14:]

Interest of the National Bank for advance payment in Gold and Silver Coins, at 3 per cent yearly.[107]

L.V. Lagneau, *Die Kunst alle Arten der Lustseuche zu erkennen, zu heilen, u[nd] sich dafür zu <hüten> sichern,* etc., etc., 4th improved edition, large 8vo, Erfurt, 5 fl. 54 kr. W.W., at Wimmer's, across from the Jägerhorn.[108]

[possibly at his apartment; possibly late morning of Thursday, April 15:]

---

[105] Unclear because of a crease in the paper; the word could also be read as *er* (he).—KH

[106] *Darangeld,* deposit upon making a contract. See Grimm, vol. 2, col. 760.—KH

[107] In 1819 this notice appeared daily in the financial reports of the *Wiener Zeitung.*—KH

[108] Excerpt from an advertisement in the *Intelligenzblatt,* No. 84 (April 14, 1819), p. 750: "To be had at Carl Gerold's Book Shop: L.V. Lagneau, *Die Kunst, alle Arten der Lustseuche zu erkennen, zu heilen, und sich dafür zu sichern. Mit besonderer Rücksicht auf deren Symptome, verschiedene Heilarten, Abänderungen und Behandlungen in Hinsicht des Alters, des Geschlechts und des Temperaments der*

Schendler.[109]

+ Shoe horn.

+ Washing sponge—very. [Blatt 41v]

[probably at a coffee house or restaurant; probably the afternoon of Thursday, April 15:]

Deutliche Anleitung zur Rechenkunst, 8vo, 3 parts, sewn binding, 3 fl., in the Himmelpfortgasse, zum kleinen Greifen [at the small Griffin], No. 1026.[110] //

OLIVA [possibly at a coffee house, later joined by Bernard; possibly the evening of Friday, April 16]: 24 fl. [//] [Blatt 42r]

You could introduce it as if you have merely had the old nobility of your family renewed.[111] [//]

BEETHOVEN: Edler von ....

OLIVA: Are you going to Mödling tomorrow? //

I want to write it for you in my office, and then you can come somewhat later to sign it. //

Kranken; wie auch des Klimas, des Jahreszeiten und der begleitenden Krankheiten, 4th improved edition, large 8vo; Erfurt; 5 fl. 54 kr. W.W." Lagneau's book was a description of and method for curing venereal diseases.

Gerold's shop was on the east side of the Graben. Franz Wimmer's shop was in the Dorotheergasse, across from the *Goldenes Jägerhorn,* No. 1173 [renumbered as 1107 in 1821] (Redl, 1820, p. 66; Behsel, p. 33, noting the *Jägerhorn* as No. 1172 [renumbered as 1106 in 1821]). The house across Dorotheergasse from the *Jägerhorn* was No. 1184 [renumbered as 1118 in 1821].

Both Gerold and Wimmer advertised on p. 750. Beethoven's citation represents an unintentional conflation: he first copied the Lagneau material from Gerold's advertisement in col. 2, and then his eye strayed immediately to the left, to col. 1, where Wimmer's address appeared, and he copied that.—KH/TA

[109] An added dot over the first "e" (by another hand) transforms this entry to Schindler. Beethoven probably did not know Anton Schindler by name until ca. September, 1822; see Blatt 45v below.—KH

[110] Excerpt from an advertisement in the *Intelligenzblatt,* No. 85 (April 15, 1819), p. 762: "Brand new, to be had from Felix Stöckholzer v. Hirschfeld, I.R. priv. Book Dealer, in the Himmelpfortgasse, zum kleinen Greifen, No. 1026: *Deutliche Anleitung zur Rechenkunst,* 8vo, 3 parts, sewn binding, 3 fl." The same advertisement also appeared on April 19 and 23, 1819.

No. 1026 [renumbered as 968 in 1821] was on the south side of Kärntnerstrasse, connecting around the corner to Himmelpfortgasse, and was called the *Erzherzog Karl* in 1829 (Behsel, p. 29). The Himmelpfortgasse entrance was seemingly called the *Kleiner Greif* (Small Griffin).—KH/TA

[111] On December 11, 1818, Beethoven declared before the Lower Austrian *Landrecht* (Provincial Court) that he had no patent or diploma of nobility. On the basis of this, the guardianship proceedings were transferred to the Viennese *Magistrat* on December 18, 1818. See Thayer-Deiters-Riemann, IV, pp. 553–554; Thayer-Forbes, pp. 708–711.—KH/TA

[Blatt 42v]

BERNARD [joining Oliva and Beethoven, and writing on the *verso* sides]: It concerns the "van." If he [Karl] is of the nobility, then it must first [go] to the *Hofstelle*.

BEETHOVEN [writing, so as not to be overheard]: Should I say [something] about the *Non*-nobility? [//] [Blatt 43r] that you agree as to the guardianship? //

OLIVA: Yesterday[112] the Englishmen brought me your letter, & the previous evening I received another one for you[113] through Fries.[114] // The second Englishman,[115] the friend of Smith,[116] gave me a new commission. A Mr. Donaldson[117] in Edinburgh wishes to know whether you would concern yourself with writing for him 1 Trio

---

[112] Beethoven had seemingly last seen Oliva probably on Tuesday, April 13. If "yesterday" was Thursday, April 15, and "the previous evening" was Wednesday, April 14, that would make chronological sense here.—TA

[113] Edinburgh publisher George Thomson's letter dated April 5, 1819 (Albrecht, *Letters*, No. 258). Because of his experiences during the Continental Blockade, Thomson customarily sent letters to Beethoven in multiple copies, even by way of Malta.—TA

[114] Count of the Realm Johann Moritz von Fries (1777–1826), banker, art collector, and patron of the arts. He belonged to the Board of the Chamber of Commerce (*Grosshandlungsgremien*) and was director of the Austrian National Bank. His banking house arranged monetary business for Beethoven and forwarded letters to England. See *Hof-und Staats-Schematismus*, 1819, I, p. 33; Redl, 1820, p. 17; Wurzbach, vol. 4, p. 362; Clive, pp. 120–121; Beethoven's letter to Thomson, February 21, 1818 (Anderson, No. 892; Brandenburg, *Briefwechsel*, No. 1244).—KH/TA

[115] The *Wiener Zeitung*'s lists of "Arrivals" were often selective and (probably following the City's official practice) usually listed only one person in a party traveling together. A survey of such arrivals from April 1 to 15 reveals only one that matches the criteria implied: David MacCarthe [MacCarthy?], nobleman from Ireland, arrived from Brussels on April 12, and lodged at Landstrasse No. 27 (*Wiener Zeitung*, No. 84 [April 14, 1819], p. 335). Landstrasse No. 27 was in the Gärtnergasse, next to No. 26, where Beethoven had technically lived from late April to late September, 1817. At this time (April, 1819), the composer's residence was around the corner to the southwest, Landstrasser Hauptstrasse No. 268 (which, confusingly enough, today bears the number 26). See Klein, pp. 96–97, 100–101.—TA

[116] John Smith also brought a letter from publisher George Thomson in Edinburgh, dated April 5 (Albrecht, *Letters*, No. 258), and took letters dated May 25, 1819, back to England for Thomson and Ferdinand Ries. See also Cooper, pp. 32–33. Smith (and probably MacCarthy along with him) seems to have departed Vienna on May 29; see entries of ca. April 30 – May 1 (Blatt 61r below).—TA

[117] James Donaldson (1751–1830), owner and editor of the *Edinburgh Advertiser* and founder of the Donaldson Hospital in Edinburgh. See *Dictionary of National Biography*, ed. Leslie Stephen, vol. 15, pp. 210–211.—KH

for 3 pianos, [Blatt 43v] difficult,[118] and in the style of your Quintet in E-flat.[119] He wishes that this will be made known as his property. The fee that you ask for it will be paid to you in whatever manner you yourself choose. The parts of the Trio must all three be obbligato. If you perhaps do not want to designate the price now, you can merely determine a time when it will be finished, and write directly to Donaldson in Edinburgh about it. [//] [Blatt 44r]

These Englishmen speak of nothing but that you must simply come to England; they assure [you] that if you were to be in England, Scotland, and Ireland, for a single Winter from September to about May, you would earn so much that you could draw interest on it for the rest of your life. [//]

[Oliva presumably departs.]

[Blatt 44v]

BERNARD **[continuing]**: You will soon receive it, because it has already left the City Government. But it has not been granted, and you must therefore appeal it. Because the Supreme Guardianship Authority did not agree to it. **[continuing on Blatt 46v→]**

[Blatt 45r: no writing.]

[Blatt 45v]

---

[118] The German word *schwer* is not modified by *nicht*, but amateur publisher George Thomson's correspondence from Edinburgh frequently complains that Beethoven's folksong arrangements are too difficult, and implores the composer to make them easier (see Albrecht, *Letters*, Nos. 255 and 258 for recent examples). Therefore, given this environment and the nature of the proposed commission, one might presume that Donaldson wants a piece that is *not* difficult, but if his model is Joseph Czerny's arrangement of the Quintet, Op. 16, as suggested below, then the parts would indeed be difficult by amateur standards in Edinburgh.—TA

[119] The model to which Donaldson refers is most likely the two-piano arrangement of Beethoven's Quintet for Piano and Winds, Op. 16. The arrangement, made by Joseph Czerny (with the original piano part intact, and the second piano part reflecting the winds), had appeared from Simrock in Bonn in 1817 (see Kinsky-Halm, pp. 37–38). Otherwise, possibly a reference to the Piano Trio in E-flat, Op. 63, arranged from the String Quintet in E-flat, Op. 4, itself arranged from the Wind Octet in E-flat, Op. 103.—TA

SCHINDLER[120] [finding blank pages after Beethoven's death; falsified entries begin→]: Beethoven.[121] // Inquire at Schindler's, in the Deutsches Haus, 3rd Stock [4th floor, American].[122] [←falsified entries end]

[Blatt 46r: no writing.]

[Blatt 46v]

BERNARD [continuing from Blatt 44v]: He said that it absolutely allows no delay, and he would forward the matter to the agency; but the permission of the Supreme Guardianship Authority must be obtained. You must therefore instruct Tuscher most submissively and very soon. [//]
[End of conversation with Bernard, probably on Friday evening, April 16.]

[Blatt 47r]

BEETHOVEN [probably in a coffee house or restaurant; probably the afternoon of Saturday, April 17]:[123]
Apartment, Holzgasse in Mödling, No. 213.[124]

[120] As noted elsewhere, Schindler and Beethoven did not really become acquainted until ca. September 1822. Their actual friendship did not begin until November 1822.—TA
[121] Written in a calligraphic hand.—KH
[122] This is Schindler's first *fingiert* (or falsified) entry in the conversation books. Since Heft 2 was chronologically the earliest booklet in Schindler's possession, he staked his claim to Beethoven's friendship by its midpoint, locating three successive pages that (other than the unidentified name "Beethoven, also possibly entered by Schindler") had been left blank during Beethoven's lifetime and would stand out prominently to a later reader.
It cannot be established with certainty that Schindler ever lived in the *Deutsches Haus* (or *Deutschordens-Haus*), the house of the Teutonic Order, just southeast of St. Stephan's Cathedral. This building was No. 933 in 1819, renumbered as 879 in 1821; the Conscriptions-Bögen for this building are cataloged as Stadt No. 879 in the Stadt- und Landesarchiv (Vienna), and Schindler's name does not appear among its surviving census sheets.
The German editors, however, evidently looked at the Conscriptions-Bögen for Stadt No. 933, as it was numbered in 1821. That building had been No. 991 in 1819 and was located in the Rauhensteingasse, two blocks south of the Deutsches Haus. The German editors believed that they had found Anton Schindler living there in 1830, but a closer reading of that 1830 census sheet (933/13 in the new collation) reveals that the resident was, in fact, one Anton Schneider, born in 1774.
One name of interest that the German editors overlooked in Rauhensteingasse No. 933, however, was newspaper editor Joseph Carl Bernard (933/9 in the new collation), probably living there about this time (before his marriage on November 25, 1823; see Blatt 4r above) because of its proximity to the *Wiener Zeitung*'s offices.—KH/TA
[123] It is also possible that Beethoven did not read Saturday's newspapers in coffee houses until the following Sunday or Monday.—TA
[124] See the *Intelligenzblatt*, No. 87 (April 17, 1819), p. 277 (Apartment Advertisements). The same advertisement had also appeared on April 15, 1819, but Beethoven's seemingly simultaneous copying of

Dr. Mayer, Landstrasse [suburb], in the Elisabethiners' House, No. 317.[125]

    1 fl. 30 kr.

        48

        30

         4

    2   52

[Blatt 47v]

OLIVA [presumably in a coffee house or restaurant; seemingly the afternoon or evening of Sunday, April 17]: Something's burning near here. [//]

BEETHOVEN: 148 [= 1 fl. 48 kr.?] [//]

[Blatt 48r]

OLIVA: If only the Mother didn't learn it earlier through the guardian.[126] [//]

If you wanted [to go to Mödling] some afternoon this week,[127] I can do it every day except Wednesday; but I must know the day before. [//]

[Blatt 48v]

BEETHOVEN [at a coffee house or restaurant; presumably the afternoon of Monday, April 19]:

At Seb[astian] Spitäler and Joh[ann] Sartori's, Rothe Thurmstrasse

Mayer's advertisement (immediately below), which first appeared on April 17, suggests the latter date as the earliest for this entry.—KH/TA

[125] Excerpt from an advertisement in the *Wiener Zeitung*, No. 87 (April 17, 1819), p. 347: "Sulphur-Fumigation Institution, combined with an Electro-Vibration machine, under the direction of Dr. Meyer [*sic*], in the Landstrasse, in the Elisabethiners' House, No. 317 … The electro-vibrations machine, whose effect is increased through the supplement of electricity in a considerable strength, will now, as before, as well as by itself, be employed in stubborn rheumatic and gouty conditions, for ringing in the ears, hardness of hearing, and deafness with similar symptoms …, Vienna, April 15, 1819, Carl Joseph Meyer, Doctor of Medicine and Surgery; also practicing physician." The same advertisement also appeared on April 24 and May 1.

The Elisabethiners' Chapel and Hospital survive today on the west side of Landstrasser Hauptstrasse, in the block north of its intersection with Beatrixgasse (formerly Bockgasse) and therefore approximately three blocks north of where Beethoven was living in April, 1819.—KH/TA

[126] German *wann* instead of *wenn*; probably a reference to the scheme to take Karl from Vienna to Landshut for his schooling.—TA

[127] This would have been written on Sunday, April 18, or possibly as late as Monday, April 19, 1819.—TA

[Rotenturmstrasse], No. 772, a new type of English water closet, of which the whole construction is molded.[128]

In the Kohlmarkt, Michaeler House, No. 1220, at reduced prices in bank notes, *Anarcharsis* [*sic*] *Reisen*, etc., 7 parts complete, Schrämbl edition; 10 fl.[129]

[Blatt 49r]

BERNARD [at an undetermined location with Schickh present;[130] late afternoon of Monday, April 19, or possibly midday dinner on Tuesday, April 20]: It has to matter little to the Magistrat, whether Karl is taken to Melk,[131] or to Bohemia, or to Landshut. If the guardians consider such arrangements to be good, and the administration agreed to it, then no-one can have anything against it. [//] [Blatt 49v] A mother would indeed have to agree, even if there were no grounds to reproach her. [//] Similar cases surely occur frequently, where children are removed from the parental home. [//] Tomorrow morning, let's go to see Herr v[on] Tuscher, [Blatt 50r] and then let's see what is to be done.

[Blatt 50v]

SCHICKH:[132] My friend needs very little time, and in case he should meet you today, just give him a few minutes, because he doesn't need any more. [//] If I should not be present when you visit, then please tell the news to my [business] partner.[133] //

[Blatt 51r]

---

[128] See the *Intelligenzblatt*, No. 88 (April 19, 1819), p. 783 (Advertisements). The same advertisement also appeared on April 21, 23, and 26, 1819.—KH

[129] Excerpt from an advertisement in the *Intelligenzblatt*, No. 88 (April 19, 1819), p. 793: "The following books are to be had at Philipp Herzl, privil. Book Dealer, in Vienna on the Kohlmarkt in the Michaelerhaus, No. 1220, across from Count Clary's house, at reduced prices in bank notes: 63. *Anacharsis Reisen durch Griechenland*, 7 parts, complete, 8vo, 1793, beautiful out-of-print Schrämbl edition with copperplates, in 7 new half-leather volumes, 10 fl."
This citation concerns Jean Jacques Barthélmy (1716–1795), *Reise des jungen Anacharsis durch Griechenland*. Franz Anton Schrämbl (1750/51–1803) was the Viennese publisher of the German-language edition; see Wurzbach, vol. 31, pp. 254–255. My gratitude to Othmar Barnert, librarian, Österreichisches Theatermuseum, for his assistance.—KH/TA

[130] This could have taken place at the office of Schickh's *Wiener Zeitschrift*, with which Bernard was also involved at the time, or possibly at a restaurant or coffee house.—TA

[131] Original phonetic spelling: Mölk. A well-known Benedictine abbey and monastery in Lower Austria. In the monastery were a public *Gymnasium*, a boarding school for forty students, and a music school for eight choir boys. See Raffelsperger, vol. 4, pp. 888–889.—KH

[132] Identity of the handwriting established by Schindler in Heft 10, Blatt 40v.

[133] The public partner in Schickh's fashionable clothing business was Jakob Regenhart. See Redl, 1818, p. 36.—KH

BERNARD: If she hears of it, your sister-in-law will tell what has happened, that the Magistrat has entered into a conspiracy against her. // I told Herr von Tuscher [that] you would have wanted to tell him about the matter first, if you had the certainty [....] [//] He himself very gladly sees that it would happen [....] [//]

[Blatt 51v]

BEETHOVEN [at a coffee house or restaurant; presumably the afternoon of Tuesday, April 20]:
Apartment on the Judenplatz, No. 437, on the first [American second] floor; 5 rooms, etc.; inquire at the coffee house on the first [American second] floor.[134]

[possibly at his apartment; possibly late morning of Wednesday, April 21:]
Veal?
Coffee?
Sugar?
[at a coffee house or restaurant; presumably the afternoon of Wednesday, April 21:]
Abtritts Gruben der Herren Cazeneuve und Compagnie, etc.; Weimar, 1819; 45 kr. C.M.; on the Bauernmarkt, No. 629.[135] [Blatt 52r]

$$2 \quad 15 \quad 45$$
$$45$$
$$45$$

[Blatt 52v]

UNKNOWN [at an undetermined office; possibly Thursday, April 22]: <In the large Weighing House[136]> A request to the Court Commission for Studies that [Karl] Beethoven may add his examinations later,[137] and the reason that one refuses to examine him is because he had not been enrolled as a private student, when he had [Blatt 53r] stopped studying in public schools. [//]

---

[134] See the *Intelligenzblatt*, No. 89 (April 20, 1819), p. 797 (Advertisements). The same advertisement also appeared on April 22, 24, and 27, 1819.—KH

[135] Excerpt from an advertisement in the *Wiener Zeitung*, No. 90 (April 21, 1819), p. 360: "To be had at Heubner und Volke, book dealers, on the Bauernmarkt, No. 629: *Die beweglichen und nicht stinkenden Abtritts-Gruben der Herren Cazeneuve und Compagnie. Eine für Hausbesitzer und Bewohner sehr wichtige leicht ausführbare Erfindung*, According to Reports by Herren Dubois, Kuzard, Hericart de Thury to the Central Agricultural Society in Paris. 8vo, with 3 copper tables; Weimar, 1819; 45 kr. C.M."—KH

[136] City, No. 682; guardian Mathias Tuscher lived here.—KH/TA

[137] For students who were instructed by private teachers with the object of being qualified for the University, an examination was compulsory every year in all subjects, administered by the professors in the *Gymnasia*. See Pezzl (1826), p. 302.—KH

BEETHOVEN [noting potential avenues of assistance in the Court Chancellery]:
I.R. Court Commission for Studies, Wipplingerstrasse 415. Commission member,
Count Guicciardi, in the Mölkerhof.[138]

Türkheim, Seilerstatt 855.[139] [Blatt 53v]

Saurau,[140] President. //

OLIVA [at an undetermined location; possibly as early as the evening of Friday,
April 23]: The coachman got overturned yesterday in the street.[141] [//]

BEETHOVEN:

20   for 24 kr.
4   16 kr.

OLIVA: I heard the opera twice here; Campi[142] is not a good match for this role, &
the whole thing loses .... [//] [Blatt 54r]

You must extricate yourself from it. // But then everything will quiet down, &
you can have a continuous influence on Karl. // He is young, and new and better
environments can bring forth many good things. // You can immediately meet with
measures against it there. [//] [Blatt 54v]

---

[138] Count Franz Joseph Guicciardi, Treasurer and Court Councillor in the United Court
Chancellery, who lived in the Melkerhof No. 111 [renumbered as 103 in 1821], was still noted in the
Schematismus of 1818 as member of the Court Commission for Studies, but no longer in 1819. See Hof-
und Staats-Schematismus, 1818, I, p. 83; 1819, I, p. 224.—KH

[139] Baron Ludwig von Türkheim (1777–1846), physician, Court Councillor at the United Court
Chancellery. In 1819 he was a member of the Court Commission on Studies, as well as vice director
of "Medical and Surgical Studies," personal physician of the family of Archduke Carl, and, in 1829,
Rector magnificus of the Vienna Hochschule. He lived at Seilerstatt No. 855 [renumbered as 805 in 1821].
See Hof- und Staats-Schematismus, 1819, I, p. 225, and II, p. 85; Frimmel, Handbuch, II, pp. 341–343;
Wurzbach, vol. 48, pp. 88–89.—KH

[140] Count Franz Joseph von Saurau (1760–1832), State and Conference Minister, seniormost
member of the Court Chancellery, Minister of the Interior, lived at Wipplingerstrasse No. 415
[renumbered as 384 in 1821]. See Hof- und Staats-Schematismus, 1819, I, p. 223; Wurzbach, vol. 28,
pp. 279–281.—KH

[141] Original, umgeworfen, could also mean that he had been knocked down.—TA

[142] Antonia Campi, née Miclasiewicz (1773–1822), was chamber singer to the King of Poland as
early as 1788, and in 1792 married the singer Gaetano Campi. She came to Vienna upon the opening
of Schikaneder's Theater an der Wien on June 13, 1801. When the administrations of the Theater
an der Wien and the Court Theaters were united (1814), she sang in both theaters. Possibly Fidelio
was the topic of conversation here; Campi sang the role of Leonore on January 23 and March 2,
1819, at the Kärntnertor Theater. If the soprano sang or acted in a questionable way, perhaps it was
because she was pregnant: over the years, she bore roughly seventeen children while maintaining her
career—including four sets of twins and one set of triplets—therefore roughly eleven pregnancies!
See Court Theater Zettel [posters] (Bibliothek, Österreichisches Theatermuseum); Wurzbach, vol. 2,
p. 247.—KH/TA

I recently took your *Adelaide* to Herz;[143] she really sings well. [//] He has property *per se*, & several houses.

[Blatt 55r]

BEETHOVEN [noting Oliva's seemingly new apartment]: Blutgasse, No. 897, first floor [second floor, American]: Oliva.[144]
   [End of conversation with Oliva.]

[Blatt 55v]

UNKNOWN [seemingly in an office; possibly Monday, April 26]:[145] The good opinion of the Magistrat goes back to the City Government, from there to the Administration [*Regierung*], then to the Police Department [*Polizei Hofstelle*]. Now the Police Department decides that this decision is in order, as it goes up again to the Magistrat, who notifies us and the Mother by decree, and I'll bet 1000 to one that she will then appeal against it, and, at about that time, through the delivery of an appellate report, according to its disposal, bring _____ against [....] [//]

[Blatt 56r]

OLIVA [possibly at his apartment in the Blutgasse; possibly Tuesday, April 27]: I'm going out just before noon.

---

[143] Presumably Pauline Herz, *Edle* von Liebenberg, a supporting (non-performing) member of the Gesellschaft der Musikfreunde, living at the Bauernmarkt, No. 616 [renumbered as 577 in 1821]. See Ziegler, *Addressen-Buch*, 1823, p. 167. See also Leopold von Herz, living in nearby Bauernmarkt No. 620 [renumbered as 581 in 1821]; see Behsel, p. 18; Heft 5, Blatt 3r.—KH/TA

[144] Franz Oliva is not listed in the surviving Conscriptions-Bögen for the house at City, Blutgasse No. 897 [renumbered as 847 in 1821]. He is entered only in an undated apartment Bogen (census sheet) of the house on the Haarmarkt, No. 777 [renumbered as 731 in 1821], Wohnpartei 7. See Conscriptions-Bogen, Stadt, No. 731 (Wiener Stadt- und Landesarchiv).
   Blutgasse essentially runs east–west, one block south of Stephansdom; in 1819 its eastern terminus was Schulerstrasse; today it is the former Kleine Schulerstrasse, now Domgasse, therefore around the corner from the entrance to the so-called "Mozart *Figaro* House." In 1829 the building in the Blutgasse (as 847) was owned by Count Leopold von Harnoncourt. The building in the Haarmarkt was located at the south side of today's Lugeck (Gutenberg Platz), two blocks east of St. Stephan's Cathedral; a statue of Gutenberg now stands in front of the later building at that location (Behsel, pp. 22 and 25). Oliva's apartment in the Blutgasse was essentially a twenty-minute walk north from Beethoven's current apartment in Landstrasser Hauptstrasse.—KH/TA

[145] The following entry is written in ink, suggesting that it was made in some official's office rather than in a restaurant or coffee house.—KH/TA

BEETHOVEN [**probably at his apartment; possibly late morning of Wednesday, April 28**]:

$$\begin{array}{rl} 168 & \text{Housekeeper, yearly} \\ \underline{84} & \text{Attendant} \\ 252 & \end{array}$$

Linen—3 Elle [yards].
Sponge.
Blotting paper.

[Blatt 56v]

OLIVA [**possibly at a coffee house or restaurant; possibly early afternoon or evening of Wednesday, April 28**]: Is the rental of your apartment already in order? But is the payment of your apartment in Mödling ...? // The Archduke [Rudolph] has so many carriages, he ought to lend one for the short journey. // I shall write the transport routes out for you in addition to the amounts for the postal fees. [//] [Blatt 57r]

In Bavaria there is an easy monetary system in which the following is valid:

1.10 kr.	12 kr. in silver
1.20 "	24 kr. "
2.20 "	48 kr. "

Except for Thalers, the other coins are merely small coins in easy money.[146] //

But she [Johanna van Beethoven] is not escaping her punishment; she is now held in contempt at all offices. // [Blatt 57v] But she has to have been deluded and persuaded by her friends, otherwise her impulsiveness appears impossible to me. //

What time is best to meet the Lobkowitz cashier?[147] I already know him from earlier times. At that time he could do nothing, but at least he was courteous. [//] [Blatt 58r]

She is setting everything into motion, and the Court must do everything in order to disarm her. // He often remains out. [//]

He [Bernard] has a loved one at the *Theater an der Wien*, who is departing

---

[146] The denomination "xr" (kreuzer) was entered later.—KH

[147] Prince Lobkowitz's cashier was Anton Richter, who lived in suburban Alsergrund No. 7. Perhaps the subject here was the annual pension that Beethoven was granted by Archduke Rudolph and the Princes Lobkowitz and Kinsky in 1809. See *Wiener Zeitung*, No. 44 (February 24, 1819), p. 175.—KH

very soon [and] with whom, however, he is said to be very preoccupied.   [//]
<Willmann>[148] [//]

Forenoon. //

In Olmütz, things will be different.[149] [//] [Blatt 58v]

I shall speak with Artaria[150] about it, so that they publish the work in the most beautiful manner, because that way [the] most is done for it. // Ries,[151] however, deals *directly* with the music dealers in London himself. // Write to Ries; I shall take care of the rest in sending the letter through business channels, whatever is best.

---

[148] Caroline (actually Maria Anna Magdalena) Willmann (1796–1860), singer, daughter of music director Johann Ignaz Willmann (b. 1739, d. 1815 in Breslau), who had been a friend of the Beethoven family since his activities as a court musician in Bonn (from 1767). After her first engagements (in Breslau and elsewhere), Caroline Willmann performed, from 1816, at the court theaters in Vienna, Munich, and Stuttgart. In 1820 Carl Maria von Weber secured her for Dresden. On April 26, 1819, the singer traveled from Vienna to Munich. See Karl Maria Pisarowitz, "Willmann," *MGG*, vol. 14, cols. 692–694; *Wiener Zeitung*, No. 96 (April 28, 1819), p. 383.

The acquaintance with this name also clarifies the wordplay in Beethoven's letter from 1819 to J.C. Bernard (Brandenburg, *Briefwechsel*, No. 1306; Anderson, No. 983). Brandenburg editorially dates the letter as Mödling, probably June 9, 1819. After a salutation to "Bernardus non Sanctus," the letter begins: "Man will oder will man?" (One wants or does one want?), continues with business concerning Karl's guardianship, and then ends with a similar wordplay, this time with considerable good-humored word repetition. Without benefit of the conversation books for comparison, Anderson did not understand the reference to Willmann, and her translation is therefore flawed. Another reference to Bernard and Willmann occurs in Heft 4, Blatt 13v, probably dating from December 8, 1819.—KH/TA

[149] Archduke Rudolph had been installed as Archbishop of Olmütz on March 24, 1819. The reference is probably not to any changes that Rudolph might make in his Moravian seat, but instead, decisions he might make or influences that he might exert on Beethoven's behalf concerning the guardianship of Karl.—KH/TA

[150] Artaria, a music publishing family with many branches. Since 1769, the Viennese firm had been located in the house "Zum englischen Gruss" at Kohlmarkt No. 1219. From the beginning of the nineteenth century, the owner was Domenico (III) Artaria (1775–1842); from 1807 to 1824, his partner was Carlo Boldrini. From 1795 onwards, many works of Beethoven had appeared from this publisher. See Frimmel, *Handbuch*, I, pp. 21–23; Weinmann, *Wiener Musikverleger*, pp. 14 and 26–27; Clive, pp. 8–10.—KH

[151] Ferdinand Ries (1784–1838), pianist and composer. Probably in early 1802, he came to Vienna, where he became Beethoven's piano student until 1805, when he went back to Koblenz and Bonn. After a stay in Paris, he came back to Vienna in 1808–1809, and then in 1813 settled in London, where he directed the concerts of the Philharmonic Society and worked on Beethoven's behalf in many ways. See Frimmel, *Handbuch*, I, pp. 65–67; Reinhold Sietz, "Ries," *MGG*, vol. 11, cols. 490–494; Clive, pp. 284–287.—KH/TA

// [Blatt 59r] He has quite certainly received the music.[152] // Should I speak with Artaria concerning the Variations?[153]

If you want to retire,[154] you can be sure for now that bank shares will bring you several percent more, and that at any given moment, you are still the lord of your property. [//] [Blatt 59v] You sell them when you want stock shares. But it would be friendly of you if you tell him before the maturity date that you no longer want to extend it. [//]

[Blatt 60r]

BEETHOVEN [at a coffee house or restaurant; presumably the afternoon of Thursday, April 29]:
Forte-piano Schule by Müller, at Steiner's, 7th improved edition, with an appendix on general-bass, 7 fl. [*sic*] C.M. or 14 fl. W.W.[155]

[Blatt 60v]

OLIVA:[156] But if the letters perhaps came addressed to your brother [Johann]? [//] Then how did they come into her hands? // If it is cleverly introduced, she can be persuaded, on the part of the Police, to deliver up the letters. // and to make her [feel] secure, you could write to her; she would make up her mind in several days. [//] [Blatt 61r] She has certainly deceived the most powerful offices, and there isn't much in this. // The copper [small] money belongs to you. Why do you want to have it exchanged? //

---

[152] In December 1818 or very early January 1819, Beethoven had evidently sent the String Quintet, Op. 104, and the "Hammerklavier" Sonata, Op. 106, to Ries in London for publication in England, since he mentions them as probably having arrived in his letter to Ries of January 30, 1819 (Anderson, No. 935; Brandenburg, *Briefwechsel*, No. 1285). On May 25, 1819, Beethoven wrote to Ries, saying that he had not received any acknowledgement of receipt for these two works (Anderson, No. 944; Brandenburg, *Briefwechsel*, No. 1302). Artaria had published the Quintet in February 1819 and would publish the Sonata (both presumably with rights for German-speaking lands) in September 1819 (Kinsky-Halm, pp. 287 and 294).—TA

[153] Probably the *Sechs variierten Themen für Klavier mit beliebiger Begleitung von Flöte oder Violine*, Op. 105, which appeared from Artaria in September, 1819, although the Variations by Archduke Rudolph could also be meant (see Heft 5, Blatt 34v). See Kinsky-Halm, pp. 288–290.—KH

[154] The verb *zurückziehen* is expressed as a reflexive, indicating retirement rather than, say, withdrawal of funds, which is also a potential topic here. See Blatt 63r below, where Beethoven jots down advertisements for a house and even 53 acres of land.—TA

[155] Excerpt from an advertisement in the *Wiener Zeitung*, No. 97 (April 29, 1819): "To be had at S.A. Steiner and Co., I.R. priv. Art Dealers in Vienna, on the Graben at Paternostergässchen No. 612, just arrived from Leipzig: *Fortepiano-Schule, oder Anweisung zur richtigen und geschmackvollen Spielart dieses Instruments, nebst vielen praktischen Beyspielen und einem Anhange vom Generalbass*, by Aug[ust] Eberh[ard] Müller, late Kapellmeister in Weimar; seventh improved edition. Price 6 fl. C.M. or 14 fl. W.W." The same advertisement appeared on May 1, 5, 10, and 17, 1819.—KH

[156] The following conversation largely concerns sister-in-law Johanna van Beethoven.—KH

The gentleman is going directly back to London next Friday [May 7];[157] he wants to take your letter to Ries with him and deliver it personally, because he is well acquainted with Ries. In this way, the matter will be in order.

[Blatt 61v]

BEETHOVEN [at a coffee house or restaurant; presumably the afternoon of Friday, April 30]:
Die Krankheit des Gehörs, etc., etc.; 10th small volume, 8vo, Cologne, 1819, sewn binding, 1 fl. 15 kr., across from the *Goldenes Jägerhorn* [Golden Hunting Horn].[158] //

OLIVA [seemingly at Beethoven's apartment;[159] probably the evening of Friday, April 30]: You must do it [write to Ries] quickly, however, because he [the messenger] leaves on Friday morning,[160] and the opportunity is too good to let it go by. [//] But the letter may not be sealed. [//] [Blatt 62r]
The letter [presumably a different one], though, must be in the form of a petition to the Archduke.[161] // If he grants it, then the passport will be prepared directly upon this decree. [//] In Stoll's case,[162] it was utterly rejected by all the offices, &

---

[157] This appears to be John Smith of Glasgow, who seems to have taken Beethoven's letters, dated May 25, 1819, to Ries in London (Anderson, No. 944) and George Thomson in Edinburgh (Anderson, No. 945) back to England with him. Actually, Smith remained in Vienna another four weeks after this entry and, noted as an "English *Partikulier* [man of private means]," departed in the direction of Munich on Saturday, May 29; see the *Wiener Zeitung*, No. 124 (June 2, 1819), p. 495. In the event, Smith did not deliver Beethoven's letter directly to Ries, and (from an annotation on the autograph) may have inadvertently kept it in his possession until late October, 1819.—TA

[158] Excerpt from an advertisement in the *Intelligenzblatt*, No. 98 (April 30, 1819), p. 901: "Just arrived at Franz Wimmer's: A completely revised and improved edition by a practicing physician, *Die Krankheiten des Gehörs, oder sichere Mittel, das Sausen vor den Ohren, Harthörigkeit und Taubheit zu mindern, und nach und nach ganz zu heilen. Nebst Anweisung u. Mitteln, Ohren u. Gehör gut zu erhalten, Fehler der selben zu verbessern, ihnen vorzubeugen, u. dem lästigen sogenannten Ohrenzwange gänzlich abzuhelfen* [The Illnesses of Hearing ...] edited by Dr. G.W. Becker, practicing physician in Leipzig; tenth small volume in his Little Medical Writings; 8vo; Cologne, 1819; costs 1 fl. 15 kr., sewn binding." The same advertisement also appeared on May 7, 1819. For the *Goldenes Jägerhorn*, see Blatt 41r above.—KH/TA

[159] Oliva relays a message from a cook on Blatt 6v below.—TA

[160] Since "today" is already presumably Friday, April 30, Oliva is probably referring to Friday, May 7, 1819.—TA

[161] This concerns the petition to Archduke Ludwig to allow Nephew Karl to go to study in Landshut. See Blatt 15r, above.—KH

[162] Joseph Ludwig Stoll (b. Vienna, March 31, 1777; d. Vienna, June 22, 1815), poet, was theater director for a short time during Palffy's administration, and was acquainted with Beethoven, who set his poem "An die Geliebte" (two versions, as WoO 140) in December, 1811. Together with Baron Leo[pold] von Seckendorf (1775–1809), he edited *Prometheus, eine Zeitschrift, der höheren Bildung des Menschen gewidmet* (Vienna, 1808). Through a misreading of the abbreviation "Jos.," Stoll's first name is often given as Johann, but it is clearly spelled out as Joseph on the title page of his *Poetische*

by permission of the Emperor, he immediately received the permission to be out of the country for a year. [//] [Blatt 62v] According to her tale, everything would already be in order; perhaps the judge himself does not know how the matter stands, & therefore one must go into the community house [suburban administration building] and inquire. //

The cook (woman) says that the landlord wanted to speak with you today, and the wife of the building superintendent already knew that an inquiry had been made. [//]

[Blatt 63r]

BEETHOVEN [at a coffee house or restaurant; presumably the afternoon of Saturday, May 1]:

Mödling: house for sale on the Kapuzinerplatz, No. 58.[163]

Auction: of the Augustinerwald in the Gradental near Sooss near Baden: [it] has 53 Joch [acres] and 1553 square Klafter [fathoms] in surface measure; black (Scots) pine is the predominant species of wood. The proclaimed price is 632 fl. 55 kr. C.M.[164]

Dr. Mayer, Landstrasse, in the Elisabethiners' House, No. 317, whose [Blatt 63v] electro-vibrations machine, whose effect [is increased] through the supplement of electricity, etc., for stubborn rheumatic ringing in the ears, hardness of hearing, and deafness.[165]

[Blatt 64r]

BERNARD [possibly joining Beethoven; presumably the afternoon of Saturday, May 1]: Was Tuscher with you at the Police Direction? [//] Do you already have lodgings? [//] Tuscher must now insist that the Magistrat expedite the matter, for nothing more is to be accomplished with this boy. [//] What is the Court copyist's

---

Schriften (1811). See Frimmel, *Handbuch*, II, p. 261; Kinsky-Halm, p. 608; Thayer-Deiters-Riemann, III, pp. 189–190; Thayer-Forbes, pp. 521, 531, and 604; Clive, pp. 356–357; Wurzbach, vol. 39, pp. 157–159.—KH/TA

[163] See *Intelligenzblatt*, No. 99 (May 1, 1819), p. 905 (advertisement).—KH

[164] See the *Amtsblatt* of the *Wiener Zeitung*, No. 35 (May 1, 1819), p. 119 (advertisement). The same advertisement had also appeared on April 24 and 28, 1819.

Sooss is located a mile or two south of Baden, halfway between that resort and Bad Vöslau. See Blatt 59r above, where Beethoven may have been speaking about retiring. There are similar references in his Tagebuch; see Solomon, "Beethoven's Tagebuch," in his *Beethoven Essays*, pp. 233–295 and 356–358; diary entries Nos. 41, 66, 86.—KH/TA

[165] Excerpt from an advertisement in the *Wiener Zeitung*, No. 99 (May 1, 1819), p. 396. On April 17 Beethoven had made a brief note from a similar advertisement about Mayer on Blatt 47r above. He passed by the Elisabethiners' hospital every time he walked from his apartment into the walled City.—KH/TA

name?[166] [Blatt 64v] Karl denies that he said it; but his mother would have found this [meaning] in it. Kudlich says that the letter naturally contained the opposite, which you can easily imagine. [//] First we must get the Magistrat's decision, and then can we take all the necessary steps. [Blatt 65r] The Government must issue the passport.

OLIVA [**possibly at Beethoven's apartment in the Landstrasser Hauptstrasse; possibly late morning of Sunday, May 2**]:

Mödling, Herrngasse No. 76, at the potter's.[167] // When do you want to move out there? //

He [John Smith] would also be glad to take along a letter for Thomson;[168] you can tell me what is to be written, & tomorrow I'll give him the letter. [//] [Blatt 65v]

Is Bernard going along [to Kudlich's school] today? //

All of them [drivers] ask 12 fl., & say that it's all the same to them whether you go now or later; perhaps it can be negotiated down a bit, but if you want to go today, it will certainly cost 10 or 11 gulden. [//] 11 fl. [gulden] [//] [Blatt 66r]

In any case, it is better if we eat here. //

NEPHEW KARL [**during Beethoven's visit at Kudlich's school in the Erdberggasse with Bernard; presumably the afternoon of Sunday, May 2**]: H[err] v[on] K[udlich] had wanted to lead me there, so that I should tell him my true sentiments. // that I should, on the whole, answer his questions [Blatt 66v] as I think. // She believed that some trouble could arise there with Kudlich. [//] [Blatt 67r] Our teacher of mathematics is the same one whom H[err] v[on] Bernard recommended to you. He teaches very well. [//]

---

[166] Presumably Court copyist (or drafter of documents) Jacob Hotschevar, a relative of Karl's mother Johanna. On her behalf, he had directed a letter to the Lower Austrian Landrecht on December 11, 1818; in it he laid the foundation for Johanna's proposal to place Karl in the University's Konvikt (secondary school). See Frimmel, *Handbuch*, I, pp. 223–224; Thayer-Deiters-Riemann, IV, pp. 113 and 543–545, and V, pp. 499–500; Thayer-Forbes, pp. 707–711; Clive, pp. 170–171; Weise, p. 21.—KH/TA

[167] German *Hafner*. In 1819 Beethoven occupied the courtyard rooms in the house of the master potter Jakob Tuschek, Mödling No. 76, from May 12 on. See Frimmel, *Handbuch*, I, p. 423; Klein, p. 104.—KH

[168] George Thomson (1757–1851), musician and publisher in Edinburgh. He collected Scottish folksongs and published folksong collections. He had sent Beethoven a request for compositions as early as 1803 and a little later gave him a commission to write introductions and accompaniments to Scottish folksongs, such as Haydn had already composed for him. These commissions occupied Beethoven for several years. The fifth volume of Thomson's Folksong Collections included twenty-five songs (Op. 108) with accompaniments by Beethoven. Thomson played an important role in the musical life of Edinburgh. See Stephen, *Dictionary of National Biography*, vol. 56, p. 242; Frimmel, *Handbuch*, II, pp. 319–321; Clive, pp. 365–367; the correspondence between Beethoven and Thomson in Anderson and Albrecht, *Letters*.—KH/TA

BERNARD: He practices at the City Government and has only a few hours to give. [//]

[Blatt 67v]

NEPHEW KARL: He just recently gave 3 lectures. //

BERNARD: The woman did not want to hand over the hat, but H[err] Kudlich ordered that the hat be brought. // <The woman> //

NEPHEW KARL: You will have seen that Kudlich always [verb] her .... [//] [Blatt 68r] 12 – 1 – //
Lectures:
  3. Geography
  4. History
  5. Mathematics
  6. Physics
  Piano lessons
  Free until 9. [Blatt 68v]
  Mornings until 11. // But I can do it [practice piano] in the evenings. // As long as I want.

BEETHOVEN:
  20
  130
  $\underline{4}$
  154

[Blatt 69r]

They are still waiting for her/it. //
[Presumably the end of Beethoven's Sunday visit to Kudlich's school.]

OLIVA **[at Oliva's apartment, Blutgasse 897;**[169] **presumably late morning or early afternoon of Monday, May 3]**: I shall go there today. I cannot speak at all today,[170] therefore I have stayed in bed at the same temperature. In any case it will probably

---

[169] For the location of Oliva's apartment, see Blatt 55r above. To get there Beethoven would have walked from his apartment in Landstrasser Hauptstrasse, across the Glacis, through the Stubentor, directly north on Wollzeile, then jogged two blocks west at a point where it was nearly even with the "east" side of the Dom, a walk of about twenty minutes. Beethoven's first written comment on Blatt 69r may, for some reason, have been made to Oliva.—TA

[170] Oliva's hoarseness is also mentioned three weeks earlier on Blatt 31r above.—TA

still continue a long time. [//] I don't believe that you will get away before the end of the month. // Lämmel[171] from Prague is here; I shall go to see him, [Blatt 69v] & turn the receipt in earlier. [//] P. Egmund.[172] [//]

BEETHOVEN [presumably at a coffee house; late afternoon of Monday, May 3]:
For the first time, I am asking for an authoritative decision against injustice. [Blatt 70r]
Open carriage [Stellfuhr] at Mödling, No. 47 (shortage of common carriages [Vulgenz]). At 6 in the morning from Vienna and at 4:30 in the afternoon from Vienna, from the Matschacker Hof to M[ödlin]g; and then at 6:30 in the morning and at 6:30 in the evening from the Bathhouse at Mödling to Vienna.[173] [Blatt 70v]
Boot polish.
Blotting paper.
Hand soap.
Linen.
[Blatt 71r]
In the Wollzeile, at the Stork, in the newly-established Perfume Shop, steel [razor] blades, etc.[174] //
Neuestes Postreise-Buch by Ant[on] Lenz, I.R. High Court Post Office Official,

[171] Simon Edler von Lämmel (1766–1845) founded a wholesale/banking business in Prague and possessed a wholesale trade authorization in Vienna; his office was at Kärntnerstrasse No. 1076. He was also a member of the Banking Commission. On April 6, 1819, he traveled to Prague. See Redl, 1822, pp. 9 and 20; Wiener Zeitung, No. 80 (April 8, 1819), p. 319; Wurzbach, vol. 13, pp. 477–478.—KH

[172] If this discussion has to do with Beethoven's submitting a receipt for his stipend (possibly from Prince Kinsky's estate in Prague through Lämmel; see also Blatt 78r), then a priest would certify that the recipient was still alive. Therefore this may have been Pater Egmund. See Albrecht, Letters, Nos. 275 and 280, for sample receipts for funds from the Lobkowitz and Kinsky estates. A priest by this name cannot be located in the Rochus or Schotten parishes at this time.—TA

[173] See the Intelligenzblatt, No. 100 (May 3, 1819), p. 911 (advertisement). The same advertisement also appeared on May 8 and 15, 1819. Stellfuhren (the term used here) were mostly vehicles similar to open carriages, which drove to less-frequented places for fixed prices. See Schmidl, Wien 1833, p. 269.

The Matschaker Hof, No. 1157 in 1819 [renumbered as 1091 in 1821], fronted on the Seilergasse, but also had another entrance on Spiegelgasse, included both hotel and apartments. It was three houses closer to the Graben than Salieri's house (No. 1154 [renumbered as 1088 in 1821]). The part of the building facing Spiegelgasse today still bears a prominent inscription with its name. See Czeike, IV, p. 200; Behsel, p. 32.—KH/TA

[174] See the Intelligenzblatt, No. 100 (May 3, 1819), p. 911. The advertisement, which, among other items, noted "Hair and shaving needs, English steel blades and powder, gold and silver cleaning powder," appeared several times in this paper from March to May, 1819. The Stork was noted as located "in Baron von Bartenstein's building, next to the Schmeckender Wurm [No. 772], and across from the Zwettelhof [No. 868];" thus, the east side of the street, four buildings south of Bischof Gasse; see Behsel, pp. 23 and 25.—KH/TA

bound, 4 fl., at [the shop of] Kaulfuss und Armbruster, Singerstrasse, No. 957.[175] [//] [Blatt 71v]

C. Ph. Funke's *Kleines Real-Schul-Lexikon*, etc. *for the Understanding of the Ancient Classics*, inexpensive edition in 2 volumes, sewn binding, 7 fl. 30 kr., Gerold's Book Shop, Stephansplatz, No. 665.[176] [//]

[Blatt 72r]

BERNARD [possibly joining Beethoven at a coffee house; late afternoon or evening of Monday, May 3]: I don't believe that you should make any changes at all, before the matter concerning the journey [Karl's projected journey to study with Sailer at Landshut] is decided. [//] Otherwise, they will immediately take the opportunity again [to raise] all kinds of complaints against you. [//] [Blatt 72v] It has already gone up to the government administration, and we are to apply to Baron Kaiserstein.[177] [//]

[Blatt 73r]

BEETHOVEN [probably at his apartment; probably late morning of Tuesday, May 4]:
Duscheck, [Mödling] No. 76, at the potter's. [//] [Blatt 73v]
Along with [guardian Mathias] Tuscher.
Kugelhupf[178] [baking] form.

OLIVA [probably at his office; probably ca. 12 noon on Tuesday, May 4]: The [second English] gentleman is writing to Donaldson in Edinburgh today. The reply can be here *in 4 weeks*, and this gentleman will also remain here that long.[179] //
Bernard wants to eat in the Rossau;[180] that is too far away. [//] [Blatt 74r]

---

[175] Excerpt from an advertisement in the *Intelligenzblatt*, No. 100 (May 3, 1819), p. 922: "To be had at Chr. Kaulfuss and C. Armbruster, Book Dealers, in the Singerstrasse, No. 957, across from the Golden Apple: *Neuestes Postreisebuch durch ganz Europa* by Ant. Lenz, I.R. High Court Post Office Official, bound, 4 fl."—KH

[176] Excerpt from an advertisement in the *Intelligenzblatt*, No. 100 (May 3, 1819), p. 922: "The following interesting work, to be had in Carl Gerold's Book Shop …: C. Ph. Funke's *kleines Real-Schullexikon, ein bequemes Hülfsmittel fürdie studierenden Jugend zum Verstehen der alten Classiker.* Inexpensive edition in 2 volumes. Price 7 fl. 48 kr.; sewn-binding version 30 kr. more."—KH

[177] Baron Franz Joseph von Kaiserstein (ca. 1763–1830), treasury official and Government Councillor, lived in the Untere Breunerstrasse, No. 1193. See *Hof- und Staats-Schematismus*, 1819, I, p. 380; Schmidt, *Nekrolog*, vol. 8, p. 966.—KH

[178] Also *Gugelhupf*, a popular round cake, characteristic of Vienna.—TA

[179] For Donaldson's request for a composition, see Blatt 43r.—TA

[180] Rossau, a suburb of Vienna, almost directly north of the walled city. See Kisch, II, pp. 554–556. If Beethoven was living in the Landstrasse (south) and Oliva in city center, the destination might have seemed unnecessarily remote to go for early afternoon dinner. This sequence of entries might

State how much you demand [from Donaldson for a composition]; when it could be finished; and in what manner you want to receive the money. He is very anxious to get a composition of yours, and one would therefore never think of delaying it. [//] It is always a large-scale work. If you get 40 Ducats for the Sonata, then he can probably pay 100. // By then, the reply from Edinburgh can be here. //

[Blatt 74v]

BERNARD [presumably at a restaurant; possibly over mid-day dinner, ca. 2 p.m. on Tuesday, May 4]: The prior[181] says that we ought to make an effort, so that the Magistrat settles the matter as soon as possible. If that doesn't happen, then we ought to go to Baron Reichmann, so that he issues a memo of urgency[182] to the Magistrat. Otherwise, the prior cannot praise Professor Sailer enough, and says that [Blatt 75r] no greater salvation could befall the boy than to spend a couple of years under his supervision.[183] [//] Hochwürden.[184] [//] If the permission from the Magistrat is here, and all the travel arrangements are already made, so that he can leave immediately on the next day following confession.[185] [//] [Blatt 75v] <This prior ....> Write to him, and ask him once again for his opinion about your intention, considering the circumstances prevailing here, to take the boy to Prof[essor] Sailer. [//]

[Blatt 76r]

BEETHOVEN [probably at a coffee house in the City; late afternoon of Wednesday, May 5]:
Apartment, [Leopoldstadt,] Jägerzeile, No. 551, [available] this coming Michaelmas [September 29], 2 rooms and 1 small room, looking over the street, and 2 rooms looking into the courtyard; with an entry hall and nice kitchen, etc. Inquire

exemplify Beethoven's routine: A shopping list at home in the morning, then dinner plans with friends.—KH/TA

[181] *Don* Ignatius [Ignaz] Thomas (b. 1781), since 1818, the prior (*Propst*) at the Court Parish Church of the Barnabites of St. Michael (Michaelerkirche), on Michaelerplatz, at the east end of the Kohlmarkt, facing the Hofburg. He was the priest who, on May 5, 1814, married Karl Peters and Josepha Julianna Hochsinger. See Conscriptions-Bogen, Stadt, No. 1139 (Wiener Stadt- und Landesarchiv); Pfarre St. Michael, Trauungs-Register, 1804–1824, fol. 136.—KH

[182] *Urgens*: A note of urgency, a reminder or admonition.—KH

[183] On April 23, 1819, Beethoven had applied for a passport for Karl for the duration of two years, so that he could go to study with Sailer in Landshut. The application was turned down by the Magistrat in a letter of May 7, 1819. See Thayer-Deiters-Riemann, IV, pp. 140–142; Thayer-Forbes, pp. 724–725.—KH/TA

[184] A form of address or salutation, possibly for a letter to the Prior.—TA

[185] Religious confession to a priest before setting out on a potentially dangerous journey.—TA

at the building superintendent there and at Kohlmarkt, No. 265, on the first floor [2nd floor, American].¹⁸⁶ [//]

[Blatt 76v]

BERNARD [**probably joining Beethoven**]: It is not necessary that you send the letter back unopened; instead, after looking at the contents, you can reply that, after having set Herr von Tuscher up as guardian, you have nothing more to negotiate in this matter with the Magistrat. [//] [Blatt 77r] Now, the main thing is to obtain the Magistrat's verdict as soon as possible. [//]

BEETHOVEN [**at his apartment; probably mid-to-late morning on Thursday, May 6**]:
Candles.
For an exception under these circumstances.
Ask Oliva about things on the floor, and leaving the furniture, etc. here [at the apartment in the Landstrasse]. [Blatt 77v]
Perhaps to Mödling on Sunday [May 9].¹⁸⁷
Piano transportation with Steiner.¹⁸⁸
Discuss the capital at Steiner's.

UNKNOWN: Schindler. //

[Blatt 78r]

---

¹⁸⁶ See the *Intelligenzblatt*, No. 102 (May 5, 1819), p. 937 (advertisement), where the correct house number was 531. The same advertisement appeared on May 3 and 7, 1819.—KH

¹⁸⁷ Probably Sunday, May 9, 1819. In his calendar of 1819, Beethoven entered "arrived in Mödling on May 12!!!" See Calendar, Staatsbibliothek zu Berlin, mus.ms.autogr. Beeth. 35,87a. May 12 was a Wednesday.—KH/TA

¹⁸⁸ Sigmund Anton Steiner (1773–1838), Viennese music publisher, bought the Chemische Druckerei in the Singerstrasse, No. 932, in 1803, and in 1805 moved it to the Paternostergässchen, No. 612, a short, narrow street that branched from the Graben at its northeasternmost extremity. One year later he received permission to establish the music business. In 1814 Tobias Haslinger became a partner in the firm. Many of Beethoven's works appeared from Steiner's press, and he himself maintained friendly relations with Beethoven. Later, their relationship was troubled by financial disagreement. In mid-1819 Steiner paid Beethoven a sum of 4,000 fl. C.M. See Frimmel, *Handbuch*, II, p. 253; Alexander Weinmann, "Steiner," *MGG*, vol. 12, cols. 1241–1243; Clive, pp. 352–355; Thayer-Deiters-Riemann, IV, p. 213; Thayer-Forbes, p. 767; Alexander Weinmann, *Wiener Musikverleger*, p. 32.—KH/TA

OLIVA [presumably at his office; probably late morning on Thursday, May 6]:
If I take care of the receipt to Prague,[189] you would not, in any case, get the money *immediately*, but instead at the earliest in 10 or 14 days. [//]

BEETHOVEN [same day?]:
Napkins.
Chalk.

[Blatt 78v]

BERNARD [at a restaurant, possibly in the City; at midday dinner on Thursday, May 6]: The government administration works in an absolutely *obstructive* manner in our case, and only wants to isolate us constantly, that is the error through which we have been set back.[190] [//]

Yes, Eulogius Schneider was also in Bonn.[191] [//] [Blatt 79r] Savigny;[192] he is now a member of the State Council. [//] Daniels[193] is also in Berlin as a State Councillor. He was also very highly regarded during the Napoleonic period. [//] [Blatt 79v]

I don't believe that, after the letter from the guardian, [schoolmaster] Kudlich will allow any more communication with Karl's mother. He has given his word of honor about that. [//]

How much does midday dinner cost you when you are alone? [//] [Blatt 80r]

Grossmann was Director in Bonn? [//] His *Sechs Schüsseln* is still a fine old comedy.[194] // I think he had no property. They were chamber servants to the nobility. // It is an indolence of the heart and spirit. [//] [Blatt 80v]

---

[189] Probably the receipt mentioned on Blatt 69r, probably for his stipend from Prince Kinsky's cashier.—TA

[190] Possibly a reference to the rejection of the proposal to send Karl to Landshut.—TA

[191] Eulogius Schneider (1756–1794), Franciscan monk, came as Professor of Classical Literature and Greek to the University of Bonn, where Beethoven attended his lectures. He was a staunch adherent of the French Revolution and in 1791 went via Mainz to Strassbourg. In 1794 he was guillotined. See *Allgemeine deutsche Biographie*, vol. 32, pp. 103–105; Frimmel, *Handbuch*, II, pp. 136–137; Clive, pp. 320–321.—KH/TA

[192] Friedrich Carl von Savigny (1779–1861), legal scholar, married Kunigunde Brentano, the sister of Bettina and Clemens Brentano. In 1808 he came to the University that had been transferred from Ingolstadt to Landshut and made the acquaintance of Sailer. In 1817 he was a member of the Justice Department of the newly-created Prussian State Council in Berlin and in 1819 the Privy *Oberrevisionsrat* of the *Kassationshof*. See *Allgemeine Deutsche Biographie*, vol. 30, pp. 425–427.—KH

[193] Heinrich Gottfried Wilhelm Daniels (1754–1827), philosopher and jurist, was Professor of Law at the University of Bonn in 1783. With the arrival of the French he lost his Bonn positions, but in 1804, became an official in Paris and in 1813, General Procurator in Brussels. In 1817 he entered the Prussian service as Privy State Councillor. See *Allgemeine Deutsche Biographie*, vol. 4, pp. 735–736.—KH/TA

[194] Gustav Friedrich Wilhelm Grossmann (1744–1796), jurist, embassy councillor, and actor. In 1788 he took over the directorship of the Electoral Court Theater in Bonn and, from winter 1792, was also municipal director in Bremen. His *Nicht mehr als sechs Schüsseln*, a domestic play in 5 acts,

All of the structural models in the Polytechnic Institute are by Wiebeking. 10 rooms are full of them.[195]

You are an *Ichthyophage*, a fish-eater.

In those days, the [exchange?] officials all speculated and gained very much with bank notes on a daily basis. [//] [Blatt 81r] Many of them gained 400–600 fl. in bank notes in a week. With it they lived extravagantly, and believed that it would always be so. [//] Through the exchange rate with the exchange businesses[196] and such. [//] [Blatt 81v] <Such> [//] <Such people live ....> //

How much do chamberlains make? // The younger sons, who can make nothing else of themselves.[197] [//] [Blatt 82r] If the nobleman has no money, it's all over for him. [//] <Here they will .... They are ....> [//] They are slaves of the Court, in order to play one gentleman off against another. // Spiritual culture is completely lacking here now. [//] [Blatt 82v] He has sacrificed his time. [//] Was he stingy, then? [//] Steigentesch[198] gives his chamber servants a pension of 600 fl. C.M. yearly. [//] [Blatt 83r] He had a stroke. [//] It was always a scandal. [//] In the end, they just live sensually. In this respect, the monasteries were actually very harmful. // [Blatt 83v]

In Berlin a public "League [*Bund*] for Truth and Law" has now been formed, as opposed to the secret "League of Virtue."[199] [//] The speech by the student Riemann[200] is extremely noteworthy. [//] The matter is as trivial as they would

originated in 1777, and was published in Bonn in 1780. See Goedeke, vol. 4, pt. 1, pp. 664–665.—KH

[195] Karl Friedrich (Ritter) von Wiebeking (1762–1842), architect and engineer. He was known for his topographical maps and for them received a call to Vienna as Court Councillor and Director of the Water-Works Department. From 1805 to 1817 he was in Munich, as Director of Bridge- and Street-Works. His collection of 50 models of machines to assist in bridge- and water-works went to the Polytechnical Institute in Vienna. See Meusel, vol. 4, pp. 541–543; Neuwirth, p. 477; Wurzbach, vol. 55, pp. 281–282.—KH

[196] Bernard uses the term *Eskomptorien*.—KH

[197] In a society governed by primogeniture, the younger sons in a noble family seldom had a function or financial means.—TA

[198] Baron August Ernst Steigentesch (1774–1826), Major General, dramatic poet. At the Congress of Vienna he was Adjutant General of the King of Denmark, Adjunct I.R. Ambassador at the Danish Court. See Wurzbach, vol. 38, pp. 7–9.—KH

[199] The *Augsburger Allgemeine Zeitung*, No. 123 (May 3, 1819), p. 492, published this report from Prussia: "Here, they are speaking of a public League for Truth and Law, Freedom of Opinion, and Legal Justice, with which one wants to oppose another League that justified just these words with its talk, but refuted in its actual deeds. God grant it success." See Sydow's poem in Schickh's *Wiener Zeitschrift* 1, No. 4 (February 25, 1816), p. 31.—KH/TA

[200] Heinrich Arminius Riemann (1793–1872) a leading representative of the German *Burschenschaft* (student society). Bernard mistakenly writes his name as "Rittmann." At the Wartburg Festival, on October 18, 1817, he gave the plenary speech in the Minnesänger Hall, in which he held the princes and their lackeys guilty of having betrayed the ideals of the War of Liberation (against Napoleon). The (Viennese) *Beobachter* (November 26, December 25 and 26, 1817, and January 14, 1818) had reported on it.—KH/TA

gladly like to make it. [//] [Blatt 84r] It has become exaltation. [//] They are the only ones who do not want to know what went before, or what kind of spirit moves among the people [*Völker*]. [//] There are now 38 (sovereign)[201] lords in Germany. [//] One cannot make jokes with the Deputies; they are the spiritual power of the people. [Blatt 84v] [//] In 50 years, it will consist only of republicans. Until the French are more practical and the English are more speculative than the Germans. The Germans lack nothing but unity in order to have the superiority. [//] [Blatt 85r] Since Adam it has always been that way. //

[presumably at Beethoven's apartment in the Landstrasser Hauptstrasse:]

The accommodations here are really very nice and spacious. [//] Have you sent to Mayer?[202] [//]

One cannot reject your petition. // He [Pater Ignatius, the Prior of the Michaelerkirche] has already agreed to it from the beginning. Your letter is only a courteous invitation. [//] [Blatt 85v] He is perhaps the most enlightened and at the same time most unassuming religious figure in Vienna. [//] He is enthusiastic about him [Sailer?]. If I were to reflect for 100 years, he said, I would not be able to conceive anything better than to entrust the boy to Prof[essor] Sailer. [//] [Blatt 86r] If he would also make errors sometimes, he would have to perceive immediately who means him well, as soon as he considers it maturely. [//] It is a great mistake that Kudlich behaved violently. Weakness. His is a subordinate spirit. [//]

[End of the long conversation with Bernard on Thursday, May 6.]

[Blatt 86v]

BEETHOVEN **[at a coffee house, possibly in the City; presumably the late afternoon of Friday, May 7]**:

Joseph Blöchlinger's[203] Educational Institution for Boys,[204] in Count Choteck's

---

[201] Word added later.—KH

[202] Bernard is possibly referring to Dr. Carl Joseph Meyer, whose Sulphur-Fumigation Institute (to include treatment for deafness) they would have passed if they had walked south on Landstrasser Hauptstrasse together.—TA

[203] Joseph Blöchlinger von Bannholz (1788–1855), a friend of Johann Heinrich Pestalozzi, whose educational principles he applied as Director of an Educational Institution for Boys. Karl attended this Institution from June 22, 1819, until August 1823. See Frimmel, *Handbuch*, I, pp. 50–52; Frimmel, *Studien*, II, p. 107; Clive, pp. 36–37.—KH/TA

[204] Excerpt from an advertisement in the *Intelligenzblatt*, No. 102 (May 5, 1819), p. 935: "Joseph Blöchlinger's Educational Institution for Boys, which until now was located in the Kaiserstrasse [today's Josephstädter Strasse] No. 8 in the Josephstadt, across from the Cavalry Barracks, has, effective May 1, this year, moved to the house of Count Chotek, No. 26, where Herr Ellmauer's Educational Institution formerly was." The same advertisement also appeared on May 3 and 7, 1819. Beethoven most likely read the issue of May 7.

Blöchlinger's former location, No. 8, was technically in the suburb of Altlerchenfeld, slightly southeast of the Cavalry Barracks, which were on the north side of Kaiserstrasse, three blocks in from

house, No. 26 in the Josephstadt, where Ellmaurer's Educational Institution formerly was. [//]

[Blatt 87r][205]

BERNARD [seemingly joining Beethoven]: Pat[er] Ig[natius][206] has also said that the matter is going very slowly at the Magistrat's. [//]

[Blatt 87v]

BEETHOVEN [possibly replying so as not to be overheard]: Once authority exists, it influences everything against the majority, which it is not. [//] [Blatt 88r]

[at a coffee house or restaurant, reading the newspapers; presumably the afternoon of Saturday, May 8:]

An der Wien, beyond the Theater, at the *Goldener Kegel* [Golden Bowling Pin], No. 36, in the second floor [third floor, American], from Michaelmas, a large room, 2 [regular] rooms, 4 small rooms, etc.[207] Schuster, No. 7[208] [//]

[Blatt 88v]

BERNARD [presumably joining Beethoven at a coffee house or restaurant; late afternoon and evening of Saturday, May 8]: He [possibly Archduke Rudolph] will probably get 500,000 Gulden in yearly income. [//] Thereby you have become a

---

the *Linie*. The new location, No. 26, was technically in the suburb of Strozzi Grund, also on the south side of Kaiserstrasse, just east of today's intersection with Strozzi Gasse. The so-called Strozzipalais was built in 1702 for Countess Maria Catharina Strozzi, came into the possession of Count Carl Chotek in 1753, and remained with his family until ca. 1841. Over the years, through 1918, several educational institutions were located there. Today the building (its northern facade somewhat altered and its address now Josefstädter Strasse No. 39) houses the Finanz-Amt (financial offices) of suburban Josephstadt. See Behsel, pp. 181 and 188; Czeike, *Das grosse Groner*, pp. 793–794 (with illustration); Faber, pp. 32–33 (with illustrations); Klusacek and Stimmer, photo facing p. 23 (current facade); Messner, *Die Josefstadt*, p. 50.—KH/TA

[205] The lower half of Blatt 87 has been torn out.—KH

[206] See Blatt 74v above.—TA

[207] See the *Intelligenzblatt*, No. 105 (May 8, 1819), p. 969 (Apartment advertisements). Beethoven made a rare slip of the pencil, writing *oder* instead of *ober*. The location was on the north side of the Wien River (today's Linke Wienzeile), one building east of Pfarrgasse (roughly today's Laimgrubengasse) and therefore two modern blocks further out from (therefore *ober*, beyond, or upstream from) the Theater an der Wien (see Behsel, p. 139).—KH/TA

[208] This addition might have been a name or occupation (shoemaker) and a *Wohnpartei* (apartment) number, possibly at Laimgrube No. 36 [renumbered as 37 in 1821]. Conscriptions-Bogen (census sheet), Laimgrube 37 (new collation 37/27), Bogen of 1805, layer no. 5 (just before 1820) includes a shoemaker, Franz Streicher (b. 1776), and his family. The Bogen for *Wohnpartei* 7 in this era seems not to survive.—TA

Godfather. [//] It will certainly give him great joy. In general it is good if such a man understands more than usual about the matter. [//] [Blatt 89r]

I occasionally eat at her place.[209] A week ago he ate there. She is extremely good-natured and benevolent. She has taken in a poor girl, whom she is bringing up entirely as if she were her daughter. Her income, however, also amounts to over 20,000 Gulden yearly. [//] [Blatt 89v] Last year, the [*Wiener*] *Zeitung* brought in over 60,000 Gulden in net profit, of which she gets a third. [//]

His wife has a half share, because her brother gets just this much.[210] [//]

Baumann[211] has 6 children; obviously, that also gives him concern for the future. [//] [Blatt 90r]

In the meantime, they will someday inherit the property of the Salmy woman[212] and of the Zimmer woman,[213] who is very rich. [//]

He, however, would like to have everything to himself, and right now. [//]

Have you told the Archduke [Rudolph] what it says in the *Allgemeine Zeitung*?[214]

---

[209] Seemingly members of the Ghelen *Erben* (heirs), a family of owners of the *Wiener Zeitung*, of which Bernard will soon be chief editor. See also Heft 64, Blätter 18r–19r (May 1, 1824); Czeike, II, p. 540, and V, p. 648.—TA

[210] This seemingly pertains to Rosalie Baumann, *née* von Rambach (noted below) and her brother, who were among the so-called "Ghelen Heirs." See also Heft 3, Blatt 49 v, and Heft 12, Blatt 5r.—TA

[211] Carl Baumann (b. 1765), "silent partner" in the I.R. priv. Himberg Paint and Dye Factory, whose owner was Romain Baboin. The store was at Franziskanerplatz No. 976. He lived at Weihburggasse No. 980 [renumbered as 924 in 1821] with his wife Rosalie (b. 1786) and six children: Carl (b. 1805), Alexander (b. 1814), Rosalia (b. 1806), Wilhelmine (b. 1808), Eva (b. ?), and Maria (b. 1816). See Conscriptions-Bogen, Stadt, No. 924, Wohnpartei 7 (Stadt- und Landesarchiv, Vienna), and Redl, 1820, p. 128; Behsel, p. 27; Heft 12, Blätter 5r–5v.—KH/TA

[212] A Franziska Salmy (b. 1788), wife of the business partner Joseph Salmy, can be found in the Conscription Census. Possibly she is the same person as the Fanny (diminutive of Franziska) von Salmy, supporting member of the Gesellschaft der Musikfreunde, listed without further identification in Ziegler. See Conscriptions-Bogen, Stadt, No. 1062 (Stadt- und Landesarchiv, Vienna); Ziegler, *Addressen-Buch* (1823), p. 181. Stadt, Plankengasse No. 1126, became 1062 in 1821 (Behsel, p. 32).—KH/TA

[213] Possibly one of the two amateur pianists, Therese and Marie Zimmer, who lived in the Kärntnerstrasse, No. 1017. See Ziegler, *Addressen-Buch*, p. 60.

Stadt, Kärntnerstrasse No. 1079, became No. 1017 in 1821 (Behsel, p. 30). Conscriptions-Bogen Stadt No. 1017, Wohnpartei 5 (new collation 1017/7), Bogen of 1818, layer no. 1, lists Johann von Zimmerl (b. Vienna, 1760), Appeals Councillor and Consultant to the Court Commission in Legal Matters; his wife Theresia (b. 1770); niece Theresia Schüller (b. 1793); niece M[aria] Anna von Gerstenbrand (b. 1807); nephew Johann Georg Schüller (b. 1783), a Rural Affairs Councillor; and Franz Schüller (b. 1792), a bookkeeper at the National Bank (Wiener Stadt- und Landesarchiv). If Bernard meant one of these (not a foregone conclusion), it must have been the wife of the household.—KH/TA

[214] In the *Augsburger Allgemeine Zeitung*, No. 124 (May 4, 1819), p. 496, there appeared the following "correspondence report" from Vienna, dated April 26: "Archduke Rudolph, Archbishop of Olmütz, will also depart for his residence [in Moravia] soon. It is said that he has engaged the

[//] [Blatt 90v] It will give him ideas, though, concerning his relationship with you. [//]

I don't talk about such matters with anyone, least of all with [guardian] T[uscher], to whom I am merely courteous. [//] [Blatt 91r]

He[215] is a person without spirit, and subordinates [himself]. [//] He is very ill and must always have his own apparatus for sitting in a carriage. I believe that he suffers from chronic tenesmus.[216] [//] [Blatt 91v]

Who was his teacher,[217] then? [//] If only he [Archduke Rudolph] had a nice library. The library, however, must be in Vienna. In the meantime, the reverend and faithful Chapter[218] will already feed the sheep. [//] [Blatt 92r] He has affection for you; otherwise, he appears to be a simple man. [//]

I asked whether it is still raining. It is shining from the kitchen.[219]

First we want to cut through the present matter. [//] [Blatt 92v] At age 12 a child is not so far developed that he cannot still improve a great deal, if he receives proper guidance. He [Karl] will be subject [to guidance] at least another 6 years, though, and if this is done with purpose, [Blatt 92a-recto] it will be impossible to go wrong. // As it appears to me, Tuscher means merely that no one is to have priority, which obviously is ill applied here. [//] I believe that he has always meant it well, but he often speaks without thinking about it first. [//] [Blatt 92a-verso] The entire Magistrat suffers from a Philistine viewpoint. [//]

---

famous Beethoven as his Kapellmeister there." Rudolph was chosen for the position of Archbishop on March 24, 1819, and Cardinal on June 4 of that year, but his installation in Olmütz did not take place until March 9, 1820.—KH/TA

[215] Possibly Tuscher or Kudlich (see Blatt 86r), neither of whom Bernard particularly liked.—TA

[216] Original German *Zwang* (or *Stuhlzwang*), a condition in which the sufferer constantly feels the need for a bowel movement. This sentence may also refer to Archduke Rudolph, but his primary affliction was epilepsy, which would probably have been termed *Fallsucht*. In the original, the word *Zwang* is repeated again, below, for emphasis.—TA

[217] Probably a reference to Archduke Rudolph and his teacher Baumeister, because Baumeister is mentioned on Blatt 94v.—TA

[218] Presumably the ecclesiastical Chapter in Olmütz; Rudolph would not take office there for another ten months.—TA

[219] Although May 7–10 were generally overcast or cloudy, official reports (made at 8 a.m., 3 p.m., and 10 p.m. each day) indicate rain only at 3 p.m. on Sunday, May 9; see the *Wiener Zeitung*, No. 107 (May 11, 1819), p. 427, among others. Bernard's remark, however, indicates the possibility of changing weather, and indeed Viennese weather often varies quickly—from cloudy to sunny to rain showers and back—throughout the day. Therefore the weather reports do not provide conclusive evidence for dating this entry.—TA

Haven't you been to Herr von Schmerling's yet?[220]

It was only here, in order to escape the tensions from both sides.

If the boy is out [of school] sometime, [Blatt 93r] you can seek to reestablish the entire matter in its previous standing, and with the greatest calm and assurance.

I told Pater Ignaz that we asked Court Councillor Ohms[221] beforehand, and that he placed in our hands the manner and means of introducing the matter; because he [Blatt 93v: no writing] [Blatt 94r] saw absolutely no obstacle in this matter. If that is so, said Pat[er] Ig[natius], we can also count on the happiest success if Court Councillor Ohms could render complete judgment in the case. [//] At most, it can only be another 14 days until everything is decided. [//] [Blatt 94v] But it must be a generally applicable decree, otherwise everyone would do as he pleased. [//] <that is, if ....> [//] Such a position is always very advantageous, because it requires very little work, provides spare time, is independent, and lasts for life. [//]

Perhaps Baumeister[222] is only a titular Government Councillor. [//] [Blatt 95r]

Have you heard nothing from Troxler[223] for a long time? He has married. Nothing more by way of his literary work has become known for a long time. He upset Schelling[224] in his last work about life and its problems, so that he became

[220] Joseph Ritter von Schmerling (1777 – ca. 1827), doctor of law, was the brother of Leopold Schmerling, the husband of Anna Giannatasio. While he was named Provincial Councillor to the Lower Austrian *Landrecht* in 1818, he appeared in the 1819 *Schematismus* as Appellate Councillor of the Appellate and Criminal High Court. See Conscriptions-Bogen, Stadt, No. 968; *Hof- und Staats-Schematismus*, 1818, I, p. 567, and 1819, I, p. 551; Wurzbach, vol. 30, p. 186; Clive, pp. 128–129.—KH

[221] Concerning Ohms, see Blatt 22r above. He is not to be confused with Ohmayer (Blatt 6a-recto above).—TA

[222] Joseph Anton Ignaz Edler von Baumeister (1750–1819), jurist, Lower Austrian Titular Government Councillor. From 1792 to 1801 he was tutor to the princes Ludwig and Rudoph, later librarian to Archduke Rudolph and lived in Prince Lichtenstein's house in the Vordere Schenkenstrasse No. 53. He published several works on history. See Gräffer-Czikann, I, p. 207; *Hof- und Staats-Schematismus*, 1819, I, pp. 184 and 386; Wurzbach, vol. 1, pp. 190–191.—KH/TA

[223] Ignaz Paul Vitalis Troxler (1780–1866), philosopher and medical man. He attended Schelling's lectures in Jena in 1800, but, with his book *Blicke in das Wesen des Menschen* (Aarau, 1811), alienated himself from Nature philosophy as Schelling taught it. In 1815 he spent time at the Congress of Vienna as an ambassador from Switzerland and, in 1820, became Professor of Philosophy and History in Lucerne. He then went to Aarau as a practicing physician and, from 1830, taught philosophy in Basel. See *Allgemeine Deutsche Biographie*, vol. 38, p. 667.—KH

[224] Friedrich Wilhelm Joseph Schelling (b. Leonberg, Württemberg, 1775; d. Bad Ragaz, Switzerland, 1854), German romantic pantheistic Nature philosopher, ennobled in 1808. See Czeike, V, p. 74; Garland, p. 789.—TA

embattled with the famous Professor Oken[225] over several [Blatt 96r][226] philosophical ideas, which Oken is said to have stolen from him, whereby he has likewise become famous. Both have quarreled terribly about it, and each has declared that the other one has stolen the ideas from him.

She [singer Caroline Willmann] will have arrived about a week ago.[227] They say that she is performing guest roles. [//] [Blatt 95v] She would like to stay in Munich, but also has an engagement in Braunschweig. This daughter is very beautiful and well educated; she has one of the best proportioned and most beautiful faces here. [//] She has not yet reached her majority and has the famous Prof[essor] Steffens in Breslau[228] as her guardian.[229] She has property from her mother amounting to ca. 30,000 fl. [//]

[End of Bernard's long conversation; presumably the evening of Saturday, May 8.]

[Blatt 96v]

BEETHOVEN **[possibly alone in Mödling, inspecting an apartment; Sunday, May 9]**:[230]

Ground-level kitchen, spacious. Chicken coops on the ground level. Ceiling, etc. Twine.[231]

---

[225] Lorenz Oken (1779–1851), philosopher and medical man, belonged among the leading romantic Nature philosophers. From 1807 to 1809 he taught in Jena, where his most significant Nature philosophical and Nature historical works originated. In 1817 he was a participant of the Wartburgfest (see Blatt 83v above) and proponent of the liberal-democratic *Burschenschaft* movement. In May 1819, presented with the alternative of assuming the editorship of the magazine *Isis, oder Encyclopädische Zeitung* or giving up his professorship, he decided to resign his teaching position. See *Allgemeine Deutsche Biographie*, vol. 24, pp. 216–218.—KH

[226] The rectos of Blätter 95 and 96 were apparently both filled before their respective versos.—TA

[227] Oliva noted above (Blatt 58r) that Bernard was reputedly carrying on an affair with Caroline Willmann, a singer at the Theater an der Wien (and whose family Beethoven had known since Bonn). On April 26, 1819, she had left Vienna for Munich. See *Wiener Zeitung*, No. 96 (April 28, 1819), p. 383. On November 25, 1823, Bernard ended up marrying another woman, Magdalena Grassl, who also had property in the Wieden (Blatt 4r above).—TA

[228] Heinrich (Henrik) Steffens (1773–1845), Nature philosopher and poet, was one of the closest adherents and friends of Schelling. From 1811 to 1831 he taught in Breslau as a Professor of Physics and Philosophy and was also active in the liberation struggle against Napoleon. Steffens's wife Johanna was a daughter of composer-conductor Johann Friedrich Reichardt (1752–1814), who had visited Vienna in 1808–1809. See *Allgemeine Deutsche Biographie*, vol. 35, pp. 555–557.—KH/TA

[229] Born in 1796, Willmann would reach her majority in 1820. For the family's Breslau connection, see Blatt 58r above.—TA

[230] On Thursday, May 6 (Blatt 77v above), Beethoven had noted that he might spend Sunday in Mödling.—TA

[231] Beethoven's original *Spagad* (from spaghetti) is defined as *Bindfaden* or twine.—KH/TA

Piano[:] Steiner or the old piano tuner.[232]

[at a coffee house or restaurant in Vienna; presumably the afternoon of Monday, May 10:]

In all bookshops: *Friedrich Christians Vermächtniss an seine Söhne*, etc., etc. [Blatt 97r] by J.M. Sailer; 2 parts with the author's portrait; 2nd improved and expanded edition; 1 fl. 30 kr. W.W.

By the same author: *Goldkörner der Weissheit u[nd] Tugend zur Unterhaltung für edle Seelen*, in 2 parts, 3rd improved and expanded edition, [Blatt 97v] 1 fl. 12 kr. W.W.

By the same author: *Krankenbibel*, 3rd expanded and improved edition, 1 fl. 30 kr. W.W.[233]

Housekeeper who cooks well, etc.; submit address with [the code] A.W. at the Hohe Brücke, <No. 854> [Blatt 98r] [No.] 151 in the Lottery Collector's Office.[234]

[possibly in his apartment; possibly late morning of Tuesday, May 11:][235]

New writing book.[236]

Wax candles.

This evening at Karl's, ask where the piano tuner lives.[237] [//]

[Blatt 98v]

[232] See the reference to the piano tuner on Blatt 98r below.—TA

[233] Excerpt from an advertisement in the *Intelligenzblatt*, No. 106 (May 10, 1819), p. 985, with all three titles of religious and inspirational books by Sailer, with whom Beethoven hoped that Karl might study in Landshut. The same advertisement also appeared on May 14, 1819.—KH/TA

[234] See the *Intelligenzblatt*, No. 106 (May 10, 1819), p. 976 (Advertisements). The woman who placed this advertisement also noted that she would be happy working in the country, which might have appealed to Beethoven, about to move to Mödling. Stadt No. 151 would be renumbered as 144 in 1821. The same advertisement also appeared on May 7 and 12, 1819. The stray "854" (which Beethoven crossed out) was accidentally copied from an advertisement immediately below this one.—KH/TA

[235] Beethoven is noting the errands to be run before his move to Mödling on Wednesday, May 12.—TA

[236] Beethoven's note to himself to buy another blank book (*Schreibe-Buch*) to use as a conversation book.—TA

[237] Beethoven will have his final visit with Karl at Kudlich's school, that evening, May 11. See the reference to the piano tuner on Blatt 96v above.—TA

BERNARD [probably at a coffee house or restaurant; possibly the afternoon of Tuesday, May 11]: Baron Sala[238]—He himself will speak with Baron Haan,[239] so that both positions press the matter mutually. You have no objection if it goes to the Government, then whether it will be allowed will depend upon the highest [= Imperial] decision. [//] [Blatt 99r] The Police Department has nothing to decide, but will only [be] <urged> asked whether it has nothing to state against it.[240] [//] One is more likely to prevail with the Government, since no such obscure men occupy the positions, as they do among [Blatt 100r] the lower officials. Also nothing remains to be done, as happens with the Magistrat; instead everything will be dispatched on the spot. [//]

[Beethoven moves to Mödling on Wednesday, May 12.]

[Blatt 99v]

COACH STATION PROPRIETOR OR COACHMAN [presumably at the coach stop in Mödling; possibly Thursday, May 13, or Friday, May 14]:
½ day [costs] 5 fl. 30 kr.
[Carriage with] 2 horses to Vienna, a full day, [costs] 8 fl., including toll and tip. //
[Carriage with] 1 horse, ditto, [costs] 5 fl., [including] toll and tip. [//]

[Blatt 100v]

BEETHOVEN [probably at a coffee house or restaurant in Mödling; probably the afternoon of Saturday, May 15, or possibly Sunday, May 16]:[241]
3 chairs in Karl's room. Also 3 boards [shelves?].
Wiener Zeitung of May 15, 1819: "France. In France, a private insurance company

---

[238] Baron Felix von Sala (ca. 1786–1840), Chamberlain and Lower Austrian Governmental document drafter to the Provincial Government to Archducal Austria below the Enns, lived in the City, No. 470. See *Hof- und Staats-Schematismus*, 1819, I, p. 382; Schmidt, *Nekrolog*, vol. 18, p. 1350.—KH/TA

[239] There seem to be three possible identifications: (1) Joseph *Edler* von Haan, Appellate Councillor, living in the City, Fischerstiege No. 198. See *Hof- und Staats-Schematismus*, 1819, I, p. 550; (2) Joseph Georg *Edler* von Haan, Lower Austrian Provincial Councillor at the Landrecht, living in the City, Dorotheergasse No. 1171; or (3) Baron Joseph von Haan, Lower Austrian Governmental Councillor and Vice City Administrator, living in the City, Kärntnerstrasse No. 1004. See *Hof- und Staats-Schematismus*, 1819, I, p. 386.—KH

[240] Beethoven and his nephew were indeed under Police surveillance during this period. See the report concerning Karl's family background and progress in school that Police chief Count Joseph Sedlnitzky submitted to Emperor Franz on June 20, 1820, in Albrecht, *Letters*, No. 270, and the sobering portrait of Count Sedlnitzky (between pp. 144 and 145).—TA

[241] The Viennese newspapers of Saturday, May 15 (quoted below), may have arrived in Mödling that day, but surely by Sunday, May 16.—TA

has been established to support soldiers ....".[242] To give Akademies [concerts] for this purpose would be very [Blatt 101r] beneficial and worthy of imitation.

Houses at 1,200 fl. W.W. and 2,000 fl. W.W. are for sale in Döbling; inquire at Herr Hofmann's, Johannesgasse in Fünfhaus, from 3 to 4 o'clock.[243]

Cook combined with servant[244] would be best for you. [Blatt 101v]

At Hochberg's Factory in the Rossau, Servitengasse No. 89, all types of machines useful for fishing are to be had.[245]

[in Mödling; probably jotted over several days after ca. May 16:]

Spend whole days on the Lichtenstein Hills in Mödling.[246]

Matzleinsdorfer Linie.[247]

Linen.   Metronome. [//] [Blatt 102r]

The unfortunate Editor, as a gallant Don Giovanni.[248]

Occasional piece on Lichtenstein's Soldiers Monument.[249]

Fantasie in C minor.[250]

No prelude.[251]

Transport the easy chair from the city.

Barber razor. [Blatt 102v]

---

[242] Extract from the *Wiener Zeitung*, No. 111 (May 15, 1819), p. 441. The lengthy report notes that in France a private insurance company will enroll boys from two to six years. Their yearly capital will contribute to a common fund. When they reach their adolescence and are subject to military service, those exempted from service will forfeit their funds, while those who serve in the military will receive not only their own, but a portion of the moneys forfeited by the others.—KH/TA

[243] See the *Intelligenzblatt*, No. 111 (May 15, 1819), p. 1033. The same advertisement also appeared on May 13 and 18, 1819. Fünfhaus, a wine village west of Vienna, between Mariahilf and Penzing; incorporated into the fifteenth Bezirk of Vienna in 1892. See Groner, p. 123.—KH/TA

[244] Beethoven uses the masculine, rather than the feminine forms of these nouns.—TA

[245] See the *Intelligenzblatt*, No. 111 (May 15, 1819), p. 1033. The same advertisement also appeared on May 3 and 22, 1819.—KH

[246] Several hills near Mödling: the lower Anninger, the Kalenderberg, and the Maaberg.—KH

[247] The *Zeiselwagen* (common carriages for about ten passengers) drove from the Matzleinsdorfer Linie (southwest of Vienna) to Mödling. See Weidmann, pp. 273–275.—KH

[248] Difficult to read: "*Re___*" [Ed—itor] written swiftly over other words. Beethoven might have been imagining a little satirical piece about his friend, the editor Bernard, infatuated with the singer Caroline Willmann.—KH/TA

[249] In 1813 Prince Johann von Liechtenstein (1760–1836) had erected a small Greek temple on the lower Anninger. Designed by architect Joseph Kornhäusel (1782–1860), Liechtenstein's building director from 1812 to 1818, it was white with Doric columns and was dedicated to Austria's military glory. In the temple was a statue of Bellona (the mythological goddess of war) and under it the grave vault of five Austrian soldiers who had rescued the Prince at the Battle of Aspern (May 21–22, 1809). Beethoven would later provide the music (*Die Weihe des Hauses*) when Kornhäusel's redesigned Theater in the Josephstadt opened in October, 1822. See Weidmann, pp. 273–275; "Kornhäusel," Czeike, III, pp. 579–580; Filek, pp. 62–63, with illustration by Max Frey.—KH/TA

[250] Possibly Mozart's Fantasia in C minor, K.475, or a projected composition of his own.—TA

[251] See Beethoven's earlier reference to the organ prelude before a Kyrie (Blatt 101 above).—TA

The road from Mödling to Vienna goes through Atzgersdorf.[252] [Blatt 103r][253]
Shoe-horn and boot jack.
Wax candles. [//]

[Blatt 103v]

BERNARD [probably in Vienna, when Beethoven visited back in the City; probably before ca. June 1]:[254] Then he can take serious measures only if it got through the offices to its decision. [//] [Blatt 104r: no writing] [Blatt 104v] If the Appellate Court has it go back to the Government Administration, then you ought to turn to the Archduke. But if it goes to the political offices, you ought to wait until [it] is back from this one.

[Blatt 105r]

TUSCHER [?][255] [probably in Vienna; during the same visit as the entry immediately above]: My domestic situation is not like that. [//] The old (weak!) woman who is at my place. [//] My little daughter. [//] My constant preoccupation ....
[//]

BEETHOVEN:
   6
   4
   6
  12
  15[256]
  10

End of Heft 2

---

[252] Beethoven spelled it "Azersdorf." Atzgersdorf is a village southwest of Vienna.—KH
[253] The top halves of Blätter 103 and 104 have been torn off.—KH
[254] When Beethoven lived in the country in the summers, he usually visited back in the City every week or two.—TA
[255] Same handwriting as on Blatt 6a-verso. Earlier German editor Georg Schünemann thought that the writer might be Mathias von Tuscher, who served as Karl's guardian from March 26 to July 5, 1819. See also Blatt 6r above.—KH
[256] Beethoven originally wrote 30.—KH

Heft 3

(November 20, 1819 – ca. December 6, 1819)

[Inside front cover]

BEETHOVEN [probably at his apartment in the Ballgasse; probably late morning, Saturday, November 20, 1819]:[1]

---

[1] Beethoven customarily worked through the morning in his apartment, then went out in early/ mid-afternoon to eat midday dinner in a restaurant. On this occasion (November 20), as on many others, he was joined by newspaper editor Joseph Carl Bernard; therefore his list of errands was probably made in the morning before he left his apartment.

In June 1819 Beethoven's nephew Karl changed schools and now studied at Joseph Blöchlinger's institute in the west-northwestern suburb of Josephstadt, on the south side of Kaiserstrasse (today's Josefstädter Strasse) in the former Strozzi Palace (no longer visible behind the former Finanz-Amt), roughly five blocks west of the Glacis. At some time while spending the summer of 1819 in Mödling, and with the intention of being near Karl's boarding school, Beethoven leased a new apartment, also in the Josephstadt, on the Glacis, across the street from and just north of the Auersperg Palace, and therefore about six blocks from Blöchlinger's school. Customary of the time, Beethoven's lease would have essentially run from Michaelmas (September 29), 1819, to St. George's Day (April 24), 1820. It appears, however, that the apartment was not ready for occupancy, and on October 10 he wrote from Mödling to his friend Bernard in Vienna, asking him to have his apartment painted, preferably light green (Anderson, No. 976; Brandenburg, No. 1340).

The apartment on the Josephstädter Glacis was still not ready when Beethoven returned to Vienna from Mödling on ca. October 15, so he was forced to take temporary quarters (possibly secured for him by Bernard) in the City, in the house "Zum alten Blumenstock," to which he himself referred in diminutive form, the "Blumenstöckl," located on the Ballgasse (or diminutive Ballgassel), No. 986 [renumbered as 930 in 1821] about three blocks southwest of the Stephansdom. Ballgasse ran a semicircular course from roughly the midpoint of Rauhensteingasse (east of the house where Mozart had died) south, and then turned east to meet Weihburggasse at Franziskanerplatz. The later building on that site is Ballgasse 6 today. On the corner of Ballgasse and Rauhensteingasse, facing the latter [No. 983, renumbered as 927 in 1821] were the offices of the *Wiener Zeitung*, of which Bernard became editor on October 4, 1819. Therefore, Beethoven lived within a block of Bernard's newspaper office and within three blocks of his level-headed friend Franz Oliva.

Even though Beethoven may have partially moved into the Glacis apartment by the end of November 1819 (which could account for Fanny Giannatasio del Rio's diary reference to Beethoven's move to the Josephstadt by December), further renovations (seemingly including a new second stove) continued slowly in the cold winter, and Beethoven kept his temporary quarters in the Blumenstöckl (which he gave as his legal address on October 30, 1819, and January 7, 1820) until Candlemas (February 2), 1820, when he finally finished his move to the Josephstadt. See Behsel, p. 28; Klein, pp. 108–109; Thayer-Forbes, p. 743.—TA

Pick up the watch today.[2]

Pen-knife.

Tooth powder.

[Blatt 1r]

BERNARD [probably in a restaurant at midday dinner; ca. 2 p.m. on Saturday, November 20]: I just put an article about the last examination of the pupils at the Singing Institute in the *Zeitung*.[3] [//]

When will you write to Weissenbach?[4] // You should press them to notify you of the difficulties that are used as an excuse, so one can refute them. // But there is always gossip. [//] [Blatt 1v] I doubt that he should be in agreement, but it is certain that he could have done more. [//]

Tomorrow [Sunday, November 21] at midday, there is a theatrical entertainment at the Kärntnertor at 12:30;[5] for this reason, I cannot have the honor of eating at

---

[2] See Beethoven's conversation with the watchmaker, a week or so later, on Blatt 30v below.—TA

[3] The following article appeared in the *Wiener Zeitung* (which Joseph Carl Bernard had now edited since October 4, 1819), No. 268 (November 23, 1819), p. 1069: "On the 8th of this month, the second public examination of the pupils at the Institute, which the Gesellschaft der Musikfreunde des Oesterreichischen Kaiserstaates has established, took place ... under the direction of Herr Hauschka. The first part pertained to theoretical matters, the second consisted of performance .... This is all supported by the dues from the members and benefit concerts, ... [such as one] on the 28th of this month, ... featuring *Das befreyte Deutschland* by the poetess Caroline Pichler, set to music by Ludwig Spohr. A second and similar grand work [*Der Sieg des Kreuzes*, poem by Bernard] is expected from Ludwig van Beethoven, which this famous composer has agreed to write for the Gesellschaft." See Frimmel, *Handbuch*, I, p. 36.—KH/TA

[4] Aloys Weissenbach (1766–1821), physician and author in Salzburg. During his journey to Vienna in 1814, he met Beethoven, and a copy of his book *Meine Reise zum Congress, Wahrheit und Dichtung* [My Journey to the Congress: Truth and Fiction] (Vienna, 1816) was in Beethoven's estate. For the Congress of Vienna, Weissenbach wrote the text to Beethoven's cantata *Der glorreiche Augenblick*, Op. 136, premiered on November 29, 1814. The original text bears a ban on performance (dated February 17, 1814) in the hand of Friedrich Gentz. From this it may be concluded that Bernard did not have to rework the libretto only because of the bombastic text (as Schindler described it), but also for political reasons.

At this time (see Blatt 4r below), Weissenbach had been drawn into Beethoven's plans to have Karl educated abroad. See Frimmel, *Handbuch*, II, pp. 413–415; Kinsky-Halm, p. 413; Schindler-MacArdle, p. 172; Clive, pp. 394–395.—KH/TA

[5] On Sunday, November 21, 1819, a midday entertainment "for the benefit of Herr Töpfer and Herr Kettel" [a wordplay on *Topf* (pot) and *Kessel* (kettle), therefore "Mr. Pot and Mr. Kettle"] took place at the Kärntnertor Theater, at which *Der Tagesbefehl*, a drama in 2 acts by Carl Töpfer was premiered. See the *Wiener Zeitschrift*, No. 138 (November 18, 1819), p. 1126, and No. 141 (November 25, 1819), pp. 1148–1150.

No *Zettel* (poster) has survived for the midday benefit performance itself. Called *Der Tagsbefehl* on later surviving Zettel, it was performed again on Monday, November 22; Thursday, November 25; Sunday, November 28; and several more times through the end of the year (Bibliothek, Österreichisches Theatermuseum; courtesy of Othmar Barnert).—KH/TA

the Strong One's [at Starke's].[6] Don't you want to go to the Kärntnertor, too? [//] [Blatt 2r]

He wasn't certain what to find in these matters; therefore the uncertainty in his behavior.[7] [//]

The two actors Töpfer[8] and Kettel[9] have a free-will admission fee. [//] The management doesn't want to lose anything because of this act of kindness.[10] [//] When are you going to see Mad[ame] Weissenthurn?[11] [//] [Blatt 2v]

I told the lawyer that such gossip was absolutely inappropriate to the authorities. [//] Have you written to him that you have not received the decision with the number? [//] He has probably been here for 15 or 16 years now. [//] He has a pair of *gray* pantaloons from Manchester, which he wears everywhere. [//] [Blatt 3r] A specific decree must finally follow, after which the matter can be continued without change. [//] He is a short man, with thin hair, some 50 years old. [//] If it doesn't work in the present manner, nothing is more purposeful than to appeal as soon as possible [Blatt 3v] Cuckold maker [next to it, a pencil sketch of a woman's head in profile]. [//] She [Johanna van Beethoven] is a child of Vienna. [//] It appears to me, though, that <the Magistrat> the Provincial Judge had prearranged the matter in this way after [lawyer Joseph von] Schmerling's departure. For how, after two

---

[6] Friedrich Starke (1774–1835), hornist, composer, military band director, piano teacher, and sometime self-publisher. Beethoven was fond of puns, and Bernard was merely making a wordplay on Starke's name; *stark* means strong. From 1812 to 1822 Starke was a hornist (supposedly at Beethoven's recommendation) in the Kärntnertor Theater's orchestra and had played in the 1814 revival of *Fidelio*. In ca. 1815 he was nephew Karl's piano teacher. His *Wiener Pianoforte-Schule in III Abtheilungen*, Op. 128, appeared from 1819 to 1821. Part 2 appeared in June 1820 and included the Andante and Rondo movements from Beethoven's Piano Sonata in D, Op. 28. See Frimmel, *Handbuch*, II, pp. 248–250; Hans Jancik, "Starke," *MGG*, vol. 12, col. 1189; Clive, pp. 348–349; *Wiener Zeitung*, No. 133 (June 12, 1820), p. 528.—KH/TA

[7] Possibly a reference to the first volume of Starke's *Wiener Pianoforte Schule*, published at his own expense in 1819.—TA

[8] Karl Töpfer (1792–1871), court actor, author, and dramatist, was a member of the Burgtheater in Vienna from 1816 to 1824. See *Portrait-Katalog*, pp. 300 and 355; Wurzbach, vol. 45, pp. 237–239.—KH

[9] Johann Georg Kettel (1789–1862), actor, was a member of the Burgtheater in Vienna from 1816 to 1825. See *Allgemeine Deutsche Biographie*, vol. 15, pp. 669–670; *Hof- und Staats-Schematismus*, 1819, I, p. 128.—KH

[10] A sarcastic reference to the fact that the management gave these two actors a midday time for their benefit performance, rather than the regular 7 p.m. hour. That evening, the Burgtheater gave Ernst Raupach's tragedy *Die Fürsten Chawansky*; the Kärntnertor Theater performed Mozart's *Don Juan* (in German); while a masked ball was given in both Redoutensäle to benefit the Widows and Orphans of Fine Artists (*bildende Künstler*). See the Zettel for the evening activities (Bibliothek, Österreichisches Theatermuseum).—TA

[11] Johanna Franul von Weissenthurn (*née* Grünberg), poet and court actress, 1773–1847, born in Koblenz. In 1789, after her first engagement in Munich, she came to the Court Theater in Vienna, where she remained until 1842. Several volumes of her plays appeared in print. See Wurzbach, vol. 4, pp. 341–342; Clive, p. 195.—TA/KH

years, would she only now have come to think of asking about your nobility? [//] [Blatt 4r]

Nothing better than [sending Karl] to Salzburg. There will already be skillful teachers and pedagogues there, as well.[12] [Pencil sketch of a head in profile.] [//] One cannot distance himself from it enough. [//]

Here is the upper house, where authentic wine is drunk; below is the lower house, where bad wine is drunk.[13] [//] [Blatt 4v]

The Magistrat is merely concerned with Karl. [//]

I shall now go to the Alservorstadt and give [Starke] my regrets concerning tomorrow.[14] [//][15] I really cannot, because of the midday [theatrical] entertainment. [//] He [actor Karl Töpfer] is very fine. [//] He [Starke?] also has only you to thank for it. [//] Merchants. [//] [Blatt 5r] He gets more for your works than you do. [//]

[There seem to be no conversational entries for Sunday, November 21, when Beethoven has dinner with Friedrich Starke at the latter's apartment in the *Rotes Haus* on the Glacis in the Alservorstadt.][16]

BEETHOVEN [**Sunday, November 21, or Monday, November 22**]: She [Johanna van Beethoven] must be brought there, so she can no longer create disturbance and harm to herself; only then will it be possible for humanity to deal with her justly. Otherwise, there are already more situations where the mother is excluded. [Blatt 5v] The exclusion of the mother is the consequence of being excluded by the Magistrat. [//] How will that now be bound with the pension? If she were to die today, what remains to him?[17]

[Blatt 6r]

---

[12] This was surely the reason for asking Beethoven when he was going to write to Weissenbach at the beginning of this conversation on Blatt 1r above.—TA

[13] Bernard's wordplay continues: Oberhaus and Unterhaus; Echtes and Schlechters.—TA

[14] Bernard writes "Alstervorstadt," which the suburb was popularly called because of the *Elster* (magpie) depicted on its seal. Starke lived in Prince Esterházy's so-called *Rotes Haus* (Red House), the large complex where Beethoven's friend Stephan von Breuning also lived, on the Glacis, No. 197. See Böckh, *Merkwürdigkeiten*, p. 381; Kisch, vol. 2, pp. 550–552.—KH/TA

[15] Beethoven seemingly asked Bernard if he wanted to have midday dinner on Sunday.—TA

[16] This suggests that Beethoven's hearing was still good enough to carry on a reasonable conversation in private quarters.—TA

[17] Possibly thoughts that Beethoven wanted to express (presumably to Bernard or Oliva) without being overheard, but more likely a draft for a letter or memorandum.—TA

OLIVA [possibly at Oliva's office in the banking firm of Offenheimer & Herz, Bauernmarkt No. 620;[18] probably ca. noon on Monday, November 22]: The music has been delivered to Adamberger,[19] who may have already taken care of its transport to England. [//] I asked at Fries's about a month ago, but nothing was there. I'll go there today, though.[20] [//] Are you already finished with the Mass?[21] [//] You will find no comfort there; then it is also too expensive. [//] I paid 1 fl. 30 [kr.] per day for a bad room in the courtyard on the 3rd floor [4th floor, American]; facing the street, it probably would have cost 2 fl. or even more; then there is expensive heating [and] service. [//]

I asked recently; he wanted 15 fl. for the whole day. [//] [Blatt 6v] I don't believe that you will get along with the person from the [woman] building superintendent, since she has always dealt with this one. [//]

BERNARD [probably at his *Wiener Zeitung*'s office, Rauhensteingasse No. 983; shortly after noon on Monday, November 22]: 1 pocket Mass [knife], 5 fl.[22] [//]

BEETHOVEN [copying an ad from that day's newspaper]: Official's widow [seeks employment] as housekeeper; inquire at the chocolate shop, Rothgässel, No. 682.[23] [//]

BERNARD: Sometime on a Sunday we'll go to Klosterneuburg.[24] [//]

[Blatt 7r]

---

[18] Oliva worked for the Offenheimer Brothers (aka Offenheimer & Herz), Bauernmarkt No. 620 [renumbered as 581 in 1821]. This conversation could also have taken place in his apartment in tiny Blutgasse, two blocks south of the Cathedral. Concerning Oliva, see Brandenburg, Nos. 617 and 654; also Heft 2, Blatt 13r.—TA

[19] Presumably Joseph Adamberger, a finance official in the Deposits Office, living at Haidenschuss No. 243. Haiden Schuss was on the Freyung, the three or four buildings next to Palais Harrach, in the direction of Am Hof. As a violoncellist he was also a performing member of the Gesellschaft der Musikfreunde. See *Hof- und Staats-Schematismus*, 1819, I, p. 679; Ziegler, *Addressen-Buch*, p. 144.—KH/TA

[20] Therefore, "today" is a business day.—TA

[21] The *Missa solemnis* was originally planned for the enthronement of Archduke Rudolph, which took place in Olmütz on March 9, 1820.—KH

[22] Bernard's original entry reads: "1 Taschen Messe" [1 pocket Mass], to which the German editors added an editorial "r" to render it "1 Taschen Messe[r]," which would mean "1 pocket knife." Bernard was known to engage in wordplay with Beethoven, and this entry probably falls into that category. Rauhensteingasse No. 983 was renumbered as 927 in 1821 (Behsel, p. 28).—TA

[23] See the *Intelligenzblatt*, No. 267 (November 22, 1819), p. 968. The same advertisement also appeared on November 24 and 26, 1819.—KH

[24] Klosterneuburg, a town ca. 10 miles north of Vienna, with a large Augustinian Monastery. In the steeply elevated upper town were the monastery's school, a private educational institution for boys and a similar institute for singing boys. See Weidmann, pp. 14–16.—KH/TA

SCHICKH [probably in his *Wiener Zeitschrift's* office, Kohlmarkt No. 268, on Monday, November 22]: So what's going on with my Lieder? Shall I have the good fortune, then, of receiving one of them? // Count Loeben[25] is tormenting me about it, and will consider himself very honored to be immortalized through you. // Do you still have the Lieder [texts]—all three or four?[26] [//]

Perhaps in carpentry shops or at sculptors'. //

[Blatt 7v]

BERNARD [possibly at *Zur Stadt Triest;* probably at midday dinner, ca. 2 p.m. on Monday, November 22]:[27] No coat and no overcoat. [//] It is unfortunate that he has never been able to bring himself to give lessons. He has always said: I want to live and die as a poor baron [*Freyherr*]. I shall not leave Vienna, for only in Vienna is there true life.[28] [//] [Blatt 8r]

Gunz.[29] [//] In Laibach, Gunz is revered as a saint. Of the opinion that he was doing a work pleasing to God, he ate and drank nothing more. He was found completely naked, praying in the church. His father and sister were present at his death; absolutely no trace of madness was noted, except that he addressed his sister as Your Grace. [//] [Blatt 8v] As a scholar he was very excellent; he put out a superb mathematical work, and very much distinguished himself in all the other specialties,

---

[25] Count Otto Heinrich von Loeben (1786–1825), writer, studied in Wittenberg and Heidelberg, visited Vienna in summer 1810, but spent most of his life in his native Dresden or the region to its east and southeast. His first volume of poetry appeared in 1810. After 1816, as his Protestant views became more mystical, he began publishing in distant journals, including those in Vienna. See *Allgemeine Deutsche Biographie*, vol. 19, pp. 40–42; Goedeke, vol. 6, pp. 108–110; *Neue deutsche Biographie*, vol. 15 (1987), pp. 23–25.—KH/TA

[26] Johann Schickh was projecting publishing songs by Beethoven among the musical supplements in his *Wiener Zeitschrift für Kunst, Literatur, Theater und Mode*. He had done so as early as "Das Geheimnis," WoO 145 (February 29, 1816); his next such work by Beethoven was the *Abendlied unterm gestirnten Himmel*, WoO 150 (poem by H[einrich] Goeble) on March 30, 1820. See Kinsky-Halm, pp. 614 and 621.

On December 13, 1819 (Heft 5, Blatt 1r), Schickh asks Beethoven for a Loeben setting "recht sehr bald" (very very soon). The next song that Beethoven sent him, based on a manuscript dated March 4, 1820, was the "Abendlied" by "H. Goeble," a text that had appeared in Bäuerle's *Allgemeine Theater-Zeitung* on May 11, 1819. It becomes apparent that "H. Goeble" is a previously unknown pseudonym of Otto H̲einrich G̲raf von L̲ o̲eb̲ e̲ n (Otto Heinrich Graf von Loeben, noted in the previous footnote). See Albrecht, "Poetic Source," pp. 7–32.—TA

[27] For dating see Blätter 9v and 26r below.—TA

[28] Possibly a reference to Esterházy librarian and violinist Georg von Gaal. In 1829 the owner of Ballgassel No. 930 (where Beethoven was living in 1819) was *Freyinn* (Baroness) von "Gall." See Blätter 16v–17r below and Behsel, p. 28.—TA

[29] Leopold Gunz (1785 – July 20, 1819), mathematician, professor in Laibach (Ljubljana) from 1811. In 1815 his book *Theorie der parallelen Geraden* appeared in Graz. In 1819 he declined into religious madness. See *Slovenski biografski leksikon*, vol. 1, p. 275.—KH

especially in languages, old as well as new. It is a great loss that he came to such an end. [//] [Blatt 9r]

Very good. He [Schneller] is interesting, a bit eccentric, but he has a sort of genius, a great deal of historical and literary knowledge. He is absolutely not a historian, however. [//] Last year, he gave a supper here,[30] to which Weissenbach and I were invited. Court Councillor Lehmann[31] told his jokes the whole [Blatt 9v] evening, at which Schneller[32] constantly laughed out loud; Weissenbach, however, was nearly irritated to death. [//]

She is now to be endured. [//] [Frau] Drosdick.[33] // Yesterday [Sunday, November 21] I ate entirely alone at Fr[au] v[on] S[almy's][34] along with a young lady. She also [Blatt 10r] spoke of Frau v. Dr[osdick], because she quite recently sat near Weissenbach and me in the theater. Frau Schneller was also there. She spoke about her in such a way as if she were shy only the presence of her husband in order to flirt all the more. It appears as if she is not the way that Weissenbach has praised her. Also, Frau Schneller says that you only imposed somewhat on Weissenbach. [//] [Blatt 10v] It appears that she does not love her husband.[35] [//] I heard from Fr[au]

[30] Possibly *Zur Stadt Triest* (corner of Neuer Markt and Plankengasse), or some other establishment that crossed the lines between coffee house, wine house, and restaurant.—TA

[31] Franz Caspar Lehmann (b. 1769), Court Councillor and Consultant in the Imperial War Council. After studying theology and law, he came to Vienna where he first taught in private homes and then accepted a teaching position in statistics, Austrian history, and general history. He was also active as a writer. See Gräffer-Czikann, I, p. 386; *Hof- und Staats-Schematismus*, 1819, I, pp. 51 and 271; Wurzbach, vol. 14, pp. 312–313.—KH

[32] Julius Franz Borgias Schneller (1777–1833), writer, professor of history and philosophy. Born in Strassburg, he came to Vienna in 1796 and joined the literary circle around Caroline Pichler (1769–1843). He was acquainted with Beethoven, presumably through the friend of his youth, Baron Ignaz von Gleichenstein. In 1806 he became professor at the *Lyceum* in Graz, and maintained friendly contact with his student, the pianist Marie Koschak (later married to Pachler). From 1823 he was active as a University teacher in Freiburg, where he also published the fifth volume of his *Geschichte Österreichs*, forbidden by the Austrian Censor. See Frimmel, *Handbuch*, II, pp. 137–138; Goldschmidt, *Franz Schubert*, pp. 391–392.—KH/TA

[33] Therese Malfatti (1792–1851), who had married Baron Wilhelm von Drosdick in 1817. This opinion cannot have been good news to Beethoven, who, a decade earlier, had thought quite highly of her. At the time of their marriage, Drosdick was a councillor in the Court Chancellery, a holder of the Silver Cross, and a consultant in the Commerce Commission. See Frimmel, *Handbuch*, I, pp. 384–385; Clive, pp. 222–224; *Hof- und Staats-Schematismus*, 1817, I, pp. 47, 218, and 241.—KH/TA

[34] For confirmation of this dinner date with Frau Franziska von Salmy, see Blatt 26r below.—TA

[35] At least three women are the topic of conversation here. It is possible that the woman discussed on Blatt 10v—rather than Frau Drosdick—could be Josephine Brunsvik, now married to Count Stackelberg. Rita Steblin has made an interesting case for her as the "Immortal Beloved" of 1812. See Steblin, "Auf diese Art," 147–180; Clive, pp. 61–63.—TA

v[on] Janitschek[36] that she is nothing less than domesticated, and [also] that she was away from her husband this summer. One must therefore be cautious. [//]

In the Landstrasse, where we have eaten.[37] [//]

[End of entries for Monday, November 22.]

[Blatt 11r]

BEETHOVEN **[at his apartment in the Ballgasse; morning of Wednesday, November 24]**:

Chamber toilet, like Bernard's.[38]

Candles.

You must [pay?] a servant and also the housekeeper from Mödling

	36 [kr.]
M [?]	36
	36
	36
	2 [fl.] 24 [kr.][39]

[Blatt 11v]

BERNARD **[presumably at the office of the *Wiener Zeitung* or at a restaurant; mid-day on Wednesday, November 24]**: Bach[40] says [that] the co-guardian is, in any case, just a figurehead, and all instructions originate from you. In addition, no

---

[36] Antonia Janschikh (born probably 1794 or 1795), wife of Franz Janschikh, lived from 1814 to 1820 at Landstrasse No. 289 [renumbered as 323 in 1821, and 364 in 1830], the northeastern corner of Ungargasse and Bockgasse. Beethoven must already have known her husband Franz by this time; he first appears in the surviving conversation books on Wednesday, November 24. See also Blatt 20v below and Behsel, p. 78.—KH/TA

[37] Possibly a reference to the Gasthaus *Zur goldenen Birne* (Golden Pear), across Landstrasser Hauptstrasse and three or four buildings south of Beethoven's recent residence there. (See the map in Klein, p. 99).—TA

[38] This suggests that one of Beethoven's recent conversations with Bernard may have taken place in the editor's apartment (No. 8) in the Rauhensteingasse No. 991 [renumbered as 933 in 1821], where he might have observed this device. Bernard's residence was in the building called the *Österreichische Krone*, on the north side of Rauhensteingasse, the second building east of Himmelpfortgasse (and Jahn's restaurant), and essentially across Rauhensteingasse from the *Wiener Zeitung*'s office.—TA

[39] Four times 36 kr. equals 144 kr., with 60 kr. per florin; therefore Beethoven's addition was correct. See Blatt 15v below for similar computations.—TA

[40] Dr. Johann Baptist Bach (1779–1847) had been an Imperial and Court Attorney in Vienna since 1817 and, in fall 1819 took over Beethoven's representation in the guardianship matter. According to Schindler, he "was feared by his colleagues as an opponent," and yet was a man "with a multi-faceted education and, in addition, was a practicing music lover." See Frimmel, *Handbuch*, I, pp. 26–27; Schindler-MacArdle, p. 27; Thayer-Forbes, pp. 728–729; Wurzbach, vol. 1, pp. 109–110; Clive, p. 11.—KH/TA

objections can be made against such instruction, because he does not have all the facts in the matter and, moreover, is a teacher himself. [//] [Blatt 12r] There will be a 2nd Assembly meeting[41] very soon, when you yourself [will] appear; the day has not been determined yet. [//] You/She. [Drawing of a head in profile.] [//] The present guardian Nusbek[42] himself hopes that you [will] assume the guardianship, but, since your deafness creates some [Blatt 12v] difficulty,[43] it is hoped that you have *someone* in reserve. Herr v[on] Bach says that Herr Nusbök is a very accommodating man for this purpose; I said, however, that I had already spoken to you about *Peters*.[44] [//] [Blatt 13r] Herr v[on] Bach says that your getting the sole guardianship cannot be brought about, because your deafness is a legal reason. [//] If Peters is an upright and insightful man, then we needn't fear any intrigues from him, especially because he has no strange interests. [//] [Blatt 13v] I can assure you that, so far,

[41] The Assembly (*Tagsatzung*) before the Viennese Magistrat mentioned here (with a convening date determined by the government) was fixed for December 7, 1819. See below, Blatt 61r; Weise, p. 28.—KH

[42] Leopold Nussböck, City Sequestrator, was installed as co-guardian of Nephew Karl on September 17, 1819, succeeding Tuscher. On April 8, 1820, he and Johanna van Beethoven were again excluded from the guardianship through a decision of the Appellate Court. See Frimmel, *Handbuch*, II, p. 463; *Hof- und Staats-Schematismus*, 1819, I, p. 678; Thayer-Deiters-Riemann, IV, pp. 145, 566–567; Thayer-Forbes, pp. 727–728.—KH/TA

[43] From this entry and others, it appears that the court could legally have refused Beethoven's sole custody on the basis of his hardness of hearing.—TA

[44] Karl Peters (b. Prague, April 16, 1782; d. Vienna, November 9, 1849) became tutor in the household of Prince Franz Joseph Maximilian Lobkowitz on April 1, 1810, with a salary of 1,200 Gulden, raised to 1,500 already in 1811. On May 5, 1814, he married Josephine Hochsinger (b. Wiener Neustadt, February 16, 1790; d. Peggau, March 28, 1866). When the elder Prince Lobkowitz died on December 15, 1816, Peters remained as tutor. Although Beethoven wrote a letter to Peters as early as January 8, 1817, he probably knew him casually at best up to the end of 1819. Bernard influenced the composer to propose Peters as co-guardian. In any case, given the sexually explicit nature of table conversations in the interim months (see, for instance, Heft 6), Beethoven probably regretted the co-guardianship even before it was made by the Court on April 8, 1820. The new reigning Prince Lobkowitz, Ferdinand, reached his majority (twenty-four years) on April 13, 1821, and at Easter 1825 Peters was reassigned to official duties in Prague, thus also occasioning the end of his co-guardianship of nephew Karl.

See Macek, pp. 393–408, specifically 393–394, 405; also citing St. Heinrich (Prague), Geburtsmatrikel N. 14, p. 383 (1782) [Stadtarchiv Prag]). Also Frimmel, *Handbuch*, II, pp. 15–16; Clive, pp. 260–262; Thayer-Deiters-Riemann, IV, p. 566; Anderson, No. 734; Brandenburg, No. 1058; Heft 4, Blatt 25r (for Josephine).

Peters was seemingly appointed through the influence of Bernard. Once Beethoven and Bernard were regularly joined at dinner by either Peters or Janschikh or both, the general level of table conversation often descended to "locker-room" levels. Another casualty of these associations may have been the closeness of Beethoven's friendship with Bernard himself. Earlier in 1819 he had been commissioned by the Gesellschaft der Musikfreunde to compose an oratorio to a text by Bernard. When Bernard at last delivered the text of *Der Sieg des Kreuzes*, Beethoven, in January 1824, refused to set it.

In his *Handbuch* article (I, p. 239), "Janschikh," Frimmel said that this (unsavory) dinner circle needed more study. For examples of the unsavory conversations themselves, see Heft 6.—TA

Peters has never altered his views in the least. He is too noble to depend on petty things. [//] [Blatt 14r] He said that you should take the documents with you to the Assembly meeting. [//]

Lend me 20 kr. [//]

Then you can immediately make the most appropriate arrangements. [//] *One plan must be accepted for Karl to receive his education systematically for several years.* [//]

[Blatt 14v]

OLIVA [at his apartment in the Blutgasse or office; midday of Wednesday, November 24]: I only need to take another step beforehand, however, that will not be delayed.[45] // She says that she had always been quite healthy, and this illness lasted the entire summer.[46] [//] [Blatt 15r] She was at home; her mother said that she only recently finished with the kitchen. [//] She has to take care of the entire service in the rooms. // It was merely from the great exertion in the summer. // She didn't have Dr. Sarenk[47] as her physician, but instead the surgeon <illegible word crossed out>. // Now she would have to stay another 4 weeks.

[Blatt 15v]

BERNARD [at the grocery and wine shop *Zur Stadt Triest*, on the Neuer Markt, corner of Plankengasse; possibly late afternoon of Wednesday, November 24]:
They have wild boar here.

SEELIG:[48] For you, 1 fl. 48 [kr.]

BERNARD: Choice.

---

[45] To the right: drawings of two heads.—KH

[46] The remainder of this conversation seems to refer to the Mödling housekeeper whom Beethoven had mentioned on Blatt 11r above.—TA

[47] Dr. Johann Sarenk was a practicing physician in Mödling. He wrote the *Geschichte und Topographie des Marktes in Mödling* (Vienna, 1817).—KH

[48] Heinrich Seelig hailed from Würzburg and was proprietor of the grocery and wine shop *Zur Stadt Triest*, on the Neuer Markt, No. 1124, in Vienna. Even so, it becomes clear from the context of these entries that one could eat and drink here, as well.

As numbered in 1819, No. 1124 [renumbered as 1160 in 1821] was on the northwest corner of the intersection with Plankengasse (Behsel, p. 32). It is not to be confused with a similarly named restaurant in the Wieden. Seelig's handwriting is confirmed by Schindler on Heft 6, Blatt 13r. His portrait appears in Köhler *et al.*, *Konversationshefte*, vol. 2, facing p. 97. See also Frimmel, *Handbook*, II, p. 176; Klein, p. 162; and Heft 6, Blatt 78v.—KH/TA

BEETHOVEN: BERNARD:

54   Delicate.

$\dfrac{54}{18}$ [= 108]⁴⁹

//

BERNARD: The Magistrat must be ashamed to issue such an order, because, as the Doctor [Bach] says, Herr Nusböck has taken care of horses and children, all mixed up. [//] [Blatt 16r] Prudent people have allowed themselves to be deceived by this woman [Johanna]. [//]

I believe that he has had it engraved. [//] He plays your sonatas; but *how?* he hasn't said. [//] He is a cultivated person. [//]

The younger attorneys are already, for the most part, of a nobler stripe. I believe that the study of philosophy and aesthetics contributes much to it. [//]

[Blatt 16v]

SEELIG: v[on] Gaal⁵⁰ sends his best regards; he hopes to meet you some evening at my establishment. [//] He often eats here.⁵¹ //

BERNARD [arriving at *Zur Stadt Triest*; ca. 8:30 p.m.⁵² on Wednesday, November 24]: A friend to all. [//] He [presumably Gaal] does not figure into the situation. [//] [Blatt 17r] It appears as if he wants to exist merely as a teacher, and is therefore a neutral person. It doesn't seem believable to me, however, that he has done something against you. [//]

The Indian illusionist performed his skillful pieces at the Kärntnertor Theater

---

⁴⁹ To clarify the arithmetic of this transaction: the wild boar meat cost 1 fl. 48 kr. per weighed portion. At 60 kreuzer per florin, this totaled 108 kr. Beethoven and Bernard evidently split a portion at 54 kr. each. In adding them, Beethoven wrote "18," neglecting to add the "0," but was surely *thinking* in terms of "1 hundred 8."—TA

⁵⁰ Georg von Gaal (1783–1855), writer. He appeared as a dilettante in theatrical performances and, since 1811, had been librarian in the library of Prince Nikolaus Esterházy. As a violinist, he had also participated in Haydn's musical productions. His poetry appeared frequently in Schickh's *Wiener Zeitschrift*. See Böckh, *Merkwürdigkeiten*, p. 94; Gräffer-Czikann, II, pp. 256–257; Wurzbach, vol. 5, pp. 43–44.—KH/TA

⁵¹ Seelig's location in the Neuer Markt is only a five- or ten-minute walk south of the Esterházy Palace in the Wallnerstrasse, although the prince's library of 20,000 volumes seems to have been housed in the family's suburban palace in Mariahilf, a mile or so to the west.—TA

⁵² If the Indian illusionist's act began at 7 p.m. and took half the evening (see immediately below), then it was probably finished by about 8 or 8:15. Depending upon how Bernard walked through or around the *Bürgerspital* apartment complex in between, Seelig's *Zur Stadt Triest* on the Neuer Markt was no more than five or ten minutes from the Theater.—TA

today [November 24].[53] The house was jam-packed full, and he was called back at the end. [//] [Blatt 17v]

Have you ever been up in the *Stephansturm*?[54] [//] The whole wide horizon of Vienna lies like a panorama at our feet. The *Münster* [cathedral] in Strassburg is a little higher. The [unfinished] tower in Cologne is not as high by far as the *Stephansturm*.[55] [//] [Blatt 18r] I was up in the tower in Cologne. The Cathedral, however, is really extraordinarily fine in its layout.[56]

They are from Italy. [//] We are also Athenians. [//] [They] are of the best. [//] [Blatt 18v]

[Joseph Czerny seemingly walks into *Zur Stadt Triest*:]

Herr Joseph Czerny, famous piano teacher.[57] [//] Zmeskall[58] is said to be so ill for the past 3 months. [//] Halm[59] is there. [//] Herr Czerny is the teacher of

[53] Since October 7, 1819, Thomas Bauleau from Madras had demonstrated his talents in the I.R. Kleiner Redoutensaal. "He calls himself the 'famous Indian.'" The entry was made on November 24, 1819, when Bauleau appeared at the Kärntnertor Theater at 7 p.m., followed, after intermission, by the ballet *Lisa und Colin* by D'Auberval, arranged by Aumer. Other performances in this theater took place on November 16 and 28, as well as December 1, 5, 8, and 12, 1819. See Theater Zettel (Bibliothek, Österreichisches Theatermuseum, Vienna); *Wiener Zeitschrift*, No. 125 (October 19, 1819), p. 1022, calling him "Bouleau" once, but "Bauleau" three times.—KH/TA

[54] The tower of St. Stephan's Cathedral.—TA

[55] The completed south tower of the *Stephansdom* (or "Steffel") is 136 meters high. Until the second half of the nineteenth century the tower of the Strassburg *Münster*, at 142 meters, was the highest church tower in the world. At that time the tower of the Cologne Cathedral, at 55 meters, remained unfinished; only in the second half of the century were Cologne's two west towers brought to a height of 157 meters.—KH

[56] Beethoven may have reminded Bernard that Cologne and its thirteenth-century Cathedral were only a short distance north of his native Bonn, and that he retained some fondness for them, resulting in Bernard's compliment for the Cathedral itself, whose nave would also remain unfinished for another half century.—TA

[57] Joseph Czerny (1785–1831) already made a brief appearance in Heft 1, Blatt 1v (ca. February 26–27, 1818). Unless Beethoven did not recognize him for some reason, Bernard's remarks and tone suggest a certain cynical humor. See Clive, p. 82.—TA

[58] Nikolaus Zmeskall von Domanovecz, also Domanowetz and Domanovitz, here spelled "Smetskal" (1759–1833), Court Secretary of the Hungarian Court Chancellery, lived at the Bürgerspital, No. 1166. He was a good violoncellist and a member of the Board of Directors of the Gesellschaft der Musikfreunde, and organized regular Sunday morning concerts in which works by his long-time friend Beethoven were frequently played. See Frimmel, *Handbuch*, II, p. 474; Clive, pp. 404–405; Frimmel, *Studien*, II, pp. 85–87; *Hof- und Staats-Schematismus*, 1819, I, p. 233, and II, p. 340; Thayer-Deiters-Riemann, II, pp. 113–115; Ziegler, *Addressen-Buch*, pp. 113 and 190.—KH/TA

[59] Anton Halm (1789–1872), composer and pianist, was active in the Austrian military service until 1811, and then as an esteemed music teacher in Vienna. In 1814 or 1815, through the recommendation of Franz von Brunsvik, he became acquainted with Beethoven. See Frimmel, *Handbuch*, I, pp. 192–193; Thayer-Deiters-Riemann, III, p. 526; Thayer-Forbes, pp. 690–691; Clive, pp. 146–147; Wurzbach, vol. 7, p. 257.—KH/TA

little [Leopoldine] Blahetka,⁶⁰ to whom you recommended him. [//] [Blatt 19r] According to the assurances of Herr Czerny, the young Lobkowitz, Joseph,⁶¹ has a great deal of talent for music and already plays compositions of yours. He is a pupil of Herr Czerny. [//] 16 years old. [Blatt 19v] He has taken great pains. [//] He says that you look so enterprising today. [//]

The timpani and trumpets must avenge themselves. [//] [Blatt 20r]

This one in the overcoat is called Grandjean,⁶² and was secretary to Count Oels, or Eltz,⁶³ who was in Brazil. [//]

Tomorrow [Thursday, November 25] is *Idomeneus*.⁶⁴ [//] *Idomeneus* was not Mozart's first composition.⁶⁵ [//] [Blatt 20v] *<Der Baum der Diana>*⁶⁶ //

⁶⁰ Anna Maria Leopoldine Blahetka (born 1809 according to the baptismal record in the parish of Guntramsdorf), died 1887, daughter of Joseph Blahetka and Barbara Sophia *née* Träg (a fine *Harmonika* player). On March 28, 1819, she gave her first independent concert and later became a significant pianist, who also appeared with her own compositions. See Frimmel, *Handbuch*, I, p. 50; Gräffer-Czikann, I, pp. 306–307; Wurzbach, vol. 1, pp. 421–422; Clive, p. 36.—KH/TA

⁶¹ Joseph Franz Karl von Lobkowitz, born in 1803 as the third son of Prince Joseph Franz Maximilian Lobkowitz and Princess Maria Carolina Schwarzenberg. He entered the Imperial Army at an early age. See Wurzbach, vol. 15, p. 325.—KH

⁶² In the Viennese census sheets, a Mathias Grandjean, "born 1789, from Sprimon in France, Riding Scholar in the Theresianum, tall," may be traced in the Laurenzergasse, No. 761 [renumbered as 716 in 1821]. According to an annotation, he became (by decree of October 1, 1818) a "tobacco dealer and lottery collector." See Conscriptions-Bogen, Stadt, No. 716 (Wiener Stadt- und Landesarchiv).—KH/TA

⁶³ Count Emerich Joseph von Eltz, Privy Councillor and Chamberlain, was Ambassador Extraordinary to Brazil in 1818. See *Hof- und Staats-Schematismus*, 1819, I, p. 208.—KH

⁶⁴ On November 25, 1819, after a long time, "*Idomeneus*, tragic opera in 3 acts. Freely adapted from the Italian by F[riedrich] Treitschke, music by Mozart. For the benefit of Madame Waldmüller" was performed in the Kärntnertor Theater. The opera was to be repeated on November 27 and 30. The Zettel, however, indicates that on the 27th, Madame Waldmüller was "suddenly indisposed," and Boieldieu's popular staple *Johann von Paris* was performed instead. *Idomeneus* did play on November 30 (with Madame Waldmüller), as well as on December 18 and 28.

Only the performance of November 25 can be meant here, since the 27th was that "Saturday" to which Bernard referred on Blatt 25r. See Kanne's *Wiener AmZ* 3, No. 97 (December 4, 1819), cols. 779–781; *Beobachter*, Nos. 329, 331, and 344 (November 25, 27, and 30, 1819); Schickh's *Wiener Zeitschrift* 4, No. 146 (December 7, 1819), pp. 1207–1208.—KH/TA

⁶⁵ Mozart's *Idomeneo, re di Creta*, had been premiered in Munich on January 29, 1781, just before he moved to Vienna. It was perhaps his eighth or ninth completed opera.—TA

⁶⁶ Probably a reference to *L'arbore di Diana*, an opera by Vicente Martín y Soler (1754–1806), set to a libretto by Lorenzo Da Ponte. Premiered in Vienna on October 1, 1787, it became one of the most popular operas of its day, in the original Italian as well as in German translation, thus its association with Mozart here. It had been produced in German in Stuttgart in January 1819, but there seem to have been no performances in Vienna at about this time. Loewenberg, col. 447 (Stuttgart); Bauer, *Theater an der Wien*, pp. 303–306; Hadamowsky, *Die Wiener Hofoper, 1811–1974*, pp. 24 and 42.—TA

JOSEPH CZERNY: Zmeskall now listens to no music other than your Sonata, Op. 106,[67] which I have already played for him several times. [//]

JANSCHIKH:[68] When does the *Dies irae* seize Mankind? [//] Who will play the *Tuba* and on what tones?[69] [//]

[Blatt 21r][70]

---

[67] Piano Sonata in B-flat, Op. 106 (Hammerklavier), published in Vienna by Artaria in September, 1819.—TA

[68] From the contents of this and similar entries, especially the reference in Heft 6, Blatt 45v, it may be concluded that this writer is Franz Xaver Janschikh (also Janschig and Janschek), born in Linz in 1776 or 1777, the son of Franz Janschikh, a master embroiderer, and Elisabeth Eidenberger. Janschikh first appears in Vienna's state directories in 1812 as an actuary in the *Bancalgefällenen-Administration* of Lower Austria, living in one of the Main Customs Buildings, No. 709 (the other, adjoining, was 708) in the Alter Fleischmarkt. By 1814 he was a Customs Office Comptroller and had moved to Landstrasse, No. 289 [renumbered as 323 in 1821]. This building was the *Schöne Sklavin* (Beautiful Slave Girl) at the northeast corner of Ungargasse and Bock- [later Beatrix-] gasse, where Beethoven would live in 1824. By 1821 Janschikh had moved back to the Main Customs Building on the Alter Fleischmarkt, probably in a better apartment, now in No. 708 [renumbered as 664 in 1821]. Here he lived, rising in seniority in his position, until his retirement or death in 1838.

On February 6, 1814, Janschikh married Antonia Mainolo, born in Baden in 1794 or 1795, the daughter of Franz Mainolo, a master chimney sweep, and his wife Anna Petrossia. At the time of their marriage, Antonia was living in the Rothes Haus, Alservorstadt No. 173, and (although the marriage was registered in her parish, the Dreifaltigkeits Kirche), they were married in the Karlskirche. In the marriage record his surname is spelled Janschick.

Janschikh had a daughter Antonie (Antonia Franziska Josepha), born, or at least baptized, on August 2, 1815. See Pfarre St. Rochus, Tauf-Register, Tom 6 (1813–1819), fol. 134. See Frimmel, *Handbuch*, I, pp. 238–239; Conscriptions-Bogen, Stadt, 1. Reihe, No. 664; Pfarre Alservorstadt, Trauungs-Register, 1809–1817, fol. 168; *Hof- und Staats-Schematismus*, survey including 1812, p. 413; 1816, p. 432; 1818, I, p. 494; 1819, I, p. 484; 1820, I, p. 481; 1821, I, p. 480; 1830, I, p. 467; 1838, I, p. 504 (his last listing); Behsel, pp. 20 and 78. I am grateful to Dr. Joachim Tepperberg and the Director, Dr. Leopold Auer, for access to the stacks of Vienna's Haus-, Hof- und Staatsarchiv (June, 2006), to make this survey of the *Schematismen*.

Bernard first mentions Frau Janschikh a day or two before, on Blatt 10v above, in connection with gossip concerning Theresia Malfatti (now von Drosdick). For Janschikh's own personality, see the note immediately following.—KH/TA

[69] The tone of many of Janschikh's entries suggests that he may have been an unsavory character and perhaps a trifle mentally unbalanced. His arrival, along with that of Peters, in Beethoven's circle (both seemingly at Bernard's behest) signaled an embarrassing frequency of "locker-room" conversations concerning their own wives and possibly other women, as well as other sexually oriented topics that Beethoven seemingly found offensive or at least uncomfortable. With the chronological gaps in the surviving conversation books it is difficult to establish when these associations began and how long they lasted, but Beethoven seems to have distanced himself from Janschikh by the end of February, and certainly by mid-March, 1820 (see Heft 8, Blatt 5r; Heft 9, Blatt 72v and Blatt 91r; Heft 10, Blatt 23v).—TA

[70] Pencil sketch of a house in the upper three quarters of the page.—KH

BERNARD: <Herr Janitschek asks why you are not giving an Akademie? // Women are fragile; they are often sick for no reason.> // He is going to watch over the sick. He is sitting up with a friend. [//] [Blatt 21v][71] But he is leaving his wife alone.[72] [//]

[Seemingly the end of entries for Wednesday, November 24.]

[Blatt 22r]

OLIVA **[probably at Beethoven's apartment in the Ballgasse; possibly the morning of Thursday, November 25]**: <Do take a> [//] You have already taken the [housekeeper] away from Mödling for several weeks; you cannot take an ordinary person [female]; a male servant would be the best. [//] Such a [male] servant does not come cheap. [//] Where can he sleep, then? Do you have a bed for him? [//] Does this [male] person please you? [//] At the same time he will be an office servant, but if your housekeeper leaves, you must still have *someone*, though. [//] [Blatt 22v] One could inquire at the Invalids' Home.[73] [//]

BEETHOVEN **[probably at his apartment in the Ballgasse, then possibly walking out of the City through the Carolinentor, west on the Glacis to the Tandelmarkt, possibly with Oliva, reentering the City through the Kärntnertor; possibly around noon on Thursday, November 25]**:[74]

Comb for salve,[75] 42 kr.

Warm trousers that retain warmth, at the Tandelmarkt.[76]

---

[71] Drawing of heads in profile in the upper two thirds of the page.—KH

[72] The German terminology indicates that the sick friend is a man. The demeaning attitude toward women in general and the leering implication that Janschikh's wife Antonia is alone and receptive to male visitors (and that Bernard seems happy enough to pass along these messages) are typical of Bernard's tone when he is with either Peters or Janschikh. Beethoven may have departed their company at this point.—TA

[73] The I.R. Military Invalids' House in the Landstrasse, No. 1 (on the Glacis) was erected through the expanded construction of the Johannisspital (St. John's Hospital) in 1783–1786 under Joseph II. See Kisch, vol. 1, pp. 390–391.—KH

[74] The day's entries go to Blatt 30v.—TA

[75] Beethoven's term is *Salfkamm*. A *Kamm* is a comb, and *Salf* is salve or ointment. One of his two apartments during this period may have been infested with bedbugs, fleas, or lice. Therefore, an extra comb might have been warranted to apply salve or ointment against such vermin. In Heft 4, Blatt 4v (December 8), nephew Karl refers to lice, but whether either he or Beethoven is troubled by them is not clear.—TA

[76] The *Tandelmarkt* or *Trödelmarkt* (rag market), consisting of the stalls of second-hand clothing dealers, was, until the 1820s, located on the Glacis before the older Kärntnertor, from the point where Wiedener Hauptstrasse joined the Glacis, extending southeast, almost to the Karlskirche. The area was essentially in front of the Polytechnic Institute, built in 1817, which Karl later attended and which still stands today. See Czeike, III, pp. 414–415; Degen, Map, 1809 (Brandenburg, *Briefwechsel*, suppl. to vol. III).

OLIVA [?]: Gulden

BEETHOVEN: 42 [kr. for a comb]
              38 [kr. for used trousers?]

The iron sheets of the stove must, for the most part, be heated inside. How, if it smokes? For that reason, the stove will be [Blatt 23r] ventilated in the room through the [outside] wall, and the doors <remain> open and shut; it will, however, be cold.[77]

Above, on the Tandelmarkt, is a fine stove, also a particular type that I don't know. [//] Ask the secondhand dealers what a table costs and a sewing table, a [portable] writing box, likewise as a model for the carpenter. [//]

[Blatt 23v]

BERNARD [probably at a restaurant; probably midday, ca. 2 p.m., on Thursday, November 25]: Every month is a school examination, and semiannually are the main examinations. Whether he [Karl] takes a prescribed course or ½ year depends upon the arrangements of the public schools. [//] He has to make up for the lost year. [//] [Blatt 24r] He must follow the normal path of prescribed studies, and if he is not to be held back, he must be enrolled in order to take the monthly examinations. If he only enters now, he must continue to follow this path until the course is completed, which happens at Easter. Then the new arrangements can take place. [//] [Blatt 24v] Now it is necessary that he continues his studies, and therefore he cannot be removed before the completion of the course. [//] You must ask what kinds of subjects ought to be taught to him for it; from that it will be seen how necessary this engagement of a teacher is. [//] [Blatt 25r] To pay a half year in advance is not a small thing. [//]

On Saturday [November 27], I have been invited by the two actors, Töpfer and Kettel, who received their proceeds on Sunday [November 21].[78] [//]

This location is not to be confused with a later one, between the Carolinen Tor (a gate for foot traffic opened in the city walls at the southern end of Weihburggasse in 1810) and the Heumarkt, east of the Karlskirche (which they called "not far from the Karlskirche," an element that described the 1819 location), essentially between today's Schwarzenbergplatz and the Konzerthaus. See Groner (1922), p. 489; Pezzl (1826), p. 258.—KH/TA

[77] Beethoven may have been reflecting here on stoves seen the day before (Wednesday, November 24). He is concerned about properly ventilating a "Franklin" type stove to the outside. Even with a pipe chimney leading through a wall, it was still wise to leave a door or window open to insure against the accumulation of deadly carbon monoxide. See his conversation with Oliva, Blätter 28r–29r below.—TA

[78] Double bill at the Burgtheater on Saturday, November 27, at 7 p.m.: Babo's *Standesproben*, a comedy with Töpfer; preceded by August von Kotzebue's idyll *Marie* with Kettel (Theater Zettel, Bibliothek, Österreichisches Theatermuseum). As noted on Blatt iv above, these actors had given a benefit performance for themselves at the Kärntnertor Theater at midday on Sunday, November 21.—TA

You must insist that she [Johanna] may not see Karl anywhere except at your place. [//] [Blatt 25v] Now there is no more time to lose concerning the schools. Once and for all, he must embark on a secure path for several years, so that he gains continuity in his studies. [//] Besides, I don't come into any contact with this class of people. [//] [Blatt 26r]⁷⁹ Room and board can always be set at 600 fl., service and so forth. //

It is already known that you signed yourself as "*Selbstvertreter*" [self-representative].⁸⁰

On [last] Sunday [November 21], he wanted to have me to dinner at Madame W[eissenthurn]'s,⁸¹ but I had already been invited to Frau von Salmy's.⁸² He will invite us soon. [//] [Blatt 26v] Weissenthurn is really no ordinary woman, and has a great deal of simplicity and naturalness in her social graces. [Salzburg physician-poet] Weissenbach was at one time in love with her, and sang her praises that she had been very beautiful. [//]

They are very delicate; she [Johanna] has not arrived there and, I'll wager that she doesn't go there at all. [//] [Blatt 27r]⁸³ You can pay nothing, and therefore happily remain away entirely. [//] They have servants for this purpose, and thus they can summarily refuse. [//] That must finally end it all. [//] Rather that they turn to

---

⁷⁹ Doodle with the word "Prague" in the upper left corner of this page.—KH

⁸⁰ This concerns the letter that Beethoven wrote in reply to an inquiry from Prince Innocenz von Odescalchi, representing the Gesellschaft der Musikfreunde. As vice-president (probably expressed something like "Präses Stellvertreter," i.e., deputy, or representative of, the president's position, or *Stelle*), Odescalchi had recently written Beethoven a letter, inquiring about his progress on the oratorio that the society had commissioned from him in 1815 and paid for in August, 1819. In reply Beethoven wrote a letter (now lost) later quoted (or possibly summarized) by Ignaz von Seyfried, thus: "I have not forgotten. Such matters cannot be hurried. I shall keep my word." In response to Odescalchi's signing his letter as "Stellvertreter," Beethoven (in a typical good-humored wordplay) signed his: "Beethoven, Selbstvertreter," meaning that he was representing or deputizing for himself. Beethoven's letter had been discussed at the most recent meeting of the Gesellschaft's officers on Monday, November 22, 1819, therefore three days before this conversation book entry was written.

From the context of Bernard's matter-of-fact entry here, it appears that the officers were not amused by Beethoven's pun. While surely recognizing the good work that the Society was doing for middle-class music-making and music education, Beethoven was also aware of its sometime humorless self-importance and punnily dubbed the Gesellschaft der Musikfreunde (Society of the Friends of Music) as the Gesellschaft der Musikfeinde (Society of the Enemies of Music). Further references to Beethoven's letter are found below in Heft 4, Blatt 28v ("They took your 'Selbstvertreter' badly") and Heft 5, Blatt 59r.

See Anderson, No. 981 (excluding the pun from the signature); Brandenburg, *Briefwechsel*, No. 1356 (with pun and substantial discussion), as well as Heft 2, Blatt 13r.—KH/TA

⁸¹ Johanna Franul von Weissenthurn (*née* Grünberg), poet and court actress, 1773–1847, born in Koblenz. See Blatt 2r above. The proposed dinner would have had to take place on the previous Sunday, November 21, because on the upcoming Sunday, November 28, Weissenthurn would be onstage at 7 p.m. in Carl Töpfer's *Der Tagsbefehl* (Zettel, Bibliothek, Österreichisches Theatermuseum).—TA

⁸² Franziska (Fanny) von Salmy (b. 1788), supporting member of the Gesellschaft der Musikfreunde. See Heft 2, Blatt 90r; as well as Blatt 9r above.—TA

⁸³ Drawing of a head in profile in the upper left corner of the page.—KH

you as guardian in all matters. In this way they will not run all over him again. [//]
[Blatt 27v]

When will you write to Weissenbach? [//]

[Blatt 28r]

OLIVA [presumably at Beethoven's future apartment on the Josephstadt Glacis; evening of Thursday, November 25]: The small stove in the other room is made of cast iron, therefore much better than the one that we saw yesterday and which is only made of sheet iron.[84] // I examined the stove only today. // It appears to me, however, that you will not save any wood, if you close this room to the entry room, because it must always be heated, and you cannot do this with a stove. [//] [Blatt 28v] As is generally known, an iron stove provides no lasting warmth: it will be warm quickly, and it will be cold again just as quickly. For your purposes, a so-called Swedish stove, made of clay, which is not too expensive and also makes the best effect, would appear better to me. These are large enough that they would heat both rooms; I myself have already seen [Blatt 29r] a shop here that sells such stoves in all sizes, but I don't know where. [//] But no iron stove for lasting warmth; you'd be spending your money for nothing. [//] With little wood and warmth that lasts. [//] They are to make a heating-fire in the room. I want to inquire about the details. //

Things take longer here; people are far behind, and the Viennese are complacent; if it's not burning above their heads, they don't bestir themselves. [//] [Blatt 29v] One sees the trouble they take in gathering leaves.[85] //

Have you seen his antiquities here? [//] In the city in the Kohlmarkt. [//] He has mummies from Egypt that are older than Moses—he himself advertises it that way.[86] // They are often wrong. //

---

[84] See the discussion of various kinds of stoves on Blätter 22v–23r above.—TA

[85] Oliva seems to be speaking sarcastically here; unraked leaves at the end of fall could have posed a fire hazard. In practical terms, these comments may refer to the protracted length of time that it was taking to get Beethoven's new apartment ready for occupancy: the painting mentioned in a letter to Bernard on October 10, finding a chamber toilet, installing a second stove, buying inexpensive furniture (possibly for a live-in servant), etc.—TA

[86] The "Collection of Egyptian Antiquities and Other Artistic and Natural Rarities" of Franz Wilhelm Sieber (1789–1844), physician and nature scientist. From August 1819 it had been exhibited in the Josephstadt, No. 42 on the Glacis [renumbered as 45, in today's Lenaugasse], and from the end of October 1819 to the end of January 1820, in a building on the Graben, No. 657 [renumbered as 616, just east of the *Pestsäule*, in 1821]. See the *Conversationsblatt* [a newspaper], No. 32 (October 19, 1819), p. 657; *Wiener Zeitung*, No. 245 (October 25, 1819), p. 980; Behsel, pp. 191 and 19 [similarity of page numbers correct]. Therefore, Oliva seemingly confused the Graben location for the nearby Kohlmarkt. Further discussion in Heft 6, Blatt 18v (ca. January 11, 1820), with correct location.

Kanne's *Wiener Zeitschrift*, No. 104 (August 31, 1819), pp. 853–854, reports on this exhibition: "[F.W.] Sieber has placed upon open exhibit the rare antiquities and notable objects collected on his

[Mozart's] *Idomeneus* was given again today [Thursday, November 25].[87] [//] [Blatt 30r] It is one of the first operas by Mozart. [//] Therefore it, too, probably cannot please. //

Concerning the stove, I will inquire tomorrow. Concerning the servants, I am getting an answer tomorrow, because I have given a commission; if it doesn't work, then I will look into the Invalids' Home. // So you need no servants now? [//] [Blatt 30v]

[leaving an entry for the sleeping Beethoven:]

You sleep so calmly that I don't want to waken you.[88] We'll see each other tomorrow.

[Oliva steals away quietly; end of entries for Thursday, November 25.]

WATCHMAKER **[at his shop, presumably in the City; probably near midday of Friday, November 26]**:[89]

The repeating watch, N 3 gold, with golden face, very good work, 250 fl.

A more ordinary repeating watch, 180 fl.

The 2 silver watches, [@] 80 fl.

   Comes to 100 fl.

A good [watch], 40 fl.

[An] ordinary [watch], 30 fl.

[Blatt 31r]

OLIVA **[at** *Zur Stadt Triest,* **Neuer Markt; afternoon of Friday, November 26]**: People pay very little when they buy used iron. Concerning the Swedish stove it is

---

journey to Crete, Egypt, and Palestine, and has thereby provided the public with an educational and enjoyable pastime. This collection, perhaps the only one of its kind, is notable for many items worth seeing, especially three complete and particularly well preserved mummies and their sarcophagi, also displayed with unpublished paintings of interest to the researcher of antiquity. One of the mummies may well have been embalmed before the time of Moses ....""

The exhibit was located in three rooms on the ground floor of the Schauenstein house, on the Josephstadt Glacis, No. 42 [renumbered as 45 in 1821], next to (actually behind) the salt storage building. Hours were 10 a.m. to 1 p.m. and 3–6 p.m.; admission was 2 fl. W.W. See also Behsel, p. 191, noting the owner as Schauerstein.—KH/TA

[87] See Blätter 20r–20v: This surely designates the performance of Thursday, November 25, rather than that of Saturday, November 27. The past tense also suggests that this entry was made late in the evening.—KH/TA

[88] Beethoven must have nodded off to sleep. Oliva's comments here suggest that the hour was late.—TA

[89] The following entries are not suggestive of a Sunday, so must have followed Thursday, November 25, rather than Saturday, November 27.—TA

most necessary first to find the warehouse for it,[90] then let's go and make reservations with the man in your apartment [building]. //

You should buy a chamber toilet with a removable element attached; it doesn't cost very much. <and> <in> [//] They do not close well, but you can have such a chamber toilet in your bedroom without the least odor. [//] [Blatt 31v] There are now weekly auctions,[91] where people make a profit and [yet] everything is very inexpensive. It hardly costs a quarter hour's time; one asks beforehand at which hour the items that he has chosen will be auctioned. [//] An association of used-goods dealers holds these auctions. //

[School director] Blöchlinger himself writes that Karl is lazy. [//] [Blatt 32r] An ordinary fellow, who lets things go their own way. [//]

Has the Magistrat's decision already been announced? [//] It appears to me that he already knows that the case has been altered. // If it doesn't trouble you, then you should settle Kudlich's bill; it doesn't amount to much. // Concerning the receipt, it is difficult, but you can raise money from the bank shares without difficulties. [//] [Blatt 32v] There are few people who know that for certain, and to move among money-lenders is evil and costly; you will avoid all of this by raising money at the bank. // Hypothetically, if you put in 3 bank shares, you get at least 500 fl., C.M., for them; that amounts to 1200 fl. in paper money [W.W.], against 4 or 5 percent interest. [//] [Blatt 33r]

I have run around today concerning the stoves, and really couldn't ascertain anything yet. The warehouse is said to be in the suburbs, where I shall learn further details tomorrow [Saturday] morning,[92] in order to tell you further details around noon.

BERNARD [seemingly joining Beethoven (and possibly Oliva) in late afternoon, Friday, November 26]: The Melniker wine[93] is already taken care of. Peters says that it costs nothing more than your allowing [him] to drink it at your place now and then. [//] [Blatt 33v]

<Weir> Weissenbach's piece [play] will never come to performance. It is said to be

---

[90] On Blätter 28v–29r, presumably the day before, Oliva said that he recalled seeing such stoves for sale but could not recall where.—TA

[91] The word used is *Licitation*, the Austrian term for *Versteigerung*, an auction. *Licitation* notices appear daily in the *Wiener Zeitung*'s *Intelligenzblatt* during this period.—KH/TA

[92] The context confirms that "today" is Friday, and not Saturday or Sunday, given the opening days for business implied.—TA

[93] Peters seems to have given Beethoven a quantity (probably a case) of wine from Melnik in Bohemia.—KH/TA

too prolix and too long. // Koch,[94] with whom I ate at midday today, has read it; but Schreyvogel[95] is also of this opinion. // I have not read it and therefore cannot judge. [//] [Blatt 34r] The actors only look for roles, and judge the piece accordingly. //

Yesterday I spoke with Stegmayer,[96] who was coming from the rehearsal of [Spohr's] *Das befreyte Deutschland*.[97] He very much complained, though in confidence, that it went badly. [//] [Blatt 34v] He is afraid that if the main performance fails in such a way, no one will come for the second one. //

This <Erlauer> Adelsberger is the best wine this year. //

I must also leave now, because I haven't done my editorial work for the [*Wiener*] *Zeitung* yet. [//] [Blatt 35r]

It does not work well for guests to be present at a monthly examination [in the school], because the examination is only given in written form, and therefore it

---

[94] Friedrich Koch was born Siegfried Gotthilf Eckardt in Berlin in 1754. By his early twenties he had become a noted actor, one of the first to appear in Shakespeare's plays (newly translated by Eschenburg, etc.) on the German stage, and had adopted the name Koch. August von Kotzebue had invited him to become a member of the Burgtheater's company in 1798, and he debuted in Iffland's *Die Advocaten* on October 1 of that year, and was noted as a big eater. With his wife, *née* von Bruckenfeld, he had two daughters: Elisabeth [Betty] (1778–1808), who married the actor Friedrich Roose (1767–1818), and Henriette (ca. 1775–1828), as well as three sons, Friedrich (ca. 1791–1831), August (b. ca. 1794), and Gustav Eckardt (also known by Koch, b. ca. 1796/97). Highly honored, Koch retired as a director at the Burgtheater in 1830, and kept his residence in Vienna, but died during his summer vacation in Alland near Baden in 1831.

It is noteworthy that Koch was a Protestant (Lutheran rather than Reformed), and yet Bernard— who was prejudiced against Protestants—seems to have enjoyed his dinner with him. Bernard was something of a *Schnorrer* (a moocher) and it is possible that Koch paid the bill.

See Gräffer-Czikann, III, pp. 232–233; Seyfried, *Rückschau*, pp. 298–299; Wurzbach, vol. 3, p. 419. None of the various Totenbeschauprotokolle and Verlassenschafts-Abhandlungen in the Wiener Stadt- und Landesarchiv, death records of the Evangelische- Lutherische Kirchengemeinde Wien, Theater Zettel in the Bibliothek, Österreichisches Theatermuseum, or *Hof- und Staats-Schematismen* (especially 1807 and 1808), has thus far revealed the first name (or even a death record) of Koch's wife, who reportedly died in 1803.

[95] Joseph Schreyvogel (1768–1832), author, sometime publisher, secretary, and dramatic advisor to the Burgtheater; see Clive, p. 325.—TA

[96] Matthäus Stegmayer (1771–1820), actor, writer, composer. In 1792 he came to the Josephstadt Theater, went to Schikaneder's Theater auf der Wieden four years later as a comic actor in local pieces, and then, in 1800, to the Court Theater. In 1804 he became choral director at the Theater an der Wien. Later he was choral director and opera director at the Kärntnertor Theater and simultaneously administrator of the Court Theater's Music Publishing House. See Wurzbach, vol. 37, pp. 327–329.—KH/TA

[97] Cantata by Louis Spohr (1784–1859), to a text by Vienna's Caroline Pichler (1769–1843), was performed by the Gesellschaft der Musikfreunde at the Grosser Redoutensaal on Sunday, November 28, and Tuesday, November 30, 1819. The rehearsal must have taken place on Thursday, November 25. See also Blatt 1r above. See Kanne's *Wiener AmZ* 3, No. 99 (December 11, 1819), cols. 795–797, and No. 100 (December 15, 1819), cols. 806–807; Clive, p. 346.—KH/TA

always takes some time to establish calm for these exercises. It is different with the semiannual [examinations], which are conducted orally.

[Blatt 35v]

OLIVA [seemingly at *Zur Stadt Triest*; presumably at midday dinner[98] on Saturday, November 27]: <Peters has cons[ented].>

[Blatt 36r]

SEELIG: Since you are a lover of Melniker wine, I shall provide you with one. // I get one & then a friend gives me one. // *Votre serviteur* [Your servant]. [//] [Blatt 36v] The Count has a means of restoring hearing & he wishes for someone to tell you about it. [//]

[Blatt 37r]

OLIVA: The gentleman over there [across the room in *Zur Stadt Triest*], a foreign Count, has told of a discovery which he applied to his wife who had lost her hearing, and got it back through a simple means. He asked me to write it out for you: One takes fresh horseradish, yes horseradish,[99] as just-pulled from the ground, and rubs it onto cotton, which is quickly twisted around and stuck into the ear. This [Blatt 37v] must be repeated as often as possible, always with fresh horseradish. He himself was witness that his wife regained her hearing in 4 weeks by this simple means. // At least it couldn't hurt anything, opined the man sitting next to him, [who is] a doctor. //

The first oratorio that he [Spohr] performed here 6 years ago[100] was make-work without inspiration. [//] [Blatt 38r] He has a great knowledge of instrumentation, but that is only external work.[101] //

I have just had the desire to drink wine, which otherwise seldom happens, because at midday I usually drink water. // But it disturbs you, during your work, to walk through the city; especially in the best restaurants, one can get [dinner] until after three o'clock. //

---

[98] See Oliva's reference to midday on Blatt 38r below.—TA

[99] Oliva uses two German words for horseradish—*Kren* and *MeerRettich*—in succession for emphasis.—TA

[100] Composer and violinist Louis Spohr was concertmaster and sometime conductor at the Theater an der Wien from 1812 to 1815. His oratorio *Das jüngste Gericht* was performed in Vienna on January 21 and 24, 1813. See the *Allgemeine musikalische Zeitung* 15, No. 7 (February 17, 1813), cols. 116–117.

[101] Beethoven, of course, paid considerable attention to orchestrating his own works and may have told Oliva so, or simply changed the topic of conversation at this point.—TA

BEETHOVEN: Can these men hear what I am saying to you? [//]

OLIVA: No, you are speaking softly. [//] [Blatt 38v] The one asked me how old you were; he thought that you were about thirty-six.[102] // He was amazed at your youthfully healthy appearance, which he seldom finds in Vienna. //

Is the poem of your oratorio [*Der Sieg des Kreuzes*] finished? No-one will learn a word of our conversation from me.[103] // <already in the> Sometimes you aren't cautious of others & therefore it could happen. [//] [Blatt 39r] In August he [Bernard] told me that he was completely finished, and was now copying it into a bound book, which he showed me. He promised then to allow me to read it. // He did not count on that; he is happy that others take the things that you didn't want— such as *Libussa* and *Faust*,[104] but otherwise certainly not. // Will you get busy with it immediately after the Mass [*Missa solemnis*]? // The [*Diabelli*] Variations for piano are also not yet completely finished?[105] [//] [Blatt 39v] Unpardonable on the part of [Ferdinand] Ries. [//] He is said to be rich already. [//]

Veal is good. [//]

Anecdotes by the Crown Prince. [//]

Razor, 5 fl. 6 kr. //

I got here a few minutes later than you, and was delayed that long by important business. Pardon me; unfortunately, I am not always the master of my [own] time. I wasn't in a rehearsal, but had to wait for someone [Blatt 40r] who was to bring me news about a position, and he came so late. // What was being rehearsed? Perhaps the oratorio?[106] It interests me neither in rehearsal nor in performance. [//] It was not that way, but instead the way I wrote it to you. //

Are you going? // It is better at the [Three] Lions.[107] // One cannot say a word without being bothered. [//] [Blatt 40v]

---

[102] Beethoven would turn forty-nine on December 16.—TA

[103] Oliva conveniently forgets that Bernard frequently writes in these books and could easily see Oliva's question. And then, in the next sentence, Oliva notes that Beethoven is sometimes inconsiderate of others.—TA

[104] Bernard's libretto *Faust* had been set by Louis Spohr (performed by Carl Maria von Weber in Prague in 1816), and his *Libussa* would be set by Conradin Kreutzer (performed in 1822 at Vienna's Kärntnertor Theater).—KH

[105] Possibly the 33 Variations (C major) for Piano on a Theme by Anton Diabelli, Op. 120. Beethoven began work on it in 1819; it was published by Cappi & Diabelli in Vienna in 1823. See Kinsky-Halm, pp. 348–350.—KH/TA

[106] Spohr's cantata *Das befreyte Deutschland*. See Blätter 34r and 34v above.—KH/TA

[107] Anton Schneider's wine dealership *Zu den drei weissen Löwen* (At the three white Lions), Kärntnerstrasse No. 1139 [renumbered as 1073 in 1821]. Stadt 1139 was at the intersection with Weihburggasse and across the street from and two buildings east from "Zum wilden Mann" (No. 942 in 1821), therefore conveniently within Beethoven's customary path to and from his monthly apartment in the Ballgasse. See Pezzl (1826), p. 244; Redl, 1820, p. 57; Behsel, p. 32; Klein, pp. 108–109.—KH/TA

[possibly while waiting to pay the bill:]

Is His Highness[108] on the path to recovery? // Who is around the Archduke when he is ill? [//]

[Beethoven and Oliva leave *Zur Stadt Triest*.]

BEETHOVEN **[possibly shopping in the vendors' stalls on the Neuer Markt, probably accompanied by Oliva]**:[109] This would-be[110] lady[111] *believes* that she wants to pick a fight with me. She wants to take offense because I asked for wax candles. [//]

[End of entries for Saturday, November 27.]

[Blatt 41r]

OLIVA **[at *Zur Stadt Triest*; seemingly ca. 1 p.m. on Sunday, November 28]**: I give you my word of honor that I was at home until 12:30 p.m., and then came directly from home to here; just after you had left. [//]

I had neither means nor desire to go and hear the oratorio.[112] //

And, moreover, a miserably bad person. [//] [Blatt 41v] It's his fault that Wieland[113] had to leave. Wieland saved the library for the Prince when the French were here [in 1809], and Gaal[114] had run off to Hungary. He [Gaal] later placed

---

[108] Archduke Rudolph, who suffered from epilepsy.—TA

[109] Beethoven would not have written this unless he did not want to be heard and he was with someone who was literate, presumably Oliva. This also assumes that the woman who ran the candle stall was illiterate or semiliterate, and would not have seen (or at least not comprehended) what he wrote here.—TA

[110] Beethoven's term: "*sollende oder wollende Dame*," meaning a cultivated lady.—TA

[111] Seemingly a candle vendor.—TA

[112] Spohr's cantata *Das befreyte Deutschland* was being performed (presumably at 2 or 3 p.m.) by the forces of the Gesellschaft der Musikfreunde at the Grosser Redoutensaal on Sunday, November 28, and would be again on the evening of Tuesday, November 30, 1819. At dinner the day before (see Blatt 40r above), Oliva had already said that he had no interest in hearing the work. On Blatt 55r below, Bernard says that he himself had waited for Beethoven until 1:30 p.m. This suggests that the performance began at 2 or 3 p.m. See the *Allgemeine musikalische Zeitung* 22, No. 4 (January 26, 1820), col. 56; Blätter 34r–34v above.—TA

[113] Ludwig Friedrich August Wieland (1777–1819), writer, son of the poet Christoph Martin Wieland (1733–1813). In 1800 he went to Bern to live with his brother-in-law Heinrich Gessner; from 1809 to 1811 he was librarian to Prince Nikolaus Esterházy; then he lived independently in Vienna and Weimar, and published numerous political writings, stories, and dramas. See Goedeke, vol. 6, pp. 104–105.

On Christmas Day 1819 Bernard told Beethoven that Wieland had died recently (Heft 5, Blatt 51v), and told him the same thing again the next day (Heft 5, Blatt 54r). Oliva is obviously sympathetic to Wieland, who was originally a pietistic Protestant, but Bernard may not have been.—KH/TA

[114] Presumably librarian Georg von Gaal. On Blätter 16v–17r above Bernard seems to have had an altogether more positive opinion of him. It also seems that Beethoven is more inclined to share Oliva's opinions.—KH/TA

himself under the protection of the *Maitresse* [Princess], the Prince re-installed him, and Wieland received a pension of 300 fl., while Gaal associated with him daily in a friendly way. // [Blatt 42r]

Noah, twenty performances.[115]

Nothing since August; then he [Bernard] wanted to revise it [the oratorio libretto *Der Sieg des Kreuzes*] over several weeks and have it completely ready. // It must be entirely finished before you write a line. // If you explain it to him very firmly, then he will quickly make provisions. The matter has become too well known, and he must be ashamed. [//] [Blatt 42v]

I don't know about the small post offices in the suburbs, but in the city, it is in the building of the large Post Office. //

[End of entries for Sunday, November 28.]

KANNE [?][116] **[first at Beethoven's apartment in the Ballgasse, then moving to a restaurant; early afternoon of Monday, November 29]:**

The hall [Grosser Redoutensaal] was not even full;[117] There were empty seats in the middle. No one from the Court was there, also few of the nobility, perhaps because of the subject matter of the poem.[118] // In general it has excited no interest at all, and could not, because the composition is without any poetic life. [//] [Blatt 43r] It is strange that he [Spohr] himself has overlooked [places] where the subject matter in the poem could have become grand passages [in the music]. The whole thing is

[115] The Leipzig *Allgemeine musikalische Zeitung* 21, No. 48 (December 1, 1819), col. 825, contains this note concerning the Theater an der Wien: "Since October 19, *Noah*, a new Biblical drama with music by Opera Director, Herr [Ignaz von] Seyfried, has been performed incessantly, perhaps ca. 20 times, and day-in, day-out, still fills the house as well as the cashier's box."

The libretto was by Eckschlager, revised by ballet master Friedrich Horschelt. Premiered on October 19, it was repeated almost daily, reaching its 20th performance on November 8. On Sunday, November 28, 1819, roughly the day when this entry was written, *Noah* received its 24th performance. It would be given two more performances on November 1 and 2, 1820 (for a total of 26), and then dropped from the repertoire. See Seyfried, "Journal."—KH/TA

[116] The following is a first-person account by someone who had attended the Spohr concert. Oliva had twice (Blätter 40r and 41r) made it clear that he was not going to attend the performance, and the tone of these critical remarks and the content of the complementary entries are not consistent with Oliva's. The author notes that bass Anton Forti came to stand near him (Blatt 44v), so he is recognized in the musical community, but he is not Bernard, who is mentioned in the third person on Blatt 47r. Moreover, the report here reads very much like a draft for the review of the concert that appeared in Kanne's *Wiener AmZ* 3, No. 99 (December 11, 1819), cols. 795–798, and No. 100 (December 15, 1819), cols. 806–807. Therefore, the author of the entries from this point through Blatt 48r seems to be composer, author, and editor Friedrich August Kanne (1778–1833).—TA

[117] This report concerning the performance of Spohr's *Das Befreyte Deutschland* at the Grosser Redoutensaal on Sunday, November 28, lasts, with interruptions, from Blatt 42v through at least Blatt 48r.—TA

[118] The "nobility" meant were probably Austrian generals who might have been mentioned in the text.—TA

piece-work; there is not a single trace of inspiration. Almost the best pieces in it are a trio modeled after that in *Die Zauberflöte* and an aria modeled after that of Pamina in the second act. He was guilty of many things in the recitatives: they were often incomprehensible, often entirely contrary to sense, often contrary to [the meaning of] the poetry. // The Overture is poor. [//] [Blatt 43v] The principal motive is an ordinary figure, which is repeated ad nauseam in all the voices. The secondary theme is ordinary and pleased him so greatly that he brought it back in the 2 choruses. // The finale of the first part makes the greatest effect, but then he himself has spoiled it. // The first chorus is pretty, but then comes a Russian March and, at the end, a dull Chorale. [//] [Blatt 44r] If he had unified these three choruses,[119] something good might have come from it; at the beginning of the chorus everyone was attentive and at the end silence. [//] The instrumentation does not seem to me to have been done with that knowledge that one could demand of him. In the choruses, the voices were completely covered. [//] That is so commonly arrogant. // People here have a taste for better things. [//] [Blatt 44v] Forti[120] came to stand near me; he acted as if he were delighted, because he wants to give *Faust* for his own benefit very soon. When he noticed the general apathy, however, he became more moderate. // Tomorrow [Tuesday, November 30] it will be empty.[121]

But Cherubini is very mannered.

[seemingly still at Beethoven's apartment:]

The carpenter who is waiting outside told her another place, and she got this wine there. [//] [Blatt 45r]

Then he took the ordinary secondary theme of the Overture, which is not worth much, & the recitative is very poor. [//] That is the *only thing* that brought forth a visible effect. //

There should be a *Receipt* there that belongs to the landlord; you would like to give it back? //

---

[119] The chorus of Russians was accompanied by a second instrumental ensemble consisting entirely of winds. See Kanne's *Wiener AmZ* 3, No. 100 (December 15, 1819), col. 806.—TA

[120] Franz Anton Forti (1790–1859), singer at the Court Opera until 1834. He initially played viola in the orchestra of the Theater an der Wien, and was employed as a chamber musician to Prince Esterházy. His wife was the singer Henriette Teimer (1797–1818), whose father Philipp had been a noted bass singer and English horn player. Her grandfather, oboist Ignaz Teimer, had played piccolo (!) in the premiere of Mozart's *Magic Flute* in 1791.

Spohr's *Faust* (1813), to a libretto by Joseph Carl Bernard (!), had been premiered at the Estates Theater in Prague, under Weber's direction, in 1816. It was not presented at the Theater an der Wien during this period, but the Court Theaters mounted it on August 7, 1827, with Forti as Faust. See Wurzbach, vol. 4, pp. 293–294; Albrecht, "Die Familie Teimer …," *Wiener Oboen-Journal* No. 24 (December, 2004), pp. 2–10; No. 25 (March, 2005), pp. 3–9; No. 27 (October, 2005), pp. 6–7; *Allgemeine Theater-Zeitung* 20, No. 101 (August 23, 1827), p. 414; Clive, p. 113 (Forti).—KH/TA

[121] Therefore "today" is Monday, November 29, the day before the second performance of the cantata.—TA

If only I had found even *one* new thought, or just one clever use of an old one! [//] [Blatt 45v] At the end is a dull fugue. //

Something secure that won't change again; 2,000 fl. [C.M.] are now 5,000 fl. [W.W.], though. [//] The other one can stay.[122] So far you don't have a title page for your Exhibit [on behalf of Karl's guardianship?] //

If he [Archduke Rudolph] wants the honor of having you *entirely alone* at his apartment, he ought to count [sentence ends]. [//] [Blatt 46r] As they say, your relationship is world famous. // He cannot survive.[123] //

[seemingly at a restaurant:]
It has been roasted too long. [//]

He [Spohr] wrote an Octet or Nonet,[124] that was performed at [Count] Brunsvik's in Pesth,[125] but Brunsvik said that it was real trash. // I have known him [Brunsvik] for a long time and always in the best way. [//] [Blatt 46v] He is a truly good person, calm, but very good-natured. [//] It would really be good fortune for Karl if this man were to take much and active interest in his education. //

Professor Klein[126] from Pressburg was at your apartment twice; he wishes to have your large Sonata,[127] and is coming back here soon. [//] [Blatt 47r]

It [Caroline Pichler's libretto for Spohr] is absolutely half-hearted and without any manly strength. Bernard can certainly do something better. // That is also [true] among the weak, but understood in reverse. //

[Concerning the Spohr performance:] There was no resonance shell;[128] it is possible that they had something of an acoustical device under the orchestra, because the orchestra was raised very [far] upwards. One noticed no effect from it, however, because everything sounded jumbled in ensemble pieces, and [Blatt 47v] sometimes

---

[122] Beethoven must be speaking of his financial investments.—TA

[123] Possibly a reference to Archduke Rudolph's frail health. See also Oliva's remark on Blatt 66v below.—TA

[124] Louis Spohr's Nonet in F, Op. 31, which was performed by Franz Clement and colleagues in a morning concert in Vienna's Augarten Hall on May 5, 1819. See Kanne's *Wiener AmZ*, No. 39 (May 15, 1819), col. 315.—KH/TA

[125] Count Franz von Brunsvik (1777–1849), a friend of Beethoven's, on whose estates Beethoven often spent time in his earlier years. In 1819 he took over the management of the City Theater in Pesth (Budapest), which closed in 1822. See Frimmel, *Handbuch*, I, p. 82; Clive, pp. 63–64.—KH/TA

[126] Heinrich Klein (1756–1830), composer, pianist, and organist, was a music teacher at the Hauptschule and at the Royal Institute for Noble Girls in Pressburg (Bratislava). Beethoven reportedly visited him in Pressburg, and he, in turn, remained in contact with the composer for many years. See Frimmel, *Handbuch*, I, p. 278; Wurzbach, vol. 12, pp. 49–50.—KH/TA

[127] Piano Sonata in B-flat, Op. 106 ("Hammerklavier").—TA

[128] A *Resonanz-Kuppel* had been used for concerts in the Burgtheater as early as 1807 or 1809, but it proved cumbersome and was auctioned off in 1827. See Pohl, *Tonkünstler-Societät*, pp. 36–37, and sundry Viennese reports in the *Allgemeine musikalische Zeitung*, starting with vol. 12 (January, 1810), col. 266.—TA

the wind instruments could not even be distinguished. Perhaps the unequal strength in the parts was to blame, because as long as the *concertino* group played,[129] the effect was good, but always the opposite in the *tutti* sections. It appears to me that the hall [Grosser Redoutensaal], though, is always mostly to blame, because it has too great a reverberation. [//] In the soldiers' choruses, he added a monstrous drum, [Blatt 48r] which made a poor effect and contributed the most to the incomprehensibility and confusion. The interest that the audience took in all this was really very limited. //

Only when he manages to do it.[130]

[Seemingly the end of entries for Monday, November 29.]

OLIVA **[at Beethoven's apartment in the Ballgasse; probably shortly after noon on Tuesday, November 30]**:[131] It's this way with the stove. The best worker in the field lives in the Tiefer Graben; I was there and looked at his products. A stove must first be made to fit your purposes, which can be done soon. [Blatt 48v] He must look at the placement, & will come out[132] with me this evening at five o'clock. // If you want to look at his products first, you could go with me now. //

[probably at the stove maker's shop in the Tiefer Graben:] An unglazed one costs only 40 fl., and the painter could paint it. The green one costs 60 fl.; the white one 100 fl. [//] [Blatt 49r]

[at a restaurant, possibly *Zum schwarzen Kameel*,[133] **eating midday dinner, ca. 2 p.m.:]** Perhaps he [Bernard] still presumes that I am here, and therefore doesn't come. // With this regular income it is completely incomprehensible. // He pays for no public entertainment; [he] is not well & attractively clothed. // In the boarding house, he is in very good circumstances; [he] has been seen there.

---

[129] A *concertino* group, especially a smaller group of strings, with some use of single winds, would still have been used for accompanying vocal soloists. It is also possible that this is a reference to the wind ensemble that accompanied the chorus of Russians.—TA

[130] Unclear reference, possibly to Spohr or Bernard.—TA

[131] Noted as "the last day of the month" on Blatt 50v below.—TA

[132] The verb *herauskommen* suggests that the apartment that is being fitted with a new stove is the one on the Glacis in suburban Josephstadt, not Beethoven's temporary residence in the Ballgasse within the City's walls.—TA

[133] If Beethoven were walking directly from Tiefer Graben to his Josephstadt apartment, then his path would have taken him through the Freyung, Teinfaltstrasse, and out of the City through the Franzenstor. In that case, he would have walked past the upscale Hotel *Zum römischen Kaiser*, and may have stopped for dinner there. More likely, however, is that Beethoven would have had errands in his customary neighborhood in the City until meeting the stove maker at the Josephstadt apartment, and Oliva would have returned to his banking office until then. Therefore they probably walked south on the Freyung, through Am Hof and possibly had dinner in the *Schwarzes Kameel* (Black Camel) in the Bognergasse that connects Am Hof with Tuchlauben. This would have been near to the *Rother Igel* in the Tuchlauben, with its boarding house, that became the subject of their conversation.—TA

// There is, I believe, a secondary factor for it. // [Blatt 49v] The master of the house is the lover of [Rosalie] Baumann;[134] it is generally known; the way that people always know such things;—but I would hope that you would not tell it further, as I have. // The two women in the boarding house are very fine and very good-natured;[135] I can say that they treat me extraordinarily well and ease my situation to a large degree.[136] // Paumgarten's wife[137] is already elderly; therefore he seeks someone somewhat younger. [//] [Blatt 50r]

You are having too much cooked; I am already full. //

From earlier times on, he had no reason to behave in this way toward me; and it is mean-spirited of him that he now would like to undo what was earlier so pleasing to him, though, without my ever giving him any kind of cause for it, because that is certainly not my way. [//] [Blatt 50v]

[after dinner, Oliva and Beethoven may have gone their separate ways, meeting again at Beethoven's future apartment on the Josephstadt Glacis; ca. 5 p.m.[138] on Tuesday November 30:]

The *Inspektor* [building manager] says that from here on, there will be no quarters vacant; Count Herberstein[139] lives on the first floor [second floor, American] with a contract; the landlord on the 2nd floor [third floor, American]; and a tenant on the 3rd floor [4th floor, American], likewise with a contract.[140] //

---

[134] Rosalie Baumann (b. 1786), wife of Carl Baumann (b. 1765), partner in a prosperous paint and dye factory. They lived in Weihburggasse No. 980 [renumbered as 924 in 1821] and had six children. Rosalie, *née* von Rambach, was one of the so-called "Ghelen Heirs," historically the family of printers who owned the *Wiener Zeitung*, of which Bernard was editor. See Heft 2, Blatt 89v, and Heft 12, Blätter 5r–6r.—KH/TA

[135] Baroness von Born and her sister, the wife of a Captain Paumgarten or Baumgarten, operated a *Kosthaus* (boarding house) in the *Rother Igel*, Tuchlauben No. 598 [renumbered as 558 in 1821], certainly a different business than the famous restaurant in the same building. See Thayer-Deiters-Riemann, IV, p. 211; Thayer-Forbes, p. 776. Other mentions occur in Heft 7, Blätter 65v (both women) and 68v (Born); Heft 12, Blätter 64r and 70r (Born); Heft 14, Blatt 71v (the Paumgarten husband, whose son may have attended Blöchlinger's school after April, 1820). See the reference to "Paumgarten's wife" in the next entry.—KH/TA

[136] On Sunday, January 30, 1820 (Heft 7, Blatt 9r), Bernard reported having seen Oliva at dinner at the boarding house that day: "They cooked special dishes for him." Therefore, Oliva (who in one report was noted as hunchbacked, but may have just been blind in his right eye) may have suffered from food allergies or perhaps even diabetes.—TA

[137] Possibly the sister of Baroness von Born. See an unclear reference to a Paumgarten (Heft 2, Blatt 17r).—TA

[138] For the time, see Blatt 48v above.—TA

[139] Count Carl von Herberstein (b. 1763), Canon of Salzburg, lived at Josephstadt No. 5 [renumbered as 6 in 1821], Wohnpartei 11. See Conscriptions-Bogen, Josephstadt No. 6/11; Bogen from 1819 (Wiener Stadt- und Landesarchiv); *Hof- und Staats-Schematismus*, 1819, I, p. 77.—KH/TA

[140] Presumably Beethoven had rented this apartment from *Michaeli* (Michaelmas, September 29), 1819, to *Georgi* (St. George's Day, April 24), 1820, and was in the process of making improvements, but now learned that there would be no possibility of extending his lease beyond late April, 1820.—TA

The woman who carries wood and washes clothes for you is here and, because today is the last day of the month [Tuesday, November 30], would like her monthly payment; her husband is sick.[141] [//]

[Beethoven probably walks back to the City with Oliva; they probably go their separate ways again, and then Beethoven meets Bernard, Wolf, Janschikh, and Joseph Czerny for coffee or wine.][142]

[Blatt 51r]

BERNARD [probably at *Zur Stadt Triest*; evening of Tuesday, November 30]:[143] I waited for you in order to go to the oratorio with you.[144] Since you didn't come and since I also didn't see you in the Redoutensaal, I believed that you had been prevented from coming, and therefore would also not eat at home. [//] [Blatt 51v] I believed that you wanted to come and get me. I didn't see you in the hall, since I came too late, and so I believed that you were not there. [//] [Blatt 52r] How did you like the oratorio?[145] [//]

WOLF [?]:[146] When will your oratorio appear, then? // We have several old Italians—Zarlino.[147] // Stadler is writing a history of music in Austria.[148] [//]

BERNARD: No news from [lawyer] Dr. Bach? [//]

---

[141] Even if Beethoven was not living in this apartment, it is apparent from some of the discussions about stoves that he occasionally heated it, which would have been practical if paint needed to dry in the late fall weather. If laundry came with the wood service, Beethoven would certainly have used it here rather than duplicate it in the City.—TA

[142] Oliva had little respect or affection for Bernard; they seldom met socially. See, among others, his comments on Blätter 59v–60r, below.—TA

[143] His first documented meeting with Beethoven since Friday, November 26 (Blätter 33r–35r, above).—TA

[144] On Blatt 55r below, Bernard said that he had waited until 1:30 p.m. This suggests that the performance began at 2 or 3 p.m.—TA

[145] There is no indication that Beethoven attended either performance of Spohr's cantata. Bernard's implied call for accountability may have irritated the composer.—TA

[146] This writer is probably the same as "Wolf" (Johann Wolf), who is mentioned later several times. Böckh lists a "Herr Wolf, former royal Imperial Books Revisor at Frankfurt am Main," as director of the Library of Prince Johann von Liechtenstein, Herrngasse No. 251. See Böckh, *Merkwürdigkeiten*, pp. 110–111; as well as Heft 5, Blatt 53v, and Heft 11, Blatt 67v.—KH/TA

[147] Wolf may be referring to the holdings of the Liechtenstein library. Gioseffo Zarlino (1517–1590), music theorist and composer, published his most important theoretical work, *Istitutioni harmoniche*, in 1558. See Claude V. Palisca, "Zarlino," *MGG*, vol. 14, cols. 1017–1022.—KH/TA

[148] Abbé Maximilian Stadler (1748–1833), composer, honorary canon and Consistory Councillor at Linz. An autograph manuscript with materials for a history of music exists in the Handschriften-Sammlung of the Austrian National Library, cataloged as Ser. Nova 4310. For an edition, see *Abbé Maximilian Stadler*, ed. Karl Wagner (1974); and Clive, pp. 347–348.—KH/TA

[Blatt 52v]

JANSCHIKH: There is only *one* voice and full of everyone's expectation—with the complete confidence and the declaration—that Beethoven will provide us with something much better [than Spohr's *Das befreyte Deutschland*]. [//] *Fiat voluntas Tua, et verbum factum est.*[149] [//]

BERNARD: A new piece by Managetta[150] was hissed off the stage yesterday [Monday, November 29].[151] [//]

[Blatt 53r]

JOSEPH CZERNY: Blahetka[152] himself is a reviewer, and his wife [is] very vain. Therefore, the reviews [of Leopoldine] must be very favorable. // I am not at all satisfied with her.[153] //

---

[149] *Fiat voluntas Tua* (Thy will be done) from the Lord's Prayer (Matthew 6:9–13) and an incompletely quoted *et verbum caro factus est* (and the Word became flesh) from John 1:14. The omitted word is *caro* (flesh), rendering the remainder as something like "and the word became deed."—KH/TA

[150] Johann Wilhelm (Ritter) von Managetta und Lerchenau (1785–1843), General Secretary of the Austrian National Bank and amateur poet. He studied philosophy and law and, in 1816, became *Hofkonzipist* at the united Court Chancellery. At the time, he was director of the Managetta Family Trust.

On Monday, November 29, 1819, his *Das Haus Mac-Alva*, a drama in 3 acts, had been performed at the Burgtheater, but without the author identified. It was performed again on November 30, and December 2, 5, 8, and 28, 1819. See *Wiener Zeitschrift*, No. 146 (December 7, 1819), pp. 1205–1206; Wurzbach, vol. 16, pp. 381–382; Theater Zettel, Bibliothek, Österreichisches Theatermuseum.—KH/TA

[151] Therefore, "today" is still Tuesday, November 30, 1819.—TA

[152] Joseph Blahetka (1783/86 – after 1847) had evidently been the manager of a paper factory in Guntramsdorf, Lower Austria, ca. 10 miles south of Vienna (on one of the routes to Baden). His current (and second) wife was Barbara Sophia Traeg (b. 1787, called Babette), niece of the Viennese music publisher Johann Traeg (Senior); she was a good glass *Harmonika* player and gave daughter Leopoldine (1809–1887) her first piano instruction. By this time Joseph Czerny had become her teacher, presumably at Beethoven's recommendation. Beethoven supposedly became acquainted with Blahetka through Dr. Johann Bihler, tutor to the children of Baron Puthon.

About 1821 Böckh listed him as an author and professor of stenography, living in the Josephstadt, Florianigasse No. 49 [renumbered as No. 52 in 1821], at the intersection of Florianigasse and Buchfeldgasse. From the mid-1820s they lived in the City, No. 591 [renumbered as 551 in 1821], in the *Weisser Hirsch*, next to the *Rother Igel* in the Kammerhof.

For a conflicting set of documents, see Conscriptions-Bögen, Stadt No. 551 (Wiener Stadt- und Landesarchiv); Böckh, *Merkwürdigkeiten*, p. 8; Behsel, p. 17 and 171; Deutsch, *Schubert-Dokumente*, p. 69; Hüffer, pp. 28–29 (citing a letter from Joseph Blahetka to Schindler, September 8, 1839); Ziegler, *Addressen-Buch*, p. 5; Brandenburg, Nos. 1280 and 1281.—KH/TA

[153] The Blahetka family's young daughter, pianist Leopoldine (1809–1887), was Czerny's student. See Blatt 18v above, and Heft 7, Blatt 20r, among others.—TA

JANSCHIKH: When are you giving the concert?[154] That is the sincerest wish of all your friends. //

[Blatt 53v]

JOSEPH CZERNY: About one fugue fewer. // Frau Streicher[155] has already studied your last Sonata for 3 months and still cannot [play] the exposition.[156] She complains the most about the beginning:[157]

$$\begin{array}{c} 8 \\ 3 \end{array}$$
b b – – [//]

BERNARD: Herr v. Janitschek insists that you give an Akademie.[158] [//] [Blatt 54r]
Czerny knows a widow who loves you very much and who should marry you. [//] Stein. [//] I am a rival of yours at the Stein woman's;[159] we are both going there soon with Czerny. [//] [Blatt 54v] Witness. [//] Czerny is also married, has 3 children, and lives a very pleasant life. He has a very pretty, agreeable wife. [//] That would be a mistress, where a wife is not also [Blatt 55r] to be found. [//]
You said that you wanted to fetch me; I waited until 1:30—<Before also> Before the Akademie [with Spohr's *Das befreyte Deutschland*]. [//] It is the truth, as it can be placed in the [*Wiener*] *Zeitung*. [//] [Blatt 55v]

---

[154] On Blatt 21r above (Wednesday, November 24) Bernard wrote that Janschikh had just asked this question. Now, less than a week later, Janschikh asks essentially the same question, which (because it was a sensitive subject to begin with) cannot have failed to irritate Beethoven.—TA

[155] Nannette (Maria Anna) Streicher, *née* Stein (1769–1833), daughter of the Augsburg piano maker Johann Andreas Stein, was married to Johann Andreas Streicher (1761–1833), who had been a friend of Friedrich Schiller in their youth. She was a pianist and also learned piano building, so that, after the death of her father in 1792, she and her younger brother Matthäus Andreas could take over the piano factory. She lived in the Viennese suburb of Landstrasse, Ungargasse No. 371 [1821 numbering]. Beethoven had been acquainted with the Steins since 1786 and remained a friend of Nannette Streicher's. See Conscriptions-Bogen, Landstrasse, No. 371 (Wiener Stadt- und Landesarchiv); Frimmel, *Handbuch*, II, pp. 262–264; Guetjahr, pp. 150–151; Thayer-Deiters-Riemann, II, pp. 554–556, and IV, pp. 483–485; Clive, pp. 357–359.—KH/TA

[156] Piano Sonata in B-flat, Op. 106, which had appeared from Artaria in September, 1819. Czerny uses the then customary term *erster Teil* (first part) for the exposition. The Sonata, Op. 106, is especially known for its abundance of fugues. See Kinsky-Halm, pp. 290–292.—KH/TA

[157] Shorthand for the anacrusis and first chord of Beethoven's Piano Sonata in B-flat, Op. 106.—TA

[158] By this time Beethoven must have been furious at Janschikh's repeated questioning about his giving a concert, nor can he have been happy with subsequent conversational topics.—TA

[159] Bernard probably refers to the piano maker Nannette Streicher, *née* Stein; it is possible that she was planning to host a multiple-piano performance of Starke's *Die Schlacht bei Leipzig* (The Battle of Leipzig); see Blatt 62r for reference to a performance probably on Saturday, December 4, 1819. It is also possible that the name Stein refers to the widow mentioned on Blatt 54r.
Bernard would marry Magdalena Grassl at the Paulanerkirche in the Wieden on November 25, 1823.—KH/TA

It will come to a Czernin.[160] // The artists must be at its head, under the directorship of the Archduke.[161] [//] Little darlings. [//] [Blatt 56r] Zmeskall has already had a great deal of vexation, says Czerny, because of the narrow representation.[162] [//]

Is it necessary, then, that so many of them participate in the singing? // It doesn't work that way; you must lose. [//] [Blatt 56v] At that time, Gentz[163] did not allow the Cantata.[164] Now it would be allowed. [//] I believe it would have been better than *Das befreyte Deutschland*! [//] [Blatt 57r] The poem by Frau v. Pichler[165] is pure prose.

I believe that the present poem [Bernard's *Der Sieg des Kreuzes*] will very much suit your purposes; I have reworked everything with a great deal of consideration, without displacing the poetry. [//] [Blatt 57v]

The girls among the pupils in the Conservatory were mostly absent because of poverty, because they lack the basic necessities. [//]

He[166] says you are unique, the *Generalissimus*. [//] [Blatt 58r]

You can write to him that you first would have consulted the attorneys about this matter, and that you could not decide anything about Karl's half-year stay there until the matter was decided at the Magistrat's, which will not take much longer. Until

---

[160] Presumably Count Johann Rudolph Czernin (1757–1845), chamberlain, supporting member of the Gesellschaft der Musikfreunde. After graduating in studies in law and art, he was partly a founder and partly an active sponsor of most of the educational institutions and beneficial societies in Vienna, was manager of the Burgtheater and, from 1823, became director of the Imperial Academy of Fine Arts. See Gräffer-Czikann, I, pp. 650–651; *Hof- und Staats-Schematismus*, 1819, I, p. 64; Wurzbach, vol. 3, pp. 101–102; Ziegler, *Addressen-Buch*, p. 158.—KH/TA

[161] Archduke Rudolph was the official Protector of the Gesellschaft der Musikfreunde.—TA

[162] A comment concerning the Gesellschaft der Musikfreunde's makeup and organization. Now increasingly incapacitated by arthritis, Zmeskall had been an accomplished amateur violoncellist.—TA

[163] Friedrich [von] Gentz (1764–1832). Born in Breslau and educated in Berlin and Königsberg, he came to Vienna in 1785 as Privy Secretary in the office of Minister Schulenberg, then became War Councillor in the General Directory, and then Court Councillor in Extraordinary Service in Austria. He worked closely with Chancellor Metternich, energetically asserting the tendencies for royal restoration and severe censorship. Gentz was never ennobled in either Germany or Austria, but received an honorary Swedish knighthood. See *Allgemeine Deutsche Biographie*, vol. 12, pp. 577–579; Gräffer-Czikann, II, pp. 306–308; *Hof- und Staats-Schematismus*, 1819, I, pp. 25 and 50; Wurzbach, vol. 5, pp. 13–18.—KH/TA

[164] Beethoven's cantata *Der glorreiche Augenblick*, text by Weissenbach, premiered at the Congress of Vienna on November 29, 1814. See Blatt 1r above.—KH/TA

[165] Caroline Pichler, *née* von Greiner (1769–1843), poet and author, for many years constituted the center of the Viennese literary circle. See Goedeke, vol. 5, p. 484; Wurzbach, vol. 22, pp. 242–244.—KH/TA

[166] Possibly Janschikh.—TA

then, he/it would still like to take care of the boy. The special circumstances that prevail here deserve this consideration [two illegible words]. [//]

[End of entries for Tuesday, November 30.]

[Blatt 58v]

BEETHOVEN **[probably at his apartment in the Ballgasse; probably the morning of Thursday, December 2]**: Blotting paper. //

OLIVA **[possibly in a restaurant; early or mid-afternoon, probably Thursday, December 2]**:[167] I am to give piano lessons to a little boy. Which method is better, the one by Pleyel[168] or by Clementi?[169] He is an Italian who will remain here only a few months. //

He [Bernard] was in the boarding house yesterday, already before two o'clock.[170] [//] I have inquired [//] [Blatt 59r] too early[;] until <I> the matter is completely ended at the Magistrat's, you should not write to Weissenbach, though. // Weissenbach is and remains the best [solution]. Peters's is, in all events, only for the present.[171] [//] [Blatt 59v] He is so unhelpful in expressing his thoughts therein in writing. //

If the Mass goes *out from here*, it is an easy one.[172] [//]

Henry VI—[it] also comes in *King John*.[173] // If you come to my place, you shall see. //

---

[167] More than one day seems to have passed since Oliva last saw Beethoven on the afternoon of Tuesday, November 30.—TA

[168] Ignaz Joseph Pleyel (1757–1831), composer and piano manufacturer, pupil of Johann Baptist Vaňhal and Joseph Haydn. Together with J.L. Dussek, he wrote a *Nouvelle Méthode de Pianoforte, contenant les principes du doigté* (Paris, 1797). His name is correctly pronounced "Ply-el," with emphasis on the first syllable. See Frimmel, *Handbuch*, II, pp. 23–24; Josef Klingenbeck, "Pleyel," *MGG*, vol. 10, cols. 1353–1359; Clive, pp. 268–269.—KH/TA

[169] Muzio Clementi (1752–1832), famous piano manufacturer, pianist, composer, and publisher, had been personally acquainted with Beethoven since 1807. Clementi published several works of piano instruction, among them his *Einleitung in die Kunst das Pianoforte zu spielen* (Vienna, 1802), and *Vollständige Clavierschule nebst 50 Lectionen*. See Frimmel, *Handbuch*, I, pp. 97–98; Hans Engel, "Clementi," *MGG*, vol. 2, cols. 1487–1496; Clive, pp. 74–76.—KH/TA

[170] Oliva's observations here seemingly pertain to Wednesday, December 1 (see Blatt 61r). Concerning the boarding house, see Blatt 49v above.—TA

[171] Oliva is referring to nephew Karl's guardianship; it is obvious that he has reservations about the less-than-savory Peters, whose candidacy Bernard seems to be promoting.—TA

[172] Perhaps Beethoven's relatively easy Mass in C, Op, 86, was envisioned as a substitute for a new work at Archduke Rudolph's upcoming enthronement at Olmütz on March 9, 1820.—TA

[173] The original German reads "Heinrich 6" and "*Johann* ohne Land," and certainly refers to William Shakespeare's dramas *Henry VI* and *King John*. The youngest son of Henry II and Eleanor of Aquitaine, King John (1167–1216) originally stood to inherit very little (therefore called "Lackland"), but after the death of his elder brother, Richard the Lionheart, in 1199, he succeeded to the throne. The

I never speak there in the [boarding] house—neither about Bernard, nor about you and your affairs. [Blatt 60r] And I often do not speak a word with Bernard in a week. // For the most part, he comes late, when everyone is already at the table, and leaves earlier than I do. // He also does not know Italian, and his French is poor. //

Not true, the technical term for *Tact* [bar] in Italian is *misura*. // Isn't that the *Taktschlagen* [beat], I mean the correct speed [*Zeitmass*]? // [Blatt 60v]

If you perhaps go along, then the moment would soon come. // It will be finished tomorrow. //

Henickstein[174] had a session [meeting?] at the bank in the morning; one may meet him in the afternoon at 5 o'clock; I shall go there. [//] [Blatt 61r]

[later, after 5 p.m. on Thursday, December 2, probably at Beethoven's apartment on the Glacis:]

Henickstein had been invited somewhere at midday, and left word that he would not return to the office in the evening. He had them tell me that I could speak to him tomorrow morning at 9:30; I shall go there. //

I was at the attorney's. He sent word that you should not be concerned, that everything will turn out well. The Assembly will be on the 7th of this month, therefore this coming Tuesday. [Blatt 61v] Then you should go with Peters to see him at about 11 o'clock, but not later, in order to go to the Magistrat and fight the matter out. // But Peters must go with you. //

You must decide concerning Henickstein, because I must now go to the City,[175] and tomorrow morning [probably Friday, December 3], I am going out at about 9 o'clock. [//]

[Blatt 62r]

BEETHOVEN: Wine shop in the Tuchlauben,[176] 2 fl. 21 kr. owed. //

---

historical King Henry VI (1421–1471) merited three plays by Shakespeare. Oliva seems to be drawing Beethoven's attention to a common element in the Henry and John dramas (possibly Prince Henry, the later Henry III [1207–1272]), and possibly sparked by the previous reference to the Mass.—TA

[174] Joseph (Edler) von Henikstein, occasionally Henickstein (1768–1838), Viennese banker, member of the Gesellschaft der Musikfreunde, lived in Kärntnerstrasse No. 1001 [current numbering]. On December 1, 1819, Beethoven turned to Henikstein in a letter concerning a loan. See Böckh, *Merkwürdigkeiten*, p. 353; Frimmel, *Handbuch*, I, pp. 208–210; Redl, 1820, p. 18; Thayer-Deiters-Riemann, III, p. 204; Clive, pp. 158–159.—KH/TA

[175] This phrase indicates that they are in a suburb, presumably Beethoven's apartment on the Josephstadt Glacis.—TA

[176] In the street called Unter den Tuchlauben were the following: the wine dealerships of Mathias Trausmüller in the house *Zum blauen Igel*, No. 597, and of Stephan Ferrich in No. 601. In house No. 474 was the grocery dealership of Joseph Reich. Possibly Beethoven meant the restaurant *Zum roten Igel*, which was located in a house with passageway between the Kammerhof and Tuchlauben No. 598. All of the above are house numbers current in 1819. See Guetjahr, p. 26; Pezzl (1826), p. 244.—KH/TA

OLIVA: It has been badly handled by the government administration, therefore he complains without always hitting upon the actual truth. [//]

BEETHOVEN [**probably at his apartment on the Glacis; probably the morning of Friday, December 3**]: Foot warmers.[177] [//]

BERNARD: Tomorrow [probably December 4] is *Die Schlacht von Leipzig*.[178]

[Blatt 62v]

OLIVA [**probably at his apartment on the Glacis; late morning[179] or early afternoon of Friday, December 3**]: Henickstein said that, in this case, he is not able to make such a transaction. When I remarked that it is nothing, I couched the matter in such terms that would not incriminate you. He reserves for himself to answer you and to excuse himself to you. [//] [Blatt 63r] Now it appears to me that it would be best for me to go to Prince Lobkowitz's cashier [Anton Richter] this afternoon; perhaps he will supply the money immediately, and then we would have time to think of something else. [//]

[Blatt 63v]

BEETHOVEN: General of the Cavalry, Baron von Stipsics.[180] [//]

BERNARD [**at Beethoven's apartment; seemingly late morning or early afternoon of Saturday, December 4**]: It appears that he now has the expense for the lessons there. [//] He is indeed like a storm with lightning and thunder and refreshing rain. [//]

Peters does not have much time this evening to go there and remain awhile;

---

[177] Beethoven may have spent the night at his under-heated apartment and found that he needed foot warmers. See also Blatt 66r below.—TA

[178] Friedrich Starke had composed *Die Schlacht bei Leipzig* (The Battle of Leipzig), a "tone painting" for five military bands, in 1816. A performance of it in that form in Vienna during this time cannot be traced, but it is possible that Nannette Streicher hosted a performance on multiple pianos at her showroom in the Ungargasse that would not generally have been advertised or reviewed. See Blatt 54r, where Bernard says they are going there soon.—KH/TA

[179] Oliva had an appointment to see the banker Henikstein (mentioned here) at 9:30 that morning; see Blatt 61r above.—TA

[180] Baron Joseph von Stipsicz zu Ternowa (1755–1831) was an I.R. Lieutenant Field Marshall, Privy Councillor, General of the Cavalry, second owner of the "King Friedrich Wilhelm" Hussar Regiment No. 10. See *Hof- und Staats-Schematismus*, 1819, I, p. 270; *Militär-Schematismus*, 1819, pp. 7, 37, 77; Wurzbach, vol. 39, pp. 53–55.—KH

therefore we'll want to go there already at 6 o'clock. [//] [Blatt 64r] The Prince [Lobkowitz] has returned from Bohemia.[181] //

OLIVA [at Beethoven's apartment; possibly the afternoon of Saturday, December 4]: I had to wait a long time. He [presumably Lobkowitz's cashier] looked through all the documents and the testimonials were not there. He was persuaded that they had *not* been received. Perhaps they are still with you. Does Bernard perhaps have them? [//] Given the many regulations that these business people observe, isn't it probable that he would have received them? [//] [Blatt 64v] He looked through all the papers concerning you in my presence; the testimonials were not there. Ask at [publisher] Steiner's. // It would be good, though, if you yourself went to [lawyer] Bach. // There is still time for a registered letter. // He has saved every one of your letters. // Tomorrow [Sunday, December 5] or Monday [December 6]; it will be difficult to meet him this evening; he left at the same time as I did. [//] [Blatt 65r] The sheets concerning your interest in the pension [from the three nobles], then several resolutions. // Nothing more than perhaps a little [monetary] incentive. Every professor certainly put himself down for that every year. //

WOLF [?] [possibly in a coffee house; late afternoon of Saturday, December 4]: Have you seen the Indian? // He does things that are almost unbelievable.[182] //

As a citizen of Vienna, you can already speak more freely. [//] [Blatt 65v] The secretary [of the Gesellschaft der Musikfreunde] wants to know whether the oratorio [*Der Sieg des Kreuzes*] will be given soon. // Grillparzer[183] has also finished an opera text. He told me. // I shall inquire about what its content is. // He has written a tragedy—entitled *Die Machabäer* [The Maccabees].[184] //

Are you satisfied with Blöchlinger? [//] [Blatt 66r] Can you maintain him? // I would have paid nothing more. [//]

[181] Prince Lobkowitz arrived from Prague on Saturday, December 4; see the *Wiener Zeitung*, No. 280 (December 7, 1810), p. 1120.—TA

[182] The Indian illusionist Thomas Bauleau from Madras (see Blatt 17r above) had recently performed on November 16, 24, and 28; he would perform again on December 5, 8, and 12 (Zettel, Bibliothek, Österreichisches Theatermuseum).—TA

[183] In 1818 Franz Grillparzer had written an opera fragment with the title *Penelope*. From 1819 to 1860 he busied himself with the plan for a tragedy *Die Nazaräer*. See Goedeke, vol. 8, pp. 317–319.—KH

[184] Possibly Zacharias Werner's *Die Mutter der Makkabäer*, tragedy in five acts, whose publication by Wallishausser was first announced in the *Wiener Zeitung*, No. 37 (February 16, 1820), p. 148. Scenes from the still unpublished work were printed in the *Conversationsblatt* (a newspaper that appeared from Wallishausser), Nos. 45 and 46 (June 4 and 8, 1819).—KH

BEETHOVEN [possibly at his still cold apartment on the Glacis; Saturday, December 4]: Woolen foot warmers, also leather ones.[185] //

BERNARD [probably in Beethoven's apartment on the Glacis, with food arriving from the *Birne* coffee house below; possibly late on Saturday, December 4]: The Schnitzels are here. [//]

PETERS[186] [possibly at a wine house in the City; Sunday, December 5, or Monday, December 6]: It will take little trouble to be finished with the gentlemen of the Magistrat. [//] Just always keep me in line.[187] [//] [written vertically on the right side→] 1/8.

[Blatt 66v]

OLIVA [Sunday, December 5, or Monday, December 6]: It must be done in such a way that his [Archduke Rudolph's] allowance will be as assured to you then as it was earlier; otherwise you could lose it upon his death. Given his weak health, you should probably watch out for this. //

This week there is a holiday [Wednesday, December 8],[188] so we should go [for an excursion]. [//] Hetzendorf.[189] //

[Blatt 67r]

BEETHOVEN [while shopping in the Tuchlauben; possibly Monday, December 6]: Per bottle of Regensburger beer: 24 kr. [//]

PETERS: According to the laws, you absolutely cannot refuse the guardianship without significant grounds; moreover, you are still the person who is paying [for Karl]. [//] The Magistrat compromises itself. [//] [Blatt 67v] The mother [Johanna] creates nothing but confusion, and her entire influence concerning the education of your nephew must be removed. [//] Very malicious. [//]

Joseph Lobkowitz forgets his handkerchief very often. //

---

[185] See also Blatt 62r above.—TA

[186] Handwriting identified by Schindler in Heft 4, Blatt 1a.—KH

[187] Peters (a friend of Bernard's) may have been engaging in some poetic wordplay on the name of editor Johann Schickh (Bernard's former partner): "Machen Sie mich nur / immer zum Schik."—TA

[188] Immaculate Conception of Mary, Wednesday, December 8, 1819.—KH

[189] Hetzendorf, a village south of Schönbrunn, part of Vienna's twelfth Bezirk since 1891. Beethoven stayed in Hetzendorf several times. For example, his stay in the little Schloss of Baron Pronay from mid-May until mid-August, 1823. Schloss Hetzendorf was also a popular place to go for a walk; Beethoven's Bonn patron, Elector Max Franz, lived here until his death. Possibly Archduke Rudolph had quarters here as well. See Frimmel, *Handbuch*, I, pp. 212–214; Groner (1922), p. 165; Klein, pp. 126–127.—KH/TA

BERNARD: I am just saying that the Magistrat is making everything known; [Blatt 68r] for example, that she [Johanna] said that you were in love with her. [//]

He belongs to a sect of mystics, of which he is one of its strongest [adherents]. [//]

[Blatt 68v] [No writing.]

End of Heft 3

Heft 4

(December 7, 1819 – December 12, 1819)

[Blatt 1r]

BACH [immediately before the beginning of and during the *Tagsatzung* (Assembly);[1] the morning of Tuesday, December 7]: We must still wait for the current guardian [Leopold Nussböck] and even the widow [Johanna]. [//] If you want to come [back] at 11:30, we might not have to wait. [//]

PETERS [continuing]: I shall give my declaration, since you give me [your] trust that, after considering the existing laws and sparing you vexations, I take upon myself the responsibility to notify the Magistrat about everything [Blatt 1v] concerning the education of your nephew according to the existing regulations! [//] I implore you to go to [Blöchlinger's] Institute with me. After that I shall report to you every time about the smallest detail and the changes that are perhaps necessary to be undertaken. // I shall already be finished with her [Johanna] in the most courteous manner. [//] [Blatt 2r] The horrible part lies in the fact that the honorable Magistrat made the matter more difficult than easier for you. //

Better than at the *Biber*.[2] // Is she beautiful?[3] //

How old is your nephew now?[4] // The young [Joseph Franz Karl] Lobkowitz is 16 years old and is studying the first year of Law with great success. [//] He will be treated like the others. // 6 years of Latin at the *Gymnasium* do not count. [//]

---

[1] For the nature of this legal convocation concerning the guardianship of nephew Karl, see Weise, p. 28; Thayer-Forbes, pp. 725–729.—KH/TA

[2] Probably a reference to the restaurant *Zum Biber* (At the Beaver), on the Glacis, No. 21 [renumbered as 22 in 1821] in the Josephstadt, one block north of Beethoven's new residence. See Heft 7, Blatt 47r (February 8, 1820), where Beethoven himself writes a brief entry about its wine.

A remote possibility is Johann Leopold Biber, Court Secretary in the High Police and Censor's Office, attached to Anton von Ohms. Biber lived in the City at Neubad, No. 311 [renumbered as 289 in 1821]. See *Hof- und Staats-Schematismus*, 1819, I, p. 267; Behsel, pp. 9 and 190.—KH/TA

[3] See Blatt 45r below, where Peters offers to procure the girl at the *Birne* (one block south of the *Biber*) for Beethoven, and the composer declines.—TA

[4] Karl had turned thirteen on September 4, 1819.—TA

[Blatt 2v]

BEETHOVEN [**writing so as not to be heard**]: What is the talk about? [//]

PETERS [**replying**]: About the annual expense for the boy. Now we have to await the decision. [//] [Blatt 3r] The Magistrat's Councillor is for the inclusion of the mother and said that her earlier [legal] offenses, which I indicated were troublesome, would be viewed entirely as insignificant.[5] [//] He, who has Counsel, also mentioned the beautiful clothes that you gave your nephew, and about which the mother has made pointed remarks. [//] [Blatt 3v] To [Blöchlinger's] Institute together? [//]

BERNARD: At an earlier time he wanted to supply his reviews to the *Mode-Zeitung*; I cut out the first one, and so then he by chance got into the *Sammler*.[6] //

Peters wanted to come; therefore I came this way. [//] [Blatt 4r] Peters asks where you eat at midday. // Peters wants the three of us to eat together somewhere, tomorrow [Wednesday, December 8] at midday. // Peters wants to fetch you at home at 1 o'clock. [//]

[Blatt 4v]

NEPHEW KARL [**confined to bed at Blöchlinger's Institute in the Josephstadt; probably early afternoon of Wednesday, December 8 (Immaculate Conception)**]: She [his mother Johanna] told me that she herself hoped that I would stay here; that it would be a hardship for her, however, to raise 1200 fl. now, instead of 900 fl. // Why? // Can't you raise yours, then, rather than she takes the pension? //

I don't know where the many lice are coming from now. // But it is healthy to have lice.[7] [//] [Blatt 5r]

So, how did the gentlemen of the Magistrat conduct themselves? // Wasn't yesterday [Tuesday, December 7] the *Tagsatzung* [Assembly]? // Schmerling is there.[8] // Have you already accepted Peters as co-guardian? // Absolutely nothing

---

[5] See Brandenburg, "Johanna van Beethoven's Embezzlement," pp. 237–251.—TA

[6] Probably Friedrich Wähner (1786–1839). His polemical article against Ernst Benjamin S[alomo] Raupach's tragedy *Die Fürsten Chawansky*, signed with his full name, appeared in the *Sammler*, No. 142 (November 27, 1819), p. 568; continuation in No. 144 (December 2, 1819), pp. 575–576, and further issues. Another article, signed "F.W.," appeared in No. 137 (November 16, 1819), p. 548. See Clive, p. 383.—KH/TA

[7] See Beethoven's possible reference to a comb for salve in Heft 3, Blatt 22v.—TA

[8] Joseph (*Ritter*) von Schmerling (1777–1828), active as an appellate judge from 1819, was the brother of the wholesaler Leopold von Schmerling. Leopold, in turn, was married to the former Anna Maria (Nanny) Giannatasio del Rio, whose sister was the doting diarist Franziska (Fanny) Giannatasio del Rio, and therefore known to Karl from the family's school. See Clive, pp. 128–129.—KH/TA

like that can happen here [at Blöchlinger's Institute], because there is the strictest supervision. // *Secretly*, never. // [Blatt 5v] 9:30. //

The day after tomorrow, I shall probably be able to get up. // Once my frozen feet are *properly healed*, they will *never* come *again*. // I have 5 corns on each foot.[9] // [Blatt 6r] He operated on the frozen toe today. //

BERNARD [probably at *Zur Stadt Triest*, with Peters; ca. 2:15 or 2:30 p.m.[10] on Wednesday, December 8 (Immaculate Conception)]: The Wranitzkys had a very full concert.[11]

The Magistrat has merely placed in the record what has been carried forward, and will now hold the session to decide about it. [//] [Blatt 6v] It is already assumed that you are to have the guardianship, with the assistance of a second. Nothing more has been spoken against it. [//] Since no objection has been raised against Peters, the matter will have no difficulty. [//] [Blatt 7r]

It has been gotten from the beer house.[12] [//]

---

[9] In January 1823, Bernard noted that another student had frozen feet (see Heft 20, Blatt 2r).—TA

[10] Bernard and Peters had attended the Wranitzkys' concert that lasted until ca. 2 p.m. *Zur Stadt Triest* was only a five-minute walk from the Redoutensaal and, depending upon how much post-concert conversation took place at the hall, they might have arrived by 2:15 p.m. or so. In fact, Beethoven may have arrived to find them already there, as Peters seemingly pays the bill on Blatt 12r.—TA

[11] On December 8, 1819, occasioned by the Immaculate Conception holiday, the Wranitzky brothers (both members of the Burgtheater's orchestra) gave a musical Akademie in the Kleiner Redoutensaal at the mid-day hour (12:30 p.m.). Anton Wranitzky (b. Vienna, ca. 1795/96; d. Vienna, 1829) played a Violin Concerto of his own. His younger brother Friedrich (b. Vienna, 1798; d. Dresden, 1840) played the first movement of a Violoncello Concerto by Nikolaus Kraft as well as a Rondo of his own composition. Their sister Anna Wranitzky (b. Holtschütz, Bohemia, 1799/1801; d. Wiesbaden, 1851), a member of the Kärntnertor Theater, sang a scene and aria from Rossini's *Sigismondo* and, together with Herr Babnigg, a duet from Rossini's *Armida*. The Overture to *Carlo Fioras* by Ferdinand Fränzl (1767–1833) rounded out the program. The music itself probably lasted 60–65 minutes; the five breaks between the pieces may have taken 3 minutes each for a total of 15 minutes. Therefore the concert would have been over by ca. 2 p.m. Bernard's comment referred to the size of the audience. Beethoven had been friends with the elder generation of the Wranitzky family (concertmasters Paul and Anton) since at least 1795; see Clive, pp. 402–403.

See the Leipzig *Allgemeine musikalische Zeitung* 22, No. 4 (January 26, 1820), cols. 56–57; Kanne's *Wiener AmZ*, No. 100 (December 15, 1819), col. 807; Schickh's *Wiener Zeitschrift*, No. 149 (December 13, 1819), p. 1231; Roland Würz, "Fränzl," *New Grove*, vol. 6, pp. 806–807; Heft 15, Blatt 39r.—KH/TA

[12] If this conversation took place at the wine house, grocery, and restaurant *Zur Stadt Triest*, then it is conceivable that beer and associated products were not on the customary menu and would have been brought in from other sources. Even today, many Viennese *Heurigen* (which specialize in "new wine") sell beer only in bottles, and not on tap.—TA

PETERS:[13] The matter will be brought to order entirely according to your wishes, and my humble self will deal with Herr Blöchlinger. The mother may not, without your presence. Four times per year at the Institute is already enough. [//]

BERNARD: Not even the guardian? // The Magistrat has really compromised itself. [//] [Blatt 7v]

I was in her box [at the theater] yesterday [December 7]; I believe that the chamber servant will finally be jealous.[14] [//]

PETERS: The Magistrat will reject it and compromise himself; i.e., the mother will always want to be included. Because the Magistrat perceived the matter incorrectly.[15] // [Blatt 8r][16] Perhaps she has captivated the gentleman by her representations. [//]

BERNARD: To which people of education and knowledge would it occur to have it take place at the Magistrat's? And if one of them is present, then he will certainly endeavor to place it in another location. [//] [Blatt 8v] It is an irrational notion that the Magistrat .... //

PETERS: I live much better than you do in my domesticated Lobkowitzian circumstances;[17] but for doing so, I shall also be completely dead when once I die. [//]

BERNARD: It will also be that way for many other people. He can take comfort in that. [//]

[Blatt 9r]

PETERS: Bernard will get married,[18] and then let's go to his place for our meals. //

---

[13] As tutor to the Lobkowitz family, Peters would have attended the Wranitzkys' concert as well, because the three young musicians' father, violinist Anton (1761–1820), had been the late Prince Lobkowitz's Kapellmeister for nearly twenty years.—TA

[14] On December 6 and 7, the Burgtheater gave the first two performances of *Die seltsame Entführung* (freely adapted from the French). One of the characters was Minna, a chamber servant (*Kammermädchen*), played by Dlle. Teimer. The chamber servant (*Kammerdiener*) in Bernard's entry, however, was a man (possibly even someone with the surname Kammerdiener), so this element remains unclear. Also on the double bill was Kotzebue's *Die deutsche Hausfrau*, one of whose stars was Bernard's friend, actress/playwright Johanna Franul von Weissenthurn (whose daughter also played the daughter onstage). Therefore Bernard probably sat in Madame Weissenthurn's box. See Zettel, Bibliothek, Österreichisches Theatermuseum.—TA

[15] Drawing of a head in profile in the left margin.—KH

[16] Cropped photo of this page in Köhler *et al.*, *Konversationshefte*, vol. 1, facing p. 49.—TA

[17] Peters means that he has a respectable and decently paid position with the Lobkowitz family, and has a relatively wealthy wife, but no children of his own.—TA

[18] The address of Magdalena Grassl, Bernard's future wife, in Heft 5, inside front cover (ca. December 13, 1819), indicates that (although they would not marry until November 25, 1823) Bernard

BERNARD: Goethe says:
   The place [*Stelle*] where a good man walked,
   Remains consecrated for all times.[19] //
So let us strike against him. [//]

[Blatt 9v]

PETERS: He is not popular because he does not like to appear in salons. [//]

BERNARD: Here is chicken, if you would like to eat some.[20] //

PETERS: My 6-year-old nephew, whom I have now gotten from the mountains, also has frozen feet. [//] Oysters. //

BERNARD: Peters asks whether you eat oysters? [//]

[Blatt 10r]

PETERS: You already know his secret. //

BERNARD: Are you satisfied with this wine, or do you want to drink *another* kind? // Isn't it cool to you? //
   He has learned nothing at all. //
   They just this moment arrived. [//] [Blatt 10v]
   That is magnesia.

PETERS: I don't know him [Blöchlinger] ! [//] I want to give you the account of it in writing. //

BERNARD: They must be the baptismal witnesses.[21] // [Blatt 11r]
   Recht zum Schicken bin ich geboren, drum heiss' ich der Schick auch, [I was born for adaptability, therefore my name is Skill,] ... //

PETERS: I shall go out there [to Blöchlinger's] tomorrow, then you talk and come to an understanding with Blöchlinger, that the mother is to be kept at a distance as long as it takes for the whole business to be put in order. He can demand that, <and> without her taking it badly. [//]

---

is already involved with her, despite the talk about singer Caroline Willmann (Blatt 13v below) and Peters's wife (Heft 6, Blatt 1r) later on.—TA

[19] Goethe, *Torquato Tasso*, Act 1, Scene 1: "The place [*Stätte*] where a good man walked is consecrated; after a hundred years, his word and his deed resound to his grandchildren."—KH

[20] *Poularde* (in Austria mostly *Poulard*): cut-up young fattened chicken.—TA

[21] Next to this entry and under it: a head in profile and picture of a woman from chest up.—KH

[Blatt 11v]

BERNARD:

> Der *Schickh*.[22]

Recht zum Schicken bin ich geboren, drum heiss' ich der Schick auch,
Bin zu allem geschickt, werd' auch nach allem geschickt!
Will's mein Geschick, so werd' ich wohl gar von der *Zeitung der Moden*,
Oder vom Redakteur in den April noch geschickt![23] [//] [Blatt 12r]

> <Soon> [//]

Peters has indeed fêted us. If we get together again, you ought to entertain us
with oysters. [//]

[Dr. Christoph Zang seems to have stopped by their table briefly:]

The Prof[essor][24] says you should not drink any *Ausbruch* wine.[25] [//]

Antipathy. [//]

[End of entries for Wednesday, December 8 (Immaculate Conception).]

[Blatt 12v]

PETERS **[in the upstairs of a restaurant, probably *Zur Stadt Triest*,[26] late dinner
on Thursday, December 9]**: Our house doctor [for the Lobkowitz family] is very
fine. If you'd like, he himself could go and take a look. He expresses great joy when I
consult him. [//] For [Karl's] feet. [//]

---

[22] Poem entered vertically on the page.—KH

[23] Extended wordplay on the name of editor Johann Schickh: Schicken (adaptability), Schick
(skill), geschickt (meaning both the adjective "skillful" and the participle "sent"), Geschick (fate), and
again geschickt (sent). Roughly translated, it means: "I was born for adaptability; therefore my name
is Skill. I am skillful in everything, so I am sent to everyone! If my fate wills it, I shall probably be sent
from the *Fashion Journal* or (away) from the editorship already in April!" In the journal itself during
this time, Schickh is noted as *Herausgeber* (editor) and Bernard as *Redakteur* (publisher), though both
words can signify editorial activity, and the roles of each are by no means clear.

Elsewhere it is evident that Beethoven liked Schickh personally and respected him professionally;
thus, he might have taken Bernard's deprecating tangent as his cue to end the evening's festivities.—TA

[24] Christoph Bonifazius Zang (1772–1835), doctor of pharmaceutics and wound medicine,
professor of surgery, living in the Josephs-Akademie, Alservorstadt No. 198 [renumbered as 221 in
1819]. Later in the 1820s Zang, living alone and listed as a widower (his son, b. 1807, must have been
independent by then), lived on the Schottenbastey No. 107 (Conscriptions-Bogen, Stadt, No. 107/2
(new collation 107/1); Wiener Stadt- und Landesarchiv); Behsel, p. 201. See Blöchlinger's estimate of
him as brilliant but peevish in Heft 9, Blätter 53r–53v. For a portrait of Zang by Waldmüller (ca. 1820),
see Husslein-Arco and Grabner, p. 35. See also Böckh, *Wiens lebende Schriftsteller*, p. 58; Wurzbach,
vol. 59, pp. 165–167.—KH/TA

[25] A type of wine made from the best berries [*Beeren*], grown especially for this purpose. See
Loritza, p. 16.—KH

[26] Heinrich Seelig, proprietor of *Zur Stadt Triest*, seems to have imported oysters, mentioned
several times during the conversations of December 8 and 9, 1819.—TA

Bernard is not coming. //

If my situation were not so uncertain, I could immediately take him [Karl] to be with me, but I don't know whether I'll stay here in the summer. [//] Blöchlinger, though, will allow him [Karl] to have dinner with [Blatt 13r] me and the young Prince. I believe that this environment will have a favorable effect on him. // The nobleman is at least good-natured. // [He] is still too young. Nevertheless, it [nobility] has certainly not corrupted him. // The oysters were from him. // For me, it is a fancied delicacy. [//] [Blatt 13v] I have not taken my wife to any restaurant yet. // Bernard likes to eat them [oysters]. //

By Mail. //

<Bernard will marry [singer Caroline] Willmann.[27]> //

One of my acquaintances became crazy from love; he was [Blatt 14r] taken to the *Allgemeines Krankenhaus*.[28] I have had to run more than 60 errands in order to get him out of there and to bring him under suitable treatment. He was a raving fool and has now nearly recovered. // Without my care, he might have been lost in the insane asylum forever. // [Blatt 14v]

Countess Herberstein[29] must pay 500 fl. monthly for my craziness. // He is crazy from love with her, and she has obeyed my successive representations. // The crazy scratched on the wall. I am suffering death from love and from being sworn to secrecy. // [Blatt 15r]

He [Nussböck?] wanted to come in ½ hour. // A guardianship that has no accountability. //

[Joseph] Czerny is a good piano teacher! Prince Joseph [Lobkowitz] has made progress. //

I must drink a mild wine. //

JOSEPH CZERNY [joining Peters]: Blahetka.[30] //

---

[27] See Heft 2, Blatt 58r; Heft 4, Blatt 9r; Heft 5, inside front cover.—TA

[28] Since the 1780s Vienna's General Hospital had actually been one of the most modern and progressive such institutions in Europe. Although primitive by today's standards, the *Narrenturm* (so-called Fools' Tower), a circular building behind the several airy courtyards of the hospital proper, nevertheless witnessed state-of-the-art treatment for the mentally ill in Beethoven's time. Today an eastern side wing of the "old" *Allgemeines Krankenhaus* houses the offices, lecture halls, and library of the University of Vienna's Faculty of Musicology.—TA

[29] The *Hof- und Staats-Schematismus*, 1819, I, lists the following countesses: Countess von Herberstein, *née* Countess von Stürgkh (p. 148); the Privy Councillor's widow, Countess von Herberstein, *née* Countess von Kolowrat (p. 163); and the Privy Councillor's widow Countess von Herberstein Moltke, *née* Countess Krakowski von Kolowrat (p. 152). It is not clear what Peters's duties with Countess Herberstein were, but 500 fl. was approximately equal to the *annual* salaries of rank-and-file orchestral musicians at the Court Theaters. For further information concerning Countess Herberstein, Peters, and her tutor, see Heft 8, Blatt 45v.—KH/TA

[30] As noted elsewhere, young Leopoldine Blahetka was Joseph Czerny's prize student.—TA

[Blatt 15v]

PETERS: The wine is too intense [*feurig*]. [//]

BERNARD **[joining Peters and Czerny]**: You are making him [the proprietor] angry. It is his wife who is downstairs. He says that he delivered the finest Erlauer [wine], and that the lemons and the sourness of the seafood are to blame that the taste is different. [//] [Blatt 16r] Prof[essor] Zang also says so. [//] Sometime we have to take an oyster excursion to Triest and Venice. // When, then, do you want to go to the doctor's tomorrow? Where should we all meet? //

PETERS: I shall have your nephew ride around in the *cabriolet* [open carriage] with P[rince] Joseph; that will provide him diversion.[31] [//] [Blatt 16v] On Sundays— they don't do anything anyway in the Institute on Sundays. // I want to conform entirely to your viewpoint, because my temperament always carries me in a different direction. [//]

BERNARD: Honor the Ladies.[32] [//] [Blatt 17r]
The late actor Roose[33] once gave a banquet that lasted from 1 o'clock at midday to 12 o'clock at night. When they got up from their seats, his father-in-law, the actor Koch, said: "It's just too bad that it won't continue like this for 3 weeks." It's almost the same with us today. [//] [Blatt 17v]
The oysters arrived today on the express postal coach. // St. George's wine is too intense [*feurig*]. We ourselves have passion [*Feuer*] enough. //
Let's pay tomorrow. [//] We're paying nothing [today]. [//] [Blatt 18r] We want to drink coffee. // We want to pay tomorrow. [//] [Blatt 18v]
It is the Civil Senate, which consists of many Councillors, chosen this way and that. They make decisions according to the presentation of the reviewers and the contents of the record. //
About 15 fl., near the Roter Turm, where I've bought all my hats for years.[34] [//] [Blatt 19r]
Peters says that he made a presentation that was very good and to the point. [//]

---

[31] This seemingly took place the next Sunday, December 12 (see Blatt 43v below).—TA

[32] Original "Ehret die Frauen," a toast over wine.—TA

[33] Friedrich Roose (1767–1818), called "Rose" here, together with Siegfried Gotthilf Koch (1754–1831) and his daughter Elisabeth (1778–1808), later Roose's wife (married ca. 1799), were (in 1798) hired by Kotzebue for the Court Theater, where he became stage director in 1802. Koch was a Protestant, yet Bernard seemed to enjoy his company. See Wurzbach, vol. 26, p. 338; Heft 3, Blatt 33v.—KH/TA

[34] Possibly Andreas Werner, municipal hatmaker, who had his shop in the Rotenturm Strasse, in the house *Zur goldenen Sonne*, No. 772 [renumbered as 726 in 1821]. See Redl, 1822, p. 147; Behsel, p. 22.

There was nothing about which you yourself needed to speak; the attorney himself has transmitted everything. [//] [Blatt 19v]

He asks whether he may accompany you home.[35] //

JOSEPH CZERNY: Let Peters do it now. // Who instructs him in music? [//]
[Presumably the end of entries on Thursday, December 9.]

BEETHOVEN **[presumably at his apartment on the Glacis, the morning of Friday, December 10]**: <Joseph Metzger,[36] N[umber] ....> [//]

[Blatt 20r][37]

BACH **[at his office; later on the morning of Friday, December 10]**: If we want to allow the widow [Johanna] to be named as co-guardian, the matter would be subject to fewer difficulties. [//] As co-guardian she would not actually have *dominion* over anything, but instead merely have the honor of taking part in the guardianship. [//] [Blatt 20v] She would remain merely a *figurehead*. [//] At present, I have proposed that she must remain completely away. [//] I have not accepted her. [//] [Blatt 21r] Send me the [house] number of your residence. //

BERNARD **[possibly not at *Zur Stadt Triest*; presumably at midday dinner, ca. 2 p.m., on Friday, December 10]**: As soon as one right is conceded to her, she will always make troubles. If she were legally made to stay away, one could always take her into consideration, as soon as she behaved herself well. [//] [Blatt 21v] He can do nothing except await the decision. // Then it will be appealed. // It will not last much longer. [//] Turkish justice is sometimes very appropriate to this purpose. //

Haven't you seen Peters today? [//] [Blatt 22r]

You lose nothing. //

Did you feel alright this morning? [//] I felt quite alright. But we stay too long in these houses where people take note of everything and always listen attentively to what is said. // As a municipal businessman, the landlord took it very badly that [Blatt 22v] you looked for him high and low that way. // Because you complained

---

[35] Beethoven may have had too much to drink at this get-together. See Bernard's inquiry, presumably the next day (Blatt 22v below), about how the composer felt that morning, but Bernard himself was not too coherent on Blätter 17v and 18r.—TA

[36] Joseph Metzger, municipal wild game dealer, had his sales shop in the multi-faceted house *Zum roten Igel* (Red Hedgehog; individual house sign *Zum Wildente* [Wild Duck]), bordering on the Wildpretmarkt, No. 1318 [renumbered as 550 in 1821]; see Behsel, p. 17, where the street is called Kammerhof. He advertised frequently in the *Intelligenzblatt*. Venison was and is a popular dish in Vienna at this time of year.—KH/TA

[37] Photo of this page in Köhler *et al.*, *Konversationshefte*, vol. 1, facing p. 64.—TA

about his wine and called him a scoundrel [*Lumpenkerl*], who cheated and played roguish tricks.[38] //

On our side, they have merely been pensioned. General Mack[39] has recently been restored to all of his honors and titles. [//] [Blatt 23r] Mack was dismissed because of the surrender and capitulation of Ulm. // He had Imperial instructions, and acted accordingly. Moreover, there was a large faction of generals against him because he is only of common origins. //

Prince Dietrichstein[40] is very popular; he was at my place two times already. [//] [Blatt 23v] He has knowledge and can provide his signature. // Not Moritz,[41] but rather the reigning prince. [//]

BEETHOVEN [in a coffee house; late in the afternoon of Friday, December 10]: Seilerstadt [*sic*]: Apartment with 4 rooms; No. 855, on the 2nd floor [3rd floor, American].[42] [Blatt 24r] Across from the walls.[43] [//]

---

[38] Beethoven and his circle seem to have had too much to drink at *Zur Stadt Triest* the night before. See Blätter 12v–19r above.—TA

[39] Carl Mack, Baron von Leiberich (1752–1828), Lieutenant Field Marshall. After the French victory at Memmingen on October 14 and 15, 1805, he had withdrawn to Ulm for the defense of the city, but already on October 17 had to capitulate. While his soldiers were taken prisoners by the French, he was set free upon his word of honor. In Vienna he was arrested, placed before a War Court, and sentenced to death. The Emperor commuted his sentence to imprisonment. On December 3, 1819, on the grounds of renewed legal proceedings, he was rehabilitated. See Gräffer-Czikann, III, pp. 515–516; Wurzbach, vol. 16, pp. 211–213.—KH

[40] Prince Franz Joseph Johann Dietrichstein-Proskau-Leslie (1767–1854), statesman, Privy Councillor, and Chamberlain. In 1809 he became High Steward of Archduke Franz von Este in Galicia, and thereafter Court Commissioner. Later he lived in England for several years. See *Hof- und Staats-Schematismus*, 1819, I, pp. 12, 55, and 65; Wurzbach, vol. 3, pp. 300–301.—KH

[41] Count Moritz Dietrichstein-Proskau-Leslie (1775–1864), manager of the *Hofkapelle* and song composer. In 1815 Emperor Franz I chose him to be the educator of the Duke of Reichstadt [i.e., Franz's grandson, the son of Napoleon and Archduchess Marie Louise], and he was also *Hofmusikgraf* (Court Music Administrator), 1819–1826, and Court Theater Director, 1821–1826. Thus, in terms of primogeniture, the Prince Dietrichstein known to Beethoven, Schubert, and Salieri scholars was not the *reigning* prince (whose role was central to the Imperial administration), but instead a *younger* prince or count (assigned to education and arts administration). See *Hof- und Staats-Schematismus*, 1819, I, pp. 55 and 67; Gräffer-Czikann, I, p. 716; Wurzbach, vol. 3, pp. 303–304; Clive, pp. 91–93.—KH/TA

[42] See the *Intelligenzblatt*, No. 282 (December 10, 1819), p. 1105. The full advertisement reads: "Apartment for Rent. At the Seilerstatt No. 855 on the 2nd floor, is apartment of 7 rooms, of which 4 face the street, 3 of them with parquet flooring and newly painted; with kitchen, large spit, cellar, bath, and large wood storage; to be rented from St. George's Day, 1820. Further information may be had at that location."—KH/TA

[43] On this next recto page, Beethoven adds: "Zu der *Mariage vis a vis*," a curious combination of German and French, not in the original advertisement. Building 855, facing the Seilerstatt, between Weihburggasse and Singerstrasse, became No. 805 in the 1821 renumbering. Across the street was a branch of the Imperial Arsenal that had once held a Chapel of the Three Kings, and behind that, the City Walls (Behsel, p. 24). Therefore it seems probable that when Beethoven wrote down this advertisement, he knew its location (five minutes southeast of his Ballgasse apartment). As for "across from

OLIVA **[possibly joining Beethoven in the coffee house, and ordering herring]**:
Common.[44] //

I was at the attorney's twice. He was never at home and had a meeting elsewhere.
Because I would also like to speak with him, I didn't leave the letter, and shall go to
see him tomorrow morning about 10 o'clock, when he is supposed to be at home.
[//]

The potter [stove maker] will appear tomorrow [Saturday, December 11]. [//]
[Blatt 24v]

At the Goethe Celebration, there was only the last part of your Overture to
Egmont, the concluding Symphony [of Victory].[45] // I'm glad that the little piece
made a greater effect than the most tiresome composition by t[?][46] // *Egmont* could
be given again now, if only Schröder's elder daughter[47] were somewhat more trained
on the stage. //

Neustadt near Baden.[48] [//] [Blatt 25r]

In the adaptation by Goethe himself, not by Schiller, the Archduchess of Parma is
completely left out. The whole is said to be made even more confused by it. Goethe
was never lucky in the adaptations of his works for the stage. //

As a girl, she [Frau Peters][49] had a special gift for comprehending the spirit of a

---

the *Mariage*," Beethoven seems to be making a pun on the word "wall," either in German (*Mauer*)
or in French (*mur*), in combination with the standard marriage/*mariage*, resulting in something like
Maueriage or *muriage*—in any case meaning "across from the City's walls."—TA

[44] Written in the right margin: *gemein*, possibly a comment on Beethoven's attempt at a pun,
above.—KH

[45] The celebration of Goethe's seventieth birthday that took place in Frankfurt am Main on
August 27, 1819. The program included: 1. Tributes by Dr. Clemens and Herr Göntgen; 2. Monologue
of Iphigenia and the poem "Zueignung," performed by Dlle. Ursprung and Herr Hegel; 3. a new
Overture by Spohr, which "did not generally meet with a good response;" 4. *Schluss-Symphonie*
[Concluding Symphony] from *Egmont*; 5. Jomelli's *Te Deum*. From a report by N. Fürst (from the
Elegante Zeitung, No. 203) in the *Sammler*, No. 147 (December 9, 1819), p. 588. Oliva may not have
known that the coda of the Overture and the actual final "Symphony" (*Siegessymphonie*) in *Egmont*
were slightly different in their introductory material.—KH/TA

[46] Unless Oliva somehow knew Jomelli's work, he is likely referring here to the Overture by
Spohr, whose *Das befreyte Deutschland* had recently made very little effect in Vienna. See Heft 3,
Blätter 42v–44v, for an extensive report on Spohr's cantata.—TA

[47] The elder daughter of the I.R. Court actor Sophie Schröder (1781–1868), Wilhelmina Schröder
(1805–1860) had made her debut as Aricia in *Phädra* by Racine-Schiller on October 12, 1819, and
would assume the title role in *Fidelio* in the revival of November, 1822. See Wurzbach, vol. 31,
pp. 321–322 and 337; Clive, pp. 325–326.—KH/TA

[48] Wiener Neustadt, city in Lower Austria, about 25 miles south of Vienna and about 10 miles
south of Baden. Karl Peters's wife Josephine was born there, so this conversational topic seems to
continue on the next page.—KH/TA

[49] Josephine [Josepha Julianna] Hochsinger (February 16, 1790 – March 28, 1866) was born in
Wiener Neustadt, the daughter of licensed merchant Zacharias Hochsinger and his wife Theresia, *née*
Manker (ca. 1755/58–1811). Her passport indicated that she was energetic, slim, with a well-developed

vocal piece and performing it. I have known her for 15 years. [Blatt 25v] She is the daughter of a merchant in Wiener Neustadt and, after the death of her father, came here with her mother. // Peters became acquainted with her much later; only when her mother died, about 7 years ago. Bernard knows about it. // Stupidity person-ified. //

It appears to me that he is really having a good effect on his studies. // Peters could look into that the best. // [Blatt 26r]

Do you want another herring? A better one, or an eel? He will get it. //

A miserable person. // The good man there has the habit, if one speaks of something in generalities, of always bringing up something that pertains to his humble self in boring examples. //

One must say: *Oberkammeramt* [Office of the Lord High Chamberlain]. [//]

[End of entries; late afternoon or evening of Friday, December 10.]

[Blatt 26v]

BEETHOVEN **[probably at his apartment; possibly the morning of Saturday, December 11]**:

Blotting sand.

[possibly in a coffee house; possibly late morning of Saturday, December 11:]

For rent: Landstrasse, Ungargasse, No. 391; beautiful apartment of 3 rooms, 1 entry room, kitchen and attic, may be had now and later, also half-yearly—No. 391.[50] [//]

[Blatt 27r]

---

figure, a round face, brown hair, and blue eyes. After the father died (by ca. 1807), the family moved to Vienna, living in the Kohlmarkt No. 1218 [renumbered as 1150 in 1821 (Behsel, p. 34)], two houses east of the old Michaelerhaus on the Kohlmarkt. Theresia died on April 27, 1811, leaving a substantial estate to Josephine and her sister Anna Maria (born ca. 1788). On May 5, 1814 (having reached her majority of 24 years), Josephine married Karl Peters in the Michaelerkirche, with P. Ignaz Thomas (often cited as a moral authority by Bernard in the conversation books) performing the ceremony. When they married, Lobkowitz provided them with an apartment in his Summer Palace at Ungargasse 309 [renumbered as 347 in 1821 and 388 in 1830 (Behsel, p. 79)], where they officially lived until Easter, 1825, when they moved to Prague. Josephine was reputed to be a good singer. For a possible brother in Gumpendorf, see Heft 6, Blätter 1r, 7r, and 33r. See Macek, pp. 393–408; Conscriptions-Bogen, Stadt, 1. Reihe, Haus No. 1150 [numbered 1218 in 1819]; Wurzbach, vol. 22, p. 80; Pfarre St. Michael, Trauungs-Register, 1804–1824, fol. 136; also Heft 3, Blatt 12v (for Karl Peters).—TA

[50] See the *Intelligenzblatt*, No. 283 (December 11, 1819), p. 1116, col. 1. The same advertisement appeared in No. 287 (December 16, 1819), p. 1156, col. 2. Beethoven copied the advertisement accurately enough, but it contained a typographical error: Landstrasse No. 391 [renumbered as 438 in 1821] was actually in the Waaggasse; see Behsel, p. 82. The error remained in the December 16 issue.—KH/TA

BERNARD [possibly joining Beethoven for midday dinner; ca. 2 p.m. on Saturday, December 11]: Yesterday[51] it was decided that you ought to give an Akademie on the holy Christmas Days [December 25 and 26] or on another day. Count Stadion[52] will provide the venue, and Schickh, [Joseph] Czerny, and Janschikh will take care of the rest. In it, there should be a symphony, the Gloria from your Mass [*Missa solemnis*], your new [Piano] Sonata [Op. 106], played by you, and a grand [Blatt 27v] Closing Chorus; everything by you. You are guaranteed 4,000 fl. // Only one movement of the Mass should be performed. //

Can the following solo parts and choruses [from *Der Sieg des Kreuzes*] be combined at the same time?

Hate and Discord:
    If it [the World]
    Never becomes reconciled, [and is]
    Consumed in blood,
    We reap the glorious reward of Victory.

Belief, Hope, Love:
    Place hope in the Lord! Whoever trusts in Him
    Has built upon secure ground! [Blatt 28r]

First Christian Chorus:
    The heart's Belief builds securely upon Him!

Second [Christian Chorus]:
    He does not allow us to be robbed by derision!

All:
    He will turn around,
    He will end
    The bitter pain of this trial!
    But may His will only be done!

---

[51] If this was written on Saturday, December 11, it implies that Beethoven did not see Bernard (or possibly anyone else in Bernard's circle) later on Friday, December 10. Other than seeing Oliva later, Beethoven may have been home with the "potter," who may have come about the new stove for his apartment.—TA

[52] Count Johann Philipp zu Stadion-Thannhausen und Warthausen (1763–1824), Minister of Finance since 1815. He was a patron of the poet Franz Grillparzer, who later worked as a Ministry *Konzipist* at his Ministry. See *Hof- und Staats-Schematismus*, 1823, I, p. 246; 1824, I, pp. 248–249; Gräffer-Czikann, V, p. 120; Wurzbach, vol. 37, pp. 37–39 [*sic*].—KH/TA

Chorus of Heathens:
    (Their multitudes approach during the previous chorus):
    The onslaught of the multitudes
    Roars this way like stormy waves;
    The hour approaches; may Zeus send us victory,
    Shame to the transgressors! // [Blatt 28v]

— ∪ ∪ —   These are choral iambics.
— ∪ ∪ —

If it[53] itself [incomplete sentence]. // They [the Gesellschaft der Musikfreunde] took your "Selbstvertreter" badly, and believed that I knew about it or would have read the letter beforehand.[54] //

I already want to bring out the musical sound and rhythm in such a manner that I would fear no one. // [Blatt 29r] I am taking the Heathens in a strict and rhymeless measure throughout, but the Christians are rhymed. [//] The effect, if it is technically correct, is also not to be despised. //

The banker Rothschild[55] from Frankfurt has taken hotel accommodations here in 11 rooms. // He immediately made his visit to Prince Metternich.[56] [//] [Blatt 29v] Metternich and Hardenberg[57] are certainly taking the Jews under their wings. //

---

[53] The pronoun is "sie" (feminine), probably referring to the word "Gesellschaft" (also feminine), implied in the following sentence.—TA

[54] The Gesellschaft der Musikfreunde had sent Beethoven a letter inquiring about his progress on their oratorio and signed by Prince Odescalchi as *Stellvertreter* (Vice President). Beethoven replied that the matter could not be hurried and, never able to resist a pun, humorously signed himself as *Selbstvertreter* (Self-Representative). See Blatt 26v above. The organization and Odescalchi may not have appreciated the humor, but on December 28, Peters told Beethoven (Heft 5, Blatt 59r) that its president, Count Friedrich Egon Fürstenberg, enjoyed the letter and kept it.—KH

[55] The banking house of Rothschild was managed by the five brothers Anselm (Amschel Mayer) in Frankfurt am Main, Solomon in Vienna and Berlin, Nathan in London, Carl in Naples, and Jakob in Paris. The *Wiener Zeitung*, No. 283 (December 11, 1819), p. 1132, lists among the arrivals of December 9: "Herr C.M. v. Rothschild, banker, and wife, and Herr S. v. Rothschild, banker, all three from Frankfurt (Stadt No. 145)." City No. 145 [renumbered as 138 in 1821] was the Hotel zum Römischen Kaiser, at the juncture of Renngasse and the Freyung (Behsel, p. 5). As noted elsewhere, the family name (meaning Red Shield) is correctly pronounced "Rote Shield," not "Roth's Child."—KH/TA

[56] Prince Clemens Wenzel Lothar von Metternich (1773–1859), statesman; he had been Minister of the Exterior since 1809, and from 1821 to 1848 was Chancellor of State. Through an absolutist police regime, he sought to preserve feudal-absolutist conditions.—KH

[57] Prince Carl August von Hardenberg (1750–1822), Prussian statesman; as Chancellor of State, he introduced several of Stein's reforms and represented Prussia at the Congresses of the Holy Alliance. After the Karlsbad Decrees, he lost all political influence.—KH

In the *Literarisches Wochenblatt* is an essay entitled "Hepp! Hepp!"[58] along with epigrams on the members in Mainz.[59]

<The Police Administration [Blatt 30r] is sending it to the Chancellery of State and the Chancellery to the Police Administration.> //

I would have eaten already, if I still had the desire. // <I really can.> //

These great bankers have all the Ministers in Europe in their hands, and can overturn governments in embarrassment as often as they want. One can no longer conclude any political business [Blatt 30v] without them. // They have also made an appearance in Aachen,[60] and have disputed the money for all payments and to [all] confederations of the various Courts. [//] European politics have taken such a path that, without money and bankers, nothing more can be settled. // [Blatt 31r] Taken together, they have no ideas. With the conquest of Paris, these [ideas] seem to have vanished from all of Europe. [//] The nobility who reign have learned nothing and have forgotten nothing. //

[End of entries for the afternoon of Saturday, December 11.]

SEELIG [at *Zur Stadt Triest*; after ca. 7 p.m.[61] on Saturday, December 11]: Veal with some ham and tongue. [//] [Blatt 31v] v[on] Bernard, Peters, [and] Czerny[62] were here and are coming back after the theater to find you.—S[eeli]g. //

JANSCHIKH [at *Zur Stadt Triest*; **alternating and overlapping conversational segments with Czerny; evening of Saturday, December 11**]: You ought to furnish

---

[58] In the nineteenth century, "Hep, hep!" was an anti-Semitic cry of derision. An essay "Die Hep Heps in Franken und anderer Orten" (The Hep Heps in Franconia and Other Places) appeared in the *Literarisches Wochenblatt*, No. 50 (December, 1819), p. 393. It is apparently not the item meant here, because it contains no epigrams on the members of the Zentral-Untersuchungs-Kommission in Mainz.—KH/TA

[59] Probably because they contained negative comments about the Jews, the end of this line in the manuscript, as well as three and a half additional lines, have been so heavily crossed out that they are no longer legible. The passage that follows is still legible, but is crossed out by a different hand.—KH

[60] The Holy Alliance held its first Congress in Aachen from September 29 to November 21, 1818. There it was resolved to withdraw the troops stationed in France since 1815, and to lower the ceiling of the war reparations, in order to promote the stability of the reactionary Bourbon domination. Moreover, measures were established to suppress any revolutions that might flare up.—KH

[61] See Czerny's indication of the time that Bernard left on Blatt 32v below.—TA

[62] Apparently Bernard had gone to the Theater, but, from the ensuing conversation with Janschikh and Czerny, it appears that Peters was visiting someone named Frank, and that Czerny may have gone to visit Zmeskall, who lived in the nearby Bürgerspital and whom he mentions twice, and had now returned.—TA

the Library with a musical monument.[63] // Now the Prince has also bought the Kahlenberg.[64] [//]

[Blatt 32r]

JOSEPH CZERNY [continuing]: Bernard is coming. [//] [He is] in the Theater. // Hempflingen.[65] // Zmeskall['s health] is better. [//]

JANSCHIKH: Didn't Bernard tell you anything about the arrangement for the Akademie? Your friends are inclined to begin, and to prepare everything for you. [//]

BEETHOVEN [writing so as not to be overheard]: It is too late for Christmas, but it could be during Lent. [//] [Blatt 32v]

JANSCHIKH: *Impedimentum invi[n]cibile.*[66] *Petrus* [Peters] is at Frank's.[67] [//] [conversation continued on top of Blatt 33r]

JOSEPH CZERNY: Doctor Bihler[68] at Puthon's[69] thinks of you often. //
    Alone. // Bernard was here; at 7 o'clock he went to the Theater. // I'll accompany you.
    It makes me and also Zmeskall happy that ... [sentence continued on Blatt 33r]

---

[63] The library mentioned here could be that of the Gesellschaft der Musikfreunde, the organization that had recently been offended by Beethoven's humorous wordplay (see Blatt 28v), or possibly the sumptuous library of Prince Lichtenstein (mentioned in the next entry).—TA

[64] In 1819 the Kahlenberg (previously Schweinsberg, Josephsberg, and, in local parlance, the Kaltenberg), ca. 8 miles north of Vienna, belonged to Prince von Liechtenstein. In the valleys at the foot of the mountain lie the villages of Heiligenstadt and Grinzing, and Weidling.—KH/TA

[65] Possibly Franz Hempfling (1761–1838), Prince Liechtenstein's Economic Councillor, and Johann Hempfling (1753–1822), Stall Master of Count Starhemberg. See also Heft 5, Blatt 54r, where Hempfling is mentioned by Liechtenstein's librarian Wolf, suggesting that the former identification is the correct one.—KH/TA

[66] An insurmountable obstacle.—KH

[67] Unclear reference: possibly an associate of the wholesale house of Franck & Comp. or even the venerable Dr. Johann Peter Frank (1745–1821); see Heft 10, Blatt 8r.

[68] Johann Bihler (whose name Czerny spells Bühler) was house teacher to the wholesaler Baron von Puthon, and later tutor to the sons of Archduke Karl. See Frimmel, *Handbuch*, I, p. 41; Thayer-Deiters-Riemann, IV, pp. 40–41; Heft 25, Blatt 32v.—KH/TA

[69] Baron Johann Baptist von Puthon (1773–1839), wholesaler and house owner in Vienna. From among the directors of the licensed Austrian National Bank, he was chosen as director of the banking house of J.G. Schuller & Co. in 1823.
    He lived in the house *Zur grossen Weintraube*, Am Hof No. 357 [renumbered as 329 in 1821]. His wife Antonie (d. 1824), the daughter of General Baron von Lilien, took piano lessons from Clementi, and numbered among Beethoven's friends. See Kysselak, "Memorabilien Österreichs, Verstorbene 1814–1839," fol. 171 (Tresor, Wiener Stadt- und Landesarchiv); Frimmel, *Handbuch*, II, p. 31; Clive, pp. 273–274; *Hof- und Staats-Schematismus*, 1823, I, p. 706; Behsel, p. 11.—KH/TA

[Blatt 33r]

JANSCHIKH [**continuing from above**]: *<Membra inter se cohaerent.>*[70]

JOSEPH CZERNY [**continuing from Blatt 32v**]: … you have turned to Peters. He will certainly give you satisfaction, because he is a sensible and noble person. // Peters is also of the opinion that there must be an appeal, and you can leave it to him; if he agrees to do something, then he does it. He is reliable and knows the routine. [//] [Blatt 33v] Perhaps he has been bribed by the mother? // The most important matters often lie on the Emperor's desk 2 to 3 years without resolution. // It is everywhere the way it is here. // That will soon be done. [//] [Blatt 34r]

I must take great pains in order to live. // I have been able to enjoy more of your compositions in Pesth than here, because I must always give lessons here. // The singular [*einzige*] Countess Kolowrath[71] pays me 4 fl. [//]

[**Beethoven departs** *Zur Stadt Triest* **before 8 p.m. on Saturday, December 11.**][72]

[Blatt 34v]

OLIVA [**probably at Beethoven's apartment in the Ballgasse; seemingly early on Sunday, December 12**]: I was in the wine house at around 8 o'clock, until around 9 o'clock [last evening]. [//]

One could not speak with Doctor Bach [lawyer] the whole day yesterday; because of the election of the *Rector Magnificus*.[73] I was at his office morning and afternoon; he had everyone who came given an appointment for 11 o'clock today.[74] //

I want to go to the potter's [stove maker's] again today. // [Blatt 35r] I want to

---

[70] "The limbs [or bodily members] hold together among themselves" (possibly a comment about the Jews). This entry was presumably made before Czerny's conversation surrounding it.—KH/TA

[71] The noble family of Kolowrat had many branches; this reference remains unclear. See also Blatt 14v above, and Heft 9, Blatt 2v.—KH/TA

[72] Beethoven had probably grown impatient with Czerny's, and especially Janschikh's, conversation. For the time element, see Oliva's comment on Blatt 34v immediately below.—TA

[73] In the *Wiener Zeitung*, No. 283 (December 11, 1819), p. 1129, there appeared a long report about the election of the Rector at the University. According to the article, the election of "national procurators" had taken place on November 4, 5, and 6; among them Dr. Johann Baptist Bach was named "Austrian Procurator." On November 19 the new procurators elected *Edler* Johann Debrois von Bruyck as *Rector Magnificus*, who was to be solemnly announced as such by Dr. Bach in the University Saal on November 30. On December 8 the *Rector Magnificus* and the Deans who had been newly elected on December 6 and 7 took part in a solemn Mass at St. Stephan's Cathedral. From these dates it cannot be determined to which activity Oliva referred. Possibly Dr. Bach was still obligated to activities connected with the election of the Rector after December 8.—KH

[74] Lawyer Johann Baptist Bach seems to have held regular Sunday consultations and even made office appointments for Christmas Day as well (see Heft 5, Blatt 47r).—TA

try to speak to him tomorrow, but I need the receipt in order to do it. // I want to come somewhat earlier—after 6 o'clock. [//]

[Blatt 35v]

BLÖCHLINGER[75] [at his Institute; probably late morning or noon on Sunday, December 12]: She [Johanna] was here on the same day that I wrote to you that she had not been here for a long time, but she has not come back since then. [//]

PETERS [seemingly visiting the Institute with Beethoven]: On Wednesday [December 15], I shall attend the examination. H[err] Blöchlinger is satisfied with his [Karl's] progress. [//]

[Blatt 36r]

NEPHEW KARL [possibly still recuperating[76] in his room at Blöchlinger's Institute]: *Twisted (linen)* stockings and, over them, woolen socks. // I only need the woolen ones, because I already have linen ones. // Do you want to take a stocking with you as a model? [//]

[Blatt 36v]

PETERS [probably at mid-day dinner, possibly at *Zur Stadt Triest* after leaving Blöchlinger's Institute; ca. 2 p.m. on Sunday, December 12]: Very much has already been gained, since the boy['s progress] is now consistent with the public studies again. It also appears to me that Blöchlinger, if not exactly very ingenious, is still good. [//] The set-up in the public school would be chains for him. [//]

Do you already have a housekeeper? [//] [Blatt 37r] The life of eating in restaurants is too high for you. If Bernard knew, he would already be here.[77] [//]

Your nephew looks good; handsome eyes, charm, a striking physiognomy and excellent posture. I would like to bring him up for just 2 years. [//] [Blatt 37v]

This coming Sunday [December 19], should we make an excursion with your nephew, perhaps with Bernard? [//] Because the examination will be over. [//] ¼ hour. // He [Blöchlinger] is always present, and so she [Johanna] cannot [Blatt 38r] be harmful. But it is understood that she ruined the boy. // If the guardianship is exclusively yours, then you designate it and he will follow. Your views are excellent, but not always compatible with the miserable world. [//] [Blatt 38v]

---

[75] Handwriting identified by Schindler in Heft 13, Blatt 46r.—KH

[76] Karl had undergone a foot operation, possibly for corns, on the previous Wednesday, December 8 (see Blätter 5v–6r above).—TA

[77] Peters's reference to Bernard seems to confirm that even his friends regarded him as a *Schnorrer* (moocher).—TA

Blöchlinger wanted to take a young man into his school. The fellow called upon me, and I had to say that I simply could not recommend him. A contentious meeting for the young man; he already settled into the Institute this week. // Blöchlinger thanked me emotionally. // This person has some 100 excellent references, also from me, [Blatt 39r] but only concerning his instruction in the Bohemian language. //

If only all the people could understand and appreciate your love for your nephew. // The public studies must continue uninterruptedly, though, as long as you do not designate him exclusively for one profession. // The *Gymnasium* instruction [here] isn't worth much. Prague is far more excellent. [//] [Blatt 39v]

Are you going with the Archduke?[78] // 4,000 fl. [C.]M. yearly. // Auersperg[79] gives 2,000 fl. [C.]M. to his tutor, who is mediocre. // And he [Rudolph] is famed in the 4 quarters of the world for having kept you in Vienna. For him that is both very much and very little. [//] [Blatt 40r] 3.45 4–5 [percentage points] //

Do you drink Ofner [wine]? //

I believe that, on the whole, 4,000 is too little. // From whom? // The Archduke must immediately compensate for it. // That lies in his earlier intentions. // They [the three princes] have consented. // The sum may not be lessened. H[is] I[mperial] High[ness] motivated the whole [stipend]. [Blatt 40v]

If you journey to England, I shall go with you. I can speak English. // The eldest Prince[80] also wants to go to England. // His grandfather[81] used up his revenue there. // You must promise me to come to Eisenberg[82] with your nephew for 2 or 3 months. [//] [Blatt 41r] I'll take you on a *Relais*[83] throughout all of Bohemia. // Hunting, riding, [and] to be level-headed. Vacation. // If only the Archduke were not jealous of the Prince. //

---

[78] This question refers to the opinion that had spread, that Beethoven would be going with Archduke Rudolph to Olmütz as Kapellmeister. See also Heft 2, Blätter 90r–90v.—KH

[79] Spelled "Auersberg" here, possibly Prince Carl Auersperg, who was married to Maria Josepha von Lobkowitz (1752–1822).—KH

[80] Prince Ferdinand Joseph Johann von Lobkowitz (1797–1868), the eldest son of Beethoven's late patron Joseph Franz Maximilian. In 1823, on the occasion of his twenty-sixth birthday, Beethoven composed his *Lobkowitz Cantata* for solo voice with chorus and piano accompaniment, WoO 106. See Kinsky-Halm, pp. 596–597; Richard Schaal, "Lobkowitz," *MGG*, vol. 8, col. 1071.—KH

[81] The grandfather of Ferdinand Joseph Johann von Lobkowitz was Ferdinand Philipp Joseph (1724–1784), who was musically gifted, associated with C.P.E. Bach and C.W. Gluck and was himself a composer. He spent from 1745 to 1747 in London, where he frequently attended operas and concerts. See Schaal, "Lobkowitz," *MGG*, vol. 8, cols. 1069–1070.—KH

[82] Eisenberg, a castle of the Lobkowitz family "with a beautiful garden and a theater," near Saaz in Bohemia. See Raffelsperger, vol. 2, p. 301.—KH

[83] Spelled *Relée* here, the exchange of horses in postal coach terminology, but probably meaning a general tour in this context.—KH/TA

I received a letter of yours from the late Prince,[84] in which I read: "If Your Serene Highness only employs the instruments to this extent, then <I shit on it.">[85] [//] [Blatt 41v] I have read it. // Prince Lobkowitz appreciated you properly, and this has remained in his children. // His environment in his youth included exotic birds. // It lacked a dog. // He was difficult to deal with. His wife was excellent, but [Blatt 42r] he could not bear any opposition, especially not from Field Marshall Karl.[86] // I often meet with the Princess, the widow;[87] she often consults me about her son, but it doesn't do much good, because old [Prince] Auersperg pays for everything; and he who pays is always right. // That will be the case from now on. //

In the evening the wine is already bottled sour; [but] it is not lost. [//] [Blatt 42v] **[possibly writing on behalf of Bernard, who has just arrived:]**

Werner[88] gave the sermon today. [//] First they [the nobility] must be afraid for themselves and then improve the states [of Europe]. [//] I believe that he meant

---

[84] Prince Joseph Franz Maximilian von Lobkowitz (1772–1816), passionate lover of music and admirer of Beethoven. The Prince, to whom several of Beethoven's works are dedicated, took part, with Archduke Rudolph and Prince Kinsky, in providing Beethoven with an assured yearly pension of 4,000 Gulden (fl.), in order to keep Beethoven in Vienna. After the national bankruptcy and money devaluation of 1811, he could no longer keep up with his payments. In 1792 he had married Caroline von Schwarzenberg (1775–1816). See Frimmel, *Handbuch*, I, pp. 367–369; Thayer-Deiters-Riemann, III, pp. 491–493; Wurzbach, vol. 15, pp. 325 and 337; Clive, pp. 212–215.—KH/TA

[85] Beethoven must have protested that he did not write such a thing, thus Peters's next comment of affirmation. The alleged letter, however, is consistent with the anecdote that the artist Joseph Wilibrord Mähler told Thayer about an incident during a rehearsal of *Fidelio* in 1805, where a "third bassoon" (probably the contrabassoon) was not present and the Prince tried to humor the frustrated Beethoven. As the artist and composer walked back into and through the city, they passed the Lobkowitz Palace, and Beethoven shouted into the doorway: "Lobkowitzian Ass" (see Thayer-Forbes, p. 384).—TA

[86] Archduke Karl of Austria (1771–1847), third son of Emperor Leopold II, married since 1815 to Henriette von Nassau-Weilburg (1797–1829). He became Imperial Field Marshall in 1796 and, despite his heroic but often futile efforts against Napoleon, was alternately in and out of Imperial favor. See Wurzbach, vol. 6, pp. 372–374.—KH/TA

[87] Princess Marie Sidonie von Lobkowitz, *née* Princess Kinsky (1779–1837), widow of Anton Isidor Lobkowitz (1773 – June 1819). She had three sons: August Longin (1797–1842), Joseph August (1799–1832), and Franz Georg (1800–1858). See Wurzbach, vol. 15, pp. 307–309.—KH

[88] (Friedrich Ludwig) Zacharias Werner (1768–1823), theologian and dramatic poet. Born in northern Germany as a Lutheran, he joined the Catholic faith in 1810 and began to study theology. In 1814, he was consecrated as a priest and came to Vienna, where he became the topic of conversation through his political sermons. Werner did not hold a regular position with any church in Vienna. At about this time, he was living in suburban Hernals (beyond Alservorstadt), and at the end of his life the Augustinians provided him with a refuge in their cloister in the City. If Peters spent much of Sunday up to this point with Beethoven, one wonders when and where Werner preached that day. See Wurzbach, vol. 55, pp. 72–74; Clive, p. 395. Werner's portrait, an engraving by Johann Ender, appears in Deutsch, *Franz Schubert. Sein Leben in Bildern*, p. 140, but is frequently reproduced elsewhere.—KH/TA

Metternich, because he also spoke about whores. [//] That can only redound to Werner's success. [//] He is the best religious speaker here. [//]

BERNARD [having joined Peters and Beethoven briefly, writing for himself]: Salieri[89] is not my man. [//]

[Blatt 43r]

PETERS [continuing at *Zur Stadt Triest*; before 3:30 p.m. on Sunday December 12]: Is [Abbé Maximilian] Stadler a good psalm composer? // If you lose the book, I shall be locked up. //

Goethe should not write any more. It is the same with him as it is with singers.[90] // Still, he remains Germany's foremost poet. // [Blatt 43v]

Prince Lobkowitz will be ready at 3:30.[91] //

He [presumably Seelig] has miscalculated by 2 kr. // It is more expensive here than at Paro's.[92] //

[Karl's progress at Blöchlinger's school] appears better than at Giannatasio's. // Hand-kissing is worth nothing. [//] [Blatt 44r] The boy will be excellent; everything coarse will be driven from him. He was too young. // Blöchlinger was glad to see me. // I shall come to various classes; if he is dissatisfied with that, he is wrong. [//] The boy is too good in himself. [//] [Blatt 44v] Only if the negative has a good effect on him. // I cannot be humble toward common people; therefore I am still no Christian with people. //

Will my wife already have asked where we are? [//]

According to unanimous judgement, Bernard is the best critical head. [//] [Blatt 45r]

Do you play billiards? Chess? Pagat?[93] Whist? [//] All of them [are] boring. Chess would be the best. //

---

[89] Antonio Salieri (1750–1825), composer and Court Kapellmeister. In 1793 Beethoven took instruction from him, to learn how to set Italian texts. Possibly a Mass by Salieri had been given in the church where Werner had preached that day. See Frimmel, *Handbook*, II, pp. 95–97; Rudolf Angermüller, "Salieri," *MGG*, vol. 11, cols. 1295–1297; Clive, pp. 302–303; Thayer, *Salieri.*—KH/TA

[90] Peters means that as singers age, their voice muscles do too; therefore they generally cannot sing as well as they did in their prime, and he is applying that model to Goethe, who had turned seventy on August 28, 1819. A poem by Goethe, addressing his admirers on the occasion of his birthday, had appeared in Schickh's *Wiener Zeitschrift* 4, No. 140 (November 23, 1819), p. 1141.—TA

[91] This Sunday outing had been proposed on Thursday, December 9 (Blätter 16r–16v).—TA

[92] Perhaps Peters means Jakob Partl, former owner of the *Schwarzes Kameel* in the Bognergasse, one of Beethoven's other favorite haunts for wine and coffee. Beethoven's friends occasionally commented that Seelig's prices at *Zur Stadt Triest* were higher than elsewhere.—KH/TA

[93] Spelled "Bagadl" (possibly a diminutive) here, meaning the trump card in Tarot.—KH/TA

The girl at the *Birne*[94] wasn't bad. // I shall procure her for you. // You disdain all of them.[95] // [Blatt 45v]

The boys are too different. // Your nephew is the *only one* who studies in the 2nd Class [grade], which makes having his own teacher necessary. It would be better if there were at least 3 or 4. [//] The only one. // There is no one [with scores] higher than his, and no one lower. [//] Not good. [//] [Blatt 46r] If there were 20, and if your nephew were the best or among the better, then it would be better. //

[End of entries for the afternoon of Sunday, December 12.]

SCHINDLER[96] [falsified entries begin→]: It is true that Court Councillor Peters chatters a great deal; but he means you well, though. // I know him all too little. // I must now prepare for major examinations—first in Natural Law. // For that I must leave all music alone, because absolutely no time remains for me. [←falsified entries end]

[Blatt 46v] No writing; crossed through with red pencil.

End of Heft 4

[94] When he lived in south suburban Landstrasse (through spring 1819), Beethoven frequently visited the restaurant *Zur goldenen Birne* (At the Golden Pear), Landstrasser Hauptstrasse No. 42 [renumbered as 52 in 1821]. See Frimmel, *Handbuch*, I, p. 160; Groner (1922), p. 42.

Beethoven's new apartment was in another house designated *Zur goldenen Birne* on the Josephstadt Glacis No. 5 [renumbered as 6 in 1821]. Perhaps Peters refers to the coffee house or restaurant on the ground floor of that building. On Blatt 2r above, Peters also seems to refer to a girl as better than one at the *Biber* (Beaver), one block north of the *Birne* in the Josephstadt. See Behsel, pp. 71 and 190.—KH/TA

[95] By now Beethoven must have realized that Peters, the supposedly reputable tutor to the Lobkowitz family, a person whom Bernard had persuaded him to nominate as co-guardian of nephew Karl, had twice within five days made suggestive remarks about waitresses and even offered to procure one for him.—TA

[96] At this time Schindler may have seen or even met Beethoven at lawyer Bach's office, but the two would not become closely acquainted until perhaps early November, 1822.—TA

Heft 5

(December 13, 1819 – December 30, 1819)

[Inside front cover]

PETERS [presumably upon departing a restaurant in the walled City; probably ca. 3 p.m., after midday dinner, Monday, December 13]: Children![1]

BEETHOVEN [possibly after leaving his apartment on the Josephstadt Glacis, walking into the City; probably shortly after noon on Monday, December 13]:

WÄHNER[3] [in the offices of the *Wiener Zeitschrift* and the *Sammler*, Kohlmarkt No. 268; probably early afternoon of Monday, December 13]: Alte Wieden, not

---

[1] Possibly entered immediately following Peters's entry at the very end of Blatt 1r. By writing here, Peters would not have had to turn the page of the book. Therefore this entry is probably out of chronological order.—TA

[2] A sketch for the "Miserere" passage in the Gloria of the *Missa solemnis*. The sketch above looks like it might have been modeled after a "Miserere" passage in the Agnus Dei of the Mass in C, Op. 86.—KH/TA

[3] Friedrich Wähner (1786–1839), aesthetician and ingenious critic, originally a Protestant preacher, came to Vienna in 1818 and was a collaborator in numerous newspapers and magazines, among them the *Aglaja*, the *Stuttgarter Morgenblatt*, the *Jahrbücher der Literatur*, the *Halle Literaturzeitung*, the *Sammler*, and, in connection with this entry, the *Wiener Zeitschrift*, edited by the next conversational entrant, Schickh.

On October 3, 1818, Wähner began to publish *Janus, eine Zeitschrift für 1819*, which, however, had already ceased to appear in June 1819. In the mid-1820s, he was expelled from the city by the Police, but he returned in 1835. See Gräffer-Czikann, I, pp. xv and 544–546; Wurzbach, vol. 52, pp. 62–63; Clive, p. 383.

The handwriting was identified through a comparison with a letter of Wähner's from June 13, 1834, in the Wiener Stadt- und Landesbibliothek, I.N. 8814.—KH/TA

far from the Karlskirche: *Zur weissen Rose*. I don't know the [house] number. It's a corner house.[4]

[Blatt 1r]

SCHICKH [**also in the offices of the *Wiener Zeitschrift*, following up**]: I implore you to set a Lied by Count Loeben *very* very soon. If you come back, I'll give you another one that I have just received from him.[5] //

Do you already have the entire oratorio [libretto to *Der Sieg des Kreuzes*] from Bernard? <Is the S> [//]

---

[4] Beethoven evidently asked Wähner about Bernard's whereabouts, and this was the reply. The house *Zur weissen Rose* (the White Rose) was in the suburb of Wieden, Altwiedner Hauptstrasse, No. 191 [renumbered as 256 in 1821 and 469 in 1830]. In the middle of a row of houses, it did not occupy a corner, but instead was directly west, across Wiedner Hauptstrasse, from the corner of Wiedner Hauptstrasse and Kirchen Gasse. The church at that particular intersection is the Paulanerkirche, but the Karlskirche is indeed "not far," only two blocks to the east. The owners were Joseph Hammerschmid (b. 1763) and his sister, Theresia Grassl. They also owned the house next door, the *Eiserner Mann* (Iron Man), Altwiedner Hauptstrasse, No. 192 [renumbered as 257 in 1821 and 470 in 1830], which Theresia presumably occupied with her husband Franz Grassl (who died by 1823). Their daughter Magdalena Grassl (b. 1797) would marry Bernard in the Paulaner Kirche on November 25, 1823 (Paulaner Kirche/Pfarre Wieden, Trauungs-Register, Tom 5, 1817–1826, fol. 137). Therefore, despite the earlier discussion that Bernard was romancing singer Caroline Willmann, and later ones where he is noted as being in a position to "inherit" Peters's wife, Bernard may have already been seeing Magdalena Grassl and spending some time at his future in-laws' house. See also Guetjahr, p. 175; Behsel, p. 94.—TA

[5] Beethoven seems to have been visiting the offices of Schickh's *Wiener Zeitschrift* when this entry was written. Schickh had already given Beethoven one or more Loeben poems earlier (see Heft 3, Blatt 7r, ca. November 22–23, 1819), but the composer may have found them uninspiring. Perhaps the poem newly received from Dresden was the "Abendlied unterm gestirnten Himmel," WoO 150, that Beethoven next set for Schick, although the "Abendlied" text had already appeared in Bäuerle's *Allgemeine Theater-Zeitung* 12, No. 56 (May 11, 1819), p. 222. The song's draft autograph is dated March 4, and it was published on March 28, 1820. In any case, Schickh asks for the Loeben song "recht sehr bald" here, with the word "bald" (soon) written over several times for emphasis. See Albrecht, "Poetic Source," pp. 7–32.

In 1821 the *Wiener Zeitschrift*'s offices were located on the Petersplatz, No. 612, corner of the Jungferngässchen (in the *Goldener Stern*), with a subsidiary across the Graben at Dorotheergasse, No. 1108 [1174 before the 1821 renumbering]. The latter address was also home to the *Sammler*, the *Wiener Allgemeine musikalische Zeitung*, the *Wanderer*, and the *Beobachter*. See Böckh, *Merkwürdigkeiten*, pp. 60–69.

In 1819, however, the *Wiener Zeitschrift*'s offices were still at Kohlmarkt No. 268 [renumbered as 257 in 1821], and this address probably served other journals, as well. Given the presence of Wähner in the entry immediately preceding Schickh's, one may conclude that these particular entries were made at their shared office. From context, one might also speculate that Schickh received the poem at the Petersplatz address and would have it available the next time that Beethoven came to the Kohlmarkt office. It is also possible that Schickh meant for Beethoven to accompany him back to Petersplatz (only a five-minute walk east) to get the new Loeben Lied.—TA

BERNARD [at a restaurant in the walled City; presumably at midday dinner, ca. 2 p.m., Monday, December 13]: They are both valid. //

PETERS [continuing]: In the interest of domestic order, I must go home.[6]

[Blatt 1v]

OLIVA: This [entry ends]

BEETHOVEN [presumably on a walk through the inner City, book shopping;[7] midafternoon of Monday, December 13]:
[at Doll's book shop, probably corner of Kramergasse and Lichtensteg:]
At Doll's, next to the Lichtensteg:[8] *Der Millionkünstler*, etc., etc.; bound; 3 fl. W.W.[9]
[at Schaumburg's book shop, Wollzeile No. 821:]
At Schaumburg's: Friedländer, *Über die körperliche Erziehung des Menschen*, etc., from the [Blatt 2r] French, etc., 2 fl. 30 kr., C.M.[10]
[possibly reading newspapers at *Zur Stadt Triest*; late afternoon of Monday, December 13:]

---

[6] The "domestic order" may have occasioned the exclamation "Children!" entered on the inside of the front cover. That way, Peters would not have had to turn the page to write his explanation. That way, the inner cover and Blatt 1 all belong to a part of the day before Beethoven met Oliva, who seems not to have gotten along with the sometimes unsavory circle around Bernard and Peters.—TA

[7] The German editors could not locate any advertisement for a work entitled *Der Millionkünstler* in the *Intelligenzblatt* and only a week-old one for the Friedländer book. This, along with the fact that the Bäuerle play was over a year old, suggests that Beethoven saw these two items (and certainly thumbed through the Bäuerle) while on a walk through the City. Indeed, Schaumburg's shop was no more than a five-minute walk from Doll's.—TA

[8] *Lichtensteg* is the short street that runs between Lugeck and the Hoher Markt. Even today, there is a bookshop on the west side of Lichtensteg, where the Kramergasse intersects with it. Beethoven probably noted the location to differentiate it from Doll's bookshop on the Stephansplatz. See Czeike, IV, p. 51, for a view (ca. 1820) of the east side of Lichtensteg, with its meat stalls.—TA

[9] "Der Million-Künstler" is not a title, but instead a term coined in Act 2, scene 8, of Adolf Bäuerle's farce *Der neue Don Juan*, premiered at the Theater an der Wien on October 24, 1818, and then at the Leopoldstadt Theater under the title *Moderne Wirthschaft und Don Juans Streiche* on October 17, 1821. In it, the character Fanny says: "Reich ist er ... Über eine Million hat er mitgenommen; der betrügerliche Tausendkünstler" (He is rich; he has taken more than a million, that deceitful thousand-trickster); to which the character Longinus replies: "Nu ... den soll man keinen *Tausend-* sondern einen *Million-*Künstler heissen" (Well, then he shouldn't be called a *thousand-* but instead a *million-*trickster). Although the play was included in *Komisches Theater*, an 1823 compilation of Bäuerle's works, Beethoven must have seen an earlier printing of it, bound with other plays, to command a price of 3 fl., even in W.W. Therefore, Beethoven not only engaged in wordplay himself, but appreciated it in others.—TA

[10] Excerpt from an advertisement in the *Intelligenzblatt*, No. 279 (December 6, 1819), p. 1084: "To be had at Carl Schaumburg and Co., Wollzeile No. 821: [Michael] Friedländer, *Über die körperliche Erziehung des Menschen* [On the Physical Education of Man, for Parents and Educators]; [transl.] from

General Inquiry and Information Bureau, on the Michaelerplatz, across from the Imp[erial] Burg [Palace], No. 3, on the 1st floor [2nd floor, American].[11]

For Karl: a medal on the Kohlmarkt.[12] [//]

[Blatt 2v]

OLIVA [possibly at *Zur Stadt Triest*; late afternoon or evening of Monday, December 13]: B[ernard] was not there [at the boarding house] yesterday when I was;[13] he was at Baumann's.[14] // Roast veal is good otherwise. [//]

BEETHOVEN [writing, so as not to be overheard]: I called the hunchback Serapis of Egypt,[15] if you know what that is. //

OLIVA [continuing]: What's more, there were 6–7 people there [at lawyer Bach's] yesterday [Sunday, December 12] who wanted to speak with him.[16] [//] [Blatt 3r]

Tomorrow I'll go to see Herz;[17] I believe that he'll probably do it, unless the

the French by Dr. Eduard Oehler, 8vo, 2 fl. 30 kr., C.M." The same advertisement also appeared on December 13, 1819. The book had been published by Voss in Leipzig in August 1819. Wollzeile 821 was renumbered as 775 in 1821; a Morawa bookshop occupies the site today; see Behsel, p. 23.—KH/TA

[11] See, for example, the *Intelligenzblatt*, No. 284 (December 13, 1819), p. 1125 (Advertisements). The same advertisement appeared frequently in the *Intelligenzblatt*.—KH

[12] See an advertisement in the *Wiener Zeitung*, No. 284 (December 13, 1819), p. 1136, in which Joseph Kern, "municipal gold- and silver-worker," on the Kohlmarkt No. 268, offered: "chronological medals for the new year and other occasions in fine gold and fine silver" and "well-made achievement medals for students in the German, Latin, and Art schools … in various sizes in fine gold and silver at the most reasonable prices." The same advertisement also appeared on December 1, 7, and 10, 1819. Kohlmarkt 268 was renumbered as 257 in 1821, and in 1819 was also the address for the *Wiener Zeitschrift*'s editorial office; see Behsel, p. 8.—KH/TA

[13] From entries in earlier conversation books, it appears that Oliva and Bernard ate at the same boarding house, at slightly different but often overlapping, times. They evidently acknowledged each other's presence, but seldom spoke. Bernard was not with Beethoven on Sunday, December 12, either, as the composer spent much of the day with Peters.—TA

[14] Carl Baumann and his wife Rosalie; see Heft 2, Blatt 89v.—TA

[15] Serapis (also Sarapis), a late Egyptian god (associated with Osiris) that survived into Greek and even Roman culture, was portrayed as a bearded man with bull's or ram's horns and a headpiece shaped like a basket or jug.

It is not clear whether Beethoven called the hunchback Serapis to his face, or whether he had simply referred to him as looking like Serapis; the latter is more likely. Interest in Egyptian culture was high in Vienna: the Egyptian antiquities exhibit mentioned in an earlier conversation book was still showing on the Graben, in the building just east of the Pestsäule.

Nearly a decade earlier, a member of Goethe's circle had described the visiting Oliva as hunchbacked, but it seems (from his passport application) that his physical limitation was actually a clouded right eye; even so, Oliva himself continues the labeling on Blatt 3v below.—KH/TA

[16] See Heft 4, Blatt 34v.—TA

[17] Leopold *Edler* von Herz, I.R. licensed wholesaler, had his "business office on the Bauernmarkt, No. 620, in his own house." His public partners in 1820 were Samuel M[arcus?] and Ignaz M. von Neuwall (Redl, 1820, p. 18). In 1822, Redl, p. 22, listed Ignaz M. *Edler* von Neuwall as Herz's partner,

change in his dealership that occurs at the end of this month prevents it. His partners are pulling out and he remains alone. If he says *no*, then what do you want to do? // I want to attempt everything that is possible at his place and, as I said, I almost don't doubt that he'll do it. [//] [Blatt 3v]

The person who is sitting across from us and looking over here so stupidly is the son of the singer Simoni.[18] //

This short, bent fellow was formerly a dealer in Nürnberg wares, & is called Plötz.[19] I know from earlier times that he was a very rich man and lost a great part of his property through alchemy. [//] [Blatt 4r]

<He is> Why is he [Archduke Rudolph] accepting such a dedication? It appears to me that you would not endure it for long [as his Kapellmeister]. // Then just put an end to the Mass. // He will do something, but it won't be much. // This one is his favorite and will remain so;—because of *other secondary reasons*.[20] [//]

Freedom. [//] [Blatt 4v]

Don't speak so loud. Your relationship [with Rudolph] is too well known. One unpleasant aspect of public places is that one is so inhibited in everything. *Everyone* hearkens and hears. // Count Waldstein[21] was also nearby. // Does he live here? [//] [Blatt 5r]

---

while Marcus *Edler* von Neuwall had his own business office in the Schulhof, No. 414. Bauernmarkt No. 620 was renumbered as 581 in 1821; conversely, Schulhof No. 414 in 1821 had been No. 447 in 1819 (Behsel, pp. 13 and 18). For Pauline (von) Herz, who lived at Bauernmarkt No. 616 [renumbered as 577 in 1821], see Heft 2, Blatt 54v.—KH/TA

[18] Joseph Simoni, actually Schimon (1764–1832), a tenor at the Kärntnertor Theater from 1796 to 1804, as well as in the Hofkapelle until his death. See Reichardt, vol. 1, p. 140; Wurzbach, vol. 34, p. 343.—KH/TA

[19] Julius Joseph Plötz dealt in "Steel and commercial wares from Nürnberg and the hereditary lands." He lived at *Zum goldenen Meerfräulein* (the Golden Mermaid), Kärntnerstrasse No. 1106 [renumbered as 1043 in 1821]. See Redl, 1820, p. 44; Behsel, p. 31.—KH/TA

[20] Oliva's cryptic passages here may imply that Rudolph was homosexual, and that his favored musical advisor (rather than Beethoven) occupied that position because the advisor, too, was homosexual. The Counts Troyer (see below) might bear research in this connection.—TA

[21] Count Ferdinand Ernst Waldstein (1762–1823), one of the closest adherents among the Viennese aristocracy to the Enlightenment. He had been called to Bonn by the enlightened Elector Max Franz in 1788, met Beethoven there and promoted his cause before and, evidently, after his move to Vienna. From 1795 to 1805, he was in the British military service, married in 1812, widowed in 1818, and now lived partially in Vienna and partially on his Bohemian estates. In 1805 Beethoven dedicated his Piano Sonata, Op. 53, to Waldstein. It is curious that Oliva noticed Waldstein, but that the count and composer seemingly did not acknowledge each other. Perhaps Waldstein was already suffering from the financial embarrassment of his last years. See Kinsky-Halm, pp. 124–126; Richard Schaal, "Waldstein," *MGG*, vol. 14, cols. 148–149; Clive, pp. 385–387.—KH/TA

Yesterday [Sunday, December 12] was Moscheles's concert.[22] Have you heard nothing about it? At the end, the Jew improvised. [//] He—and improvising? //

Last week, the Archduke baptized a whole family of Jews.[23] [//] 6 or 7 persons, all at once.[24] [//] T.[25] has a very commonplace manner in social conversation. [//] [Blatt 5v]

The wine is too strong for me.[26]

[End of entries for Monday, December 13.]

OLIVA **[presumably at Beethoven's new apartment on the Glacis; probably late morning of Tuesday, December 14]**: We have hope. Herz was very busy today, and because tomorrow is a Post day,[27] I made an appointment for Thursday morning at his residence.[28] I believe that it will work out, one way or another. // If you transact this [business] in a bank, they will know how [Blatt 6r] to do it better,

---

[22] On Sunday, December 12, 1819, Ignaz Moscheles gave a Grand Musical Akademie in the Grosser Redoutensaal. The program included, among other works, a new Concerto in E-flat for piano and orchestra by Moscheles, a new French Rondo Concertant for piano, violin and orchestra, and, to close the concert, a free Fantasie, into which he wove the "Abschied des Troubadours." See Kanne's *Wiener AmZ* 3, No. 99 (December 11, 1810), col. 800 and No. 101 (December 19, 1819), cols. 811–812. The Leipzig *Allgemeine musikalische Zeitung* 22, No. 4 (January 26, 1820), col. 57, noted that Moscheles's concert did not meet expectations; see also Blatt 19v below.—KH/TA

[23] Archduke Rudolph had been made a priest during the summer of 1819, and was consecrated as a bishop in the Augustiner Kirche on September 19, and as cardinal there on September 28. These telescoped functions were viewed as mere formalities, and Kaiser Franz even ordered that the music for them be limited. See Hofmusikkapelle, Akten, K. 11, 1819, fols. 112 and 119; 1820, fol. 84v (Haus-, Hof- und Staatsarchiv, Vienna). If Rudolph baptized a family of Jews, it did not take place in the Augustiner Kirche.—TA

[24] order for their members to hold certain positions or to own property, Jewish families often converted as a group: the Mendelssohns to Lutheranism in northern Germany, the Lewys in Catholic Vienna. Elias Lewy (1792/96–1846) arrived in Vienna probably in November 1823, to become the principal hornist at the Kärntnertor Theater. When, a decade later, he aspired to membership in the Hofkapelle (which played for Imperial church services), he (adopting the name Eduard Constantin), along with his wife and four musical children (including pianist Carl, hornist Richard, and harpist Melanie), converted as a family at the Peterskirche on June 24 (Feast of St. John the Baptist), 1835. See Pfarre St. Peter, Tauf-Register, 1826–1837, p. 241 (housed in the Michaelerkirche).

Similarly, Father Paschal Kelesich, a Capuchin priest, baptized Solomon (Sigismund) Fischer, 25, on December 8 (Feast of the Immaculate Conception), 1819, in his own church, but recorded it in the nearby Augustinerkirche's Taufbuch, 1814–1830, fol. 60. Therefore, the baptism that Rudolph performed (possibly in the Hofkapelle) probably also took place the previous Wednesday, December 8.—TA

[25] Original "Der T-": possibly Count Ferdinand Troyer (b. 1780) or Count Franz Troyer (1783–1854). Both brothers were amateur clarinettists (at least Ferdinand was a student of the Theater an der Wien's Joseph Friedlowsky), and both were in the service of Archduke Rudolph.—TA

[26] Oliva indicated elsewhere that he drank very little wine.—TA

[27] Either Herz's private banking business or Oliva's own job must have kept him busy on mail days.—TA

[28] For Oliva's report on that meeting, see Blatt 14r below.—TA

because the matter will go through several hands there, which would not be the case here. Otherwise it is certainly the same. // One bank share, then, gives you 500 fl. 20 kr. [C.M.] or 1,250 fl. W.W., which, then, you can expect from the sale of the Mass [*Missa solemnis*]. // You still receive the interest from the bank share, and, for the loaned one [another bank share], [Blatt 6v] you then pay the interest that one gets, which, however, will not bear much. Then you only take the money for 2½ months. //

It occurs to me that there is a restaurant not far from you that was excellent several years ago; I don't know how it is now. It is directly across from the Piaristen and is called *Zu den drei Hacken.*[29] [//] [Blatt 7r]

Are you going into the City now?[30] //

BERNARD [seemingly at a seldom visited restaurant[31] in the City, with Bernard, Peters, and Oliva;[32] probably at midday dinner, ca. 2 p.m. on Tuesday, December 14]:[33] That is the poet Captain Philipp,[34] who once sent me a poem entitled "Der Grosshändler der Gelehrsamkeit." // Tomorrow we must make an appearance at this friend's place. //

[Blatt 7v]

PETERS: Therefore tomorrow [Wednesday, December 15] is an examination. // I have to. // I'll send word out in time, because Blöchlinger did not know whether it would be in the morning or afternoon. //

---

[29] The old Gasthaus *Zu den drei Hacken* (later called *Hackeln*) in the Josephstadt, across from the Piaristenkirche and Gymnasium, at the southeast corner of Pfarrgasse and Piaristengasse. See Groner (1922), p. 143. In 1819 the building was numbered 122; in 1821 it became No. 125 (Behsel, p. 193); in later years Anton Bruckner occasionally ate there. The restaurant was a ten-minute walk from Beethoven's apartment, which was also in the parish of Maria Treu, the Piaristenkirche.—KH/TA

[30] The wording here confirms that this conversation took place in a suburb, presumably the Josephstadt, and suggests that Beethoven would soon walk to the walled City for midday dinner.—TA

[31] On Blatt 10r Peters notes that the restaurant is expensive, suggesting that he had seldom (or never before) eaten there. The restaurant *Drei Hacken* was also expensive, but it was in suburban Josephstadt, whereas Beethoven and his friends were seemingly within the walled City.—TA

[32] Oliva did not usually socialize with Bernard and his circle.—TA

[33] The conversation lasts through Blatt 11r.—TA

[34] Carl Philipp, I.R. Captain in Vienna, published numerous poems, among others a *Zeitgedichte. Ein Geschenk beym Wechsel des Jahres 1816. Österreichs Patrioten geweiht* (Poem of the Age. A Gift upon the Turn of the Year, 1816; dedicated to Austria's Patriots). See Goedeke, vol. 6, p. 592; Meusel, vol. 19, p. 131.—KH

OLIVA: Your portrait. // Not a success—the painting [of you and Karl] is much better. I saw it in the Freyhaus auf der Wieden; it is in Berlin.[35] [//] What is the artist's name? // The copper engraving has shadows that are too dark // [Blatt 8r] Very successful; I know him and her. // He has [drawn] only the Emperor of Austria and you from life. //

His [Karl's] mother is the vile scum of the earth. // Isn't it true that Karl knew that she slept with her lover while your dead brother was in the house? //

PETERS: I'll bring you the answer myself.

[Blatt 8v]

OLIVA: Too hot.[36] [//]

BERNARD: In stone? // How does the guardian personage present himself? // He is an actor in Leipzig. // Costs. [//] [Blatt 9r]

PETERS: He does not read music. [//] I believed that there would be texts there. //

BERNARD: Weissenbach's tragedy[37] will not come [to the stage]. From a dramatic consideration, it is too full of errors. Not bad, just not suitable for performance. [//] [Blatt 9v] Who is supposed to correspond with him? He will only [consider] an order from the H[igh Guardianship Administration].[38] [//]

---

[35] This concerns the painting—now lost—that August Karl Friedrich Kloeber (1793–1864), painter of historical scenes, upon commission from his brother-in-law, Baron Skrbenkski, made in Mödling in 1818, that showed Beethoven and his nephew in a landscape. The comparison here is between Klöber's oil painting and an engraving of Beethoven's head that was based on it. The life-size chalk drawing of Beethoven's head, dating from 1817, served as a preparatory study for it. Schickh's *Wiener Zeitschrift* 3, No. 139 (November 19, 1818), pp. 1134–1135, published the following report: "Vienna. Herr Klöber from Breslau has recently completed the portrait of our great master of music Ludwig van Beethoven in oils …. It appears to us that this likeness, in its conception and execution, is the most successful and most accurate of all that we have had the occasion to see, and we are glad to be able to invite the friends and admirers of Beethoven's muse to view it. Herr Klöber … lives in the Wieden, in the Freyhaus, Courtyard 5, Stairway 24, on the 1st floor [2nd floor, American]." See *Allgemeine Deutsche Biographie*, vol. 16, pp. 200–201; *Allgemeine musikalische Zeitung* (Leipzig), New Series, vol. 2, No. 18 (May 4, 1864), 324–325; Frimmel, *Beethoven Studien*, I, pp. 72–74; Thieme-Becker, vol. 20, p. 530; Clive, pp. 187–189.—KH/TA

[36] Depending upon context, this could also mean too hot-headed or (in the case of wine) heady.—TA

[37] Possibly *Der Brautkranz*, tragedy in 5 acts (Vienna: Wallishausser, 1810). See Goedeke, vol. 6, p. 661.—KH

[38] The last part of this entry is difficult to read; it follows the reconstruction of the German editors.—KH/TA

BEETHOVEN [**writing so as not to be overheard**]: What do you think of this Chinese man? //

PETERS [**replying**]: I don't know him. His physiognomy is deceptive. [//]

[Blatt 10r]

BERNARD: I get up every morning at 5:30. [//]

OLIVA: Because you always speak about the wife, the husband will recognize any child of his who possesses musical talent to be *your* child.[39] //
    Where the *talare* [Thalers?] are calculated. //

PETERS: It is very expensive here. [//]

[Blatt 10v]

OLIVA: You yourself should come, to pass on your regards to the wife. [//]

BERNARD: Coffee. [//]

OLIVA: What have you decided about raising the money? I want to try to put an end to the matter tomorrow. [//] [Blatt 11r] Because it is late. [//] The gentleman promised tomorrow, because he was occupied out of the house today. // I sit across from you for an hour, and you sleep. //

BERNARD: How is it for tomorrow [Wednesday, December 15] at midday? I should think that we would be out of there [presumably Blöchlinger's Institute] at 2 o'clock. [//]
    [**Bernard and Peters depart; Oliva and Beethoven possibly repair to a coffee house; probably ca. 4 p.m.**[40] **on Tuesday, December 14.**]

[Blatt 11v]

OLIVA: There is also capon ready. //

---

[39] In 1988, following upon Solomon's "Immortal Beloved" theory, Susan Lund proposed that Antonie Brentano's last child, Karl Joseph (b. March 8, 1813), was Beethoven's biological son. She and her husband Franz Brentano, living in distant Frankfurt, remained friends with Beethoven. Similarly, in 2007, Rita Steblin proposed Josephine von Brunsvik (1779–1821) as the "Immortal Beloved" and her child Minona ("Anonim" spelled backwards, b. 1813) as Beethoven's biological daughter. At the time, Josephine was married to Christoph Stackelberg. See Lund, "True 'Fleshly Father,'" pp. 9–10; and Steblin, "'Auf diese Art,'" pp. 147–180.—TA

[40] On Blatt 13v Oliva mentions that stove workers are coming to Beethoven's new apartment on the Glacis that evening at 7 p.m.—TA

UNKNOWN: What is Wagner[41] doing in Berlin? //

OLIVA: The gentleman wishes to know what Wagner is doing in Berlin. He was a captain and was earlier [employed] at Count Schönfeld's.[42] He is a major in Prussia. //

Many of the best Ofener wines cost 4, or at least 3 fl.—even 2 fl. [Blatt 12r]

I hear that one cannot eat here at midday, but the gentleman knows a good restaurant, right next to the Theater [in der Josephstadt], below the house *Zum Hänchen*.[43] // We were in the Theater building.[44] //

[He/it] is from Münster. [//] <I nee> The gentleman is writing a history of the War.[45] // Isn't the short officer's name Pannasch?[46] [//] [Blatt 12v] Rothkirch[47] is

---

[41] Probably Captain Wagner, staff member of the *Österreichischer militärische Zeitschrift*, 1811–1813 (see also Blatt 12v below). He is presumably the same person who wrote a review of Kanne's Mass in G, composed for the birth of the King of Rome (son of Napoleon and Marie Louise, and later Duke of Reichstadt), performed in the Augustiner Church on Saints Peter and Paul Day, 1811. See the *Allgemeine musikalische Zeitung* 13, No. 30 (July 24, 1811), cols. 505–507. Given Georg August Griesinger's connection with *AmZ* and the Saxon Ambassador Count Schönfeld, the two Schönfelds could be related or even identical—possibly Saxon father, Viennese chamberlain son. See Count Johann Hilmar Adolph von Schönfeld (born 1743), Electoral Saxon Ambassador in Vienna, in Brandenburg, *Briefwechsel*, Nos. 119, 137, 327, and 1470; Anderson, Nos. 73 and 167; Albrecht, *Letters to Beethoven*, Nos. 50 and 291.

Schünemann presumed that this was Major August Wagner, officer in the Grand General Staff in Berlin, living at Unter den Linden 14. See *Adresskalender f. d. kgl. Haupt- und Residenzstadt Berlin und Potsdam*, 1819, p. 120.—KH/TA

[42] Count Johann Heinrich Schönfeld was a Treasury official. See *Hof- und Staats-Schematismus*, 1819, I, p. 75.—KH

[43] The restaurant *Zum weissen Hahn* was in the Josephstadt, Kaiserstrasse, No. 101 [renumbered as 104 in 1821]. On the north side of today's Josephstädter Strasse, it was almost equidistant between Lange Gasse and Piaristengasse, two buildings east of the Theater in der Josephstadt. See Guetjahr, p. 315; Behsel, p. 192.—KH/TA

[44] The restaurant *Zum goldenen Strauss*, located in the building facing the street in front of the Theater in the Josephstadt, No. 99 [renumbered as No. 102 in 1821]. The theater itself was located at the back of a small courtyard behind the restaurant. With succeeding renovations, perceptible even today, the courtyard was covered to expand the theater's lobby, and the "Strauss-Saal" was moved to the east of the complex. See Behsel, p. 192.—KH/TA

[45] In this connection, see also the entries in Heft 11, Blatt 35r, where a historian of the Turkish War (1788–1791) is identified as Mengen, although it is possible that two different military historians, writing about two different wars, were meant.—TA

[46] Anton Pannasch (1789–1855) was a Captain in the Infantry Regiment of Archduke Karl and wrote works with historical settings for Vienna's Burgtheater. See Gräffer-Czikann, IV, p. 147.—KH

[47] Count Leonhard von Rothkirch und Panten (b. 1773), Privy Councillor. In 1806, Archduke Karl called him to Vienna to write *Beiträge zum praktischen Unterricht im Felde* (Contributions to Practical Instruction in the Field). At the outbreak of war in 1809 he was on the Quartermaster General's staff, and he was wounded in the Battle of Aspern (May 21–22, 1809). Thereupon followed his promotion to Lieutenant Colonel. In 1811, with Schels and Wagner, he began publication of the *Österreichische militärische Zeitschrift*, which was suspended in 1813, but continued again in 1818. See Gräffer-Czikann, IV, pp. 100–102 and 421–422.—KH

very skillful as a military man. // The gentleman is most sincerely glad to see you. // The gentleman became a captain at the Battle of Aspern. // The gentleman is of the opinion that you would have received presents from England for the *Battle* [*Wellington's Victory*].[48] [//] [continued on next page→]

BEETHOVEN [entered later, at the bottom of the page]: Barber for shaving beard. [//]

[Blatt 13r]

OLIVA [continuing from above]: The gentleman is also of the opinion that if you went to England, you would never again return here. [//] 1816, in July. // They are playing Charades there. // He remains in Prague and is hailed there.[49] // [He] writes at home. [//] [Blatt 13v]
  The potter [stove maker] chastised me because no one was at home. This evening at 7 o'clock, the master will come with journeymen in order to look into the matter, and to adjust it in the best way. Therefore, if you cannot be at home, you must make arrangements so the maid lets them in. // [Blatt 14r]
  [End of entries for Tuesday, December 14; no later than ca. 6:30 p.m.]

  [No identifiable entries from Wednesday, December 15.]

OLIVA [probably at Beethoven's apartment on the Glacis; probably late morning or early afternoon, Thursday, December 16]:
  Compliments and hot air at Herz's![50] But I have another route without going to the Bank. Today I took a new position, and everything will certainly go well there, so much so that I have already spoken [about it], and perhaps will take care of everything today. It appears to me that the separation [of the partners] that took

---

[48] *Wellington's Victory, or the Battle of Vittoria*, Op. 91, premiered in Vienna, to great applause, on December 8, 1813]. Beethoven had sent a copy to the Prince Regent in England, but never received any gifts for it.—KH/TA

[49] Possibly the oboist, composer, and conductor Joseph Triebensee (1772–1846), music director at the Prague Opera since October 1, 1816. Triebensee was the son of Vienna Court oboist Georg Triebensee (1746–1813), for whom Mozart had written solos in his *Die Entführung aus dem Serail* (1782) and Beethoven in his *Die Geschöpfe des Prometheus* (1801). The younger Triebensee had studied oboe with his father and composition with Albrechtsberger. He was named music director to Prince Liechtenstein in Vienna in 1809, and music director to the Theater in Brünn in 1811. When Carl Maria von Weber resigned from the music directorship in Prague in summer 1816, Triebensee was named his successor, effective that fall. He remained in Prague until his death. See, among others, Karl Maria Pisarowitz, "Triebensee," *MGG*, vol. 13, cols. 663–665.—TA

[50] On Blatt 5 (Tuesday, December 14) Oliva said that he could get an appointment with Herz on Thursday the 16th.—TA

place at Herz's occasioned him to do it. He summoned me so often in order to tire me out. [//]

Is a dog [used] as a rabbit for the hunt? + + − [//] [Blatt 14v]

You must especially call the situation with the stove to the potter's attention: as it stands now, all the heat goes into the walls and none of it into the area of the room. It appears to me that the main thing is that it [the stove] will be placed standing further out into both rooms, and that the wall above the stove will be broken out, the way it also is here. Otherwise it cannot warm the room, [Blatt 15r] rather only the tile wall that is around it. [//] The potter believes that his journeyman committed an error, otherwise this absolutely could not have been the case, considering the acknowledged goodness of this stove. // Let him break it down right away. [//] [Blatt 15v] I know that this type of stove is universally praised, but in your case it is warming the wall and not the room. **[possibly continued on Blatt 16r→]**

[In light of the entries above and below, it appears that Beethoven spent the evening of his birthday, Thursday, December, 16, with Oliva (and possibly others), and that no conversation book entries survive from that occasion.][51]

BEETHOVEN **[at a coffee house; possibly late afternoon of Friday, December 17]**: Augustinergasse, at Grund's, [House No.] 1226, *Corbeille de fleurs*, etc., with copperplate title page, sewn binding, 1 fl. W.W.[52] [//]

[Blatt 16r]

OLIVA **[possibly continued from Blatt 15v]**: In the future, I shall doubtless be on my guard—It [finding the stove] was done in [with] the best intention. I could not foresee that what all other people find to be good (of which I have many examples), [would] not be feasible in your case. //

[possibly late afternoon, Friday, December 17:]

It [the *Sparkasse*] is organized according to English models.[53] // As often as he

---

[51] If Beethoven hosted a birthday get-together at his apartment on the Glacis, he could have had food delivered from the *Birne* on street level, below, or from the *Biber*, one block north. Because they would have been in private quarters, with windows and doors closed in the December weather, Oliva and any other guests could have spoken to him in raised voices without the aid of the conversation books.—TA

[52] Excerpt from an advertisement in the *Wiener Zeitung*, No. 288 (December 17, 1819), p. 1151: "To be had in Franz Grund's Book Shop, Augustinerstrasse No. 1226: *Corbeille de Fleurs, ou choix de Maximes et sentence morales. Cadeau pour l'année 1820. Dediée à la jeunesse d'un age mûr.* With illustrations. Title page copperplate, tastefully sewn-bound, 1 fl. W.W." The same advertisement also appeared on December 24, 1819.—KH/TA

[53] The *Erste Österreichische Sparkasse* (First Austrian Savings and Loan), which had been founded at the beginning of September 1819 with the purpose "to provide for factory workers, handworkers, day laborers, country people and domestic servants, and in general every thrifty person, the means of

desires, a person can invest monetary payments [of] 5 fl. there, this capital will be [Blatt 16v] paid as interest to everyone who deposits [money] at 4%, the interest will be paid to capital every quarter year, and this accumulated capital again pays interest anew, so the poorest class, in the course of several years, can collect a nest-egg for their old age, because each person will take every increase of the capital [Blatt 17r] itself at the rate of so-and-so many Gulden per day. // The bank share amounts to 500 fl. and several Gulden without interest; if you therefore take 450 or perhaps 400 fl. on that, then the value is always fulfilled and the entire procedure in connection with this is only that your bank share must not appear as if [it had been] *sold*, which is always the case at the Bank. [//] [Blatt 17v] The concern is only that your name does not appear in this connection at the Bank; otherwise, this is a well-known and respected house, for you wouldn't think that I could accept a position where there isn't some assurance of ca. 500 fl. // At most 6 to 7%; at the Bank [it is] 5%; it doesn't amount to much for a few months. [//] [Blatt 18r] I am almost assured that they aren't going to make me wait; it is going easier with this matter than I imagined after the 2 negative replies. [//]

The *Correspondent von und für Deutschland* is said to be forbidden from January 1 onward.[54]

I just ate beef and roast veal, and paid over 2 fl. //

But not here. An official here made paper [money] and Obligations, [Blatt 18v] fled, and was captured in France. // He was seen in Prague, where he continued his journey to Hamburg; he had 2 days' advantage and has probably [sailed] for North America. [//] [Blatt 19r] Tomorrow [Saturday, December 18], maybe even before noon, I shall try to get the matter in order. To do that, though, I need the bank share and then a sheet of paper with your signature to be able to write the assurance for the money received. I would like to have both of these tomorrow, and I must go out at 9 o'clock. // You will get a copy of this note or [Blatt 19v] especially the receipt. //

I drank somewhat more [than usual] last night [Thursday, December 16][55] & slept badly the whole night. Wine is not healthy for me. //

putting back, from time to time, a little capital from their earnings at interest, in order to apply it, in later days, for better care, for dowries, for assistance in illness and old age." The smallest deposit possible was 25 kr. C.M., the largest 100 fl. C.M. See Pezzl (1826), pp. 511–513.—KH

54 The Nürnberg newspaper, the *Correspondent von und für Deutschland*, which, however, appeared further after 1819. Perhaps a special prohibition for Austria is meant here. Upon a command from Metternich's government, dated January 13, 1820, it was forbidden to display German and French newspapers in Viennese coffee houses and restaurants from January 22 on. However, "for this quarter year, private individuals were still allowed to receive certain German newspapers." See the *Augsburger Allgemeine Zeitung*, No. 23 (January 23, 1820), p. 92.—KH/TA

55 As noted above, Beethoven's birthday, possibly at a celebration at his apartment.—TA

He is said to have gotten more than 5,000 fl., even though the Akademie turned out badly.[56] In general people were dissatisfied as much with his compositions as with his playing. [//] [Blatt 20r] He makes variations on some common theme, rather like Hummel, but worse.[57] // *Tancredi* and *Othello*—he [Rossini] has some genius that cannot be denied, but he is a scribbler without taste.[58]

[End of entries for Friday afternoon, December 17.]

OLIVA **[probably at a bank in or near Untere or Obere Bäcker Strasse;[59] morning of Saturday, December 18]**: When is the potter [oven maker] coming?[60] //

Did you bring a sheet of paper?[61] //

[written in ink,[62] therefore on a formal writing desk, through Blatt 21r:] You have to pay interest for the loan. Against that, your bank share lies inactive at the lender's, and they enjoy the full use of the earning that results from the bank share [Blatt 20v] through the interest, through the dividends. That is only because of the procedure. Anyhow, you will indeed receive the greatest part of the sum. // As much as you receive; because the same business affairs will never be equal, if compared completely hypothetically. [//] What is the least amount that you need? The exchange rate always remains the same. [//] 1000 [fl.] By the end of February you will indeed get 150 fl. again. If you take less, then you will also need to pay less. //

I think that you should write earlier than when you deliver the Mass [*Missa solemnis*]. He [Archduke Rudolph] already knows what you expect.

40   20 –

30
──────
120/0

---

[56] Presumably Ignaz Moscheles's Akademie of Sunday, December 12. See Blatt 5r above.—KH

[57] Johann Nepomuk Hummel (1778–1837), piano virtuoso, Kapellmeister and composer, student of Mozart, and successor to Haydn in Eisenstadt, now (since 1819) Kapellmeister in Weimar, was an off-and-on friend of Beethoven's. See Clive, pp. 172–174.—KH/TA

[58] Gioacchino Rossini's opera *Tancredi* had been performed on December 2, 1819, in the Kärntnertor Theater; his *Othello* was scheduled for December 21.—TA

[59] Beethoven later seemingly walks from Schaumburg's bookshop in the Wollzeile to Bauer's in the Schottenhof, to *Zum römischen Kaiser* for dinner. A banking house in the Bäcker Strasse seems a possible beginning for this journey across the inner City. At about this time Oliva began working for Nathan Mayer & J.G. Landauer (wholesale silk and linen merchants), Untere Bäckerstrasse No. 798 [renumbered as 752 in 1821].—TA

[60] It is not clear whether this question is the final element in the foregoing conversation or the first element of the next.—TA

[61] Mentioned the day before on Blatt 19r above.—TA

[62] The previous dividing line was also written in ink.—KH

[Blatt 21r]

N.7.A. <399>. 3099. July 13, 1819.[63] [//] You have the interest from July 13, & then you don't receive the dividend that begins from January 1, 1820, until the last day of June, 1820. With these bank shares there is a double interest rate. From the Thousand Gulden W.W. that was paid, the same were cancelled, and for which the Emperor gave the Bank an Obligation of 2½ [%] interest. The Bank made business with the former C[onventions] Geld, transactions which then constitute the dividends. Every half year the balance will be drawn and the entire resultant earning will be distributed on every bank share. [//] Every bank share carries 5 kreuzer C.M. *daily* on the accumulating interest. **[End of entries in ink.]** [//]

[Blatt 21v]

BEETHOVEN **[at Schaumburg's book shop, Wollzeile No. 821; late morning of Saturday, December 18]**: Trattnick, custodian of the I.R. Natural History Collection, *Plant Life of the Austrian Empire.*[64]

Austrian Wreath of Flowers, by the same author, at Schaumburg's.[65]

[presumably at a coffee house, reading the day's newspapers,[66] after leaving Schaumburg's:]

At Bauer's in the Schottenhof: *Neuer National-Kalender, etc., etc, for the Leap Year*

[63] Two of Beethoven's bank shares from his *Nachlass* (estate) are preserved in the Wiener Stadt- und Landesbibliothek, with their original numberings: Folio 3099, Nos. 4 and 5, dated July 13, 1819.—KH

[64] Leopold Trattnick (1764–1849), botanist, was custodian of the United Court Natural History Collections from 1808 to 1835. Between 1812 and 1824 he published *Flora des österreichischen Kaiserthums*, in 24 issues or 2 volumes. He also published poems in Schickh's *Wiener Zeitschrift* during this period. See Böckh, *Wiens lebende Schriftsteller*, p. 52; Kayser, vol. 5, p. 465; Wurzbach, vol. 46, pp. 281–283.—KH/TA

[65] Excerpt from an advertisement in the *Wiener Zeitung*, No. 277 (December 3, 1819), p. 1108: "*Oesterreichischer Blumenkranz* by Leopold Trattnick. With this poetical pocketbook, which, for its form as well as its content, may be recommended as a friendly companion for walks in the country, the publisher flatters himself to make a friend, not only of admirers of the Muses, but also all educated people, lovers of beautiful Nature, especially those who are occupied with the moral and aesthetic cultivation of youth. This pocketbook may be had in the book shop of Carl Schaumburg and Co. in the Wollzeile, No. 821, and, bound on printing paper, costs 3 fl. W.W., and on vellum postal paper, 4 fl. 30 kr. W.W." The same advertisement had already appeared several times in November. *Wollzeile* No. 821 was combined with 822 and renumbered as 775 in 1821; see Behsel, p. 23.

The lack of a current newspaper advertisement and the pattern of entries on Blätter 1v–2r above suggest that Beethoven actually examined these two items in Schaumburg's bookshop.—KH/TA

[66] Beethoven accurately copied the following two items from the *Intelligenzblatt*, so there is no question that he read them there, rather than seeing the *Kalender* first at Bauer's.—TA

1820, etc., by Christian Carl [Blatt 22r] André (10th annual edition, 40 folded sheets), Prague, bound quarto, 6 fl. 18 kr. W.W.[67]

Polish for patent leather is now [available] only in the city, Kärntnerstrasse at the small grocer's next to the spice [and grocery] shop *Zum rothen Rössel*, etc., etc, [and] in the Josephstadt in the I.R. Lottery Collector's Office, above the Theater.[68] [//]

[resuming the day's activities that may have taken him to Bauer's bookshop[69] before meeting Oliva again.]

[Blatt 22v]

OLIVA **[seemingly at *Zum römischen Kaiser*; seemingly later in the afternoon[70] on Saturday, December 18]**: I still do not have any money today. [//] It became known today that the quantity of bank shares designated by the Bank would be decreased, so that the Bank is to issue no more *new* bank shares. If this is true, one may presume that the bank shares will increase sharply in price, and therefore they wanted me to designate [your] bank share for sale at the present exchange rate, which is now understood to be less, because you can earn more otherwise. [Blatt 23r] These merchants are the Devil's handiwork.

This afternoon, however, I turned to a private person, whom I know and who is rich, and I shall do it there tomorrow [Sunday, December 19], so that you have the money by about 11 o'clock. By doing so, you will make money in terms of interest and procedure of the matter. //

Bernard is said to have published several very beautiful poems in the *Aglaja*;[71]

---

[67] Excerpt from an advertisement in the *Intelligenzblatt*, No. 289 (December 18, 1819), p. 1183: "To be had at B. Ph. Bauer's: New National Calendar for the Entire Austrian Monarchy, for the Leap Year 1820, for Catholics, Protestants, Greeks, Russians, Jews, and Turks. For the instruction and pleasure for sacred and secular individuals, teachers, officials, city dwellers and country folk, compiled in a comprehensible manner by Christian Carl André," with other details as Beethoven copied them. The advertisement had first appeared in the *Intelligenzblatt*, No. 283 (December 11, 1819), p. 1123, and, in the meantime, had appeared again on December 15.—KH/TA

[68] See the *Intelligenzblatt*, No. 289 (December 18, 1819), p. 1175 (Advertisements). The advertisement listed fourteen locations where the wax was available; Kärntnerstrasse was No. 3; Josephstadt was No. 14. In the advertisement the *Rössel* was distinctly "red," but *Zum fliegenden* ("flying") *Rössel* was located at Kärntnerstrasse No. 1101 [renumbered as 1038 in 1821]; see Behsel, p. 31. The designation "above" the Theater in der Josephstadt presumably means "west" of it.—KH/TA

[69] Bauer's bookshop was in the Schottenhof, to the north of the Schottenkirche's entrance, and *Zum römischen Kaiser* faced the Freyung, two buildings behind and to the east of the church.—TA

[70] On Blatt 23r below Oliva notes having already had dinner, presumably at the Born and Paumgartner boarding house in the *Rother Igel*.—TA

[71] The *Aglaja. A Pocket Book for the Year 1820*, vol. 6, contains the following poems by J.C. Bernard: "Preis der Geliebten" (pp. 78–79), "An die Sterne" (p. 131), "Inschriften. Unter Bildnisse deutscher Dichter" (Inscriptions. Under portraits of German poets) (pp. 300–302). These last were

people were complimenting him about it today at the table [in the boarding house]. [//]

[Blatt 23v]

BEETHOVEN: Cajetan Koschazki,[72] town chaplain in Jägerndorf; poem by him to Trattnick. //

OLIVA: After Schlegel's translation [of Shakespeare], many want to say that there could only be something *like* it, but not *better* than it. [//]

BEETHOVEN: <Cest> qu'est ce qu'il parle cet homme la.[73] [//]

[Blatt 24r]

OLIVA: He is an officer, and is telling far and wide about the capture of the Austrian Corps at Ulm [in October, 1805]. //

How long are you staying at home tomorrow morning [Sunday, December 19]? I am not coming before 11 o'clock.[74] //

One never pays the hypothetical value in full. I've heard that the Bank is to have specified that they would not accept bank shares in exchange for money. The Bank, however, gives only ⅔ of it in Obligations. [Blatt 24v] You can sell it immediately, but if what is being said right now is true, it would be at a loss. // Everything is taken care of for the *best*. [//] The lender has given 450 fl. C.M. for 4 months. This is therefore to be repaid on April 18,[75] when you then receive your bank share back in its original state. [//] [Blatt 25r] The lender is a very rich man who possesses 5 houses in the City; thus you may also be reassured by this. I negotiated the interest at such a reasonable rate that I myself would not have believed possible. In toto, I paid only 10 fl. C.M., which makes ca. 7%. In addition, you therefore have no loss at all, because [Blatt 25v] the interest on your bank note, at 5 kreuzer per day, during the 4 months, will bear precisely these 10 fl. for you.

---

verbal (not visual) portraits of Caroline Pichler, Aloys Jeitteles, Franz Grillparzer, Theresa Artner, and Georg von Schall. The annual volumes for 1818 and 1819 contained no contributions by Bernard. See also Blatt 49v below.—KH/TA

[72] Cajetan Koschatzki, monastery chaplain in Jägerndorf, belonged to the Agricultural Society in the Margraviate of Moravia. See *Hof- und Staats-Schematismus*, 1819, II, p. 314.—KH

[73] The French text means: "What is that man saying?"—KH

[74] Similar to other occasions during this period, there are no conversation book entries for this projected meeting at Beethoven's apartment.—TA

[75] This suggests that the loan was made on December 18 (Saturday), but possibly as early as Friday, the 17th, or as late as Monday, December 20, 1819.—TA

He lent   450 fl. [C.M.]
Less interest   10 fl.
You receive   440 fl.
Which makes about 1,100 in W.W.

425
 15
440

[Blatt 26r]

Your bank share bears 5 kreuzer every day for you; in one month this makes 2 fl. 30 [kr.]; therefore 10 fl. in 4 months—exactly as much as you have just paid as interest on the money that was lent. //

BEETHOVEN: In the *Römischer Kaiser*,[76] 4 fl. 13 kr.
    [End of dinner with Oliva at *Zum römischen Kaiser*, seemingly late afternoon, Saturday, December 18.]

[Blatt 26v]

PETERS **[at *Zur Stadt Triest*, also with Bernard; afternoon or evening of Sunday, December 19]**:[77] No one has opened it. [//]
    The Greek examination turned out well, although he [Karl] was prepared for it only a couple of days before. He really has a great deal of talent. The professors have really treated him with consideration. //
    He is receiving no instruction in *fortepiano*. If you find [Joseph] Czerny appropriate, he will be happy to do it. He would have time in the evening hours. // [Blatt 27r] Have you seen him since that time?[78] //
    I have merely come here to see you. This week, I am going to Blöchlinger's again. He will certainly take great pains, because at the same time it brings him honor to

---

[76] The hotel *Zum römischen Kaiser* was located two buildings behind the Schottenkirche in the Renngasse, No. 138 [as numbered in 1821], and was widely known. It gained literary fame through the lectures that Friedrich von Schlegel gave there in 1812 and 1827, and was also a favorite location for recitals and chamber music concerts during this period. See Groner (1922), p. 144; Pezzl (1826), p. 240.—KH/TA

[77] According to Blatt 36r below proprietor Seelig told Oliva that Beethoven had enjoyed himself at *Zur Stadt Triest* on Sunday, as represented in this conversation with Bernard and Peters that lasted through Blatt 33v.—TA

[78] Czerny taught piano to the Lobkowitz family. His most recent entries in the conversation books were made at *Zur Stadt Triest*, probably on the evening of December 11 (Heft 4, Blätter 32r–34r). Peters's use of the term *fortepiano* suggests that he was not particularly current in musical terminology.—TA

further a talented boy in his education. // He is now very much at one with you. [//] That is true. // Calm and consistency. [//]

[Blatt 27v]

BEETHOVEN: 24

BERNARD: I have received a letter from Salzburg that was very thick and therefore should have been paid for at double the rate. I took it to be only a single, however, and sent it back. Since the Post Office insisted upon it, someone opened it there, but no-one read it. [//]

[Blatt 28r]

PETERS: I must write him[79] immediately for so many beautiful things. Because I still remain so much in his debt, he could rightly say *Petrus non sanctus*. [//]

[Blatt 28v]

BERNARD: Because the paper is somewhat rougher, just estimate a doubled letter and weigh it. I recently had to pay 28 kr. C.M. for a letter from Prague that also merely had thicker paper. [//]

Haven't you been well? I have not been able to get away to visit you.[80] [//]
[Blatt 29r]

I talked to [Don Ignatius Thomas,] the Prior at the Michaelerkirche the day before yesterday and told him the story about Karl. He said that he is not lost, and that he [Thomas] has found [the] correct comprehension of honesty in him. //

[Blatt 29v]

PETERS: He [Karl] will not become a failure. The relationship will be reestablished again. What has happened was fatal, but he was too young to behave himself any other way, and those around him[81] were not clear about the entire incident. // Integrity certainly, but human weaknesses. // He is still always [Blatt 30r] brighter than the entire body of Magistrat officials. // Very long ago, I explained [to] Blöchlinger exactly what you just said. // Boys who enjoy better education up to their 18th year are often worthless. Your nephew will successfully work out

---

[79] Presumably Aloys Weissenbach (1766–1821), a deaf physician in Salzburg; he came to Vienna for the Congress of 1814–1815 and wrote the text for Beethoven's *Der glorreiche Augenblick*, Op. 136. See Clive, pp. 394–395.—TA

[80] Bernard's most recent entry was on Blatt 11r (December 14). This suggests that he had not seen Beethoven in five days and was *not* present at the get-together with Oliva on December 16.—TA

[81] After this, an added word: "Plechlinger."—KH

all of his disgusting behavior and will drive everything crude from himself. [//]
[Blatt 30v] You are ten times better than I am; if my nephews do not completely act
according to my wishes, I'll send them into the country to a farmer's life under strict
supervision. [//]

BERNARD: Herr Pflanze (*Pianta*),[82] though, was a good creature [*Kraut*]. [//]
Persecutions by his colleagues. [//] [Blatt 31r]

[Weissenbach's play] is forbidden by the Censor. I wrote to Weissenbach about it.
He appeared to be hurt about it. [//] Church rites and a miracle worker appear in
it. [//] The other is also suitable for the [Theater an der] Wien. [Blatt 31v] If you
want to have a reserved seat near the stage, you need only send [word] each time.
[//] The [Theater] an der Wien must remain exactly as it is, because you called
the Count[83] a "miserable Excellency." [//] [Blatt 32r] It is a <lasae> Crimen lasae
Excellentiae.[84] // For all eternity. //

I recently encountered Frau von Janschikh; she did not look beautiful at all. She
reproached us that we never visit her. I had promised her [Blatt 32v] to go out there
with you this afternoon, if the weather permitted it. //

One must first await the decision before anyone can think about Salzburg [for
Karl's schooling]; even then, however, [it] can be treated without consideration.
[//] [Blatt 33r] It cannot last much longer. [//] They [the Magistrat] are probably
ashamed that they should repeal an order.[85] // S [//]

[Blatt 33v]

PROPRIETOR SEELIG: Bread—4 [kr.] // Wine—3 fl.

You had:	1 bottle	2 fl.
	Small "	1 fl.
	[total]	3 fl.

---

[82] Leopold Joseph Pianta, Magistrat's Councillor in the Senate for Municipal Legal Affairs,
lived in the walled City, Rauhensteingasse No. 993. The building was renumbered as 935 in 1821,
and in 1829 was owned by Johanna Pianta. See *Hof- und Staats-Schematismus*, 1819, I, p. 657; Behsel,
p. 28.—KH/TA

[83] At that time, Count Ferdinand von Palffy-Erdöd (1774–1840) was the owner of the Theater
an der Wien. According to a report by Ludwig Spohr (who had served as concertmaster there for
a period), Beethoven, in 1813, had offended him with loud insults in the Theater. See Frimmel,
Handbuch, II, pp. 231–232; Spohr, I, p. 177.—KH/TA

[84] Crime of the insulted Excellency.—KH

[85] Contrary to Beethoven's deliberations to have Karl educated abroad, the Viennese Magistrat
sided with the mother (Johanna) and, on May 7, 1819, had denied the issue of a passport. See Thayer-
Deiters-Riemann, IV, pp. 140–141.—KH

[Then]	Bread	4 kr.
	Veal	30
	Nessmüller[86]	30
	3 lemons	36
	Oysters	4 fl. 48 kr.
[Grand total]		9 fl. 28 kr.

[End of the afternoon or evening at *Zur Stadt Triest*, Sunday, December 19.]

[Blatt 34r]

BEETHOVEN **[possibly at his apartment or even on his walk into the City; around noon on Monday, December 20]**:

[Blatt 34v]

JOSEPH CZERNY **[presumably at a restaurant with Beethoven and Janschikh; early to midafternoon, Monday, December 20]**: Wolf[88] asks why you did not give

---

[86] Nessmüller, Hungarian wine from Neszmély; see also Heft 10, Blatt 16r.—KH/TA

[87] Sketches for "Et vitam venturi" and "Et sepultus est" in the Credo of the *Missa solemnis.*—KH/TA

[88] Probably Prince Liechtenstein's librarian Wolf; see Heft 3, Blatt 52r.—KH/TA

the Variations by Archduke Rudolph[89] to Artaria. // They were already promised to Artaria. [//] [Blatt 35r] Is Diabelli[90] also waiting for 2 manuscripts? //

<He believes> [He] presently has no position. // He is retired. //

JANSCHIKH: Are you still thinking about the concert during Lent?[91] //

JOSEPH CZERNY: I already found a copy at Peters's. [//] [Blatt 35v] The Censor does not allow it. //

Peters says that your nephew's examination turned out well. // One is always happiest when working. [//]

[Blatt 36r]

OLIVA [possibly at the *Kameel*, Bogner Gasse; shortly after 7 p.m.[92] on Tuesday, December 21]: Yesterday [Monday, December 20], I was in the Plankengasse on the Neuer Markt[93] about 8 o'clock. I spoke to Peters.

I now leave [my apartment] at 9 o'clock every day except Sunday. Today I would like to show you the place where I can be found during the days.[94] //

The charming proprietor[95] told me that you were at his place on Sunday [December 19] and had really enjoyed yourself. [//] [Blatt 36v]

---

[89] This concerns the *Aufgabe, von Ludwig van Beethoven gedichtet, vierzig Mal verändert und ihrem Verfasser gewidmet von seinem Schüler R. E.H.* [Rudolph Erzherzog] (Forty Variations on a Theme by Beethoven), published by Steiner in Vienna in 1819. Both Artaria and Steiner had stated that they were willing to print the work. See Thayer-Deiters-Riemann, IV, pp. 166–168.—KH/TA

[90] Anton Diabelli (1781–1858), pianist, composer, and music publisher. After apprenticeship with Sigmund Anton Steiner, he founded, with Pietro Cappi, the firm of Cappi & Diabelli on the Kohlmarkt, No. 300, on December 10, 1818. From 1824, he had his own firm as Diabelli & Co. Nos. 300 and 301 were combined as No. 281 in 1821. See Frimmel, *Handbuch*, I, pp. 107–108; Willi Kahl, "Diabelli, Anton," *MGG*, vol. 3, cols. 388–391; Clive, pp. 89–90; Thayer-Deiters-Riemann, III, p. 500; Weinmann, *Wiener Musikverleger*, p. 17; Behsel, p. 9.—KH/TA

[91] Janschikh's recurring refrain must have irritated Beethoven!—TA

[92] Oliva had just recently begun his job at the firm of Nathan Mayer & J.G. Landauer (wholesale silk and linen merchants), Untere Bäckerstrasse No. 798 [renumbered as 752 in 1821]. Combining the information here with what he told Beethoven on Blatt 62r below, his hours there were roughly 9 to 12, then a dinner break and back to work until 7 p.m. Therefore, this entry would have been made after 7 p.m. on Tuesday, December 21.—TA

[93] Heinrich Seelig's grocery and wine shop *Zur Stadt Triest*, on the corner of the Neuer Markt and Plankengasse, No. 1124 [renumbered as 1060 in 1821].—KH/TA

[94] This does not take place until Tuesday, December 28; see Blatt 62r below.—TA

[95] The original German reads "Herr Kaufmann," literally "Mr. Merchant," but consistent with terminology sometimes used for the *Triest*'s proprietor, Heinrich Seelig. For conversations during the afternoon or evening in question, see Blätter 26v–33v.—KH/TA

He[96] very much praises Karl in his examination. // I would [like] to be paid, but you must now pay Kudlich a trifle. // About 2 fl. 3 kr. more. [//]

[Blatt 37r]

BEETHOVEN:
 Hauschker'l   [little Hauschka]
 Pauschker'l   [Bulky fellow]
 Sauker'l   [Piggish fellow]

OLIVA: Only [his] offended vanity, and not the subject itself, is spoken of at his place because he has been demoted. // Something is to happen, but it will be little. // Because of him,[97] I do not like to come here. [//]
 [End of get-together with Oliva; evening of Tuesday, December 21.]

[Blatt 37v]

PETERS **[probably at *Zur Stadt Triest*; midday dinner, ca. 2 p.m., on Wednesday, December 22]:**[98] Bernard is making corrections [for the *Wiener Zeitung*] and has promised to come here. // They have never yet been so beautiful. [//]

BERNARD **[joining them]:** Have you seen the *Schwan*[99] in its transformed state yet? The restaurant above it is new and elegantly appointed. [//]

[Blatt 38r]

PETERS **[continuing]:** Haven't you seen [lawyer] Bach? // It will still take 6 weeks for the appeal. //

---

[96] On Blatt 35v above Joseph Czerny had related a similar report, originally from Peters; therefore it is not clear whom Oliva is quoting.—TA

[97] Possibly a reference to Bernard, although the previous two sentences may also refer to Archduke Rudolph (see Oliva's similar entry on Blatt 4r). In Bernard's case, "here" may still refer to *Zur Stadt Triest*, Seelig's wine house on the Neuer Markt. In Rudolph's case, no counterpart can be identified.

Another, even stronger possibility in the context of Beethoven's wordplay immediately above, is Vincenz Hauschka, at whose apartment Beethoven had dinner on St. Stephan's Day, December 26 (see Blatt 54r below). We do not know what wine houses Hauschka might have frequented, but the *Kameel* (occasionally visited by Beethoven) was roughly halfway between Oliva's new workplace and Hauschka's residence. If Hauschka was demoted, it is not reflected in the contemporary *Hof- und Staats-Schematismen*.—TA

[98] This conversation goes through Blatt 42v.—TA

[99] As early as 1700 the restaurant *Zum weissen Schwan*, Kärntnerstrasse No. 1107 [renumbered as 1044 in 1821], was a well-known restaurant and overnight hotel. The property also faced Neuer Markt, as it does today.—KH/TA

BERNARD: I don't believe that they will allow it to come to an appeal. // If it comes to appeal, however, it is all the better because her [Johanna's] stupidity must then be to her shame. [//] [Blatt 38v] For Doctor Bach it is all the more preferable if [it is] appealed, because all the preliminary arrangements are such that she must approve everything that is reasonable. I shall go to see him on Saturday [December 25, Christmas Day!]. // The satisfaction consists of the fact that justice will be done to you. [//] [Blatt 39r: written vertically] It would also go no faster. Thereupon, he would likewise have had to place the same request. //

[Blatt 39v]

PETERS: My wife has not been in a wine house yet. [//] I told her that you would certainly be here, and that *Bernardus* was *non sanctus*. [//] Yesterday [Tuesday, December 21] between 8 and 10.[100] //

Just arrived by the express carriage.[101] //

I want to be pensioned and move with my wife to your place. I shall educate your nephew with all care. [Blatt 40r] If you want to make alterations to the good apartment, then we'll remain in the Lobkowitz house. //

BERNARD: On Sunday [December 26, St. Stephan's Day], we will eat dinner at Hauschka's.[102] //

Böhm[103] hopes that you might give him another sitting. //

Herr Schwarzböck,[104] choral director of the [Theater an der] Wien, is sitting next to you and asks me to tell you of his admiration. [Blatt 40v] At one time, earlier, he

---

[100] On Tuesday, December 21, shortly after 7 p.m., Beethoven had met Oliva elsewhere, possibly at the *Kameel* (see Blatt 36r above); or this may refer to Sydow's arrival, immediately below.—TA

[101] This may refer to Baron Theodor von Sydow, who arrived from Munich on Tuesday, December 21, and was staying in the City at the Matschaker Hof, No. 1157; see "Arrivals," *Wiener Zeitung*, No. 293 (December 23, 1810), p. 1171. Sydow is mentioned by name on Blatt 49r below.—TA

[102] The next Sunday was December 26, St. Stephan's Day. For conversations at dinner, see Blätter 54r–56r below.—TA

[103] (Joseph) Daniel Böhm (1794–1865), medal designer and sculptor, studied at the Viennese Akademie in 1813. In 1821–1822 and 1825–1829 he undertook journeys to Italy, and later became Chamber Medal Designer and Director of the Engravers Akademie at the Imperial Coinage Office in Vienna. Böhm fashioned a medal with Beethoven's portrait. See Clive, pp. 37–38; Frimmel, *Handbuch*, I, pp. 52–53; Frimmel, *Beethoven im zeitgenössischen Bildnis*, pp. 47–49 and plates 17–18; Thieme-Becker, vol. 4, p. 194. The medal is depicted in Frimmel, *Bildnis*, plate 17; Böhm's drawings of Beethoven out walking are reproduced in Bory, *Beethoven*, p. 198; Landon, *Documentary Study*, pp. 338–339; Comini, p. 43 and Figures 14 and 15. See also Heft 10, Blätter 7r and 56v–57v (the latter for a visit to Böhm's studio in the Wieden, Alleegasse 55, on March 29, 1820).—KH/TA

[104] Ludwig Schwarzböck (b. Hungary, 1782/83; d. Pesth, 1839), member (actor) of the Kärntnertor Theater from July 15, 1816, and Choral Director at the Theater an der Wien. He was also director of the Music School for Boys that Count Palffy established in 1821, but which lasted only until 1825. His daughter Beatrix, the wife of the actor Carl Fischer, was also a singer. Later, Schwarzböck was a

directed [the chorus] at an Akademie of yours [at the Theater] an der Wien, and is sincerely glad to see you again. //

In Bremen you are considered to be a god.[105] In the *Bremer Zeitung*, the day before yesterday, there was an inquiry about why the local [Viennese] newspapers are entirely silent about you, which is not true, though.[106] [//] [Blatt 41r]

Then the word is: *Sapientis est tacere*.[107] [//]

Serviteur, Serviteur, I am the secretary. //

Don't you hear anything from those around the Cardinal [Rudolph]? //

PETERS: W[_____] Krog.[108] //

BERNARD: Janitschek [Janschikh] declares that you would have to make 20,000 fl.[109] C.M. from a [concert] tour of two years. [//]

---

choral director and singing teacher at the German Theater in Pesth. See Bauer, *150 Jahre*, pp. 103–104; Böckh, *Merkwürdigkeiten*, p. 380; *Portrait-Katalog*, p. 355; Wurzbach, vol. 32, pp. 320–321; Gugitz, Conscriptions-Bögen, p. 259.—KH/TA

[105] Largely through the efforts of Wilhelm Christian Müller (1752–1831), music director at Bremen's Cathedral and organizer of the city's concert series, as well as his daughter Elise (d. 1849), Bremen had become the center of a Beethoven cult some years before. They enlisted the aid of historian-theologian Ernst Moritz Arndt (1769–1860), who taught at the University of Bonn, in locating Beethoven's baptismal record of December 17, 1770. In conjunction with the perceived birthday on December 17, 1819, they collaborated with Dr. Carl Iken, editor of the *Bremer Zeitung*, sending to Beethoven a poem and an essay by Iken, as well as a second poem by a young local admirer, totaling ten pages. See Albrecht, *Letters to Beethoven*, No. 266.—TA

[106] The *Bremer Zeitung* of December 8, 1819, said: "The public examination at the local *Musikschule*, which presently draws 65 pupils of both sexes, took place again recently. Why, though, does one so seldom hear anything by the greatest composer of our time, the superb Beethoven? Strange—he himself is deaf, and people are dumb [silent] about him! Could it be true, then, that the Viennese find his music not to their taste? That can hardly be believed, because even the English have presented him with gifts and rewarded him in a princely fashion. Let us hope, though, that the Viennese newspapers will occasionally give us reports about this rare virtuoso!"

Bernard's reference to "the day before yesterday" is surely meant in terms of the December 8 issue of the *Bremer Zeitung*, which must have arrived in Vienna two days before this entry was made, seemingly on December 21. On December 29 or 30 Bernard asked whether Beethoven had heard from Bremen (see Blätter 67v–68r).—KH/TA

[107] A wise man is usually silent.—KH

[108] Schünemann (in his incomplete World War II-era edition of the *Konversationshefte*) gives the following possibilities: (1) Fr[an]z Georg von Krogh, lieutenant colonel, who died at Cappeln [Kappeln, Schleswig-Holstein, west side of Schlei inlet] in 1830; and (2) Fr[iedrich] Ferdinand von Krogh, who published several literary works and died in Hadersleben in 1829 (from Schmidt, *Neuer Nekrolog*, vols. 7 and 8). Also (3) Franz Krog, a perfume manufacturer in Vienna (from Redl, 1820, p. 177). See the term "Grog," possibly a drink, in Heft 8, Blatt 64r.—KH/TA

[109] The German edition gives the currency as "Gl." (Gulden?).—TA

OLIVA: I would also like to go with you.[110] [//]

[Blatt 41v]

PETERS: Krog. [//] Bernard is of the opinion that the co-guardian is left behind. //

BERNARD: On Saturday [December 25], on holy Christmas, we are to have dinner at Janitschek's [Janschikh's].[111] //

Janitschek believes that Rupprecht[112] would now resolve [to go] on a tour with you. [//] [Blatt 42r] I think that he's a worthless person, whose physiognomy is completely debased and without shame. I believe that he himself thinks badly of his

---

[110] The level-headed Oliva seldom associated with Bernard and his circle, so he may not have been present on this occasion, but instead may have added this comment at the bottom of the page as he leafed through the book at a later meeting with Beethoven.—TA

[111] For this awkward occasion see Blätter 47v–54r below.—TA

[112] Johann Baptist Rupprecht (1776–1846), writer, and Book Censor, became one of Vienna's most prominent horticulturists. Earlier in the 1810s, as a municipal merchant, he had lived in the City, Köllnerhof, No. 784 [renumbered as 738 in 1821], with his wife Elisabeth (b. 1780). By this time he may already have lived in his own house in Gumpendorf, Hauptstrasse No. 53 [renumbered as 54 in 1821, remained 54 in 1830], where he organized flower exhibitions each year. In 1829 the house was listed under Elisabeth's name, as were five lots in the adjacent Marchettigasse (as her *Baustelle*), doubtless the location of an extensive commercial nursery (Behsel, p. 128). He was a member of the Agricultural Society in Vienna, as well as many learned and agricultural societies in Austria and abroad.

In 1814–1815 Beethoven had set Rupprecht's *Merkenstein*, a nostalgic poem in three stanzas in praise of Schloss Merkenstein, a Romantic castle ruin near Baden, not once, but twice! The first, a sixteen-bar solo song (E-flat major, 6/8) with piano accompaniment, WoO 144, dates from November–December, 1814; Beethoven noted in his diary that it was written on December 22. It appeared at the end of 1815 as a musical supplement in *Selam, An Almanac for Lovers of Variety, for the Leap Year 1816*, edited by Ignaz Franz Castelli, and printed by Anton Strauss (the same firm that printed Schickh's *Wiener Zeitschrift*). The second setting, a fourteen-bar vocal duet (F major, 3/8) with piano accompaniment, was sketched with the first, but was worked out only early in 1815. It appeared from Steiner & Co. in September, 1816, as Op. 100, with a dedication to Count Joseph Karl von Dietrichstein-Hollenburg-Finkenstein (1763–1825), who owned Merkenstein (see Wurzbach, vol. 3, pp. 296–297). Dietrichstein had been Vice Chancellor of the United Bohemian, Austrian, and Gallician Chancelleries, and lived at Herrengasse No. 33 [1819 numbering] (see *Hof- und Staats-Schematismus*, 1808, p. 175). When he died in 1825, he was last of his line, and Merkenstein castle was sold. For members of the more commonly cited Dietrichstein-Proskau-Leslie branch, see Heft 4, Blätter 23r–23v.

During this period (1819–1820), Rupprecht still contributed poems and translations to Schickh's *Wiener Zeitschrift*. See Frimmel, *Handbuch*, II, pp. 91–92; Thayer-Deiters-Riemann, IV, p. 439; Thayer-Forbes, pp. 863–864; Clive, pp. 297–298; Wurzbach, vol. 27, pp. 272–274; Kinsky-Halm, pp. 277–278, 310, 613–614; Anderson, No. 1022; as well as Heft 11, Blatt 41r, and Heft 12, Blatt 64v.

N.B.: The *Hof- und Staats-Schematismus*, 1819, notes a potential source of confusion: I, p. 279, lists a Johann Ruprecht, k.k. Amtsrath, Bürgerspital No. 1166. He was in the *Hofkriegsrath*, whose head, though many echelons above Ruprecht, was Prince Carl von Schwarzen*burg*. Vol. II, p. 317, however, listed Johann Baptist Rupprecht (no address given), a merchant in Vienna, who was also a member of the Gesellschaft of Agriculture in Moravia. The latter is the Rupprecht meant here.—KH/TA

superior, as much as I have been able to determine from several [of his] statements.[113]
//

I am going with Peters. [//]

BEETHOVEN: "*Van* specifies nobility and patrician status [Blatt 42v] *only* if it comes between two proper names, for example, Bentink Van Dieperheim, Hooft Van Vreeland," etc., etc. One would obtain the best information about this *insignificant significance* from Netherlanders. [//]

BERNARD: There is only Pomeranian goose at the boarding house.[114] [//]
[End of dinner with Bernard and Peters; Wednesday, December 22.]

[Blatt 43r]

BEETHOVEN **[probably at his apartment;[115] late morning of Thursday, December 23]**:
Night stool [toilet].
Chests for items that now hang on wooden pegs,[116] or also the clean linens in these. First one has to take the design from the present chest of drawers.
1 or 2 chests for linens (N.B.) and clothes.
Writing-box.
N.B.: a sofa
A hanging chandelier; or, instead of that, several night lights. [Blatt 43v]
Machine on which glasses, coffee cups, etc.
15 fl. taken from it today.
Tomorrow, new books.
[in a coffee or wine house, reading newspapers; probably late afternoon of Thursday, December 23:]

---

[113] Beethoven had known Rupprecht since at least November 1814 and seemingly continued to value his talents as a poet and proposed translator of his Scottish Songs well into 1820. Bernard's reference to Rupprecht's physiognomy is unclear. Although married, Rupprecht may have been a visually obvious homosexual who wrote poetry and managed a flower show! If Beethoven still valued him for his talents after knowing him for at least five years, he may have found Bernard's remarks (and by extension Janschikh's presence) irritating, making the prospect of Christmas dinner with them unpleasant.—TA

[114] Possibly disgusted by Bernard's condemnation of Rupprecht and the implicit agreement on Janschikh's part, Beethoven may have tried to beg out of Christmas dinner at Janschikh's by saying that he would simply go to the boarding house where Bernard and Oliva (separately) often ate their early afternoon meals. Bernard, then, may have tried to persuade him to join them at Janschikh's by pointing out the relatively meager fare at the boarding house.—TA

[115] It is not immediately apparent *which* apartment.—TA

[116] This is obviously a "working" list of furniture; the entries concerning the *Kasten* (chests) are partially crossed out.—KH/TA

Potatoes at 2 fl. W.W. per peck, No. 1187 on the Graben; inquire at the house manager's between 10 and 12 in the mornings, and afternoons between 3 and 6 o'clock.[117] [Blatt 44r]

62

35

OLIVA [probably at the *Birne* on the ground floor of Beethoven's new apartment on the Glacis;[118] probably shortly after noon on Friday, December 24]:[119] There are fresh pickled lampreys.[120] // He [the proprietor?] says that when Bernard ordered them for you, there was always oil with them. //

How do you want to arrange it with Blöchlinger? I don't want to pay more? Why should you hinder yourself in other ways? It is a sure thing for him. Also, I believe that he will accept it without further ado. [//] [Blatt 44v] Why, then? It is enough if he gets it each month in advance. Otherwise you really don't know which deposition will hit you. // For now, leave it at the old one's.[121] //

The proprietor says that the carpenter Götz in the Schauffler Gasse,[122] next to the Burg, is the best. [//] [Blatt 45r]

Concerning Blöchlinger, just tell me if you want me to .... // I will come tomorrow [Christmas Day] about 1 o'clock.[123] // This evening, I cannot; therefore I will go now, and because it is getting late for me, I'll eat in the City.[124] Just tell me now what you want at Blöchlinger's and I'll go immediately. //

---

[117] See the *Intelligenzblatt*, No. 293 (December 23, 1819), p. 1217 (Advertisements). The same advertisement had also appeared in the *Intelligenzblatt*, No. 291 (December 21, 1819), p. 1196, and would appear again on December 27, 1819.—KH/TA

[118] For the location, see two indicators on Blatt 45r below.—TA

[119] The weather had been below freezing for several days, but on Friday afternoon, December 24, the temperature rose to 3 degrees Reaumur (ca. 38 degrees F.) and remained above freezing through December 27—thus relatively pleasant weather (if relatively consistently overcast, with nighttime snow showers) for Beethoven and his friends to walk around town. On December 28 the temperatures headed downwards, and, from January 1, were well below freezing and, by January 9–10, bitterly cold. See *Wiener Zeitung*, No. 292 (December 22, 1819), p. 1167, through No. 8 (January 12, 1820), p. 31 for daily weather reports.—TA

[120] *Bricken*: lampreys (sucking eels), baked and pickled in vinegar. See Campe, vol. 1, p. 620.—KH/TA

[121] Unclear: Oliva could also be telling Beethoven to leave something in the old apartment in the Ballgasse for now.—TA

[122] Master carpenter Joseph Götz in the Schaufflergasse No. 31 [renumbered as 24 in 1821] had a shop arranged with all varieties of wooden furniture. See Redl, 1822, p. 220; Behsel, p. 11.—KH/TA

[123] Therefore, Beethoven was projecting a visit to see nephew Karl at Blöchlinger's Institute at 1 p.m. on Christmas Day.—TA

[124] This wording indicates that this conversation took place in a suburb.—TA

[returning later from Blöchlinger's Institute:]
She is asking you for the money for 3 days of milk, 24 kreuzer. Then she is asking for some money in advance for the holidays,[125] about 3 fl. [//] [Blatt 45v]

There is nothing more to be paid at Blöchlinger's except small expenses for which he will again give you a bill. // He[126] was not well and I had to wait for over a quarter of an hour until His Lordship became visible; therefore I am late. //

30 fl. per year results in 5 kreuzer per day. [//] [Blatt 46r]

BEETHOVEN [**initial computations**]:

30	6
30	60
30	6
50	6
	6

OLIVA [**writing over them**]: His name is Petz.[127] //

I cannot say for certain whether I can come [to Christmas dinner at Janschikh's] tomorrow evening. It has occurred to me that I was invited halfheartedly, when I cannot refuse it. If I don't come, how shall we arrange it concerning Sunday? // [Blatt 46v] If I am not at your place [in the Ballgasse] by 8 o'clock, then I am not coming at all.[128] [//]

BEETHOVEN [at *Zur Stadt Triest*; later on **Friday, December 24**]: From January 3 on, the usual interest on the bank shares pays 30 fl. per bank share per year. [//] Whoever has 20 shares* is a "shareholder."[129] //

---

[125] Possibly the entire period between Christmas and Epiphany, judging from the amount, if the 24 kreuzer figure represented milk money for a single day, rather than three. Such a conversation would have taken place at the *Birne* or elsewhere in Beethoven's apartment house on the Glacis.—TA

[126] It is not clear whether this refers to Blöchlinger (above) or Petz (below).—TA

[127] It is not clear who is meant here.—KH

[128] In the event, Oliva did not accompany Beethoven to Christmas dinner at the Janschikhs', but Bernard did—probably following much the same schedule as Oliva projected, essentially meeting Beethoven at his Ballgasse apartment (close by for either Bernard or Oliva) at 8 p.m., then walking south to the Janschikhs' in the Landstrasse, arriving at about 8:30 p.m.—TA

[129] The *Wiener Zeitung*, No. 294 (December 24, 1819), p. 1173, reported: "that for the collected bank share letters, which are based on deposits that were made after March 31, 1819: beginning from January 3, 1820, at the bank share cashier's office, that payment of the usual annual dividends can be withdrawn at thirty Gulden per bank share, which belong proportionately to them from the date of the original deposit until December 31, 1819." An appended list indicated the names of fifty "Aktionaere" shareholders who had to possess at least twenty bank shares in order to be accepted on the Bank's Board, in addition to the fifty major shareholders already chosen.

The person who owned twenty bank shares would therefore make 600 fl. per year in interest, an amount equivalent to the salary of an established orchestral player at the Kärntnertor Theater at this time.—KH/TA

BERNARD: Seelig [the proprietor] will place something before you that you are to eat up very quietly.[130] //

BEETHOVEN [**clarifying his previous entry**]: *in the Bank is a shareholder. [//]

[**Christmas Day, Saturday, December 25, 1819, ca. 1 p.m.: Beethoven (as projected on Blatt 45r) presumably visits nephew Karl at Blöchlinger's Institute; no conversation book entries survive from that occasion.**]

[Blatt 47r]

[**Christmas Day, Saturday, December 25, ca. 8 p.m.: Beethoven has presumably walked from the Josephstadt to his old apartment in the Ballgasse. Bernard possibly meets him there and gives him the news concerning his meeting with lawyer Bach. Then the two walk south, leave the City by the Carolinentor, across the Glacis, then east on Rabengasse to Janschikh's residence at the northeast corner of Ungargasse and Bockgasse (later Beatrixgasse).[131] It is also possible that Bernard just pulled Beethoven aside after he arrived at Janschikh's by about 8:30 p.m.**]

BERNARD:[132] Peters is ill; therefore I was alone. The friendly Doctor [Bach] sends his best regards. There was a Board of Inquiry where the Queen of the Night[133] was summoned. She declared that she would gladly submit to this directive. Otherwise she admitted very little, [Blatt 47v] and will gladly submit to everything. If the Magistrat should not agree, then the Doctor will proceed most rigorously at the Appellate Court, and put the Magistrat completely to shame. He had me tell you [Blatt 48r] that he will do everything possible to be equal to your trust. You just need to have patience for a few more days. //

---

[130] Because it was Christmas Eve, Seelig probably made a special or favorite dish that was otherwise not on his menu, just for Beethoven, and did not want it broadcast around the restaurant.—TA

[131] This is the building where Beethoven would live at the time of the premiere of the Ninth Symphony in May, 1824.—TA

[132] The following conversation (to Blatt 53r) may have taken place on Saturday, December 25, 1819, since Bernard had designated this day for his visit to Dr. Bach (announced on Blatt 38v) as well as the date projected in the invitation to Beethoven (Blatt 41v).—KH

[133] Probably the hearing date at the Magistrat on December 14, 1819, to which Beethoven's sister-in-law Johanna (whom he repeatedly called the "Queen of the Night") was invited, since she had remained absent from the *Tagsatzung* (Assembly) on December 7, 1819 (see Heft 3, Blatt 12r). See Thayer-Deiters-Riemann, IV, p. 565; Thayer-Forbes, pp. 750–752.—KH/TA

BEETHOVEN: Von [*sic*] Himmel hoch, da komme ich her [From Heaven above to Earth I come].[134] [//]

[Blatt 48v]

BERNARD: Your Mass has been performed in Graz, and delighted everyone.[135] // The early services are now at <10 o'clock> 5 o'clock in the morning. //

ANTONIA JANSCHIKH [**proposing a toast**]:[136] To Weissenbach's health. // Flattering remarks have had a very bad effect on him. // [Blatt 49r]

BERNARD: On account of his poem "Das alte und neue Rom" [The Old and New Rome],[137] Grillparzer has received a reprimand from the Police Minister, because, as a Christian, he should not have written such a poem; because he, as an I.R. pensioner

[134] Whether quoting a well-known Christmas hymn by Luther himself or likening his own arrival to Christ's, Beethoven might have been having his own joke in Janschikh's household, where the prevailing religious sentiment seems to have been fairly liberal. Indeed, much of the following conversation, at least as the staunchly Catholic Bernard carries it forward, involves Protestants who have become Catholic (which might seem to favor Catholicism), but whose fortunes have subsequently declined (thus possibly their rewards for conversion).—TA

[135] Bernard calls the city Grätz. Beethoven's Mass in C, Op. 86, was performed in Graz's Church of the Brothers of Mercy (Barmherzige Brüder) at a St. Cecilia Festival on Friday, November 26, 1819. (St. Cecilia's actual feast day had been Monday, November 22.) Schickh's *Wiener Zeitschrift* reported: "The wondrously lovely setting of the Mass, in the good performance, did not fail to make an effect in the responsive hearts of the boys and girls, as well as the cultivated men and women here. The submissive *Adoramus te* after the rousing *Benedictus te* and the exulting *Laudamus te* hit the praying people like an electric shock; they all felt the worship in submissiveness proper to the Supreme Being. The striking *Miserere, Miserere* was all the more touching, since the related tones were already, but not easily, known to the listener. See *Wiener Zeitschrift*, No. 153 (December 23, 1819), pp. 1265–1266.—KH/TA

[136] From the content of the entries here and on Blatt 41v, also coordinated with those on Heft 6, Blätter 67r–68r, and Heft 7, Blätter 42r–43r, one can conclude with fair certainty that the writer is Antonia Janschikh.—KH/TA

[137] Probably Grillparzer's poem "Die Ruinen des Campo Vaccino in Rom." Grillparzer had received a five-year income for his tragedy *Sappho*, which he used for a journey to Gastein and Italy. Here he wrote the poem upon the ruins of Campo Vaccino, which was subsequently rejected by the Censor in 1819, and was cut out of the *Aglaja*, in which it had already been printed. The lines that were understood as an attack on Pope Pius VII (ruled 1800–1823) were:

Must you still carry the cross
On which, Lordly One, you die!
Take it away, this Holy symbol!
All the world yea belongs to you;
Everywhere, except where these Departed lie,
Stand everywhere, just not here.

This was a reference to the cross that Pius VII had had placed on the Colosseum in the memory of the Christian martyrs. See Goedeke, vol. 8, p. 320.—KH

[appointee], should have taken that fact into consideration; and because he had had the honor of traveling to Italy in the Emperor's retinue. //

Your brother [Johann] is here and has bought a large estate near Krems; he also wants to buy a house here. Your neighbor has spoken to him. // Your brother has really become an Italian.[138] [//] [Blatt 49v]

Sydow[139] has also brought you regards from Linz. //

Wähner[140] looks a great deal like Doctor Luther.[141] //

I have a distich on him [Werner?] among the "Inscriptions" in the *Aglaja*; he took it so badly, that he in return made one about me.[142] [//] [Blatt 50r]

---

[138] Beethoven's brother Nikolaus Johann van Beethoven (1776–1848) had bought the estate *Wasserhof* at Gneixendorf, north of Krems, on August 2, 1819. Johann had owned an apothecary's shop in Linz and had made enough money from war profiteering in Army medical supplies that he could buy the aforementioned estate in relatively remote Gneixendorf, which would have cost him less than a similar farm and mansion house close to Vienna. The epithet "Italian" probably refers to Johann's love for the tasteless display of luxury, which irritated Beethoven. See Frimmel, *Handbuch*, I, pp. 172–174; Thayer-Deiters-Riemann, IV, p. 165; Thayer-Forbes, pp. 739–740; Clive, pp. 24–26.—KH/TA

[139] The wording of the entry might imply Sydow's possible association with brother Johann in Linz. Baron Theodor von Sydow (b. Berlin, March 13, 1773; d. Graz, April 8, 1855), poet and orator, was in the Prussian Army by 1806, belonged to the Lützow Corps (immortalized in poetry by Theodor Körner and in music by Weber) in 1813, and then went with Karl von Holtei to Graz.

On February 8 (Ash Wednesday), 1815, Sydow participated with two declamations on a Foundlings Benefit concert of mixed media, given at the Kärntnertor Theater by the Society of Noble Women: first "The Return of the Adored Father of His Country (Emperor Franz) to His Residence (Vienna)," and later "Saul and David" by Mahlmann. See *Allgemeine musikalische Zeitung* 17, No. 13 (March 29, 1815), cols. 216–217.

Sydow published a six-line poem "Der Tugend-Bund. Impromptu" in the *Wiener Zeitschrift* 1, No. 4 (January 25, 1816), p. 31. Schünemann mentions a Baron Sydow, named in the Secret Police records in Linz in 1817 and 1818. Sydow had arrived in Vienna from Munich on Tuesday, December 21, 1819, and was staying in the City, at the Matschakerhof, Spiegelgasse/Dorotheergasse No. 1157 [renumbered as 1091 in 1821]; see Peters's possible note of the fact on Blatt 39v above.

See Wurzbach, vol. 41, p. 87; *Deutsches Literatur Lexikon*, vol. 21 (2001), cols. 489–490; *Wiener Zeitung*, No. 293 (December 23, 1819), p. 1171; Behsel, p. 32.—KH/TA

[140] Bernard may have spoken aloud to Beethoven, who initially confused Wähner with Werner, which led to the discussion of both.—TA

[141] The editor Friedrich Wähner (see entry inside front cover of Heft 5 above), who edited the *Aglaja* and collaborated in the *Wiener Zeitschrift*, had been a Protestant minister before coming to Vienna in 1818. See also the epigram concerning Wähner on the inside of the back cover (Blatt 71r). On Saturday, February 26, 1820 (Heft 8, Blatt 14v), Bernard notes that Wähner is "very plump." Most portraits of Luther likewise portray him as plump.—TA

[142] This possibly refers to the distich dedicated to Zacharias Werner in the "Inschriften (Inscriptions). Under Portraits of German Poets," *Aglaja* (1820): "Werner. Sparsely coming into flower, late-blooming roses. The landscape vanishes in fog, the misty air of autumn touches gently. Warm me, flame of the hearth!" Whether the distich written against Bernard in reply was ever printed remains open to question.—KH

Wallishausser[143] visited me today and said that Schlegel[144] does nothing but eat, drink, and read the *Bible*. He thinks that Werner[145] will become crazy, because no one goes to his sermons any more. //

Fri[e]drich Leopold[146]—I knew him well. While I was in Münster, he usually invited me to visit him three times a week. // [Blatt 50v]

Ch. [?][147] Trout. //

That was an excellent family. When I departed, the countess sent me the Thomas à Kempis[148] with a charming inscription, as a remembrance. [//] [Blatt 51r]

This Fall at Prince Schwarzenberg's,[149] 15,000 rabbits, pheasants, and partridges were shot[150] within 4 days. //

[143] Johann Baptist Wallishausser the Younger (1790–1831), well-known book dealer and publisher, lived on the Hoher Markt, No. 584 [renumbered as 543 in 1821]. Bernard spelled his name "Wallishauser." In his conversation book jottings from newspaper advertisements, Beethoven had already noted books available from Wallishausser, and would do so again in the future. See Böckh, *Wiens lebende Schriftsteller*, p. 400; Wurzbach, vol. 52, pp. 273–274; Behsel, p. 17.—KH/TA

[144] Friedrich von Schlegel (1772–1829). Friedrich was the younger brother of August Wilhelm von Schlegel (1767–1845), known, among other things, for his German translations of Shakespeare. Sons of Lutheran pastor Johann Adolf Schlegel, August Wilhelm remained largely in northern Germany, teaching at Jena and, especially, Bonn, while Friedrich married Dorothea (1763–1839) the eldest daughter of Moses Mendelssohn. In 1808 Friedrich and Dorothea converted to Catholicism, and in 1809 he was appointed Court Secretary at the headquarters of Archduke Karl in Vienna.—KH/TA

[145] Originally a Protestant, Zacharias Werner became Catholic in 1810 and a priest in 1814, then came to Vienna, where he combined political views in his popular sermons. He often seemed mentally unstable. See Heft 4, Blatt 42v.—TA

[146] Friedrich Leopold, Count zu Stolberg-Stolberg (1750–1819), member of the Göttingen Dichterbund (Poets League), published *Plato, Auserlesene Gespräche* (Selected Speeches), translated by Friedrich Leopold, Count zu Stolberg, in three parts (Königsberg, 1796/97). Encouraged by Princess Galitzin, he converted to Catholicism in 1800, and thereafter moved to Münster to be near the Princess. After the death of his first wife, Agnes von Witzleben (1761–1788), he married Countess Sophie Charlotte Eleonore von Redern (b. 1765). See *Allgemeine Deutsche Biographie*, vol. 56, pp. 350–352; Kayser, vol. 4, p. 358.

Bernard told Beethoven the same story on March 29, 1820 (see Heft 10, Blatt 66v).—KH/TA

[147] Possibly C.h. or C.H., meaning *Confession Helvetica*, the Reformed Protestant religion.—TA

[148] Presumably the *Imitation of Christ*, the most famous work of the medieval theologian Thomas à Kempis (Thomas Hemerken, from Kempen in the Rheinland, ca. 1380–1471).—KH

[149] Prince Joseph Johann Nepomuk Schwarzenberg (1769–1833), brother of Princess Caroline Lobkowitz (d. 1816), married to Princess Caroline Iris von Arenberg-Archot, and Privy Councillor since 1804. He was second Deputy from Bohemia at the United Reparations and Repayments Deputation, and lived on Neuer Markt, No. 1118 [renumbered as 1054 in 1821]. See Gräffer-Czikann, IV, p. 617; *Hof- und Staats-Schematismus*, 1819, I, p. 362; Wurzbach, vol. 33, pp. 86–88; Behsel, p. 31.—KH/TA

[150] In the original manuscript, the German word here was *geschoffen*, but the meaning was probably *geschossen* (shot), possibly an intentional play on the handwritten f and the handwritten "long" s. On a similar theme, as late as February 23, 1827, Beethoven's brother noted: "The day before yesterday, there was a brilliant ball at Geymüller's; the asparagus alone cost 6,000 fl. W.W." (Heft 138, Blatt 23v).—KH/TA

Mlle. Weber[151] is a young actress in the Court Theater; she now has much to do. Therefore, one asks: why is Mamsell Weber now coming up in this way? Thereupon it can be   [Blatt 51v]   answered: because the others are going down [i.e., giving birth].[152] [//]

[Frau] Karsch;[153] Sophie Brentano;[154] Friedrike Brunn, née Münter.[155]   //   [pg. 170→]

In England, there is a sect whose members obligate themselves to eat nothing but vegetables. //

Women are always only *negative* as poets, and in the first lines I can already tell whether it originated from a woman. [//]

Wieland has died.[156] [//] [Blatt 52r]

I have written the following Wine Song:

Say, why is the Moon so pale,
And how the frogs and toads are singing,
O so plaintively in the pond?
They have drunk water![157]

[151] Born in ca. 1803, Louise (Aloysia) Weber, daughter of Thomas Weber, a municipal wigmaker, had become an actress at the Burgtheater in 1816, playing naïve and sentimental roles. Her first role, on July 26, 1816, had been Juliet in Shakespeare's *Romeo and Juliet*. She made guest appearances at the Hoftheater in Munich in 1822, returned to the Burgtheater, and died of a premature stroke at age twenty-three at her father's home, *Zum Wolf in der Au*, Salzgries No. 214, on October 19, 1826. See *Hof- und Staats-Schematismus*, 1820, I, p. 130; Flüggen, *Biographisches Bühnen-Lexikon*, p. 321; Totenbeschauprotokoll, 1826, W, fol. 42v (Wiener Stadt- und Landesarchiv).—KH/TA

[152] A play on words: *aufkommen* (to come up, to come into prominence) and *niederkommen* (to go down, to descend, to give birth). According to the research of Carol Padgham Albrecht (University of Idaho), Court opera singers (and probably actresses, by extension) customarily received five weeks of maternity leave.—TA

[153] Anna Louise Karsch (1722–1791), north German poet, grandmother of Wilhelmine von Chezy. She wrote poetry exclusively. See *Allgemeine Deutsche Biographie*, vol. 15, p. 421.—KH

[154] Sophie Brentano (1761–1806), author, daughter of a Count's secretary and high tax counselor Gotthelf Schubart. After her marriage to Friedrich Ernst Karl Mereau, she belonged to the literary circles in Jena. After their divorce in 1801, she married Clemens Brentano in 1803, and, a year later, went to Heidelberg. In 1792, Beethoven had set her poem "Feuerfarb," Op. 52. See *Allgemeine Deutsche Biographie*, vol. 21, pp. 420–421; Goedeke, vol. 6, p. 63.—KH

[155] Friederike Sophie Christiane Brun (1765–1835), author, came to Copenhagen at an early age with her father, the Pastor Münter. Here, in 1783, she married the Conference Councillor Brun, with whom she undertook numerous journeys through Europe. Since 1810 she had lived again in Copenhagen. See, Schmidt, *Nekrolog*, vol. 13, pp. 312–314.—KH

[156] See Heft 3, Blatt 41v, for identification. Ludwig Friedrich August Wieland, originally a pietistic Protestant, died in Jena on December 12, 1819. Bernard tells Beethoven the same news again the next day (Blatt 54r below).—KH/TA

[157] Bernard quotes this much of his poem again on Heft 6, Blätter 39v–40r.—TA

Recke.[158] [Blatt 52v][159]

But look at the Sun!
Can you perceive the moral?
It drinks wine on its course,
Then dips into the sea to cool itself.
Sun and Moon and frog and toad,
Away with water; let's drink wine!

[Blatt 53r] <She wanted to say that> she is very fond of you ....

ANTONIA JANSCHIKH:[160] <like your mother. [//] Back then. [//] Don't be so sad, otherwise I will be, too. [//] I hope that you will come to see us again very soon.>

[Blatt 53v]

WOLF:[161] The vinegar dealer[162] is coming in January. [//]

JANSCHIKH: *Bernardus non sanctus!* [Bernard: not a saint!] // [pg. 171➔]
 [**End of Christmas dinner at the Janschikhs'; Beethoven attempts to make an exit, possibly in the company of librarian Wolf.**]

---

[158] Elisa von der Recke, *née* von Medem (1754–1833), poet, influenced by Cagliostro, initially surrendered herself to religious enthusiasm. After 1784, under the influence of Nicolai, Bürger, and Stolberg, she turned away from this and wrote *Die entlarvte Cagliostro* (1787). She spent 1804 and 1807 in Italy with Christian August Tiedge. Beethoven had set Tiedge's "An die Hoffnung" twice: in 1804 (Op. 32) and again in 1813 (Op. 94). Böttiger published her *Diary of a Journey through Germany and Italy* (4 vols.) in 1815/17. Beethoven presumably met her in Teplitz in 1811. See Thayer-Deiters-Riemann, III, p. 276; Thayer-Forbes, pp. 513–514; Clive, pp. 278–279.—KH/TA

[159] Doodled sketches of two heads in profile in the upper left corner.—KH

[160] Already the subject of the foregoing potentially leering sentence, Frau Janschikh evidently grabbed the conversation book away from Bernard in order to clarify her own intentions, possibly as Beethoven was departing.—TA

[161] Johann Wolf, Prince Lichtenstein's librarian (see Heft 6, Blätter 49r–49v, for a strong circumstantial identification). If Johann Wolf had previously been an Imperial Book Inspector in Frankfurt, that would explain how he might have known Neberich, from nearby Mainz.—TA

[162] German, *der Essighändler*, presumably a joking wordplay on Adam Neberich's profession as wine dealer. The *Wiener Zeitung*, No. 14 (January 19, 1820), p. 55, reports the arrival (on January 17) of "Adam Neberich, merchant of Mainz, coming from Darmstadt." Beethoven had been acquainted with Neberich since at least March, 1816; see his letter to Franz Brentano of March 4, 1816 (Brandenburg, *Briefwechsel*, No. 914; Anderson, No. 619). The allusion here is to a one-act operetta, *Der Essighändler* by Giovanni Simone Mayr (1763–1845), among five new productions at the Theater in der Leopoldstadt in June, 1816. See *Allgemeine musikalische Zeitung* 18, No. 30 (July 24, 1816), col. 513.—KH/TA

WOLF [possibly walking home after leaving Janschikh's apartment; late on Christmas Day, Saturday, December 25]: As long as they are not printed, documents belong in archives and not in libraries. // You know, though, that Abbé Stadler is writing the History of Music in Austria? From the oldest times under Friedrich III[163] until our times. [//] Not only people born in Austria, but instead everyone who has written in Austria, will be covered. [//] [Blatt 54r]

His name is Hempfling.[164] //

[Wolf and Beethoven seemingly walk their separate ways home.]

BEETHOVEN [possibly at his apartment in the Ballgasse; morning of St. Stephan's Day, Sunday, December 26]:[165]

Chests for clothing.
Night stool [toilet].
Eating table. //

[St. Stephan's Day dinner at the residence of Vincenz Hauschka, City, No. 111,[166] across Herrengasse from the Cloister of the Schottenkirche.]

BERNARD [as above, at Hauschka's; presumably ca. 2 p.m. on Sunday, December 26]: Wieland died recently.[167] // Do you know the satirist Friedrich? He drowned himself in the Elbe in Hamburg.[168] [//]

[163] Wolf originally wrote "Friedrich IV," but then corrected the IV to III. For more on Stadler's projected history, see Heft 3, Blatt 52r. Friedrich III lived from 1415 to 1493. In a striking parallel, the coverage in George Grove's first edition of his *Dictionary of Music and Musicians* began in 1450.—KH/TA

[164] Probably Franz Hempfling (1761–1838), Prince Liechtenstein's Economic Councillor. See Heft 3, Blatt 32r.—TA

[165] St. Stephan's Day, the "second day of Christmas," was and is a national and religious holiday in Vienna.—TA

[166] Vincenz Hauschka, Treasury Councillor, Accountant, and amateur violoncellist in the Gesellschaft der Musikfreunde. He lived in the Melkerhof, Schottengasse No. 111 [renumbered as 103 in 1821]. Located between Herrengasse and the Mölkerbastei, the building was owned by Stift Melk. Any possible demotion in his position (Blatt 37r above) is not reflected in the *Hof- und Staats-Schematismen*. See also Böckh, *Merkwürdigkeiten*, p. 352, and Ziegler, *Addressen-Buch*, p. 112; Behsel, p. 4; Clive, pp. 153–154.—TA

[167] Bernard had told Beethoven the same thing the day before (see Blatt 51v above). Perhaps these notes were prompted by Beethoven's referring to or quoting from Wieland.—TA

[168] Theodor Heinrich Friedrich (1776–1819), dramatic poet and jurist. In 1806, he was councillor of the Provincial Court in Stettin, served in the Lützow Corps in 1813, and had lived in Hamburg since 1817. He drowned himself in the Elbe on December 12, 1819. See Goedeke, vol. 6, p. 391.—KH

[FRAU] WEISSENTHURN [?] [continuing social conversation]:[169] I was in Karlsbad for only one day, but I had read von der Recke's *Reise durch Deutschland* [Journey through Germany][170] only recently, and found this woman very charming. [//] [Blatt 54v] Are you coming to Marienbad[171] this coming summer? It is very inexpensive there. [//] Not as bad as is said; they have given *Das Waisenhaus*[172] very well. [//]

BERNARD: We are speaking about Wähner and his bravery. [//] Lucullus.[173] [//]
[after the meal proper:]
Hauschka asks whether you are full. [//] [pg. 172] [Blatt 55r] Menescher [wine].[174] //

[FRAU] WEISSENTHURN [?]: He is drinking no more wine now. [//] I have given it to him to take with him, and invite you to eat a piece of it at my place. [//]
[Beethoven presumably declines the invitation.]

BERNARD [continuing]: One must pay homage to the beautiful lady. //
[*Pater* Ignatius Thomas,] Prior of the Michaelerkirche. [//]
The question concerns Werner: will you set something by him to music?[175] [//]

---

[169] This round of conversations took place at Vincenz Hauschka's on December 26, 1819 (see Blatt 40r). Schünemann's opinion that this writer was Hauschka must be doubted, because Hauschka was on a "du" footing with Beethoven. See Brandenburg, Nos. 1026 (late 1816/early 1817) and 1882 (September 23, 1824); Anderson, Nos. 716 and 1309; no letters from Hauschka to Beethoven have survived.

The writer is possibly Johanna Franul von Weissenthurn (poet and Court actress; see Heft 3, Blatt 26r), since, according to Bernard's remark (Blatt 56r), she appears to have been a participant in this conversation and was connected with Hauschka (see Heft 6, Blatt 34v).—KH/TA

[170] For Recke, see Blatt 52r above.—TA

[171] Marienbad, Bohemian resort town, ca. 20 miles south-southeast of Karlsbad, noted for its cold waters and mud baths.—TA

[172] The Singspiel *Das Waisenhaus* (The Orphanage) by Joseph Weigl, dating from 1808.

[173] Lucius Licinius Lucullus (lived from about 117 B.C. to 58–56 B.C.), Roman general, fought Mithradates VI from 74 to 66 B.C., and defeated Tigranes in Armenia in 69 B.C. He was a gallant general, but handled his men badly, and, after his return to Rome in 66 B.C., lived in great extravagance.—TA

[174] *Menescher*: Méneser, fine Hungarian red dessert wine. See Hamm, p. 277; also Heft 9, Blatt 71v.—KH/TA

[175] Zacharias Werner (Protestant turned Priest), whose name also appears in a list of opera librettists prepared by Beethoven. Between 1792 to 1801, Werner entered into three marriages, each of which lasted only a short time. See *Allgemeine deutsche Biographie*, vol. 42, pp. 67–69; Thayer-Deiters-Riemann, IV, p. 5; Clive, p. 395.—KH/TA

[Blatt 55v] His three wives are still alive. // At the Congress [of Vienna], the Grand Duke of Weimar[176] voluntarily offered to deliver the pension. //

When do you believe that your Mass [*Missa solemnis*] will be performed? [//] [Blatt 56r] Frau v[on] Weissenthurn wishes to hear some of the ideas that you are using as the basis for your composition of the Mass. [//] *Gloria, incarnatus.* [//] For the soul. [//] We are saying that the usual church music has almost degenerated into operatic music.[177]

[At this point, Beethoven presumably departs from the dinner at Hauschka's, St. Stephen's Day, Sunday, December 26.]

[Blatt 56v]

BEETHOVEN **[presumably at a coffee house, possibly *Zur Stadt Triest*; on Monday, December 27]**: Dr. von Liederskron[178] in Erlangen, proprietor of a notable Institute. On the average, the cost for one student is around 450 fl. (Rhenish). [//]

JANSCHIKH: Otherwise are you well, and did you sleep well?[179] //

OLIVA: 1 fl. Rhenish is 550 [*sic*] kr.[180] [//] [Blatt 57r]
     10 kr. per *Lot* [½ ounce]. // Isn't he making any reservations? //
     I haven't been there in more than a month, and at that time no one said anything about you; in general, I restrain myself from speaking about your affairs with someone or anyone. //

---

[176] Karl August of Sachsen-Weimar-Eisenach (1757–1853) met Goethe in 1774, and in 1775 called him to Weimar. At the Congress of Vienna, his duchy was raised to the level of an archduchy, and enlarged to include Weida and Neustadt.—KH

[177] Beethoven was sensitive about discussing when the *Missa solemnis* (or any of his works) might be finished or performed. He might also have been sensitive about comparisons between operatic and church music, because his *Christ on the Mount of Olives* had been likened to operatic music fifteen years before. In any case, Beethoven may have found this turn in the conversation cause to depart Hauschka's.—TA

[178] Dr. Karl Leopold von Liederskron (actually Liederer von Liederskron), born in Grätz, had studied in Vienna and was at first involved with social life, and later served as a volunteer in the Campaigns of 1805 and 1809. In 1814 he went to Erlangen and founded a widely known educational institution that enjoyed the special support of King Max Joseph of Bavaria. Without the composer's knowledge or permission, publisher Breitkopf und Härtel dedicated the Choral Fantasy, Op. 80, to this monarch in 1811. Noted in *Die Erziehungsanstalt des Dr. von Liederskron zu Erlangen*, by its Board, Parents, and a number of the Students themselves (Erlangen, 1826); Vogel, pp. 146–148; Kinsky-Halm, p. 215.—KH/TA

[179] Wherever Beethoven was at the moment, Janschikh seems to have encountered him by chance. Janschikh's brief entry seems to imply that it was made the day after Beethoven ate Christmas dinner at his apartment. It also appears that Beethoven was already in the company of Oliva and did not encourage Janschikh to join them.—TA

[180] Oliva certainly meant either "50 kr." or "55 kr."—TA

His Highness [*Hoheit*: Archduke Rudolph] therefore does not behave himself very highly [*hoch*: in an elevated manner]? // [Blatt 57v] Was Bernard there, too?[181] You will finish the Mass for him, though? // Even now. //

The common way of thinking manifests this behavior. //

How, then, did he come by his money? //

If I cannot come tomorrow evening [Tuesday, December 28] before about 9 o'clock, and you want to go out [to the Josephstadt], where can I meet you? [//] [Blatt 58r] If you were to go to the *Hacken*[182] in the Josephstadt, I could find you there. // She would certainly come; if she weren't coming, she would have written you. We were of one mind that she *certainly* would come, and I consider her to be too upright that she would decide to the contrary without writing it. [//]

[Blatt 58v]

BEETHOVEN [**possibly at his apartment in the Ballgasse; probably morning of Tuesday, December 28**]:
   Blotting sand.
   Bookbinder.[183]
   Soap.[184] //

[**At *Zur Stadt Triest*, Tuesday, December 28. Beethoven seems to have visited the Archduke Rudolph, possibly without success, and then comes to the coffee house, seemingly in midafternoon, first joined by Peters, then Oliva. Janschikh joins them, then he and Peters depart, leaving Beethoven alone with Oliva.**]

PETERS [**as noted above**]: Fräulein Spitzenberger[185] played the 40 Variations by the Archduke [Rudolph] for me today. // I don't understand it. But it appears to be heavily corrected by you; even the critics want to declare that. //

[Blatt 59r]

---

[181] Probably a reference to the St. Stephan's Day dinner, where Bernard was present during a well-meaning, but probably irritating interrogation concerning Beethoven's progress on the *Missa solemnis*. This sequence suggests that Beethoven was complaining to Oliva about the incident.—TA

[182] See Blatt 6v above. The restaurant was located across Piaristengasse from the Piaristenkirche.—TA

[183] Original German: *Buchbinder*, the name of a prominent interpreter of Beethoven's piano works.—TA

[184] Under this an illegible word pressed into the paper with the nub of a pencil.—KH

[185] Perhaps the daughter of Baron Zesner von Spitzenberg. See *Hof- und Staats-Schematismus*, 1819, I, p. 69.—KH

PROPRIETOR SEELIG: The tankard: 1 fl. 48 [kr.]

BEETHOVEN: 30
                        24[186] //

PETERS [**continuing**]: Fürstenberg[187] showed me a letter where you signed yourself as "Selbstvertreter."[188] // Fürstenberg has the greatest joy in possessing the letter. [//] [Blatt 59v]

My two nephews give me more trouble than the princely pupils. // Considering his talent, your nephew would be recreation for me. //

OLIVA: None actually. [//]

JANSCHIKH: Have you seen Weissenbach's [work] as revised by Böhm at Schickh's? [//] Only the breath of life is missing, and Weissenbach lives and spins. [//] [Blatt 60r] Three words for superb [literary] composition: Error! Confusion! Inspiration! // For further compositions: *Abivit, Excessit, Erupit, Evasit.*[189] [//]

OLIVA: 4,000 Thaler are the equivalent of 15,000 fl. here [=W.W.?] [//] [Blatt 60v]

Fresh Venetian arsenal oysters are coming tomorrow [December 29] and every Wednesday. //

This improved version [of a play] was already given here a year ago & has very much displeased. // Auerbach's Keller in Leipzig.[190] // It also had to do with the Magistrat. [//] [Blatt 61r]

I told [the tailor] Lind that you need some nice black trousers; he sends word in passing, asking you just to come to him and he will take care of it immediately; it goes without saying that you are now embarrassed because of money. // 40 to 50. // The performance. [//]

---

[186] Beethoven originally wrote 12 rather than 24.—KH

[187] Friedrich Egon von Fürstenberg-Weitra (1774–1856) was High Ceremonial Master and Privy Councillor. From 1817 to 1825 and 1842 to 1853 he was president of the Gesellschaft der Musikfreunde, Assessor of the "Court Commission over the Imperial Court Council's Acts." In 1801 he married Princess Therese von Schwarzenberg. See *Hof- und Staats-Schematismus*, 1819, I, p. 221, and II, p. 290; Perger, p. 279.—KH

[188] See Heft 3, Blatt 26r.—TA

[189] This last is a quote from Cicero (106–43 B.C.); the first word is actually *Abiit*. There are several plausible translations, among them "He has left, absconded, escaped, and disappeared." In any case, Beethoven probably did not appreciate the slogans that Janschikh implied as models for his compositional process.—TA

[190] Auerbach's Keller, a noted tavern in Leipzig, dating from 1530, and the locale of a famous scene in Goethe's *Faust*, from which Beethoven extracted the "Song of the Flea," Op. 75, No. 3 (Leipzig: Breitkopf und Härtel, October, 1810), although the work had been sketched as early as 1791–1792.—TA

BEETHOVEN: *Geschichte der Teutschen* [History of the Germans], for Schools and [Blatt 61v] Self-Instruction, by Johann Heinrich Voss; Elberfeld [published] by Schaub. 18 Groschen.[191] [//]

[Blatt 62r]

OLIVA: I believe that the housekeeper will come anyway by Sunday or Monday [January 2 or 3]. //

I now want to show you where I can usually be found until 12 [noon] and then until 7 in the evening. The firm is called *Mayer und Landauer;*[192] they are wholesale dealers who do business in silk, in the Backerstrasse [*sic*]. [//]

[Late afternoon, Tuesday, December 28: Beethoven and Oliva leave the *Triest*, walk from Neuer Markt to Untere Bäckerstrasse 798, where Oliva's new job is, then to Lind's tailor shop on Hohe Brücke 149, intersection with Renngasse.]

[Blatt 62v]

LIND[193] **[writing with red pencil in his tailor shop, Hohe Brücke, with Oliva present; late afternoon of Tuesday, December 28]**: It will be all right in the wash. [//]

The most exact price is 10 fl. [//]

These come to 8 fl. 30 kr.

With *St.*,[194] 9 fl.

About 30 kr. cheaper.

It stretches because it is woven.

[Beethoven and Oliva leave Lind's tailor shop.]

[Blatt 63r]

[191] Excerpt from an advertisement in the *Augsburger Allgemeine Zeitung*, No. 278, Supplement No. 165 (October 5, 1819), p. 659: "*Geschichte der Deutschen für Schulen und den Selbstunterricht*, by Johann Heinrich Voss; Elberfeld: Johann Eckhardt Schaub … The history begins with the oldest times and goes to the Exile of Napoleon to St. Helena."—KH

[192] The firm of Nathan Mayer & J.G. Landauer had its "office and store with raw silk and linen in the Untere Bäckerstrasse No. 798 [renumbered as 752 in 1821], next to the Regensburger Hof [No. 797, renumbered as 751 in 1821], across from the *Weintraube* [No. 816, renumbered as 770 in 1821]" See Redl, 1820, pp. 21–22, and Behsel, p. 23.—KH/TA

[193] On the basis of Oliva's entry on Blatt 61r, master tailor Joseph Lind is accepted as the writer. Lind's shop and residence were on the east side of Hohe Brücke, No. 149 [renumbered as 142 in 1821], at the corner of Renngasse. See Frimmel, *Handbuch*, I, p. 364; Behsel, p. 5; Heft 2, Blätter 12r and 18v.—KH/TA

[194] Meaning of the abbreviation unclear.—TA

OLIVA [before entering his apartment in the Blutgasse; evening of Tuesday, December 28]: Give me a couple matches to light the candles; I forgot to buy some today. //

OLIVA [at an undetermined location, probably in the City;[195] probably between noon and 2 p.m.[196] on Wednesday, December 29]: A fiacre to Mödling gets 8 fl. because of the poor road; maybe you could get one for 7 fl. They don't want to drive with sleighs, because they don't know whether there are sleigh lanes on the country roads. [//] [Blatt 63v]

It is ready. //

Because of his thorough Theater reviews, Bernard is very much praised in the *Oppositionsblatt*.[197] //

If you want to send Ries a proprietary document for England, you must find me the formula that Thomson sent, and which I gave you for safekeeping. [//] [Blatt 64r] It would come attached on certain forms, about which I do not know by heart. //

Are you going to the Archduke again now?[198] & without compensation for your many troubles? // It is certain, however, that on account of his own honor, he *cannot* separate himself from you. Therefore you are not doing the right thing if you don't press for the stabilization of a complete income. [//] [Blatt 64v] It should be made known. // That is good and right;[199]—because his behavior must degrade him in everyone's eyes. // Through this series of years. // It remains a weakness that is not noble. // Press for that which is owed to you; & for what is certainly very commensurate with your services rendered. [//] [Blatt 65r] He doesn't believe that; therefore, that's the way he is. It also appears that his minions set his mind at rest about the break with you. //

There you are wrong; I drink nothing in the evening.[200] //

If you discourage [it], then who would have courage to do so? All the world

---

[195] Beethoven might have accompanied Oliva to the Born and Paumgartner boarding house in the *Rother Igel*, where Ries had a midday dinner contract.—TA

[196] Oliva's approximate dinner break from his new job; see Blatt 62r above.—TA

[197] In the *Oppositionsblatt, Weimarische Zeitung*, No. 269 (November 12, 1819), cols. 2149–2150, under the heading "Miscellen," there is a brief review of the "Journals in Vienna." Among other things, it says here: "The *Zeitschrift für Kunst, Literatur, Theater und Mode* provides pleasant and good items ... Among the complementary newspapers are the *Sammler* and the *Theaterzeitung* .... The reviews in both newspapers are worthwhile in other respects; Herr Bernard in the *Zeitschrift für Kunst*, etc., is, especially, a skillful reviewer."—KH

[198] This would suggest that these entries were made during daytime hours.—TA

[199] Original: *Das ist gut, und recht*—possibly an allusion to a response "Dignum et iustum est" in the Catholic Mass, during the Preface before the Sanctus, especially appropriate here when applied to the future Cardinal, Archduke Rudolph.—TA

[200] This wording does not mean that the entry was made in the evening.—TA

would take pains to make your life pleasant for you. [//] [Blatt 65v] Procurer. // Just don't let the matter languish again. // You have so many miserable supporters that it can take years until something good is accomplished. //

The wine does it. // In Hungary, the *best wine* costs 28 for a glass that is larger than here. [//] [Blatt 66r]

I was very busy—8 to 10 hours per day—and merely lived with the family where I was. // But only at the end, shortly before my departure. Earlier he was always on his estate. At that time, he was not avaricious; I was with a group of people there, where it was incredible. //

[Blatt 66v]

BEETHOVEN [at his apartment, possibly in the Ballgasse; probably the morning of Thursday, December 30]:
[Note] to Oliva concerning baths.—Bookbinder.—Ask the Archduke.
Tailor Lind concerning me and Karl.
Soap. Bookbinder. Bernard—Peters
Steiner, 7 fl.
Large iron nails. [Blatt 67r]
[at a coffee house, reading the newspapers; late morning of Thursday, December 30:]
Der Vampir, a Tale from the English, etc., by Lord Byron, 40 kr. C.M. at Schaumburg's.[201]

$$2 \text{ fl. } 50 \text{ kr.}$$
$$\underline{25}$$

36	36
36	36
36	36
1 fl. 48 kr.	45
	42

Gottes Vorstellung by Motall, or some such.[202]
Oliva: cut pens. //
Curtains

---

[201] Excerpt from an advertisement in the *Intelligenzblatt*, No. 298 (December 30, 1819), p. 1269: "To be had at Carl Schaumburg and Co.: *Der Vampyr*. A Tale from the English of Lord Byron, along with an account of his stay in Mytilene. 8vo. 40 kr. C.M." The same advertisement also appeared on January 7, 1820. Beethoven accurately copied selected details from this advertisement, rather than copying them from a copy of the book examined at Schaumburg's.—KH/TA

[202] The surname may be Mottal, but the identity of this entry remains unclear.—KH/TA

Sonatas and Variations at Artaria's.[203]

Carpenter: [hang] the curtain in the large room. [Blatt 67v]

How much is a *Louis d'or* worth?

To do: [take] the blue coat to Lind. //

BERNARD [at *Zur Stadt Triest*, Neuer Markt; probably midday dinner with Peters, ca. 2 p.m. on Thursday, December 30]: Haven't you received anything from Bremen? In Bremen your birthday has been celebrated with great solemnity by a group of enthusiasts, and there is a long article about it in the *Zeitung* there. They have [Blatt 68r] sent you poems and other items from the occasion.[204] //

PETERS: Tomorrow [Friday, December 31],[205] I shall congratulate your Nephew and the Director [Blöchlinger], and then, in humility, I shall visit you to express my good wishes.[206] // I take the boy in whatever way is necessary. [//] [Blatt 68v]

In the *Conversations* [*Lexikon*]. //

BERNARD: This morning I absolutely decided about Schickh, and wrote him about it, and my conditions are such that I believe that he will be completely frightened. He has misused my kindness very inconsiderately, and committed the most unauthorized acts in my name. I have demanded 100 Ducats [= 450 fl.] per year honorarium,[207] [Blatt 69r] with a 4-month advance in salary, 10 Ducats [45 fl.] honorarium per sheet of theater reviews, and 6 Ducats [= 27 fl.] for other essays. In addition, all the interference from foreigners that he allows ought to be removed,

---

[203] Beethoven's *Six Varied Themes* [i.e., Six National Airs with Variations, for piano and flute or violin], Op. 105, composed in 1818/1819 for George Thomson in Edinburgh, and the Piano Sonata, Op. 106, composed in 1818; both appeared from Artaria & Comp. in September, 1819. See Kinsky-Halm, pp. 288–290.—KH

[204] The following report on the December 17 celebration of Beethoven's birthday in Bremen appears in Kanne's *Wiener AmZ* 4, No. 2 (January 5, 1820), cols. 14–15: "To give the genius composer the most sincere indication of our admiration on this day, a congratulatory letter, accompanied by several poems and other supplements, were sent to him. In these, they sought to express the sentiments of devotion and the hope that he will still work among us for a long, very long time and observe our widely felt joy." See Albrecht, *Letters to Beethoven*, No. 266 and illus. (vol. 2); Blatt 40v above.—KH/TA

[205] The regular visitation day at Blöchlinger's Institute was Thursday (and the dating here might be a day off), but the German editors likewise believed that Peters planned to bring New Year's greetings, presumably on December 31. Peters's congratulations, however, could concern Karl's passing the recent examinations. Peters planned to visit Karl and then Beethoven, both presumably in the Josephstadt, the latter at his apartment on the Glacis.—TA

[206] Perhaps Peters means New Year's greetings.—KH

[207] The title page of the *Wiener Zeitschrift* indicated that it was published at the expense of the editor.—TA

and the Directorship of the journal with the addition of an assistant ought to be left to me alone.[208]

I am leaving for a moment, but am coming right back. [//]

[Blatt 69v]

PROPRIETOR SEELIG: Roughly what a little piece weighs. [//] 1 fl. 15 kr.—or 1 fl. 30 kr. with oil and vinegar. //

PETERS: How is His Highness [Archduke Rudolph]? //

The error is already corrected. I asked Bernard whether [the statement] that you were a natural son of the King of Prussia [Blatt 70r] had not yet been corrected in the *Conversations Lexicon*.[209] // Such things must be corrected, though, because you have no need of reflected glory from the King; just the opposite is the case. [//]

[Blatt 70v]

OLIVA: Don't you know the story in Teplitz?[210] //

BERNARD: "Grillparzer?"[211] asked Count Czernin, when he heard the name, "Is that the poet?—*Jean!* [Idiot!][212] I've already had some!" When eating, he meant. *Jean.* [Idiot.] [//] [Blatt 71r = inside the back cover]

Then when will you go to the theater?

Isn't he hungry? He only eats out of courtesy.[213] //

---

[208] This report may have dismayed Beethoven, who seems to have enjoyed working with the Catholic Schickh and his Protestant friends.—TA

[209] The 1819 *Conversations-Lexicon* that appeared from F.A. Brockhaus says: "Beethoven (Ludwig von) ... born at Bonn, 1772, a son of the former tenor of the Electoral Kapelle; according to another opinion by Fayolle, however, a natural son of Friedrich Wilhelm II of Prussia." *Allgemeine deutsche Real-Encyclopädie*, vol. 1, p. 621.

Indeed, nine years earlier, Choron and Fayolle, vol. 1, p. 60, had already noted Beethoven's birth year as 1772, and that he was said to be "fils naturel de Frédéric-Guillaume II, roi de Prusse." Thus the *Conversations-Lexicon*'s misinformation may have been old news to Beethoven by this late date, and Peters's insistence upon a correction more an irritant than anything else. See further references in Heft 7, Blätter 39r–39v.—KH/TA

[210] The Bohemian spa, northwest of Prague, where Vienna's wealthy often spent part of their summers, and where Beethoven himself even visited in 1811 and 1812. Oliva asks Beethoven the question, then Bernard seems to have related the story.—TA

[211] The introduction of the poet Grillparzer's name here is difficult to connect with the surrounding anecdotal material.—TA

[212] The original *Jean* probably means *Jeannot* (dunce, stupid fellow).—TA

[213] Left of this line: a drawing of a head in profile. To the right of the line, someone has added in faint pencil: "man muss" (one must).—KH

We now have the following epigram about Wähner![214]

I am shy of water and am going mad [*rase*],[215]
    though I do not rage [*ras'*] against water,
No, I often dash away [*ras'*] from [drinking] wine,
    more often from its own poison.
But [if] anger commands me, then give me journal and verse,
Give me comedies quickly, otherwise I'll tear myself to pieces.
[End of entries for Thursday, December 30.]

[No conversation book entries seem to have survived for the week from New Year's Eve, Friday, December 31, 1819, until Epiphany, January 6, 1820. During this period, Beethoven seemingly lived in his poorly-heated new apartment on the Glacis, while the temperatures outside remained consistently, though not yet alarmingly, below freezing.]

End of Heft 5

---

[214] The Protestant journal editor, Friedrich Wähner. At Christmas dinner (Blatt 49v above), Bernard had likened him to Martin Luther, possibly a reference to his weight as much as his religion. Another reference to his weight appears in Heft 8, Blatt 14v.—TA

[215] Bernard originally played with the word *raste* [rest] here; other significant wordplay on *rase*.—KH

Heft 6

(ca. January 7, 1820 – January 26, 1820)

[Blatt 1r]

PETERS [**at a restaurant or coffee house (possibly *Zur Stadt Triest*) with Bernard; possibly Friday, January 7, 1820**]:[1] Bernard resents me that I have a wife and want to go home;[2] I believe that he is jealous. //

---

[1] Working back chronologically from the first datable entry, ca. Tuesday, January 11 (or possibly a day later), on Blatt 17v, we find that Beethoven's dinner with nephew Karl on Blätter 6r–6v probably took place on a Sunday (in this case, January 9), rather than on a normal Thursday school visitation day, which would have been January 6 (Epiphany). Thus, this conversation book appears to have been begun once all of the Christmas-related holidays were over, ca. Friday, January 7, 1820.—TA

[2] As tutor to the Lobkowitz children, Peters had received an apartment in the Lobkowitz Summer Palace in suburban Landstrasse, Ungargasse No. 309 [renumbered as 347 in 1821, and 388 in 1830] upon his marriage on May 5, 1814, and retained it until early in 1825 (Macek, p. 395). On February 24, 1820 (Heft 8, Blätter 3r–4r), he noted that "in the winter, the building is not warm enough."

It seems logical that Peters would also have received a room in House No. 1226 [renumbered as 1157 in 1821] at the corner of Dorotheergasse and Augustinergasse, directly behind the Lobkowitz Palace. In the surviving Conscriptions-Bögen for Stadt No. 1157 (Wiener Stadt- und Landesarchiv), Peters does not appear as a regular resident of the building, and there are no surviving *Fremden-Bögen* (where a person with another residence elsewhere might be listed) before 1830.

Josephine Peters's maiden name was Hochsinger (as it was spelled in documents surrounding her mother's death and her own marriage; see Heft 4, Blätter 25r–25v). When her mother died in 1811, she left a substantial middle-class estate and only two surviving children: Josephine (b. 1790) and her older sister Anna Maria (b. ca. 1788), but no son. Depending upon Anna Maria's actual birthdate, a guardian may have been appointed for both of the sisters, because the age of majority was 24 years.

Blatt 33r below, however, indicates that Josephine had a brother; Blatt 7v implies that Josephine had a residence separate from Peters's; and Blatt 7r associates her with suburban Gumpendorf. Heft 7, Blatt 11r (ca. January 31, 1820), likewise implies that Josephine maintained a separate residence, one large enough to accommodate a large bulldog that she intended to adopt on Beethoven's behalf.

Therefore it seems possible that, although Peters's and Josephine's primary residence was probably at the Lobkowitz Summer Palace, Peters also received a room or small apartment in a Lobkowitz building in the City to assure his proximity to his pupils in the family. If the Summer Palace apartment was not warm in winter, Josephine may have retained one of her family's earlier apartments (which *could* be warmed) in the City. With these choices the more logical, any speculation that the Peterses also maintained a well-appointed apartment in Gumpendorf (or possibly Margarethen, see below) becomes less probable.

Behsel (1829), p. 134, lists one Johann Höpfinger (as spelled consistently in the documents) as the

BERNARD [continuing]: He concerns himself too little about his wife. She says that I am her vice-husband, and I always say that if Peters dies, I shall inherit her.[3] [//] [Blatt 1v]

Today he [Schickh] spoke very sorrowfully with me, and wants to clear everything up with me tomorrow. I cannot escape, but I shall obtain my freedom, though. [//] [Blatt 2r] He has no position if I abandon him, so he doesn't know what to do. // <Who was ....> //

I want to copy out a song by Lessing for you that you ought to compose.[4] [//]

BEETHOVEN [**figuring the bill for refreshments,[5] maybe in hopes of escape**]:
    1 [fl.] 30 [kr.]
    <u>   45</u>

---

owner of a house in Gumpendorf, Hirschgasse No. 299 (No. 262 before the 1821 renumbering, and 377 in the final renumbering of 1830). Conscriptions-Bogen, Gumpendorf No. 377 (new collation: 377/1 and 377/2) from 1832, lists Johann Höpfinger, a municipal silk cloth maker, b. 1785 in Margarethen, present since 1807, with his wife Franziska (b. 1792), and five children, born between 1811 and 1824. It appears that he owned the house in 1827, but lived in Margarethen (directly across the River Wien) at that time.

Behsel, p. 118, also lists the House *Flucht in Egypt*, Margarethen, Garten Gasse No. 60 (No. 59 before 1821), owned by Joseph Höpfinger.

Hochsinger and Höpfinger are two distinct spellings, but they look very similar in Kurrentschrift; stranger confusions have occurred in the literature. *If* there is a correlation, then Höpfinger (b. 1785) may have been a son of Zacharias Hochsinger by a first marriage, in which case he would not necessarily have appeared in widow Theresia's Verlassenschafts-Abhandlung of 1811.—TA

[3] From March 21 through August 20, 1822, John Russell (ca. 1796–1846), a young Scottish lawyer, would visit Vienna and observe: "To hear the nonchalance with which a party of respectable merchants or shopkeepers speak of their amours, you would think them dissolute bachelors; yet they are husbands and fathers, and … it never enters their heads that their conduct has anything improper in it."

As early as December 8, 1819 (Heft 4, Blatt 9r), Peters and Bernard had begun writing suggestive bits of banter. By now, a month later, the conversations had become more explicit and involved Janschikh and Joseph Czerny. Beethoven never seemed comfortable in these situations. On March 1, 1820, Bernard once again wrote that if Peters died, he would inherit his wife (Heft 8, Blatt 48v), and on March 2 Bernard told Beethoven a lurid tale of a maid sold into slavery, facilitated by a Jew (Heft 8, Blätter 54r–55r). Thereafter, Beethoven started to dissociate himself from this circle of friends.

See John Russell, *Tour in Germany, and Some of the Southern Provinces of the Austrian Empire, in 1820, 1821, 1822*. 2 vols. (Edinburgh: Constable, 1828), vol. 2, pp. 201–203; facsimile reprint with Introduction by William Meredith, *Beethoven Journal* 29, No. 2 (Winter 2014), pp. 67 and 75.—TA

[4] Gotthold Ephraim Lessing (1729–1781), *Lob der Faulheit* (Praise of Laziness, 1751), had already been set to music by Haydn (Hoboken XXVIa: 22) in the early 1780s. A setting with slight textual variants also appeared from composer Georg Benda (1722–1795). The only text by the north German Protestant author, philosopher, and aesthetician Lessing that Beethoven set was "Die Liebe," Op. 52, No. 6, dating from the early- or mid-1790s.—TA

[5] He would spend exactly the same amounts on ca. Thursday, January 27, also with Bernard; see Heft 7, Blatt 1r.—TA

[Blatt 2v]

BERNARD [copying the poem]:

> Lob der Faulheit
> [*Praise of Laziness*]⁶

> Faulheit! Endlich muss ich dir
> Auch ein kleines Loblied bringen!
> Ach, wie sauer wird es mir,
> Dich nach Würden zu besingen—
> Doch ich will mein Bestes tun,
> Nach der Arbeit ist gut ruh'n! [Blatt 3r]

> Höchstes Gut!—wer—dich nur—hat—
> Dessen ungestörtes Leben—
> Doch ich—gähn'—und werde—matt—
> Drum wirst du es mir vergeben,
> Dass ich dich nicht singen kann,
> Du verhinderst mich ja dran!

[Blatt 3v]

BEETHOVEN [left alone after the above exchange, or at his apartment; possibly Friday, January 7]:

25 Scottish Songs, among them a duet and 4 with choruses.⁷ [//]

NB: Can't one also garnish *her* pension? And doesn't compensation for damages, as much as possible, have to be made to me, [Blatt 4r] in addition to the half of the [princes'] pension, which is now outstanding for more than a full year?⁸ NB:

---

⁶ Roughly translated: "Laziness! Finally I must bring you a little song of praise! Ah, how unpleasant it is to me to sing unto you in a worthy manner. But I will do my best; after work it's good to rest! Most Worthy One! Whoever possesses you has an untroubled life. But I'll push on and remain dull. So you'll forgive me if I cannot sing unto you; you prevent me from doing so!"—TA

⁷ 25 Scottish Songs, with accompaniment for piano, violin, and violoncello, Op. 108. The duet is No. 8 ("Behold my Love"), the four Lieder with chorus are No. 1 ("Music, Love and Wine"), No. 13 ("Come fill"), No. 19 ("O swiftly glides the bonny boat"), and No. 22 ("The Highland Watch"). Beethoven composed the accompaniments to songs for George Thomson in Edinburgh (see Heft 2, Blatt 65r). See Kinsky-Halm, pp. 300–302.—KH/TA

⁸ On May 10, 1817, Johanna van Beethoven had legally bound herself to pay half of her pension as her contribution to Karl's education. As it emerges from Beethoven's *Denkschrift* (Memorandum) to the Court of Appeals on February 18, 1820, he had received no payment from her since the middle of 1819, because she could "not withdraw" her pension and Beethoven could "raise [the sum] only after she did." See Thayer-Deiters-Riemann, IV, pp. 555–557. See Anderson, III, pp. 1388–1408 for the text of the draft Memorandum; also Weise's facsimile edition.—KH/TA

Since I have pension sheets in hand, can you, for instance, raise the money from the guardian? If she dies, he has nothing; and [if] I do not take care, [Blatt 4v] not only does he lose everything from me, [but] moral corruption also hangs over him. The simple question is whether the Magistrat is empowered to overrule that which the Landrecht has done? And whether I can't bring action against it? [//]

[Blatt 5r]

PROPRIETOR SEELIG [at *Zur Stadt Triest*, Neuer Markt; probably the evening of Saturday, January 8]: von Bernard and Peters were here until just now & pass along hearty greetings. //

JANSCHIKH [joining Beethoven]: Philosophy of Life: you have that, and that is enough. [//]

BEETHOVEN [writing so as not to be heard]: The money for [Karl's] education belongs to me, and, as a remaining indemnity, a charge ought to be made against her pension. [//]

[Blatt 5v]

JANSCHIKH [continuing]: Then how did the matter come to the Magistrat, since the *Landrecht* should also speak as a competent authority? // Then isn't it possible to make an *exception fori* [application for change of venue]? // Then can't the case be handled at the *Landrecht*?[9] [//]

[Blatt 6r]

NEPHEW KARL [at a relatively expensive restaurant in the Josephstadt;[10] midday dinner, ca. 2 p.m. on Sunday, January 9]: 1 pair of fur-lined shoes // I am to be at home [at Blöchlinger's school] at 7 o'clock. // He [Blöchlinger] also said that it would not matter if I came about ½ hour late. // Lately he has said *absolutely* nothing. [//] [Blatt 6v]
I am very hungry today. // Today the prefect and several professors from the *Piaristen* [School] are eating at Herr von Blöchlinger's.[11] //

---

[9] Once again, Janschikh can only have irritated Beethoven by his repeated questions and insensitive lack of perception.—TA

[10] Possibly the *Hacken* on Piaristengasse, across from the Piaristen Church, or the *Strauss*, to the east of the Theater in der Josephstadt.—TA

[11] The Piarists—members of an Order whose purpose was school instruction, founded in Rome in 1597 by Joseph Calasanz (1556–1648)—operated several schools in Vienna. This reference could be to Prefect Leonhard Seitz, as well as professors Anton Rössler, Joseph Walch, Joseph Tranz, Joseph

BEETHOVEN [**so as not to be overheard**]: This restaurant is only for *Leckermäuler* [gourmets]. //

NEPHEW KARL: I have little time to read.[12] //
[Beethoven presumably accompanies Karl back to Blöchlinger's Institute by 7 or 7:30 p.m. (or even earlier), Sunday, January 9.]

PETERS [**at** *Zur Stadt Triest,* **Neuer Markt; probably sometime before 5 p.m., Monday, January 10; Oliva joins them briefly, then Bernard joins for a long conversation**]: Up to now, he [Karl] has had no reason to be satisfied with me.[13] [//] [Blatt 7r]

At 5 o'clock, I must go to Gumpendorf with my wife.[14] //

I would like to go to Sieber's [exhibition];[15] Bernard will go with us, but another time. [//]

If you had not taken a firm hand, he [Karl] would really have become a failure. [//]

BEETHOVEN [**jotting notes to himself**]:
Blotting sand.
Do not lose the flyer [*Zettel*] from Sieber's.[16] [//]

[Blatt 7v]

Kirchmayer, Franz Heissenberger, Franz Hauer, and Adam Hauer from the Academic Gymnasium of the University of Vienna. They also cared for the k.k. Konvikt in which Karl, at the wish of his mother, was to have been accepted.

More likely, however, given geographical proximity and familiar terminology, the reference concerns the prefect of the Piarist Gymnasium in the Josephstadt, the Piarist Joseph Czizek, as well as its professors Anton Schuller, Franz Xaver Kaneider, Anton Hofer, Franz Xaver Branzl, Caspar Kriczenski, Pius Strauch, and Joseph Holzmann. See Groner (1922), pp. 358–359; *Hof- und Staats-Schematismus,* 1820, II, pp. 120–121; Pezzl (1826), pp. 291–292.—KH/TA

[12] Beethoven may have suggested that Karl accompany him on an after-dinner walk, occasioning this excuse.—TA

[13] Peters was being suggested as co-guardian of nephew Karl; here he means that Karl hardly knows him.—TA

[14] Gumpendorf, a suburb about a mile west-southwest of the City, just beyond Mariahilf. Haydn had bought a house there in 1797. It is remotely possible that Peters's wife had an apartment in the suburb, more extensive than the room or two that he probably received from Lobkowitz. See Groner (1922), pp. 141–142. See Blatt 1r above.—KH/TA

[15] For Franz Wilhelm Sieber's Egyptian exhibition on the Graben, see Heft 3, Blatt 29v.—KH

[16] Whether this entry concerns the Egyptian exhibition of Sieber or Baron Franz Seraphicus von Siber, High Director of the High Police Direction (as Schünemann suggested), remains unclear. See *Hof- und Staats-Schematismus,* 1819, I, pp. 591 and 593.—KH

PETERS [continuing]: Do you want to sleep at my wife's place?[17] [//] It is so cold.[18]

OLIVA [joining Beethoven and Peters briefly]: He [Bernard] was at dinner [at the boarding house] today. For the first time in a week. //

BERNARD [joining Beethoven and Peters after Oliva departs, through Blatt 17r]: Who is the consultant, then?[19] [//]

Schickh does not show himself and always signs with the name-stamp, without settling his account with me from the previous year [Blatt 8r] or properly making the new agreement. //

When did Schmerling[20] indicate that he was going to come here? [//]

BEETHOVEN [writing so as not to be overheard]: … as the incident when I caused him [Karl] pain, not by striking him, but instead by pulling him from his chair, though without the least injury. [//]

[Blatt 8v]

---

[17] It has been repeatedly asserted that, in this passage, Peters is offering Beethoven a sexual visit with his wife (Solomon, *Beethoven*, 1977, pp. 262 and 362; rev. 1998, pp. 340 and 475), but it is probably just a teasing reference consistent with the Viennese middle-class proclivity for sexual banter, discussed by Scottish visitor John Russell in March–August, 1822, as cited in a footnote to Blatt 1r above.

Otherwise, in the context of Beethoven's chronic problems in heating his Glacis apartment, the documented extreme cold of January, 1820, and even Bernard's question about the cold on Blatt 8v, Peters is merely offering Beethoven the opportunity of spending a night or two at his financially secure wife's presumably warmer apartment, probably nearby. If Josephine Peters retained one of her apartments (in the Kramergasse or Wallner Strasse) within the City after her marriage [see Blatt 1r above], then Peters's offer while he and Beethoven were in *Zur Stadt Triest* makes more geographical sense than offering Beethoven a place to stay in distant Landstrasse, Gumpendorf, or Margarethen.

For further contextual problems regarding sexual favors, see Blätter 12r, 56r, 57r. Unfortunately, in light of the conversations in Heft 7, Blätter 71v–75r, the possibilities of suggestive double entendres in tasteless "locker-room" banter cannot be ruled out. The fact that Beethoven had essentially dropped Janschikh (the worst of the offenders) from his circle by the end of the winter suggests that the composer did not approve of this sort of conversation.—TA

[18] The end of November 1819 had been marked by extreme cold, accompanied by snowfalls at the beginning of December. Shortly before Christmas, it had become warmer, but at the beginning of January 1820 the temperatures sank once again, and remained low until January 22. On January 9 the temperatures ranged from –12 to –14 degrees Réaumur (+5 to 0 degrees, Fahrenheit), with the skies becoming clear and therefore not holding in the heat overnight, and on the 10th—probably the day that this entry was written—the temperatures ranged from –15½ to –12 degrees Réaumur (–4 to –5 degrees, Fahrenheit). See *Wiener Zeitung*, No. 7 (January 11, 1820), p. 28, and No. 8 (January 12, 1820), p. 31. See Strömmer, pp. 277–278.—TA

[19] On Blatt 13v below Bernard refers to the consultant as Appellate Councillor Winter.—TA

[20] Appellate Councillor Joseph von Schmerling; see Heft 2, Blatt 92a-verso, for details.—TA

BERNARD: What is your apartment like in this cold [weather]? //

It was possibly all the easier [to cause Karl pain], since he already had the hernia.[21] // He already knows what he has to do. Only when he sets to work with a heavy heart will he learn the hard lesson of [the value of] money. [//] [Blatt 9r] Now the matter will finally be successful, though on a firm decision for the future, since the Court of Appeals takes a firm hand. // He is very seldom to be found in the afternoon; [find him] mornings up to 8:30. //

Haven't you written him [Weissenbach?] everything that has happened? Concerning the Court of Appeals too, of course. The Doctor [Bach] is also doing his. [//] [Blatt 9v] In general, the situation will be judged only as an entity; the Court of Appeals cannot go into details. [//] The orders that are given now must receive the approval of the Appellate [Court], as opposed to the decrees of the Magistrat, seen in such a poor light, and so the choice is not difficult. [//] [Blatt 10r]

He will soon feel himself again and observe what kinds of people surround him. //

PETERS: I spent the whole evening with them; the only pieces played and sung were by Beethoven.[22] //

BERNARD: It is Seyfried's style,[23] then, instead of which [sentence ends]. //

My good colleague. He was proposed before me [as editor] of the *W[iener] Z[eitung]*, but the State Chancellery rejected him. [//] [Blatt 10v]

Spontini recently had a new opera, *Olimpie*, after Voltaire, performed in Paris; it received great approval. // You know that he has been employed in Berlin. In Paris there were many intrigues against him. [//] [Blatt 11r] It is strange enough that the King has employed a French Kapellmeister in Berlin.[24] //

[21] This probably refers to the aforementioned incident when Beethoven pulled Karl from a chair. Dr. Smetana operated on Karl's hernia at Giannatasio del Rio's Institute in 1816.—KH/TA

[22] Possibly Zmeskall, who lived in the Bürgerspital complex, essentially across the street (or, technically, the square) from the Lobkowitz Palace. Joseph Czerny, who played at Zmeskall's regularly, reported his almost exclusive fondness for Beethoven's works, and also his acquaintance with and approval of Peters. See Heft 3, Blatt 20v; Heft 4, Blätter 32v–33r.—TA

[23] Ignaz *Ritter* von Seyfried (1776–1841), composer, student of Albrechtsberger and Mozart, was Kapellmeister at the Theater an der Wien from 1797 to 1827; afterwards he was still active as a music teacher, composer and musical author. He edited the *Wiener Allgemeine musikalische Zeitung*, published by Steiner, from October 6, 1819, to December 30, 1820, to be succeeded by Friedrich August Kanne. See Gräffer-Czikann, V, pp. 27–29; Wurzbach, vol. 34, pp. 176–178; Clive, pp. 335–336.—KH/TA

[24] Gaspare Luigi Pacifico Spontini (1774–1851), significant Italian opera composer. He had come to Paris in 1803, and two years later became court composer and conductor. His opera *Olimpie* had its Paris premiere on December 22, 1819. Because he had been a loyal adherent of the King since the Restoration, he had a strong liberal party against him.

On September 1, 1819, Spontini had entered into a contract with Friedrich Wilhelm III in Berlin, as a result of which he would be employed as "First Kapellmeister and General Music Director" and

Austria comes from *Austern* [oysters], so why shouldn't an Austrian or Oystrian eat oysters? [//] [Blatt 11v] One will say that you are making him into a gourmand. [//]

She is now more beautiful than ever, and as intelligent as a beautiful woman needs to be. [//]

BEETHOVEN: Count Troyer.[25] [//]

[Blatt 12r]

PETERS: [He] plays flute. //

[BEETHOVEN: "No, he plays clarinet."]

BERNARD: All of these matters do not belong in my department and never pass before my eyes. //

PETERS [at *Zur Stadt Triest*; shortly before 5 p.m. on Monday, January 10]: I still have to get cleaned up and fetch my wife. [//]

BERNARD: *Husband*. Philistine. Rembrandt. // [Blatt 12v]

Sankt Petrus ist kein Fels,
Auf ihn kann man nicht bauen. //

Bernardus war ein Sankt,
Der hatte sich gewaschen,
Er hat der Hölle nicht gewankt,
Und nicht zehntausend Flaschen.[26] [//] [Blatt 13r]

---

named as "High General Administrator of the Royal Music" there starting on February 1, 1820. See Wilhelm Pfannkuch, "Spontini," *MGG*, vol. 12, cols. 1078–1090.—KH/TA

[25] Count Ferdinand Troyer (b. 1780), Privy Councillor, Gentleman of the Chamber, and High Chamberlain to the Archduke Rudolph, was an excellent clarinettist. He studied privately with Joseph Friedlowsky (1777–1859), who came from Prague as principal clarinettist at the Theater an der Wien in 1802 and who, in 1821, would also be named Professor of Clarinet at the Gesellschaft der Musikfreunde's Conservatory (possibly through the influence of Archduke Rudolph). In 1818 Troyer performed at a concert of the Gesellschaft der Musikfreunde. His younger brother Franz Anton (1783–1854) was a Major and likewise a Gentleman of the Chamber to Archduke Rudolph and a clarinettist. See Wurzbach, vol. 47, p. 251; Ziegler, *Addressen-Buch*, p. 149; Pohl, *Gesellschaft der Musikfreunde*, p. 127.—KH/TA

[26] These stanzas feature wordplay on the names of Bernard and Peters in context with their religious origins, the concept that St. Peter was the "rock" on which Christ would build his church, and so forth:

PETERS: Too bad about your Canon,[27] which is perhaps already erased. It would have immortalized me. //

[Peters presumably departs.]

PROPRIETOR SEELIG: Those are morello cherries, Spanish raisins, preserved with fine spices & v[ery] f[ine] rum. It is made this way for the house. //

[Blatt 13v]

BERNARD [at *Zur Stadt Triest*; **probably late afternoon of Monday, January 10, remaining, after Peters departs; conversing to Blatt 17v**]: He has already spoken about the matter/case with the consultant, Appellate Councillor Winter,[28] who has already also been instructed by the *Landrecht* here, where he was [employed] earlier. A report about his proceedings will now be demanded by the Magistrat, and hereupon the matter/case decided at the Court of Appeals. He asked whether Herr Nussbeck [*sic*] has already resigned. If not, then it would be good if Dr. Bach were to append to the letter that has already been submitted a written renunciation of this at the Court of Appeals. [Blatt 14r] Dr. Bach has already said earlier that Nussbeck would gladly stand down, and so the matter/case would suffer no added difficulty from this side. Hereupon it is still to [be] noted whether you earlier withdrew from the guardianship altogether or only in favor of Tuscher, in order better to effect the distancing of the mother. [//]

BEETHOVEN [**writing so as not to be overheard**]: I named Tuscher as guardian of the named individual.[29] [Blatt 14v] On the same day that Tuscher [Blatt 15r] withdrew, I took over the guardianship again. [//]

Saint Peter is no rock; one cannot build upon him.
Bernard was a Saint, who washed himself. He stood firm in the face of Hell, and ten thousand bottles.
With a probable wordplay on "nicht weichen und nicht wanken."—TA

[27] The riddle canon, WoO 175, whose upper voice reads, "Sanct Petrus war ein Fels!" and whose lower voice reads, "Bernardus war ein Sanct??". Beethoven sent it in an undated letter (presumably early in 1820) to Court Councillor Karl Peters. See Kinsky-Halm, pp. 680–681; Thayer-Deiters-Riemann, IV, pp. 189–191.—KH

[28] Karl Winter, living at Kärntnerstrasse No. 1108 [the so-called *Mehlgrube*, which was renumbered as 1045 in 1821 (Behsel, p. 31)]. In the *Schematismus* of 1820 he is still listed as a Lower Austrian Provincial Councillor (*Landrat*), but in 1821 as an Appellate Councillor. Winter was active as a consultant in Beethoven's guardianship trial at the Court of Appeals. See *Hof- und Staats-Schematismus*, 1819, I, p. 553, and 1821, I, p. 548; Thayer-Deiters-Riemann, IV, pp. 181, 183, and 185.

[29] From Blatt 14 to Blatt 16 several sentences are partially on one page, partially on another, possibly as the booklet was passed between Beethoven and Bernard. The renderings below preserve the sense of the sentences, as determined by the German editors, following Beethoven's own annotations "Vi-" and "de."

[Blatt 14r]

BERNARD [continuing]: Then the manner in which Tuscher abdicated, and whether you [Blatt 14v] have been instructed with regard to the order not made here by the Magistrat. [//]

BEETHOVEN [likewise continuing and commenting]: This is not clear. [//]

BERNARD: Then it is necessary to act—in the most moderate manner possible—so that it does not look as if passion prevailed; also one will attack the mother as a point of honor only in the most extreme case. [Blatt 15r] The whole thing is to be made relevant on the principle that one could not allow her any influence concerning his education now, because a woman is not equipped to do so when a boy reaches this age. Further, it is necessary that you, if it should be extended, declare that you are covering the expenses of his education in perpetuity, whereupon ...

BEETHOVEN: This is self-evident. [Blatt 15v]

BERNARD: ... then the worst case could result in the threat that your hand would be entirely removed. He thinks that you might perhaps be reproached about the time that you have had little Karl at your place; ... [Blatt 16r]

BEETHOVEN: ... if the mother and, to an extent, the natural inclination of the boy himself [were] not to blame ... [Blatt 15v]

BERNARD: ... because the priests have gotten mixed up in it, and the opposition party has seized upon this in order to raise difficulties. Dr. Bach is to inquire concerning Nussbeck, [Blatt 16r] so he receives the appended declaration concerning the resignation. He believes that still another Commission would take place at the Magistrat's, with which this report to the Court of Appeals about the mutual declarations could be made, in case the proceedings could not be exhibited. [Blatt 16v]

I believe that, in order to eliminate every subterfuge even now, you should not take little Karl into a restaurant [*Gasthaus*] to eat, because it immediately suggests that you are taking him to taverns [*Wirtshäuser*], because everyone takes notice of you, and everything will be distorted through gossip and false interpretation. [//]

When, then, will you go to see Doctor [Bach]? [//] [Blatt 17r] You already know everything; even he himself ought to write moderately in his submissions, because, as Schmerling says, he likes to write in a cutting manner. [//]

[End of long conversation at *Zur Stadt Triest*, Monday, January 10, probably after 5 p.m. by now.]

[Beethoven probably spends the snowy night of January 10–11 in his apartment in the Ballgasse in the City, rather than the poorly heated apartment on the Glacis.][30]

BACH [presumably at his office; relatively early the next day, Tuesday, January 11]: All of this has been considered and touched upon in the time period for the appeal.

[Blatt 17v]

BEETHOVEN [at a coffee house; presumably Tuesday, January 11]: Emmerich von Legradi, Court Agent of the Hungarian Court Chancellery, owner of a mummy from Thebes, etc., and such.[31] //

WOLF [?]: Staudenheim sends you greetings, and asks that you send him the book back. It doesn't belong to him.[32] //

Tomorrow [presumably Wednesday, January 12], your neighbor [i.e., the person sitting near you] is presenting 3 hearing machines to State Councillor Stifft,[33] and wants you [Blatt 18r] to come and see him, and to see whether you can use any

---

[30] The night before had been colder (probably because of clear skies on Sunday, going into Monday), but the night of Monday–Tuesday, January 10–11, was characterized by snow, with temperatures between –12 and –10¼ degrees Réaumur (between ca. 5 and 10 degrees Fahrenheit) overnight, rising by a degree the next day. See *Wiener Zeitung*, No. 8 (January 12, 1820), p. 31; No. 9 (January 13, 1820), p. 35.—TA

[31] Emerich von Legrady (b. 1778), researcher in ancient history, Court Agent at the Royal Hungarian Court Chancellery, provincial and court lawyer, possessed a large collection of ancient items, Egyptian antiquities, and so forth. The *Conversationsblatt*, No. 4 (January 11, 1820), p. 29, included an article, "V. Legrady's Art Collection in Vienna," which said that "here, in particular, there is a well-preserved female mummy from Thebes, which would bring honor to a collection like that of our worthy Sieber." See *Hof- und Staats-Schematismus*, 1819, I, p. 374; Schmidl, *Wien*, 1833, p. 180; Wurzbach, vol. 14, pp. 311–312.—KH

[32] Jacob Staudenheim, often called "Staudenheimer," as in this entry (1764–1830), Beethoven's physician. Born in Mainz, he had studied in Paris and Augsburg, as well as with Maximilian Stoll in Vienna. In 1812 he had recommended that Beethoven visit the curative spas northwest of Prague and to alternate treatments at Teplitz, Carlsbad, and Franzensbad. Later he was also the personal physician of the Duke of Reichstadt (the son of Napoleon and Marie Louise of Austria). He lived in the Palace of Count Harrach, who had greatly promoted him, on the Freyung, No. 247 [which became No. 239 in 1821]. See Frimmel, *Handbuch*, II, pp. 250–252; Wurzbach, vol. 37, pp. 250–251. For more about the borrowed book, see Blätter 21v and 54r.—KH/TA

[33] Andreas Joseph von Stifft (1760–1836), physician, was State and Conference Councillor, first Personal Physician to Kaiser Franz I, and President of the Medical Faculty of the University. He lived at Ballhausplatz No. 29 [renumbered as 22 in 1821]. See *Hof- und Staats-Schematismus*, 1820, I, pp. 118–119; Wurzbach, vol. 39, pp. 250–251.—KH/TA

such devices. He calls himself Wolfsohn,[34] lives on the Bauernmarkt No. 629, and is at home between 11 and 1 o'clock. // If you have your own [hearing] devices, he would like to see them. He believes that he could surely supply you with something appropriate. [//]

[Blatt 18v]

BEETHOVEN: No. 903, Dr. Bach,[35] across from the Post Office.

No. 682, Tuscher, Haarmarkt.[36]

Collection of Egyptian antiquities, on the Graben No. 657, 1st floor [2nd floor, American], in back of the Dreyfaltigkeits [Trinity] Church [sic], from 10 o'clock in the morning [Blatt 19r] to 5 o'clock in the afternoon; admission 2 fl.[37] //

---

[34] Sigmund Wolfsohn (b. London, 1767; d. Vienna, December 30, 1852), practicing physician specializing in ruptures, came to Vienna in ca. 1795, and became owner of an I.R. privileged Surgical Machines Factory, supplying bandages and inventing mechanical devices from trusses to adjustable beds. During the Napoleonic Wars, this became a lucrative business. The hearing device that he showed Beethoven was just one of dozens of such inventions. In 1807 he had built the Apollosaal, a dance hall complex in western suburban Schottenfeld, but was forced to sell it in the wake of the national bankruptcy of 1811. Throughout this period, however, he remained in the business of medical supplies.

His ancestry may have been Jewish, but by 1800, Wolfsohn (also called Wolfssohn in some sources) was a Catholic and remained so. He lived at Hohe Brücke, No. 386, until 1804, then moved to Bauernmarkt, *Silbernes Rössel* [Small Silver Horse], No. 629 [renumbered as 590 in 1821], remaining there at least through 1825. He seemingly retired in ca. 1826, and died in poverty. See *Hof- und Staats-Schematismus*, 1800–1838, specifically 1820, II, p. 128; Wurzbach, vol. 59, pp. 47–48; *Wiener Zeitung: Lokalblatt*, No. 5 (January 7, 1853), p. 19.—KH/TA

[35] From 1816 until 1822 Beethoven's lawyer, Dr. Johann Baptist Bach (1779–1847), lived in the Grosse Schulerstrasse, No. 903 [renumbered as 853 in 1821]. See *Hof- und Staats-Schematismus*, 1820, I, p. 700; II, p. 111, and similar annual issues, 1816–1822. From 1823 to 1827 he lived at Wollzeile, No. 863. See the *Schematismus*, 1823, II, p. 111, and similar annual issues.

Conscriptions-Bogen, Stadt 853, apartment 14 (Bogen of 1807 [filled in later], new collation 853/7) and apartment 2 (Bogen of 1830) reveal an Albert Bach, born in Mallerstadt near Würzburg, 1774 or 1779, and his family: wife Catharina (b. 1794/95, in Hallen, Bohemia), and a total of five children born between 1819 and 1827. Numbered as 846 before 1795, this building is the Camesina Haus or so-called *Figarohaus*, where Mozart lived when composing his *Marriage of Figaro*. See Messner, *Die Innere Stadt*, I, pp. 163–164.—KH/TA

[36] Matthias Tuscher (see Heft 2, Blatt 19r).—KH/TA

[37] Excerpt from an advertisement in the *Wiener Zeitung*, No. 3 (January 5, 1820), p. 12: "The interesting collection of Egyptian antiquities and other rarities of art and nature, visited by connoisseurs and the interested public, to be found in the City, on the Graben No. 657 [renumbered as 616 in 1821], 1st floor, in back of the Dreyfaltigkeitssäule (Trinity Column, also known as the *Pestsäule* or Plague Column), and may be seen daily from 10 o'clock in the morning to 5 o'clock in the evening, until the end of January, for an admission fee of 2 fl. W.W."

The same advertisement appeared almost daily during the month of January 1820. Beethoven absent-mindedly wrote *Kirche* (Church) instead of *Säule* (Column), though he certainly knew the location of the Dreifaltigkeitskirche, the parish church of suburban Alservorstadt, from which he

WOLF [?] **[continuing]**: Herr Wolfsohn says that his machines are optically engineered. //

I am guardian and, at the same time, administrator of a book dealership. [//]

BEETHOVEN **[now alone at the coffee house; possibly late afternoon into the evening of Tuesday, January 11, through part of Blatt 25r]**:[38] Since the L[and]r[echte] positively wanted him to enter an [educational] institution, then it is appropriate that as soon as I am no longer guardian, I shall have to be compensated. [Blatt 19v]

Karl's own nature is to blame that one cannot place him everywhere, as the professors themselves maintain that he would not do well in the Gymnasium. He was placed at the University because it was believed that study there was the best. I could do just as little for his nature as the others had, for he remained the same when the *Hofmeister* [Peters] [Blatt 20r] and I fetched him as when he was at Giannatasio's. Otherwise this *person* [Johanna], as the [female] plaintiff, should be heard very little, because whoever has such a criminal record deserves little trust or demonstrates absolutely none in this matter, also the § 191[39] in addition inspired her evil interest in enjoying the pension. If I, here too, *should* have made a mistake which must have been shown, then I deserve respect and consideration for my [Blatt 20v] constantly demonstrated support and participation. When Tuscher was guardian, I myself paid for everything out of my own pocket, [but] had more vexation than before, because she always had more influence over him [Tuscher] against me and her son.

The various time periods demonstrated that this is the most important. First, Giannatasio [Blatt 21r] could and would not keep him—all the testimonials from me are good—everyone knows how it happened at Kudlich's [school], where he

---

would be buried in 1827. The admission price was only 48 kr. when expressed in C.M. See also Heft 3, Blatt 29v.—KH/TA

[38] The following entries (through Blatt 25r, with a few diversions), as well as similar ones in later Hefte, are Beethoven's early drafts for his painstaking and often painful *Denkschrift an das Appellationsgericht* (Memorandum to the Appellate Court) of February 18, 1820.

Normally one can detect a certain pattern in Beethoven's entries: a shopping and errand list in the morning or before going out in early afternoon, dinner with friends, newspaper advertisements in a coffee house later. The entries from this point through roughly the middle of Blatt 25r, however, feature draft ideas for the *Denkschrift* alternating with making a list of shopping or errand items, and then back to the *Denkschrift*. This suggests a long single session alone, possibly accompanied by several cups of coffee or even glasses of wine.—KH/TA

[39] *Das Allgemeine bürgerliche Gesetzbuch für die gesammten Deutschen Erbländer der Österreichischen Monarchie* (Vienna: k.k. Hof- und Staats-Druckerey, 1814), Teil 1, Hauptstück 4, provides the legal direction for all guardianship cases. In § 191 (p. 41), it says, among other things: "Unfit for guardianship are those [...] who are known to be guilty of a crime, or those from whom a decent education of the orphan or a purposeful use of the inherited property are not to be expected."—KH

could have been out the whole day; strange that one can thrash the benefactor from all sides; on the contrary, really bad [things] can begin, everything outrageous against good things. I cannot make a pest of myself everywhere, as this lazy woman can.—

During the period when I was in Mödling and Karl was at Kudlich's, she [Johanna] ran to Tuscher, [and] always pressed him. [Blatt 21v]

On May 12, [1819,] I arrived in Mödling. Tuscher had already resigned.

On June 22, Karl came to Blöchlinger's [school]; from November on, 100 fl. per month.

[errand items added later:] Blotting paper, candles, [blotting] sand, Bernard, book,[40] restaurant.[41]

[resuming:] Why isn't Frau Beethoven's first letter as guardian mentioned? From the very beginning, the Magistrat has demonstrated itself to be biased in her favor and only [Blatt 22r] pitched into me—and how?

Several other counts and barons have left Giannatasio, and all of them have gone to the University.

[drafting an errand list:]

Carpenter, housekeeper.

Piano tuner.

Bank. Karl—

[resuming:] Education positively demands a similar path. No sooner had she been forbidden to see him, than [Blatt 22v] the contrary [took place] to excess.

[continuing the list:]

Go to the consultants with the lawyers.

Juniper wood.

Broom and dust pan.

[resuming:]

2 times he [Karl] went to her [Johanna], where he committed the worst [deeds]. [Blatt 23r]

Since I paid the money once, thereby his education will be promoted. Therefore it is natural that this purpose must be attained.

[continuing the list:]

Night candles.

Plankengasse.[42]

[resuming:]

---

[40] Possibly Staudenheim's book, which he needed to return.—TA

[41] The word in the original is *wirths*, with an unclear letter or sign (possibly *h*) after it, to make the word *Wirthshaus*.—KH

[42] Beethoven phonetically writes "Blankengasse." Several businesses were located in this street, including Traeg's music shop; the restaurant *Zur Stadt Triest* was located at its intersection with Neuer Markt.—TA

Everything against her would not be deemed worthy.

The letters of Giannatasio only against me.[43] [Blatt 23v]

One can think that [Dr.] Smetana would not allow me to suffer a misfortune, since he declared that the case would be dispatched quickly.

[continuing the list:]

Schlemmer.[44]

Paper.

[resuming:]

The character of his mother [Blatt 24r] was never kept secret from my nephew. Out of constantly evil immorality and prejudice, the Magistrat wanted to know nothing about it, even though my nephew was guided in the appropriate degree of respect for his mother. [Blatt 24v]

[concluding the list:]

Blotting paper. [//]

PETERS: Countess Erdödy, Kärntnerstrasse 1138, 2nd floor [3rd floor, American].[45]

BEETHOVEN: I committed several errors, but not enough to take children away from a father (which I was and am), any more than if an oversight takes place in an educational house. This raises just *as little hope*, that [Blatt 25r] one could take the guardianship from me <an outrage>, because now I have only behaved myself appropriate to the purpose.

[43] If Giannatasio wrote letters that could have been used against Beethoven, one wonders if his daughter Fanny had any idea that he had done so. By her account Beethoven evidently still brought the family a copy of his new *Abendlied unterm gestirnten Himmel*, WoO 150, on April 9, 1820.—TA

[44] Wenzel Schlemmer (b. Skutsch/Skutec, Bohemia, 1758; d. Vienna, August 6, 1823), Bohemian-born copyist, held in high esteem by Beethoven. He lived with his second wife Josepha (1781 – November 4, 1828) and his two children, Anna (b. 1810) and Alexander (b. 1815) on the Kohlmarkt No. 1216 [renumbered as 1148 in 1821]. Schlemmer also regularly copied church and concert music for the Hofkapelle during this period. See Verlassenschafts-Abhandlung, Fasz. 2: 4682/1823 (Stadt- und Landesarchiv, Vienna); *Wiener Zeitung*, No. 262 (November 12, 1828), p. 1092; Behsel, p. 34; Frimmel, *Handbuch*, I, p. 292, and II, p. 120; Clive, pp. 315–316.—KH/TA

[45] Countess Anna Marie Erdödy, *née* Niczky (1779–1837), had been married to Count Peter Erdödy since 1796, and had been a trusted friend of Beethoven's since ca. 1803. In 1820 she was banished from the country. Because only four sheets of Conscriptions-Bögen survive from this period, Countess Erdödy cannot be traced in the census for Stadt, Kärntnerstrasse No. 1138 [renumbered as 1072 in 1821]. See Frimmel, *Handbuch*, I, pp. 123–124; Clive, pp. 101–102; Thayer-Deiters-Riemann, II, pp. 548–549; Conscriptions-Bögen, Stadt No. 1072 (Wiener Stadt- und Landesarchiv).—KH/TA

The *Descriptive Catalogue* of Sieber's Egyptian Antiquities is to be had at Gräffer's for 1 fl. 30 kr.[46] [//]

[Probably the end of entries of Tuesday, January 11.]

JOSEPH DANIEL BÖHM **[undetermined location; possibly midday or early afternoon on Wednesday, January 12]:** It [the medal of Beethoven] will soon be ready in steel, and then stamped in metal.

[two lines written sideways on the page and with a circle around them:]
(Such a large   *Mode* [fashion]
Medal   Yesterday.)[47]

[Blatt 25v]

OLIVA **[at a restaurant or possibly even the boarding house in the *Rother Igel* in the Tuchlauben; early/midafternoon, possibly Wednesday, January 12, or possibly that evening, after he was finished with work]:** The anecdote about the 2 drunken pianists who kissed your hair here [at this establishment] is already known everywhere.

Frank[48] is chatting thoughtlessly—[//] about religion, rapture, fanaticism, about Pater Werner and his stupid common manner.

Rothschild, a Jew[49]—the greatest banker in Paris and London. [//] [Blatt 26r] He has 4 banking houses,—and he is said to have profited 7 million through the last state operation in France.[50] [//] The bank shares are increasing a great deal [in value] because of him. One does not know whether it will last; one says that he wants to take over the number of bank shares that are still outstanding from the plans of the Bank; this explains the increase in price of the bank shares. [//] [Blatt 26v]

He [Bernard?][51] has been invited as a guest today. //

The W[iener] W[ährung] is said to be lessened [in value] through the deposits at

---

[46] In the almost daily advertisements in the *Wiener Zeitung* (see Blatt 18v above) it says further: "The Descriptive Catalogue (*Catalog Raisonnée*) of this Collection, which contains a satisfying and entertaining explanation of the various interesting objects in it, and a new treatment concerning the origins, purpose, and manner of preparation of the mummies, is to be had at the exhibit as well as at Gräffer's Book Shop in the Weihburggasse, for 1 fl. 30 kr."—KH/TA

[47] These two lines in parentheses were enclosed by a circle in the manuscript.—KH

[48] Probably a merchant, see Heft 4, Blatt 32v.—TA

[49] See Heft 4, Blatt 29r for the distribution of this family as it branched out of Frankfurt and arrived in Vienna on December 19, 1819. The correct pronunciation is "Rote shield," not "Roth's child."—TA

[50] The family's brilliant, cunning, self-centered, and even cruel rise to power has received two contrasting histories in Morton, *The Rothschilds*, and Ferguson, *The House of Rothschild*.—TA

[51] Bernard and Oliva ate early afternoon dinner at the same boarding house, though they seldom actually spoke. Bernard also prided himself that he was often invited to have dinner with prominent members of Viennese society.—TA

the Bank;—therefore, if all of a sudden the amount of funds of the Bank are filled, and thereby all of a sudden the paper money goes out of circulation more, then it is a profit for the institution itself and for the State in general. [Blatt 27r]

I will speak with him tomorrow.[52] [//]

It appears to me that he [Karl] did not want to speak with me much. I asked him about several things, and he hardly answered. I ascribe that to the calculation of his mother. //

B[ernard] is coming *daily* to eat [at the boarding house], a sure sign that he is short of money. // With his secure income, this lifestyle incomprehensible. [//] [Blatt 27v] And he understands the nature of study. [//]

Are you far along with the Mass [*Missa solemnis*]? //

You have already paid from time to time, & I don't like it when I *can* avoid it. //

Tomorrow I shall see about the bank shares; you will merely have to sign the receipt, [Blatt 28r] and then there will be no delay;—but because, at the beginning of January, so many people are now getting their money at the Bank, it would be good if you could just wait a little bit. But you can always have the money immediately, as soon as you want it. [//]

50, 49, 38, and 50 again—already for a year. [//]

[End of entries for Wednesday, January 12.]

[Blatt 28v]

BEETHOVEN **[possibly at his apartment in the Ballgasse; the morning of Thursday, January 13, or Friday, January 14]**:

Coffee.

Oliva [at] banking house of Nathan Mayer [and] I.G. Landauer, Untere Bäcker Strasse.[53]

Send [a message] to [piano maker] Stein, that he [should] come tomorrow.[54]

[Blatt 29r]

---

[52] It is not clear whether Karl, Rothschild, or some other person is meant here.—TA

[53] The entry from "Oliva" to "Strasse" is framed by a pencil line in the original.—KH

[54] Either at this time or shortly thereafter, Stein must have come (presumably to Beethoven's new apartment on the Glacis) and examined the composer's Broadwood piano. See Heft 7, Blatt 81r (ca. February 17, 1820).—TA

Baggy thick trousers, lined with water-proof cloth.[55]

Swanskin.[56] //

2 busts on Stephansplatz.[57]   UNKNOWN:[58]   15 fl.

12

PROPRIETOR SEELIG [at his restaurant _Zur Stadt Triest_, Neuer Markt; in the evening, probably Thursday, January 13, or no later than Friday, January 14]:[59]

I won't add any vinegar. // von Peters must be ill? // Arrived today.[60] //

[Blatt 29v]

BEETHOVEN: Fame //

PROPRIETOR SEELIG: Is it true that you won the year's Grand Lottery? [//] In the Silver Lottery for 50 fl.? // von Peters must be ill; von Bernard is in the Theater.[61] [//] [Blatt 30r]

The 2 gentlemen are from Nürnberg and assigned transactions at the Congress

---

[55] Original: _Barchet_, Beethoven's spelling of the French participle _bâché_ (covered with tarpaulin) or the noun _bâche_ (tarpaulin, oilcloth, or waterproof cloth in general). See Clifton and Grimaux, _Dictionary_, p. 86. Beethoven also mentions the term in Heft 2, Blatt 12r.—TA

[56] Original: _Moldon_, Beethoven's spelling of the French _molleton_, swanskin or a kind of blanket. See Clifton and Grimaux, _Dictionary_, French-English, p. 705.—KH

[57] If Beethoven bought these busts, perhaps one of them is visible in Johann Nepomuk Hoechle's drawing of his apartment, made on March 29, 1827. They seem not to have been auctioned in Beethoven's _Nachlass_ (estate) (Thayer-Forbes, pp. 1074–1075). See also the discussion in Alessandra Comini, _The Changing Image of Beethoven_, pp. 44–45, and figs. 20–24, and the entry by "Unknown" that follows.

On ca. May 19, 1824, contralto Caroline Unger noticed two Cossack figures at Beethoven's apartment and asked if she might own one of them (Heft 68, Blatt 2r). It is possible that Beethoven sold or even gave it to her.—TA

[58] The German editors speculated cautiously that these two amounts might have already been written by Seelig, but given the two relatively high, but similar prices, as well as the fact that Beethoven had just indicated "2 busts on Stephansplatz," it is just as likely that they were prices quoted by a seller of plaster busts (either itinerant or, more likely, in a peddler's stall) on the Stephansplatz. See "Figurini," in Czeike, II, pp. 301–302, and Krammer, pp. 14–15; both use Georg Emanuel Opitz's engraving, Krammer's reproduction larger and in color. For further illustrations of figurine peddlers see Kos, _Wiener Typen_, pp. 27 (figurine vendor, ca. 1825) and 249 (Italian figurine vendor, 1777).—TA

[59] See Blatt 34v below for reasoning of dating.—TA

[60] Never all-inclusive, the _Wiener Zeitung_ does not reveal the arrival of anyone known as significant to Peters or Beethoven. The arrival, therefore, may have been food, perhaps fresh oysters.—TA

[61] This suggests that the entry was made at or after the 7 p.m. curtain time.—TA

[of Vienna]. // The one's name is Schnell, a merchant from Nürnberg;[62] the other is Professor List from Stuttgart.[63]

My cap is because of the *cold*.[64] [//] [Blatt 30v]

16 fl. 40 kr.

It is open from

    7 to 9 o'clock

    11 to 1

    4 to 12 midnight //

Are you eating at his place? //

WOLF [?]: The vinegar dealer[65] is coming in a few days and is bringing you something from Frankfurt. [//] [Blatt 31r]

In the Theater in the Josephstadt,[66] one eats well and has an extra room.[67] //

---

[62] Johann Jakob Schnell, merchant from Nürnberg, where he had owned a manufactured wares dealership and a house, and lived at No. L. 209. As with List (see following footnote), he belonged to the Business and Trade Society, and arrived in Vienna on January 5, 1820. Here he lived in the walled City, in the Trattnerhof on the Graben, No. 659 [renumbered as 618 in 1821]. See *Wiener Zeitung*, No. 5 (January 8, 1820), p. 20.—KH/TA

[63] Friedrich List (1789–1846), political economist, obtained the Professorship in the Practice of Statesmanship at the University of Tübingen in 1818, but in 1819 had to relinquish his post because of his progressive political ideas. He took the position of a consultant to the Business and Trade Society, which he had co-founded, and was editor of this Society's *Zeitschrift*. He was one of the Deputies who had to visit various cities with noble residential seats, and therefore was in Karlsruhe and Munich in summer 1819, and Vienna in January 1820, where the conference from Karlsbad was continued. Here, on February 15, he presented a new Memorandum concerning the removal of the German inland customs tax. From 1825 to 1832 he lived as an emigrant in America. List arrived in Vienna on January 5, 1820, and (as did Schnell) lived in the walled City, in the Trattnerhof on the Graben, No. 659 [renumbered as 618 in 1821]. He departed back to Stuttgart on May 17, 1820. See *Allgemeine Deutsche Biographie*, vol. 18, p. 761; *Wiener Zeitung*, No. 5 (January 8, 1820), p. 20, and No. 114 (May 19, 1820), p. 455.—KH/TA

[64] The temperatures of alternate evenings (Tuesday the 11th, Thursday the 13th, and Saturday the 15th) ranged from –10½ to –12 degrees (Réaumur), two to four degrees lower than on Wednesday and Friday. Even so, this information is not particularly conclusive in dating the entry, because in such extreme cold a proprietor such as Seelig could understandably add clothing on any of these days. See weather reports in the *Wiener Zeitung*, No. 9 (January 13, 1820), p. 35, through No. 13 (May 18, 1820), p. 52.—TA

[65] Adam Neberich, wine dealer from Mainz, arrived in Vienna on January 17. The wordplay on wine dealer/vinegar dealer is an allusion to an operetta *Der Essighändler* by Giovanni Simone Mayr (see Heft 5, Blatt 53v).—KH/TA

[66] In the building in front of (i.e., to the east of) the Theater in the Josephstadt, Kaiserstrasse No. 12, was Wolfgang Reischl's restaurant *Zum goldenen Strauss*. See Groner (1922), p. 482; Ziegler, *Josephstadt*.—KH/TA

[67] Anton Schindler related that, "in his later years, Beethoven often visited restaurants and coffee houses, which he always entered by a back door—where he could sit in a private room." See Schindler-MacArdle, pp. 386–387.—TA

He is said to live in the Archbishop's palace.[68] // *Suffering from dropsy.*[69] //

He [Franz Brentano] wrote it to Stieler.[70] // He certainly wants to have your portrait painted life-size by Stieler.[71] [//] [Blatt 31v] Beautiful, but with a moderate amount of property.[72] //

I believe that Baron Doblhof[73] has it. We [the Liechtenstein family library]

[68] Since the wine dealer Neberich stayed in the City at *Zur ungarischen Krone* (Hungarian Crown), No. 1018 [renumbered as 961 in 1821], as he had in the previous year, this entry could refer to Zacharias Werner, who had lived in the house of the Viennese Archbishop, Count Sigmund Anton von Hohenwart, since November 1819. See *Allgemeine Deutsche Biographie*, vol. 42, p. 74.—KH

[69] Werner died at the Cloister of the Augustinians (City, No. 1158) at 2 a.m. on January 17, 1823. The cause of death was *Lungeneiterung* (a discharge of pus in or from the lungs). Totenbeschauprotokoll, 1823, W, fol. 3v (Wiener Stadt- und Landesarchiv). See also Wurzbach, vol. 55, pp. 72–74.—TA

[70] Joseph Karl Stieler (1781–1858), portrait painter. Born in Mainz, he went to Würzburg in 1798, and from there to the Akademie in Vienna. In 1812 he became Bavarian Court Painter and, in 1816, returned to Vienna upon commission of the King of Bavaria, in order to paint a portrait of Kaiser Franz I. Here, in 1818, he married the Moscow-born Pauline Becker (Luise Beckers, according to the Thieme-Becker *Lexikon*). On March 27 and 28, 1820, Beethoven, with conversation book in hand, sat for the portrait in which the artist painted him as a half figure with the score of the *Missa solemnis* (see Heft 10, Blätter 35v and 39r). In mid-1820, Stieler moved back to Munich. See *Allgemeine Deutsche Biographie*, vol. 36, pp. 187–189; Frimmel, *Studien*, I, pp. 88–90; Thayer-Deiters-Riemann, IV, pp. 207–209; Clive, pp. 355–356.

Another portrait of Beethoven ascribed to Stieler exists in a private collection and, if authentic, may date from the artist's later years. It shows a frontal view of the composer from waist up, looking down at some music. The portrait differs greatly in style from the generally known depiction with the *Missa solemnis* score; indeed it seems almost proto-Impressionistic and is cast in a greenish-yellowish hue. In ca. 1977 it was used for the cover of a Deutsche Grammophon LP recording of the Piano Sonatas Opp. 101 and 106 played by Maurizio Pollini, and was retained (severely cropped) for its CD re-release, Deutsche Grammophon 429 569-2.—KH/TA

[71] The person who commissioned the Stieler portrait of Beethoven with the *Missa solemnis* was Frankfurt banker Franz Brentano (1765–1844).—KH/TA

[72] If the foregoing sentences refer to Franz Brentano, then this sentence presumably refers to his Viennese-born wife, Antonie Brentano, *née* Birkenstock (1780–1869). Antonie was the daughter of Johann Melchior *Edler* von Birkenstock (1738–1809), former Minister of Education, who arranged her marriage to Brentano in 1798. Birkenstock's art collection, assembled over a lifetime, was evidently a strange mixture of valuable and worthless items, and it took Antonie over two years and multiple auctions to dispose of the estate. Even so, she retained ownership of the large family home, Landstrasse No. 98 [renumbered as 93 in 1821] in the Erdberger Hauptstrasse at least through 1829. Solomon, *Beethoven Essays*, pp. 166–189, specifically p. 180; Behsel, p. 72. Solomon has posited that Antonie Brentano may have been Beethoven's "Immortal Beloved" of 1812. After the mention of Franz Brentano and Stieler above, Beethoven may have noted that Brentano's wife was beautiful, resulting in Wolf's comment about her *Vermögen* (property), which would have been very moderate indeed in relation to the fabulously wealthy Liechtenstein family (with their incredibly vast art collections) for whom Wolf worked.

[73] Baron Karl von Doblhoff-Dier (1762–1837), composer, was a pupil of Albrechtsberger and Salieri. His library went to the Gesellschaft der Musikfreunde. See Gräffer-Czikann, I, p. 724.—KH

have the Zarlino. // It is called *Dodecachordon*.[74] // Look for it in the Imp[erial] Library. //

UNKNOWN: I am from Turkey[75] and have Turkish, Greek, and Wallachian dances and melodies. If you wish, I will bring them sometime. // The primary song is called *Postref*,[76] with which the Turks are fascinated. [//] [Blatt 32r] The written notation of the Greek singers is completely different from our notation; it is heavily spun out and decorated with flourishes. // Because they consider it beneath their dignity to sing. Serfs have always been restrained from doing it. They dance just as little, but allow themselves some simple dancing. // I am not musical. // Both Turkish and Greek [song] are very similar to Jewish song. [//]

[Blatt 32v]

OLIVA [presumably at a coffee house or restaurant; the evening of Friday, January 14]:[77] What do you think is so funny? // Frank [merchant] says that he did not know whether the laughter concerned him; that's why he asked. //

I was detained and could not get away from the office until nearly 2 o'clock. [//] Because it would have become too late for me to get back into the City for dinner. //

I was there [at the lawyer's][78] this morning, but, because one could not speak with him, then again in the afternoon. [//] [Blatt 33r] He said that today he could not reserve a time for me, because he has too much to do on the first days of next week. He wanted to designate a day and time for you, but I asked him to come again on Monday [January 17],[79] and we left it that way. //

[No obvious conversational entries from Saturday, January 15. It is possible that Beethoven invited Peters and Bernard to his apartment on the Glacis, and

---

[74] Wolf omitted one syllable and originally wrote "Dodechordon," but he meant the important work by humanist and music theorist Heinrich Glarean (1488–1563) that appeared in Basel in 1547. The theory of twelve accepted church modes was taken over by, among others, Zarlino in the first two editions of his book *Istitutioni harmoniche*. See Hans Albrecht, "Glarean(us)," *MGG*, vol. 5, cols. 215–221.—KH/TA

[75] The writer's references to the Turks in the third person in the next entry suggests that he is a European who was born or has lived for an extended period in Turkey, rather than an ethnic Turk himself.—TA

[76] Correctly *Peśrev*, an instrumental overture in four parts, each of which is followed by a refrain. See Kurt Reinhard, "Türkische Musik," *MGG*, vol. 13, cols. 964–965.—KH

[77] For a clue to dating, see Blatt 35v below.—TA

[78] The generic lawyer (*Advokat*) noted here and later is not Beethoven's lawyer, Dr. Johann Baptist Bach, but seemingly a lawyer for the state who needed to be apprised of the case. In Beethoven's legal matters, it is always wise to consult Thayer, who would have known all the terminology because he himself was a lawyer.—TA

[79] This wording suggests that the entry was written no later than Saturday, January 15.—TA

sent out for food, possibly including capons (see Blatt 34v, below). Most of the conversation could then be carried on in loud speech. On this evening, Oliva went to *Zur Stadt Triest* and did not find Beethoven there (see Blatt 35r, below).]

PETERS [Saturday, January 15, or Sunday, January 16]: My wife's brother.[80] //

[Blatt 33v]

BEETHOVEN [at a coffee house; presumably the early afternoon of Sunday, January 16]:
Öhlzweige, 7 fl. W.W. yearly; Dorotheergasse No. 1174.[81]
General Vandamme,[82] from Cassel (that looks fine).[83] //

[Blatt 34r][84]

NEPHEW KARL [possibly at Blöchlinger's Institute or a restaurant; probably the afternoon of Sunday, January 16]: She [Johanna van Beethoven] has said so much to me, that I cannot withstand her any more. I am sorry that I was so weak then, and for that reason beg forgiveness. But now I shall certainly be misled no longer. I did not know what kind of result it would have when I spoke to the Magistrat that way. But if it comes to another inquiry, I shall renounce everything untrue that I said then! //

[Blatt 34v]

[Evening, presumably Sunday, January 16, at *Zur Stadt Triest*, ca. 7 p.m.;[85] Beethoven seems to be joined by Bernard, Peters, and (strangely enough) Oliva,

---

[80] Possibly Johann Höpfinger (Behsel, p. 134), but see the discussion in Heft 4, Blätter 25r and 25v, and on Blatt 11, above.—TA

[81] Excerpt from an advertisement in the *Beobachter*, No. 16 (January 16, 1820), p. 78: "*Öhlzweige*, a periodical sheet; First Volume 1819; 8vo; 438 pp. Price 7 fl. W.W. in the shop of the Sacred Lending Library, Dorotheer-Gasse No. 1174." See Bernard's comment about it on Blatt 38r below.—KH/TA

[82] Dominique René Vandamme, Count of Hüneberg (1770–1830), French General of Flemish origins, distinguished himself under Napoleon, but his career was severely flawed by his penchant for excessive looting and corruption, beginning with his first campaigns in the Netherlands and the Rheinland in the 1790s (thus Beethoven's impression of him might not have been positive). From 1815 to 1819 he lived in exile in America. Concerning his return, the *Beobachter*, No. 16 (January 16, 1820), p. 76, published the following notice: "General Vandamme arrived at Lille on December 29, from which he immediately departed for his birthplace, Cassel." The Cassel mentioned here was in the French *Département Nord*, therefore not to be confused with Kassel, north of Frankfurt.—KH/TA

[83] The context of Beethoven's own parenthetical phrase is unclear; it could also mean "beautiful" or "handsome," as if Beethoven had also seen one of the many published portraits of Vandamme.—TA

[84] Cropped photo of this page in Köhler *et al.*, *Konversationshefte*, vol. 1, facing p. 65.—TA

[85] See Bernard's comment on the time on Blatt 38v below.—TA

who generally does not associate with Bernard. Conversation continues through Blatt 40r, by which time warm food is no longer available.]

PETERS: The capon yesterday [presumably Saturday, January 15] was quite good.[86] [//]

BERNARD: Saturday [January 22] is a ball and supper at Hauschka's. // Only several young girls, friends of Mlle Weissenthurn.[87] //

PETERS: Fürstenberg's father[88] owns Weitra, the only estate. [//]

[Blatt 35r]

BERNARD: Did you sleep well? //

OLIVA: Is His Highness [Archduke Rudolph] healthy again? [//]

PETERS: All the better. //
[Peters probably departs at this point or shortly thereafter.]

OLIVA: Tomorrow after dinner, I shall again inquire at the lawyer's. Yesterday [presumably Saturday, January 15],[89] I waited here [at *Zur Stadt Triest*] until 9:30. [//]

PROPRIETOR SEELIG: With oil and little vinegar. [//]

[Blatt 35v]

BERNARD: He is bringing you a smoked herring without vinegar and oil. [//]
First shouldn't we see whether it will come so far? [//]

---

[86] This entry suggests that Peters was at *Zur Stadt Triest* on Saturday, January 15, but Beethoven was not. Peters was absent on Blätter 29r and 29v above, which therefore could be no later than Friday, January 14. Similarly, Oliva (Blatt 35v below) implies that he was at the *Triest* on Saturday the 15th, but Beethoven was not. Thus, there seem to be no conversational entries for Saturday, January 15.

An alternative scenario is that Peters's remark here is a compliment to Beethoven, who might have hosted him and Bernard (but seemingly not Oliva, who had a weak stomach) for dinner at his apartment on the Glacis on Saturday. Such an occasion, as mentioned earlier, would have left few or no conversation book entries.—TA

[87] Bernard means the daughter of actress Johanna (Franul) von Weissenthurn.—KH

[88] The father of Friedrich Egon von Fürstenberg, president of the Gesellschaft der Musikfreunde (see Heft 5, Blatt 59r), was Joachim Egon von Fürstenberg-Weitra (1749–1828), who "occupied several Court offices" (Wurzbach, vol. 5, pp. 15 and 17).—KH/TA

[89] Therefore, Oliva did not see Beethoven at the *Triest* on the evening of Saturday, January 15 (see Blatt 32v). Collectively, the comments concerning Beethoven's absence suggest that he may have remained at home alone on Saturday.—TA

BEETHOVEN [**writing so as not to be overheard**]: Won't we know what the Magistrat objected to before a decision is made? [//]

[Blatt 36r]

BERNARD: The appeal had to do only with the Magistrat, no longer with the mother. The lawyer has to refute all that; it will be judged only according to the minutes of the Magistrat and her complaint. [//] This assertion must be made known to the lawyer, so he can refute the complaints in all situations. [//]

[Blatt 36v]

BEETHOVEN: In this event, the bad fellows themselves say that one noticed that he lied, in that he always made an assertion, where one contradicted the others. On this occasion, you said that the nephew lied—Shouldn't the Pastor of Mödling[90] be detained [Blatt 37r] to prove his assertion, or publicly declared to be a scoundrel [?] //

OLIVA: Just try something with lemon.[91] //

BERNARD: He has no one, since the people are not at hand. He would very gladly do everything. You need only to invite them; Oliva will advise.[92] [//] [Blatt 37v] He says that he learned everything from you, just not cooking. //
    [**Oliva probably departs at this point or shortly thereafter.**]

I was at Voss's in Heidelberg;[93] as soon as he heard that I was a Catholic, he began to agitate vehemently against Catholic spirituality. He is highly intolerant. [//] [Blatt 38r, all written sideways:]

---

[90] Johann Baptist Fröhlich, pastor in Mödling, had instructed Karl for a short time in summer 1818. He had asserted at the *Landrecht* [that] Beethoven had stopped his nephew from speaking only deprecatingly about his mother. See Frimmel, *Handbuch*, I, p. 156; Thayer-Deiters-Riemann, IV, pp. 97 and 548–549.—KH

[91] Perhaps Oliva is suggesting that Beethoven, who seemingly does not like a great deal of vinegar, try some lemon as a substitute. Next to this entry is a pencil sketch of a head in profile.—KH

[92] Bernard's word is *braten* (to roast, in the sense of cooking), but he also seemingly intends a pun on *beraten* (to advise) in this context. This is apparent from the word *kochen* at the end of the next sentence. From entries elsewhere, it appears that Oliva had a delicate stomach and could eat only certain dishes, and Bernard knew this.—TA

[93] Johann Heinrich Voss (1751–1826), poet, translator, and philologist, had been in Heidelberg since 1806. He belonged to the Göttingen Poets League and was, for a time, editor of the *Musenalmanach*. He is especially important for his transcriptions of ancient texts. Voss made a firm stand against Catholic obscurantism and mysticism. See *Allgemeine Deutsche Biographie*, vol. 4, pp. 334–336; also Heft 10, Blatt 67r.—KH/TA

It [*Öhlzweige*] is a mystical-poetic-religious sheet. Schlegel and Werner also work diligently on it.[94]

Kanne has written a carnival piece for the [Theater an der] Wien; it is called *Jockerl, der Spion von Mazelshausen*. It went to the Censor's Office in the Court War Council because the subject concerns a spy. [//] [Blatt 38v] We still laugh about the spy.[95] [//]

We have been here since nearly 7 o'clock and want to go now. [//] We only wanted to stay a half hour. // [Blatt 39r] Seelig [proprietor] may have nothing warm.

We shall meet there very soon. [//] [Blatt 39v]

Frau von Janitschek [Janschikh] likes the composition of the Drinking Song that I wrote for you then.[96]

Sagt was ist der Mond so bleich?

Und wie singen Frösch' u[nd] Unken?

[Blatt 40r]

Ach so kläglich in dem Teich?

Wasser haben Sie [*sic*] getrunken. [//]

[Bernard's doggerel (or froggerel) ends the evening of Sunday, January 16.]

BEETHOVEN **[presumably in a coffee house; presumably late afternoon of Monday, January 17]:**

[94] Perhaps a reference to the *Öhlzweige*, a journal that Beethoven had noted on Blatt 33v, and which was condemned in enlightened circles. See also *Überlieferungen zur Geschichte unserer Zeit* (1819), No. 23/24, p. 599. This magazine appeared in Vienna from 1819 to 1823 (Vols. 1–5). The publisher and editor was G. Passy, the owner of the Sacred Lending Library, Dorotheer-Gasse No. 1174. The contributions to the *Öhlzweige* were very seldom signed. The collaboration of Friedrich von Schlegel may be surmised from the abbreviation "F.S." (No. 104 [December 29, 1819], p. 436). An anonymous handwritten note in the copy at the Austrian National Library refers to F. v. Schlegel's authorship in the article "Anfangsgründe des christlichen Nachdenkens" (No. 19 [March 8, 1820], p. 77). (Friedrich Ludwig) Zacharias Werner is at least represented with an excerpt from his "Geistliche Uebungen für drey Tage" (No. 23 [March 22, 1820], pp. 106–108).—KH/TA

[95] Nothing is known of this piece. It was not produced at the Theater an der Wien (Seyfried, "Journal;" Bauer, *Theater an der Wien*, pp. 303–311). At one time a play called *Jocko, the Brazilian Ape* had been popular in Vienna. If Bernard and his friends laughed at the concept of a spy's causing concern, possibly the "spy" in this comedy turned out to be an ape or similar creature called "Little Jocko."

On September 3, 1825, *Joko, der brasilianische Affe*, a play (with music) in 2 acts by Carl Meisl after the French, was premiered at the Theater in der Josephstadt (Anton Bauer, *Theater in der Josefstadt* [Vienna: Manutius, 1957], p. 209). *Danina, oder Joko der brasilianische Affe*, a ballet by Lindpaintner, was performed at the Kärntnertor Theater on August 10, 1826 (Hadamowsky, *1811–1976*), p. 90.—KH/TA

[96] See Heft 5, Blätter 52r–52v (Christmas dinner, 1819, at the Janschikhs' apartment). Except for tiny details Bernard quotes his masterpiece accurately.—TA

Hänke, natural historian from Bohemia, dead in South America.[97]   [//]
[Blatt 40v]

Oliva, concerning trousers, lamps, etc.[98]

That he himself should come with the housekeeper.

Syrup or brown sugar for the h[ousekeeper].

Peck of potatoes for the h[ousekeeper].

2 coffee cups. [Blatt 41r] for the h[ousekeeper].

Swanskin[99] for an indoor overcoat. [//]

[Blatt 41v]

PETERS [presumably with Oliva at *Zur Stadt Triest*; presumably the evening of Tuesday, January 18]: He [Bernard] appears somewhat displeased about the Schickh business.[100] // The journal is good, but Schickh won't keep it that way for long. // Wähner has gone into partnership with him. // If I had money, I might give Bernard 2000 fl. in order to see whether he then might straighten out with time and occupation; for work that is worthy of him. [//]

[Blatt 42r]

OLIVA [continuing]: The lawyer will speak with you next Friday afternoon [January 21]; he is leaving the hours between 4 and 6 o'clock open for you, where he will not accept other appointments; & asks that you just notify him whether you want to come at 4 or 5. I told him about Karl's recantation. He very much wishes to speak with him and believes that such a discussion could be important for the outcome of the case. [//] [Blatt 42v]

In Hungary, very near Pressburg, there is a peasant uprising that is said to be very serious.[101] Three battalions of the Viennese Garrison with 12 cannon depart

[97] Excerpt from a notice in the *Beobachter*, No. 17 (January 17, 1820), p. 82: "Obituary. All friends of Thaddäus Hänke, the famous natural historian from Bohemia, heard with deep feeling the report of his death, which was first made known by the *Morning Chronicle*."—KH

[98] Oliva became ill on Monday, January 17, and did not meet with Beethoven; see Blatt 46v below.—TA

[99] As on Blatt 29r, Beethoven spelled *molleton* as *Moldon*.—TA

[100] Reference to the conflict between Schickh and his editor Bernard. In the *Wiener Zeitschrift* 5, No. 10 (January 22, 1820), p. 80, Bernard published the following notice: "Since I hereby give notification that I shall no longer participate in the editorship of this journal, I ask everyone who has heretofore honored me with communications and reports to turn to the publisher in the future. Vienna, January 20, 1820. Jos. Karl Bernard."—KH

[101] A report from Vienna, dated January 21, 1820, concerning the peasant uprising of Malaczka in the County of Pressburg and its suppression by Austrian troops appeared in the *Augsburger Allgemeine Zeitung*, No. 26 (January 26, 1820), p. 104.—KH

today. 8,000 peasants from the estates of Prince Palffy[102] are said to be assembled; and one battalion from the Alexander Regiment is said to have been deployed. [//] [Blatt 43r] Prince Palffy is guilty of too great a suppression. In many ways more harmful than serfdom. //

PETERS [continuing]: Our mercantile friend! [//] 4 Seidel are my limit.[103] [//] Ofener [wine][104] tears me apart and gives me headaches. //

Frank [merchant] is glad that the tobacco is pleasing; he will offer a continuation. [//]

[Blatt 43v]

JANSCHIKH [joining them and interrupting]: How is the canon going? [//] Then Bernard's Drinking Song?[105]

Are you coming here [to *Zur Stadt Triest*] tomorrow evening? [//] My question about tomorrow is for a reason, because I hope to see you at my place on Sunday [January 23], along with Peters and Bernard.[106] [//]

[Blatt 44r]

OLIVA [continuing at *Zur Stadt Triest*]: Sitting across from [banker] Henickstein's business associate is a Jew, who was a supplier for the French here in 1809, and, himself, was imprisoned by the French. For the past year the man has made an enormous amount of money on the Stock Exchange here, and, because he has money, Henickstein goes with him, although he is a most common and ignorant fellow. [//] His name is Kallmann.[107] [//] [Blatt 44v] He is sitting with his back toward you, the first from the mirror. //

The lawyer [Bach] is very obliging & has especially taken note that Karl himself

---

[102] Presumably Prince Joseph Franz Palffy (1764–1827), hereditary High Administrator of the County of Pressburg. See Wurzbach, vol. 31, p. 208; Clive, p. 267.—KH/TA

[103] A *Seidel* is roughly three-tenths of a liter; a *Krügerl* roughly half a liter, and is customarily used to measure beer, but possibly referring to wine in this instance.—TA

[104] The vineyards in the area around Ofen (or Buda, united with Pest as Budapest since 1872) for the most part produced heavy white and red wines. See Hamm, p. 226.—KH

[105] For Janschikh's proposed canon concerning oysters, see Blatt 57v; Bernard's drinking song about toads, etc., appears frequently in his own conversation. One can almost hear Beethoven's largely monosyllabic replies to Janschikh's questions, as irritating as ever.—TA

[106] Janschikh asks about the invitation again, presumably the next evening, on Blätter 56r–56v.—TA

[107] Presumably Leon Kallmann, b. 1788, "Israelite merchant from Pressburg," living in the Gundelhof, Bauernmarkt No. 627 [renumbered as 588 in 1821]. See Conscriptions-Bogen, Stadt, No. 588 (Wiener Stadt- und Landesarchiv).—KH/TA

should contribute to it, in order to confound the mean tricks. [//] Don't forget to come on Friday [January 21].[108] [//] Today is *Tuesday* [January 18]. [//]

[Blatt 45r]

JANSCHIKH: He is my Flesh and Blood,[109] like Beethoven. //

PROPRIETOR SEELIG [**responding to an inquiry from someone at the table**]: I received them [oysters] today [Tuesday, January 18], but they are frozen and are here at your convenience![110] // Saturday, too. [//]

[Blatt 45v]

JANSCHIKH [**resuming**]: We shall definitely eat fresh and roasted oysters and drink champagne. [//]
   In the Fall, he will come back and will lodge at my place, because by then I shall live in the City in the Treasury Building, namely in the large *Mautgebäude* [Customs House].[111] [Blatt 46r] He [artist Böhm][112] did Weissenbach['s portrait] so well that only the breath of life was missing in it. //
   [**Janschikh presumably departs.**]

OLIVA [**continuing**]: Several hundred Gulden W.W. // I encountered Haslinger[113] from Steiner's shop today. He has had a splendid hand copy of your works in score made;[114] he wishes to have your portrait with it, and the very skilled miniature

---

[108] For reference to the upcoming meeting, see Blätter 49v–50r below.—TA

[109] Janschikh uses this phrase again on Blätter 56v and 91v below, in connection with nephew Karl. The phrase "Blame it on the flesh" (Heft 7, Blatt 54v; quoted in Solomon [1977], p. 262), may have to do with a visit to Tuscher on the Haarmarkt, in connection with Karl's guardianship. By 1998 (p. 340), Solomon had changed the translation to "Blame it on someone else," with no explanation.—TA

[110] This circle of Beethoven's friends had discussed a possible oyster party as early as December 8, 1819 (Heft 4, Blätter 9v and 17r) and as recently as ca. January 9–10, 1820 (Heft 6, Blätter 11r and 11v).—TA

[111] The *Hauptmauth* (Central Customs House) was on the old Fleischmarkt, No. 708/709 [renumbered as 664/665 in 1821]. See *Hof- und Staats-Schematismus*, 1820, I, p. 481.—KH/TA

[112] Artist and medal sculptor Joseph Daniel Böhm (see Heft 5, Blatt 40r).—KH

[113] Tobias Haslinger (1787–1842) had received a good musical education in Linz under Franz Xaver Glöggl. In 1814, he became a public partner in the Viennese music publishing house of S.A. Steiner, which he took over in 1826. He and Beethoven were friends throughout these years. See Frimmel, *Handbuch*, I, p. 197; Weinmann, *Wiener Musikverleger*, p. 32; Clive, pp. 151–152.—KH/TA

[114] Böckh writes about Tobias Haslinger: "A laudable undertaking of the proprietor [...] is that he is having the collected works of Ludwig van Beethoven hand copied in large folio format, in score, and on the finest English drawing paper. An expert in the field (Herr M. Schwarz) has copied for several years, and every single line of music is drawn with a rice pen, for clarity and sharpness. The skillful calligrapher, Herr Fridrich Warsow [...] has made the title pages and inscriptions for it. This work consists of 60 large folio volumes, containing 4,000 sheets of music."

painter Daffinger,[115] from here, has offered to make your portrait in [Blatt 46v] a single sitting. Haslinger will ask you for an hour. //

I became ill at suppertime yesterday, and am going home immediately.[116] // I am making every effort very urgently. //

The Bank has adjusted the deposits of the bank shares; it doesn't accept any more money; therefore the [value of the] bank shares is rising very significantly, [and] [Blatt 47r] you are profiting from it. // You can buy, because the greater portion of it is always in circulation; but it always shows that this institution has sealed off the things that must increase the State's credit. //

I have an interesting *reading* today. [//] From someone close to me, I learned that no-one knows it. [//] The Police here are [Blatt 47v] going into all the bookshops and *visiting*; in the case of all forbidden books that are printed in this country, they are taking the copies away and are even inventorying the books in stock. In a fearsome way, the obscurantists have here the upper hand. // I know such an example of a statistical book [Blatt 48r] that was printed in Prague & had been allowed several months ago. // Görres[117] has been ruined forever because he dared to tell the truth; he had to flee to France, and one knows how Germans are treated there. //

I am not well and already wanted to go a half hour ago.[118] [//] [Blatt 48v] Business manager in a wholesale dealership [banking establishment]. [//]

This splendid edition, in which the portrait of Beethoven by Höfel-Létronne (1814) was inserted before the dedication, went to the Archduke Rudolph for the sum of 4,000 Gulden, and, ultimately, to the Gesellschaft der Musikfreunde, in whose Archiv it is to be found, even today.

See Böckh, *Merkwürdigkeiten*, p. 98 and (1823), p. 140.—KH

[115] Moritz Michael Daffinger (1790–1849), originally a porcelain painter, but a portrait painter since 1809. See Gräffer-Czikann, I, p. 659; Thieme-Becker, vol. 8, pp. 260–262; Wurzbach, vol. 3, p. 127.—KH

[116] This accounts for no entries by Oliva on Monday, January 17 (see Blatt 40v above).—TA

[117] Johann Joseph Görres (1776–1848), Rhenish writer and journalist, edited *Das rote Blatt*, a political-satirical magazine, for a short period from 1797. In Heidelberg in 1806 he developed associations with Ludwig Tieck, Achim von Arnim, Clemens Brentano, and Jean Paul [Richter]. Through the editorship of *Der rheinische Merkur* from 1814 to 1816 he actively participated in the patriotic movement of the German *Volk*. After his principal work, *Teutschland und die Revolution*, appeared in 1819, Görres, as a consequence of demagoguery, had to flee from Koblenz to Strassburg, and then to Switzerland. In 1827 he was called to the University of Munich, where, transformed from his former national-democratic posture, he became a representative of reaction. See *Zur Literatur der Befreiungskriege*, ed. the Kollektiv für Literaturgeschichte im volkseigenen Verlag Volk und Wissen (Berlin, 1958), pp. 45–47.—KH

[118] In light of his subsequent illness, it must be noted that Oliva felt unwell already on Monday, January 17; see Blatt 46v above.—TA

JOSEPH DANIEL BÖHM [unexpectedly joining Beethoven and Oliva]: To the little Karl Beethoven: Next time we must draw your portrait.[119] //

OLIVA [making his escape]: Middays 12 o'clock; evenings 7 o'clock.[120] //
[Oliva departs.]

JOSEPH DANIEL BÖHM [continuing]: I've already been here a fairly long time; I am glad that I've met you, because my medal continually nears completion. I want to place [part] the hair this way in the middle, somewhat less and longer than now. I shall let you see it [Blatt 49r] before I finish it. My compliments.
[Böhm departs; end of entries for Tuesday, January 18.]

JOSEPH CZERNY [possibly at *Zur Stadt Triest*; relatively late in the evening of Wednesday, January 19]: Peters had to be at a ball today;[121] perhaps Bernard as well. //

WOLF[122] [interrupting and presumably delivering a package]: The vinegar dealer [Neberich] has arrived [on January 17][123] and has brought it. // He doesn't know your address. [//] Number? [//]

[Blatt 49v]

JOSEPH CZERNY [continuing]: There should be a letter in the package that Wolf gave you. Wouldn't you take a look at it? [//]
[End of entries for Wednesday, January 19.]

BEETHOVEN [probably at his apartment and while running errands in the City; presumably late morning of Friday, January 21]:
Ask about the wine.

---

[119] Böhm's verb was *zeigen* (to show), but he probably meant *zeichen* (to draw). Indeed the artist Klöber had recently included young Karl in a portrait with his uncle (now lost). Böhm later asked for another sitting with Beethoven to take place in early February 1820 (see Heft 7, Blatt 4v).—TA

[120] As Oliva had noted in Heft 5, Blatt 62r, concerning his new job at Mayer and Landauer, he took his dinner break at 12 noon and finished his duties at 7 p.m. on weekdays.—TA

[121] On Wednesday, January 19, 1820, a "Masked Society Ball" took place in the I.R. Redoutensäle. Such balls, also noted on the theatrical playbills during Carnival season, customarily began at 9 p.m. and ended at 5 a.m. See Schickh's *Wiener Zeitschrift* 5, No. 11 (January 25, 1820), pp. 85–86; Zettel, Bibliothek, Österreichisches Theatermuseum (courtesy Othmar Barnert).—KH/TA

[122] Czerny's entry immediately following almost certainly identifies the writer as Johann Wolf, Prince Lichtenstein's librarian; see also Heft 5, Blatt 53v.—TA

[123] Adam Neberich, wine dealer from Mainz, arrived in Vienna on January 17 (see Heft 5, Blatt 53v).—KH/TA

Did the Dr. [Bach] receive the letter[124] from Bern[ard]. [Blatt 50r] The consultant himself told Bernard that Blöchlinger should not admit the mother; in other respects, everything chronological today [Friday].[125] [Blatt 50v]

Struwe[126] is in Hamburg.

Chargé d'affaires

1820

Chladni's *Akustick*.[127]

For the Graben.[128]

[Blatt 51r]

UNKNOWN SHOPKEEPER: Including skis, 6 fl.; poles[129] alone, 2 fl. 30 kr. [//]

PETERS [**possibly at a coffee house with Bernard and Beethoven; early afternoon on Friday, January 21**]: I was at the Institute.[130] Blöchlinger is very satisfied, but he says that someone must spur little Karl on a bit, which, once he is accustomed to it, will also not be necessary in the end. [//]

---

[124] This refers to Beethoven's *Denkschrift*. A draft dated February 18, 1820, was found in Bernard's estate. Beethoven had asked Bernard to revise the material, and Dr. Bach, in a letter, presumably written at the beginning of February 1820, asked for copies of the draft to have this one reach the Appellate Councillors Schmerling and Winter. See Brandenburg, *Briefwechsel*, No. 1367; Anderson, No. 1007, and pp. 1388–1408; Thayer-Deiters-Riemann, IV, p. 181; Weise, pp. 7–9.—KH/TA

[125] On Tuesday, January 18 (Blatt 44v above), Oliva noted that there was to be a meeting with lawyer Bach on Friday, presumably January 21.—TA

[126] Possibly Heinrich von Struve, Imperial Russian State Councillor, Resident Minister and General Consul in Hamburg, who published several mineralogical writings in Hamburg. See Meusel, vol. 20, p. 683.

Beethoven possibly made this annotation upon the occasion of Struve's resignation from the position, since the *Beobachter*, No. 21 (January 21, 1820), p. 97, reported from Russia that "Dr. Sieveking, Resident Minister in the free city of Hamburg" had delivered his credentials to the Austrian Emperor on December 19, 1819.—KH/TA

[127] This work was not advertised in the Viennese newspapers in January 1820, but instead in the *Intelligenzblatt*, No. 91 (April 22, 1819), p. 826, and No. 94 (April 26, 1819), p. 858: "New book to be had at C. Haas, book dealer in Vienna: *Akustik* by E.F. Chladni; 2 vols. with 22 copperplates; 1802–1817; 4to; Leipzig; 25 fl. W.W." See also Heft 2, Blatt 11r (ca. April 2, 1819). Therefore Beethoven may have seen a copy of it in a bookstore (possibly a bookstore on the Graben) and noted it in his conversation book.—KH/TA

[128] Unclear reference to this long, heavily-trafficked marketplace.—TA

[129] German nouns here are *Bret* and *Spill*. The latter is also the German *Spindel*. In this context, skis and poles seem a plausible solution if Beethoven is considering renting or purchasing equipment (possibly for nephew Karl) for the snowy winter.—TA

[130] Visitation day at Blöchlinger's Institute was probably still Thursday, so Peters (as Karl's co-guardian) had been there and at the Piarist Gymnasium the day before in preparation for Friday's meeting.—TA

I also visited his Professor from the Piarists, who praised him extraordinarily and looks forward with pleasure to giving him examinations again soon. //

BERNARD [**changing the subject**]: I don't know what to do concerning the invitation, because, since the day before yesterday, I am already engaged for Sunday, and, just a short while before, had turned down [an invitation] there. [//] [Blatt 51v] At Herr v. Franck's mother's residence. She had already invited me for the Sunday after New Year, when I had to turn her down. Janitschek [Janschikh] should postpone it a week. //

There is a most remarkable tightrope walker here, who surpasses everything in his daring. Shouldn't we go and see him sometime? He is playing [at the Theater] an der Wien.[131] [//]

[Blatt 52r]

BEETHOVEN [**continuing the conversational thread from Peters**]: As I am disposed to Confession, one can deduce from it that I myself led Karl to the Abbot of St. Michael[132] for Confession. He [the Abbot], however, declared that, as long as he [Karl] has to frequent the mother, all the Confession would not be of any help. //

PETERS: Out of *respect*—because I didn't want to disturb you in the morning. //

BERNARD [**resuming his subject**]: I have been invited to Frau v. Salmy's[133] [for dinner] every Friday. // [Blatt 52v]

I have ended everything with Schickh.[134] The whole business has not once

---

[131] The "equilibrist" Franz Bevilacqua and his gymnastic family performed first from January 5, 1820, in the Leopoldstadt Theater, and then, in order to have more space for their act, in the Theater an der Wien on January 14, 1820, with further performances there on January 16, 17, 19, 20, and 24, March 15, April 6, 14, 23, and 24, and again on July 25 and 26, 1820, for a total of thirteen appearances there, usually sharing an evening with a one-act comedy. Bevilacqua's wife Katharina died in Vienna in 1821. See the daily *Beobachter*, Nos. 19–20 (January 19–20, 1820), pp. 92 and 96, resp.; as well as Seyfried, "Journal;" summarized in Bauer, *150 Jahre Theater an der Wien*, p. 306.—KH/TA

[132] The clergyman is Father Ignaz Thomas, prior of the Michaeler Church (see Heft 2, Blatt 74v). Beethoven seems never to have lived in St. Michael's Parish. Aloys Weissenbach's letter to Beethoven of November 15, 1819, mentions a father confessor as a means of getting to the Empress for intercession. See Albrecht, *Letters to Beethoven*, No. 264.—KH/TA

[133] See Heft 2, Blatt 90r (May, 1819).—TA

[134] In the *Wiener Zeitschrift* of January 22, 1820, Bernard (in a note dated two days earlier) announced the termination of his association with the journal. See Heft 6, Blatt 41v, and its footnote.

Since late November 1819 Bernard's conversation book entries often suggest that he (a staunch Catholic) was prejudiced against Protestants, Jews, and women poets. A survey of the *Wiener Zeitschrift*'s contents from 1816 to 1821 reveals that the year 1819 marked a high point in Schickh's inclusion of poetry by Protestants (especially Germans, whom Bernard labeled "foreigners"), Jews, and women, possibly influenced by Schickh's friendship and collaboration with Friedrich Wähner, a

amounted to 1,000 fl. for the whole year, though it has robbed me of so much time. Today, though, he already asked me again to write something for him, because W[ähner] has already created a fiasco. // I still needed to receive 100 fl.; [Blatt 53r] I had to send [requests] to him four times since yesterday, and finally went to get it myself. //

Prince Palffy's peasants in Hungary have rebelled against their officials and driven them from the estates, because they have been so oppressed. Military forces have departed from here; [Blatt 53v] the matter, however, has reached a very peaceful outcome. [//]

He has no position and lives from his writings; the King of Prussia has given him the title of Court Councillor. [//] He lost his position through the partition of Saxony. [//] [Blatt 54r]

I've already eaten. [//]

This letter is from Schunke,[135] probably stamped[136] with the intention of drawing some attention to himself. [//]

BEETHOVEN: Volumes for binding.

Bernard concerning Staudenheim's book;[137] concerning the wine house near to me. [//]

[Blatt 54v]

BACH [probably at his office in the *Figaro* House; probably mid-to-late afternoon on Friday, January 21]: Pose your questions and I shall answer them here [in the booklet]. [//] As long as [it takes] until he has given up. [//] Gladly, because I myself heard some information from him. [//] [Blatt 55r] I was of the understanding that you had already been to the Councillors. [//] At Schmerling & Winter's. [//] Because they have done it voluntarily. [//] He will not give up

---

Protestant pastor turned secular author and editor. Even so, Bernard advocated Beethoven's setting a text by Lessing on Blatt 2r above.—KH/TA

[135] Karl Schuncke (1801–1839), pianist. According to contemporary reviews, he was a student of Johann Nepomuk Hummel, but all the lexica since Schilling note him as a student of Ferdinand Ries! In fall 1819 Schuncke and the violinist Adolph Wiele undertook a tour from Stuttgart, which led them to Vienna. There they gave concerts on November 14, 1819, and February 27, 1820, among others. He is not to be confused with hornist Carl Schuncke, born in 1811 and active in Stuttgart. See Kanne's *Wiener AmZ* 4, No. 19 (March 4, 1820), p. 148; *Conversationsblatt*, No. 41 (November 19, 1819), p. 487; Helmuth Hopf, "Schuncke," in *MGG*, vol. 12, col. 326. He might be confused with the slightly older Schwenke, who wrote Beethoven an undated attention-getting letter; see Albrecht, *Letters to Beethoven*, No. 281.—KH/TA

[136] On Blatt 69r below, nephew Karl refers to an officially stamped folio.—TA

[137] For the borrowed book, see Blatt 17v above.—TA

freely without a court's order. [//] [Blatt 55v] Sunday, 10, 11–12 o'clock.[138] [//] On Monday, [January 24,] then, let's go to Winter.[139] [//]

BEETHOVEN [after the meeting with Bach, above]: Tomorrow morning, write to Bernard, [telling him] what splendid morality was promised for [Blatt 56r] ingratitude toward me. //

JANSCHIKH [probably at *Zur Stadt Triest*; evening of Friday, January 21]: I greet you![140] O Adonis! [//] Have you spoken yet with Bernard and Peters about [this coming] Sunday? [//]

BEETHOVEN: Leave the false Bohemians![141] [//]

JANSCHIKH: This determination lies with your purpose. [//] [Blatt 56v] You, however, will certainly come on Sunday with your young Flesh and Blood [Karl].[142] [//] On Sunday at precisely 2 o'clock. [//] Let us live and drink in good friendship, striving for our health and for Weissenbach's.[143] [//]

NEBERICH [joining Beethoven and Janschikh]:[144] I have also brought St.[145] along again. [//]

JANSCHIKH: You come on Sunday with your Flesh and Blood [Karl], and then, on some day in the following week, let's get together with the others. [//] [Blatt 57r]

---

[138] From previous references, lawyer Johann Baptist Bach seems to have held office hours on Sunday and even holiday mornings.—TA

[139] See Blätter 13v, 69r–72v.—TA

[140] In his greeting Janschikh uses the familiar *Du* here in a poetic context, but then reverts to the customary formal *Sie* in his question concerning Bernard and Peters.—TA

[141] Bernard, who was born in Hradetz, Bohemia, is noted in a Conscriptions-Bogen as coming "from Prague." Peters had actually been born in Prague. Beethoven may also have been referring to the Lobkowitz family or the Bohemian nobility in general.—KH/TA

[142] Janschikh means nephew Karl. He used this phrase on Blatt 45r above, and would again, immediately below, and on Blatt 91v. It is crucial to an accurate interpretation of the citations in Solomon's biography (1977), pp. 262 and 362.—KH/TA

[143] A toast, if only rhetorical, originally in Latin: *Nos vivimus et bibimus in bona amacitia et certamus pro Sanitate nostra et Weissenbachii.* Indeed, their friend Dr. Weissenbach in Salzburg was seriously ill.—TA

[144] On the basis of its content, it may be concluded that this entry was made by the Mainz wine dealer Adam Neberich, who would later deliver Beethoven's letter of March 23, 1823, to E.T.A. Hoffmann in Berlin. See Heft 8, Blatt 76r (and footnote), and Heft 10, Blatt 69r; Brandenburg, No. 1373; Anderson, No. 1014.—KH/TA

[145] Possible completions: St[ieler] or St[audenheim]. Dr. Staudenheim and the artist Stieler were both from Mainz (see Blätter 17v and 31r, resp.). The arrivals for January 17, as selectively noted in the *Wiener Zeitung*, No. 14 (January 19, 1820), p. 55, do not reveal anyone of note traveling with Neberich. He could also simply mean that he had brought Staudenheim or Stieler along with him to the *Triest* again.—KH/TA

You look very enterprising today. Therefore a protest against the single visit to my wife!¹⁴⁶ [//]

NEBERICH: Herr Staud[enheim] has no time to have himself painted; likewise Herr v. B-n also none. [//]

[Neberich presumably departs.]

JANSCHIKH **[alone with Beethoven at** *Zur Stadt Triest;* **continuing well into the evening of Friday, January 21]**: The oysters are already in the oyster bank; that is, in the ice storage. [//] At your pleasure. [//] Just specify the day now. [//] [Blatt 57v]

Indeed the oysters want to sing a canon, which goes: "We are born, fruits to be eaten."¹⁴⁷ [//] "It is finished."¹⁴⁸ [//]

[Come on Sunday] at 2 o'clock.

I know several fine and noble men among the Magistrat's Councillors.¹⁴⁹ [//] There are 70 Councillors divided in 3 different Senates. [//] [Blatt 58r] *Civil— Justice*—and *Criminal* Senates. [//] Only 3 persons have an effect in your affair: 2 Councillors and the Vice-Mayor.¹⁵⁰ [//] "Justice [must] be done, or the World will go to ruin" was the motto of Emperor Karl.¹⁵¹ [//]

---

¹⁴⁶ At this point there is only one documented previous visit to Janschikh's apartment, Christmas evening dinner, December 25, 1819. At the end of it, Antonia Janschikh touchingly invited Beethoven to come and visit again (see Heft 5, Blätter 47r–53r). Janschikh's phrase "bei meiner Frau" used here is the same that Peters used on Blatt 7v above, and may simply refer to the apartments which the two men shared with their respective wives. It is possible that there were no sexual connotations meant, but entries in Heft 7 (Blätter 18v and 42r–42v) suggest a sexually promiscuous way of life including wife-swapping. At the very least, Janschikh seems to have enjoyed sexually-oriented banter, with which Beethoven was not particularly comfortable.

For further clarification about the visits, see Heft 7, Blätter 30v–31r and 42r–43r, where it seems possible that Antonia Janschikh was somewhat empty-headed. In that case, if Janschikh's "alleinige" above meant that Beethoven had somehow been invited to a midday dinner with her alone for less than honorable purposes, he might have been both embarrassed and resentfully angry. Indeed he generally does not seem to have been happy in her presence (see Heft 7, Blatt 43r).—TA

¹⁴⁷ Original: *Nos fruges consumere nati* (from Horace). Janschikh had also referred to a canon on Blatt 43v; it is possible that he is trying to persuade Beethoven to give him a sample of his handwriting. He writes it again in Heft 7, Blatt 50r (February 8), where his purpose in asking for a composition is clear.—KH/TA

¹⁴⁸ Original: *Consum[m]atum est,* from the final words of Christ in the Bible, but here also a pun on consume, as to eat: "it is eaten."—KH/TA

¹⁴⁹ This acquaintance might be the reason why Beethoven, for the moment, tolerated this high-spirited, garrulous, irritating, and often crude member of Bernard's circle of friends.—TA

¹⁵⁰ The Vice Mayor for Legal Affairs was Joseph Anton von Hober, I.R. Councillor, Himmelpfortgasse No. 1011 [renumbered as 954 in 1821]. See *Hof- und Staats-Schematismus,* 1819, I, p. 655; Thayer-Deiters-Riemann, IV, p. 568.—KH/TA

¹⁵¹ Original: *Fiat Justitia aut pereat Mundus.* This motto was said to have originated with Emperor Ferdinand I (1503–1564), the younger brother of Emperor Carl V (1500–1558).—KH/TA

What's happening with the Akademie and your preparations for it?[152]   [//]
[Blatt 58v] Then make Germany rejoice with a new opera. [//] In you there is still a
great deal of Slavic sensibility and the craft and variety springing from it. [//]

At that time [the Congress of Vienna, 1814–1815], they only quarreled about
souls and privileged rights—thereby, however, the well-being of humanity and its
improvement were trampled underfoot. [//] [Blatt 59r][153]

If Napoleon were to come again, he could expect a better reception in Europe.[154]
[//] He was acquainted with the spirit of the time, and knew to keep a tight rein on
things. [//] Our posterity will value him more highly. [//]

As a German, I was his greatest enemy, but with the passage of time, I have
become reconciled to it.[155] [//] [Blatt 59v] Promised loyalty and belief are past.
[//] His word counted for far more. [//] He had a sense of art and science and
hated the darkness. [//] He would have valued the Germans more and ought to
have protected their rights. [//] In the final days [of his regime], he was surrounded
[Blatt 60r] by traitors, and the spirit had deserted the Generals. The best Field
Marshalls had retired. [//] The children of the Revolution and the spirit of the time
demanded such an iron will, though he overturned the feudal system in general and
was the protector of rights and of law. [//] [Blatt 60v]

His marriage to Princess Louise[156] was the highest culmination point. [//]
Here the intention was to provide world peace and good laws, and the desire to
undertake no more conquests. [//] Greatest good fortune and, through arrogance,
greatest misfortune. [//] An old torn garment that can no longer be repaired. [//]
[Blatt 61r] Instead of becoming wise through experience, they have become even
more eccentric. [//] Privileges do that. [//] How can one inherit the nobility of the
heart? [//] The privileged class have dissolved the Social Contract, and they speak
of rights. [//]

Are you coming tomorrow?[157]   [//]   In any case, the arrangement for Sunday is

---

[152] By this point in their acquaintance, Beethoven must have dreaded this oft-repeated question
during his meetings with Janschikh.—TA

[153] Cropped photo of this page in Köhler et al., Konversationshefte, vol. 1, facing p. 112.—TA

[154] Although irretrievably in exile on remote St. Helena, Napoleon would live until May 5,
1821.—TA

[155] This Blatt 59r is illustrated in Köhler et al., Konversationshefte, vol. 1, facing p. 112.—TA

[156] In 1810, Napoleon married Marie Louise (1791–1847), daughter of Emperor Franz I. After the
downfall of Napoleon, she took over the administration of Parma in 1816. In 1821 she married Count
Albert Adam von Neipperg. His family name (also spelled "Neuberg") was translated as Montenuovo
in succeeding generations and became musically influential in Mahler's Vienna.—KH/TA

[157] Beethoven might have replied in the negative, and indeed there are no conversation book
entries for Saturday, January 22, 1820.—TA

still good. [//] [Blatt 61v] I enjoy my life when you visit me. [//] I am getting an apartment with 5 rooms.[158] //

[Janschikh departs *Zur Stadt Triest*.]

UNKNOWN **[a random encounter]**: My sister-in-law Caroline, the sister of my late wife, is ill and almost without hope [for recovery]. //

There was a small riot in the Akademie.[159] //

[Blatt 62r]

PROPRIETOR SEELIG: Do you want grilled pickled herring?[160] // Not very. [//]

BEETHOVEN **[remaining at *Zur Stadt Triest*; rambling musings concerning Karl, etc.]**: One will reproach me for having done this and that; only in the case of a thorough investigation can I overcome. <Illegible word> primary concern, to what degree …. [Blatt 62v]

I omit the retractions! Meeting minutes appended of …. [I] must discover … what more … to append to this …. I leave it more to the general one …. It is impossible to put confidence in a woman who [has] this [criminal] record in the past, that she would as soon alter. [Blatt 63r]

I omit the mistreatment to which I was exposed from all sides, and one will note how secure and imperturbable I was. *Socrates* and *Jesus* were my models.[161] From the Meeting minutes, about which *I myself* said, in order to be responsible. Erroneous opinion of the guardian and her [Blatt 63v] son, to have [him] at her place— was always there, and still others who[m] one does not want to mention. Europa Steht.[162] On this, don't dwell on the period when Herr G[iannatasio] [Blatt 64r] did not want her in his Institute, and this person …. //

---

[158] At this time Janschikh lived in suburban Landstrasse, at the corner of Ungargasse and (today's) Beatrixgasse, but would soon move to the Mauthaus (Customs House, in connection with his employment there) at the south end of the Fleischmarkt in the walled City.—TA

[159] This entry must have been made by ca. Friday, January 21 (if on the day of Janschikh's immediately previous entries), but in any case no later than Saturday, January 22. No riots had been mentioned in recent concert reports, although the annual concert to benefit the *Bürgerspital* (the Home for the Elderly Poor) in suburban St. Marx, held in the Grosser Redoutensaal on the evening of December 25, 1819, was reported as unusually full well before the beginning of the program. See Bäuerle's *Allgemeine Theater-Zeitung* 13, No. 1 (January 1, 1820), p. 4.—TA

[160] An appropriate Friday night supper, given Beethoven's rare pious pronouncements earlier in the day (see Blatt 52r).—TA

[161] This sentence is occasionally cited out of context to imply an exalted philosophical meaning that Beethoven did not intend.—TA

[162] The word "Steht" (translated as "dwell" in context) really belongs to the next sentence, but Beethoven (ever fond of wordplay) places "Europa" in front of it, rendering it as "Europa steht"

PROPRIETOR SEELIG: I believe that it is better that the dried codfish is outside rather than here inside. // What is your dear little nephew doing? [//]

[Blatt 64v]

BEETHOVEN [concluding his rambling musings]: No guardian, for anyone who took the trouble to counsel [him] to love only the Good. I was to gain because of my desire for money. That I committed nothing that could make me forfeit the guardianship was proof that I would be recognized as guardian. [//]
   [End of entries at *Zur Stadt Triest*; probably late evening of Friday, January 21.]

[Blatt 65r]

[Midday dinner at Janschikh's apartment, Landstrasse, northeast corner of Ungargasse and Beatrixgasse, probably accompanied by nephew Karl; 2 p.m.[163] on Sunday, January 23.]

JANSCHIKH: You are from Bonn! Is it true that, in a Nuns' Cloister, the male organ of Jesus is shown as a relic?[164] // Among the miraculous works of St. Benno[165] is one relating that, even after his *death*, he appeared to Duke Albert of Bavaria in a dream and put one of his eyes out. [//] [Blatt 65v]
   The Jesuits wanted us to transfer to Indostan and found the caste system. [//] The Ponzen Brahmin priests were the ones who threw pure belief into the shade in all cities. // Confucius. [//]
   58 years. [//] For three years, I was in his house every day.[166] [//]

[Blatt 66r]

(Europe stands!), the first words in his 1814 cantata *Der glorreiche Augenblick*, Op. 135, with libretto by Weissenbach, who was often mentioned in the conversation books of this period.—TA
   [163] The time was specified on Blatt 57v above.—TA
   [164] Beethoven must certainly have found such questions annoying and Janschikh himself obnoxious.—TA
   [165] Benno (1066–1106), Bishop of Meissen, was canonized in 1523, which occasioned Luther's writing *Wider den neuen Abgott und alten Teufel, der zu Meissen soll erhoben werden*. In 1576 the bones of the Saint were transferred to the Duke Albrecht V of Bavaria, who, influenced by the Jesuits, preserved them in the Frauenkirche in Munich. See Höfer *et al.*, *Lexikon für Theologie und Kirche*, vol. 2, col. 200.—KH
   [166] Linz's Cathedral Kapellmeister Franz Xaver Glöggl (mentioned on Blatt 67r below) would have been about fifty-five in 1820; Janschikh was born in Linz and could well have visited Glöggl on a daily basis.—TA

BEETHOVEN [**writing so as not to be overheard**]: Don't say anything about our Bohemians; this man is also one of them.[167] [//]

Everything can be deduced merely from her K. [//]

[Blatt 66v]

UNKNOWN: [Drawing of a tree.][168] *Adelaide.*[169] [//]

[Blatt 67r]

JANSCHIKH: He ate at my place this Fall. He is a Cathedral Kapellmeister and is called Glöggl.[170] [//]

A dish from Frankfurt. [//] They are not salted. //

ANTONIA JANSCHIKH: <He may never know what he had to eat at midday. The Steigner.[171]> [//] A very old wine. [//] [Blatt 67v] That is not my brother, rather my brother's son.[172] [//]

JANSCHIKH: Ruprecht[173] has drafted a superb sketch for an opera. Entitled: "The Founding of Pennsylvania, or The Arrival of Penn in America." [//] His plan was

---

[167] This entry of Beethoven's suggests that Janschikh had just made a disparaging comment about the Bohemians, loud enough for the composer to hear it and be embarrassed by it.—TA

[168] Photo of this page in Köhler *et al.*, *Konversationshefte*, vol. 1, facing p. 128.—TA

[169] *Adelaide*, Op. 46, a song by Beethoven from 1795–1796, was so popular that (like the Septet, Op. 20) it became an almost unattainable standard for the composer's later works.—TA

[170] Franz Xaver Glöggl (1764–1839), City Music Director in Linz since 1790, and its Cathedral Kapellmeister since 1798. He was a teacher of Tobias Haslinger and wrote several theoretical works. Beethoven became acquainted with him in Linz in fall 1812 and composed the *Equale* for trombones for All Souls Day (November 2).

Franz Xaver Glöggl would have been about fifty-five years old in 1820, therefore possibly the person mentioned above as being fifty-eight years old. His father Joseph had been born in Baden in ca. 1739, had moved to Linz in ca. 1763 and, having essentially handed his professional activities to his son, had retired back to Vienna in ca. 1790. He then played viola in the orchestra of the Theater auf der Wieden by ca. 1794, and trombone in the Court Theaters by 1801, possibly playing part-time at the Theater an der Wien when Beethoven premiered *Christus am Ölberge* (with trombones) there in 1803, and died in 1806. Thus the "younger" Glöggl, if he visited his father in Vienna, may have met Beethoven by 1803 or so. See Frimmel, *Handbuch*, I, p. 171; Thayer-Deiters-Riemann, III, pp. 351, 355, and 358; Wurzbach, vol. 5, pp. 218–219; Clive, pp. 132–133.—KH/TA

[171] Unclear reference because it is crossed out and because the surrounding subjects change rapidly: possibly a family named Steigner or a female member of it; possibly a food dish or wines (plural) from a so-named family or region.—TA

[172] Antonia Janschikh's maiden name had been Mainolo, therefore presumably her brother's name as well. See Heft 3, Blatt 20v.—TA

[173] Johann Baptist Rupprecht (1776–1846), florist and amateur poet. Beethoven and Janschikh seemingly thought highly of him; Bernard did not. See Heft 5, Blatt 41v. The original German title:

to give you the words for musical composition. [//] Too bad that it has not yet [Blatt 68r] been performed. [//]

Did you know Süssmayr?[174] My wife asks you about it. [//]

Early in the year, we are going to Baden. //

[After Sunday dinner with the Janschikhs, Beethoven and Karl return to the City, probably through the Carolinentor, stop at *Zur Stadt Triest* on the Neuer Markt, and encounter Bernard, possibly also Peters.]

BERNARD: Peters has a sick wife, to whom he is taking oysters home with him. [//]

[Beethoven and Karl continue to Blöchlinger's Institute in the Josephstadt, and they possibly arrive after the school's 7 p.m. curfew.][175]

[Blatt 68v]

NEPHEW KARL: The door of the adjoining room, where Herr v. Blöchlinger sleeps, is always open. // What time will you come to get me tomorrow? //

[Beethoven leaves Karl and walks home.]

BEETHOVEN **[presumably at his apartment; either late on Sunday, January 23, or early on Monday, January 24]**: Concerning Karl:

1. About the Commission as he went away.

2. Concerning the Confession, when, instead of going to Confession, he ran to her.

3. Lies, that he <went to> came from Mödling on foot.

4. That the mother urges him to neglect his studies. [//]

[Blatt 69r]

Die Begründung von Pensilvanien, oder Die Ankunft des Penn in Amerika. The subject was William Penn, 1644–1718 (correction courtesy of Grita Herre). See also Clive, pp. 297–298.—TA

[174] Franz Xaver Süssmayr (1766–1803), composer, pupil of Mozart. From 1794 he was Kapellmeister of the German Opera in the I.R. Court Theater next to the Burg (designated as National Theater in 1774). Carl Czerny gave evidence of a personal encounter between Beethoven and Süssmayr in 1801. See Othmar Wessely, "Süssmayr," *MGG*, vol. 12, cols. 1697–1698; Thayer-Deiters-Riemann, II, p. 295; Ziegler, *Addressen-Buch*, p. 67 (theater's history).—KH

[175] The uninterrupted walking time between Janschikh's apartment and Blöchlinger's Institute was ca. 70 minutes. The 7 p.m. school curfew (and Karl's possible overstaying it by thirty minutes on visitation days) is noted above on Blatt 6r. In this case, they seemingly arrived after Blöchlinger was asleep.—TA

NEPHEW KARL [**presumably at or shortly after leaving Blöchlinger's Institute; possibly late morning of Monday, January 24**]:[176] I have received red wine with water one single time because of diarrhea. //

I slept very well yesterday. //

On an officially-stamped folio.[177] //

The magnet pulls with a very great strength. [//] [Blatt 69v]

Yes, no one is learning natural history. // Two [students] are becoming acquainted with animals; but when they come to minerals, then he [Blöchlinger] will certainly provide them. // When I learned physics, materials were provided from the apothecary's. [//]

[Blatt 70r]

BEETHOVEN [**probably in a coffee house in the City with Karl, reading newspapers; possibly midday of Monday, January 24**]:

Bohemian pheasants, Herrengasse No. 68;

Zur wilden Ente [At the Wild Duck] in the Wildpretmarkt; Metzger, wild game dealer.[178] [//]

[Blatt 70v]

NEPHEW KARL [**similarly looking at newspapers**]: We have not walked so much today.[179] //

A new book about law.[180] [//]

He [Blöchlinger] says that at present he has no piano teacher. [//] It would be good. [//]

[Blatt 71r]

---

[176] See Dr. Bach's proposal that they go and see Winter on the coming Monday (Blatt 55v).—TA

[177] For another seeming reference to stamped paper, see Blatt 54r above.—TA

[178] See the *Intelligenzblatt*, No. 18 (January 24, 1820), p. 119, and No. 24 (January 31, 1820), p. 158 (Advertisements). Immediately under the advertisement for pheasants in both of these issues is the advertisement of Joseph Metzger (see Heft 4, Blatt 19v).

Herrengasse No. 68 [renumbered as 60 in 1821] was directly across the street from the back of the Harrach Palace and was owned by Prince Trautmannsdorf.

Metzger and the *Ente* were both on Wildpretmarkt/Kammermarkt, No. 1318 [renumbered as 550 in 1821], one block south of Tuchlauben (Behsel, pp. 3 and 17); see also Heft 4, Blatt 19v.—KH/TA

[179] This suggests that Karl and Beethoven walked a great deal the previous day, Sunday, January 23, possibly from Blöchlinger's Institute in the Josephstadt to Janschikh's apartment in the Landstrasse, and back. "Today," Monday, they would walk only from Blöchlinger's Institute to lawyer Bach's office in the so-called *Figaro* House, and back to the Josephstadt again, about two thirds of the previous day's distance.—TA

[180] Karl may have found an advertisement for such a book in a newspaper.—TA

BACH [at his office in the *Figaro* House; probably early afternoon on Monday, January 24]:[181] His memorandum leads to nothing, because he is still an orphan [i.e., a minor]. Today it already went off course about the report from the Appellate Court to the Magistrat. [//] I must have the testimonials concerning his studies. [//] [Blatt 71v] One can get duplicates of the testimonials; be so good as to take care of those. [//] Let's go to the consultants', if the report goes up. [//] But I shall go to Piuk.[182] [//] [Blatt 72r] I am going for myself in order to lend more weight to the matter. The best is in the afternoon from 3 to 6 o'clock. [//]

[Blatt 72v]

NEPHEW KARL [after leaving lawyer Bach's office; probably midafternoon on Monday, January 24]: He [Bach] asked me how old I am.
Whether I want to have you as my guardian.
Whether I am convinced that you want only my best interests.
Whether I know the guardian.
Whether he [the guardian] had concerned himself about me.
In which school I am enrolled. [//]
    [Beethoven walks back to the Josephstadt with Karl.]

[Blatt 73r]

PETERS [at *Zur Stadt Triest* with Bernard; after Beethoven takes Karl back to Blöchlinger's Institute; probably late afternoon of Monday, January 24]: You are giving your co-guardian (honorary guardian) nothing at all to do. I am envious of Bernard.[183] [//]

[Blatt 73v]

---

[181] Although Bach seems to have held Sunday morning office hours (see Blatt 55v), this meeting seems to have taken place on Monday.—TA

[182] Franz Xaver Piuk (whom Bach phonetically spells as "Biuk"), Magistrat's Councillor for Municipal Legal Cases, lived in the Himmelpfortgasse No. 1011 [renumbered as 954 in 1821]. Beethoven began corresponding with him concerning the contest over Karl's guardianship already in 1819. As an authorized consultant, Piuk turned down the request for Karl to be given a passport to Bavaria. See Frimmel, *Handbuch*, II, p. 23; *Hof- und Staats-Schematismus*, 1819, I, p. 655; Thayer-Deiters-Riemann, IV, p. 144; Weise, p. 25. See Blatt 58r for Hober (Vice Mayor for Legal Affairs) at the same address, though certainly a different apartment in the large building.—KH/TA

[183] Peters was a much closer acquaintance, even friend, of Bernard's than Oliva was, but Peters's remark adds substance to Oliva's disapproving observation that Bernard had too much spare time in his professional life (see Heft 2, Blatt 13r, ca. April 5, 1819).—TA

BERNARD [continuing]: You must give Peters a decree and a certain sphere of activity (as co-guardian). The lawyer can do nothing about the progress of activity. If it depended upon him, he would end it on the spot. [//]

[Blatt 74r]

PETERS: Today the settlement of a petition to Prince Lobkowitz was handed down, [a petition] that was made to the Lower Austrian *Landrecht* 2 years ago. // Your affairs are going astonishingly fast. [//]

[Blatt 74v]

BERNARD: The lawyer knows the nature of the proceedings of the trial; one cannot persuade him here. [//] The interpretation of the Minutes does not depend upon the Magistrat, but rather upon the Appellate Court. The Magistrat [Blatt 75r] appears only as a [disinterested] party here. [//] The lawyer will already cite that, because he certainly makes the opposite point as your representative. There will also perhaps be a commission where Karl will appear, [Blatt 75v] and therefore the questions of the lawyer are good, because he must be informed about everything, therefore even about the way in which the boy thinks. // This is his business. [//] [Blätter 76 and 77 are missing.] [Blatt 78r] These people acquire great skill in comprehending so many different kinds of incidents. // Just as with the Magistrat, that is a trifle. Until now it has had no judge appointed over it. [//]

[Blatt 78v]

PROPRIETOR SEELIG [joining them at their table]: But materialist. //
   Drink some tea with me! With rum? //
   I am indeed from Würzburg, wine territory.[184] [//] [Blatt 79r]
   Just try some; it is white *Apaya* rum! //

JANSCHIKH [joining the group]: How did you sleep? //

NEBERICH [also joining the group]: When can you do Stieler and me the honor, if you will, of having midday dinner with us at his place? [//] 11 various kinds? // Staudenheimer will also come, if we know the day beforehand. // Stieler is leaving [Vienna] soon, and you already promised last year[185]—upon his promise to return— but you forgot it. Now [Blatt 79v] you must make good on it. The excellent woman

---

[184] Würzburg, in south central Germany, is surrounded by high hills and vineyards.—TA
[185] Neberich had visited Vienna almost exactly a year before: "Herr Adam Neberich, Grand-ducal Hessian State Pensioner from Mainz" arrived in Vienna on January 11, 1819, and lodged in the City, *Hungarian Crown*, No. 1018 [renumbered as 961 in 1821]. In 1820, now listed as a *Kaufmann*

must meet you before she goes to Russia! // Which day? // It is very nice at Stieler's place, and we will be disturbed less than in a restaurant. // He is healthy, but his daughter is still sick. [//]

JANSCHIKH: The husband [man] is the Lord of Creation. [//] My father and I, his son, are from Linz in Upper Austria. Earlier generations are unknown to me. [//]
[End of entries at *Zur Stadt Triest*; late afternoon of Monday, January 24.]

[Blatt 80r]

OLIVA **[at his apartment in the Blutgasse, evidently confined to his bed; possibly still on Monday, January 24]:**[186] I have suffered terribly with peritonitis, but it is better now. I hope to go out again in a few days. I've been in bed since Friday [January 21]. //

The day before yesterday [probably Saturday, January 22], in the afternoon, a young man was here from Hessen-Kassel, and he had a little packet to deliver to you. He looked for you in vain everywhere, and accidentally learned that you often came here. The packet is lying there on the chest.[187] [//] [Blatt 80v]

When I am healthy again, I will take care of it; right now, I can do nothing. // I don't know which formality it needs; I believe that it must be a stamp. Altogether it should arrive in 2 or 3 days. By Thursday [January 27], I'll go out. //

I became ill on the same evening when we were together the last time; otherwise everything was already cared for. [//] [Blatt 81r]

This Herr Dr. Wekbeker from Koblenz[188] is a cousin of yours on your mother's side; he is happy to have such a great relative. He made your acquaintance earlier

---

(merchant) from Mainz, he arrived on January 17. See *Wiener Zeitung*, No. 9 (January 13, 1819), p. 35, and No. 14 (January 19, 1820), p. 56; Clive, p. 246.—KH/TA

[186] In context it appears that Beethoven has not seen Oliva in at least four days and probably more. Oliva's most recent conversation book entries had been on Blätter 46r–48v, probably Tuesday, January 18, nearly a week before. His apartment was no more than a five-minute walk from *Zur Stadt Triest*.—TA

[187] Possibly a packet from Dr. Georg Christoph Grosheim (1764–1841), a music teacher in Kassel, who had written to Beethoven as recently as November 10, 1819, sending his letter via the Electoral Legation's secretary Weissenborn, who was staying at the home of the Electoral Ambassador, Baron von Münchhausen; see Brandenburg, *Briefwechsel*, No. 1352; Albrecht, *Letters to Beethoven*, No. 263; Clive, pp. 141–142.—TA

[188] According to Schmidt-Görg, the physician Dr. Weckbecker may have been a distant relation of Beethoven's, since the composer's maternal grandmother was Anna Clara Keverich, née Westorff. At most, the mother of the doctor might have been a cousin of Beethoven's mother. At the period in question, the name Weckbecker is encountered both in Ehrenbreitstein and in Koblenz (across the Rhein River from one another). See Schmidt-Görg, *Die Geschichte seiner Familie*, pp. 234–235. Eventually Oliva complained to his own doctor about Weckbecker's rude bedside manner. See Heft 7, Blatt 29r.—KH/TA

at Czerny's. // The Doctor's mother was born a Wistorf. // There was a Wistorf family here that died out. [//] **[conversation continues on Blatt 81v]**

[Blatt 81v]

BEETHOVEN **[musings probably written earlier]**:[189] ... where one would have wished that I would remain away from him entirely, where he [Karl] [verb: was] absolutely not obedient to me, only to his mother, because I, as before [verb missing] all cares, etc. //

OLIVA **[continuing conversation from Blatt 81r]**: He was a Privy Councillor to the Elector of Trier. //

This man [still Weckbecker] is the substitute[190] for my physician, who is ill; he appears to be skillful. [//] [Blatt 82r] It appears to me that the son knows nothing about it. //

Is the Archduke [Rudolph] restored to health yet? // But for you, that is good; then you can work undisturbed. [//] Will the Mass [*Missa solemnis*] be finished soon? //

The lawyer really picked up on the case. //

Less than a serious Police transgression, it is between Criminal and Simple Police transgression. [//]

[Seemingly the end of the conversation with Oliva, begun on Blatt 80r.]

[Blatt 82v]

BEETHOVEN **[more musings, intermittently through Blatt 87v]**: she must be unable to do harm; only then can consideration take place. In other respects a means should be found, so the Pension can [Blatt 83r] also be raised without her. [//] Finally I obligate myself [to that] which is always understood in me anyhow, to have an [Blatt 83v] investigation made. In addition to time, so much money, and so much exertion have been lost. Also her intrigues extended to my home; the son ran away when he had committed an error, and then found protection with her. [Blatt 84r]

Then it was learned that my brother was not of the Nobility.[191] It is remarkable,

---

[189] Beethoven's rambling notes concerning nephew Karl's guardianship may be found on Blätter 52v (top), 62r (long, beginning close to top), 64v (top), and now 81v (top), suggesting that he often began these notes on a nearby page that was empty. Therefore, he had probably made this entry before visiting Oliva, who then wrote his entries on either side.—TA

[190] *Substitut*: in modern terminology, an assistant.—KH

[191] The Viennese often confused the Dutch "van" in Beethoven's family name (meaning "from" a place) with the German and Austrian "von," a designation of nobility that was also used to flatter a commoner. Families like the Webers had even adopted the "von" for self-aggrandizement.—KH

so much is certain that there was a serious gap here, which should <not> be filled, because I accordingly do not belong by nature among these plebes.[192] [Blatt 84v]

[at a coffee house, presumably in the City; probably late afternoon of Wednesday, January 26, 1820:]

At Gerold's on Stephansplatz: [published] 1818, *On the Use of Cold and Luke-warm Waters through Showers or Baths in Illness with Fever*, etc., 1 fl. 30 kr. W.W.[193] [//]

Bank Direction [will pay to bank share owners] "whose deposits earned the full legally-claimable dividend [from December 18] until March 31, 1819, etc. [Blatt 85r] 8 fl., as documented proportion of the profit achieved for every bank share, based on 23 fl. as the full semiannual amount."[194] [//]

Merchant's young widow as housekeeper, inquire in the Allgemeines Auskunfts Comptoir, No. 3 on Michaelerplatz.[195] [//] [Blatt 85v]

[returning to his musings about Karl:]

The last *Tagsatzung*.[196]

It can be about clothes again; the mother said it has just made a suitable *Be-g* [*sic*]—which also has the appearance of being against me. It may easily be refuted; everyone who ever had [anything] to do with education can imagine [Blatt 86r] that there is certainly a terrible purpose in such opposition.

How little obedient.

The guardian does not show up, and the woman is [illegible word]. It therefore also proves that one has agreed with me in matters that are essential. [Blatt 86v]

In case the appeal is not won, then I shall also, at this time, pay out the arrears— Such is the nature of this social level, this rabble for whom no one can have respect, and that, in general, is the character of this miserable Mother. H[?]—as I am inclined to send the <illegible word> back, because just such a Mother honors nothing and knows nothing. [Blatt 87r]

---

[192] There is the first letter or two of a new word here, difficult to read, but possibly *M* or even *Ke*.—KH

[193] Excerpt from an advertisement in the *Wiener Zeitung*, No. 20 (January 26, 1820), p. 80: "The 1818 book *Von dem auffallenden Nutzen des kalten und lauwarmen Wassers durch Uebergießungen, oder Baden in hitzigen Krankheiten* is to be had, in commission, at Carl Gerold's on the Stephansplatz for 1 fl. 30 kr. W.W." This is a book by "Herr Court Physician Dr. Fröhlich." Although this advertisement appeared several more times, only January 26 is relevant here, since it may be concluded from the two advertisements that follow immediately afterwards that all of the advertisements were extracted from the same newspaper.—KH

[194] Excerpt from an announcement from the Austrian National Bank in the *Amtsblatt* of the *Wiener Zeitung*, No. 7 (January 26, 1820), p. 20; it had also appeared in No. 6 (January 22, 1820), p. 15.—KH

[195] See *Intelligenzblatt*, No. 20 (January 26, 1820), p. 133 (Advertisement). The same advertisement appeared on January 19 and 21, 1820.—KH

[196] December 7, 1819; see Heft 4, Blatt 1r, etc.—TA

At that time, she wanted him [to go] to Kudlich. I wanted to leave him at Giannatasio's, but she knew that she found there a man who certainly had my principles, since *this* with her consent <also> ....

As soon as one does not retain me in the position this year, I won't pay a *Heller* [Blatt 87v] for my nephew and this guardian! I want to see, though, whom they will name for me. What has once been determined for his education cannot be removed. Thus the Magistrat makes another type of intentional agitation. [//]

[Blatt 88r]

OLIVA [presumably at his apartment in the Blutgasse; probably later in the afternoon of Wednesday, January 26]: I have been out of bed today already, and hope to be able to go out yet this week. [//] My doctor has prescribed for me a good Spanish or Tokay wine; therefore I shall have to turn to Herr Seelig [proprietor of *Zur Stadt Triest*]. [//]

The food is worse than the drink [in the boarding house]. [//] [Blatt 88v] One can take only a Seidel.[197] [//]

It is detestable that Bernard is such a gourmet. // [We] are both Bohemians. The one, however, has more soul than the poet. // He is indeed prideful now. // I never speak with him about you and your business affairs, if I am not directed by you. [//] [Blatt 89r] At that time we spoke about the boarding house, then about the book by Görres.[198] // I noted then that you wrote something to yourself in your book and turned the page; then later, he took the book in order to say something to you, and read the passage that struck him; perhaps this was the reason. // I saw very well that it was not right with you that he read it. [//] [Blatt 89v]

Weissenbach has an extremely favorable opinion of him. //

Is everything alright between him [Bernard] and Schickh? // A goddamned pretension![199] // Oh, he [Bernard] whitewashes himself very much with your friendship. [//] It goes back to the article that Wähner placed in the *Morgenblatt*, where he is called your closest friend over many years.[200] [//] The article was

---

[197] Roughly three-tenths of a liter.—TA

[198] See Blatt 48r.—TA

[199] Original: *eine verfluchte praetension* (also "Goddamned arrogance!"). Oliva was not fond of Bernard.—TA

[200] The *Morgenblatt für gebildete Stände* (Tübingen: J.C. Cotta's Buchverlag), No. 266 (November 6, 1819), p. 1064, says: "Our Beethoven, who certainly is just as fine a musician as Goethe is a poet, has undertaken to compose a cantata for the Musikverein [Gesellschaft der Musikfreunde] here, whose author is the tasteful Herr Bernard, his trusted friend of many years, editor of the *Wiener Zeitung* as well as of the *Wiener Zeitschrift*. According to reports, this work has been interrupted for a short time by other projects, since the Archduke Rudolph wishes for a new Mass from our composer. As ever, Beethoven enjoys the encouraging good will of this noble Patron of Music ...."—KH

suggested by him. [//] [Blatt 90r] He himself said something from which I inferred it. He spoke of the very correct and good way that Wähner comprehended, and mentioned[201] thereby that he always helped him in these essays, however; but that essay is by Wähner. // He wants to make a name for himself in foreign countries, and that will be easier for him because of your celebrity. [//] [Blatt 90v]

Are you going to Archduke [Rudolph's] tomorrow? [//] Just see the Mass through to the end. [//] You will see: with every explanation [from you], he is still waiting until he has it. //

Then the highest [Bureau of] Justice, where a very fine man is President and who is accessible to Everyman—Fechtig.[202] [//]

BEETHOVEN: Already at Giannatasio's, malicious designs, which one only considers a severe judgement. Such things, where he mostly gave way to this cruel mother? [//]

[Blatt 91r]

OLIVA [continuing]: Just recommend to him that, tomorrow, he sends *something better* if I send .... [//]
[Beethoven leaves Oliva's apartment.]

[Blatt 91v]

JANSCHIKH [at *Zur Stadt Triest*, as Beethoven comes in and soon leaves; the evening of Wednesday, January 26]: You appear as if you are leaving already, because I make the payment. What's new?[203] [//] What is your Flesh and Blood [Karl][204] doing? [//] Where are you going now? [//] What's the status of the Trial business? [//] Have you spoken with anyone about the appeal? [//] Schmerling is a noble and imperturbable man, who has great trust [Blatt 92r] and much influence. [//]

Come tomorrow; I am going now into the other room, because I have associates

---

[201] Original *erwähnte*, a word-play when used in conjunction with Wähner.—TA

[202] Baron Ferdinand von Fechtig (b. 1756) was First Vice President of the High Bureau of Justice from 1805 to 1817, and President of the Appellate Court since 1818. He lived on the Alter Fleischmarkt No. 734 [renumbered as 690 in 1821 (Behsel, p. 21)]. In 1824 he became second President of the High Justice Department and in 1829 High Justice President. See Gräffer-Czikann, II, pp. 105–107; *Hof- und Staats-Schematismus*, 1817, I, p. 258, and 1818, I, p. 564.—KH/TA

[203] Beethoven may have gone to *Zur Stadt Triest* briefly to have the prescribed Spanish or Tokay wine sent to the housebound Oliva.—TA

[204] See Blätter 45r and 56v (twice) for use of this phrase.—TA

there and am still going to the Ball with them today [at 9 p.m.].[205] [//] Do you have a commission for some ladies or masks? [//]

He [Karl?] has a bright and strong look in his eye, and, in his appearance, seems to proclaim acumen and stability. [//]

[Blatt 92v: no writing on this page.]

End of Heft 6

[205] "Today" is Wednesday, January 26, and the ball at the Redoutensäle begins at 9 p.m. and ends at 5 a.m. Such balls began on Sunday, January 23, and were held on each Sunday and Wednesday, from 9 p.m. to 5 a.m., through Sunday, February 6. The final four balls were held on Tuesday, February 8; Thursday, February 10; Sunday, February 13 (as usual, from 9 p.m. to 5 a.m.), and then on Tuesday, February 15 [Fat Tuesday, *Mardi gras*], when the ball began at 8 p.m. and ended at 12 midnight. See Court Theater, Zettel, Wednesday, January 26, 1820; others from January 23 through February 15, 1820 (Bibliothek, Österreichisches Theatermuseum; courtesy Othmar Barnert).—TA

Heft 7

(ca. January 27, 1820 – February 22, 1820)

[Inside front cover]

BEETHOVEN [possibly away from his apartment; probably ca. Thursday, January 27]:

[Blatt 1r]

BERNARD [possibly at a coffee or wine house; probably ca. Thursday, January 27]: The reason he still says that is, therefore, because the matter is not yet finished with the Magistrat; and the decision of the Court of Appeals would have to be set aside because of that. [//] 6 fl. [//]

BEETHOVEN [reckoning cost of refreshments]:[2]

 1 [fl.] 30 [kr.]
 45
 ———
 2 15

[Blatt 1v]

---

[1] Sketch for the rushing violoncello/contrabass accompaniment in the "Amen" of the Gloria from the *Missa solemnis*. See the *Gesamtausgabe*, Series 19, No. 203, p. 87, bar 5 (beginning the second half of the bar).—TA

[2] He had spent exactly the same amounts on ca. Friday, January 7, 1820, also with Bernard; see Heft 6, Blatt 2r.—TA

[probably left alone, drafting a memorandum:]

I admit that the behavior of my nephew could have been better. That was a first case, and one sees that *she* [Johanna] has a great deal of influence, but acknowledges no guilt.[3] But one must take away his own complete dependence upon his mother and then have patience with his poor development, which even Karl cannot relish, and one must always be happy that he already acknowledges better things and wants to vouch for his future.

[Blatt 2r]

OLIVA **[confined to his apartment in the Blutgasse; possibly Friday, January 28]**:[4] I thank you for the wine, but I cannot drink it. It is so bad that it is shocking; I would become completely sick from it. A connoisseur says that a third of this bottle is ethyl alcohol. Only 1½ glasses have been taken out. You should give the rest back. //

The case is therefore going well at the Magistrat's. Dr. [Bach] [sentence ends] //

BEETHOVEN: What you should believe, what and how much, examine that.—As a guest, do not be curious.—Yield to the people, but do not obey them.[5]

[Blatt 2v]

OLIVA: Tomorrow I am going out. [//] The amount of interest from the bank shares doesn't come to much. On which day were they issued? // Where do you want to have it earlier, then? And with bank shares you can get all your money at a moment's notice. Then the security, and then you received 9% interest last year. // You are getting the dividend at the end of June. You will never find a better, more useful, [Blatt 3r] and more secure way to invest your money. [//]

One organ after another is coming into the building, and my headache cannot endure it.[6] //

Have you been to the Archduke [Rudolph's] yet? //

---

[3] Beethoven seemingly writes "Geduld" (patience) here, but probably means "Schuld" (guilt). He may have been thinking ahead to a more appropriate use of "Geduld" in the next sentence.—TA

[4] Following the chronology established in Heft 6, Beethoven had already brought Oliva the supposedly medicinal wine from *Zur Stadt Triest* at least a day before. If Heft 6 ended on Wednesday, January 26, then this visit to Oliva was probably on the following Friday.—TA

[5] Original in Latin: *quid credere debeas / quid et quantum / vide—hospes ne / curiosus.—populo cede, non pare.* In copying such proverbs, Beethoven still treats the conversation books as an extension of his old *Tagebuch* (diary).—KH/TA

[6] Small house organs seem to have been popular. At one time Beethoven even jotted down an advertisement for one. The building in the Blutgasse where Oliva was living still stands today. It has two or three small courtyards and at least three stories; several small pipe or even reed organs within this confined space could have created a considerable cacophony.—TA

<That> It is a very special piece. He [Shakespeare] made it at the request of Queen Elizabeth. Fallstaff pleased her, so she wanted to see him in circumstances of love; therefore he used several characters from *Henry*.[7] [//] [Blatt 3v]

What else I can do will be done. When and where shall I see you? It is important that I conserve my strength. //

The Tokay is not from him [Seelig at *Zur Stadt Triest*]; I saw that from the seal [on the bottle]. It is not smart to send such a thing to a sick person. // Price out the other wine that will do you some good; it will work like medicine on you.[8] [//] [Blatt 4r]

On Monday [January 31], I'll inquire at the Bank. It would be good if you were to come and see me on Monday evening after 7 o'clock, and bring with you your bank shares and the number of the one that you disposed of. //

I am sending the wine back. [//]

[End of conversation; possibly Friday, January 28.]

BEETHOVEN **[probably not at Seelig's establishment, possibly the evening after he visited Oliva; or possibly still on Friday, January 28, continuing to draft a memorandum]**: Things are being changed at State institutions everywhere. Should it be less in the case of education? Earlier, I already had the plan of moving my nephew away from me. <but> Because I saw the terrible difficulties under such a guardian, I considered it best to remove him from here. [//]

[Blatt 4v]

SCHICKH **[presumably in the office of his *Wiener Zeitschrift* in the Kohlmarkt; possibly Saturday, January 29]**:[9] Böhm [artist] may need you again in the second week. //

I need something from you as soon as possible.[10] // <Epigrammatist.> [//] I recommend [Wähner] to you as the new *Redakteur*.[11] // [Blatt 5r] With *him* [Wähner?], as your own experience shows, everything remains as of old. //

---

[7] *The Merry Wives of Windsor*, in which William Shakespeare, reportedly upon the express wish of Queen Elizabeth, incorporated the character Sir John Falstaff, who had already appeared in the play *Henry IV*.—KH

[8] See Beethoven's subsequent discussion with Seelig on Blatt 5v. On Blatt 16r it becomes apparent that Seelig had actually sent a Menescher, rather than the prescribed Tokay wine.—TA

[9] Schickh's handwriting established by Schindler in Heft 55, Blatt 11r.—KH

[10] Beethoven would compose *Abendlied unterm gestirnten Himmel*, WoO 150, for the embattled editor Schickh and his *Wiener Zeitschrift* in the first days of March 1820.—TA

[11] Through No. 9 (Thursday, January 20, 1820), p. 72, the staff line in the *Wiener Zeitschrift* read: "Herausgeber: Joh. Schickh; Redakteur: J.C. Bernard." From No. 10 (Saturday, January 22, 1820), p. 80, it indicated: "Herausgeber und Redakteur: Joh. Schickh." *Herausgeber* would usually be understood as publisher, while *Redakteur* would be the editor. Schickh's entry could pertain to

BERNARD [presumably in the office of the *Wiener Zeitung*, where pen and ink were present; possibly Saturday, January 29]:[12] The judge lives in the Lange Gasse, where the Althan woman is.[13] You merely write: "Because I have determined not to retain my present apartment longer [than the current lease], I hereby give notice to that effect."[14] [//]

[Blatt 5v]

PROPRIETOR SEELIG [upon Beethoven's arrival at *Zur Stadt Triest*; probably the evening of Sunday, January 30]: My Tokay is certainly good and *generally* acknowledged as such. Indeed you yourself have drunk it. Von Oliva should send the rest back to me, though. Especially because he said that my seal was not on it, I want to [Blatt 6r] exchange it. // Von Peters is a wine connoisseur who should also examine my Tokay, because the judgement of the Doctor is incorrect. S[eeli]g. //

[Blatt 6v]

BERNARD [at *Zur Stadt Triest*; probably late evening, Sunday, January 30]: A new comedy by the Court actor Töpfer was given today; it pleased very much.[15] [//]

What is [long space] Oliva doing?[16] [//] He lacks a passion for life; he is worn out. //

Now I must completely finish the oratorio [text for *Der Sieg des Kreuzes*]. Until

---

Friedrich Wähner, who ultimately succeeded Bernard as *Redakteur* of the *Wiener Zeitschrift*. Bernard had withdrawn as *Redakteur*, and it is often difficult to distinguish which duties the two had. It seems, however, that Schickh was responsible for determining the content, while Bernard may have done the actual editing of the assembled materials.—KH/TA

[12] The following paragraph is written in ink.—KH

[13] In this sentence "der Richter" could mean someone named Richter, but in context it more likely refers to the judge to whom Beethoven will submit a document. The final phrase, "wo die Althane ist," could mean "where the balcony is," but the noun "Altan" is masculine, and the construction here is decidedly feminine singular. Ziegler, *Addressen-Buch*, p. 152, lists a Countess Althan, Lady to the Empress, City, Bischofgasse No. 768, and there were several other highly placed ladies with that surname.—TA

[14] This entry concerns Beethoven's cancellation notice of his troublesome apartment in the Josephstadt, on the northwest corner of the Glacis and Schwibbogengasse No. 5 (about 300 feet east of Lange Gasse); he intended to spend the summer in Mödling.—KH

[15] *Zwey Tableaux für Eins*, a comedy in four acts by Carl Töpfer, was performed in the Burgtheater on Monday, January 24, 1820, at 7 p.m., "for the benefit of the [four] stage directors." See *Wiener Zeitschrift* 5, No. 13 (January 29, 1820), pp. 102–103. The same new play was performed again on Tuesday, January 25; Thursday, January 27; and Sunday, January 30. Another new play by Töpfer, *Der Tagsbefehl*, was premiered on Friday, February 4 (see Zettel, Bibliothek, Österreichisches Theatermuseum). A close comparison of Theater Zettel and the entries on Blätter 8r–8v and 10r below strongly suggest that "today" was Sunday, January 30.—KH/TA

[16] The original reads "Was macht Oliva?" with a large space between the words "macht" and "Oliva."—KH

now it [Blatt 7r] was really impossible, since, in the evenings, I was obligated to go to the Theater and in the mornings to write about it. [//]

Anyhow, you will go to the country again next Spring. [//] I myself shall take a room in Döbling. [//] Döbling, however, is considered to be very healthful, and especially the air. [//] [Blatt 7v]

I hope that you will find the working [of the oratorio text] to be suitable for composition.[17] [//] Since the poem has no other purpose, it goes without saying that I shall gladly undertake any alteration of it in order for you to find it appropriate to your purpose. //

[Blatt 8r]

WOLF [**encountering them briefly**]: Staudenheimer requests the return of his book.[18] //

BERNARD [**continuing**]: Weissenbach is very ill; he has nose polyps that have expanded into the pharynx [throat]; he must have an operation. // Only excerpts [of plays] and reviews of them. //

On Tuesday, [February 1,] Meyerbeer's new opera will be given at [the Theater] an der Wien.[19] [//] [Blatt 8v] It is better suited to the [Court] Opera [at the Kärntnertor Theater]. //

He[20] must pay him 150 fl. monthly and honor what he writes. // He [Wähner], however, laughed at Schickh, and will leave him in the lurch as soon as he doesn't need him anymore. [//] [Blatt 9r]

---

[17] By March 1820 Beethoven had become disillusioned with Bernard and in January 1824 declined to set the only recently completed text.—TA

[18] See Blatt 15v for the possible identification of this book, for whose return Staudenheim has been asking for some time.—TA

[19] A performance at the Theater an der Wien on February 1, 1820: "*Emma von Leicester, oder: die Stimme des Gewissens*, grand heroic opera in two acts, with dancing, from the Italian of Rossi by Herr Joseph Seyfried; music by Meyerbeer. For the benefit of the singer Herr Joseph Seipelt." *Wiener Zeitschrift* 5, No. 17 (February 8, 1820), pp. 133–135. From its wording, this entry cannot have been made any earlier than Wednesday, January 26, and was likely made four days later. Blatt 16r definitely dates from Wednesday, February 2.—KH/TA

[20] This paragraph concerns Johann Schickh and Friedrich Wähner.—TA

<Schickh married a publicly known whore.[21] Seelig knows her very well, and I believe that she even earned something from him.[22]> [//]

Bach has married a beautiful young wife.[23] //

[Possibly the end of entries for Sunday, January 30.]

BERNARD [at *Zur Stadt Triest* with Peters; possibly the evening of Monday, January 31]: Oliva was at [midday] dinner [at the boarding house] today [Monday, January 31]; he looked very bad. They cooked special dishes for him.[24] [//]

[Blatt 9v]

PETERS: Even well-bred people don't know to refuse everything. //

BERNARD: He merely maintained that the witnesses were present; otherwise he said nothing, because it was not an actual Commission. [//]

[Blatt 10r]

PETERS: If I am not at home, I shall be replaced by highly gifted friends. //

---

[21] By calling Schickh's wife an "öffentliche Hure," Bernard, who obviously had no respect for his former business associate, was engaging in scandalous gossip. On August 19, 1818, in the Kirche am Hof, Johann Schickh had married Anna von Arvay, the daughter of an official in one of the noble houses. He gave his age as 47, hers as 22, and both were listed as Catholic and single (previously unmarried). They seemingly had no children: none were baptized in the Kirche am Hof or the Peterskirche through 1825, or the Michaelerkirche through 1824, and none survived when Schickh died in Gastein on August 1, 1835. An official from Prince Palm's administration signed their mutual Testament, dated January 2, 1821, so it is possible that Anna's father was associated with that house. In any case, there is no suggestion in any of the surviving documents examined that Anna Schickh had any history of moral or legal impropriety. See Pfarre Am Hof, Trauungs-Register No. 3 (1801–1824), fol. 213 (housed at the Michaelerkirche, Vienna); Verlassenschafts-Abhandlung (Johann Schickh), Fasz. 2: 5426/1835 (which includes numerous additional documents, including the Testament of January 2, 1821; Wiener Stadt- und Landesarchiv); Totenbeschauprotokoll (Johann Schickh), 1835, S, fol. 47v (death on August 1 in Gastein, "an der schwarzen Krankheit").—TA

[22] This entry suggests that Beethoven and Bernard were in Seelig's *Zur Stadt Triest*, and that Bernard may have written it for Seelig to read, as well, and join in the joke or gossip at Schickh's expense.—TA

[23] On January 22, 1820 (therefore only eight days before), Beethoven's lawyer, Dr. Johann Baptist Bach, had married in St. Stephan's Cathedral. His wife was Katharina Feicht, born in Temesvar on March 29, 1804, the daughter of the Stadt Lieutenant Gabriel Feicht. See Pfarre St. Stephan, Vienna; Trauungs-Buch, Tom 84 (1816–1821), fol. 266. Bernard describes lawyer Bach's wife as a "junge Frau," therefore also implying that—in contrast to Schickh's wife—she had the virtue of being a virgin. See also Heft 11, Blätter 39v and 72r.—TA

[24] This may have been Oliva's first day out of the house since being ill, or it may just have been the first day that Bernard had seen him at the boarding house after his return. For Oliva's report concerning food, see Heft 3, Blatt 49v.—TA

Czerny is really fine. I am giving him 3 fl.[25] //

BERNARD: It really appears to me that I have something common. //

Don't forget: Wednesday [February 2, Candlemas,] at 10 o'clock [in the morning]. //

<Berlin> //

I asked him whether you already knew him. It appears that he was embarrassed. [//] [Blatt 10v]

It appears that the actor Lembert[26] has edited this letter for him.[27] // He believed that he could make a great sensation here. [//] It appears that his father[28] is also a musician, because they were under Hieronymus[29] in Kassel.

[Blatt 11r]

PETERS: I can fetch you beforehand, because I will be passing by .... // The second examination will go even better. //

My wife took a large black bulldog into her residence[30] and intended him for you; but after 3 days, his Master came to get him. // It cost 10 Ducats. [//]

[Blatt 11v]

OLIVA [seemingly at his office at the bankers Mayer & Landauer, Untere Bäckerstrasse No. 798; presumably Tuesday, February 1]: I have put in a request [at the boarding house] concerning a housekeeper and have received the most reassuring

[25] Joseph Czerny was piano teacher to the Lobkowitz family, and Peters was in charge of the children's education.—TA

[26] Johann Wilhelm Lembert, pseudonym of Wenzel Tremler (1780–1838), Court Actor and poet. Called from Stuttgart to the Vienna Court Theater by Treitschke and Schreyvogel in 1817, he was active as an actor until 1833, and personnel manager and legal advisor thereafter. See Wurzbach, vol. 14, pp. 349–351.—KH

[27] Karl Schuncke (see Heft 6, Blatt 54r).—KH

[28] Karl Schuncke's father, Johann Michael (1778–1821), a well-known horn virtuoso, was a court musician in Kassel and Stuttgart. See Helmuth Hopf, "Schuncke," *MGG*, vol. 12, cols. 325–327; Heft 6, Blatt 54r.—KH/TA

[29] From 1807 to 1813 Napoleon's youngest brother Jerome (1784–1860) resided in Wilhelmshöhe near Kassel as King of Westphalia. In this capacity he had offered Beethoven the position as his Kapellmeister in 1808–1809, resulting in the composer's annual stipend from the Archduke Rudolph and Princes Lobkowitz and Kinsky as an inducement to remain in Vienna. From 1816 until 1827 Jerome lived in Austria as Prince Hieronymus von Montfort, then went to Italy and Switzerland, and, after the February Revolution of 1848, back to France.—KH/TA

[30] Peters's original was *zu sich nehmen*, implying, once again, that she maintained a residence separate from his day-to-day lodgings. As for her judgement in attempting to adopt a dog on Beethoven's behalf, Oliva had already characterized her the previous December 10: "Stupidity personified." See Heft 4, Blatt 25v.—TA

information that they have already sent for a fine old person who is known to them, and tomorrow perhaps I shall receive my answer. Now the question is where you want to speak with her. [//] [Blatt 12r] I was told that the demands in price were very uneven, but that the most expensive [housekeeper] would be 18 fl. //

Concerning the bank, it is necessary that I have the bank shares themselves, in order to produce them, and after that to be able to provide the receipt. I'll do it for you tomorrow afternoon. [//] [Blatt 12v] But you must bring me the bank shares here [presumably at Oliva's office] at 3:30, where I'll copy everything & probably have the money for you by 6 o'clock. [//] I shall try, if possible, to get it for all; I am known there. // Perhaps you can bring them in the morning; I'll be at home until 9:30. [//] [Blatt 13r] Then the copy must be transcribed, because the number is noted on it. // Just decide how you [will] have the papers furnished to me, because if you are not coming, then I shall not go home at that hour; it will lead me out of my way. // Then let us determine right away where or when I am to give you the money, or, if you prefer, [Blatt 13v] go with me to the bank. I have brought you a slip. [//]

PETERS [at *Zur Stadt Triest*, Neuer Markt; presumably Tuesday, February 1]: Oliva's health must gradually be restored through careful diet, moderate exercise in fresh air, and bathing. //

PROPRIETOR SEELIG [serving them]: It is only cold; meanwhile, I'll bring you another. //

[Blatt 14r]

PETERS: His *dreyer* from Ofen is the best wine.[31] //

PROPRIETOR SEELIG: Just leave something out. The red wine must be warm. //

PETERS: Prince Ferdinand Lobkowitz wants to travel to Sicily.[32] [//] He's already passed his exams in Law. // He's 23 years old. [//] I believe that his guardian, Prince Joseph Schwarzenberg, does not want [him to do] it. [//] [Blatt 14v] He (P[rince] Schwarzenberg)[33] did not want Prince Ferdinand to take charge of his estates in Bohemia until he was 28, and because the young prince has certainly not

---

[31] Original *Ofener dreyer*, seemingly a mixture of three wines from Ofen (Buda) in Hungary.—TA
[32] Prince Ferdinand von Lobkowitz (1797–1868) departed for Venice on March 9, 1820. See *Wiener Zeitung*, No. 58 (March 11, 1820), p. 232. The age of majority was twenty-four years.—KH/TA
[33] This clarification was added to the manuscript later.—KH

done that, I have had a great deal of worry. // [The younger daughter] to Prince Schönburg; the oldest [daughter] to Prince Windischgr[ätz].[34] //

Certainly you will now put things to rights with Karl; even Blöchlinger is, so to speak, enamored of you, [Blatt 15r] and appears to be attentive to Karl with joy and seriousness. // Efficient use of time takes place at Blöchlinger's. //

Pepi Lobkowitz[35] said: Beethoven was really right. I must play [piano] more. // Czerny is teaching [Leopoldine] Blahetka a Concerto in B-flat major of yours.[36] [//]
[Blatt 15v]

People know that you have catarrh. //

WOLF: The librarian is asking for the *Praeadamiten*[37] for Doctor S[taundenheim?]. //

PETERS: Baron Puthon[38] would very much like to see you. [//]

JANSCHIKH: If Weissenbach brings it, then everything is customs-free. [//]
[End of conversation at *Zur Stadt Triest*, Tuesday, February 1.]

[Blatt 16r]

---

[34] The eldest daughter of Prince Joseph von Schwarzenberg, Marie Eleonore Philippe (1795–1848), was married to Prince Alfred Windisch-Grätz. The second daughter, Marie Pauline Therese (1798–1821), married Prince Heinrich Eduard Schönburg-Waldenburg; after her death, he married her sister, Aloisia Eleonore (b. 1803). See Wurzbach, vol. 33, p. 88 and the second *Stammtafel* (genealogical chart) after p. 2.—KH

[35] Young Prince Joseph, b. 1803.—KH/TA

[36] Leopoldine Blahetka played Beethoven's Piano Concerto in B-flat, Op. 19, at the Landständischer Saal at the customary "midday hour" (12:30 p.m.) on April 3, 1820. See Schickh's *Wiener Zeitschrift* 5, No. 43 (April 8, 1820), p. 348.—KH/TA

[37] Probably the book *Praeadamitae* by Isaac de La Peyrère (1600–1676), which appeared in 1655. In this work as well as his *Systema theologicum ex Praeadamitarum hypothesi I* (also 1655), La Peyrère presented for the first time the hypothesis of pre-, co-, and postadamites, i.e., men who were said to have lived before, at the same time as, and after Adam, as well as being unrelated to and independent of him. On the basis of these perceptions, the Calvinist La Peyrère became a victim of the Inquisition. After a journey to Rome, he had to recant his teachings and convert to Catholicism. See Höfer-Rahner, vol. 6, col. 797, and vol. 7, col. 652.

Perhaps this is the book that Dr. Staudenheim has repeatedly asked Beethoven to return to him, most recently on Blatt 8r above.—KH/TA

[38] Wholesaler Baron Johann Baptist von Puthon (1773–1839), phonetically called "Button" here. See Heft 4, Blatt 32v.—KH/TA

OLIVA [presumably at his apartment in the Blutgasse, Candlemas; before 9:30 a.m.[39] on Wednesday, February 2]: He [Seelig] sent Menescher rather than Tokay.[40] //

You must open the package. Inside is the receipt that you sign in your own hand. No seal is necessary. The receipt amounts to 112 fl. [C.M.] or roughly 280 fl. W.W. I have made it so that we are getting the money for all 8, and that the bank shares may never be produced. [//] You will get the money tomorrow, because today [February 2] is a holiday.[41] [//] [Blatt 16v]

The form costs 3 kreuzer in silver coin [C.M.]. [//] The official himself filled out the form for me. //

He was somewhat cocky. [//] It is a parade of rudeness, [//] and carries over into the restaurant.

Have you already been to see His Highness [Archduke Rudolph]? //

There is a letter from Vienna in the December issue of the *Überlieferungen*, where there is also something about the Archduke.[42] [//] [Blatt 17r][43]

When and where shall I see you tomorrow concerning the money, [//] and am I to exchange it for you immediately on the Graben?[44] [//]

BEETHOVEN [possibly after visiting the *Wiener Zeitschrift*'s office on the Kohlmarkt; Wednesday, February 2]: "*The Moral Law in us, and the starry Heaven above us.*" … *Kant!!!*[45] [//]

---

[39] See Oliva's note that he will be home in the morning until 9:30 (Blatt 12v above).—TA

[40] During Oliva's recent illness his doctor had prescribed a Spanish or Tokay wine. When Beethoven learned of this (Heft 6, Blatt 88r, January 26 or 27), he went directly to *Zur Stadt Triest* (Heft 6, Blatt 91v) and presumably had Seelig send some Tokay to Oliva, who then became even more ill on the wine (Blatt 2r above). Now it becomes evident that Seelig sent a Hungarian *Menescher* wine instead of Tokay. It is evident from many entries up to this point that Oliva has a rather delicate digestion.—TA

[41] Wednesday, February 2, 1820, was Candlemas, the feast of the purification of Mary after the birth of Jesus.—KH/TA

[42] In the December issue (Nos. 23 and 24) of the 1819 volume of the *Überlieferungen zur Geschichte unserer Zeit* (compiled by Heinrich Zschokke), p. 599, there was a "Letter from Vienna, December 8, about Life, Music, and Literature there," which spoke, among other things, about the relationship between the Emperor and the Pope, and said: "Indeed the Holy Father made a brother of the Emperor into a Cardinal; but when the latter wanted to know how much the honor had cost him, the Emperor considered the matter settled."—KH

[43] Blatt 17r, with the quote from Kant, is illustrated in Köhler *et al.*, *Konversationshefte*, vol. 1, facing p. 129.—TA

[44] Presumably Oliva means the jewelry and banking firm of Hackl & Co., Graben No. 1200. See Heft 8, Blatt 32r. On the corner of Untere Bräunerstrasse and the Graben, it became No. 1133 in 1821 (Behsel, p. 34).—KH/TA

[45] In Schickh's *Wiener Zeitschrift* 5, No. 13 (January 29, 1820), pp. 97–99, and No. 14 (February 1, 1820), pp. 105–107, there appeared an essay by Joseph Littrow under the title "Kosmologische Betrachtungen," at whose conclusion (p. 107) he cited Kant: "There are two things

Littrow,[46] Director of the *Sternwarte* [Observatory]. [//]

[Blatt 17v]

OLIVA [presumably at Beethoven's apartment on the Josephstädter Glacis; early evening of Thursday, February 3]: I wondered why you made it so late;[47] I found the weather very poor toward evening.[48] [//] Have you eaten in the City? [//] 24 kr. //

My physician's name is Franck.[49] He is skillful and has known me since my 15th year.[50] Weckbecker [his assistant] was so unpleasant to me that I wrote to Franck and refused to tolerate the visits by his assistant. [//] [Blatt 18r] He has such unpleasant things about himself; he is curious and wants to know everything; then he is not clean—a most unfortunate man to be a physician. [//] He has a type of headache

that raise Man above himself and lead him to eternal, ever increasing admiration: The Moral Law in us and the starry Heaven above us."
    Beethoven's next completed composition (ca. March 4, 1820) would be the *Abendlied unterm gestirnten Himmel* (Evening Song under the Starry Heaven), WoO 150, with a text by Otto Heinrich von Loeben (writing under the pseudonym H. Goeble), a north German disciple of Kant's philosophy. See Albrecht, "Otto Heinrich Graf von Loeben," pp. 7–32.—KH/TA
    [46] Joseph Johann Littrow (1781–1840), astronomer, became Director of the Observatory on the Blocksberg near Ofen [Budapest] in 1816, and from 1819 was both Director of the Observatory and Professor of Astronomy in Vienna. See *Hof- und Staats-Schematismus*, 1819, II, pp. 246–247; Wurzbach, vol. 15, pp. 286–288. Beethoven wrote over the letters "row" (in his name) a second time.—KH
    [47] If Thursday was still a visitation day at Blöchlinger's Institute, Beethoven may have spent the day there with nephew Karl. Or, given the discussion about the apartment later in this group of entries, February 3 might have marked Beethoven's final move from his monthly rental in the Ballgasse out to the Josephstadt.—TA
    [48] On the day before, Wednesday, February 2, the skies had been clear in the morning, but became overcast by midafternoon, with rain by evening and temperatures just above freezing. See the *Wiener Zeitung*, No. 27 (February 4, 1820), p. 107.—TA
    [49] Possibly the famous physician Johann Peter Frank (1745–1821), who came from Pavia to Vienna in 1795, and became Director of the Viennese Hospitals and Professor at the University. Beethoven had consulted him in 1801. In 1804, Frank went to Vilnius, Lithuania, and later to St. Petersburg, but returned to Vienna in 1811. See Frimmel, *Handbuch*, I, pp. 163–164; Gräffer-Czikann, II, p. 167; *Hof- und Staats-Schematismus*, 1820, II, p. 112; Wurzbach, vol. 4, pp. 320–322; Clive, pp. 114–115.
    This could also mean his son, Dr. Joseph Salesius Frank (1771–1842), married since August 20, 1798 (when he lived in Alservorstadt, No. 130), to the amateur singer Christine Gerhardi, and now a member of the Medical Faculty, living at Naglergasse No. 325 [renumbered as 298 in 1821]. See *Hof- und Staats-Schematismus*, 1820, II, p. 115; Brandenburg, *Briefwechsel*, VII, p. 215; Thayer-Deiters-Riemann, II, p. 133 (marriage record, Pfarre Alservorstadt); Clive, pp. 114–115; Heft 10, Blatt 8r–9r.—KH/TA
    [50] Oliva was born in 1786 and is specific about his fifteenth year (age 14). Therefore, Frank would have known him since ca. 1800, a date that could apply to either father or son. An 1811 description of Oliva as hunchbacked might have been exaggerated, but he had a film over his right eye and his digestion was delicate, so his health may have needed closer supervision than usual.—TA

that distorts his eyes in such a way that one sees nothing but the whites; [he] was almost nasty to me from the time I first saw him. //

Therefore do you want to keep this apartment over the Summer? [//]⁵¹ Then you must take everything with you, and nothing of yours remains here. [//] [Blatt 18v] The [woman] superintendent says that one could give notice at Candlemas and that is now. //

I cannot promise to be home before 7 o'clock in the evening, because I must go to the office tomorrow. [//]

JANSCHIKH [at *Zur Stadt Triest* with Peters; possibly slightly later on the evening of Thursday, February 3]: Sit at our table later; my wife will also come. // I am engaged with a social group, of which 2 men are escorting my wife here. [//] [Blatt 19r] Then why didn't you come? There was a cheerful, merry social group there. [//] You are welcome under all circumstances and conditions. //

PETERS [continuing]: I just came perhaps to see you. At first, I thought that you were sitting with Herr Janitschek, when I was [sitting] with the librarian.⁵² [//] Now I'm occupying my time here with [Janschikh's] beautiful wife, who asks about you every moment. [//] [Blatt 19v]

When you were at my place on the second floor [third floor, American], I was on the first [second, American]! I ran after you, but in vain. //

Anyone who is not dense in the head must uphold your wish. //

He has a recommendation from Wildfeuer.⁵³ //

---

⁵¹ Beethoven must have answered, "No," or "Probably not."—TA

⁵² Presumably Johann Wolf, Librarian to Prince Liechtenstein; see Blatt 15v above.—KH/TA

⁵³ Wilhelm Wildfeyer, a *Hofmeister* (house tutor), b. 1783. In a *Fremden-Tabelle* (census sheet listing servants, visitors, and other temporary residents) from 1824, he is listed as first among nine *Fremden* (in this case, mostly maids) in the apartment of Count Kollowrath, Wohnpartei (apartment) No. 13 in the building Dorotheergasse No. 1182 [renumbered as 1116 in 1821]. See Conscriptions-Bogen, Stadt, No. 1116 (new collation 1116/20) (Wiener Stadt- und Landesarchiv); Frimmel, *Handbuch*, II, pp. 436–437 (where he is called "Wildfeger," an easy confusion of "g" and "y" in *Kurrentschrift*). For a letter from Beethoven, perhaps two years later, see Brandenburg, No. 1498.

In Heft 9, Blatt 2v, Joseph Czerny identifies Wildfeyer as being at Kollowrath's. The Count had been promoted to *wirklich Kämmerer* in 1804 (*Hof- und Staats-Schematismus*, 1819, I, p. 71).

Kollowrath's apartment was Wohnpartei 3 (new collation 1116/3), Census sheet begun in 1810, probably fourth layer of residents (with no clue to dating, other than an 1811 birth in an earlier layer). The family consisted of Count Franz Xaver Collovrad (phonetic spelling), b. 1784 [1783–1855]; wife Juliana, b. 1787 [Julia, 1785–1849]; sons Leopold, b. 1805 [1804–1863]; Theodor, b. 1807 [1806–]; Ferdinand, b. 1808 [1807–]; daughters Xaverine, b. 1809 [1808–]; Leontine, b. 1811 [1812–]; Valeria, b. 1821 [1821–]; Julia, b. 1823 [Juliana, 1823–]; and Maria, b. 1826 [1825–]. Dates in brackets from Wurzbach, "Kollowrath," vol. 12 (1864), *Stammtafel* IV (between pp. 396 and 397), and allow the reader to judge the relative accuracy of the Conscriptions-Bögen of the period.

Reading the Conscriptions-Bögen is often a complicated matter. Given the stability of a noble family like the Kollowraths, the apartment numbered 3 in 1810 was the same as numbered 13 in 1824.

[Beethoven seemingly made a move to leave.]

Frau v[on] Janitschek [Janschikh] is not satisfied with me without you. [//]
[Blatt 20r]

He [Joseph Czerny] is going to see [Leopoldine] Blahetka; [//] in the neighborhood of [Blöchlinger's] Institute.[54] // In the evening, Blöchlinger has said. [//]
Czerny also has time in the evening from 7 to 8. That is the time when Karl can
[take piano lessons]. [//]

[End of entries of Thursday, February 3.]

BEETHOVEN **[presumably at his apartment on the Josephstädter Glacis;
morning of Friday, February 4]**:

Large dust mop.

Bowel movement bowl or shit-shovel.

Juniper wood.

Bernard.

Oliva.

Steiner.

Peters. [Blatt 20v]

Education of an uncle against a miserable guardianship. [//] [Blatt 21r]

My godmother may have been called Frau Bongard or Baumgarten.[55] [//]

[Blatt 21v]

PETERS **[presumably at a coffee house; midday on Friday, February 4]**: You
disappeared suddenly yesterday.[56] //

Himmelbrand tea.[57] //

If the consultant knew the matter accurately through you, then the primary

---

The "new collation" is supplied by the Stadt- und Landesarchiv staff to the surviving Bögen of any
given house, generally in approximate chronological and organizational order from 1805 to ca. 1856.

In any case, Kollowrath had a large family that seemingly needed a tutor.—KH/TA

[54] Blahetka lived in the Josephstadt on the south side of Florianigasse, No. 49 [renumbered as
52 in 1821], at approximately the point where it intersects with today's Buchfeldgasse. Therefore,
Blöchlinger's Institute was ca. 5 blocks southwest of Blahetka's residence. Ziegler, *Addressen-Buch*
(1823), p. 5; Behsel, p. 171.—TA

[55] Beethoven's godmother was Gertrud Baum, *née* Müller. Already in 1810 he expressed the
opinion that his godmother's name was "Baumgarten." See Schmidt-Görg, *Beethoven*, p. 62; Thayer
(original), I, pp. 105–106; Thayer-Deiters-Riemann, I, p. 122; Thayer-Forbes, p. 53.—KH/TA

[56] As noted elsewhere, Beethoven seems to have developed a limited tolerance for Antonia
Janschikh's company.—TA

[57] *Himmelbrandtee*, from the leaves of *Verbascum thapsus* (high taper, mullein or mulen, often
called figwort) were used as folk medicines against dropsy, stones, and kidney illnesses. See Loritza,
p. 63.—KH

consideration has already been taken care of. // If only our Philosophical studies were better. // The Professor of Logic does not understand this himself, but there are still 3 years until then. [//] [Blatt 22r]

Bernhard [*sic*] owes a great deal to his stays in other countries. //

The Engineering Akademie is poorly organized; [a school] where so many means stand at their disposal. // Karl must still study for 10 years. //

You are staying home[?] // An apartment in solitude. // The apartment has a very great deal; it has *you*. // The business [of moving into the apartment] has cost you a great deal—hardly believable. [//] [Blatt 22v]

We have a woman superintendent; her name is Kobold.[58] She is very sweet and charming—but also so hateful that I had to tell her [that] if she did not behave better, I would report her wickedness. // She is a mixture of bestiality and excellence. [//] [Blatt 23r]

We have the works of <Handel [and] Haydn.> [//] [He] makes 120 fl. monthly [from] piano lessons.[59] // Pepi [young Joseph Lobkowitz] is studying a Trio of yours with accompaniment.[60] // The music collection is very large. // I shall show you the catalogue. I don't understand it. // I liked many things in the *Passion* by Weigl.[61] [//]

Barley water and tea. [//] [Blatt 23v] Staudenheim is very fine. [//]

---

[58] No one by this name could be traced in the surviving Conscriptions-Bögen of the Palais Lobkowitz, Stadt, No. 1167 [renumbered as 1101 in 1821].

Many of the Lobkowitz employees did not live in the official palace (where the reigning prince lived with his family), but in the house directly behind it, on the corner of Dorotheergasse and Augustinergasse, No. 1226 [renumbered as 1157 in 1821] also owned by Lobkowitz. In fact, in 1807 Princess Gabriella (b. 1745) [Maria Gabriele, b. 1748], the mother of then-reigning Prince Franz Joseph Maximilian (1772–1816) occupied Wohnpartei 1 in this house—the building where Peters, as family tutor, probably had a room or small apartment later on (although, it, too, cannot be traced). From 1807 the successive *Hausmeister* (superintendents) living in apartment 19 (also numbered 20, 14, 10, and, by 1830, No. 1!) were Matthias Kandel (b. 1755), Anton Straberger (b. 1769), and, probably during this period, Anton Gebhart (b. 1775/78). All of the superintendents were married, and Gebhart's wife was Anna (b. 1788/90). See Conscriptions-Bögen, Stadt No. 1157; new collation 1157/6 and 1157/16 (Wiener Stadt- und Landesarchiv).

At the Lobkowitz Summer Palace in the Ungargasse in suburban Landstrasse No. 309 [renumbered as 347 in 1821 and 388 in 1830], near the *Linie*, the *Hausmeister* was one Matthias Juthmann or Judmann (b. 1763); see Conscriptions-Bögen, Landstrasse 388/1 and 5.—KH/TA

[59] Probably a reference to Joseph Czerny.—TA

[60] Beethoven's Trio in B-flat for piano, violin, and violoncello, Op. 97, dedicated to the Archduke Rudolph and known as the "Archduke" Trio.—KH

[61] Joseph Weigl (1766–1846), opera composer, conductor, and Court Opera director. In March 1821 his oratorio *La Passione di Gesù Cristo* (Italian text by J[oseph = Giuseppe] Carpani) was performed by the Gesellschaft der Musikfreunde twice in German translation. Until that time the work (originally composed in 1804) had been presented only at Court and once in the Lobkowitz house, the performance to which Peters refers here. See Kanne's *Wiener AmZ* 5, No. 28 (April 7, 1821), col. 222; Franz Grasberger, "Weigl," *MGG*, vol. 14, cols. 377–379.—KH

OLIVA [joining them]: 3 kr. for the form and 15 stamped impressions makes 45 kr. W.W. //

The woman where I eat [at the boarding house] has already given instructions [to find a housekeeper for Beethoven] and assured me that I shall hear in a few days. [//]

BEETHOVEN [reckoning the cost of refreshments]: 1 fl. 36 kr. //
[Peters presumably departs, leaving Oliva with Beethoven.]

OLIVA: The bank shares are increasing so much; their price stands at 550 [fl.]. You now received 4400 fl. for your 8 [shares]. [//] [Blatt 24r] What then did you want to do with the money? // If you get bank shares again, then you must spend all the money that you've gotten. // Everything else is uncertain; don't get taken in by any speculation. Your money is earning you at least 8%; you cannot hope for more. Leave the buying and selling to the Jews. We will have no luck at it; that is my advice. [//] [Blatt 24v]

And do what with the money? // In general, it is half-yearly; all *Obligations* are half-yearly. // Have the *Coupons* cashed in. // I must first see the papers; then I would tell you right away what could be done. If I come to see you, let's talk about it. [//] [Blatt 25r]

For every day from the date of issue until the 31st of December, 5 kr. for every share. A share carries cumulative interest at 30 fl. annually, which are these 5 kr. daily. Then, from the beginning of July and beginning of January, you receive the resulting dividends, which now amount to 8 fl., and thus *circa* 16 fl. annually.

Given the   30 fl.
Add the   16
Total, for each share   46 fl.
Has been over 9%. [//]

[Blatt 25v]

BEETHOVEN: 46 fl.   80 fl.   80
            46   <80>   80
            46   <24>   80
            46   <24>   80
            46   <208 fl.>
                                      24
            46   24
            46
            46

OLIVA: 46
                 8
                368 fl.
                368   BEETHOVEN: 27½
                184   27½

                920 fl.
                138

BEETHOVEN: 55 fl. C.M.
                             55
                             28
                             138 fl. C.M.

OLIVA [continuing]: As a convalescent, I am now taking it easy, and must [do so]; also I am very weak. [//] [Blatt 26r]

He ought to send me the *Überlieferungen*.[62] //

I shall recommend good Ofener wine to you. You can surely have an 1811, and then also of lesser qualities. [//] At a new wine dealer's. [//] Not a grocery dealer. [//] We shall first go there and determine the price, and only then should you get some. [//]

[Blatt 26v]

BEETHOVEN [possibly at a wine house or coffee house, jotting random thoughts for his memorandum; later on Friday, February 4]: He spent some time at my place. [//] I threatened my nephew for the 3rd time that I would abandon him, but it is so hard for one who has been led astray. I was raised in a large house[hold]. [//] About her generosity, which [she] bestowed only upon my nephew as an heir, because she entrusted none to her [illegitimate] daughter. [Blatt 27r] I admit my nephew's behavior, but I could quarrel with Giannatasio so little because of it, and blame him just as little as [I could blame] myself; all the more, since Giannatasio already deplored that he could not be taken away from his mother earlier. [//] The education of a son already belongs to the husband. [Blatt 27v] Precisely her middle-class origin appears to the M[agistrat] to her friend to …. [//]

[now reading the day's *Intelligenzblatt*; late afternoon of Friday, February 4:]

---

[62] The periodical *Überlieferungen zur Geschichte unserer Zeit*. See Blatt 16v above.—KH

Dorotheergasse No. 1181, street floor, right at the gate: cream for 1 fl. per *Maaß* [measure]; good milk for 6 kr. per measure.[63] //

From Lichtenstein zu Enzersdorf in the Mountains, apartment in the house of the Herrnhuter, [Blatt 28r] in the 1st floor [2nd floor, American] with garden, etc.[64] //

Tavern, Hungarian Wines, Himmelpfortgasse No. 1023, where, in addition to the room for guests, there are extra rooms, etc.[65] [//]

Explanation. //

OLIVA **[possibly at his apartment in the Blutgasse; possibly on Saturday, February 5]**: The wine from Seelig is as bad as the last stuff was; it burns in the chest and in the stomach. [//] [Blatt 28v]

Maids are the devil's creations; they don't pass muster. [//] It doesn't take several days. //

I beg your pardon, but I must go to the bathroom.[66] [//]

[63] See *Intelligenzblatt*, No. 27 (February 4, 1820), p. 181 (Advertisements). The same advertisements also appeared on February 7 and 9, 1820. Dorotheergasse No. 1181 was renumbered as 1115 in 1821.—KH/TA

[64] See *Intelligenzblatt*, No. 27 (February 4, 1820), p. 181 (Advertisements). The same advertisement appeared several times, including on February 7, 1820.

The house of the Herrnhuter was a large building on three lots at the eastern end of Neuer Markt, Nos. 1133–1135 [renumbered as Nos. 1067–1069 in 1821]. It was so-called because of the linen shop "Zum Herrnhuter," founded there in 1797, which bore a statue of an eighteenth-century member of the *Unitas Fratrum*, the spiritual descendants of reformer Jan Hus, also called the Moravian Brethren, given religious asylum at Herrenhut in Saxony by the Protestant branch of the Zinzendorf family, whose Catholic branch was active in Vienna. Members of the "Herrenhuter" sect became the "Moravians" who settled in Bethlehem, Pennsylvania; Winston-Salem, North Carolina; and Fulneck near Leeds, among other places in England and America. A sign on the building still proclaims the name. See also Czeike, III, p. 160.—KH/TA

[65] See *Intelligenzblatt*, No. 27 (February 4, 1820), p. 181 (Advertisements). The same advertisement appeared several times, including on February 7, 1820. Himmelpfortgasse No. 1023 was renumbered as 965 in 1821. This advertisement would have appealed to Beethoven, who reportedly preferred sitting in a room where he could not be observed.—KH/TA

[66] It is likely that Oliva is still feeling unwell from his illness in late January; he says as much on Blatt 25v.—TA

BEETHOVEN [while waiting for Oliva to return]:

18	120
18	16
18	16
18	16
18	16
18	16
18	16
18	2 fl. 14 kr
18	
18	
18	
18	

[Blatt 29r]

OLIVA [**returning**]: Either he [*Triest* proprietor Seelig] understands nothing & allows himself to be deceived, or he himself corrupts the wines, because both types are worthless;—and for exactly the same reason. // Only he shouldn't give it to anyone who is sick; [even] a healthy person still suffers to some extent. // He should not sell any more wine for 3 Gulden. [//] [Blatt 29v]

He [Dr. Weckbecker] is 32 years old. [//] But an unsuccessful physician; his outward appearance & his behavior have something fatal about them. I told this to my doctor and asked him not to send him [Weckbecker] to visit me any more.

Then it costs increasingly more [to have a servant]; I know that they [the owners of Oliva's boarding house] have already spoken with a woman [who works] in the building—but she was turned down because they want to do something good for you. [//] [Blatt 30r]

I must go to see him [Bernard]; he has not yet sent me my newspapers, [and] yet is indiscreet, as in all matters. // He will probably get more for the *Wiener Zeitung*. Then he needs to work. He is being paid enough for all the needs to be covered. [//] Because he cannot be helped. // That costs several hundred Gulden, which he can save up in a few months. //

[Blatt 30v]

BEETHOVEN [**jotting more random thoughts for his memorandum**]: They allowed the mother [Johanna] to come with him [Karl]. The Magistrat did not rest until the guardianship was given up.—Formal arrangements ceased, and I therefore also sought to distance my nephew from here [Vienna]. //

BERNARD [possibly at *Zur Stadt Triest*, first alone with Beethoven, then joined by Peters and Janschikh; late on Sunday, February 6]: I have received a tender note from Frau v[on] Janschikh, in which she begs forgiveness concerning her husband's invitation, because [Blatt 31r] he did not know that there were hindrances that made it impossible for us to eat there tomorrow. [//] She has at least written cheerfully. //

If he [Meyerbeer] had as much taste as money, he would remain in Germany [i.e., German-speaking lands]. [//] [Blatt 31v] He has too much money to compose well. [//]

The Court of Appeals does not take sides. //

He [Peters] is untroubled. // He will be in a better position if the young Prince [Lobkowitz] ever becomes the reigning member of the family. [//] [Blatt 32r]

I took a walk in Weinhaus[67] today [Sunday, February 6]. The weather outside is very beautiful.[68] //

PETERS: Seelig has a Leonardo da Vinci[69] of exceptional beauty. [//] It's worth 20,000 fl. [Conv.] Münze. // Family property. [//] You should see it. [//] A [depiction of] Christ. [//] [Blatt 32v]

I don't know her/it. //

BERNARD: Seelig has a wondrously beautiful Christ carrying the Cross by Leonardo da Vinci. //

You have promised to visit Baroness Puthon,[70] and are expected longingly. [//] [Blatt 33r]

Would you like to go with me, tomorrow afternoon [Monday, February 7] at 4 o'clock, on a picnic to Frau von Dilg's,[71] whose children always greeted you in such a friendly way in Mödling? It is a very pleasant household. The husband is an official

---

[67] Weinhaus, a village northwest of Vienna, also to the northwest of Währing, with which it is now incorporated. The area extends from the Türkenschanz Park, south to the Sternwarte, St. Josephs Kirche, and Währinger Strasse.—TA

[68] Although the day before had been foggy and overcast, Sunday, February 6, was sunny and clear for most of the day, with temperatures up to the freezing point by midafternoon. Clouds returned at night, and the next two days, although considerably warmer, were foggy and overcast again. Thus weather reports allow the dating of this entry with considerable accuracy. See *Wiener Zeitung*, No. 30 (February 8, 1820), p. 120; No. 31 (February 9, 1820), p. 123. See projected picnics on Blätter 33r, 40v, and 41v below.—TA

[69] The identity of the picture cannot be determined. On the basis of Seelig's possible connections, Frimmel referred to a possible relative of the same surname, who in 1808, as Secretary to Duke of Corigliano, offered a picture to the Viennese Court, which, however, was not accepted. See Frimmel, *Handbuch*, II, p. 176.—KH/TA

[70] See Blatt 15v above.—TA

[71] Carolin [*sic*] Dilg von Dilgskron (b. 1778), married to Johann Philipp Dilg von Dilgskron (born in the Rheinland in 1771), an official of the Privy Imperial House-, Court-, and State-Chancellery, lived in the suburb of Wieden, No. 537. She had four daughters and one son, Carl (b. 1808), who attended

in the State Chancellery. [//] [Blatt 33v] The son studies in the Theresianum[72] and is a very excellent boy. [//] His [the husband's] uncle was an Imperial Court Councillor and was ennobled. The nephew has secured this nobility for himself in order to send his son to the Theresianum. [//] [Blatt 34r] The advantage is that, upon their graduation, pupils of the Theresianum are immediately employed. // Therefore, we must eat our midday meal tomorrow at our Bonifacius's place.[73] [//]

[Blatt 34v]

JANSCHIKH: Our Heart calls you.—That is also our Postillion's horn.[74] //

PETERS: The 2 beautiful Canons[75] are certainly already erased. [//]

BERNARD [canon text]: Saint Peter is a rock; on him one must b[uild]. // Hamburg. // Salzmann[76] was in Schnepfenthal. [//] [Blatt 35r]

Starke wishes to have a short piece of music from you for the second part of his *Klavierschule*, for which he already has contributions from the foremost composers, along with short biographical sketches.[77] [//]

[Blatt 35v]

the Theresianum. See Conscriptions-Bogen, Wieden, No. 170 (Wiener Stadt- und Landesarchiv); *Hof- und Staats-Schematismus*, 1819, I, p. 201, and 1820, I, p. 203. As noted in connection with Blatt 32r above, Monday, February 7, turned out to be foggy and overcast.—KH/TA

[72] The *Theresianische Ritterakademie* (Theresianum), an institute run by the Piarist Order, that "drew noble youth from all the Catholic lands," was located in suburban Wieden, Favoritengasse No. 101 [renumbered as 156 in 1821, and 306 in 1830]. Beethoven had to give up the plan of sending his nephew to the Theresianum because of his background as a commoner. See Pezzl (1826), pp. 287–288; Thayer-Deiters-Riemann, IV, p. 553; Thayer-Forbes, p. 709.—KH/TA

[73] A reference to St. Boniface, the meaning of which is unclear. Born in England with the name Winfrid, Boniface (680–754) came to northwest and central Germany, where he converted much of the population to Christianity. In Hesse he reputedly cut down a tree sacred to the pagan god Thor. He is the patron saint of brewers and tailors; his feast day is June 5.—TA

[74] Although this entire gambit is in German, Janschikh may have been making an unwritten wordplay on *Cor* as meaning *Herz* (heart) and *Horn* (horn).—TA

[75] See Heft 6, Blatt 13r.—KH

[76] Christian Gotthelf Salzmann (1744–1811), significant pedagogue. He studied Theology and, in 1781, came to Dessau through the influence of the (woman) philanthropist von Basedow. In 1784 he founded his own educational institute in Schnepfenthal near Gotha. See *Allgemeine Deutsche Biographie*, vol. 30, p. 293.—KH

[77] The second part of Friedrich Starke's *Wiener Pianoforte-Schule in III Abtheilungen*, Op. 108, appeared in June, 1820. In it Starke published the movements Andante and Rondo from the Piano Sonata in D major, Op. 28, by Beethoven, "Die Applicatur von ihm selbst bezeichnet." In connection with it he issued an enthusiastic endorsement of Beethoven as a "Star of the first magnitude in the musical heaven." See *Wiener Zeitung*, No. 133 (June 12, 1820), p. 528. Bernard essentially repeated this request on ca. March 3, 1820; see Heft 8, Blätter 60r–61r.—KH/TA

JANSCHIKH: I beg you not to forget the Drinking Song tomorrow [dinner at Janschikh's, Monday, February 7]. In other respects, I am already quite satisfied with my reputation. [//]

PETERS: Bernard demonstrated to [Joseph] Czerny that he must drink seltzer.[78] Tomorrow he will be ruined. // It cools the stomach. [//] [Blatt 36r] Tomorrow will be a magnificent dinner. I'll hold on to my wife if you smoke. [//]

[Blatt 36v]

JANSCHIKH: My wife is already cooking oysters and falsifying the wine to champagne. [//] The fritters will also not be lacking, as well as pheasant and rabbit.[79] [//]

PETERS: Bordeaux is far stronger than Adlersberger. //

BERNARD: Czerny is a Melnicker,[80] but not the wine. [//]

[Blatt 37r]

JANSCHIKH: When will your Mass be given, then? [//] Then your concert?[81] [//]

[Blatt 37v]

BERNARD: Seyfried has received a commission to write a Mass for Napoleon on St. Helena, after he received a clergyman from Italy. [//]

[Blatt 38r]

JANSCHIKH: Correction: not Seyfried, but instead Eybler,[82] and in fact by means of a flattering letter from General Bertrand.[83] [//] A *Kapelle* for Napoleon is being

---

[78] Probably seltzer water.—KH

[79] Preparations for the social evening on Monday, February 7 (see Blätter 42r–43r below).—TA

[80] Joseph Czerny came from the Bohemian village of Horzin, near the famous wine-growing town of Melnik. See Schilling, II, p. 346.—KH

[81] On virtually every encounter with Beethoven, Janschikh asks these or similar irritating questions.—TA

[82] Joseph von Eybler (1765–1846), church composer, Court Kapellmeister, became choral director at the Barmherzige Brüder in 1792, the Schottenkirche in 1794, and music teacher to the Imperial family in 1801. In 1804 he became Vice Hofkapellmeister under Salieri, and was later his successor. See Wurzbach, vol. 4, pp. 120–121.—KH/TA

[83] Count Henri Gratien Bertrand (1773–1844), French General, loyal follower of Napoleon. He participated in most of Napoleon's campaigns, and also accompanied him to exile on Elba and St. Helena.—KH

sought through Hyronimus [Jerome]; *Canné*[84] [Kanne] is among those competing to be Kapellmeister at St. Helena. [//] He is demanding 6,000 Thaler[85] per year. Kanne has just delivered a History of Music.[86] It is still at the Censor's Office. [//] [Blatt 38v] You should compose a Hymn on the [subject of] Napoleon, who was so very misunderstood.[87] [//]

BERNARD: It is too bad about Napoleon; he was a good fellow. // He wanted to take the Continent away from the English in order to destroy them. [//]

[Blatt 39r]

JANSCHIKH: Napoleon was a Maecenas of the arts and sciences. [//]
    In the *Conversations Lexikon*, it is written that you were an [illegitimate] child of the great Friedrich. [//]

PETERS: Herr v[on] Janschikh thinks that you therefore love Frederick the Great so much because he is said to be your father.[88] // Such errors must nevertheless be corrected. You don't need to borrow anything from Friedrich. [//]

[Blatt 39v]

BERNARD: One must place an article in the *Allgemeine Zeitung*.[89] [//]
    Where shall we meet tomorrow?[90]
    [Beethoven seemingly departs. End of entries for Sunday, February 6.]

BEETHOVEN **[probably at his apartment on the Josephstädter Glacis; probably the morning of Monday, February 7]:**
    Chladni's *Akustik*.[91]
    Introduce Karl to accompanying. [//]

[Blatt 40r]

---

[84] Possibly a French-influenced wordplay on the name of composer-author Friedrich August Kanne (1778–1833), but it could also be a play on the Latin *canus* (dog).—KH/TA

[85] If Reichsthaler are meant, then the sum was roughly 9,000 Gulden.—TA

[86] This study is not mentioned in Imogen Fellinger, "Kanne," *MGG*, vol. 14, cols. 903–904.—TA

[87] German original, *verkannten*, might also be a wordplay on Kanne.—TA

[88] Beethoven had already had a similar conversation with Peters on December 30, 1819 (Heft 5, Blätter 69v–70r). He must have been offended by Peters and the frequently irritating Janschikh, and, with the change of topic, seems to have left the convivial company quite suddenly.—TA

[89] Whether Bernard means Leipzig's *Allgemeine musikalische Zeitung* or a periodical with a more general readership is not clear. In any case, Beethoven seldom protested against such errors in writing.—TA

[90] Originally in Latin: *Ubi conveniemus crastina die?*—KH/TA

[91] See Heft 2, Blatt 111.—TA

BERNARD [possibly with Peters at *Zur Stadt Triest*; probably at the midday dinner hour, ca. 2 p.m. on Monday, February 7]: Last Wednesday [February 2, Candlemas], he [Karl] had me told that in the course of the past week, he gave up. [//] Peters can go to [see] him in the school. [//]

PETERS [continuing]: We are saying that Herr Janschikh has a strict household regimen. Bernard says that I should learn that. [//] [Blatt 40v]
  <St. Blasius is insurance against vomiting, says> Bernard.[92]
  We shall soon be filled with it [presumably some food]. [//] <Glutton.> [//]

BERNARD [continuing, but well before 4 p.m.]: I must still go on a picnic today.[93] [//] [Blatt 41r]
  Emperor Leopold I[94] was a 7-month baby. In order to have him mature properly, he was constantly placed into a freshly slaughtered pig, and the meat from it afterwards given to the poor—who called it *Kaiserfleisch* [emperor's meat].[95] [//] Before Joseph I.[96] [//] The 1st [___].[97] [//] Franz I was the first Lothringer.[98] [//] [Blatt 41v] It <was> is already better with him. //

PETERS: As soon as I have my own household in order, Bernard will be my daily guest. My wife loves gifted people. [//]

BERNARD: Picnic. //

[92] Because it is heavily crossed out, this line is difficult, even impossible, to read, with "St. B" and "V" among the legible elements. The previous Thursday, however, was February 3, the Feast of St. Blasius, whose blessing is considered to be protection against disease, especially choking and diseases of the throat. Since Beethoven's friends are describing the plentiful foods and even gluttony, "St. B[lasius]" and "V[omiting]" seem logical solutions in context.—KH/TA

[93] The picnic was planned for 4 p.m. at the Dilgs's in the Wieden; see Blatt 33r above. Perhaps it was an *indoor* picnic, replicating the sunshine and warmth of the summer. After a foggy morning, the temperature at 3 p.m. was 46 degrees Fahrenheit, with weak wind and unsettled skies; see the *Wiener Zeitung*, No. 31 (February 9, 1820), p. 123.—TA

[94] Leopold I (1640–1705), second son of Ferdinand III, Holy Roman (German) Emperor from 1658.—KH

[95] In connection with this legendary incident, the term *Kaiserfleisch* was transferred to young, delicate, smoked pork as late as Beethoven's time. See Loritza, p. 70; Heft 55, Blatt 10v.—KH/TA

[96] Joseph I (1678–1711) Holy Roman (German) Emperor from 1705, was the eldest son of Emperor Leopold I.—KH

[97] The missing word here is the fragmentary "*bot.*"—TA

[98] Franz I, Duke of Lorraine (Lothringen), 1708–1765, married to Maria Theresia from 1736, co-regent from 1740, remained in any case without political influence. In 1745, as titular successor to the short-reigned Carl VII (Carl Albert of Bavaria), he became Holy Roman (German) Emperor, and, with that, founding father of the new Habsburg-Lorraine reigning line of the House of Austria.—KH/TA

We are speaking of the amenities of the Leopoldstadt Theater.[99] [//]

Petrus [Peters] is a stranger in his fatherland.[100] [//]

[Bernard departs before 4 p.m.; Peters possibly remains and accompanies Beethoven to the Janschikhs' apartment, a ca. 30-minute walk away.]

[Blatt 42r]

[The following entries were made at dinner at the Janschikhs' apartment[101] in the Landstrasse, corner of Ungargasse and Bock- (later Beatrix-) gasse; presumably on Monday evening, February 7.]

JANSCHIKH: Herr v[on] Peters appears to want to lay claim to my wife; his conduct could be dangerous to me. [//]

PETERS: Herr v[on] Janschikh and I have resolved that you are to stay with this wine. [//]

JANSCHIKH: My wife wishes that you take her under your protection today. A good glass of punch will contribute to the strengthening of the body and the soul, and my wife is [Blatt 42v] making it. //

PETERS: She says that I cannot sleep with her; the bed is too small [short]. //[102]

   What are you doing today yet? //

   Can't both of us stay here? We must draw lots. [//]

[Blatt 43r]

ANTONIA JANSCHIKH: <Why are you so sad? [//] Then I must be, too. [//][103] I am still sitting upright.> //

[Without further written conversation, Beethoven departed, evidently accompanied by Peters.[104] End of entries for Monday, February 7.]

---

[99] The Theater in der Leopoldstadt, Jägerzeil No. 452 [renumbered as 511 in 1821], which eventually became Praterstrasse No. 31, opened in 1781, and was Vienna's most successful stage for comedy and musicals, especially those in local dialect.—TA

[100] Originally in Latin: "Petrus est peregrinus in patria." Peters was from Bohemia.—KH/TA

[101] For the foods served see Blatt 36v above. It is possible that they were considered more "party foods" than dinner dishes. The whole tone of the following conversation was probably repugnant to Beethoven.—TA

[102] At this turn in the conversation, Beethoven may have attempted to leave, claiming that he still had errands to run.—TA

[103] Beethoven may have remarked that he was on the verge of falling asleep, and that it would not look good if he did.—TA

[104] See Blatt 44v below.—TA

BEETHOVEN [at *Zur Stadt Triest*; possibly midday on Tuesday, February 8, reading an advertisement of February 7]:[105] Apartment with beautiful large garden, Landstrasse, Ungargasse 339, either by the year or for the summer, 3 large spacious rooms, etc., a servant's room, may be inspected in the afternoon hours. This apartment may be occupied immediately.[106] //

[Blatt 43v]

JANSCHIKH [joining Beethoven]: These gentlemen ate yesterday with [Zacharias] Werner and Adam Müller.[107] [//] They are Protestants; Werner wants to convert them. [//]

You should also move to the Landstrasse again. [//]

How did you and Peters get home? Did you sleep well?[108] [//]

Haven't you spoken with Bernard? [//]

His name does not come to my mind now. [//] The President of the High Court Administration is presently Baron Gärtner.[109] [//]

[Blatt 44r]

---

[105] If Beethoven had gone to the Janschikhs' on the evening of Monday, February 7, then he would have caught up on his newspaper reading the next day.—TA

[106] *Intelligenzblatt*, No. 33 (February 11, 1820), p. 228 (Advertisements). The same advertisement had already appeared on February 7 and 9, 1820. Landstrasse No. 339 [renumbered as 376 in 1821] was actually in the tiny Krongasse, west of Ungargasse, about three long blocks further out from the Janschikhs' apartment. See Behsel, p. 80.

From the chronology it appears that Beethoven probably read the advertisement in the February 7 issue of the *Intelligenzblatt* at midday on Tuesday, February 8.—KH/TA

[107] Adam Heinrich Müller von Nittersdorf (1779–1829), philosopher and statesman, converted to Catholicism in 1805, and in 1815, through Metternich, was called to Austrian State service. In 1819/20, he was Court Councillor in the service of the Privy Imperial House, Court, and State Chancellery, and took part in the Conferences in Karlsbad and Vienna. As representative of the reactionary conservative viewpoint, Müller was a friend of Friedrich Gentz, Clemens Hoffbauer, Zacharias Werner, Joseph Pilat, and Friedrich Klinkowström. See *Allgemeine Deutsche Biographie*, vol. 22, pp. 501–503; Gräffer-Czikann, III, pp. 723–724; *Hof- und Staats-Schematismus*, 1820, I, pp. 205, 209, and 213; Wurzbach, vol. 19, pp. 322–324; and Blatt 72r below.—KH/TA

[108] Beethoven had evidently fallen asleep during dinner at the Janschikhs' the night before and had to be awakened to be escorted home. If to his apartment in the Ballgasse, it would have been a twenty or twenty-five-minute walk; if to the Josephstadt Glacis, probably an hour-long walk See Blätter 71v–72r, extending to 74r below.—TA

[109] Baron Friedrich Christian von Gärtner was president of the Court Commission in Judicial-Legal Affairs (Janschikh called the office the *Oberst Gerichts-Hof*) as well as Privy Councillor, Vice President of the Supreme Court and Court Commissions Assistant Judge. He lived in his own house in the City, Schulerstrasse, No. 873 [renumbered as 823 in 1821]. See *Hof- und Staats-Schematismus*, 1819, I, p. 261; Behsel, p. 25.—KH/TA

PROPRIETOR SEELIG: This is *Ruster*,[110] which will please you. Then, if you would like to see an extraordinary picture, a Leonardo da Vinci, then I beg you to give me the honor in the morning! //

[Blatt 44v]

PETERS [**joining Beethoven and Janschikh**]: Yesterday [Monday] was a beautiful evening, and a fine dinner from 2 to 10 [i.e., from soup to nuts, or: from start to finish]. I was not able to get you away from it.[111] //

Do you want me to come and get you, tomorrow [Wednesday] morning at 9 o'clock? // Many students, Professor Director Blöchlinger, and several private teachers. //

Are you going to the *Redoute* [ball] tomorrow?[112] // Frau v[on] Janschikh, too.[113] [//]

[Blatt 45r]

JANSCHIKH: The adulterated wine ought not to appease me. //

PETERS: Why are you drinking the Ruster [wine]? It goes into the blood too much. //

It is the birthday of the Empress [Tuesday, February 8];[114] nothing is happening. // I shall send an inquiry when the examination is. [//]

[Blatt 45v]

OLIVA [**at his apartment in the Blutgasse, or possibly visiting Beethoven at his apartment on the Glacis; possibly the afternoon of Tuesday, February 8**]: I am going out every day, even to the office. [//]

Between today and tomorrow, I hope to hear something about the housekeeper. [//]

---

[110] *Ruster*, a Hungarian wine from Ruszt.—KH

[111] This argues against the tone of the entries during the dinner itself. Probably Beethoven tried to leave, was persuaded to stay, and probably lost himself in eating and drinking (and seemingly even a nap), with no further written conversation.—TA

[112] There would be no balls in the Redoutensäle on the next night, Wednesday, February 9, as had been the case the previous two weeks. During the week in question, the festivities would take place on Tuesday, February 8, and Thursday, February 10, both lasting the customary eight hours from 9 p.m. to 5 a.m. See the Zettel, Hof-Theater (Bibliothek, Österreichisches Theatermuseum; courtesy Othmar Barnert).—TA

[113] Antonia Janschikh attended the ball on Tuesday, February 8, participating in a practical joke described on Blatt 55v below.—TA

[114] Empress Carolina Augusta's birthday was on February 8.—KH

Until today Herr Bernard has left me in the lurch with my Journals [daily accounting books?]; I cannot get them back and am in the most awkward position. [//] I was there twice. [//] If I am pressured, I'll go myself. [//] [Blatt 46r]

Go right ahead with the Mass. [//] But don't abandon yourself to melancholy ideas. You have to expect the best outcome in the matter. [//] Necessity knows no law.[115] [//]

It is a wine house in wholesale and retail sales, but I don't know whether it is already open. One could also get Austrian wine. [//] [Blatt 46v]

Indeed he has a servant and has promised to send her [a candidate for house-keeper] to me after a few hours. //

Kanne wanted to have the book by Goethe. I asked Bernard whether I ought to give it to him, and he said yes. Therefore it is no longer my business. [//]

[Blatt 47r]

BEETHOVEN [possibly back at *Zur Stadt Triest*, joined by Janschikh, then Peters, then finally Bernard; late afternoon or evening of Tuesday, February 8]: <There is good wine> at the *Biber*.[116] [//]

JANSCHIKH: Flower wreaths and Orpheus's lyre will someday hang on your grave. But you—in the Book of Immortality. [//]

PETERS [continuing, seemingly in the evening]: It has annoyed me very much. I received the answer when I sent the inquiry again. But there wasn't any school anywhere today. [//] [Blatt 47v] I became downright angry and still can't get over my annoyance. In former times, examinations never took place on recreation days.[117] //

<Wouldn't you rather here ....?> Have you already had something warm for [evening] supper? [//]

[Blatt 48r]

---

[115] Original in Oliva's Latin: *Necessitas non noscit legem.*—KH

[116] In the Josephstadt, on the Glacis, No. 21 [renumbered as 22 in 1821], was the restaurant *Zum Bieber* (At the sign of the Beaver), owned by Franz Schierer. It stood roughly midway between Josephsgasse and Kaiserstrasse [today's Josefstädter Strasse]. See Guetjahr, p. 312; Rotter, p. 130; Behsel, p. 190; Heft 4, Blatt 2r.—KH/TA

[117] The recreational day or holiday, Peters obviously means the birthday of Empress Carolina Augusta (see Blatt 45r). Therefore this conversation took place on Tuesday, February 8.—KH

JANSCHIKH: The Campe about whom you are speaking has died.[118] The one in Hamburg is his nephew.[119] //

PETERS: My wife is at Zizius's;[120] I shall still go and fetch her. There is music and a ball; if there is time left, then I'll go to the *Redoute*.[121] [//]

You are just as dissatisfied [with the legal situation] as I am today. [//]

---

[118] Joachim Heinrich Campe (1746–1818), linguistic scholar, pedagogue, children's author, was tutor in the house of the Humboldt family and in 1787 became Canon and in 1805 Deacon of the *Cyriacus-Stift* in Braunschweig. He took over a book and printing shop (previously belonging to the orphanage) under the name *Braunschweigerische Schulbuchhandlung*, and was the compiler of several dictionaries (*Wörterbuch zur Erklärung und Verdeutschung der unserer Spracheaufgedrungenen fremden Ausdrücke*, 1801; *Wörterbuch der deutschen Sprache*, 5 vols., 1807–1812). See *Allgemeine Deutsche Biographie*, vol. 3, pp. 733–735.—KH

[119] The nephew of Joachim Heinrich Campe was August Campe (1773–1836). With his brother Friedrich (1777–1846) he founded a book shop in Hamburg, and then took over the book shop of his father-in-law Hoffmann, now under the name "Hoffmann und Campe." In 1823 he turned the business over to his brother Julius (1792–1867).—KH

[120] Johann Nepomuk Zizius (1772–1824), Court and Legal Attorney, Professor of Political Science at the University of Vienna and at the Theresianum, member of the executive board of the Gesellschaft der Musikfreunde, lived at Kärntnerstrasse No. 1101 [renumbered as 1038 in 1821], behind the Kärntnertor Theater, in the 2nd floor (3rd floor, American), directly above the theater's rehearsal hall. The correct location, "at the end of the Kärntnerstrasse, No. 1038," is given in Leopold von Sonnleithner, "Musikalische Skizzen aus Alt-Wien," *Recensionen und Mittheilungen über Theater und Musik* 9, No. 21 (May 24, 1863), p. 322.

Previous misidentifications of Zizius's address as Kärntnerstrasse No. 1191 [renumbered as 1125 in 1821] stem from the *Hof- und Staats-Schematismus*, as early as 1816, and here as 1819, I, p. 378, and II, p. 290; 1820, I, pp. 387 and 698; as Kärntnerstrasse [*sic*] No. 1125 in *Hof- und Staats-Schematismus*, 1821, I, p. 696; 1822, I, p. 720; Böckh, *Merkwürdigkeiten*, p. 352. Before 1821 the *Schematismus* editors misread the correct 1101 as 1191, and repeatedly printed it as such. When the houses were renumbered in late 1820, the editors simply converted the erroneous 1191 into a newly-erroneous 1125. Instead of verifying Zizius's address independently, Böckh merely looked up his name in the *Schematismus*, gave his address as No. 1125, and perpetuated the error (even though the erroneous house number would lead the seeker to Untere Bräunerstrasse!).

When Zizius (from Gaudim, Bohemia), who remained single, died of repeated strokes at age 52, on April 5, 1824, he was living in the Colloredo house, No. 911, on Franziskanerplatz (Totenbeschauprotokoll, 1824, Z, fol. 6). This address is first noted in the *Schematismus*, 1823, I, p. 703, so Zizius must have moved there during the course of 1822. See also Wurzbach, vol. 60, pp. 192–193; Clive, p. 404; Behsel, pp. 31 and 34.—TA

[121] Unlike Peters's reference on Blatt 44v, there can be no confusing the date here. This ball, the first Tuesday ball in a series that had *previously* been held on Wednesday and Sunday nights, began at 9 p.m. on February 8, in the Redoutensäle, and lasted until 5 a.m. on Wednesday, February 9. See Hoftheater, Zettel, Tuesday, February 8, 1820 (Bibliothek, Österreichisches Theatermuseum; courtesy Othmar Barnert).—TA

BEETHOVEN **[writing so as not to be overheard]**: The commoner [*Bürger*] ought to be separated [Blatt 48v] from higher Mankind, and *I have fallen among them.*¹²² [//]

[Blatt 49r]

PETERS: In three weeks you won't have to have anything more to do with the commoner [*Bürger*] and the Magistrat. They will still petition for your support, and send you the friendliest service of legal process from the Court of Appeals. [//]

JANSCHIKH: Are you having your beard singed off? [//]

[Blatt 49v]

PETERS: The Salon, the balls, the social activities are just as hateful to me on behalf of Prince Pepi [young Joseph Lobkowitz], with respect to his education, as dealing with the Magistrat was for you. [//]

BEETHOVEN **[writing so as not to be overheard]**: Who is this person? //

PETERS: An *obscurus*! // An accounting councillor at the *Stift*'s bookkeeping office in Lerchenfeld.¹²³ [//]

[Blatt 50r]

JANSCHIKH: "We are born, fruits to be eaten," or "We must enjoy life."¹²⁴ [//]

---

¹²² This commonly cited passage was first quoted by Anton Schindler in the chapter "Auszüge aus Beethovens Conversations-Heften," in his *Biographie von Ludwig van Beethoven*, 2nd ed. (Münster: Aschendorff, 1845), p. 277. As can be seen in the context of Peters's reply, Beethoven is differentiating between the commoners (whose law cases were heard by the Magistrat) and the nobility (whose cases were heard by the Landrecht). He deeply resented being adjudicated in a Court that had jurisdiction over such perceived rabble as his sister-in-law Johanna, who, at this time, was five months pregnant with an illegitimate child.—TA

¹²³ The most obvious identification might be the Mechitaristen (formerly Kapuziner) *Stift* (religious order) on the north side of Am Platzl, behind the Trautson Palace, but it was not technically in Lerchenfeld. Given the often confusing proximity of the suburbs Alt Lerchenfeld, Neubau, and Am Platzl, it is difficult to isolate this location any further.—TA

¹²⁴ Latin: *Nos fruges consumere nati* (already quoted from Horace in Heft 6, Blatt 57v). To this Janschikh adds "Wir müssen uns des Lebens freuen." As in the Latin quotation already copied on ca. January 21, Janschikh is trying to get Beethoven to compose a canon or similar piece for him, as becomes obvious only a couple of lines later.—KH/TA

If you had remained silent, you would have remained a philosopher.[125] [//] The Magistrat—is a Magistrat.

I beg you to write a musical composition on these [two quotations above]. [//]

[Blatt 50v]

BERNARD: The powers that be are instituted by God;[126] one can do nothing against them. Also it's not worth the trouble to impede people of this type. [//] [Blatt 51r] The Court of Appeals will already do it. [//] It is indeed the defendant; also the other party will be heard.[127] // [Blatt 51v] After the two reports, a judgement will be made and sent to you through the Doctor [Bach], as well as to the other [party]. //
   [Presumably the end of entries for Tuesday, February 8.]

BEETHOVEN **[at his apartment on the Glacis; presumably the next morning, Wednesday, February 9]**: Volumes. [Blatt 52r]
   Writing paper.
   Pens—Hamburger.[128]
   Candles.
   Show the deposition.[129]
   Errors.
   Candles. [Blatt 52v]
   [No.] 682, Haarmarkt.[130] [//]

[Blatt 53r]

OLIVA **[somewhere in the City; at midday dinner on Wednesday, February 9]**: & is his wife pretty? [//] Are you reconciled with Frau Brentano?[131] [//] She has a very well-rounded education. //

---

[125] Originally in Latin: *Si tacuisses Ph[i]losophus mansisses* (Boethius). Presumably Janschikh making a wordplay on Beethoven's declaration before a committee of the Landrecht that he possesses no certificate of nobility. See Thayer-Deiters-Riemann, IV, p. 553.—KH

[126] Bernard is quoting from the Bible: Romans 13:1.—TA

[127] Latin: *Audiatur et altera pars* (Seneca).—KH/TA

[128] See Oliva's comment on Blatt 54r.—TA

[129] To the right, an indistinct beginning of a word.—KH

[130] The Haarmarkt and the old weighing house. Several Magistrat Councillors lived here, including Matthias Tuscher, who had been nephew Karl's guardian for a period. Note the reference to the square on Blatt 54v, and the interpretations given to it.—KH/TA

[131] Antonie Brentano (1780–1869), daughter of Court Councillor Melchior von Birkenstock. In 1798 she was married to Franz Dominik Maria Joseph Brentano, wholesaler/banker in Frankfurt, and played an important role in the communication between Beethoven and Sailer in Landshut. See Frimmel, *Handbuch*, I, pp. 63–64; Clive, pp. 47–51.
   In the 1970s Maynard Solomon put forth a compelling, but not universally-accepted, argument that Antonie Brentano was Beethoven's Immortal Beloved (Solomon, *Beethoven*, 1977, pp. 158–179,

He [Archduke Rudolph] wants the Mass [*Missa solemnis*], therefore he ought to allow you time and not make such impositions upon you. // What use is all of that?—You cannot endure it in the long run. [//] Think of the outstanding [pension] owed to you. // The expenses of the election, the expenses of a cardinal's hat. [//] [Blatt 53v]

It appears to me that there are competent creatures of Count Troyer here other than Mayseder[132] and Merk.[133] //

I remembered again, just today, and someone promised to take all pains. Two items that were considered unusable by you had already been sent back. // [Blatt 54r]

You can get really natural Hamburg quills in the stationery shop in the building where the *Österreichische Kaiserin* [Austrian Empress Hotel] is, in the Weihburggasse.[134] [//]

[Blatt 54v]

BEETHOVEN [presumably after having run some of the errands noted above; probably at *Zur Stadt Triest*; sometime after 7 p.m. on Wednesday, February 9]: Who is the man next to the one who is sleeping? [//]

JANSCHIKH: A Count whose name, however, doesn't come to my mind, but known for [his] humanitarian and liberal principles. [//]

---

among several other publications). In any case, it is apparent from her letter to Sailer of February 22, 1819, that she had very tender and affectionate feelings for the composer (see Albrecht, *Letters to Beethoven*, No. 256). For Erich Leischner's 1909 watercolor of the Birkenstock-Brentano house in Vienna's Erdberggasse, see Czeike, I, p. 460. For Ludwig Emil Grimm's drawing of Antonie Brentano and her husband's circle in Frankfurt in 1820, see Kramer, pp. 278–279.—KH/TA

[132] Joseph Mayseder (1789–1863), significant violinist, composer, and teacher; member of the Orchestra of the Kärntnertor Theater and the Hofmusikkapelle. He was also a student of Schuppanzigh's and, for a time, played second violin in his quartet. He met Beethoven through Schuppanzigh in about 1800. See Böckh, *Merkwürdigkeiten*, p. 375; Frimmel, *Handbuch*, I, pp. 397–399; Wurzbach, vol. 17, pp. 195–197; Clive, pp. 231–232.—KH

[133] Joseph Merk (1795–1852), Court Violoncellist, member of the Orchestra of the Court [Burg] Theater; teacher of violoncello at the Conservatory of the Gesellschaft der Musikfreunde. See Böckh, *Merkwürdigkeiten*, p. 373; Wurzbach, vol. 17, pp. 396–397; Ziegler, *Addressen-Buch*, p. 64.—KH

[134] The stationery and drawing materials shop of J.C. Axt, Weihburggasse No. 962 [renumbered as 906 in 1821]. See Redl, 1822, p. 259; Behsel, p. 27. A hotel by this name remains there today. Such pens had been on Beethoven's shopping list on Blatt 52r above.—KH/TA

Where were you going today on the street near the Haarmarkt[135] around 7 o'clock? [//] Put the blame on someone else.[136] [//]

[Blatt 55r]

SCHICKH [**presumably at the offices of the *Wiener Zeitschrift* on the Kohlmarkt; presumably the late afternoon of Thursday, February 10**]: When do I get the Canon? [//]

WÄHNER [**also in the same office**]: It is not allowed to answer Weidmann.[137] Then why do they generally allow conflict? // Consequence!? [//]

[Blatt 55v]

JOSEPH CZERNY [**possibly at *Zur Stadt Triest*, initially with Peters sitting at another table; presumably the evening of Thursday, February 10**]: I have made a great deal of music with Count Brunswick. What is he doing <now>?[138] [//]

---

[135] On Blatt 52v above Beethoven had noted among his projected errands a visit to Haarmarkt 682 (the old weighing house, home to several Magistrat Councillors, including Matthias Tuscher, who had been nephew Karl's guardian).—TA

[136] Originally in Latin: *Culpam transferre in alium.* The version above follows the German edition. Solomon (1977), pp. 262 and 362, translates the initial question as "Where were you going today on the street near the Haarmarkt?" with no temporal reference, and translates the following phrase (which he attributes to Beethoven himself!) as "Blame it on the flesh." Curiously, Solomon cites Nohl, *Beethovens Leben,* vol. 3, p. 828 (rather than Köhler's *Konversationshefte,* vol. 1), as his source, and then uses it as evidence that Beethoven was visiting prostitutes.

If, indeed, one were to translate *alium* as "flesh," then one must also consider that Haarmarkt No. 682, the residence of Tuscher, nephew Karl's former guardian (see Heft 6, Blatt 18v), was on Beethoven's recent list of errands, and that Beethoven may have been there at ca. 7 p.m. concerning Karl, whom Janschikh often called Beethoven's "Flesh and Blood," without any reference to his given name (see Heft 6, Blatt 45r).

Another distinct possibility is the optician Karl Joseph Rospini, who had his shop in Haarmarkt No. 688 [renumbered as 646 in 1821]. Beethoven visited him occasionally concerning eyeglasses and other instruments. See Heft 12, Blatt 1v; Heft 34, Blatt 11r; Heft 42, Blatt 5v.—KH/TA

[137] Franz Carl Weidmann (1787–1867), author. After brief activity as an actor at the Court Theater, he began to write plays, and later concentrated on reviews and contributions for sundry journals. For some time he was an editor for Schickh's *Wiener Zeitschrift.* See Wurzbach, vol. 53, pp. 262–264.—KH

[138] Count Franz von Brunsvik de Korompa (1777–1849), longtime friend of the composer's and instrumental in Beethoven's commission to supply incidental music to Kotzebue's *König Stephan* and *Die Ruinen von Athen* for the opening of the German Theater in Pesth in 1811/1812. The letters struck out are *geg,* presumably "gegenwärtig" (now, at present) judging from context, since Beethoven probably saw his old friend very seldom by this time. See Clive, pp. 63–64.—TA

SCHWARZENBERG'S BUSINESS REPRESENTATIVE [?][139] **[possibly at *Zur Stadt Triest*; ca. 9 p.m. on Thursday, February 10]**: [Bernard is] at the Theater. Without a doubt, Janschikh is at the *Redoute* [masked ball].[140] //

I played a great prank on Herren Weber[141] and Schnell at the last *Redoute* [on Tuesday].[142] Frau v[on] Janschikh and Frau Oberhauser[143] were masked, and I instructed them very exactly about the domestic relations of those gentlemen, [Blatt 56r] so that they knew [how] to specify to them the most insignificant details. Frau v[on] Oberhauser spoke Italian and reminded Herr Weber of his earlier stay in Italy, about which I had specified the details to her. The two gentlemen were almost beside themselves in amazement at this phenomenon. At the end the ladies disclosed their identities, whereupon the whole riddle became clear to the gentlemen. [//]

[Blatt 56v]

JOSEPH CZERNY **[continuing]**: The eldest [Lobkowitz son][144] is now also learning music. The younger,[145] however, will perform your Trio in B-flat [Op. 97] on Sunday [February 13].[146] // Kraft[147] and Schreiber.[148] // Unfortunately, Zmeskall is still

---

[139] This previously unknown writer knows a great deal about the members of Beethoven's circle who frequent *Zur Stadt Triest*, and is also of a social class where he feels free playing practical jokes at a ball. Therefore, he is probably Prince Schwarzenberg's business representative, identified by position on Blatt 59v below. From entries on Blätter 57r and 59v it appears that his name may be Jantschik or Janschiz (the latter spelling written by the individual himself).—TA

[140] Janschikh may have attended this ball without his wife (see Blatt 73r below). This one took place in the Redoutensäle on Thursday, February 10, from 9 p.m. to 5 a.m. See the Zettel, Hof-Theater (Bibliothek, Österreichisches Theatermuseum; courtesy Othmar Barnert).—TA

[141] The merchant Ernst Weber, who arrived in Vienna on January 16, 1820, and, along with Schnell, departed again on February 19. See the *Wiener Zeitung*, No. 14 (January 19, 1820), p. 55, and No. 42 (February 22, 1820), p. 168.—KH

[142] This would have been the ball on Tuesday, February 8. Peters mentioned Antonia Janschikh in connection with attending a ball on Blatt 44v above.—TA

[143] Probably Franziska Oberhauser (b. 1794), the wife of Joseph Oberhauser, I.R. (real) Court Secretary and Doctor of Law (b. 1782). See Conscriptions-Bogen, Stadt, No. 214, Wohnpartei 5 (Wiener Stadt- und Landesarchiv); *Hof- und Staats-Schematismus*, 1820, I, p. 246.—KH

[144] Ferdinand Joseph Johann von Lobkowitz (1797–1868); see Heft 4, Blatt 40v.—TA

[145] Joseph Franz Karl (b. 1803), called Prince Pepi. See Heft 3, Blatt 19r.—TA

[146] Because Kraft was ill, the performance was postponed until Wednesday, February 23 (see Heft 8, Blätter 5r–5v).—TA

[147] Anton Kraft (1749–1820), Bohemian-born, one of Europe's leading violoncello virtuosi, had served Prince Esterházy until 1790, then Prince Grassalkowitsch until ca. 1795, and then Prince Joseph Lobkowitz. He was the violoncellist in Schuppanzigh's earlier Quartets (ca. 1796–1807), and was the intended cello soloist in Beethoven's Triple Concerto, Op. 56. His estate record indicates that he owned a Ruggiero violoncello. See Frimmel, *Handbuch*, I, pp. 296–297; Wurzbach, vol. 13, pp. 101; Clive, pp. 193–194.—KH/TA

[148] Anton Schreiber (1766/67 – after 1830), born in Jaromirsch, Bohemia, played violin in the Prague National Theater until employed by Prince Lobkowitz in Vienna in January 1797. He gradually turned to viola and played in Schuppanzigh's String Quartet through ca. 1807. From 1813

constantly ill, and it appears that he will never again be healthy. He very much misses making music.[149] [//] [Blatt 57r]

They are getting angry, however, and even that can hurt you. // Peters says that the matter concerning your nephew must come to a conclusion completely according to your wishes. //

His name is *Jantschik*.[150] [//]

[Blatt 57v]

SCHWARZENBERG'S BUSINESS REPRESENTATIVE[151] [?]: It would be a great honor for me and my family, if you will visit us. //

JOSEPH CZERNY: Who is the man sitting next to Peters? //

She [Leopoldine Blahetka] is playing your Concerto in B-flat [Op. 19] like every virtuoso. // You are not satisfied with me?!! Why? //

PETERS: I parry every thrust. [//] [Blatt 58r]

There is no instruction in mathematics. According to the new curriculum, very little will be taught—as much as Karl learns in 3 days. // But the arrangement exists that provides Karl [his] own course in Mathematics. [//] [Blatt 58v] The curriculum in studies is for the majority—a proper Institute must compensate for that, because the number [of students] is smaller. // Multiplication and division in algebra. // Blöchlinger's Institute performs—and quite a bit, in my judgement—according to precedent. [Blatt 59r] Moreover, the curriculum that he has now is the most superior; you can make other preliminary arrangements later, if <you> they prove themselves to be good. I think that if, after some time, you want to send him to another town in a foreign country, no person [Blatt 59v] or agency will restrain you. //

---

until his retirement he played viola in the Kärntnertor Theater's Orchestra. It is obvious that, for the performance projected in this conversation book entry, Schreiber was to play violin. See Ziegler, *Addressen-Buch*, p. 79; also Albrecht, "'First Name Unknown,'" 10–18.—TA

[149] Nikolaus Zmeskall von Domanovecz (1759–1833), official in the Hungarian Chancellery, accomplished amateur violoncellist, and a friend of Beethoven's since the 1790s. Since Zmeskall lived in the Bürgerspital apartment complex, whose northern wing extended to the square in front of the Lobkowitz Palace, Beethoven had apparently suggested inviting him to the salon performance on Sunday, and this was the reply. For the first performance of the Ninth Symphony on May 7, 1824, Zmeskall had himself carried across the street to the Kärntnertor Theater, to the west of the Bürgerspital. See Clive, pp. 404–405.—TA

[150] In context this does not seem to be Janschikh's name. Given the context and the varied repetition of the name on Blatt 59v below, this seems to be the name of Prince Schwarzenberg's business representative.—TA

[151] Same unknown person as writing on Blatt 59v below.—TA

JOSEPH CZERNY [**presumably to Peters, so as not to be overheard**]: Who is your neighbor [the person sitting next to you]? [//]

PETERS [**also so as not to be overheard**]: The business representative of Prince Schwarzenberg. //

SCHWARZENBERG'S BUSINESS REPRESENTATIVE[152] [?]: I cannot attend the churches [*sic*].[153] // I have no time! [//]
   You must set the word Janschiz[154] to music. //

[Blatt 60r]

PETERS: In that you are not true to Luther, because you don't protest—that is, you make up your own mind. // I was not. //
   [**End of entries for Thursday, February 10.**]

SCHICKH [**probably at the office of his *Wiener Zeitschrift* on the Kohlmarkt; possibly the late morning of Friday, February 11**]: I ask you very, very much to give me the promised Canon soon. [//] On what text do you want to compose it, then? // [Blatt 60v] What comes from you, O superb man, is superb! // I'll gladly give you [some texts] that I have,[155] only you must protect them very cautiously for me. You can get or send for some by Hormayer[156] tomorrow. // [Blatt 61r] This is a proof sheet; the entire thing would appear in the *Zeitschrift*. // Which poets do

---

[152] The same unidentified person as on Blatt 57v above, but perhaps partially identified by Peters immediately above.

[153] The writer uses the verb *besuchen* (to visit or attend) here. It is difficult to interpret further without context.—TA

[154] This is possibly the Schwarzenberg employee's own name in his own phonetic spelling; see Blatt 57r above.—TA

[155] Beethoven must have requested song texts, rather than setting any of the canon texts proffered by Bernard or others.—TA

[156] Baron Joseph von Hormeyr zu Hortenburg (1782–1848), because of his significant scholarly activity in the area of history, became Director of the Privy Haus-, Hof- und Staatsarchiv in Vienna in 1808. From 1820 to 1829 he coedited, with Baron Mednyansky, the *Taschenbuch für vaterländische Geschichte*. See Gräffer-Czikann, III, pp. 643–645; Wurzbach, vol. 9, pp. 277–279.—KH

you want, then? [//] Which?[157] // I have nothing by Lessing except *Nathan [der Weise]*.[158] // I don't have Herder![159] [//]

[Blatt 61v]

BEETHOVEN [at a restaurant or wine house or coffee house, possibly *Zur Stadt Triest*; possibly around noon on Friday, February 11]: Pair of bellows, solely from wood without leather—at Hauptstrasse No. 198 in Neubau; Wunsch, mechanic.[160] [//] This .... //

BERNARD [seemingly joining Beethoven; before the time for midday dinner[161] on Friday, February 11]: I want to rent a room in Döbling [for the summer]. // The air is very good indeed. // [Blatt 62r] I was at the *Redoute* [ball]. //

Only the reports about the commission will be required at the Magistrat's. [//] Over all [bottom half of sheet torn off]. [Blatt 62v] The *Protokolle* [minutes] are indeed available at the Magistrat's; they must be made available for inspection. // That was only a private conversation. [//] [Blatt 63r]

After the oratorio, I am willing to write [the libretto for] a grand opera. [//] But I must make a change in my residence.[162] [//]

Is nothing yet determined about when the Mass will be performed? //

I am invited to Herr v[on] Schreyvogel's today.[163] // He lived with a Frau von Rottmann, who died this summer. [//] [Blatt 63v] He had a daughter with her,

---

[157] At this point Beethoven must have suggested Gotthold Ephraim Lessing. See Heft 6, Blatt 2r, where Bernard had offered him a Lessing text already set by Haydn.—TA

[158] Lessing's famous work with a Jew (modeled on Moses Mendelssohn) as its hero. Setting an excerpt from it, after Bernard's criticisms of Schickh, would have been too obvious an act of defiance. A cursory survey of the current season reveals performances at the Burgtheater on October 2 and November 1 (All Saints Day!), 1819, and January 11 and March 14, 1820 (Theater Zettel, Bibliothek, Österreichisches Theatermuseum).—TA

[159] Johann Gottfried Herder (1744–1803), north German writer and literary historian, influenced by Kant and, for a time, friendly with Goethe in Weimar.—TA

[160] See the *Intelligenzblatt*, No. 33 (February 11, 1820), p. 227 (Advertisements). The same advertisement also appeared on February 14 and 16, 1820.

Neubau No. 198, *Zwei goldene Zederbäume* (Two Golden Cedar Trees), technically on tiny Ungarische Krongasse, one building east of Neubau Hauptstrasse (today's Neubaugasse), was renumbered as 182 in 1821 (Behsel, p. 163).—KH/TA

[161] On Blatt 63r below Bernard notes that he is invited to Schreyvogel's, presumably for midday dinner.—TA

[162] Possibly Bernard is contemplating a move from his apartment in the Rauhensteingasse in the City to Altwiedner Hauptstrasse, across the street from the Paulanerkirche. See Heft 5, inside front cover.—TA

[163] Joseph Schreyvogel (1768–1832), prominent author and publisher, also wrote under the pseudonym West. See Clive, p. 325.—TA

who is 20 years old. The husband of this daughter; she is Frau von Mechetti.[164] Herr v[on] Schreyvogel asked me to tell you that it would give him very much joy if he could see you sometime. He seemed sorry that he has already [Blatt 64r] given the plan of his opera to Weigl. He is a very learned and profound aesthetician. // Weigl (very much) wanted to write one, and so he sent him the draft. The material is from the Spanish of Calderon, and is highly tragic. The subject is called *The Daughter of the Air*, and is actually Semiramis.[165] [//] [Blatt 64v] At first he wanted to make a tragedy out of it, and read me several scenes from it. But it seemed to him more suitable to an opera. // Schreyvogel says that himself. // He is more idyllic. // Circe?[166] // [Blatt 65r] I must go now. // The daughter is pretty, skillful, and well educated, as is appropriate for the child of an aesthetician. //

OLIVA [possibly at the *Birne* restaurant in Beethoven's apartment building on the Glacis; after ca. 2 p.m.[167] on Friday, February 11]: My health is improving very slowly; I suffer a great deal. //

You will see [that] the Archduke [Rudolph] has stated that as soon as he has the Mass, and you expressly request it [payment?]; he cannot leave you. [//] [Blatt 65v]

A housekeeper has been found, whom the two women [Born and Baumgarten] in the building where I eat[168] believe to be suitable for you. She is around 40, a widow, has had only two positions, one at a Countess's for 5 years, where she has a letter of recommendation; then at a lawyer's wife's, where she worked for 6 years, and the lady wants to give personal information. She understands how to cook *everything*. I have told her everything that is [Blatt 66r] unusual about you, such as your getting up at 5 o'clock & such;[169] she is satisfied with that. She requests 14 fl. [plus] 2 fl. tip, thus a total of 16 fl. [per month?]. [//] She is coming tomorrow morning at 9:30. [//] She looks quite respectable and strong. [//] She has a sister in the suburbs, who is the wife of a middle-class citizen; therefore she actually has more of a sense of honor than so many common maids. [//] [Blatt 66v] She still has several things to take care of at home, and thinks [that she can start] a week from this coming

---

[164] Therese Mechetti (1788–1855), wife of the art dealer Peter Mechetti (1777–1850), was born a Rothmann. Bernard was prone to passing gossip and sensational stories, and was not always accurate in his accounts. See Wurzbach, vol. 17, p. 223; Clive, pp. 232 and 283.—KH/TA

[165] In 1653 Calderón wrote the two-part drama *La Hija del Aire*, which included an adaptation of the Semiramis legend from ancient Babylon. In 1808 Bernard Romberg had produced an opera on this theme at the Theater an der Wien. See Heft 8, Blatt 65r.—TA

[166] Probably Bernard Romberg's opera *Ulisses und Circe* (1808).—TA

[167] On Blatt 67r below nephew Karl knew where to find Beethoven, and seemingly noted that it was after his own customary dinner time at Blöchlinger's Institute.—TA

[168] See Blatt 68v below.—TA

[169] This supports in principle Schindler's report that "Beethoven rose every morning the year round at dawn and went directly to his desk;" see Schindler-MacArdle, p. 385.—TA

Monday [therefore on February 21]. // In the mornings. [//] 14 days after the 2nd [of February].[170] // Hietzing, Penzing, St. Veit.[171] [//] [Blatt 67r] She has suffered a great deal; she was unhappily married for 14 years. [//]

NEPHEW KARL [seemingly coming from Blöchlinger's Institute and briefly joining Beethoven and Oliva]: We were still eating dinner. // I wanted to come today anyhow, because you did not send for me in the morning.[172] [//]

[Blatt 67v]

OLIVA [resuming]: Candlemas or Purification of Mary is the time for giving notice [concerning your lodgings] by 14 days later, therefore on the 16th. [//] By the 16th. //

Rent at least 2 rooms. You must keep the 1st room on account of your things; take all of your trunks there [to your summer lodgings] and back. [//] [Blatt 68r] You can dispose of it certainly and easily. // 2 rooms overlooking the street, the maid's room, & the kitchen. // But the expenses [for taking] everything out there and everything [back] in. // If you will completely leave it [the apartment on the Glacis], then it is better that you cancel. // At *Michaeli*.[173] [Blatt 68v]

That is Baroness von Born,[174] who assures you that you will be very satisfied with your housekeeper. // If you get the large apartment, then it is better if you move out [of the Josephstadt Glacis apartment] entirely; you can take a monthly rental room in the City. [//]

[Presumably the end of entries for Friday, February 11.]

[Blatt 69r]

---

[170] Thus Wednesday, February 16, two weeks after Candlemas, and seemingly the period in which a tenant needed to notify the landlord of his intention to vacate the premises on *Georgi* (St. George's Day, celebrated on April 24 in Austria). See Oliva's clarification on Blatt 67v.—TA

[171] Towns lying west of Vienna, almost in a line, with Hietzing closest (ca. 3 miles) and St. Veit furthest (ca. 5 miles) from the capital. Schönbrunn Palace lies perhaps a half mile south of the center of Penzing.—KH/TA

[172] This implies locations relatively close to each other; Blöchlinger's Institute was only about a 12-minute walk from Beethoven's apartment on the Josephstädter Glacis.—TA

[173] Michaelmas, September 29, the rent terminus that complements St. George's Day, April 23 (celebrated in Vienna on April 24).—TA

[174] Baroness von Born, who, with her sister, the wife of a Major Baumgarten, operated a boarding house in the *Rother Igel*, Tuchlauben No. 598 [renumbered as 558 in 1821]. Franz Oliva and, very often, Joseph Carl Bernard ate their midday meals here. See Heft 3, Blatt 49v, for a general introduction to them; also Heft 12, Blatt 64r; Thayer-Deiters-Riemann, IV, p. 211.—TA

STIELER [possibly at Beethoven's apartment[175] or possibly at Stieler's studio;[176] probably Saturday, February 12]:[177] Please seat yourself as if you were writing, to try out the pose. // When I nod to you, please remain in the pose that you have right then. //

BEETHOVEN [already at *Zur Stadt Triest* (or possibly the *Schwan*); evening of Saturday, February 12]: Buschmann,[178] a man from Cologne, in Prince Liechtenstein's Agricultural Service; he could probably help somehow in getting somewhere in the Prince's estates in the country. [//] [Blatt 69v]

[random notes concerning Karl's guardianship:]

In face of this opposition, it was necessary[;] a deposition would absolutely never have been necessary—. Moreover, I do not need my nephew. My nephew, however, [to] me, too, is only one voice about this bad business [?] [Blatt 70r][179]

It was a difficult task for [guardian] Tuscher, not with his colleagues—in general that this entire matter [___] not indigenous to the Magistrat, if my nephew and I must [be _____] from/by the [illegible], etc.; therefore this is a deficiency in the Austrian Monarchy. Moreover, only one voice from the entire of civilized Europe can prevail over this conduct of the Magistrat. [Blatt 70v]

Should it happen, then I would prefer not to live in such a land.

There will be few guardians or uncles like me.

Denkschrift [Memorandum].[180] [//]

[Blatt 71r]

---

[175] If Stieler was simply making a pencil sketch at this point, he would not have needed his paints and might have visited Beethoven at his apartment, where the composer could have donned the housecoat depicted in the portrait.—TA

[176] Böckh, *Merkwürdigkeiten*, p. 281, gives no address for Stieler, simply noting him as "part-time in Vienna, part-time in Munich." Gugitz, "Conscriptions-Bögen," has no listing for him.—TA

[177] Handwriting established by Schindler in Heft 10, Blatt 35v.—KH

[178] Baron Joseph von Buschmann, secretary at the central administration of Prince Johann von Liechtenstein, belonged to the *Landwirtschaftsgesellschaft* (Agricultural Society) in Vienna. See *Hof- und Staats-Schematismus*, 1820, II, p. 285.—KH

[179] The entries on Blatt 70r are written extremely hastily and are therefore very difficult to read.—KH

[180] Beethoven's Memorandum draft to the Court of Appeals, dated February 18, 1820, and given to Bernard to correct, but which was seemingly never sent. See Anderson, No. 1007, and pp. 1388–1408, as well as Heft 6, Blätter 49v–50r.—TA

BERNARD [**possibly at the** *Rother Igel* **in the Tuchlauben;**[181] **in the evening, lasting until after 10 p.m., presumably on Saturday, February 12**]:[182] Have you found quarters to your taste? //

The opera by Meyerbeer has failed badly. It is nothing but an imitation of Rossini.[183] //

Hasn't it been a long while since you've spoken with [the lawyer] Dr. Bach? [//] [Blatt 71v]

Calf's head. [//]

Peters tells that the cloak was pulled off at Frau v[on] Janschikh's just as it happened to Joseph at Potiphar's.[184] [//] Potiphar. You are also said to have slept at Frau von Janschikh's. [//]

[BEETHOVEN: must have protested this accusation.]

[Blatt 72r]

PETERS [**continuing**]: I am a witness. // The long period of time [the long evening at the Janschikhs'] had entirely different effects upon you and me. // I almost couldn't awaken you. // I really could not have behaved myself better.[185] //

---

[181] The discussion on Blatt 76 suggests that this establishment is definitely not the *Kameel*, and that on Blatt 77r suggests that this discussion may have been held in a business with a longer history than Seelig's *Triest*. On Blätter 81r–81v, on another occasion several days later Joseph Czerny mentions an establishment, also not the *Triest*, where he drank Cyprus wine with Peters. In Heft 8, Blätter 1r–7r (Thursday, February 24), Peters has a conversation with Beethoven at the *Rother Igel*, where prices are less than at Seelig's (Blatt 2v) and where the Cyprus wine is said to be good (Blatt 7r). Therefore, both this conversation and the one begun on Blatt 81r could plausibly have taken place at the *Rother Igel* in the Tuchlauben, No. 598 [renumbered as 558 in 1821].—TA

[182] See Blätter 76r–77r.—TA

[183] Meyerbeer's *Emma von Leicester* was given at the Theater an der Wien on February 1, 2, and 7, with no further performances. See Seyfried, "Journal" (confirmed in Bauer, *150 Jahre Theater an der Wien*, p. 306).—TA

[184] In the Lutheran and King James Bibles, he is called Potiphar (the spelling used here), but Bernard spells his name "Putiphar." The fact that Beethoven seemingly had to ask Bernard to repeat the name suggests that either he did not recognize the spelling or that he was not well versed in Bible stories.

Genesis 39 is devoted to the story that Joseph, while in Egypt, was bought as a slave by Potiphar, captain of the guard, and was made overseer of his house. When Potiphar was called away, his wife asked Joseph to sleep with her, and Joseph refused. When she repeated the request, he refused again, but she grabbed at him and was left with his garment as he departed (thus the allusion to Peters's coat at Frau Janschikh's). Potiphar's wife, however, later used Joseph's garment to accuse the man who had rejected her. One wonders whether Peters rejected Frau Janschikh's attentions, but the context suggests that ultimately he may have succumbed.—TA

[185] A reference to the dinner at the Janschikhs' attended by Peters and Beethoven on Monday, February 7. Beethoven evidently fell asleep during the evening's conversation (possibly his own escape

BERNARD [continuing, and below]: At his place, the fox is set to guard the henhouse.[186] //

PETERS [continuing, and below]: There was no objection against my marriage, and it was also performed in Vienna.[187] [Blatt 72v] I could only return the kiss to her. // Bernard says that it is unlucky if one does not continue it. //

BERNARD: I behave myself more virtuously. //

PETERS: Certainly you kiss her; what concerns me [is that] Janschikh is not disgusted by forbidden goods. [//]

[Blatt 73r]

BERNARD: Janschikh // <I am>
    Uriah went to the Ball and the Davids remained with Frau Bathsheba.[188] // Everything depends upon the storm.[189] // I myself have been more cautious. I knew his [Peters's or Janschikh's?] wife when she was still a girl, was often   [Blatt 73v] alone with her, but never kissed her. //

PETERS: Human deeds are doomed to failure.[190] //

BERNARD: I slept next to a woman's room for three weeks. Several times the door [to the next room] opened by itself, and I always closed it back again. She has very much boasted such modesty [Blatt 74r] to her husband upon his return. // Good ones are [the same] here as there. //

mechanism), and had to be awakened for Peters to escort him home. See Blätter 42v–43v for the dinner itself and comments the next day.—TA

[186] German original: *Bey ihm heissts den Bock zum Gärtner stellen*, a variant on a relatively common saying. Even with the circle's proclivity for punning, this is probably not a wordplay on the name Gärtner on Blatt 43v above.—TA

[187] Karl Peters was married in Vienna's Michaelerkirche on May 5, 1814, when he was 32 and his wife 24. Probably because Peters was then serving an internship at the Lobkowitz Palace on the Hradschin in Prague, the marriage record notes that he had Prince Lobkowitz's permission to marry; Pfarre St. Michael, Trauungs-Register, 1804–1824, fol. 136. See also Macek, p. 395. Apart from important documents in the Lobkowitz archives, much of Macek's material was derived (often out of context) from the *Konversationshefte*, and his documentation of sources is often incomplete.—TA

[188] Beethoven must have known the Biblical story of David and Bathsheba in 2nd Samuel 11: King David spies beautiful Bathsheba, wife of Uriah, and sends for her, so he can sleep with her. He then sends Uriah off to war and certain death, so that he can have Bathsheba as a wife. Janschikh may have attended the ball on Thursday, February 10, alone (see Blatt 55v above).—TA

[189] The *Sturm* here may not be meteorological, but rather medieval military: laying siege to a lady's heart.—TA

[190] Original Latin: *Mortalia facta peribunt.*—KH

I served Professor Raupach very well with his *Fürsten Chawansky*.[191] //
I didn't order it as a meal, rather just because of its taste. //
We could already be at Frau Janschikh's now.[192]

[Blatt 74v]

PETERS: I am still as much in love as I was 5 years ago, and if I am absent for 5 days, I am homesick. //

BERNARD: He is very lukewarm in his love, otherwise he would not have forgotten his wife at Frau Janschikh's. [//]

[Blatt 75r]

PETERS: I have committed no sins other than those committed in the company of Bernard; but now he no longer leads me astray. The Spirits always prevail upon weaker natures. //

BERNARD: He has only sinned when authorized. [//] [Blatt 75v]
I believe that the entire Kingdom of Andalusia is already in the hands of the insurgents. [//] Abbé de Pradt,[193] about whom the *Österreichischer Beobachter* is so embittered, says in his book, *The Congress of Carlsbad*, that the King of Spain will

---

[191] Ernst Benjamin Salomo Raupach (1784–1852), dramatic poet born in Straupitz, Silesia; lived from 1804 to 1822 in Russia, where, from 1816, he was an *Ordinarius* (Professor) on the faculty in St. Petersburg and taught German literature and history. Returning to Germany in 1824 he settled and ultimately died in Berlin. His 1810/11 tragedy *Die Fürsten Chawansky* (The Princes Chawansky), a tragedy in five acts, opened at the Burgtheater on October 21, 1819, with Madame Schröder as Sophia and Herr Lange as Prince Joan Chawansky. Further performances took place on October 22, 25, and 30, and November 21, 1819; January 28, February 25, and May 21, 1820. A cursory survey through June 1, 1820, did not reveal any further performances. In Schickh's *Wiener Zeitschrift* 4, No. 129 (October 28, 1819), pp. 1059–1061 (and continuing in No. 130), there appeared an extensive unsigned review, to which Bernard possibly alludes here. See *Allgemeine Deutsche Biographie*, vol. 27, pp. 440–441.—KH/TA

[192] Bernard probably wrote this in jest; there was no court sponsored ball on Saturday, February 12 (although it does not preclude Janschikh's attending another ball elsewhere alone).—TA

[193] Dominique Dufour de Pradt (1759–1837), Archbishop of Mecheln since 1808. In 1815 he was declared to have lost his Archbishopric because of his political stance, and thereafter he appeared as a liberal politician. His two-volume book *Le congrès de Carlsbad* appeared in 1819/20. The *Beobachter*, No. 22 (January 22, 1820), pp. 103–105, and No. 42 (February 11, 1820), pp. 203–205, printed the German translation of a polemical article, "On Herr v. Pradt's *Congress of Carlsbad*, Second Part" (reprinted from the *Journal des Débats*), which the Viennese editors had furnished with approving annotations. See also Heft 12, Blatt 16v.—KH/TA

soon wish nothing more ardently than [Blatt 76r] to be imprisoned in Valençay again.[194] //

PETERS: Seelig [proprietor of *Zur Stadt Triest*] is not as despotic as the *Kameel*,[195] where all the guests disappear at 10 o'clock [p.m.]. //

BERNARD: Seelig never counted on having such connoisseurs as we are as guests. [//] [Blatt 76v]
Herr v[on] Janschikh always has a great deal to eat and to drink. // Peters wants to drink Cyprus wine.[196] //

PETERS: *Agreed.* [//]

BERNARD: It is like a prison. [//] [Blatt 77r] In order to provide such items in this quality, old business agreements and credit are necessary, neither of which does a beginner know or have immediately. //

PETERS: The wine tastes so good to you only because the Nürnbergers[197] are not here. [//]
[End of entries for the evening of Saturday, February 12.]

[Blatt 77v]

[No datable entries for Sunday, February 13, when a private concert scheduled at the Lobkowitz Palace was cancelled.][198]

BERNARD **[late afternoon, possibly Monday, February 14]:** I was at the *Redoute* [ball] until 3 o'clock [in the morning].[199] [//] Today, until the moment when I met

---

[194] Ferdinand VII (1784–1833), King of Spain. In 1808–1814, when the Spanish people were under Napoleonic rule, he spent his time, upon Napoleon's orders and provided with an *apanage*, in Talleyrand's Renaissance castle Valençay.—TA

[195] The grocery and wine dealership *Zum schwarzen Kameel* (Black Camel), founded in the seventeenth century, Bognergasse No. 340 [renumbered as 312 in 1821], and still extant today (in a building dating from 1901), belonged, from 1818, to Joseph Stiebitz, Joseph Söhnel, and Ignaz Arlet. Adjoining the shop was a wine house that Beethoven frequently visited. Many Viennese Gasthäuser, especially those with outdoor gardens, still maintain a 10 p.m. closing time for those public areas that might cause disturbance to the neighbors. See Frimmel, *Handbuch*, I, pp. 160 and 245–246; Groner (1922), p. 210; Czeike, III, p. 439; Behsel, p. 10.—KH/TA

[196] Further references to *Zyper(n)wein* on Blatt 81v below and Heft 8, Blatt 7r, might help determine a locale.—TA

[197] See Heft 6, Blätter 30r–30v, for a discussion of Schnell and List, and their visit to *Zur Stadt Triest* a month or so before.—KH

[198] Beethoven may have kept largely to himself for several days; see Blatt 81r below.—TA

[199] The ball in question probably took place on Sunday, February 13, from 9 p.m. until 5 a.m. on Monday morning; Hoftheater, Zettel; Bibliothek, Österreichisches Theatermuseum.—TA

you, I was at home, ate cold foods at midday, and drank only water. I was chilled through and through [Blatt 78r] at home, and will probably have a head cold tomorrow. //

It is rather like when the soldiers would say, We don't need any officers, we shall wage the war, for we can load, shoot, march, make a right-face, etc. [//]

[Blatt 78v]

BEETHOVEN: Sperr.²⁰⁰ [//]

OLIVA [probably at Beethoven's apartment on the Glacis or the *Birne* below it; presumably (Fat) Tuesday, February 15]: On the contrary, I could get an admirer to sign up until *Michaeli*. // Have the notice to vacate made immediately. Tomorrow [Ash Wednesday, February 16] is the last day;²⁰¹ by tomorrow at midday. [//] [Blatt 79r]

You don't need him for that; his legal assistant will do it better and faster. //

Pardon me, I must stand up, on the toilet.²⁰² [//]

My advice is that you write Bach a little note today. The legal assistant wants to be [Blatt 79v] *at your place tomorrow by 9 o'clock.* Then he will come and, in a quarter hour, everything will be in order.²⁰³ [//] Don't get involved with the lease. //

The doctor declared me to be better, but I almost feel worse. //

[seemingly walking from the Josephstadt toward the Burgtor:]

Everything is being cleared away here. An open square and a garden for the public will be placed there.²⁰⁴ [//] [Blatt 80r]

In the City, the apartments are better at *Michaeli* because many people are in the country, but one must take care of this earlier. [//] Do you want to spend the Winter here? // The housekeeper will come on Monday [February 21]. // You always have it,—[Blatt 80v] and if you want to have this on May 2 or 3, then just have it secured. //

---

²⁰⁰ Presumably Johann Speer, Beethoven's landlord in Mödling in summer 1820. See Heft 8, Blatt 27v.—KH

²⁰¹ This entry was made on Tuesday, February 15, because the next day, February 16—fourteen days after Candlemas, February 2—would be the end of the renewal period. See Heft 7, Blatt 67v. That the deadline date happened to be Ash Wednesday was purely coincidental.—TA

²⁰² Elsewhere Oliva (ill and recovering) excuses himself to go to the bathroom; this may be a similar case. Note reference to his health four lines later.—TA

²⁰³ The appointment with the legal assistant probably took place on Ash Wednesday, February 16, but no conversation book entries survive for it.—TA

²⁰⁴ If Beethoven and Oliva are walking between Beethoven's apartment on the Josephstadt Glacis and the walled City, or even if they are looking east from Beethoven's building across the Glacis, it is probable that they are viewing the future construction site of the Volksgarten, Heldenplatz, and Hofgarten, and the replacement of the old Burgtor with the new.—TA

[No datable entries for Ash Wednesday, February 16, when Johann Baptist Bach's legal assistant visited Beethoven in the morning.]

BEETHOVEN [possibly at the *Rother Igel*;[205] presumably Thursday, February 17]: Candles on Thursday [February 17]. [//] Wine in the *Birne*,[206] best;[207] a half is 1 fl. 13 kr. //

Siegel, M. Kath., *Bayersches Kochbuch*, 3 fl. 45 kr. W.W., Regensburg, sewn binding, in the Tendler Bookshop on the Graben, in the Trattner Building.[208] [//]

[Blatt 81r]

JOSEPH CZERNY [joining Beethoven;[209] presumably Thursday, February 17]: Bernard and Peters were here yesterday, in the hope that you would be here.[210] // <He has a> [//] The wine is more expensive at Seelig's [*Zur Stadt Triest*] than here. //

That is H[err] Schuster, watchmaker;[211]—He invented the *Clavier* [piano] that cannot go out of tune. [//] [Blatt 81v] It consists of steel quills. // Stein [piano maker] says that he learned something from your [Broadwood] piano.[212] // The man is so happy that you are sitting here. //

---

[205] After the social engagement at the Janschikh apartment on February 7, 1820, Beethoven (without announcing his intentions) began distancing himself from Janschikh, Seelig, and *Zur Stadt Triest* as quickly as possible, and saw Peters and Bernard much less frequently.—TA

[206] See Heft 4, Blatt 45r: Probably no longer *Zur goldenen Birne* (Golden Pear) in the Landstrasser Hauptstrasse, but instead an establishment by the same name on the ground floor of the building on the Josephstädter Glacis No. 5, where Beethoven was currently living. See Behsel, p. 190.—TA

[207] The word "best" was entered later.—KH

[208] Excerpt from an advertisement in the *Intelligenzblatt*, No. 38 (February 17, 1820), p. 273: "In der Tendler'schen Buchhandlung […] ist zu bekommen: Siegel, Mar[ia] Kath[arina], *Bayer'sches Kochbuch*. Achte vielvermehrte und verbesserte Auflage, 2 Theile […]." The same advertisement also appeared on February 10 and 25, 1820.—KH

[209] Seemingly at the same place where Beethoven, Bernard, and Peters met on Saturday, February 12.—TA

[210] If this was written on Thursday, February 17, then it means that Beethoven did not see Bernard and Peters on Ash Wednesday, February 16, and possibly not for several days before. He may still have been saturated by the explicit conversation of (probably) late Saturday, February 12 (see Blätter 71r–77r above).—TA

[211] Franz Schuster, "Watch (pocket and small varieties) Maker" in the Schottenbastey No. 115 [renumbered as 107 in 1821], invented the *Adiaphonon* in 1818. Franz Schuster himself does not appear in the census record for Haus 107 (possibly due to lost sheets), but one Anton Schuster (b. Vienna, 1776), a business commissioner, lived in apartment 5 with his wife and 3 children.

New instruments of one sort or another were constantly being invented during this period, were played in public a few times, possibly received notice in the *Allgemeine musikalische Zeitung* or other periodicals, and then disappeared. See Conscriptions-Bogen, Stadt, No. 107, Wohnpartei 5 (Wiener Stadt- und Landesarchiv); Redl, 1820, p. 222; 1822, p. 229; Sachs, p. 3; Behsel, p. 4; Heft 12, Blätter 35r–35v.—KH/TA

[212] On January 13 or 14 (Heft 6, Blatt 28v), Beethoven had made a note to himself to have Stein come the next day.—TA

Yesterday I drank a Cyprus wine[213] here with Peters. [//] [Blatt 82r]
Stairway. //

Somewhere today, [I] played the latest Sonata with Violin by Woržischek,[214]—
and Peters's wife sang.[215] // The sonata is very good. //

Old Kraft is sick. Therefore we haven't been able to play your Trio [in B-flat,
Op. 97] at Lobkowitz's yet.[216] [//]

[End of entries for Thursday, February 17.]

[No datable entries for Friday, February 18.]

[Blatt 82v]

BEETHOVEN **[presumably in a coffee house; late afternoon of Saturday,
February 19]:** Spar's polishing wax [for patent leather]. In the Wipplingerstrasse,
next to the Wasserdichten [waterproof] Hat Shop.[217] [//] [Blatt 83r]

Machai's *Neue Erfindung eines gegen das Durchgehen der Pferde gesicherten Wagens*;
Pest, at Kilian's Book Shop; printing paper, 2 fl. W.W.[218] [//] [Blatt 83v]

[drafting a letter:]

… that you [*du*] had a lawyer in Prague; also that K[arl] is gone because of her
enticements for the 2nd time.[219] [//]

[back to reading newspapers:]

---

[213] Other references to *Zypernwein* on Blatt 76v with Peters and Heft 8, Blatt 7r.—TA

[214] Jan Hugo/Václav Voříšek (1791–1825), Bohemian composer, pupil of Tomášek, belonged among Beethoven's acquaintances. He came to Vienna in 1813 and was promoted by Court Councillor Zizius; in 1820 he figured among Vienna's significant pianists; in 1823 he became Court Organist. See Frimmel, *Handbuch*, II, p. 469; Clive, p. 382.—KH/TA

[215] Given Peters's wife's earlier visit to Zizius's (see Blatt 48r) and Zizius's patronage of Voříšek (see immediately above), it is possible that the salon concert noted here took place at Zizius's apartment in the Kärntnerstrasse (or Untere Bräunerstrasse). Given her association with the Schwarzenbergs, who were closely related to the Lobkowitzes (see Heft 8, Blatt 5v), the performance could have been at the Schwarzenbergs', as well.—TA

[216] This salon concert had been projected for Sunday, February 13 (see Blatt 56v above). Anton Kraft would die on August 28, 1820.—TA

[217] See the *Intelligenzblatt*, No. 34 (February 12, 1820), p. 235 (Advertisements). The same advertisement also appeared on Saturday, February 19, 1820. For another reference to Franz Spar, see Heft 10, Blatt 2v.—KH/TA

[218] An advertisement with this wording cannot be traced.—KH

[219] This fragment may not be a conversational entry, but rather the draft for a letter to one of the few people with whom Beethoven was on familiar *du* terms (incl. Vincenz Hauschka, see Heft 5, Blatt 54r).—TA

Kerzmann, No. 854 in his own [Blatt 84r] house, from the Weihburggasse to the Bastei [Bastion].[220] //

BERNARD [briefly joining Beethoven]: One must try his luck. Let's take it [presumably a lottery ticket] for your nephew. [//]
[End of entries for Saturday, February 19.]

[Blatt 84v]

OLIVA [possibly at Beethoven's apartment on the Josephstädter Glacis; presumably Sunday, February 20]: The housekeeper is coming tomorrow morning.[221] [//]

UNKNOWN [probably at *Zur Stadt Triest*;[222] probably late afternoon on Sunday, February 20]: Today we admired your *Sinfonia Eroica*.[223] [//] [It was] well done, but the violins [were] too weak. Not for the *Allegro* [first movement].[224] //

WOLF [encountering Beethoven, as above]: *Praeadamiten*.[225] // [Blatt 85r]
Why haven't you come to see Stieler?[226] //
The *Ruster* [wine] for 3 Gulden is better.[227] //

---

[220] Matthias Kerzmann (b. 1770 or 1773), Councillor to Prince Esterházy, "from Bonn in Prussia," lived in Vienna from 1816, and resided in the House No. 854 [renumbered as 804 in 1821], corner of Seilerstätte and Weihburggasse. His wife Josepha (b. 1778 or 1785) was listed in the Conscriptions-Bogen as co-owner of the house, along with Joseph von Bouschwa. By the time these Conscriptions-Bogen entries were made, Bonn was technically in Prussia. See Conscriptions-Bogen, Stadt No. 804, Wohnpartei 1 and 12, as well as *Fremden-Tabelle* (Wiener Stadt- und Landesarchiv).—KH/TA

[221] On Blatt 66v Oliva had told Beethoven that the housekeeper would begin a week from that coming Monday, therefore on February 21. If so, it would make today Sunday, February 20, 1820.—TA

[222] Wolf and Bernard were seemingly still regular customers at *Zur Stadt Triest.*—TA

[223] Beethoven's Symphony No. 3 ("Eroica") was performed at the concert of the Gesellschaft der Musikfreunde in the Grosser Redoutensaal, "at the midday hour" (12:30 p.m.) on Sunday, February 20, 1820. See the *Allgemeine musikalische Zeitung* 22, No. 13 (March 29, 1820), col. 217; *Beobachter*, No. 50 (February 19, 1820), p. 244.—KH/TA

[224] Possibly Beethoven asked if the repeats were taken in the *Eroica*, to which "Not for the Allegro" would be a logical reply.—TA

[225] Librarian Wolf is seeking a book about the preadamites. See Blatt 15v above.—TA

[226] Beethoven had begun to sit for a portrait by Stieler on ca. Saturday, February 12 (see Blatt 69r above). After possibly another sitting (see Blatt 86v below), Stieler notes that the paint must dry before the next sitting.—TA

[227] Seelig, the proprietor of *Zur Stadt Triest*, had served Beethoven some Ruster wine on February 8 (see Blätter 44r–45r above), to the disapproval of some of his other friends, because it entered the system too quickly.—TA

He [presumably Buschmann] has become an Economic Councillor.[228] // Like all Austrians? // He has intrigued in general. // Specht. //

BERNARD [briefly encountering Beethoven]: They are merely epicures. //

[Blatt 85v]

BEETHOVEN [presumably at his apartment on the Glacis; the morning of Monday, February 21]:
Linen 3 yards.
Writing paper.
Candles, wax candles and half-wax candles.
Schlemmer: put strings on the violin.[229]
Lambskin. [Blatt 86r]
[at a coffee house; late morning of Monday, February 21:]
Wasserkunst Bastei, Nos. 1268 and 1269, left, the stairway, apartment.[230]
Coffee cup for the housekeeper.
Linen cloth.
Pottery shaving mug. //

[Blatt 86v]

STIELER [at his painting studio; possibly 12 noon or later on Monday, February 21]: The picture must dry. When it is dry, I shall write you, if you can give me an hour again. [//]
    Koller.[231] [//] Your [portrait] must be my masterpiece. [//] 69 fl. to 250.[232] //

[228] Presumably Baron Joseph von Buschmann, whom Beethoven had mentioned earlier (Blatt 69r) and who was named an Economic Councillor to Prince Liechtenstein in 1822. This would be an appropriate topic for discussion with Prince Liechtenstein's librarian Wolf. See Böckh, *Wiens lebende Schriftsteller*, p. 10.—KH/TA

[229] Beethoven's preferred copyist, Wenzel Schlemmer (b. 1758), living on the Kohlmarkt. He was also the Court Theaters' music librarian and copyist until his death on August 6, 1823.—TA

[230] See the *Intelligenzblatt*, No. 37 (February 16, 1820), p. 259 (Advertisements). The same advertisement also appeared on February 18 and 21, 1820. Nos. 1268 and 1269, at the stairway leading up to the bastion, were combined as 1191 in the renumbering of 1821 (Behsel, p. 36).—KH/TA

[231] In the exhibition of the Wiener Kunstakademie, which took place early in 1820, Stieler displayed, next to the portrait of Beethoven, another portrait of Johanna Koller, who worked in Vienna as a dilettante in painting flowers between 1816 and 1822. See Böckh, *Merkwürdigkeiten*, p. 263; *Conversationsblatt*, No. 49 (April 25, 1820), p. 459.—KH

[232] Seemingly the price range for Stieler's portraits.—TA

BERNARD: In addition are the stories from Spain; Prince M[etternich] and the *Österr[eichischer] Beobachter* are greatly embarrassed.[233] [//]

[Blatt 87r]

UNKNOWN[234] **[possibly at a music dealership; on Monday, February 21, or Tuesday, February 22]**: He's written an opera. // I shall show you a 4-hand Sonata that will be engraved. // Herr Stiller [Stieler] is painting your/her portrait. [//]

[Blatt 87v]

BERNARD **[probably at a coffee house in the City; presumably Tuesday, February 22]**: He [Peters] will journey with the Prince [Lobkowitz] to Italy for a time.[235] //

It is the painter Daffinger,[236] who, because his portraits are accurate, is very much sought. He likewise wishes to paint you. He has now painted Grillparzer. [//] [Blatt 88r]

Now we must reach a point where you can write the oratorio [*Der Sieg des Kreuzes*] early this year. [//]

The best and cheapest. //

The consultant has asked why the Doctor [Bach] did not hold forth further about her [Johanna]. The documents [Blatt 88v] should therefore be secured from the *Landrecht*. [//] She wanted nothing more than that it would have to come this far.[237] //

Yesterday and today it was said all over that the Duke de Berry, as he was leaving

---

[233] In the *Beobachter*, No. 53 (February 22, 1820), pp. 253–254, there appeared an extensive report about the battles around Cadiz in Spain. The *Beobachter* also printed short reports in earlier numbers.—KH

[234] Probably someone connected with one of Vienna's music publishers, possibly Steiner & Co. on the Graben, where Beethoven was known to visit frequently.—TA

[235] They will depart on March 9, 1820; see the *Wiener Zeitung*, No. 58 (March 11, 1820), p. 232.—TA

[236] Moritz Michael Daffinger (phonetically called Taffinger here), portrait, miniature, and watercolor painter (b. suburban Lichtenthal, 1790; d. Vienna, 1849). He was a friend of poet/ playwright Franz Grillparzer in his youth, made a name for himself by painting the representatives at the Congress of Vienna in 1814–1815, and became one of Vienna's most significant portrait painters from the early 1820s. See Czeike, I, pp. 608–609.—TA

[237] On Monday, February 21, 1820, the Court of Appeals demanded further documentary materials from the Magistrat. Beethoven's memos to the Landrecht about his sister-in-law's petty crimes were mentioned in the reply of February 28. See Thayer-Deiters-Riemann, IV, p. 565; Weise, p. 29.—KH/TA

the Theater in Paris, was stabbed to death [Blatt 89r] by a saddler[238] whose wife had pleased him.[239] // Yesterday Prince Palffy, the two Counts Harrach, and others from the High Nobility were there.[240] [//]

One can have such written material printed in France and England. [//] [Blatt 89v][241]

The first [lottery] drawing is on March 1.[242] [//] If we win, let's go on tour immediately. [//] Very stupid people have already won. [//] I have bought a lot [ticket] for every lottery, but have never won anything. [//] [Blatt 90r] It is only an accident if one doesn't win. //

I must go now, since I must still supervise the report about the Duke de Berry at the printer's shop [for publication on February 23].[243] [//] [Blatt 90v] While getting into his carriage, he was stabbed from behind. [//] After the theater on the 13th. // He had [married] the daughter of the Crown Prince of Naples.[244] He was the only one from whom [Blatt 91r = inside back cover] there could be descendants. Now, however, the Bourbons' succession to the throne is finished. // The Bourbons

---

[238] Charles Ferdinand duc de Berry (1778–1820), second son of the Count of Artois (from 1824, Charles X), was assassinated in the night of February 13/14, 1820, by the journeyman saddler Louis Pierre Louvel (1783–1820), a Bonaparte sympathizer and political enemy of the Bourbons. On February 13, as the Duke was leaving the Opera and about to get into his coach, Louvel, acting alone, stabbed him in the right side of the chest, and he died at 6:30 the next morning. The news of the murder appeared on February 23, 1820, in both the *Beobachter*, No. 54, pp. 257–258, and the *Wiener Zeitung*, No. 43, p. 169.—KH/TA

[239] Bernard either fabricates a sensational sexual motive here or seems happy to repeat one. In fact, Louvel himself proclaimed that he had no motivation other than his love for Bonaparte and his desire to end the Bourbon lineage that might claim the French crown. See *Wiener Zeitung*, No. 43 (February 23, 1820), p. 169.—TA

[240] Presumably a memorial service for the Duke de Berry. The surviving Hofkapelle *Akten*, 1820 (Haus-, Hof- und Staatsarchiv, Vienna) do not indicate such a Mass in the Augustinerkirche or the Hofkapelle itself. Similarly, the *Wiener Zeitung* noted above does not mention such a service, merely that the official Habsburg Court mourning would begin on Friday, February 25, and last for four weeks.—TA

[241] On the upper third of the page, partially covered by the entries, is the pencil sketch of a half-figure in profile.—KH

[242] By organizing this lottery the entrepreneurs of the Theater an der Wien had hoped to be free from the debt in which the poor financial management of Count Ferdinand Palffy had placed it. One "lot" (ticket) cost 20 fl. W.W. [8 fl. C.M.]. The *Beobachter*, No. 34 (February 3, 1820), p. 164, announced the first drawing (for which 50,000 fl. W.W. had been set aside for the first prize) for March 1. Further notices appeared in the *Wiener Zeitung*, No. 34 (February 12, 1820), p. 133, and in the *Beobachter*, No. 58 (February 27, 1820), p. 284.—KH

[243] Editorial work on an article appearing on Wednesday, February 23, must have been accomplished no later than Tuesday, February 22. The initial entries in Heft 8 also suggest no break between Hefte 7 and 8.—TA

[244] The Duke de Berry was married to Princess Caroline Ferdinande Louise of Naples (1798–1870). His son Heinrich [Henri], later Count of Chambord, born on September 29, 1820, the last representative of the old Bourbon line, lived in exile after the July Revolution of 1830.—KH

are usurpers. [//] In their toilet in Koblenz, they used only new silk cloths [*Tücher*] or young chickens [instead of paper].[245]

End of Heft 7

[Heft 8 follows upon Heft 7 without a break.]

---

[245] Bernard tells Beethoven much the same thing (and thereby clarifies the context of this distasteful reference) in September, 1824; see Heft 76, Blatt 14r. On that occasion, the birds specified were doves.—TA

Heft 8

(ca. February 22, 1820 – ca. March 11, 1820)

[Inside front cover]

BERNARD **[probably Tuesday, February 22]:**[1] Thursday is set up. [//] Your Majesty. //

[No entries for Wednesday, February 23.]

[Blatt 1r]

PETERS[2] **[presumably at the *Rother Igel*; after visiting Blöchlinger's Institute on Thursday, February 24]:**[3] Karl has made great progress in Greek. [//] The whole Institute was active; I found the greatest orderliness and quiet. [//] Karl's teacher in Latin and Greek appears to be very accomplished.[4] [//] He [Karl] is studying Greek diligently and might be able to read Homer in 3 months. [//] In Mathematics they have 3 classes per week; they are now on equations. [//] I am thoroughly satisfied with the Institute. // It is an endorsement for the Institute that Karl is learning far more than is required in the school. // He must also take public examinations in Salzburg. [//] [Blatt 1v] He is learning far more at the Institute than in the school. [//]

---

[1] The final entries in Heft 7, which find Bernard editing an article that would appear in his *Wiener Zeitung* on Wednesday, February 23, cannot have been made any later than Tuesday, February 22. Here, inside the front cover of Heft 8, Bernard refers to "Thursday," which would be February 24, and indeed Peters's subsequent entries must have been made after he visited Blöchlinger's Institute on the normal visitation day (Thursday). Since Bernard does not refer to Thursday as "tomorrow," his initial entry here (like his final entries in Heft 7) must have been made before Wednesday, February 23.—TA

[2] In red pencil Schindler identified the writer as "Hohler" (a name otherwise unknown in the literature), but a comparison with the handwriting in Heft 4, Blatt 1r, confirms that the writer is Peters, as would be expected from the contents of the entries.—KH/TA

[3] This long conversation lasts through Blatt 7r.—TA

[4] At Blöchlinger's Institute, the teacher of Latin and Greek was Joseph Bergmann (later Director of the Imperial Coin and Antiquities Collections); his successor at Blöchlinger's was Pulai (or Pulay). See Frimmel, *Studien*, II, p. 116.—KH

Assuming that public instruction in Salzburg is excellent, it could probably be recommended; but that cannot be concealed.[5] [//]

I was at the *Kameel*.[6] [//]

You are leaving? [//] The worst time is past. [//]

Is he [Stieler] far along with your portrait? //

Prince Joseph Schwarzenberg[7] still has to speak with the Emperor first. // If we don't leave in a week, we will miss Holy Week in Rome and the *Miserere*.[8] [//] 8 months [on the road]. [//] [Blatt 2r] Upper [Northern] Italy, Florence, Rome, Naples, Sicily, Genoa, Turin, Switzerland. // If His Majesty says that he would prefer him [young Prince Ferdinand Lobkowitz] to go to the estates in Bohemia, then the good times are over; in order thoroughly to learn the [family's] business affairs. [//] He will reach his majority in a year.[9] [//]

BEETHOVEN [noting prices]:

At the *Rother Igel* [Red Hedgehog], Tuchlauben 598:[10]

Erlauer	2 fl. 24 [kr.]	
Nesmüller	1 fl. 30	
Schomlauer	1	12
Wazersdorfer	48	

[Blatt 2v]

PETERS [continuing, presumably at the *Rother Igel*]: At Seelig's [*Zur Stadt Triest*] one costs 30 kr., here [it is] 15 kr. //

Karl pleased me extraordinarily today [Thursday, February 24]; a truly superb

---

[5] The discussion turns to the possibility of sending nephew Karl to a school in Salzburg, to get him away from the negative influences of his mother Johanna. The reference in this clause is unclear. Perhaps in the word *verbergen* (conceal), Peters was attempting a feeble wordplay on *Bergen* (mountains), of which the area around Salzburg has many.—TA

[6] The Black Camel, grocery and wine shop (with appended wine house) in the Bognergasse.—KH/TA

[7] Guardian of the Lobkowitz children, whose mother had been born a Schwarzenberg.—KH/TA

[8] The celebrated *Miserere* by Gregorio Allegri (ca. 1582–1652), sung in the Sistine Chapel during Holy Week. Its performances outside the Vatican were rare, and the young Mozart supposedly wrote out the piece after just one hearing. In 1820 Palm Sunday fell on March 26, Good Friday on March 31, and Easter Sunday on April 2.—TA

[9] Born in 1797, Prince Ferdinand Lobkowitz would reach his majority of twenty-four on April 13, 1821; see Macek, "Beethovens Freund," p. 401.—TA

[10] The restaurant/tavern *Zum Rothen Igel* was located in a so-called *Durchhaus*, a building that led from the narrow Kammerhof (Wildpretmarkt) No. 1318 [renumbered as 550 in 1821] through to the broader Tuchlauben No. 598 [renumbered as 558 in 1821]. The location had later associations with the Gesellschaft der Musikfreunde and Johannes Brahms. See Groner (1922), p. 186; Guetjahr, p. 26; Behsel, p. 17.—KH/TA

nature. // You must have struggled to make things beneficial for Karl; such love must be explained to him; that must bind him to you forever. // In a harmful environment, such natures often go completely to ruin. [//] [Blatt 3r] He would probably have been able to go to school at his mother's, if, however, his moral and physical side had gone to ruin; because in his many fantasies, she has gladly abandoned the young soul to weakness. // Blöchlinger will make every opportunity for her to be with him difficult; he says that Karl may not be disturbed and she must leave. [//] [Blatt 3v] The whole story is really interesting for she restrains herself almost unbelievably. The Magistrat is playing a fatal role. He has not thoroughly understood. [//] The Magistrat does not appear to be adaptable for unusual cases. // Since you have distributed the evidence in such a manner that was conspicuous; and the most important legal ground against his guardianship up till now. [//] [Blatt 4r]

I have not seen Bernard. Pepi Lobkowitz met him today at the sermon at Werner's. //

Are you completely well? // Take my wife into your home during my absence.[11] // Would you like to live in the Lobkowitz garden?[12] // I shall speak to Prince Ferdinand about it! [//] <He> You can have it, and the garden is beautiful and cosy. // In the winter the building is not warm enough.[13] [//] [Blatt 4v] At the moment when Schwarzenberg was to see the Emperor. [//] Because Their Majesties were at the Burg [Theater] for Mad[ame] Korn's first performance,[14] so he will not refuse you this. [//] She was in Karlsbad and the young Schwarzenbergs noticed *that he had his horse exercise in front of Mad. Korn's windows.*[15] [//] Such a love is unfortunate; he has grown sons and the story has made the rounds of all the taverns. [//] [Blatt 5r]

Do you like to eat smoked salmon?[16] //

[11] In this context Peters seems to be offering Beethoven his wife's services as a caregiver (for the composer's health) during his absence, rather than in the sexual sense. Unfortunately, when taken out of context, it could lend credence to Solomon's implication (1977, p. 262) that Beethoven would enjoy Josephine Peters's sexual favors during her husband's absence.—TA

[12] The Summer Palace of the Lobkowitz family (originally part of the Harrach Summer Palace complex) was in the Landstrasse, Ungargasse No. 309 [renumbered as 347 in 1821], on the east side of the street, just south of today's Juchgasse, and on the approximate site of today's Höhere technische Lehranstalt. Beethoven, who had recently written down the address of an apartment just west of Ungargasse, two blocks closer to the City, must have answered in the affirmative. See Pezzl (1826), p. 165; Behsel, p. 79.—KH/TA

[13] If this apartment was not warm enough in winter, it was surely not the location that Peters offered Beethoven to spend the night, to keep warm, on January 10, 1820 (see Heft 6, Blatt 7v).—TA

[14] Wilhelmine Korn, née Stephanie (1786–1843), Court actress, married the Court actor Maximilian Korn in 1806. She made her debut at the Burgtheater in 1802 and was active there until 1830. See *Hof- und Staats-Schematismus*, 1819, I, p. 128; Wurzbach, vol. 12, p. 463.—KH

[15] The phrase in italics was originally written in French.—TA

[16] Bernard also recommends smoked salmon on Blatt 13r below.—TA

I must visit Frau von Janitschek [Janschikh] once more before my departure; it would be very discourteous [not to]. [//] "The Husband is the Lord of Creation."— Janschikh's Motto; he holds her on a very short tether. // That is no proof. // That is only a single case. //

Yesterday [Wednesday, February 23], Kraft accompanied Prince [Joseph/Pepi] Lobkowitz in the performance of your Trio [Op. 97].[17] [//] [Blatt 5v] If you ever have nothing better to do, [then] listen to it.[18] //

The former [piano] teacher Ehlinger[19] was very fine and, for 8 months, had Lobkowitz play the Variations by Hummel, which were too difficult for what he had learned. // My wife recommended Gebauer[20] at Schwarzenberg's; he [Lobkowitz] has little technique. // I have never yet mentioned your authority. [//] [Blatt 6r] He is glad if he can play something, but has no diligence. A correct feeling, if you are present; he completely lacks courage the first time. //

The Nürnbergers[21] have left Vienna and List is sleeping. // They still have need of a special recommendation to Metternich; they wasted their time. [//] [Blatt 6v]

---

[17] The violinist for this salon performance was probably Kärntnertor Theater violist Anton Schreiber, formerly in the full-time employ of Prince Lobkowitz (see Heft 7, Blatt 56v).—TA

[18] Beethoven had played the successful public premiere of the "Archduke" Trio, Op. 97, with Ignaz Schuppanzigh and Joseph Linke, at the Hotel zum römischen Kaiser on April 11, 1814; see the *Allgemeine musikalische Zeitung* 16, No. 21 (May 25, 1814), col. 355. The trio had been sketched in 1810–1811, finished by March 3, 1811, and was played, possibly for the first time, in the garden of Prince Lobkowitz's Palace (presumably the Summer Palace) on June 2, 1811, with Archduke Rudolph at the piano; see Steblin, *Beethoven in the Diaries*, courtesy Rita Steblin.—TA

[19] Possibly Sebastian Ehrlinger (b. 1778), I.R. Court Organist, living in Bischofsgasse No. 678 [renumbered as 637 in 1821]. See Conscriptions-Bogen, Stadt, No. 637, Wohnpartei 4 (Wiener Stadt- und Landesarchiv).—KH/TA

[20] Born in Eckersdorf near Glaz, Franz Xaver Gebauer (1784–1822) had been a music teacher in Vienna since 1810. From 1816 he was Kapellmeister and choral director at the Augustinerkirche. He was a member of the representative body of the Gesellschaft der Musikfreunde. In 1819, together with Ferdinand Piringer, he founded the *Concerts spirituels*, which took place every two weeks, on Fridays from 4 to 6 p.m., in the restaurant *Zur Mehlgrube* on the Neuer Markt. See Kanne's *Wiener AmZ* 5, No. 22 (March 17, 1821), cols. 172–174; No. 10 (December 25, 1822), pp. 821–822; Böckh, *Merkwürdigkeiten*, p. 367; Frimmel, *Handbuch*, I, p. 160; Thayer-Deiters-Riemann, IV, p. 218; Clive, pp. 123–124.

Glaz: Kladsko, Silesia (now Kłodzko, Poland, 35 miles south-southwest of Breslau, 8 miles east of the Czech border). In Heft 16, Blatt 7v, Gebauer told Beethoven that he had been born in Nepomuk (Bohemia, ca. 15 miles south of Pilsen). Eckersdorf, however, is now Bożków, Poland; Kreis Nova Ruda (formerly Neurode), near Fischstein (also called Forellenstein), where oboist/copyist Benjamin Gebauer had been born; see Albrecht, "Benjamin Gebauer," pp. 7–22.—KH/TA

[21] The "Departures" column of the *Wiener Zeitung*, No. 42 (February 22, 1820), p. 168, lists: "On February 19: Herr Weber and Herr Schnell, merchants, both to Nürnberg." The Nürnbergers and List are discussed in Heft 7.—KH/TA

You would eat it fresh in Raudnitz;[22] it is caught there. // If I deserved your favor—and because mankind is always interesting—it would give me great joy if you were to come with Karl to Bohemia; then we would go to the Riesengebirge—it is very educational, particularly for its minerals. [//] [Blatt 7r] If you don't go to England, then perhaps you will go to Bohemia. // I am at your service if you go. //

That [wine] is not [available] at Seelig's [*Zur Stadt Triest*]. We must go to [see] him. // Aren't you drinking anything more? // Cyprus wine is good here.[23] // Do you want to determine the cost? [//]

[End of entries for Thursday, February 24.]

BEETHOVEN **[probably at his apartment; probably late morning, presumably Friday, February 25]**:
Paper. Schlemmer.
Sharpen the knife.
Violin maker.
Ink. Spices.

[Blatt 7v]

SCHLEMMER[24] **[presumably at his home and copying shop, Kohlmarkt No. 1216;[25] presumably ca. 12 noon on Friday, February 25]**: A few days ago I spoke with Z.;[26] he told me that he doesn't know why you don't come there. [//]

---

[22] Raudnitz, Bohemia, population ca. 5,000, ca. 25 miles north-northwest of Prague, on the Elbe River, principal city of a duchy belonging to the Princes Lobkowitz. See Raffelsperger, V, p. 126. Peters is probably speaking of some variety of fish or game, probably the former, given the word "gefangen" and Beethoven's love of fish.—KH/TA

[23] For further references to Cyprus wine and Peters, see Heft 7, Blätter 76v and 81v.—TA

[24] Handwriting identified through a comparison with two authentic bills in Schlemmer's hand in the Staatsbibliothek zu Berlin: February 28, 1814 and ca. November 30, 1814 (mus. ms. autogr. Beeth. 35,83 and 35,84; Albrecht, *Letters to Beethoven*, Nos. 182 and 194). See also Bartlitz, *Die Beethoven-Sammlung*, p. 148.—KH/TA

[25] Various documents from the time of Wenzel Schlemmer's death on August 6, 1823, indicate that he lived in the City, No. 1216 [renumbered as 1148 in 1821], located on the south side of the Kohlmarkt, across from its intersection with Wallnerstrasse. See, for instance, Schlemmer, Verlassenschafts-Abhandlung, Fasz. 2: 4682/1823 (Wiener Stadt- und Landesarchiv); Behsel, p. 34.—TA

[26] Presumably Franz Joseph Zips, servant of Archduke Rudolph, also mentioned on Blatt 80r. This might also mean Zmeskall.—KH/TA

Maschek [?]²⁷ gets 5 fl. and [___] ducats for a piece. [//] *Sie kaufen Mehlmagel /
weis schmotz lad*²⁸ [//]

[Blatt 8r]

OLIVA **[probably at mid-day dinner, Friday, February 25]**: The housekeeper
was at my place to request me to give [you] her opinion of the woman. She would
advise you in no way to retain the woman; she would be of the most common and
most ungrateful disposition. [//] On the very first day she told her everything
possible in order to get rid of her. [//] She told her about your behavior toward
others. [//] [Blatt 8v] About the most recent incidents that continue, about the
less recent incidents that you would have stopped, &c. Further, the woman would
be lazy; she would not earn the money that you would pay her. She [the house-
keeper] opines that, for a lower price, you could get a type of servant who would
take care of everything in the house, and who would also be better for your daily
affairs. [//] [Blatt 9r] The [other] woman appears to be honorable; she opines [that]
her treatment would always be as one deserves; & you can count on her. //

Only she says that kitchen utensils are so lacking that she wants to talk to you
about it. // She knows such a [house] cleaner who could do everything. [//]
[Blatt 9v]

It was dangerous for several days. [//] Nervous bilious fever.²⁹ //

On April 18, you may not be able to cash in the money for the bank share; if that
were to be, then I could already prolong it [so] that you perhaps don't have to think
about if for 3 months, but, for the present, you must decide. [//] [Blatt 10r] Toward
9 o'clock. [//]

²⁷ Paul Maschek (1761–1826), composer, piano teacher, copyist, and famous glass harmonica
player. From 1813 to 1820 he was secretary of the *Tonkünstler-Societät*. Beethoven engaged him briefly
in March, 1824, to copy orchestral parts for the Ninth Symphony (see Heft 57, Blatt 40v–60, Blatt
11r). The brackets and question mark after Maschek's name originate with the German edition. The
monetary amounts are unclear. See Böckh, *Merkwürdigkeiten*, p. 373; Pohl, *Tonkünstler-Societät*, p. 99;
Wurzbach, vol. 17, pp. 78–79.—KH/TA

²⁸ The words presented here in italics are difficult to read. Some elements lend themselves to
rudimentary translation (You/They buy flour-something, white dust?), but seem meaningless in
context. Viennese dialect dictionaries do not provide a reliable key to coherent meaning.—KH/TA

²⁹ Unless Oliva suffered a more recent illness, after February 15, this probably refers to the
condition (which he then described as peritonitis) from which he suffered, beginning on ca.
January 18, and which kept him housebound for nearly two weeks and with limited activity for some
time thereafter.—TA

BEETHOVEN [possibly at the *Rother Igel*; late afternoon of Friday, February 25]:[30] Weihburggasse, Lilienfelderhof, at Kath[arina] Gräffer's: *Der Vogelfänger und Vogelwarter*, etc., etc., by D.J. Tscheiner; 8vo; 1820; 4 fl. 30 kr.[31] [//]

[Blatt 10v]

BERNARD [joining him there]: A week from Monday[32] the Archduke [Rudolph] goes to Olmütz. [//] Count T[royer][33] asked me if I hadn't seen you for a long time. The Archduke wants to write to you, you won't believe it, that you must go with him to Olmütz. [//]

[Blatt 11r]

PETERS [joining Beethoven and Bernard]: May I write to you from Naples, Palermo, and Syracuse?[34] [//]

[Blatt 11v]

---

[30] When Bernard joins Beethoven, he notes (Blatt 12r) that he had eaten midday dinner sometime earlier. At the end of his conversation (Blatt 13r below), he urges Beethoven to eat some smoked salmon, which would be appropriate as a light evening repast in a coffee house or wine house. Peters had also mentioned smoked salmon when presumably at the *Rother Igel* (Blatt 5r above), and so this conversation may have taken place there, as well.—TA

[31] Excerpt from an advertisement in the *Intelligenzblatt*, No. 45 (February 25, 1820), p. 329: "Newly published by Hartleben's Verlag and available in Vienna at Kath[arina] Gräffer, Weihburggasse, Lilienfelderhof, No. 964 [renumbered as 908 in 1821]: *Der Vogelfänger u[nd] Vogelwärter, oder Naturgeschichte, Fang, Zämung, Pflege und Wartung unserer bliebsten Sing und Zimmervögel* (The Bird Catcher and Bird Watcher, or History of Nature: Capture, Taming, Care and Observation of our most beloved song- and domestic birds). With a Calendar for Lovers of Birdsong and Enthusiastic Collectors. After Many Years of Personal Observations written by D.J. Tscheiner. With illustrations (true to Nature) of 16 songbirds, and 4 copperplates to demonstrate the capture of birds." The same advertisement also appeared on March 6 and 9, 1820.—KH/TA

[32] The coming Monday was February 28, but, since 1820 was a leap year, the Monday after that (and the day specified here) was March 6. Rudolph spent the night of Tuesday, March 7, in Wischau (Moravia) and arrived in Olmütz on Wednesday, March 8. On Thursday, March 9, his solemn installation as Archbishop took place in the city's metropolitan Church. See *Wiener Zeitung*, No. 65 (March 20, 1820), p. 257, and No. 66 (March 21, 1820), p. 261.—KH/TA

[33] As noted elsewhere, an official on Rudolph's staff and an amateur clarinettist.—TA

[34] This random entry by Peters may have been made at some other time. If, however, he was present during Bernard's conversation with Beethoven (a distinct possibility), then he made this entry in mock derision of Beethoven. From the context of several entries concerning Archduke Rudolph, it appears that Beethoven feared being impressed into the Archduke's day-to-day service as Kapellmeister and, even worse, being forced to live in distant Olmütz. Thus Peters's entry here suggested that he would write the potentially unhappy Beethoven from pleasant and sunny southern Italy and Sicily.—TA

BERNARD [still presumably at the *Rother Igel*; approaching evening of Friday, February 25]: Count Troyer says that several people in his [Rudolph's] service have not received their salary for 6 months. [//]

What is Oliva doing? [//] Haven't you seen him?[35] [//] [Blatt 12r]

Since yesterday I've had a ringing in my ears. [//]

Troyer is also not going. [//] I ate there at midday. [//]

On Sunday [February 27] I am dining with the religious community in the Kreuzerhof.[36] [//]

Tomorrow [Saturday, February 26], Fischer from Berlin is singing Figaro.[37] [//] They say that she has improved.[38] [//] [Blatt 12v]

I didn't get to sleep until 3 o'clock [a.m.] [//] It was impossible today. [//] I have only taken the incoming mail. *Ex Officio.* //

He[39] hates the Bourbons and, [Blatt 13r] as he says, has realized the necessity that they not rule France. [//]

[35] Beethoven, of course, had seen Oliva earlier that same day (Blätter 8r–10r), but, knowing that he and Bernard were not on the friendliest of terms, might have tried to be circumspect. Even so, Beethoven had probably seen very little of Oliva since February 15, possibly due to the illness described on Blatt 9v.—TA

[36] The *Heiligenkreuzerhof* between Schönlaterngasse and Grashof, which belonged to the Cistercian Monastery of Heiligenkreuz in Lower Austria and consisted of a cloister and several rental buildings; see Groner (1922), p. 159.—KH

[37] Joseph Fischer (1780–1862), bass singer, was born in Vienna and, in 1790, went with his father, the famous bass Ludwig Fischer, to Berlin. From 1814 to 1818 he was engaged at the Royal Opera in Berlin, and from there went to Stuttgart and Munich. On February 17, 1820, Fischer arrived in Vienna from Munich. "On Saturday, February 26, *Figaro*, opera by Mozart, was given at the I.R. Court Opera Theater next to the Kärntner Tor; Herr Fischer, R[oyal] Bavarian Court Singer, debuted therein as Figaro." Carl von Ledebur, *Tonkünstler-Lexicon* (1861), pp. 155–156; see also the *Wiener Zeitung*, No. 40 (February 19, 1820), p. 160; Schickh's *Wiener Zeitschrift* 5, No. 28 (March 4, 1820), pp. 222–223; Zettel, Kärntnertor Theater, February 26, 1820 (Bibliothek, Österreichisches Theatermuseum, courtesy Othmar Barnert).—KH/TA

[38] After Bernard's remark about Fischer, Beethoven must have replied in the negative concerning a female member of the cast, eliciting this reply. Joseph Fischer sang Figaro on February 26 and 27, Madame Grünbaum the Countess, Demoiselle Wranitzky the Susanna, Demoiselle Bondra the Cherubino, Madame Vogel the Marzelline, and Demoiselle Bio the Bärbchen (Barbarina); Zettel (Bibliothek, Österreichisches Theatermuseum).—TA

[39] Louis Pierre Louvel, who had assassinated the Duke de Berry as he came out of the Opera in Paris on February 13–14, 1820. See Heft 7, Blätter 88v–91r.—TA

He is at the Opera with his wife.[40] I don't have any more time today to go to the Doctor [lawyer Bach].[41] [//]

Take some smoked salmon; it is very good.[42] [//]

[Seemingly the end of entries for Friday, February 25.]

[Blatt 13v]

WOLFSOHN[43] [?] [**possibly at the** *Rother Igel;* **possibly the evening of Saturday, February 26**]: Was the person who makes the chests [of drawers] at your place? He has already made a wooden model. I saw the model in his apartment. If he doesn't come, I'll have a note sent to him today that he should come to see you tomorrow, if it is possible for him. [//] [Blatt 14r]

If he has shown you the model, it will certainly be in the works during the coming week.

Have you been to Dr. Meyer's in the Landstrasse already?[44] [//]

BERNARD [**possibly at the** *Rother Igel;* **presumably ca. 10 p.m., after the** *Figaro* **performance, Saturday, February 26**]: Fischer acts and sings with great refinement. [//] [Blatt 14v]

He [Wähner] is very plump.[45] Even though he intended to say something very

---

[40] This represents a change in subject and does not refer to the Duke de Berry, but instead probably to Peters. Curtain time at the Kärntnertor Theater was 7 p.m.; therefore, this conversation took place toward or during the evening of Friday, February 25. The performance that night consisted of Cherubini's *Der portugiesische Gasthof* (1 act), followed by Gyrowetz's ballet *Pagen des Herzogs von Vendome* (choreography by Aumer). See Theater Zettel, Bibliothek, Österreichisches Theatermuseum.—TA

[41] Beethoven evidently hoped to have Peters, but failing that, Bernard, go to see his lawyer, Dr. Johann Baptist Bach. Bernard's comment about his availability to see the lawyer on Blatt 28r below seems to confirm this.—TA

[42] Peters mentions smoked salmon on Blatt 5r above.—TA

[43] From the contents of his entries it may be concluded that the writer is Sigmund Wolfsohn (b. London, 1767; d. Vienna, 1852), a physician specializing in ruptures and owner of a surgical supplies factory. Beethoven had become personally acquainted with him on ca. January 11, 1820 (see Heft 6, Blätter 17v–18r) and later (Blatt 90v below) noted his name and address after they conversed again on ca. March 11.—KH/TA

[44] Dr. Carl Joseph Mayer's Sulphur-Fumigation Institute, in the building of the Elisabethiners' hospital, on the west side of Landstrasser Hauptstrasse, a block south of the Glacis. Beethoven had considered seeking treatment for his deafness there in April, 1819. See Heft 2, Blätter 28r and 47r, among others.—TA

[45] Friedrich Wähner, who also wrote for Schickh's *Wiener Zeitschrift.* The reference here is to Johanna Franul von Weissenthurn's tragedy *Ruprecht Graf von Horneck,* which had been performed at the Burgtheater on February 7. The review appeared in the *Wiener Zeitschrift* 5, No. 20 (February 15, 1820), pp. 158–160.—KH

nice to Madame Weissenthurn about her most recent play, she took it so badly that he may never enter her house again. [//]

Wähner has now also received a card as Honorary Member of the Commercial Society.[46] [//] [Blatt 15r] Wähner allows his reviews to extend as far as it pleases Schickh. [//] A short while ago, in the *Morgenblatt*, he trampled the local actors with both feet; now he exalts them in the extreme. //

Biller[47] ([the tutor] at Baron Puthon's) is sick. [//] [Blatt 15v]

Over 70. [//] His name is Bernard. // B [//]

We are only now living in luxury with oysters. //[48]

He would be very afraid of cannon.[49] [//] [Blatt 16r]

Tomorrow [Sunday, February 27] is the Akademie of Meister Gyrowetz [in the Grosser] Redoute[nsaal].[50] //

Czerny has made note of a half dozen composers who are wolves in sheep's clothing. Every day he looks in the Obituaries to see whether or not one of them has died. //

I received two [tickets][51] from Henikstein as a gift, and I have re-sold [Blatt 16v] one that I bought; therefore I am very thrifty. // Out of esteem and veneration, he will very gladly do it, but he cannot accept anything for it from you, from the Master of Tones. [//] [Blatt 17r]

---

[46] The so-called Fischhof Manuscript (Staatsbibliothek zu Berlin, mus. ms. theor. 285, Bl. 16v) mentions that on October 1, 1819, Beethoven was named Honorary Member of the *Kaufmännischer Verein* (Commercial Society) in Vienna.

The Commercial Society was founded in 1819 and met in the City, Bauernmarkt No. 626 [owned by Prince Liechtenstein and renumbered as 587 in 1821], "partly to acquaint themselves about business affairs, partly to enjoy themselves in a select company, and to facilitate desirable acquaintanceships among friends of this rank." In addition to the wholesalers (bankers), manufacturers, and merchants who were regular members, state officials, learned individuals, and artists could also enter the society "through distributed Honorary cards." See Johann Pezzl, *Beschreibung von Wien*, p. 613. See Brandenburg, *Briefwechsel*, No. 1337a, and Albrecht, *Letters to Beethoven*, No. 262, for the materials (now presumed lost) that the Society sent to the composer; and Behsel, p. 18.—KH/TA

[47] Dr. Johann Bihler, tutor in the house of wholesaler Baron von Puthon (see Heft 4, Blatt 32v).—KH/TA

[48] Under the dividing line, a crossed-out pencil sketch of a head in profile.—KH

[49] Possibly a play on the words "canon" and "cannon." Janschikh had urged Beethoven to write a canon on the lament of oysters about to be eaten. See Heft 6, Bl. 57v (ca. January 21, 1820); Heft 7, Blatt 50r (February 8, 1820).—TA

[50] On Sunday, February 27, 1820, a "grand musical Akademie" for the benefit of Adalbert Gyrowetz (1763–1850), Kapellmeister at the Kärntnertor Theater, took place in the Grosser Redoutensaal. The program included, among other items, an Overture, as well as a Duet and Sextet from *Il finto Stanislao*, an opera that Gyrowetz had written in Milan. In addition Anna Wranitzky sang a Cavatina by Rossini, Herr Costa played on the guitar, and visiting pianist Karl Schuncke played an Adagio and Rondo by Ries. See Kanne's *Wiener AmZ* 4, No. 19 (March 4, 1820), cols. 148–149; Schickh's *Wiener Zeitschrift* 5, No. 25 (February 26, 1820), p. 200.—KH/TA

[51] Presumably tickets to Gyrowetz's concert.—TA

If you win the Theater [Lottery] or otherwise become rich, then you ought to produce it.[52]

Otherwise, nothing will be lost if he [Czerny] can give an evening lesson [to Karl]. You should only say when he will begin. //

A Pükling [wine] costs 15 [kr.] here, 24 kr. [per glass] there.[53] [//]

[Blatt 17v]

BEETHOVEN [**writing so as not to be overheard**]:[54] Princess Lubomirska had this man[55] study composition with Haydn. [//]

BERNARD [**continuing**]: If we only have oysters and Menescher [wine], we will be able to get through the desert.[56] [//] [Blatt 18r]

I was amazed that he [Archduke Rudolph] didn't go to *Figaro*. Probably this opera wasn't written for Archbishops and Cardinals.[57] //

[Seemingly the end of entries for Saturday, February 26.]

[Blatt 18v]

BEETHOVEN [**possibly at a coffee shop, reading the previous day's newspaper; probably late morning of Sunday, February 27**]: Antiquarian Music Shop, Untere Breunerstrasse No. 1198.[58] [//]

---

[52] Reference to the Theater an der Wien's grand lottery (see Heft 7, Blatt 89v). The prime beneficiary of the fourth drawing was the Theater building.—KH

[53] After *Zur Stadt Triest*'s owner Seelig provided Beethoven's friend Oliva with an unhealthy wine on ca. January 26/27 (Heft 6, Blätter 88r–91v; Heft 7, Blatt 2r). By ca. February 12, Beethoven seems to have tried out the *Rother Igel* or *Kameel*, often noting their prices as less expensive than Seelig's (Heft 7, Blätter 81r–81v). See below (Blatt 23r) for an entry indicating that Seelig had lost his lease. For another reference to "Pükling" wine, see Blatt 55v below.—TA

[54] Possibly Hänsel was sitting nearby.—TA

[55] Since November 1791 the composer Peter Hänsel (1770–1831) had been first violinist and Kapellmeister to Princess Lubomirska in Vienna. From 1792 Hänsel studied composition for several years with Haydn. In 1802 he undertook an artistic tour to Paris, and from 1803 lived permanently in Vienna, playing in Beethoven's benefit concerts of 1813–1814. See Rudolf Klein, "Hänsel," *MGG*, vol. 5, cols. 1294–1296.—KH

[56] A pun on the words "Wüste" (desert) and "wüsten" (to squander or to live wastefully).—TA The other meaning of this clause is the improbable "we have already come through the desert," a pun on the words "Wüste" (desert) and "wüsten" (to squander or to live wastefully).—TA

[57] The space between last word and the dividing line (and covering some of both) is filled with a pencil sketch of a double profile in the style of a Janus head.—KH

[58] See *Intelligenzblatt*, No. 146 (February 26, 1820), p. 336: advertisement for the newly established "*Antiquar-Musikalien-Handlung*, in the City, next to the Graben, in the Untere Breunerstrasse No. 1198." The same advertisement had also appeared on February 19 and 23, 1820.—KH

NEPHEW KARL [**presumably at a restaurant in the City, possibly the *Rother Igel* or *Kameel*, but not the *Triest*; possibly late afternoon on Sunday, February 27**]:
I found the flyer from Sieber['s antiquities exhibit] at my place today. // I have already taken it [the tour] twice. [//] [Blatt 19r]

In the *Löwenapotheke* [Lion Apothecary].[59] // The finest red t[ooth powder];[60] a box of it costs 1 fl. //

Giannatasio.[61]

Because it was included at the confession. // In the country, they will be celebrated more than in the City. // [Blatt 19v]

Peters has not spoken with Herr v. Blöchlinger because he was sick; instead he came up to me. // I just had my Greek lesson.[62] // But a new tutor has come. // Now there are 2. // [Blatt 20r] The one who instructs me in Greek doesn't live there [at the Institute], but only comes from 10 to 12 each day. // After the semi-annual examination. // Tomorrow is the written examination. // I'll do that without errors. // [Blatt 20v] I already did one from the Greek, but not written. // But I am now more qualified for the 4th Class. //

Yesterday I had a very severe headache. I get it often; I don't know what causes it. [//] [Blatt 21r] Smetana is only a *wound* doctor. //

Most of them [maid servants] are from the country. // That doesn't matter. // I am doing it because I see it differently. // She says that everything looks that way. //

She says that she knows a man who wants to take care of everything that *she* does, and of whose [Blatt 21v] *honesty* she is convinced. She says [that],[63] // The woman sweats unceasingly and snuffs so much tobacco. //

She says, you give the woman 14 fl. per month, including bread money, but the man wants to do it for 12 fl., and you will be more satisfied with him than with the woman. [//] [Blatt 22r] <She herself wants> [//] *Everything*, better and in better

---

[59] The *Löwenapotheke* of Joseph Moser was located in the house *Zum goldenen Löwen* (The Golden Lion) in the Josephstadt, Kaiserstrasse (today's Josefstädter Strasse) No. 126 [renumbered as 132 in 1821] on the *north*west corner of Kaiserstrasse and Piaristengasse. The apothecary still exists today, across the street, at the *south*west corner of Josefstädter Strasse and Piaristengasse. See Guetjahr, p. 316; Behsel, p. 193.—KH/TA

[60] The German original has the abbreviation "Z.," which the Berlin editors believed to mean *Zahnpulver* (tooth powder).—KH/TA

[61] Karl's former teacher.—TA

[62] For the teachers Bergmann and Pulai/Pulay, see Blatt 1r (above).—KH/TA

[63] "She says [that]" was probably added to the next sentence afterwards.—KH

order. // She wants to bring him tomorrow. // She is so lazy that she carried only 1 basket.[64] //

1138.[65] //

PETERS [joining Beethoven and Karl; early evening, ca. 6 p.m. on Sunday, February 27]:[66] I was at the sermon.[67] //

Bernard and I have reserved *Zum Dachel*[68] for us—Beer house. [//] [Blatt 22v]

It is self-evident that the expenses of the journey will be reimbursed to you. // Perhaps the Archduke will stay only a very short time. //

Are you working on the oratorio? [//] Does Bernard have the text finished already? // *Der Sieg des Kreuzes?* //

If you are tired,[69] I'll accompany Karl to the Institute.[70] //

---

[64] German original reads *Butte*, an open wooden carrying basket that was carried on the back by means of straps; see Loritza, p. 32.—KH

[65] At the beginning of the line Schindler had identified the writer as Oliva. Whether the writer of the number was Oliva or still nephew Karl is uncertain. The number is presumably an address in the City. Stadt No. 1138 was the *Weisser Hahn* in the Kärntnerstrasse [renumbered as 1072 in 1821], on the north side of the street, only one building away from a short passage leading to the east end of the Neuer Markt. See Behsel, p. 32.—KH/TA

[66] Judging from entries below, this conversation began before the 6:30 p.m. curtain time at the theaters. Peters offers to accompany Karl back to Blöchlinger's Institute (perhaps a 35-minute walk from either the *Igel* or *Kameel*), presumably in time for the 7 p.m. school curfew.—TA

[67] Peters uses the term *Predigt*, presumably one of the religious-political sermons of Zacharias Werner. He would have used a different term (*Messe* or *Gottesdienst*) to designate a normal church service.—TA

[68] *Zum rothen Dachel* was the name of a famous beer house on the Alter Fleischmarkt No. 756 [renumbered as 712 in 1821], at the entrance to the Hafnersteig. It survives today as the *Reichenberger Griechenbeisel*, Fleischmarkt 11, and a plaque proclaims that it was frequented by Beethoven, Schubert, Waldmüller, Grillparzer, and, later, Richard Wagner.

Another *Zum rothen Dachel* existed on the Neuer Markt No. 1122 [renumbered as 1058 in 1821], only two doors west of Seelig's *Zur Stadt Triest*, but that seems not to have been the establishment meant here. See Groner (1922), p. 72; Groner-Czeike, *Wien, wie es war*, pp. 111–112; Messner, *Die Innere Stadt Wien*, I, p. 143, and III, p. 168; Behsel, pp. 21 and 31.—TA

If the reservation mentioned was for that night, Beethoven seems not to have joined Peters and Bernard, but instead—after Peters's final entry on Blatt 25v—accompanied Karl back to Blöchlinger's Institute.—KH/TA

[69] Beethoven may have claimed fatigue as a way of escaping the subject of Bernard's oratorio text which, by this time, he probably had little intention of setting. In any case, this entry indicates that nephew Karl was still with Beethoven and needed to go home, whether before or after the 7 p.m. school curfew.—TA

[70] The curfew at Blöchlinger's Institute was 7 p.m.—TA

NEPHEW KARL [continuing]: To whom, Schindler?[71] [//] [Blatt 23r] The assignments will be done in the afternoon.[72] //

PETERS [continuing]: He will already be gone—perhaps to the Theater. // He [an actor] acts in a very lively manner, but his voice no longer has any strength. //

Seelig has received notice [to vacate his present location]; he doesn't know where he is to go.[73] // They should be baked.[74] //

It was terribly hot at my place; therefore I didn't want to make you come up. [//] [Blatt 23v]

We miss each other frequently now. I was often at Seelig's when you were here [possibly the *Rother Igel* or *Kameel*], and vice versa. //

When the Prince [Ferdinand Lobkowitz] reaches his majority, an appropriate re-organization will be introduced at our place. The house with the few children costs 50 to 60,000 fl., and we have nothing special. My realm [of influence] will then receive another designation. // [Blatt 24r] I would have the children live better with 15,000 fl. // I could have the Court Councillor's position of the late Edelbach,[75] but he had nothing to do; 7,000 fl. and an apartment. //

Idleness is the beginning of every vice. //

What the master neglects, the pupil picks up on. [//] [Blatt 24v] They don't comprehend who is greater or lesser. //

He does not know that we are here. // Seelig will be melancholy if he learns that you are here. //

In Italy there are no excellent artists and music. // Composer. // [Blatt 25r] But the loss is great that, because of your attitude, you do not write more operas. Otherwise, I don't understand very much. // Opera has a remarkable effect on

---

[71] Anton Schindler was still essentially a clerk in the office of lawyer Johann Baptist Bach. From this reference it appears that Beethoven was already aware of his existence in February, 1820, although they probably would not become closely acquainted until summer 1822 or later.—TA

[72] From Karl's entries, it appears that Beethoven will be interviewing some sort of domestic servant the next day, presumably Sunday, February 27, and that Karl will do his assignments that afternoon. In any case, these activities produced no entries in Beethoven's conversation book.—TA

[73] In mid-October 1820, Heinrich Seelig moved his wine and grocery shop *Zur Stadt Triest* from Neuer Markt No. 1124 to the House No. 990 [renumbered as 948 in 1821] at the northeast corner of Himmelpfortgasse and Rauhensteingasse. There may have been several reasons why Seelig lost his lease on the Neuer Markt, selling mislabeled wines and staying open beyond the customary 10 p.m. City curfew among them. See the *Intelligenzblatt*, No. 238 (October 17, 1820), p. 709, and following numbers; Behsel, p. 28.—KH/TA

[74] Possibly a reference to the oysters frequently mentioned during this period.—TA

[75] Benedikt von Edlenbach, Court Agent and Court Councillor to the Princes Lobkowitz, died on July 24, 1819, aged seventy, at his apartment in Augustinergasse No. 1226 (also owned by the Lobkowitz family, at the corner of Dorotheergasse [renumbered as 1157 in 1821]); *Wiener Zeitung*, No. 170 (July 28, 1819), p. 679.—KH

people. // I wanted to say that with words. // [Blatt 25v] It is a shame for us that we do not clear away all the distractions from your path. [//]

[Presumably the end of entries for Sunday, February 27.][76]

BEETHOVEN **[at his apartment; probably early on Monday, February 28]**:
Coffee cup.
Paper.
Schlemmer.
Ink.[77]
Violin maker.
Shit shovel.
Candles.
Soap powder.
[Soap] balls.
    [Blatt 26r]
Shaving mug.
Blotting paper.
Ask Schlemmer where his knives are sharpened.
Ask at Oliva's what a room costs per month.
What do people wear now instead of an undershirt? //

[Blatt 26v]

PETERS **[presumably at midday dinner; ca. 2 p.m. on Monday, February 28]**:
You were somewhat tired.[78] [//] Bernard can be at Seelig's [*Zur Stadt Triest*].[79] //

OLIVA **[possibly at his office; the afternoon of Monday, February 28]**: Can't you extricate yourself then, for God's sake, for you[rself] and for Art! // Will the Mass [*Missa solemnis*] be finished while he [Archduke Rudolph] is still here? [//]

I am paying 24 fl. [for a room]. In the suburbs—Landstrasse, for instance—it is cheaper by half. [//] [Blatt 27r] You have no furniture there. [//]

A Cardinal's title without money, it will come about, but with time, then, his revenues are great, more than fl. 13—[seemingly 13,000 fl.]. [//]

---

[76] Beethoven may have interviewed a domestic servant earlier on that day, and he may have gotten an initial quote for the wood discussed on Blatt 44v and elsewhere. He may have devoted the rest of the day to sketching the *Abendlied unterm gestirnten Himmel*, WoO 150, whose autograph is dated the following Saturday, March 4, 1820. He may also have started his long "to do" list for the next day, which included seeing the copyist Schlemmer, possibly to alert him that the *Abendlied* would be forthcoming.—TA

[77] Entered afterwards.—KH

[78] Presumably a reference to their meeting on Sunday, March 27 (see Blatt 22v above).—KH/TA

[79] See Blätter 28r–29r and 29v–31r for that conversation.—TA

[Blatt 27v]

UNKNOWN [briefly encountering Oliva and Beethoven]: I was in Kaschau[80] and am now going to Vicenza. I hope to live for several years in pleasure in this splendid land. [//] I like the Italians. [//]

Franz [considerable space] Raimund.[81]

What is Oliva doing?[82] [//]

OLIVA [continuing]:

For 11 fl. 30 [kr.]   250

$$
\begin{array}{rr}
4 & 30 \\
4 & 30 \\
2 & 15 \\
\hline
11\ \text{fl.}\ 15\ \text{kr.}^{83}
\end{array}
$$ 4 fl. 35 kr.

70/

3   30

80 fl. 35 kr.

Are you going to Mödling again?[84] [//] [Blatt 28r]

[One is] not satisfied with 1 Seidl [of wine or beer]. //

BERNARD [at Zur Stadt Triest; after 7 p.m. on Monday, February 28]: I cannot go to the lawyer's until tomorrow morning,[85] since I could not leave from home

---

[80] Then in Hungary, Kaschau is now Košice in eastern Slovakia, ca. 10 miles north of the Hungarian border.—TA

[81] Ferdinand Raimund (1790–1836), Viennese popular poet, actor, and theater director, created the material for his tales and magical dramas from Austrian folklore. In 1814 he created a sensation appearing as Franz Moor, possibly the origin of the reference to Franz. See Wurzbach, vol. 24, pp. 254–256 and beyond.

Occasionally there was a telling crossover between popular theater and opera in Vienna. Johann Nestroy (1801–1862), the future comic playwright/actor, sang Don Fernando in the November, 1822, revival of Fidelio. See Kärntnertor Theater, Zettel (Bibliothek, Österreichisches Theatermuseum, courtesy Othmar Barnert).—KH/TA

[82] It is not clear whether the unknown author of this sentence is the same as that of the previous entry.—KH

[83] This column indicates that 4 fl. 30 kr. C.M. equals 11 fl. 15 kr. W.W. See the related figures on Blatt 31v below.—TA

[84] From the end of April or beginning of May 1820 Beethoven lived in the "Christhof" garden house, Mödling No. 116, which at that time belonged to the vine grower Johann Speer (Klein indicated his first name as Anton). See Frimmel, Handbuch, I, p. 423; Klein, pp. 111–113 and 164; Thayer-Deiters-Riemann, IV, p. 201; Thayer-Forbes, p. 740.—KH/TA

[85] On Blatt 13r above Beethoven had already seemingly asked Bernard to go and see lawyer Bach, either with him or on his behalf.—TA

today before 7 o'clock. // I was busy, without interruption, from 9 o'clock until 2:30, and from 3:15 until 7 o'clock, without being able to take a step out of the building. I only went [out] to eat. [//] [Blatt 28v] You have no idea of this work. // It is an awful prison. // Pure integrity. // I have not been able to profit for even a quarter of an hour from the beautiful sunshine today,[86] and even now would have gone for some exercise if I hadn't [Blatt 29r] promised you to come here.[87] //

PETERS [joining Beethoven and Bernard]: Wähner told me today that people in Austria [and] in Vienna do not understand drinking wine. He has always drunk 6 to 10 *Seidl* and now people consider him a drunkard. He now no longer drinks wine, just punch.[88] [//] [Blatt 29v]

My wife sings more beautifully. // *Maitre du Clavecin* [piano teacher Joseph Czerny] takes exception to Bernard. // Politics.[89] //

Tokayer Vermouth. //
Karl will play diligently. //
I am drinking sugar-water. //
[Mostly illegible word:—dom.] //

BERNARD [continuing]: You are to take Herr Czerny to your nephew on a Wednesday or Thursday afternoon. [//] [Blatt 30r] He [Peters?] may not, because of his wife. //

Herr Starke, the creator of several works, was at my place today with a short biographical sketch of you. // Starke [the strong one] writes weak works.[90] [//] [Blatt 30v]

When is he [Czerny] to come, Wednesday or Thursday? [//]
Noble Cyprus wine. //
The Bourbons are very .... //
Seelig, Seelig, Seeligkeit! [Blessed, Blessed, Blessedness!][91]
One gets the little cypress [*Cyperlein*] from Cyprus wine [*Cypernwein*]. [//] [Blatt 31r]

---

[86] On Monday, February 28, the skies were clear and sunny all day, and the temperature reached 1 degree Réaumur (ca. 34 degrees Fahrenheit); see *Wiener Zeitung*, No. 49 (Wednesday, March 1, 1820), p. 195.—TA

[87] Peters conveyed Bernard's promise to meet at Seelig's on Blatt 26v.—TA

[88] A *Seidl* is roughly one-third liter. The north German Protestant Wähner was evidently heavyset and may have been able to drink more wine than most without negative effects.—TA

[89] These two entries originally in French: *Maitre du Clavecin fait des oppositions a Bernard* and *Politique.*—KH/TA

[90] Beethoven and his circle were fond of making wordplays on Friedrich Starke's name.—TA

[91] Wordplay on the name of Heinrich Seelig, owner of *Zur Stadt Triest.*—TA

He [the assassin Louvel] has no wife at all.[92] It was nothing but political fanaticism. [//] "God is nothing more than a string puppet, who never came to earth," he said. [//]

[Probably the end of entries for Monday, February 28.]

[Blatt 31v]

BEETHOVEN **[probably at his apartment; the morning of Tuesday, February 29]**:[93]

Leave the knife at the *Kameel* [to be sharpened?].

Coffee [and] sugar.

Take there this evening.—Candles.

Buy Russian night-candles with Bernard. [//]

OLIVA **[possibly at a restaurant in the City; probably at midday dinner, ca. 2 p.m. on Tuesday, February 29]**:

$$
\begin{array}{r}
250 \\
4.30 \\
10|00 \\
1|25 \\
6 \\
\hline
1.50
\end{array}
$$

It really makes 11 [fl.] 15 [kr.] @ 250.[94] [//] In addition the Gold *agio* [exchange rate] should apply, which always amounts to 6 to 7 kr. C.M. [Blatt 32r] Otherwise the rate of exchange ought to stand higher than 250. //

If you go there, you will be served the best. His name is Hackl[95] and [he] is actually a jeweler, and in addition has a money exchange business.

$$
\begin{array}{l}
14 \\
\underline{60} \\
840 \qquad \text{29 kr. for the month of 30 days}
\end{array}
$$

You have done too much—Certainly he does everything for you. [//] [Blatt 32v]

---

[92] A reference to the journeyman saddler Louvel, who had murdered the Duke de Berry. See Heft 7, Blätter 88v–90v.—KH

[93] 1820 was a leap year.—TA

[94] See the related figures on Blatt 27v above.—TA

[95] The firm of Fr. X. Hackl & Co. was located in the house *Zum Spiegel* (At the Mirror), on the Graben, No. 1200, at the corner with Untere Breunerstrasse [renumbered as 1133 in 1821]. The public business associate of the proprietor Franz Xaver Hackl was Ignaz Zwerger. See Redl, 1820, p. 44; Behsel, p. 34.—KH/TA

5000.

He is a Lieutenant Colonel, has the Theresia Cross, and is going to Italy to his Regiment. //

Austrian wine from the *Pfau*[96] at 4 fl.—as my doctor says, a rare good wine. [//] Where we bought the wine when Tuscher was at your place, at the end of Kärntnerstrasse. [//]

[Blatt 33r]

BEETHOVEN [jotting financial figures concerning his stipend]:

4000
1200
 700
————
5900

OLIVA [continuing]: You will be able to pick up [the stipend money] at Lobkowitz's already on March 1 or 2.[97] [//] I need nothing for the present, and thank you. //

You are also impeded with the Mass [*Missa solemnis*], because the Archduke must first hear it, [Blatt 33v] [before] you can sell it, and now in Olmütz [Cardinal Archduke Rudolph's residence]. [//]

[End of midday dinner with Oliva; Tuesday, February 29.]

BEETHOVEN [possibly at a coffee house; late afternoon of Tuesday, February 29, 1820]: *Conversationsblatt* No. [__] of February 29, 1820, Herr Wolfsohn lies about me.[98] //

BERNARD [probably at the aforementioned coffee house; late afternoon of Tuesday, February 29]:[99] I was of the understanding that it [Beethoven's *Denkschrift*] will be given to the private consultant for unauthoritative use. [//] [Blatt 34r] Otherwise I have not read it [the draft of February 18] yet and shall give you my

---

[96] The restaurant *Zum goldenen Pfau* (Golden Peacock) was located in the Kärntnerstrasse No. 1102, at the corner of Comedie Gasse, behind the Kärntnertor Theater [renumbered as 1039 in 1821]. See Guetjahr, p. 47; Behsel, p. 31.—KH/TA

[97] The annual pension bestowed on Beethoven by the Archduke Rudolph in conjunction with Princes Lobkowitz and Kinsky in 1809.—KH

[98] In the *Conversationsblatt* No. 25 (February 29, 1820), p. 225, the lead article, "Technische Neuigkeiten," about the technical apparatus of the "ingenious engineer" Herr Wolfsohn, says: "The head apparatus for the hard of hearing, a clever apparatus in the form of a flat-pressed diadem, which is covered by a toupee, can be worn undetected. Wolfsohn assures me that our immortal Beethoven makes use of it with decided benefit." Despite variants such as "Wolffsohn" and "Wolfssohn," documents closest to the inventor himself most consistently spelled his name Wolfsohn, the form preferred here.—KH

[99] This long conversation ends on Blatt 43v below.—TA

viewpoint only then. I shall already see perhaps how best to handle it. [//] In the mornings I am always so torn, because I always have the thread of the news in my head and must retain it. [//] [Blatt 34v] [Letters] to the Editor. [//] Lampi[100] is only a copyist. [//]

Peters and I were at Neuling's in the Landstrasse.[101] [//] Superb, but not in the garden. // [Blatt 35r]

In the *Conversationsplan* [*sic*] it says that you are very successfully using a hearing apparatus by Wolfssohn,[102] which is stretched like a diadem over the head and covered by hair or a toupee. [//] [Blatt 35v] Shall I refute it in your name, etc.?[103] [//]

He [Peters] is staying at home today, because he went to sleep late yesterday. [//] [Blatt 36r] His wife scolded him severely because he came home so late last night. [//] That is characteristic only of a young wife, and will soon pass. [//] [Blatt 36v] I said recently that he looks somewhat thin and pale; that was not quite right with him. //

Don't you believe that Doctor Bach will handle the matter well? [//] [Blatt 37r][104]

There is no Natural Law. // People have always said that there is one, but since no natural condition exists, then there can also be no such Law. [//] [Blatt 37v] Laws arise only in society. // If I am isolated, I have no law, and no one has law over me. // [Blatt 38r] Natural condition presupposes Mankind without limitation; as soon as one enters into a social union, he has limitations and considerations, and therefore has to observe obligations towards other men; these also have to observe other [obligations] towards him, [Blatt 38v] and he can demand these, because he must also fulfill them. These are therefore his laws, which do not take place in Nature, because Man is then alone. [//] [Blatt 39r]

There is no natural condition, because then a man would have to exist entirely alone. [//] As soon as a People exists, then there are already mutual obligations and

---

[100] This reference remains unclear. It is certainly not the famous portrait and historical scenes painter J.B. (Ritter) von Lampi (1751–1830), but more likely someone employed in the office of the *Wiener Zeitung*.—KH/TA

[101] Vinzenz Neuling (1795–1846) was Court Jewelry Supplier, a representative in the Gesellschaft der Musikfreunde, and brewer and owner of a widely-known brewery garden in suburban Landstrasse, Ungargasse No. 315–317 [renumbered as 352–353 in 1821]. See Gräffer-Czikann, vol. 2, p. 332; Guetjahr, pp. 28 and 151; Behsel, p. 79.—KH/TA

[102] "by Wolfsohn" was added afterwards.—KH

[103] The following correction, unsigned, appeared in the *Conversationsblatt*, No. 29 (March 9, 1820), p. 273: "Herr Wolfsohn's assertion in the *Conv. Bl.* No. 25 that 'Herr van Beethoven makes use of this head apparatus for the hard-of-hearing' is to be corrected there, that Herr van Beethoven indeed inspected that machine, but has never made use of it."—KH

[104] On the upper third of the page: a drawing of a man's head in profile, then a dividing line.—KH

laws, therefore already a State or a System. [//] The "People" is already a State. [//] [Blatt 39r] <There is already [incomplete sentence]>

Law is a limitation; i.e., that I cannot do everything that I want to others. I can therefore demand that others also observe these considerations regarding me; these are therefore my laws. If, however, [Blatt 40r] there are no other persons towards whom I must observe and fulfill considerations and obligations, and who must do the same towards me, then all Law ceases, and a natural condition occurs, where Law is no longer possible. [//] [Blatt 40v]

All of this, however, is not in the textbooks. [//] Completely false. [//] People long believed that the Sun revolves around the Earth, but it was also not true. //

If I win 50,000 fl. [in the Theater an der Wien's lottery] tomorrow, [Blatt 41r] then I shall revoke Natural Law above all things. //

Today at midday, I wrote the following poem:

> Man Proposes, God Disposes.
> To Wähner.

Wie hab' ich, armer Freund, dich sonst gekannt!
So recht als donnerlauten Eisenhammer,
Hochofen, Strohmesmühle, Kriegesschiff; [Blatt 41v]
Doch jetzt,—wie find' ich dich nun?—Schmerz und Jammer!
Was hat dich, Freundchen, denn so umgewandt?
Wo nehm' ich Wort und Bild her, und Begriff?—
Ein Fischerkähnchen, das am Ufer streicht,
Ein Klippermühlchen, Sperlinge zu jagen,
Gluthpfännchen, das die Zofe spielend reicht,
Und Hämmerchen, den Zucker zu zerschlagen.[105] [//] [Blatt 42r]

In France a book has appeared that has already enjoyed its third printing. In it is evidence that in France there are many thousands of people who can occupy the position of the Duke of Angouleme and Berry, etc., etc. much better [than the incumbents]. [//] [Blatt 42v]

I consider it very unwise for a State newspaper to promulgate such enthusiastic essays, because they obviously instigate more than they deter.[106] [//] [Blatt 43r]

---

[105] The poem addresses Wähner's former state of confidence and strength and compares it with his current state of pain and confusion. Beethoven was painfully aware that the staunchly Catholic Bernard bore little good will for the Protestant Wähner.—TA

[106] Bernard refers here to the *Allgemeine Preussische Staatszeitung*, which, on February 19, 1820, had published "Documentary Reports Concerning the Revolutionary Activities in Germany," in which opinions of progressive-minded youths about their revolutionary goals had been quoted

It has been postponed; tomorrow [Wednesday, March 1] we shall be rich—50,000 fl.[107] [//]

BEETHOVEN:

18

18

18

6

6

BERNARD: I have invited the Apostle Petrus [Peters] for Thursday.[108] [//]

[Blatt 43v]

JOSEPH CZERNY [**briefly joining Bernard and Beethoven**]: You must also invite Peters. Then we will all be together. //

[End of the conversation with Bernard (and Czerny); afternoon of Tuesday, February 29.]

SCHLEMMER [**presumably at his copying shop, Kohlmarkt No. 1216; evening of Tuesday, February 29 (rather than the next day)**]: The cashier is not here. [//] He has already gone. [//] Herr v[on] Ridel[109] disburses [the money]. [//] The stamp must be affixed on it in the office. [//] Because I heard that the cashier was not here, I asked Herr v[on] Z. what is to be done. He has offered; has it.[110] [//]

---

verbatim from the Prussian investigation documents. The *Beobachter* reprinted this report in No. 56 (February 25, 1820), pp. 269–271, and No. 60 (February 29, 1820), pp. 289–291. Further installments appeared in Nos. 64 and 65.—KH

[107] Concerning the Theater an der Wien's lottery, see Heft 7, Blatt 89v. The four drawings of the Theater an der Wien's lottery were originally supposed to take place on December 1 and 21, 1819, as well as on January 19 and March 1, 1820. See the "Beilage" to the *Allgemeine Augsburger Zeitung*, No. 92 (June 10, 1819), p. 366.—KH

[108] Peters confirms this invitation on Blatt 46v below.—TA

[109] It is not possible to determine precisely who is meant here. In connection with Beethoven's inclination to sell a bank share, or at least to borrow money against one, it could refer to an employee in the "Effekten-Pfänder" [Bailiff] Department of the I.R. Pawn Office, Dorotheergasse No. 1178 [renumbered as 1112 in 1821]. The *Hof- und Staats-Schematismus*, 1820, I, p. 396, names the "Property Trustees" Joseph Riedl and Joseph Zöffel, as well as the "Cashiers" Anton Kofler and Joseph Paul Fieglmüller.

Joseph Riedl was also an Art and Music Dealer, Hoher Markt No. 582 [renumbered as 541 in 1821], with whom Beethoven had business dealings in April, 1820 (see Heft 11, Blätter 42r and 53r). See Ziegler, *Addressen-Buch*, p. 233; Behsel, pp. 33 and 17.—KH/TA

[110] Copyist Wenzel Schlemmer was never good with the written word; some of these entries are fragmentary, vague, and repetitious.—TA

[Blatt 44r] I asked him what is to be done to get the money, so [he] told me that I should come tomorrow afternoon; I will go to see him today. [//]

[Blatt 44v]

WOOD DEALER SWOBODA [probably at Beethoven's apartment on the Glacis; probably the morning of Wednesday, March 1]:

1 *Klafter* [cord], 36 inch-thick, Beech, split … 36 fl. 15 [kr.]

1 *Klafter*, 36 inch-thick, uncut Oak … @ 21 fl. 15 kr.

Cutting [logs]   1 fl. 30 kr.

Splitting [pieces]   1   30

                       1   30

                                        Swoboda, Neutor, Becker Platz[111]

[Blatt 45r]

BEETHOVEN [still at his apartment; probably late morning of Wednesday, March 1]: Coffee.

PETERS [at a restaurant, possibly the *Rother Igel*; presumably midday dinner, ca. 2 p.m., Wednesday, March 1]:[112] Bernard told me that you are here, and [he] should already be here. [//]

Tomorrow, Prince Ferdinand [Lobkowitz] is going to the Emperor to thank him for the Key conferred upon him as Gentleman of the Chamber and to request permission to go to Italy. //

Bernard said that he would be here right away. //

What is Oliva doing? [//] [Blatt 45v]

---

[111] Matthias Swoboda (b. 1773), "*Holzschreiber* from Martinsdorf, Oedenburger County [Hungary]," who presumably wrote out this bill for wood. A *Holzschreiber* was originally a technical official who stood directly subordinate to the manager of a forest administration. Since Swoboda cannot be traced in the 1820 *Hof- und Staats-Schematismus*, it may be assumed that *Holzschreiber* here meant an employee of a firm that supplied wood.

The *Neues Tor* (New Gate) was at the northwestern point where the Danube Canal met the city walls and led to the *Holz-Gestätte* on the Danube shoreline, where the floating nets were placed and the wood was stacked. Becker Platz is probably a river basin at that point. See later conversation with Karl (Bl. 52r–53v) about wood hacking (cutting of logs into segments) and splitting (with the grain for half pieces and a second time for quarter pieces). See also Conscriptions-Bogen, Stadt, No. 194 (Wiener Stadt- und Landesarchiv), and Groner (1922), p. 181.—KH/TA

[112] This conversation may also have taken place in the late afternoon or evening, and lasts through Blatt 50v.—TA

Try to read this letter—Doctor Görgen[113] to Countess Herberstein[114] concerning her tutor, who has now become insane for the second time. // The Countess will condemn me because I was the reason that the crazed man was taken from the hospital to this excellent and skillful, but honest physician. [//] [Blatt 46r] He has restored the daughter of Court Councillor Schwarz to health.[115] [She was the one] to whom Prince Odescalchi[116] had to give 20,000 fl. [C.] M. //

Maitre du Clavecin [piano teacher Joseph Czerny] is still coming; he is playing cards with my wife. // I have a peculiar talent for always providing my wife with social activity in my absence. [//] [Blatt 46v]

I have been invited to breakfast in your neighborhood tomorrow morning [Thursday, March 2, visiting day], and shall then inquire as to the health of Herr Blöchlinger and visit Karl. // You will become ever more satisfied with the Institute. [//] [Blatt 47r]

If Seelig runs his business with profits of 50 percent, he loses 150 fl. on us each month. //

BERNARD [joining Beethoven and Peters]: It is said that the Orientals have never once become acquainted with *Brimsen* cheese.[117] // We are nothing but thirsty fellows.[118] [//]

PETERS: In two weeks, I'll be eating oysters in Venice, without a black edge.[119] [//]

---

[113] Bruno Görgen (1777–1842), physician, member of the Medical Faculty, University of Vienna, had received permission from the Provincial Government in 1819 to build a "Private Healing Institute for those with illnesses of the mind," according to his own plans. This was first in Gumpendorf No. 155 [renumbered as 173 in 1821 and 194 in 1830] and then in the Henikstein Building in Döbling. In 1824 Görgen's daughter Helene (b. 1808), later married name Grebner, would be a young member of the Gesellschaft der Musikfreunde's chorus when it participated in the premiere of Beethoven's Ninth Symphony. See Gräffer-Czikann, II, p. 390; *Hof- und Staats-Schematismus*, 1819, II, p. 115; Pezzl (1826), p. 458; Behsel, p. 131; Kopitz and Cadenbach, I, pp. 371–373 (citing Helene Grebner's interview with conductor Felix Weingartner in 1898).—KH/TA

[114] For Peters's intercession on behalf of Countess Herberstein's tutor, see Heft 4, Blätter 13v–15r.—TA

[115] Anton Schwarz, I.R. Court Councillor (in actual service), was an assistant in the Court Commission in Justice Matters and lived in the Bürgerspital, No. 1166 [renumbered as 1100 in 1821]. See *Hof- und Staats-Schematismus*, 1820, I, p. 265; Behsel, p. 33.—KH/TA

[116] Prince Innocenz von Odescalchi (b. Rome, July 22, 1778; d. Vienna/Obermeidling, September 24, 1833), Privy Councillor, Treasurer, stockholder in the Austrian National Bank, Vice President (under Prince von Fürstenberg) of the Gesellschaft der Musikfreunde. See *Hof- und Staats-Schematismus*, 1820, I, pp. 38, 69, and 703, and II, p. 292; Gräffer-Czikann, IV, p. 78. For later references to this confusing relationship, see Blatt 55r.—KH/TA

[117] Brimsen, a sheep's milk cheese made in Austria and Hungary.—KH

[118] That is, they are not interested in eating.—TA

[119] Peters and young Prince Lobkowitz left Vienna for Italy on Thursday, March 9; see *Wiener Zeitung*, No. 58 (March 11, 1820), p. 232.—TA

BERNARD: <I shall read it today; then I shall see what is to be done with it. // The *Denkschrift* [Memorandum] of Herr v. Beethoven.> [//]

[Blatt 47v]

PETERS: They supposed Frau Janitschek [Janschikh] to be my wife. [//]

[Blatt 48r]

JOSEPH CZERNY [**briefly joining Beethoven, Peters, and Bernard**]: They are the last [of the oysters]. //

PETERS: Don't you want to give me a recommendation letter to take with me [to Italy]? //

BERNARD: It seems to me that Prince Lobkowitz will abandon his domains, and Peters will do the same to his wife, who is also his domain, in order to enjoy the beauties of Nature. [//]

[Blatt 48v]

PETERS: We have a Letter of Credit in good order. //

BERNARD: If he dies, I inherit his wife.[120] //

PETERS: I am hoarse. //

BERNARD: The luxury-loving Czerny has just ordered 12 oysters. [//] [Blatt 49r] Early in the day, he is [eats] in Italy;[121] evening in the *Kameel* or [otherwise] blessed;[122] and at night in Cyprus[123]—is anyone more fortunate? //

PETERS: Life is not a good man's most precious possession …. [//]

---

[120] Bernard had written almost exactly the same thing on ca. January 7, 1820. See Heft 6, Blatt 1r, to place this locker-room banter, which Beethoven probably found distasteful, in a Viennese context through the eyes of John Russell (ca. 1796–1846), a visiting Scottish lawyer.—TA

[121] This sentence, implying an exotic journey, involves extensive wordplay, explained here in three footnotes. *Früh ist er Intalien: Intalien* means "in Italia," with Italy the potential source of either wine or the aforementioned oysters (usually shipped to Vienna from Venice); thus *ist* (is) could also mean *isst* (eats). Czerny lived on the Schottenbastey, so there seems to be no overt association with Thalia.—TA

[122] *Abends im Kameel oder selig:* the *Kameel* [Camel] is a wine house in the Bognergasse; *selig* means blessed or blissful, but also alludes to Heinrich Seelig, owner of the wine house *Zur Stadt Triest* (another Italian or at least Adriatic allusion), where the group also ate oysters. Czerny was married, and possibly considered "blessed" by the still unmarried Bernard.—TA

[123] *und des Nachts in Cypern:* Cyprus the Mediterranean island, but also meaning Cyprus wine, which Beethoven and his friends seem to have enjoyed at the *Rother Igel*.—TA

BERNARD: Nevertheless, it is not to be disdained. [//] [Blatt 49v]

Seelig had all of them removed [to] between the bridges.[124] // One can make *Magnesia* from it.[125] [//] [Blatt 50r]

[written vertically→] He is beginning to compose in his thoughts.[[126]←written vertically]

Life is not a good man's most precious possession …—*Petrus* [//]

PETERS: … but obligation is the greatest possession of an evil one.—*Bernard*[127] [//]

BERNARD: There are so many people who do absolutely nothing out of obligation. [//] [Blatt 50v] This man absolutely does not want to yield. //

PETERS: Böhm has deeply affected you—It itself made a striking effect in the concave form. [//] It is concave in the steel.[128] //

[End of the long conversation; afternoon of Wednesday, March 1.]

[Blatt 51r]

NEPHEW KARL **[seemingly at Beethoven's apartment on the Josephstadt Glacis; visitation day,**[129] **Thursday, March 2]**: On [Sunday,] March 19, is Herr Blöchlinger's Nameday [St. Joseph's Day], and we would like to perform a play under the leadership of one of the tutors. Everyone has chipped in to have scenery, etc., made. [Blatt 51v] Therefore, I wanted to invite you to it, because a dance will also be held in conjunction with it. // It is not because of that. // Only because I shall also be one of the actors. [//] [Blatt 52r] You are at liberty. // <She [Mother?] does not want in the least that[130] it be done in a forced manner.> //

---

[124] The reference is unclear, but it seems to mean that Heinrich Seelig, proprietor of *Zur Stadt Triest*, had had all of the bad wines that had seemingly infiltrated his stock by late January thrown into the Danube between the bridges leading from the inner City to the Leopoldstadt.—TA

[125] Certain compounds, such as magnesium oxide and magnesium hydroxide, can serve as an antacid and laxative (even Epsom salts). Seelig's wine had had a severely negative effect on Oliva's stomach, and that may explain this allusion.—TA

[126] Possibly some of this wordplay was intended to stimulate Beethoven to compose canons and other ephemeral pieces.—TA

[127] Bernard and Peters are making humorous use of the (adapted) last two lines of Schiller's *Die Braut von Messina* (Act IV, Scene 4): "Das Leben ist der Güter höchstes nicht, der Übel grösstes aber ist die Schuld." Schiller's play was performed twice at the Burgtheater during the 1819–1820 season: Saturday, December 4, 1819 (with Madame Schröder as Donna Isabella, and her daughter Wilhelmine as Beatrice), and Saturday, May 21, 1820 (with Madame Neumann as Beatrice). See Zettel, Bibliothek, Österreichisches Theatermuseum (courtesy Othmar Barnert).—KH/TA

[128] Possibly a reference to the sculptor Böhm and his works. See Heft 6, Blatt 25v.—TA

[129] Thursday was evidently the day on which Blöchlinger's students could visit their families, or individuals from the outside could come and visit the students. See Blatt 53v below.—TA

[130] At this point three words have been crossed out, to the extent that they are illegible.—KH

He[131] cannot come until next week. // Is that indeed less? //

   1 fl.   Cutting [logs]

   <u>1 fl.</u>   Splitting [pieces]

   2 fl.   [Blatt 52v]

He [Swoboda][132] says that it is 2 fl. for cutting and splitting. // Now he wants 6 fl. // He will not accept it. // [Blatt 53r] He wants 2 fl. for cutting and 4 fl. for splitting twice.

   2

   <u>4</u>

   6 fl. //

I believe that it is not quite right, because on Sunday, they constantly laughed at you. // [Blatt 53v] She says that it is not worth the trouble. //

   I can come every Thursday.[133] [//]

[Karl returns to Blöchlinger's Institute.]

BEETHOVEN [short shopping list]: Blotting paper. //

BERNARD [seemingly at a coffee house; probably late afternoon of Thursday, March 2]: Doesn't his mother make an appearance there anymore? [//]

BEETHOVEN [at the coffee house, reading the current *Beobachter*; late afternoon of Thursday, March 2]: The most significant winnings [in the Theater an der Wien's lottery] fell to these 5 numbers:[134]

   28,878

   22,803

   26,119 [Blatt 54r]

   73,180

   139,452 //

BERNARD [continuing]: Here in Vienna a horrible event has taken place. Two years ago, a well-known Countess here claimed that her companion maid, who was very beautiful, was dead. Actually she sold her to a Turkish Jew, [Blatt 54v] who,

---

[131] Possibly Karl Peters, who (on Blatt 46v) had promised to visit Blöchlinger's Institute the next day.—TA

[132] For the woodcutter's earlier entry see Blatt 44v above.—TA

[133] Thus, as surmised elsewhere, today is Thursday, March 2. Evidently a discussion about wood had been held the previous Sunday, February 27, since Swoboda's entry on Blatt 44 was likely made on Wednesday, March 1.—TA

[134] The list of the primary winnings of the Theater Lottery was published in the *Beobachter*, No. 62 (March 2, 1820), p. 304.—KH

in turn, wanted to sell her to Turkey to be in a *Serail* [Harem].[135] An Englishman, however, purchased her from him, and now she comes here. In Baden, they had buried the chambermaid rather than this girl, and the doctor, who had made out the false death certificate, [Blatt 55r] hanged himself last summer in Baden. It is believed that the chambermaid was poisoned. //

She is very much like [Prince] Odescalchi with the daughter of Court Councillor Schwarz, who [anecdote ends].[136]

BEETHOVEN [beginning a shopping list; possibly the evening of Thursday, March 2]: Soap powder; hand soap; blotting paper.

[Blatt 55v]

BEETHOVEN [at his apartment, making a longer shopping list; probably the morning of Friday, March 3]:
  Ribbons for binding.[137]
  Coffee cup and coffee spoon.[138] [for a housekeeper?].
  Blotting paper.
  Shaving mug.
  Soap powder.
  Hand soap.
  Bücking.[139] //

BERNARD [seemingly at a coffee house; later in the day or evening of Friday, March 3]:[140] It is to be regarded as a promotion. He [Archduke Rudolph] is not happy to go to Olmütz. //

---

[135] Beethoven may not have appreciated this lurid story, which, typical of Bernard, exhibited his prejudice against Jews and devaluation of women.

From March 21 through August 20, 1822, John Russell (ca. 1796–1846), a young Scottish lawyer, would visit Vienna and leave an extensive description of the City that included affluent mothers willingly selling their daughters into sexual slavery. This anecdote would simply have been a variant on what Russell reported. See John Russell, *Tour in Germany and … the Austrian Empire in 1820, 1821, 1822*, new edition, 2 volumes (Edinburgh: Constable and Co., 1828), vol. 2, p. 199–201; repr. facsimile with Introduction by William Meredith, *Beethoven Journal* 29, No. 2 (Winter 2014), pp. 67 and 74–75.—TA

[136] For earlier references to this confusing relationship see Blatt 46r.—TA

[137] Possibly to bind copies of the newly composed *Abendlied unterm gestirnten Himmel*, WoO 150.—TA

[138] Possibly for a projected housekeeper, or even for nephew Karl, if Beethoven thought that he might visit often.—TA

[139] A type of wine. See Blatt 17r above.—TA

[140] Beethoven and Bernard do not eat a meal, but seemingly munch on almonds; the conversation lasts through Blatt 64r.—TA

How is Oliva? [//] [Blatt 56r] The people [at the boarding house] where he eats at midday have done him many kindnesses. //

Don't forget about your *Akademie*. [//]

In the *Brünner Zeitung* it says that his [Rudolph's] solemn entry into Olmütz will be held on [Thursday,] March 9.[141] [//] [Blatt 56v] Before he leaves he will probably give his opinion. //

JOSEPH CZERNY [**joining them briefly**]: I was also sick the day before yesterday.[142] // There is also a Gebel who is a painter.[143] //

BEETHOVEN [**writing so as not to be overheard**]: A lame government.[144] [//]

[Blatt 57r]

BERNARD [**resuming**]: I have been invited.[145] // Since Sunday [February 27], I have already been invited the 4th time; one does not have time and, eventually, must put an end to it // You will have a poor guest in Czerny; he eats very little and drinks only water at midday. [//] [Blatt 57v] <Yes, I have already been invited.> // We don't know all that. //

You are far too afraid. The nobility cannot tolerate the thing. It is that way here even now. [//] [Blatt 58r] You don't know these people. Even the young officers are that way. You don't know these people. //

The whole generation in general is like that …. That cannot be suppressed

---

[141] The *Beobachter*, No. 66 (Monday, March 6, 1820), p. 322, published this notice from the *Brünner Zeitung*. See also Blatt 10v above.—KH

[142] Perhaps the *other* person who was ill on Wednesday, March 1, was Peters, who seemingly missed his visit to Blöchlinger's Institute on Thursday, March 2.—TA

[143] Carl Peter Goebel (1791–1823), noted Viennese painter of historical scenes. He did his first original painting in 1820; before that he had devoted himself only to copying the great masters in the Belvedere. See Böckh, *Merkwürdigkeiten*, p. 254; Gräffer-Czikann, II, p. 388; Wurzbach, vol. 5, p. 234; Thieme-Becker, vol. 14, pp. 301–302.

This entry seems to indicate that Beethoven was not clear about the identity of "H. Goeble," poet of his *Abendlied unterm gestirnten Himmel*, WoO 150, whose autograph bears the date March 4, 1820. Czerny's reply here also provides a clue as to how Beethoven must have pronounced Goeble's name, possibly reflecting the composer's Rhenish origin. See Albrecht, "Otto Heinrich Graf von Loeben."—KH/TA

[144] Possibly a lame constitution, a reference to someone's health.—TA

[145] In Heft 6, Blatt 52r (ca. Friday, January 21, 1820), Bernard boasted that he had been invited to Frau von Salmy's for dinner every Friday; see also Heft 2, Blatt 90r. For Oliva's comment see Heft 6, Blatt 88v. On Friday, February 11, Bernard was invited to Schreyvogel's for dinner; see Heft 7, Blatt 63r.—TA

through similar Karlsbad Decrees.[146] // [Blatt 58v] *Brindisium suique susque usque ubique.*[147] [//] I also do not consider it good that the universities are isolated. <It ....> [//] "Happy is he who does business from afar!"[148] // [Blatt 59r]

If it is possible, I'll come by 2 o'clock. If I am not here by this time, then I am not coming at all.—One must have the freedom and the time to decline [invitations], to send [messages] and to receive replies, etc. [//] [Blatt 59v]

We shall already do it. [//] <He is a handworker/surgeon.>[149] [//] He needs none. He already has one. // You have not yet shown me your monument. // As newspaper journalists, we have [Blatt 60r] the obligation to make such a monument known to the world. // And then a grand opera.[150] //

Anyhow, it will make a paragraph in your biography. Herr Starke also wishes [Blatt 60v] a tiny bit of it[151] in his newest work [Volume 2 of his *Wiener Pianoforte Schule*]. // He also wants a few lines of your biography to go along with it. We must give him something. [//] But in all of his large-scale musical and literary [Blatt 61r] endeavors, he is always most modest, diligent, and humble. // He understands the art of compiling well.[152] // There are always weak ones [*Schwache*], I think, even

---

[146] The Karlsbad *Pasteten* or *Beschlüsse* (Decrees), which were drawn up by the Conference of Ministers of the German States in Karlsbad from August 6 to 31, 1819, and ratified by the *Bundestag* on September 20. They adhered to the University Law (according to which teachers out of political favor could be dismissed, student associations were forbidden, etc.), The Press Law (severest censorship of all journals and books), the "Law concerning the Establishment of a Central Commission of Inquiry in Mainz for the Detection and Pursuit of Revolutionary Activities," and the Execution Order. See Bartel, ed., *Sachwörterbuch der Geschichte Deutschlands*, vol. 1, p. 905.—KH

[147] "A toast, up and down and all around." An allusion to the university student movements that began as liberal and revolutionary, were suppressed by the Karlsbad Decrees as a reaction to the assassination of Kotzebue, but turned conservative after 1848.—TA

[148] Latin original: *Beatus ille, qui procul negotiis!* (Horace).—KH

[149] Bernard's original Greek: Χειρουργος (Cheirourgos: handworker or surgeon). The references to Beethoven's longtime friend, hornist and band director Friedrich Starke, and his three-volume *Wiener Pianoforte Schule* (to which the composer contributed several numbers) probably begin here. Starke's vol. 1 had appeared in 1819; the preface to vol. 2 would be dated May, 1820; that to vol. 3, dated January, 1821 (with a slightly varied reprint after Starke had moved to Oberdöbling in March, 1824). See Jones, "The *Wiener Pianoforte-Schule* of Friedrich Starke"; Clive, pp. 348–349.—KH/TA

[150] In Heft 7, Blatt 63r, Bernard indicates that after Beethoven composes the oratorio *Der Sieg des Kreuzes* (to his text), he would be willing to write an opera libretto for him.—TA

[151] Possibly a piece from the aforementioned un-composed opera or possibly whatever work had been discussed beforehand as Beethoven's "monument" (possibly the *Missa solemnis* or a setting of Bernard's libretto *Der Sieg des Kreuzes*). Ultimately Beethoven gave Starke some bagatelles and a solo adaptation of the first coda of the Piano Concerto No. 3. Bernard had made a similar request on February 6, 1820; see Heft 7, Blatt 35r.—TA

[152] Beethoven may have said that Starke did not understand the art of composition, with this sentence as Bernard's reply.—TA

among the strong ones [*Starken*].[153] // He is the fat landlord of noisy houses.[154] // [Blatt 61v]

Now, let's go home. //

The fat overfed little pig; she is a completely unspoiled child, who, in time, will also become fat and spoiled. //

He [presumably someone sitting nearby] asked whether one must also pay for the shells from [Blatt 62r] the almonds; I said No, because one must give the shells back.[155] //

Have you already looked to see whether your lottery ticket is a winner? Don't you have it with you? [//] The Orchestra [of the Theater] an der Wien has won 10,000 Gulden. [//] [Blatt 62v] Palffy [the owner of the Theater], who has 40,000 lottery tickets, has won nothing at all. [//] They were left over to him and are part of the game. // The lottery is otherwise an amoral means of regaining one's [financial] health. The individual is not [Blatt 63r] swindled, but all those who play the game are collectively swindled. Now then, let us go home. // It is still a leftover product of poor financial management. [//] [Blatt 63v]

It [presumably this coffee house] is open from 6 o'clock in the morning until 10[156] o'clock; and from 4 o'clock to 12 o'clock. // Coffee is so little important to me that I can dispense with it entirely. If, however, [Blatt 64r] one goes to a coffee house, that's what one must drink. [//]

She is the sister of our little fat friend. //

[End of long conversation with Bernard on Friday, March 3.]

[Beethoven may have spent Saturday, March 4, 1820, largely in his apartment, because the so-called "autograph" of his *Abendlied unterm gestirnten Himmel*, WoO 150, is dated that day.]

UNKNOWN: She was here. [//] Grog.[157] [//]

[Blatt 64v]

---

[153] Starke's name always invited a pun.—TA

[154] In addition to his salon pieces, Starke had also published several collections of works for "noisy" military band, including works for multiple bands.—TA

[155] This suggests that Beethoven and Bernard (with Czerny stopping by) have been sitting in this coffee house for some time, eating enough almonds to leave a significant pile of shells and invite a good-humored exchange with another guest.—TA

[156] The zero has been corrected several times, so that the number could read "11" or even "1."—KH

[157] Possible reference to a drink. See term "Krog," which the German editors presumed to be a name (Heft 5, Blätter 41r–41v).—TA

JOSEPH CZERNY [possibly at Beethoven's apartment on the Josephstadt Glacis with Bernard; presumably the afternoon of Sunday, March 5]:[158] The father of the [female] piano player Bühler[159] is Economic Councillor to Prince Liechtenstein. [//] Linke[160] is also fine. //

BERNARD [continuing]: Linke [left] has no faults except that he is *krum* [curved].[161] [//] [Blatt 65r]

I hear that [cellist Anton] Kraft has already declined somewhat.[162] [//]

I know the Romberg family[163] quite well. // [Bernhard] Romberg has a greater

---

[158] This day's conversations—at Beethoven's apartment, at Blöchlinger's, at a restaurant, and/or at Beethoven's apartment again—seem to last until Blatt 75v.—TA

[159] Franz Biller (b. 1766), economic councillor, living in the City at Löwelstrasse No. 18, had five children with his wife Magdalena (b. 1777), among them Franziska (b. 1795), noted in Ziegler (1823) as "Virtuosa on the pianoforte." See Conscriptions-Bogen, Stadt No. 12, Wohnpartei 1 (Wiener Stadt- und Landesarchiv); Ziegler, *Addressen-Buch*, p. 4.—KH

[160] Joseph Linke (1783–1837), violoncellist and composer, born in Drachenberg, Silesia, came to Count (later Prince) Rasumowsky in Vienna in 1808 and played in his string quartet under the leadership of Ignaz Schuppanzigh. After the prince dissolved the quartet early in 1816, Linke followed Countess Marie Erdödy to exile in Croatia, but soon returned to Vienna. In May or June 1818 he became solo player in the Theater an der Wien's orchestra, and, from 1831, the Court Opera Orchestra. With his wife Barbara (whom he married in ca. 1813) he lived at [Laimgrube] an der Wien, Pfarrgasse No. 60 [renumbered as 66 in 1821], one very long block west of the Theater an der Wien. Linke did much to promote Beethoven's works. See his Verlassenschafts-Abhandlung, Fasz. 2, 5201/1837 (Wiener Stadt- und Landesarchiv); Böckh, *Merkwürdigkeiten*, p. 373; Frimmel, *Handbuch*, I, pp. 364–366; Gräffer-Czikann, III, p. 453; Thayer-Deiters-Riemann, III, pp. 73–75; Thayer-Forbes, pp. 442–444; Wurzbach, vol, 15, pp. 215–216; *Allgemeine musikalische Zeitung* 20, No. 29 (July 22, 1818), col. 524; Behsel, p. 139.—KH/TA

[161] Bernard is making a pun on Linke's name (*Linke*: left) and the adjective *krumm* (crooked, curved, hunchbacked). Thus Linke is curved to the left. There is no indication in the Conscriptions-Bögen for Laimgrube No. 60 [renumbered as 66 in 1821] or No. 172 that Linke was handicapped in any way. The annotation "Gänzlich Unanwendbar" in Conscriptions-Bogen, Laimgrube 172/31 verso (made by ca. 1828) simply means that Linke, by now about forty-five years old and in the Imperial employ as a musician, was "entirely ineligible" for military service.—TA

[162] Kraft had recently been ill and would die the following August 28.—TA

[163] Among the earlier generations, the best-known members of the Romberg family of musicians (with origins in Münster) were the brothers Bernhard Anton (1742–1814), bassoonist and violoncellist, and Gerhard Heinrich (1745–1819), clarinettist and violinist, who both worked from 1776 to 1803 in the Prince-Bishop's Kapelle in Münster. Bernhard Anton Romberg had two sons pertinent to this discussion: Bernhard Heinrich (1767–1841), violoncellist, composer, and Kapellmeister, and Anton (1771–1842), a fine bassoonist who spent 1808–1814 in Vienna, working for Princes Lobkowitz and Kinsky, as well as the Court Opera. Gerhard Heinrich had a son pertinent to the discussion: Andreas Jacob (1767–1821), violinist and composer.

The two cousins Bernhard and Andreas entered the Hofkapelle in Bonn in 1790 and became acquainted with the young Beethoven. In 1795 they went on tour together to Vienna, where they met Haydn and Beethoven. In 1799 the cousins went on separate paths: violoncellist Bernhard went to Berlin and, in 1820, to Hamburg; violinist Andreas spent time in Hamburg and then went to Gotha. See Kurt Stephenson, "Romberg," *MGG*, vol. 11, cols. 855–860; Clive, pp. 291–292.

name than Kraft. // He produced an opera, *Circe*,[164] here at [the Theater] an der Wien, but it did not please. [//] [Blatt 65v] He seeks to accentuate the part at the expense of the whole [work], which is a false endeavor. [//] Incidentally, actors have the same kind of relationship to the poet. [//] [Blatt 66r] We artistic philosophers form opinions only from the point of view of the whole work. // I have never made much of a role, and therefore also not of the actors who, as a rule, are far inferior to the artist [Blatt 66v] who has brought his instrument to perfection. [//]

[Beethoven, Bernard, and Joseph Czerny walk up the hill to Blöchlinger's Institute.]

BLÖCHLINGER **[presumably at his Institute in the Josephstadt, with Beethoven, Bernard, and Joseph Czerny present; afternoon of Sunday, March 5]**: It is also going somewhat better with mathematics, but he [Karl] seldom thinks, and has become spoiled through learning by rote earlier. [//] Last week he was in bed for a day, because he complained of headaches. The next day, through appropriate diet [Blatt 67r], he was fine again. [//] Don't worry at all; I shall do everything that is necessary in every respect. [//]

How does it look for the guardianship trial? [//]

Shall I have Carl [Karl] come? [//] Carl has his semester examinations on the 14th [Tuesday, March 14, still ten days away]. [//]

[Blatt 67v]

JOSEPH CZERNY **[interjecting]**: I'll give him [Karl] the lesson at 3 o'clock; however, I only go to Hernals[165] and to [Leopoldine] Blahetka 2 times [per week]. If, however, you wish 3 lessons [weekly] for your little one, then I must come a 3rd time extra. //

Beethoven would initially have known bassoonist Anton Romberg from the time that he was employed by Prince Lobkowitz through Lobkowitz's bankruptcy in June, 1813. Thereafter, he was employed by the Court Opera at the Kärntnertor Theater (as a "Concert- und Solospieler"), probably played in Beethoven's series of benefit concerts from December 1813 to February 1814 and was surely present for the May 1814 revival of *Fidelio*. See "Status der k.k. Hof-Theater, 1814," in Hoftheater, Generalintendanz, K.6, No. 131/1814, Beilage 6, fol. 148r (Haus-, Hof- und Staatsarchiv, Vienna). Romberg is not present in a similar personnel list of March 1817.—KH/TA

[164] Bernhard Romberg's *Ulisses und Circe*, an opera in three acts (after Calderón), was premiered at the Theater an der Wien on March 5, 1808, and received a total of four performances before it was dropped. See Bauer, *Opern und Operetten in Wien*, p. 102; Seyfried, "Journal."—KH

[165] The Blahetka family lived in the Josephstadt, therefore a second pupil must have lived in more distant Hernals, a village northwest of Vienna, beyond the *Linie* (today's *Gürtel*) and north of Neulerchenfeld. It had a Calvary Hill with a *Passionsweg* (Way of the Passion/Cross), built in 1714, which were pilgrimage destinations from Vienna during Fasting periods, especially Holy Week. See Schmidl, *Wiens Umgebungen*, I, pp. 97–98; Weidmann, pp. 158–160.—KH/TA

BLÖCHLINGER [**continuing**]: Our [national] school curriculum is to blame for the poor progress in Mathematics; now it will change all its points of view.[166] [Blatt 68r] One does not know where to begin. [//] Director Schönberger is dead;[167] his school curriculum has now been rejected, and a new one is being hammered out by the government. // The curriculum of our confused [national] schools does not agree within itself at all, so that, for example, the pupils of the 3rd *Grammatical* grade take the same lessons in Arithmetic that the pupils of the 3rd *Normal* grade have already had. [//]

[Blatt 68v]

[Beethoven, Bernard, Czerny, and Karl, possibly retiring to Beethoven's apartment on the Glacis or the *Birne* wine house on its ground floor, later in the afternoon of Sunday, March 5, probably going into the evening:]

JOSEPH CZERNY: You should always send your card along to the *Kameel*. Then you will get your things correctly. //

NEPHEW KARL [**joining the group**]: Wednesdays.[168] //

JOSEPH CZERNY [**continuing**]: Bühler[169] is very fond of you. // Bühler and his Mrs. have one heart; the former, however, is melancholy. //

BERNARD: Count Bentheim,[170] who has also always played the grand absolute lord, had his [Blatt 69r] hair cut one day. His chamber servant was present; a large

---

[166] Blöchlinger engages in a bit of wordplay: "diesen Augenblick" (at this moment, now), and "alle Augenblicke" as Augen Blicke (all eye-views or viewpoints).—TA

[167] Franz Xaver Schönberger (1754 – January 20, 1820), pedagogue, priest in the Order of Pious Schools (*Orden der frommen Schulen*—the *Piaristen)*, had been Vice Director of the I.R. Gymnasium System of Schools since 1808, and Director of the I.R. *Konvikt* since 1816. Blöchlinger, who occasionally ate dinner with the faculty of the Piaristen Gymnasium and seemingly liked Schönberger, will have a similar conversation with Beethoven on Thursday, March 16, 1820 (see Heft 9, Blätter 65v–66r). See also *Hof- und Staats-Schematismus*, 1820, II, p. 120; *Wiener Zeitung*, No. 19 (January 23, 1820), p. 76; Wurzbach, vol. 31, pp. 127–128.—KH/TA

[168] Possibly the days on which outsiders could visit Blöchlinger's Institute.—TA

[169] It remains unclear who is meant here: Franz Biller, the Economic Councillor to Prince Liechtenstein (see Blatt 64v above), who (Biller) had a daughter who was a pianist; or Johann Bihler, the tutor for Baron Puthon (see Heft 4, Blatt 32v); or even Dr. Bühl (dentist Joseph Biehl? See Heft 10, Blatt 76r)—all of them mentioned by Joseph Czerny during this period.—KH

[170] Prince Friedrich Wilhelm Belgius zu Bentheim-Steinfurth (1782–1839), Lieutenant Field Marshall and I.R. Chamberlain, had been born in Burg-Steinfurt as the third son of Count Ludwig Wilhelm and Duchess of Holstein-Glücksberg (of a Danish house). He was appointed to the Austrian Army under Emperor Leopold II in 1791, and was noted as a brave, noble, and honorable soldier. He was raised from the rank of Count to Prince in 1818. He presumably met Beethoven in Teplitz in 1811. See Frimmel, *Handbuch*, I, pp. 33–34; Wurzbach, vol. 1, pp. 282–283.—KH/TA

mirror [was] in front of him, in which the Count viewed himself. One lock was too low, so he said to the chamber servant: "George, tell the barber that the right lock is too low." [//] Father. // In his audience room, he had only one chair, so that no one could sit down [Blatt 69v] in his presence. // Now they are ashamed of the middle class. //

He always seeks to bring everything into harmony; a very fine occupation. //

Indeed you have Klopstock.[171] // [Blatt 70r] At home I have a collection of Lieder [poems] that was compiled in Hamburg for the Hanseatic *Legion;*[172] in it, there are many excellent poems [suitable] for [musical] composition. //

JOSEPH CZERNY: Haven't you heard anything about my "second Blahetka" (Fanny Sallomon)? She is a child of 8½ years and has already played in the Theater [Blatt 70v] to great approbation, and who also plays your compositions in addition to the usual bravura pieces. // She has a first-class talent.[173] //

---

[171] Bernard spells the name "Klopfstock" but means the north German Protestant poet Friedrich Gottlieb Klopstock (1724–1803), whose epic *Der Messias* and other works influenced the young Goethe. A copy of Klopstock's *Werke* (Troppau, 1785), as well as other individual works, were present in Beethoven's library at the time of his death (see Albrecht, *Letters to Beethoven*, No. 483, items no. 28 and 39); Clive, p. 189.—KH/TA

[172] The Hanseatic Legion was initially made up of citizens from Hamburg under General Karl von Tettenborn in 1813, during the wars against Napoleon. They were joined by other volunteers from Bremen and Lübeck, returned home by June 30, 1814, and were decorated by their cities in 1815. See Blatt 73v for Bernard's reference to the Bohemian *Legion* in which he himself served.—TA

[173] On December 23, 1819, Fanny Sallomon (or Salomon) played piano variations by Joseph Czerny at the Theater an der Wien. In Ziegler's *Addressen-Buch* (1823), p. 41, she is listed as a "pianist of eleven years." See also Kanne's *Wiener AmZ* 4, No. 7 (January 22, 1820), p. 55. The young pianist's proper name was Franziska. In ca. 1822 she lived in suburban Alsergrund, Währinger-Gasse No. 205 [numbered as 182 before 1821], inner corner of today's Währinger Strasse and Lakierer Gasse. According to a Conscriptions-Bogen from sometime after 1814, her family included her father, Karl Salomon (b. ca. 1778), cashier for a business concern; mother M[aria] Anna (b. ca. 1780); and elder sisters Anna (b. ca. 1800) and Johanna (b. ca. 1806).

Franziska herself was listed in the Conscriptions-Bogen as being born in 1809, but ages in such census listings are often approximate (as reflected above). Because Ziegler's *Addressen-Buch*, which gives her age as eleven, was compiled in late 1822, it suggests that she was born ca. 1811, which could still make her about eight and a half years old in March, 1820, as Czerny claims above. See Böckh, *Merkwürdigkeiten*, p. 378; Behsel, p. 201; Conscriptions-Bogen, Alsergrund No. 205, Wohnpartei 12 [later numbered 9], new collation 205/12 (verso).

Her activities matured and on October 26 and November 1, 1834, she played a Beethoven Concerto (presumably the one in E-flat, Op. 73) on two benefit concerts given by hornist Joseph Rudolph Lewy at the Hall of the Gesellschaft der Musikfreunde. A little over a month later, on December 7, 1834, she played the Adagio and Rondo from Beethoven's Concerto in E-flat, Op. 73 (this time specified) on a benefit concert for the widows and orphans of the Law Faculty in the University's Hall (*Aula*); all three concerts featured an orchestra under [Georg] Hellmesberger (program file, Gesellschaft der Musikfreunde). Her playing on the Lewy concerts was termed "incomparable," and on the Law Faculty benefit "as brilliant as it was expressive." See the *Allgemeine musikalische Zeitung* 37, No. 12 (March 25, 1835), cols. 202–203.

Do you want to say something to him?[174] //

Stein [piano maker] sends you his regards and will visit you very soon.[175] [//]

[Blatt 71r]

NEPHEW KARL: The bottle has been popped open. //

JOSEPH CZERNY [continuing]: The man says that you had reached a monthly agreement with him for 2 instruments, <each> specifically <4 fl.> 6 fl. for 4 tunings. [//]

BERNARD: Indeed he demands only 6 fl., since you want to give him 12. [//] 1 fl. 30 kr. for 1 tuning. [//] [Blatt 71v] There were 3 tunings at Karl's—he demands only 1 fl. 30 kr. [each]. [//] 4 tunings [per month]—[each instrument] every two weeks. [//] Today it is the 3rd time [at Beethoven's apartment]; and 3 tunings at Karl's makes 6 tunings. [//]

[Blatt 72r]

NEPHEW KARL: He [Bernard] was at my place 3 times.[176] //

JOSEPH CZERNY [continuing]: I pay 2 fl. for one tuning; and the man from Stein's demands only 1 fl. 30 kr. //

Chattering is his natural failing. //

[Czerny may have left the group at this point.]

BERNARD [with Karl still present, but seemingly without Czerny, presumably at a restaurant near Beethoven's apartment; still Sunday, March 5]: People are not different. //

I don't need any, either. [//] [Blatt 72v]

She continued to be mentioned frequently in Viennese reports to the Leipzig *Allgemeine musikalische Zeitung* through spring, 1839, when she collaborated in a performance of Beethoven's "Kreutzer" Sonata, Op. 47, with violinist Bernhard Molique (1802–1869), visiting from Stuttgart. The *AmZ*'s correspondent termed her "seine seelenverwandte Gefährtin" (a companion related to his soul). See *AmZ* 41, No. 9 (February 27, 1839), col. 166; No. 20 (May 15, 1839), col. 389; No. 21 (May 22, 1839), col. 404 (accompanying thirteen-year-old violinist Nicolai Dmitriev Schäfer in Variations on a Russian Theme by Herz and Lafont).

After this time there seem to be no further references to Fanny Salomon in the literature. Perhaps she married and withdrew from public performance.—KH/TA

[174] Possibly nephew Karl.—TA

[175] Stein would visit Beethoven ca. Sunday, March 12 (Heft 9, Blätter 8r–10v).—TA

[176] In the upper right corner: "C.B." [Carl Bernard] drawn in the form of a monogram.—KH

He says that the coffee at your place is better than at our fat little pig's.[177] //

The professors at [my] *Gymnasium* one time excluded me from the Spring Celebration because they considered me to be a free spirit. // [Blatt 73r] I was the top prize winner in all my school classes. They took the prize away from me in a solemn assembly of the professors, and I had to sign my name into the black book. At the end of the year, though, they had to give me the first prize again, since they could not put forward any of my fellow pupils. [//] [Blatt 73v] When I went to the Bohemian *Legion*, one of my professors broke down in tears and said: "Thus all of my good teaching has not borne any fruit!" // But it is still always better than in Russia. // One fears them here as well. // [Blatt 74r] One has no right, however, to rob a Nation of its Language, because one destroys it thereby.[178] //

NEPHEW KARL: She had the bill. //

BERNARD [continuing, possibly at Beethoven's apartment on the Josephstadt Glacis]: At the Congress now here, they are working on a law in which it will be prescribed how high the birds may fly, and how fast the rabbits may run.[179] [//] [Blatt 74v] They are to promulgate the Acts that concern pedagogical activities with great diligence; they can do nothing better for the purpose toward which they work.[180] //

20 years ago, Wolff[181] was still taught almost everywhere. // Feder[182] is even

---

[177] Beethoven enjoyed making strong coffee for himself, but seemingly for his friends, as well. See Blatt 61v for a "fat little pig" and Blatt 64r for a "fat little friend." The "fat little pig" might refer to a mutual friend, but it might also refer to the proprietor of a restaurant or drinking establishment, possibly the *Stadt Belgrade* only a few houses north of Beethoven's apartment.—TA

[178] In Bernard's case, probably a reference to the Habsburg Empire's requirement that Bohemians speak German and not their own language.—TA

[179] Bernard refers to the Viennese Conference of Ministers, called by Metternich to carry out the Karlsbad Decrees, a meeting that lasted from November 25, 1819, to May 15, 1820. The result of their work, the Viennese School Acts of May 15, 1820, was declared on June 8, 1820, through the *Bundestag*, as a fundamental Statute of the German *Bund* (League).—KH

[180] See Blatt 42v above about revolutionary ideas.—KH

[181] Christian Wolff (1679–1754), philosopher and mathematician, was Professor of Natural and International Law in Halle. Already during his lifetime, his method of popularizing Leibniz's philosophy had become the reigning university philosophy. He wrote *Philosophia rationalis* (Halle, 1728), *Philosophia prima* (Halle, 1729), and *Psychologia empirica* (Halle, 1732), among others. See *Allgemeine deutsche Biographie*, vol. 44, pp. 12–14.—KH

[182] Johann Georg H. Feder (1740–1821), philosopher, became professor in Göttingen in 1768. He wrote *Grundriss der Philosophischen Wissenschaften Nesbst der nöthigen Geschichte* (Coburg, 1767/69), *Lehrbuch der Logik und Metaphysik* (Göttingen, 1769), and *Lehrbuch der praktischen Philosophie* (1770), among others. See *Allgemeine deutsche Biographie*, vol. 6, pp. 595–596.—KH

worse, but his textbook was still used until 1806. [//] [Blatt 75r] Kiesewetter[183] was more exhaustive; he lectured entirely according to Kant. //

A week ago [Sunday, February 27] I ate midday dinner with several professors from the University here at the religious community in the Heiligen Kreuz Monastery.[184] The professor of Philosophy was also there;[185] he awakened no great hopes. [//] [Blatt 75v] Also Littrow, director of the Observatory was there; he is a genuinely good fellow; but a Bohemian.[186] [//] Also the botanist Trattinik[187] was there. [//]

[Seemingly the end of entries for Sunday, March 5.]

[Blatt 76r]

NEBERICH **[presumably at Beethoven's apartment; possibly late morning of Monday, March 6]:**

1. In 14 days, I depart for Dresden & Berlin.[188] You designate now *when* we will dine together at the Archduke Carl.[189] //

2. Stieler had some head cold, but is well again. // Staudenheimer, Stieler & Wolf.—I am supplying all the wines. //

Now, on next *Friday* [March 10]? [//] So it *is still* on *Friday?* // He is certainly not that; I know it from my own experience. // She was happily in Vienna. // Please drop off the *designated* day at *Stieler's* for me. [//]

---

[183] Johann Gottfried Karl Kiesewetter (1766–1819), philosopher, follower of Kant, became professor of philosophy in Berlin in 1792. He wrote *Über die ersten Grundsätze der Moralphilosophie* (1788), *Versuch einer fasslichen Darstellung der wichstigen Wahrheiten der neuen Philosophie für Uneingeweihte* (1795), and *Grundriss einer allgemeinen Logik nach Kantschen Grundsätzen* (1796). See *Allgemeine deutsche Biographie*, vol. 15, pp. 730.—KH

[184] The Heiligenkreuzerhof, part of whose buildings had also been converted to secular apartments. The dinner presumably took place on Sunday, February 27. See Blatt 12r.—TA

[185] Ludwig Rembold (1785–1844) was professor of theoretical and practical philosophy, as well as the history of philosophy at the University of Vienna. See *Hof- und Staats-Schematismus*, 1820, II, p. 95 (giving his first name as Leopold); Wurzbach, vol. 25, pp. 273–274.—KH

[186] Joseph Johann Littrow (1781–1840); see Heft 7, Blatt 17r. Bernard was also a Bohemian by birth.—TA

[187] Leopold Trattnick (1764–1849), custodian of the Court Natural History Collections. See Heft 5, Blatt 21v.—TA

[188] The *Wiener Zeitung*, No. 72 (March 29, 1820), p. 287, notes: "Departures. March 26: Herr Neberich, State Pensioner, to Dresden." Therefore Neberich departed three weeks later (not two), on Palm Sunday, March 26.—KH/TA

[189] The traveling wine dealer Adam Neberich seemingly wanted to treat Beethoven to dinner at a relatively elegant restaurant, possibly in the company of Dr. Staudenheim, the artist Stieler, and the librarian Wolf. The restaurant *Erzherzog Carl* was established in 1806, and was located at Kärntnerstrasse No. 1026 [renumbered as 968 in 1821, and later as 29–31], on the south side of Kärntnerstrasse, between Himmelpfortgasse and Johannesgasse. See Gräffer-Czikann, vol. 2, p. 426; Behsel, p. 29; Messner, *Die Innere Stadt*, II, p. 149.—KH/TA

[Blatt 76v]

BERNARD [joining Neberich and Beethoven]: Two years ago, the friend[190] who lives above you sold his restaurant on the Schwechat [River][191] to Baron Minkwitz[192] for 40,000 [fl.]. [//]

[Blatt 77r]

NEBERICH: Your portrait [by Stieler] will be very good; everyone says so even now. //[193]
   [Neberich presumably departs.]

BERNARD [continuing]: I shall read it [the draft for the *Denkschrift*] today yet. I had already intended to do it yesterday [Sunday, March 5], but we were together too long.[194] // Are you staying longer? [//] [Blatt 77v] Indeed it will soon be decided. // But it is for the boy's sake that you take an interest. // The Institutes are not different. //

PETERS [seemingly joining Bernard and Beethoven]: We'll want to go on Wednesday evening [March 8], if everything else has been put in order.[195] // [Blatt 78r] That was good advice concerning the country. Only title. //

---

[190] This seems not to have been a person named Freund.—TA

[191] The Schwechat, tributary river on the right (south and west) side of the Danube, springs forth in the Vienna Woods and flows through the Helenental and Baden, then northeast through Mödling.—KH

[192] Baron Joseph von Minkewitz, manager of several domains, member of the National Agricultural Society in Bohemia. See *Hof- und Staats-Schematismus*, 1820, II, p. 300.—KH

[193] On the dividing line: a pencil sketch of a man's head in profile.—KH

[194] The entries of Sunday, March 5, seem to last from Blatt 64v through Blatt 75v.—TA

[195] At this late date it seems that Peters is projecting a final social evening on Wednesday, March 8, before he and Prince Ferdinand Lobkowitz depart for Italy on Thursday, March 9; see *Wiener Zeitung*, No. 58 (March 11, 1820), p. 232.—TA

CARBON[196] [at Beethoven's apartment; possibly later on Monday, March 6]: The same one? // Doll[197] sold his house in Mödling by means of auction. // Book dealer.[198] // Across from Galliano.[199] //

UNKNOWN: You have a fine lawyer, Bach. [//]

[Blatt 78v]

CARBON [continuing]: The reason I am visiting you is to learn whether you are coming to Mödling again. // Then to tell you that if you wish a house in Mödling sometime, the one that Doll owns would be much better:

1st, the same view as at Binder's[200]

2nd, everything is in good structural condition

3rd, in the 1st floor [2nd floor, American] there are 7 [normal] rooms, a large room, and a large balcony—half of which could be rented right now. [//] [Blatt 79r]

On the ground level are more apartments and [horse] stalls for rent—a nice little garden at the house, in addition to an exit from the back of the garden. // December 6. // Now it will be substantially enlarged. // In the evening, mostly small-scaled music. [//] My daughter [is] at home. [//] [Blatt 79v] End of April. //

BEETHOVEN [entered later]: *Carbon*

CARBON [concluding]: I am glad to have found you in good health, and would be doubly glad to be able to pay you homage in Mödling this year. // That would be a joy for my daughter. // But there are indeed enormous estates connected with the Bishopric. [//]

---

[196] Carbon is considered the writer here because Beethoven, possibly to aid his memory, jotted his name between the lines of the following entries. Franz Ludwig von Carbon, *Hauptmann* (probably Mayor, rather than military Captain), land and house owner in Mödling. As follows from Beethoven's letter to Sigmund Anton Steiner, October 10, 1819, Beethoven was interested in the acquisition of Carbon's house "Christhof," which was sold by auction to Johann Speer in fall 1819. See Frimmel, *Handbuch*, II, pp. 90 and 423–424; Thayer-Deiters-Riemann, IV, p. 166; Thayer-Forbes, p. 740 (where his title of "Captain" is treated as military rank); Brandenburg, No. 1343; Anderson, No. 977.—KH/TA

[197] The public auction of book dealer Aloys Doll's house in Mödling, Kapuzinerplatz No. 58, which, early in 1819, was already "for sale or for rent" (see Heft 2, Blatt 63r), was announced for March 20, 1820, in the *Intelligenzblatt*, No. 49 (March 1, 1820), p. 358.—KH/TA

[198] Aloys Doll (ca. 1767–1826) was a Viennese book dealer with a shop in the Deutsch-Ordens Haus, No. 933 [renumbered as 879 in 1821], on Stephansplatz, behind and to the southwest of the Cathedral. See Heft 11, Blatt 78v.—TA

[199] In 1786, Giacomo Cagliano established a Swiss silk ribbon factory in the building of the dissolved Kapuziner monastery in Mödling. See Schalk, p. 235.—KH/TA

[200] Binder's house lay right next to that of Aloys Doll in Mödling. See Frimmel, *Handbuch*, I, p. 423. Frimmel does not provide a first name for Binder.—KH/TA

[Blatt 80r]

SCHLEMMER [presumably at his copying shop, Kohlmarkt No. 1216; later afternoon of Monday, March 6]: Today was the rehearsal for the Grand Concert at the Court.[201] [//] He [Archduke Rudolph] departed today at 11 o'clock in the morning;[202] or so I've been told. [//] He has his [ceremonial] entry on the 9th. [//] He out/from yesterday Arch ….[203] [//] He was ill. [//] Zips[204] told me that. [//] Yesterday evening at 6 o'clock. [//]

[Presumably end of entries for Monday, March 6.]

[Blatt 80v]

BEETHOVEN [possibly at his apartment on the Glacis; probably the morning of Tuesday, March 7]: Frau [Johanna] Beethoven, "Born for intrigue, trained in deception, mistress in all the arts of pretense." //

Russian wax candles.
Shoemaker.
Barber glass [cup].
Shoemaker.
At Bernard's concerning Wolfssohn. [//] [Blatt 81r]

[201] If the pattern of February 12–13, 1820, had been followed here, the rehearsal would have taken place in the gallery of the Ceremoniensaal at 10 a. m., with the concert on the next day. See Hofmusikkapelle, Akten, K.11, 1820, fols. 29 and 45 (Haus-, Hof- und Staatsarchiv). In this case the rehearsal was indeed on March 6, but the performance was not until March 11; Schlemmer copied 110 fl. 50 kr. worth of music for it. See HMK, as above, K.11, 1820, fols. 43–44 (program) and 68 (receipt).—TA

[202] See Beethoven's letter to Archduke Rudolph, April 3, 1820. Archduke Rudolph presumably left Vienna on Monday, March 6, 1820, to travel to Olmütz, where his installation as Archbishop took place on March 9. Archduke Rudolph's departure does not appear in the Wiener Zeitung, nor does that of any highly ranking members of the Imperial house. See Blatt 10v above; Brandenburg, No. 1378; Anderson, No. 1016.—KH/TA

[203] Also unclear to the German editors: "er aus ges[t]ern Erz," even with Schlemmer's customary phonetic spellings. In any case, this entry probably duplicates information stated elsewhere in this group of entries.—TA

[204] Franz Joseph Zips was a personal chamber servant to Archduke Rudolph. See Frimmel, Handbuch, II, p. 473; Hof- und Staats-Schematismus, 1820, I, p. 125 and 186; and possibly Blatt 7v above.—KH/TA

"*Several contrabass [and] sundry other parts; just remember* the occasions with them, how [parts] were missing in the Symphony in A."²⁰⁵ [//]

N.B. Since someone is named, then he stated that [sentence ends at page turn].

[Blatt 8Iv]

SCHINDLER²⁰⁶ [finding a blank page after Beethoven's death; falsified entries begin→]: There were mistakes, but only a few, in it; but in the Sonata, Op. 106, I found extraordinarily many. // In places, the manuscript was too poorly written and so scratched out that I could not figure it out at all. // Business at the office gives me only very little time left over, also, I must always be at the ready if the Archduke has me called. // That is a different slavery, such dependence. // The

---

²⁰⁵ Beethoven is lamenting the loss of "Noten" (written music) here. Some organization had evidently borrowed his set of parts for the Symphony No. 7 and had returned them with several contrabass and various other parts missing. The implication here is that the same organization was probably asking Beethoven for another loan of his performing materials, which at this time would still have been handwritten parts. Beethoven is reminding himself to remind them to take better care of the music.

Stefan Weinzierl's appendix with the Viennese public and semiprivate performances of Beethoven's music during his lifetime allows us to narrow the possibilities and even to identify the probable culprit organization that meets the description above. While the "Theater-Poor Fund" of the Kärntnertor Theater, for instance, had produced Beethoven's Symphony No. 7 on a benefit concert on March 25, 1818, they would have done so with exclusively professional musicians and the theater's relatively careful music librarians. The culprit organization, however, had evidently had the Symphony No. 7 on multiple occasions (*Fälle*), and we can therefore narrow our search to the *Juridische Witwen und Waisengesellschaft* (Beneficial Society for Widows and Orphans of Lawyers). It had performed the popular second movement of Symphony No. 7 on a benefit concert on June 1, 1817, and the entire Symphony on January 1, 1819, indeed the Symphony's most recent performance, as of March, 1820! The Lawyers' Society would have performed the symphony with their members, who were amateur orchestral players, supplemented by professionals wherever needed. Their orchestral librarian, too, would surely have been a relatively inexperienced amateur. Moreover, in early March, 1820, the Lawyers' Society probably applied to Beethoven again for the loan of orchestral materials for their upcoming benefit concert on April 16, 1820, only five or six weeks away, and this time Beethoven lent them the *Namensfeier* Overture, Op. 115, often called *Jagdovertüre* (or "Hunting Overture") in the contemporary press. No other performing organization or concert sponsor in Vienna comes as close to satisfying the conditions implied in Beethoven's entry above as the Beneficial Society for Widows and Orphans of Lawyers. See Weinzierl, pp. 229–235.

Contemporary orchestral parts (often in multiple copies) for several of Beethoven's symphonies survive in the Archive of the Gesellschaft der Musikfreunde, and all of them are missing at least some parts. Assuming that many of these materials came from Beethoven's estate, evidence in conversation book entries such as this helps to explain the nature and history of those incomplete sets of parts.—TA

²⁰⁶ Anton Schindler did not become closely acquainted with Beethoven until ca. November, 1822.—TA

Canon[207]—Motive from the 2nd movement of the 8th Symphony—I cannot find the original. // You will probably have to do a favor and write it out again. [//] Herr Pinterics[208] sang the bass then, the Captain[209] 2nd tenor, Oliva 2nd bass. // One now hears nothing at all from Maelzel.[210] [//] Tomorrow I must go to Baden again with the Court Councillor.[211] [←falsified entries end]

[Blatt 82r]

GEORG ADAM SATTLER [?][212] [perhaps in the offices of the *Wiener Zeitung*;

---

[207] The canon "Ta, ta, ta […] lieber, lieber Mälzel," WoO 162 (supposedly originating in 1812 and used by Beethoven for the second movement of Symphony No. 8 in F, Op. 93), is now generally regarded to be spurious.—KH/TA

[208] Carl Pinterics (ca. 1780 – March 6, 1831), private secretary of Count Joseph Palffy, was closely associated with Beethoven from 1815 to 1820. They most often met in the restaurant *Zum Blumenstöckl*. See Deutsch, *Schubert-Dokumente*, pp. 256 and 544; Frimmel, *Handbuch*, II, pp. 19–20; Thayer-Deiters-Riemann, III, p. 348, and IV, p. 188; Thayer-Forbes, p. 755; Clive, p. 267; Brandenburg, *Briefwechsel*, VII, Index, p. 244. For an authentic (as opposed to a "falsified") reference to Pinterics, see Heft 10, Blatt 38v (March 27, 1820).—KH/TA

[209] Presumably Franz von Praitschopf (see Heft 1, Blatt 2v).—KH

[210] Johann Nepomuk Mälzel (1772–1838), mechanician and I.R. Court Engineer, inventor of several mechanical musical instruments, had a metronome constructed after an invention by the Dutchman J.N. Winkel patented in Paris. Upon Mälzel's instigation, Beethoven composed his "Battle Symphony," *Wellington's Victory*, Op. 91, for his mechanical instrument the *Panharmonikon* in 1813. Between 1818 and 1825 Mälzel spent long periods of time in London and Paris, where he exhibited his instruments. He had written to Beethoven from Paris on April 19, 1818, describing his activities there and urging the composer to join him for a series of concerts. See Alfred Orel, "Mälzel," *MGG*, vol. 8, cols. 1456–1458; Thayer-Deiters-Riemann, III, pp. 385–388; Clive, pp. 224–245; Wurzbach, vol. 16, pp. 248–250; Albrecht, *Letters to Beethoven*, No. 248.—KH/TA

[211] Presumably Schindler means Court Councillor Karl Peters, whose name he might have spied on Blätter 77v–78r.—TA

[212] This writer was previously "Unknown," but the contents of his conversations (see especially Heft 9, Blätter 26v and 30r–31r) lead to a near presumption that he was a publisher in the House of Artaria. Since he was not Carlo Boldrini (see Heft 9, Blatt 69v), and probably also not Domenico Artaria himself (see Heft 10, Blätter 4r–5r and 7v–10v), the writer could be an additional partner who was not publicly known.

From the wording of Bernard's following entry, the unknown writer could also be someone partially connected with the *Wiener Zeitung*, the *Beobachter*, and/or the *Wiener AmZ*. From this and the four conversations, it may be gleaned that the individual may have been from Prague; that he worked in the *Hofkriegsrath* (Ministry of War) in the early to mid-1790s and lived with someone named Frank in the Drachengassel, off the Alter Fleischmarkt; that Beethoven may have associated with his social circle and played the writer's piano in the mid-1790s; that he had been in Prague in 1790, 1792, and 1796, and may have seen Beethoven there in 1796 (and therefore was Beethoven's age or a little older); that, as a child, he had played some instrument well (presumably the piano, since he had one in his apartment in the 1790s), but no longer did; and that he had pursued several professions between the mid-1790s and 1820, and was now involved with newspapers and music publishing (specifically for Artaria), including shipments to foreign countries. He need not have been a partner, as the German editors presumed, but instead a knowledgeable and garrulous shipping clerk.

Starting with a survey of *Hofkriegsrath* personnel in the *Schematismen* of the 1790s (and beyond),

possibly Tuesday, March 7]: Moscheles pleased very much in Munich. [//] His concert took in a great deal.[213] [//]

BERNARD: A correspondent reported it to us. //

[Perhaps moving to a wine house with Sattler (but without Bernard), and meeting Czerny there; possibly Tuesday, March 7.][214]

as well as several other documents in Viennese libraries and archives, we can tentatively identify this unknown writer as Georg Adam Sattler, who seems otherwise unrecorded in the Beethoven literature.

Sattler first appears in 1791 as a *Concipist* (document drafter) in the Headquarters for Military (Food) Provisions, living at Kärntnerstrasse No. 625 (across the street from the Bishop's Palace, and technically Bischofsgasse [renumbered as 678 in 1795, and 637 in 1821]). He remained in that position through 1795, though his address changed to Bauernmarkt No. 557 [renumbered as 617 later in 1795, and 578 in 1821] in that year.

By 1796 Sattler was a *Concipist* in the Auxiliary Services of the *Hofkriegsrath*, living in Alter Fleischmarkt No. 736 (which had been renumbered as 734 in 1795 [although changes may have taken place slowly], and would become 690 in 1821). The building presumably also had a side entrance in the tiny Drachengassel, leading off the Alter Fleischmarkt. He remained in this position and at this address through 1801. These elements satisfy several conditions in the "unknown" writer's conversation of 1820. See Conscriptions-Bogen, Stadt No. 689–693, combined file; Stadt No. 1057 (not present in either in 1805 and beyond).

By the *Schematismus* for 1803, Sattler was back at the Headquarters for Military (Food) Provisions, now as Registrar and Expeditor, and living on Neuer Markt No. 1121 [renumbered 1057 in 1821]. With the French rapidly approaching from the west, there may have been some reorganization, but in any case, Sattler disappears in 1804 and does not reappear in the *Schematismen* until 1811, when he was working for the General Military Command for Lower Austria as Registrar and Expeditor, and lived at suburban Alstergasse No. 130 [renumbered as Alsergrund No. 148 in 1821]. By 1812 he had been replaced by Franz Pösler, and he appears in no further *Schematismen* through 1820.

One Georg Adam Sattler was among the members of Vienna's Masonic Lodge *zur Wohltätigkeit* (Beneficence) on June 14, 1785, the lodge of which Mozart was also a member; see Landon, *Mozart, the Golden Years*, p. 251. If this was the same individual it would suggest that he was more of Mozart's generation, perhaps ten years older than Beethoven. He may also have been related to Johann Tobias Sattler (d. Vienna, December 19, 1774), who wrote the first two choruses in Mozart's pasticcio *Thamos, König in Ägypten* (see Deutsch, *Mozart: die Dokumente*, p. 130).

Thus, having served as a civilian Registrar and Expeditor for at least two military offices, in addition to other positions in between, Georg Adam Sattler would surely have been in a position to fulfill these functions (perhaps part-time) for the music (and art) publisher Artaria in 1819–1820, as well as for Bernard's *Wiener Zeitung*, Schickh's *Wiener Zeitschrift*, and possibly other concerns, as well.—TA

[213] In the *Beobachter*, No. 72 (March 12, 1820), p. 352, there appeared, under "Wissenschaftliche und Kunst-Nachrichten," an extensive report about Ignaz Moscheles's concert in the new Royal Court and National Theater in Munich on Wednesday, February 23. On the program was a Grand Overture as well as a Concert-Polonaise with Orchestra by Moscheles; an aria by Ferdinando Paër; Variations on the Alexander March by Moscheles; Variations for Clarinet, composed and played by Heinrich Joseph Bärmann; Trio by Domenico Cimarosa; and a free fantasy on the piano by Moscheles. A detailed report also appeared in Kanne's *Wiener AmZ* 4, No. 20 (March 8, 1820), cols. 158–160.—KH/TA

[214] This conversation goes to the middle of Blatt 85v.—TA

JOSEPH CZERNY: The little fellow [Karl] was overjoyed when I came [to give him his lesson at Blöchlinger's] and asked me when I would see you. [//]

[Blatt 82v]

GEORG ADAM SATTLER [?]: If this wine costs 3 fl., what then should a Sonata by Beethoven cost? Answer: a million. // Too *difficult.* [//] [Blatt 83r] Out of curiosity, they desired the Sonata even in Milan, although not a person lives there who can play such a thing.[215] //

He is still composing something more, i.e., Variations.[216] [//] [Blatt 83v]
Every pendulum clock can be adjusted just this way.[217] //
[Sattler presumably leaves.]

JOSEPH CZERNY **[remaining and continuing]**: I believed that he [presumably either Bernard or Peters] was coming here; I have to speak with him. //

He [nephew Karl] played a Sonata by Mozart and [your] *Sonate pathétique,* [Op. 13,] for me today; [Blatt 84r] I became acquainted with him through these. Next lesson, I shall begin him with something suitable for him. //

He has 3 pensions. // 9 or 10 months. //

He [Karl] was very lovely today; he did everything that pleased me. [//] [Blatt 84v]

It will probably be finished—the tale of the Trial? // I remember that Peters said that you could rest easily, because the matter would have to come out exactly as you wished. // That must have cost a great deal of money. // The Counsel. [//] [Blatt 85r]

In what kind of conditions does she [Johanna van Beethoven] live now, and how old is she? // <It would be better if she already <sentence ends.> // Vienna is too large to get to know these people completely well. //

<I was ....> merely interest. //

It is better to be here in the summer than now. [//] [Blatt 85v]

Where might Bernard be? //

You've already paid. 3 fl. 9 kr. // You gave a 2 fl. [coin] and 1 fl. bill]. //

---

[215] Presumably a discussion about Beethoven's notoriously difficult Piano Sonata in B-flat, Op. 106 (*Hammerklavier*), dedicated to Archduke Rudolph, published by Artaria in September, 1819, with a note on its title page that it was being distributed by several foreign publishers, including Riccordi [*sic*] in Milan. This supports the German editors' belief that the writer was associated with the Artaria publishing house. For publication data see Kinsky-Halm, p. 294.—TA

[216] Abbé Joseph Gelinek (1758–1825), Bohemian composer; see Blatt 87v below.—KH

[217] Probably likening a metronome to a pendulum clock.—TA

Schi[ndler].[218] //
[End of entries; possibly Tuesday, March 7.]

[There seem to be no entries from Wednesday, March 8, or Thursday, March 9, 1820. On Blatt 77v above, Peters was planning either a farewell gathering or a departure on Wednesday, March 8. In the event, he and young Prince Lobkowitz actually departed for Italy on Thursday, March 9.][219]

BEETHOVEN **[at a coffee house, reading the *Wiener Zeitung*; presumably the late afternoon of Friday, March 10]**: Bank shares are valued at 610 [fl.] in C.M.[220] [Blatt 86r]

Arithmetically ordered lists; [lottery] drawing lists from the Theater an der Wien, etc., at Gerold's on Dominikanerplatz.[221]

[Blatt 86v]

JOSEPH CZERNY **[joining Beethoven; probably late afternoon of Friday, March 10]**: Peters was so sad that he could not come here. Your company is so pleasant for him. //

Lightweight ware. //

One of the better is Bernard, but Peters belongs among the noblest of men. //

The man who just left is nearly 80 years old. // [Blatt 87r] A rich manufacturer from France.[222] //

Upon [reading] the recommendation in the *Conversations-Blatt*, the Baroness acquired a hearing apparatus for herself from Wolfsohn. // I told her that it is not true. [//] [Blatt 87v]

---

[218] The letters "ndler" are partially written over. At a much later date Schindler himself may have altered this entry to reflect his own name.—KH/TA

[219] Their departure is noted in the *Wiener Zeitung*, No. 58 (Saturday, March 11, 1820), p. 232. Heft 9, Blatt 38r, indicates that by March 15 Bernard had received letters from Peters in the Steyermark and Mürzzuschlag, and presumed him to have arrived in Venice.—TA

[220] "Bank Shares: […] Deposits according to March 31, 1819: 610 C.M. per each," according to the *Wiener Zeitung*, No. 57 (March 10, 1820), p. 227 ("Exchange Rate of March 9, 1820"). Since the Bank exchange rates varied very much at that period, and the exchange rate was established at 610 fl. only on this one day, Beethoven's notation was clearly taken from No. 57.—KH

[221] Excerpt from an advertisement in the *Wiener Zeitung*, No. 57 (March 10, 1820), p. 228: "To be had at Carl Gerold's on Dominikanerplatz No. 771 [actually No. 711, renumbered as 667 in 1821] for 30 kr. W.W.: *Die arithmetisch geordnete Ziehungsliste der ersten Ziehung von der grossen Lotterie des k.k. priv. Theaters an der Wien, mit den Gratislosen und allen Vor- und Nachtreffern.*" The same advertisement also appeared on March 13, 1820, but since the previous notation demonstrably came from the March 10 issue, we can surmise that Beethoven read that issue fairly systematically, first reading an item from p. 227 and now an item from p. 228. See also Behsel, p. 20, for renumbering.—KH/TA

[222] See also Heft 9, Blätter 40v–41r, for a similar description of a seventy-year-old Frenchman named Bernard.—TA

But the rumor is going around that the A[rchduke], before his departure, had guaranteed you a pension of 1500 [fl.]. // Gelinek[223] was the first who told me about it. // [Blatt 88r]

I too have gotten nothing yet, and he departs tomorrow evening.[224] // 4 fl. has been agreed upon, but I have gotten nothing yet. // That is merely jealousy. // Now, however, you will have peace for a while. [//] [Blatt 88v]

But the Westphalian government[225] already ceased a long time ago. // I wanted to make some use of him at Lobkowitz's, and now it is too late. // New *financial operations* are in store for us again. [//] [Blatt 89r] The exchange rate [for bank shares] is set at 250 fl.[226] [//]

BEETHOVEN:

[*Abendlied unterm gestirnten Himmel*, WoO 150, bars 10–14]

[Blatt 89v]

[223] Abbé Joseph Gelinek (1758–1825), Bohemian composer, met Mozart in Prague and, upon his recommendation, became house chaplain and piano teacher to Count Philipp Kinsky. Presumably before 1795 he came to Vienna, where he became house chaplain to Prince Esterházy. At first he had a friendly acquaintance with Beethoven, but later this lessened perceptibly. See, for instance, Heft 9, Blätter 38r–38v, where Gelinek is reported to have complained in public about Beethoven. Gelinek's compositions are predominantly variations on favorite themes. See Frimmel, *Handbuch*, I, pp. 162–163; Karl Michael Komma and France Vernillat, "Gelinek," *MGG*, vol. 4, cols. 1630–1632; Schilling, III, pp. 175–176 (signed "—d."); Clive, pp. 124–125.—KH/TA

[224] Since Archduke Rudolph had already departed for Olmütz, this could refer to one of his staff, left behind and authorized to make expenditures. It could not refer to young Prince Ferdinand Lobkowitz, who had already departed for Italy on Thursday, March 9; see the *Wiener Zeitung*, No. 58 (March 11, 1820), p. 232.—TA

[225] In late 1808 and early 1809 the Kingdom of Westphalia under Jerome Bonaparte had offered Beethoven a position as Kapellmeister, resulting in the counter-offer of a Viennese pension funded by Archduke Rudolph and Princes Lobkowitz and Kinsky.—TA

[226] In a proclamation of March 9, 1820, the Austrian National Bank announced that, in order not to exceed the statutorily established number of 100,000 bank shares, no new bank shares would be contracted. "In order to find new ways of opening the flow of paper money, impeded until now by bankshare deposits, the Austrian National Bank, from the twentieth of March 1820, will begin [...] to take over redemption- and anticipation-bills, for two hundred fifty Gulden *Wiener Währung*, reimburse one hundred Gulden bank-value, and turn over the paper money to the High State *Verwaltung* [Administration] for destruction." See *Wiener Zeitung*, No. 57 (March 10, 1820), p. 225. See Blätter 85v and 86r above, where Beethoven had also obviously read this March 10 issue of the *Wiener Zeitung*.—KH/TA

[227] Beethoven's *Abendlied unterm gestirnten Himmel*, WoO 150, the autograph of which (actually an advanced draft) is dated March 4, 1820, presumably the previous Saturday. See Albrecht, "Otto Heinrich Graf von Loeben," pp. 17–20.—TA

NEBERICH: ... *have; thus I will ask him; Kraft [strength]; perhaps Salis.*[228] // *His portraits* express character. [//]

[On the evening of Friday, March 10, Joseph Czerny saw Bernard "bei der Peters" (at Frau Peters's), where Bernard was coughing and otherwise not well. Earlier, Peters had boasted of his talent for providing social activity for his wife while he was absent (Blatt 46r). Beethoven was not present on this occasion.]

BEETHOVEN [presumably at his apartment on the Josephstadt Glacis; the morning of Saturday, March 11]:

Brown sugar at the *Kameel.* [//]

What time? [//]

Wolfssohn.

Bernard. //

SCHICKH [presumably at the office of his *Wiener Zeitschrift*, Kohlmarkt No. 268;[229] perhaps midday on Saturday, March 11]: You don't need to send the coupon. Just cut two months off.[230] //

[Blatt 90r]

WOLFSOHN [?] [possibly at a restaurant or coffee house; slightly later on Saturday, March 11]: This gentleman places great stress on the fact that he is the I.R. Court Belt Maker.[231] // This is the reason why one cannot undertake anything here:

---

[228] Because of the fragmentary nature of this entry, it is difficult to determine who is meant here. Schünemann assumed that it concerned a member of the extensive aristocratic Salis family, but it could also be Carl von Sales, also Salis (1791–1870), a portrait painter born in Koblenz. He had been educated at the Wiener Akademie and can be traced as working in Vienna between 1816 and 1830. See Thieme-Becker, vol. 29, p. 341.—KH

[229] The editorial office of Schickh's *Wiener Zeitschrift* was directly across the street from Artaria's Art and Music Shop. Kohlmarkt No. 268 was renumbered as 257 in 1821 (Behsel, p. 8). In fact, it began using its new address already in mid-November 1820; see *Wiener Zeitschrift* 5, No. 138 (November 16, 1820), and No. 139 (November 18, 1820), for the change of address from one issue to the next.

The actual printer of the *Wiener Zeitschrift* was Anton Strauss (also a paper maker), who did a great deal of jobbing for Vienna's cultural community. His office in *Zum Augen Gottes*, No. 1248 [renumbered as 574 in 1821], faced south on to Petersplatz. It also was connected to a building (of the same name), No. 603 [renumbered as 563 in 1821], that faced north on to Spänglergasse (Behsel, pp. 17–18). His printing plant (*Schriftgiesserei/Buchdruckerei*) itself was located in suburban Laimgrube, An der Wien No. 24 (in the block between the Glacis and the Theater an der Wien). See Redl, 1820, pp. 175, 201, and 240.—TA

[230] As an act of support for his friend, Beethoven may have been subscribing to Schickh's *Wiener Zeitschrift*, in which his *Abendlied unterm gestirnten Himmel*, WoO 150, would soon appear.—TA

[231] The I.R. Court Belt Maker was Joseph Jaich, who lived in the suburban Wieden, No. 454 in the Starhemberg Freyhaus [renumbered as No. 1 in 1821; remaining as No. 1 in the renumbering of 1830]. See *Hof- und Staats-Schematismus*, 1820, I, p. 141; Behsel, p. 88.—KH/TA

if people have another occupation besides their usual work, then one cannot pay them enough, at the same time [they] want a person to elevate them to [the status of] God. // This man asked me how he was <there>. [//]

[Blatt 90v]

BEETHOVEN [as a follow-up to the above]:
Bauernmarkt No. 629, hernia physician, Wolfsohn. [//]
[then reading the *Intelligenzblatt*:]
Xenophon's Orations and *Deeds of Socrates*, 3 fl. 30 kr. W.W. at the Used Book Shop [Blatt 91r] in the Currentgasse behind the Superior Jesuit Church [am Hof].[232] [//]

SCHICKH [possibly back in Schickh's editorial office, with journalist colleague Friedrich Wähner; Saturday, March 11]: <Send it to me tomorrow. I shall already ... it.> I shall give it [*Abendlied unterm gestirnten Himmel*, WoO 150] to the copyist myself, and just ask that you send it to me tomorrow. I know where the copyist [Schlemmer] lives and ask only for his name. //
Where, then, do you have the free coupon? // Coupon? [//]

[Blatt 91v]

WÄHNER [as a follow-up]: As a rule, the stories are worth nothing. // for chamber maids. <And which of these, however, are not> //

JOSEPH CZERNY [seemingly in the *Birne* or some other establishment near Beethoven's apartment on the Josephstadt Glacis; later in the day, Saturday, March 11]: Blöchlinger sends his greetings and says that Tuesday the 14th is the examination,[233] in case [Blatt 92r] you might like to invite someone who might be interested. // I thought about Bernard. // He, however, could tell [you] how it turned out. // He has probably already forgotten something. // He [Karl] is still only a child, I think. He must still gain the experience. [//] [Blatt 92v] I consider Blöchlinger to be a fine, honorable man. // That is the 3rd or 4th bankruptcy. // <Only Zmeskal> [//]

---

[232] Excerpt from an advertisement in the *Intelligenzblatt*, No. 57 (March 10, 1820), p. 428: "Books will be bought at Johann Tauer's, antiquarian book dealer in the Currentgasse behind the Superior Jesuit Church, and will be sold at very reduced prices, *Xenophons Reden und Thaten Sokrates* (Greek with German notes), Leipzig, 1802. [...] 3 fl. 30 kr." Currentgasse was and is a very short and narrow street to the south and east of the Kirche "Am Hof." Vienna's other Jesuit Church was and is the Universitäts-Kirche, across the square from the old university.—KH/TA

[233] From this wording, the entry could not have been written later than Sunday, March 12, and—if a business day—more likely on Saturday, March 11.—TA

Too bad about your letter. The people outside [the circle] are too stupid to understand the joke.[234] [//] [Blatt 93r]

Today Blöchlinger offered me to [give] a course at his place, but I could not accept it. // I do not know how I won his confidence. // Where may Peters be now? //

Zmeskal always asks me what you are writing. What shall I tell him? [//] [Blatt 93v]

You are having a poor conversation with me? I write poorly. //

The man [sitting] at the door is saying so many nice things about you! // He completely recognizes your worth as an artist and as a human being. He is telling those around him [Blatt 94r] that you are the greatest man in Europe. // He is right. //

Business affairs are too overwhelming for you, says the porter. //

How is it going with the oratorio [Bernard's libretto *Der Sieg des Kreuzes*]? // I shall remind him subtly. [//] [Blatt 94v][235] It is already 2 years? // You should tell him what you wish. //

NEBERICH [joining Beethoven and Czerny]: In the *Phantasiestücke* of [E.T.A.] Hoffmann, you are very much the subject.[236] // Hoffmann was Music Director in Bamberg; now he is a Government Councillor. In Berlin they are giving operas that he composed. //

[Blatt 95r = inside back cover]

BEETHOVEN [continuing]: Hofmann—You are no Court Man.[237] [//]

JOSEPH CZERNY [resuming]: There are 3 in the group. The one who left is the best, however. //

11 <fl.> //

---

[234] Probably a reference to Beethoven's reply of ca. November 20, 1819, to Prince Odescalchi, the "Stellvertreter" (Vice President, literally: position-representative) of the Gesellschaft der Musikfreunde, where the composer humorously signed himself as "Selbstvertreter" (self-representative); see Heft 3, Blatt 26r. Several members of the august organization did not appreciate Beethoven's humor, but its President, Prince Fürstenberg, enjoyed it; see Heft 5, Blatt 59r; Brandenburg, No. 1356.—TA

[235] Photo of this page in Köhler *et al.*, *Konversationshefte*, vol. 1, facing p. 113.—TA

[236] With the *Fantasiestücke in Callots Manier*, published in 1814/15, E.T.A. Hoffmann laid the foundations for his fame as an author. A second printing appeared in 1819. The entry above refers to the fourth item of *Kreisleriana*, entitled "Beethovens Instrumentalmusik," consisting of an adaptation of two reviews of Beethoven's works from 1810 and 1813.—KH

[237] This wordplay ultimately became the two-voiced canon, "Hoffmann, sei ja kein Hofmann," WoO 180 (see Kinsky-Halm, p. 684). For a sketch for this canon, see Heft 9, Blatt 37v, also made after a conversation in which Neberich took part.—TA

NEBERICH [**continuing**]: He [Staudenheim or Wolfsohn?] has very many patients.

End of Heft 8

N.B. Heft 9 begins on Saturday, March II, 1820, without any perceptible break in continuity.

Appendix

Descriptions of the Conversation Books in Volume 1

N.B. The brief descriptions here are based on the full physical descriptions preceding each Heft in the German edition. All Hefte are understood to be in the Staatsbibliothek zu Berlin—Preussischer Kulturbesitz, except for Hefte 1 and 95, which are in the Beethoven-Haus, Bonn.

Virtually all of the Hefte, except for 1 and 95, bear either annotations or an inserted slip by Anton Schindler or Alexander Wheelock Thayer. Most Hefte also contain librarians' cataloging numbers, often in ink.

Many of these originally blank booklets have paper shields pasted on to the exterior of the front covers (probably standard at the time of manufacture) for the purchaser to write a title, date, or some other identifier.

Heft 1 (ca. February 26, 1818 – after March 2, 1818): Original pink cardboard cover, covered with green silk. 6 Blätter (leaves); all pages contain writing, some greatly smudged. Format 16.6 x 9.5 cm. **Significantly smaller format than all the other Hefte in this volume.**

First surviving Heft in the regularly-preserved sequence:

Heft 2 (March 17, 1819 – after May 15/16, 1819): Original gray marbled cardboard cover. 107 Blätter, 13 of which contain no writing. Schindler seems to have numbered three Blätter twice. One Blatt has been torn out from after each of Blätter 17, 53, and 77. Either the upper or lower half of three further Blätter have been torn out. Format 18.4 x 11.4 cm., although Blatt 21 is 18.4 x 7.4 cm.

Heft 3 (November 20, 1819 – ca. December 6, 1819): Original blue marbled cardboard cover. 68 Blätter; only Blatt 68v and inside back cover contain no writing. Format 18.5 x 12.3 cm.

Heft 4 (December 7, 1819 – December 12, 1819): Original blue marbled cardboard cover. 46 Blätter. Final page and interior of back cover contain no writing. Final page crossed out with red pencil. Format 18.5 x 12.4 cm.

Heft 5 (December 13, 1819 – December 30, 1819): Original blue marbled cardboard cover. 70 Blätter; all the pages contain writing. Format 18.6 x 12.1 cm.

Heft 6 (ca. January 7, 1820 – January 26, 1820): Original blue marbled cardboard cover. 90 Blätter (Schindler's numbering lacks 76 and 77); all the pages contain writing except Blatt 92v and interior of back cover. Format 18.1 x 12.2 cm.

Heft 7 (ca. January 27, 1820 – February 22, 1820): Original blue marbled cardboard cover. 90 Blätter; all the pages contain writing; lower half of Blatt 62 has been torn out. Format 18.8 x 12.1 cm.

Heft 8 (ca. February 22, 1820 – ca. March 11, 1820): Original blue marbled cardboard cover. 94 Blätter; all the pages contain writing. Format 19 x 12.2 cm.

Bibliography

Albrecht, Theodore. "Anton Grams: Beethoven's Double Bassist." *Bass World* 26 (October, 2002), pp. 19–23.

Albrecht, Theodore. "Anton Schindler as Destroyer and Forger of Beethoven's Conversation Books: A Case for Decriminalization." In *Music's Intellectual History*. Ed. Zdravko Blažeković and Barbara Dobbs Mackenzie. New York: RILM, 2009, pp. 169–181.

Albrecht, Theodore. "Beethoven and Shakespeare's *Tempest*: New Light on an Old Allusion." *Beethoven Forum* 1 (1992), pp. 81–92.

Albrecht, Theodore. "Benjamin Gebauer, ca. 1758–1846: The Life and Death of Beethoven's Copyist C." *Bonner Beethoven-Studien* 3 (2003), pp. 7–22.

Albrecht, Theodore. "Die Familie Teimer—sowie eine neuere (überarbeitete) Datierung der zwei Trios für zwei Oboen und Englischhorn (op. 87) und der Variationen WoO 28 von Ludwig van Beethoven." *Wiener Oboen-Journal*, no. 24 (December, 2004), pp. 2–10; no. 25 (March, 2005), pp. 3–9; no. 27 (October, 2005), pp. 6–7.

Albrecht, Theodore. "'First Name Unknown': Violist Anton Schreiber, the Schuppanzigh Quartet, and Early Performances of Beethoven's String Quartets, Op. 59." *Beethoven Journal* 19, no. 1 (Summer, 2004), pp. 10–18.

Albrecht, Theodore. "The Fortnight Fallacy: A Revised Chronology for Beethoven's *Christ on the Mount of Olives*, Op. 85, and the Wielhorsky Sketchbook." *Journal of Musicological Research*. Ed. F. Joseph Smith, 11 (1991), pp. 263–284.

Albrecht, Theodore, trans. and ed. *Letters to Beethoven and Other Correspondence*. 3 vols. Lincoln: University of Nebraska Press, 1996.

Albrecht, Theodore. "Otto Heinrich Graf von Loeben (1786–1825) and the Poetic Source of Beethoven's *Abendlied unterm gestirnten Himmel*, WoO 150." *Bonner Beethoven-Studien* 10 (2012), pp. 7–32.

Albrecht, Theodore. "Picturing the Players in the Pit: The Orchestra of Vienna's Kärntnertor Theater, 1821–1822." *Music in Art* 34, nos. 1–2 (2009), pp. 203–213.

Albrecht, Theodore. "Time, Distance, Weather, Daily Routine, and Wordplay as Factors in Interpreting Beethoven's Conversation Books." *Beethoven Journal* 28, no. 2 (Winter, 2013), pp. 64–75.

Allgemeine Deutsche Biographie. Ed. Rochus von Liliencron. 56 vols. Leipzig: Duncker & Humblot, 1875–1912.

[*AmZ.*] *Allgemeine musikalische Zeitung.* Leipzig: Breitkopf und Härtel, 1798–1848.

Allgemeine musikalische Zeitung mit besonderer Rücksicht auf den Österreichischen Kaiserstaat. Ed. Ignaz von Seyfried and Friedrich August Kanne. Vienna: S.A. Steiner, 1817–1824. (Commonly called the *Wiener Allgemeine musikalische Zeitung* or *Wiener AmZ.* Often cited with mention of editor Kanne to avoid confusion.)

Allgemeine Theater-Zeitung [title varies]. Ed. Adolf Bäuerle. Vienna, 1806–1860.

Amtsblatt. Separately titled supplement to the daily *Wiener Zeitung* (q.v.). Vienna, 1818–1827.

Anderson, Emily, trans. and ed. *The Letters of Beethoven.* 3 vols. London: Macmillan/ New York: St. Martin's Press, 1961.

Arnim, Bettina von. *Goethe's Briefwechsel mit einem Kinde.* 2 vols. Berlin: Ferdinand Dümmler, 1835.

Bartlitz, Eveline. *Die Beethoven-Sammlung in der Musikabteilung der Deutschen Staatsbibliothek: Verzeichnis.* Berlin: Deutsche Staatsbibliothek, 1970.

Bauer, Anton. *150 Jahre Theater an der Wien.* Zürich: Amalthea Verlag, 1952.

Bauer, Anton. *Opern und Operetten in Wien: Verzeichnis ihrer Erstaufführungen.* Graz and Cologne: Böhlau, 1955.

Bauer, Anton. *Das Theater in der Josefstadt zu Wien.* Vienna: Manutiuspresse, 1957.

Beer, Gretel. *Austrian Cooking and Baking.* London: Andre Deutsch, 1954. Repr., New York: Dover Publications, 1975.

[Beethoven, *Gesamtausgabe.*] *Ludwig van Beethovens Werke: Vollständige kritisch durchgesehene überall berechtigte Ausgabe.* Ser. 1–25. Leipzig: Breitkopf und Härtel, 1864–1890. Repr., Ann Arbor, Mich.: J.W. Edwards, 1949.

Beethoven im Gespräch. Ein Konversationsheft vom 9. September 1825. Facsimile. Ed. Grita Herre. Trans. Theodore Albrecht. Bonn: Verlag Beethoven-Haus, 2002. (Heft 95.)

Beethoven, Ludwig van. *Beethoven: Drei Skizzenbücher zur Missa solemnis. II: Ein Skizzenbuch zum Credo, SV 82. Teil 1: Übertragung.* Transcription. Ed. Joseph Schmidt-Görg. Bonn: Beethovenhaus, 1970.

Beethoven, Ludwig van. *Entwurf einer Denkschrift an das Appellationsgericht in Wien vom 18. Februar 1820.* Ed. Dagmar Weise. Bonn: Beethoven-Haus, 1953.

Beethoven, Ludwig van. *Missa solemnis, Opus 123, Kyrie: Faksimile nach dem Autograph.* Ed. Wilhelm Virneisel. Tutzing: Hans Schneider, 1965.

Behsel, Anton. *Verzeichniss aller in der kaiserl. königl. Haupt- und Residenzstadt Wien mit ihren Vorstädten befindlichen Häuser.* Vienna: Carl Gerold, 1829. (Annotated copy in the Wiener Stadt- und Landesarchiv.)

[*Beobachter.*] *Der Oesterreichische Beobachter.* Vienna, 1818–1827.

Biba, Otto. "Beethoven und die 'Liebhaber Concerte' in Wien im Winter 1807/08." In *Beiträge '76–78. Beethoven Kolloquium 1977: Dokumentation und Aufführungspraxis*. Ed. Rudolf Klein. Kassel: Bärenreiter, 1978, pp. 82–93.

Biba, Otto. *"Eben komm' ich von Haydn": Georg August Griesingers Korrespondenz mit Joseph Haydns Verleger Breitkopf & Härtel, 1799–1819*. Zürich: Atlantis, 1987.

Böckh, Franz Heinrich. *Merkwürdigkeiten der Haupt- und Residenzstadt Wien und ihren nächsten Umgebungen*. Vienna: Bernhard Philipp Bauer, 1822–1823 [reflecting 1821]; Supplement, 1823 [reflecting 1822–1823].

Böckh, Franz Heinrich. *Wiens lebende Schriftsteller, Künstler und Dilettanten im Kunstfache*. Vienna: Bernhard Philipp Bauer, 1822.

Bory, Robert. *Ludwig van Beethoven*. Zürich: Atlantis, 1960. (Available in several languages.)

Brandenburg, Sieghard. "Johanna van Beethoven's Embezzlement." Trans. Mary Whittall. In *Haydn, Mozart, and Beethoven: Studies in the Music of the Classical Period. Essays in Honour of Alan Tyson*. Ed. Sieghard Brandenburg. Oxford: Clarendon Press, 1988, pp. 237–251.

Brandenburg, Sieghard, ed. *Ludwig van Beethoven. Briefwechsel: Gesamtausgabe*. 7 vols. Munich: G. Henle, 1996–1997.

Brown, James D. *Biographical Dictionary of Musicians*. London: Alexander Gardner, 1886.

Brummitt, Eric. "The Writings of Antonio Tosoroni: Promoting the Early Valved Horn as an Orchestral Instrument in 19th-Century Italy." Paper. Early Brass Festival, New Orleans, July 24–27, 2008.

Campe, Joachim Heinrich. *Wörterbuch der Deutschen Sprache*. 5 vols. Braunschweig: Schulbuchhandlung, 1807–1811.

Castelli, Ignaz Franz. *Memoiren meines Lebens*. 2 vols. Ed. Josef Bindtner. Munich: Georg Müller, 1913.

Clive, Peter. *Beethoven and His World: A Biographical Dictionary*. Oxford/New York: Oxford University Press, 2001.

Comini, Alessandra. *The Changing Image of Beethoven*. New York: Rizzoli, 1987.

Conversationsblatt: Zeitschrift für wissenschaftliche Unterhaltung. Ed. Franz Gräffer and Ignaz Franz Castelli. Vienna: Wallishausser & Gerold, 1819–1821.

Costenoble, Carl Ludwig. *Aus dem Burgtheater, 1818–1837*. 2 vols. Vienna: Konegen, 1889.

Cooper, Barry. *Beethoven's Folksong Settings: Chronology, Sources, Style*. Oxford: Clarendon Press, 1994.

Czeike, Felix, ed. *Historisches Lexikon Wien*. 6 vols. Vienna: Kremayr & Scheriau, 1992–2004.

Davidis, Henriette. *Praktisches Kochbuch*. Ed. Gertrude Wiemann. Berlin: W. Herlet Verlag, 1907. Repr., Augsburg: Bechtermünz Verlag, 1997.

Davies, Peter J. *Beethoven in Person: His Deafness, Illnesses, and Death.* Westport, Conn.: Greenwood Press, 2001.

Deutsch, Otto Erich. *Alt-Wiener Verduten: 25 Feuilletons über Stadt und Leute.* Ed. Gritta Deutsch and Rudolf Klein. Vienna: Österreichischer Bundesverlag, 1986.

Deutsch, Otto Erich. *Beethovens Beziehungen zu Graz.* Graz: Leykam, 1907.

Deutsch, Otto Erich. *Schubert: Memoirs by His Friends.* Trans. Rosamond Ley and John Nowell. London and New York: Macmillan, 1958. Originally: *Schubert: Die Erinnerungen seiner Freunde.* Leipzig: Breitkopf und Härtel, 1957.

Deutsch, Otto Erich. *The Schubert Reader/Schubert: A Documentary Biography.* Trans. Eric Blom. London: Dent, 1946/New York: W.W. Norton, 1947. Originally: *Schubert: Die Dokumente seines Lebens.* Munich: Georg Müller, 1914. (See also under Waidelich.)

Deutsch, Otto Erich. *Schubert: Sein Leben in Bildern.* Munich/Leipzig: Georg Müller, 1913. (Never translated or reprinted.)

Deutsches Literatur Lexikon. Ed. Lutz Hagested. 35 vols. to date. Berlin: De Gruyter, 1999–.

Dorfmüller, Kurt, ed. *Beiträge zur Beethoven-Bibliographie: Studien und Materialien zum Werkverzeichnis von Kinsky-Halm.* Munich: G. Henle, 1978.

Dorfmüller, Kurt, ed. *Ludwig van Beethoven: Ausstellungs-Katalog der Bayerischen Staatsbibliothek.* Tutzing: Hans Schneider, 1977.

Eisenberg, Ludwig. *Grosses biographisches Lexikon der deutschen Bühne im XIX. Jahrhundert.* Leipzig: P. List, 1903.

Faber, Elfriede M. *300 Jahre Kunst, Kultur & Architektur in der Josefstadt.* Vienna: Holzhausen, 2000.

Ferguson, Niall. *The House of Rothschild: Money's Prophets, 1798–1848.* New York: Viking, 1998.

Filek, Egid. *Komm mit in der Wienerwald.* Vienna: Wiener Verlag, 1949.

Fischmann, Nathan L. "Das Moskauer Skizzenbuch Beethovens aus dem Archiv von M.J. Wielhorsky." In *Beiträge zur Beethoven-Bibliographie* .... Ed. Kurt Dorfmüller. Munich: G. Henle, 1978, pp. 61–67.

Fischmann, Nathan L. "Die Uraufführung der Missa solemnis." *Beiträge zur Musikwissenschaft* 12 (1970), pp. 274–280.

Fortuna: Taschenbuch des kais. kön. privil. Josephstädter Theaters für das Jahr 1824. Ed. Franz Xaver Told. Vienna: Leopold Grund, [1824].

Frimmel, Theodor [von]. *Beethoven-Handbuch.* 2 vols. Leipzig: Breitkopf und Härtel, 1926. (Abbreviated version in English as Paul Nettl, *Beethoven Encyclopedia*, 1956.)

Frimmel, Theodor [von]. *Beethoven im zeitgenössischen Bildnis.* Vienna: Karl König, 1923.

Frimmel, Theodor [von]. *Beethoven-Studien.* 2 vols. Munich: Georg Müller, 1905–1906.

Garland, Henry, and Mary Garland. *The Oxford Companion to German Literature*. 2nd ed. New York: Oxford University Press, 1986.

Gay, Ruth. *Unfinished People: Eastern European Jews Encounter America*. New York: W.W. Norton, 1996.

Giannoni, Karl. *Geschichte der Stadt Mödling*. Mödling: Stadtgemeinde, 1905.

Ginsburg, Lev. "Ludwig van Beethoven und Nikolai Galitzin." *Beethoven Jahrbuch* 4 (1959–1960), pp. 59–65.

Gluck, Franz. "Prolegomena zu einer neuen Beethoven-Ikonographie." In *Festschrift Otto Erich Deutsch zum 80. Geburtstag*. Ed. Walter Gerstenberg, Jan La Rue, and Wolfgang Rehm. Kassel: Bärenreiter, 1963, pp. 203–212.

Goedeke, Karl. *Grundriss zur Geschichte der deutschen Dichtung*. 2nd ed. 18 vols. Dresden: L. Ehlermann, 1884–1998.

Goethe, Johann Wolfgang von. *Faust*. Trans. Walter Kaufmann. New York: Anchor Books, 1963.

Goldschmidt, Harry. *Franz Schubert: Ein Lebensbild*. Leipzig: Henschel, 1960.

Goldschmidt, Harry. *Um die Unsterbliche Geliebte*. Beethoven Studien 2. Leipzig: VEB Deutscher Verlag für Musik, 1977.

Gräffer, Franz. *Kleine Wiener Memorien*. Ed. Anton Schlossar and Gustav Gugitz. 2 vols. Munich: G. Müller, 1918.

Gräffer, Franz, and Johann Jacob Heinrich Czikann, eds. *Oesterreichische National-Encyklopädie*. 6 vols. Vienna: Michael Schmidl's Witwe & Ignaz Klang, 1835–1837.

Grandaur, Franz. *Chronik des Königlichen Hof- und National-Theaters in München*. Munich: Theodor Ackermann, 1878.

Grillparzer, Franz. *Grillparzers Werke*. Ed. August Sauer. 20 vols. Vienna: Gerlach & Wiedling, 1914–1916.

Grimm, Jacob, and Wilhelm Grimm. *Deutsches Wörterbuch*. 33 vols. Leipzig: Hirzel, 1854–1971.

Groner, Richard. *Das Grosse Groner Wien Lexikon*. Ed. Felix Czeike. Vienna: Verlag Fritz Molden, 1974. (Includes biographical entries. For later editions, see under Czeike.)

Groner, Richard. *Wien, wie es war*. Vienna: Waldheim-Eberle, 1922.

Groner, Richard. *Wien, wie es war*. Rev. ed., ed. Felix Czeike. Vienna: Verlag Fritz Molden, 1965.

Guetjahr, Mathias. *Vollständiges Verzeichniss aller in der k.k. Haupt- und Residenzstadt Wien und ihren Vorstädten befindlichen Strassen, Gassen, Plätze und Häuser*. Vienna: Carl Gerold, 1821.

Gugitz, Gustav. *Das Wiener Kaffee-Haus*. Vienna: Jugend und Volk, 1940.

Gugitz, Gustav. See also Archival Documents (below).

Gurk, Joseph, and Eduard Gurk. *Wien's Umgebungen, nach der Natur gezeichnet*. Vienna: Mollo, 1827. Repr., ed. Robert Wagner. Graz: Akademische Druck- und Verlagsanstalt, 1988.

Gutiérrez-Denhoff, Martella. *"Die gute Kocherey": Aus Beethovens Speiseplänen*. Bonn: Beethoven-Haus, 1988.

Haberl, Dieter. "Beethovens erste Reise nach Wien—Die Datierung seiner Schülerreise zu W.A. Mozart." *Neues Musikwissenschaftliches Jahrbuch* 14 (2006), pp. 215–255.

Hadamowsky, Franz. *Wien, Theatergeschichte: Von den Anfängen bis zum Ende des Ersten Weltkriegs*. Vienna: Jugend und Volk, 1988.

Hadamowsky, Franz. *Die Wiener Hofoper (Staatsoper), 1811–1974*. Vienna: Georg Prachner, 1975.

Hadamowsky, Franz. *Die Wiener Hoftheater (Staatstheater) 1776–1966. Teil 1: 1776–1810*. Vienna: Georg Prachner, 1966.

Hagested, Lutz, ed. *Deutsches Literatur Lexikon*. 35 vols. to date. Berlin: De Gruyter, 1999–.

Hamm, Wilhelm. *Das Weinbuch*. 3rd ed. Ed. A. von Babo. Leipzig: Weber, 1886.

Hanslick, Eduard. *Geschichte des Concertwesens in Wien*. Vienna: Wilhelm Braumüller, 1869.

Hess, Willy. *Verzeichnis der nicht in der Gesamtausgabe veröffentlichten Werke Ludwig van Beethovens*. Wiesbaden: Breitkopf und Härtel, 1957.

Hilmar, Rosemary. *Die Musikverlag Artaria & Comp*. Tutzing: Hans Schneider, 1977.

Hof- und Staats-Schematismus des österreichischen Kaiserthums [title varies]. Vienna, 1800–1848.

Hollender, Martin. "Joachim Krüger Alias Dr. Krüger-Riebow: Bücherdieb, Antiquar und Agent im Kalten Krieg." *Bibliothek* 30, no. 1 (2006), pp. 69–75. (Detailed account of the theft of the conversation books, 1951–1961.)

Hopfner, Rudolf. *Wiener Musikinstrumentenmacher, 1766–1900: Adressenverzeichnis und Bibliographie*. Vienna: Kunsthistorisches Museum/Tutzing: Hans Schneider, 1999.

Hüffer, Eduard. *Anton Felix Schindler*. Münster: Aschendorff, 1909.

Hummel, Walter, and the Internationale Stiftung Mozarteum Salzburg. *W.A. Mozarts Söhne*. Kassel: Bärenreiter, 1956.

Humphries, John. *The Early Horn: A Practical Guide*. Cambridge: Cambridge University Press, 2000.

Husslein-Arco, Agnes, and Sabine Grabner, eds. *Ferdinand Georg Waldmüller (1793–1865)*. Vienna: Christian Brandstätter Verlag, 2009.

Hutchings, Arthur. *Mozart: The Man, the Musician*. New York: Schirmer Books, 1976.

Intelligenzblatt. Separately titled supplement to the daily *Wiener Zeitung* (q.v.). Vienna, 1818–1827.

[Israelitische Kultusgemeinde, Vienna.] *Die ersten Statuten des Bethauses in der Inneren Stadt. Facsimilie of By-Laws, 1829*. Ed. Bernhard Wachstein. Vienna: Israelitische Kultusgemeinde, 1926.

Ivanov, Georgi Konstantinovich. *Notoizdatel'skoe delo v Rossii: Istoricheskaya spravka* [Music Publishing in Russia: Historical Survey]. Moscow: Sov. Kompozptor, 1970.

Johnson, Douglas. "The Artaria Collection of Beethoven Manuscripts: A New Source." In *Beethoven Studies*. Ed. Alan Tyson. New York: W.W. Norton, 1973, pp. 174–236.

Johnson, Douglas. "Music for Prague and Berlin: Beethoven's Concert Tour of 1796." In *Beethoven, Performers, and Critics: International Beethoven Congress, Detroit, 1977*. Ed. Robert Winter and Bruce Carr. Detroit: Wayne State University Press, 1980, pp. 24–40.

Jones, Charles Howard. "The Wiener Pianoforte-Schule of Friedrich Starke: A Translation and Commentary." D.M.A. diss., University of Texas at Austin, 1990.

Kagan, Susan. *Archduke Rudolph, Beethoven's Patron, Pupil, and Friend: His Life and Music*. Stuyvesant, N.Y.: Pendragon Press, 1988.

Kayser, Christian Gottlob. *Vollständiges Bücher-Lexicon enthaltend alle von 1750 bis zu Ende des Jahres 1832 in Deutschland und in den angrenzenden Ländern gedruckten Bücher*. 6 parts. Leipzig: L. Schumann, 1834–1836.

Kaznelson, Siegmund. *Beethovens Ferne und Unsterbliche Geliebte*. Zürich: Standard-Buch Verlag, 1954.

Kerst, Friedrich. *Beethoven: The Man and the Artist, as Revealed in His Own Words*. Trans. and ed. Henry Edward Krehbiel. New York: B.W. Huebsch, 1905. Repr., New York: Dover Publications, 1964.

Kerst, Friedrich, ed. *Die Erinnerungen an Beethoven*. 2 vols. Stuttgart: Julius Hoffmann, 1913.

Kinsky, Georg. *Das Werk Beethovens: Thematisch-bibliographisches Verzeichnis*. Completed by Hans Halm. Munich: G. Henle, 1955.

Kisch, Wilhelm. *Die alten Strassen und Plätze von Wien*. 3 vols. Vienna: Frank, 1888–1895.

Klein, Rudolf. *Beethovenstätten in Österreich*. Vienna: Verlag Elisabeth Lafite, 1970.

Klusacek, Christine, and Kurt Stimmer. *Josefstadt: Beiseln, Bühnen, Beamte*. Vienna: Mohl, 1991.

Koch, Bertha. *Beethovenstätten in Wien und Umgebung, mit 124 Abbildungen*. Berlin: Schuster & Loeffler, 1912.

Köchel, Ludwig von. *Die kaiserliche Hof-Musikkapelle in Wien von 1543 bis 1867*. Vienna: Beck'sche Universitäts-Buchhandlung, 1869.

Köhler, Karl-Heinz. "The Conversation Books: Aspects of a New Picture of Beethoven." In *Beethoven, Performers, and Critics: International Beethoven Congress, Detroit, 1977*. Ed. Robert Winter and Bruce Carr. Detroit: Wayne State University Press, 1980, pp. 147–161.

Köhler, Karl-Heinz. *"... tausendmal leben!": Konversationen mit Herrn van Beethoven*. Leipzig: VEB Deutscher Verlag für Musik, 1978.

[Köhler *et al.*] *Ludwig van Beethovens Konversationshefte*. Ed. Karl-Heinz Köhler, Grita Herre, and Dagmar Beck. 11 vols. Leipzig: VEB Deutscher Verlag für Musik. Vol. 1 (1972), vol. 2 (1976), vol. 3 (1983), vol. 4 (1968), vol. 5 (1970), vol. 6 (1974), vol. 7 (1978), vol. 8 (1981), vol. 9 (1988), vol. 10 (1993), vol. 11 (2001).

Kopitz, Klaus Martin. "Wer schrieb den Text zu Beethovens Chorfantasie? Ein unbekannter Bericht über die Uraufführung." *Bonner Beethoven-Studien* 3 (2003), pp. 43–46.

Kopitz, Klaus Martin, and Rainer Cadenbach, eds. *Beethoven aus der Sicht seiner Zeitgenossen*. 2 vols. Munich: G. Henle, 2009.

Kos, Wolfgang, ed. *Wiener Typen: Klischees und Wirklichkeit. Katalog. Wien Museum*. Vienna: Christian Brandstätter Verlag, 2013.

Kramer, Waldemar. *Frankfurt Chronik*. 2nd ed. Frankfurt am Main: Waldemar Kramer, 1977.

Krammer, Otto. *Wiener Volkstypen*. Vienna: Wilhelm Braumüller, 1983.

Kysselak, Franz. See Archival Documents (below).

Landon, Howard Chandler Robbins. *Beethoven: A Documentary Study*. New York: Macmillan, 1969. (As much a pictorial as documentary biography of the composer.)

Landon, Howard Chandler Robbins. *Mozart and Vienna*. New York: Schirmer Books, 1991. (Much of the volume is devoted to Pezzl, *Skizze von Wien*, 1786–1790, q.v.)

Ledebur, Carl von. *Tonkünstler-Lexicon Berlin's von den ältesten Zeiten bis auf die Gegenwart*. Berlin: Ludwig Rauh, 1861.

Leitzmann, Albert, ed. *Ludwig van Beethoven: Berichte der Zeitgenossen, Briefe und persönliche Aufzeichnungen*. 2 vols. Leipzig: Insel-Verlag, 1921.

Lexikon für Theologie und Kirche. 2nd ed., ed. Josef Höfer and Karl Rahner. Freiburg im Breisgau: Herder, 1963.

Liess, Andreas. *Johann Michael Vogl: Hofoperist und Schubertsänger*. Graz: Hermann Böhlau, 1954.

Loewenberg, Alfred. *Annals of Opera, 1597–1940*. 3rd ed. Totowa, N.J.: Rowman & Littlefield, 1978.

Lorenz, Franz. "Franz Gläser: Autobiographie." *Die Musikforschung* 31 (1978), pp. 43–45.

Loritza, Carl. *Neues Idioticon Viennense*. Vienna/Leipzig: Josef Stöckholzer v. Hirschfeld, 1847.

Ludwig van Beethoven: Ausstellungs-Katalog der Bayerischen Staatsbibliothek. Ed. Kurt Dorfmüller. Tutzing: Hans Schneider, 1977.

Lund, Susan. "Beethoven: A True 'Fleshly Father'?" *Beethoven Newsletter* 3, no. 1 (Spring, 1988), pp. 1 and 8–11; 3, no. 2 (Summer, 1988), pp. 25 and 36–40.

Lütge, Wilhelm. "Waldmüllers Beethovenbild." *Der Bär* (1927), pp. 35–41.

MacArdle, Donald W. *An Index to Beethoven's Conversation Books.* Detroit: Information Coordinators, 1962. (Index to names in Schünemann and Prod'homme editions.)

MacArdle, Donald W. "Anton Felix Schindler, Friend of Beethoven." *Music Review* 24, no. 1 (1963), pp. 51–74.

Macek, Jaroslav. "Beethovens Freund Karl Peters und seine Frau." In *Beethoven und Böhmen.* Ed. Sieghard Brandenburg and Martella Gutiérrez-Denhoff. Bonn: Beethoven-Haus, 1988, pp. 393–408.

Maiski, Ivan Michailovich. *Neuere Geschichte Spaniens 1808–1917.* Berlin: Rütten & Loening, 1961.

Marek, George R. *Beethoven: Biography of a Genius.* New York: Funk & Wagnalls, 1969.

Mayer, Anton. *Wiens Buchdrucker-Geschichte, 1482–1882.* 2 vols. Vienna: Wilhelm Frick, 1885–1887.

Mendel, Hermann. *Musikalisches-Conversations-Lexicon: Eine Encyclopädie der gesammten musikalischen Wissenschaften.* 10 vols. Ed. August Reissmann. Berlin: Robert Oppenheim, 1877–1883.

Messner, Robert. *Die Innere Stadt Wien im Vormärz: Historisch-topographische Darstellung auf Grund der Katastralvermessung.* 3 vols. Vienna: Verein für Geschichte der Stadt Wien, 1996–1998.

Messner, Robert. *Die Josefstadt im Vormärz.* Vienna: Verein für Geschichte der Stadt Wien, 1972. (Similar one-volume suburban studies for Leopoldstadt [1962], Alsergrund [1970], Wieden [1975], and Landstrasse [1978]).

Meusel, Johann Georg. *Das gelehrte Teutschland, oder Lexikon der jetzt lebenden teutschen Schriftsteller.* 5th ed. 23 vols. Lemgo: Meyersche Buchhandlung, 1796–1831.

[*MGG.*] *Die Musik in Geschichte und Gegenwart.* 17 vols. Ed. Friedrich Blume. Kassel: Bärenreiter, 1949–1986. (Individual articles cited under authors' names in footnotes.)

Militär-Schematismus des österreichischen Kaiserthums. 2 vols. Vienna: K.k. Hof- und Staats-Druckerei, 1819–1820.

Morton, Frederic. *The Rothschilds: A Family Portrait.* Rev. ed. New York: Collier-Macmillan, 1991.

Moscheles, Charlotte, ed. *Aus Moscheles' Leben: Nach Briefen und Tagebüchern.* 2 vols. Leipzig: Duncker & Humblot, 1872–1873.

Nettl, Paul. *Beethoven Encyclopedia.* New York: Philosophical Library, 1956. (English-language condensed edition of Frimmel, *Beethoven-Handbuch* [1926], q.v., and articles from Wurzbach, q.v. Largely the work of his students at Indiana University.)

Neuwirth, Joseph. *Die k.k. Technische Hochschule in Wien 1815–1915.* Vienna: Gerold, 1915.

Nichols, Irby Coghill, Jr. *The European Pentarchy and the Congress of Verona, 1822.* The Hague: Martinus Nijhoff, 1971.

Nohl, Ludwig. *Beethoven's Leben.* 4 vols. Leipzig: Ernst Julius Günther, 1867–1877.

Nohl, Ludwig. *Eine stille Liebe zu Beethoven: Nach dem Tagebuch einer jungen Dame.* Leipzig: Ernst Julius Günther, 1875. (Excerpts from the Diary of Franziska [Fanny] Giannatasio del Rio [1790–ca. 1873/74].)

Nohl, Ludwig. *An Unrequited Love: An Episode in the Life of Beethoven (from the Diary of a Young Lady).* Trans. Annie Wood. London: Richard Bentley & Son, 1876. (Includes excerpts from the diary of Franziska [Fanny] Giannatasio del Rio [1790–ca. 1873/1874].)

Nohl, Walther. "Beethovens 'Konversationshefte': With Other Essays." *Athenaion Blätter* (Potsdam) 4, no. 1 (1935), pp. 2–28.

Nohl, Walther, ed. *Ludwig van Beethovens Konversationshefte.* Munich: O.C. Rech/ Allgemeine Verlagsanstalt, 1923–1924.

Österreichisches Biographisches Lexikon 1815–1950. 17 vols. to date. Ed. Leo Santifaller *et al.* Vienna/Graz: Böhlau, 1957–2015.

Palla, Rudi. *Verschwundene Arbeit: Ein Thesaurus der untergegangenen Berufe.* Illustrations selected by Christian Brandstätter. Vienna: Christian Brandstätter Verlag, 1994. Repr., 2010.

Parkinson, Roger. *The Hussar General: The Life of Blücher, Man of Waterloo.* London: Peter Davies, 1975. Repr., Ware, Hertfordshire: Wordsworth Editions, 2000.

Perkins, Charles C. *History of the Handel and Haydn Society of Boston.* Boston: Alfred Mudge, 1883.

Perger, Richard, and Eusebius Mandyczewski. *Geschichte der k.k. Gesellschaft der Musikfreunde in Wien.* 2 vols. Vienna: Alfred Holzhausen, 1912.

Pezzl, Johann. *Beschreibung von Wien.* 7th ed. Ed. Franz Ziska. Vienna: Carl Armbruster, 1826.

Pezzl, Johann. *Skizze von Wien.* 6 vols. Vienna: In der Kraussischen Buchhandlung, 1786–1790. (Extended excerpts in Landon, *Mozart and Vienna* [1991], q.v.)

Pfeiffer, Martina. "Franz Xafer [*sic*] Gebauer: Sein Leben und Wirken." Ph.D. diss., University of Vienna, 1995.

Phillebois, Anton, ed. *Verzeichniss aller in Wien practicirenden Doctoren der Arzney und Wundarzney, dann der bürgerlichen Wund und Zahnärzte.* Vienna, 1824.

Pichler, Caroline. *Denkwürdigkeiten aus meinem Leben.* 2 vols. Ed. Emil Karl Blümml. Munich: Georg Müller, 1914. First published Vienna: A. Pichlers sel. Witwe, 1844.

Picture of Vienna, Containing a Historical Sketch of the Metropolis of Austria, a Complete Notice of All the Public Institutions, Buildings, Galleries, Collections, Gardens, Walks, and Other Objects of Interest or Utility, and a Short Description of the Most Picturesque Spots in the Vicinity, with a Map of the Town and Suburbs. Vienna: Braumüller und Seidl, 1844.

Pohl, Carl Ferdinand. *Denkschrift aus Anlass des hundertjährigen Bestehens der Tonkünstler-Societät.* Vienna: Carl Gerold's Sohn, 1871.

Pohl, Carl Ferdinand. *Die Gesellschaft der Musikfreunde des österreichischen Kaiserstaates und ihr Conservatorium.* Vienna: Wilhelm Braumüller, 1871.

Pope, Stephen. *Dictionary of the Napoleonic Wars.* New York: Facts On File, 1999.

[*Portrait-Katalog.*] *Katalog der Portrait-Sammlung der k. u. k. General-Intendanz der k.k. Hoftheater. Zugleich ein biographisches Hilfsbuch auf dem Gebiet von Theater und Musik.* Vienna: Adolph W. Künast (Wallishausser'sche Hofbuchhandlung), 1892. (Not all of the personnel listed are represented by actual surviving portraits.)

Prod'homme, Jacques Gabriel, trans. and ed. *Les cahiers de conversation de Beethoven, 1819–1827.* Paris: Éditions Corréa, 1946.

Raffelsperger, Franz. *Allgemeines geographisches statistisches Lexikon aller Österreichischen Staaten.* 2nd ed. 6 vols. Vienna: Typo-geographische Kunstanstalt/Ignaz Klang, 1845–1853.

Redl, Anton. *Adressen-Buch der Handlungs-Gremien und Fabriken der kaiserl. königl. Haupt- und Residenzstadt Wien dann mehrerer Provinzialstädte.* Vienna: Redl, 1818–1824.

Regier, Willis Goth. *In Praise of Flattery.* Lincoln: University of Nebraska Press, 2007.

[Reichardt.] *Johann Friedrich Reichardts Vertraute Briefe, geschrieben auf einer Reise nach Wien.* Ed. Gustav Gugitz. Munich: Georg Müller, 1915.

Rietsch, Heinrich. "Aus Briefen Johanns van Beethoven." *Neues Beethoven Jahrbuch* 1 (1924), pp. 115–127.

Rietsch, Heinrich. "Nochmals Johann van Beethoven und anderes." *Neues Beethoven Jahrbuch* 3 (1927), pp. 44–50.

Rollett, Hermann. *Neue Beiträge zur Chronik der Stadt Baden bei Wien.* 13 vols. Baden: Ferdinand Schütze, 1880–1900.

Rotter, Hans. *Die Josephstadt.* Vienna: Rotter, 1918.

Russell, John. "'Vienna.' Chapter 5 of the 1828 Edition of John Russell's *Tour in Germany.* Facsimile." Introduction by William Meredith. *Beethoven Journal* 29, no. 2 (Winter, 2014), pp. 66–83. From *A Tour in Germany and Some of the Southern Provinces of the Austrian Empire in 1820, 1821, 1822.* Edinburgh: Constable, 1828.

Sachs, Curt. *Real-Lexikon der Musikinstrumente.* Berlin: Julius Bard, 1913. Repr. Hildesheim: G. Olms, 1964.

Sachwörterbuch der Geschichte Deutschlands und der deutschen Arbeiterbewegung. 2 vols. Ed. Horst Bartel. Berlin: Dietz Verlag, 1969–1970. (Used for the East German edition.)

Der Sammler, ein Unterhaltungsblatt. Vienna: Schaumburg/Anton Strauss, 1809–1846.

Sandberger, Adolf. "Zum Kapitel: Beethoven und München." In *Ausgewählte Aufsätze zur Musikgeschichte*, vol. 2. Munich: Drei Masken Verlag, 1924, pp. 258–265.

Sauer, August, ed. *Grillparzers Gespräche und die Charakteristiken seiner Persönlichkeit durch die Zeitgenossen*. 5 vols. Vienna: Literarische Verein, 1904–1911.

Schilling, Gustav, ed. *Encyclopädie der gesammten musikalischen Wissenschaften, oder Universal-Lexicon der Tonkunst*. 6 vols. and suppl. Stuttgart: Franz Heinrich Köhler, 1835–1842.

Schindler, Anton. *Beethoven in Paris*. Münster, Aschendorff, 1842.

Schindler, Anton. *Biographie von Ludwig van Beethoven*. 3rd ed. 2 vols. Münster: Aschendorff, 1860.

[Schindler-MacArdle.] Schindler, Anton. *Beethoven as I Knew Him*. Trans. Constance S. Jolly. Ed. Donald W. MacArdle. Chapel Hill: University of North Carolina Press, 1966. Reduced repr., New York: W.W. Norton, 1972. (Annotated translation of *Biographie*, 3rd ed. [1860].)

[Schindler-Moscheles.] Schindler, Anton. *The Life of Beethoven, Including His Correspondence with His Friends, Numerous Characteristic Traits, and Remarks on His Musical Works*. 2 vols. Ed. Ignaz Moscheles. London: Henry Colburn, 1841. Altered repr., Boston: Oliver Ditson, [1840s]. (Only Moscheles's name appeared on the title page.)

Schirmer, Wolfhart. "Standortberichtigung zu Beethovens Wohnstätte in Hetzendorf (1823)." *Mitteilungsblatt der Wiener Beethoven-Gesellschaft* 12, no. 1 (1982), pp. 1–3.

Schmidl, Adolf. *Wiens Umgebungen auf zwanzig Stunden im Umkreise: Nach eigenen Wanderungen geschildert*. 3 vols. Vienna: Carl Gerold, 1835–1839.

Schmidl, Adolf. *Wien wie es ist*. Vienna: Carl Gerold, 1833.

Schmidt, Friedrich August. *Neuer Nekrolog der Deutschen*. Vols. 1–19. Ilmenau/Weimar: Voigt, 1824–1843.

Schmidt, Otto. *Wiener Typen und Strassenbilder*. Ed. Helfried Seemann and Christian Lunzer. Vienna: Album Verlag Seemann & Lunzer, 2000.

Schmidt-Görg, Joseph. *Beethoven: Die Geschichte seiner Familie*. Bonn: Beethoven-Haus, 1964.

Schmidt-Görg, Joseph, and Hans Schmidt. *Beethoven*. Bonn/Hamburg: Deutsche Grammophon Gesellschaft, 1969/New York: Praeger, 1970.

Schönfeld, Johann Ferdinand von. *Jahrbuch der Tonkunst von Wien und Prag*. Vienna: Schönfeld Verlag, 1796. Repr., ed. Otto Biba. Munich: Musikverlag Emil Katzbichler, 1976.

Schreyvogel, Joseph. *Josef Schreyvogels Tagebücher, 1810–1823*. 2 vols. Ed. Karl Glossy. Berlin: Gesellschaft für Theatergeschichte, 1903.

Schünemann, Georg, ed. *Ludwig van Beethovens Konversationshefte*. 3 vols. Berlin: Max Hesses Verlag, 1941–1943.

Schwarz, Heinrich. "Die Anfänge der Lithographie in Wien." Diss., University of Vienna, 1921.

Seyfried, Ferdinand von. *Rückschau in das Theaterleben Wiens seit den letzten 50 Jahren.* Vienna: Selbstverlag des Verfassers, 1864.

Seyfried, Ignaz von. "Journal." See Archival Documents (below).

Slezak, Friedrich. *Beethovens Wiener Originalverleger.* Vienna: Franz Deuticke, 1987.

Slezak, Friedrich. "Zur Firmengeschichte von Artaria & Compagnie." *Beethoven Jahrbuch* 9 (1973–1977), pp. 453–468.

Slovenski biografski leksikon. 16 vols. Ed. Izidor Cancar *et al.* Ljubljana: Zadružna gospodarska banka, 1925–1991.

Smidak, Emil F. *Isaak-Ignaz Moscheles.* Aldershot: Scolar Press, 1989.

Smolle, Kurt. *Wohnstätten Ludwig van Beethovens von 1792 bis zu seinem Tod.* Bonn: Beethoven-Haus; Munich: G. Henle, 1970.

Solomon, Maynard. *Beethoven.* New York: Schirmer Books, 1977.

Solomon, Maynard. *Beethoven.* 2nd, rev. ed. New York: Schirmer Books, 1998.

Solomon, Maynard. "Beethoven's Tagebuch." In *Beethoven Essays.* Cambridge, Mass.: Harvard University Press, 1988, pp. 233–295 and 351–353. (One of several publications of essentially the same material.)

Solomon, Maynard. "Beethoven: The Nobility Pretense." *Musical Quarterly* 61, no. 2 (1975), pp. 272–294; rev. in *Beethoven Essays.* Cambridge, Mass.: Harvard University Press, 1988, pp. 43–55 and 310–314.

Sonneck, Oscar George, ed. *Beethoven: Impressions by His Contemporaries.* New York: Schirmer, 1926. Repr., New York: Dover Publications, 1967.

Sonnleithner, Leopold von. "Musikalische Skizzen aus Alt-Wien." *Recensionen und Mittheilungen über Theater und Musik* 7, no. 47 (November 24, 1861)–9, no. 20 (May 17, 1863).

[Sonnleithner-Vago.] Vago, Alexandra. "Musical Life of Amateur Musicians in Vienna, ca. 1814–1825: A Translated Edition of Leopold von Sonnleithner's *Musikalische Skizzen aus Alt-Wien* (1861–1863)." M.A. thesis, Kent State University, 2001.

Spohr, Louis. *Lebenserinnerungen.* Unabridged ed., ed. Folker Göthel. Tutzing: Hans Schneider, 1968.

Sporschil, Johann Chrysostomus. "Musikalischer Wegweiser." *Allgemeine Theater-Zeitung* 16, no. 137 (November 15, 1823), p. 548. (Probably documents loss of conversation books, ca. November 1, 1822.)

Stadler, Maximilian. *Abbé Maximilian Stadler: Seine Materialien zur Geschichte der Musik unter den Österreichischen Regenten: Ein Beitrag zum muzikalischen Historismus im vormärzlichen Wien.* Ed. Karl Wagner. Kassel: Bärenreiter, 1974.

Steblin, Rita. "'Auf diese Art mit A geht alles zu Grunde': A New Look at Beethoven's Diary Entry and the 'Immortal Beloved.'" *Bonner Beethoven-Studien* 6 (2007), pp. 147–180.

Steblin, Rita. *Beethoven in the Diaries of Johann Nepomuk Chotek*. Bonn: Verlag Beethoven-Haus, 2013.

Steblin, Rita. "Beethoven's Name in Viennese Conscription Records." *Beethoven Journal* 24, no. 1 (Summer, 2009), pp. 4–13. (Biographical details on housekeeper Barbara Holzmann, pp. 9 and 13.)

Strömmer, Elisabeth. *Klima-Geschichte: Methoden der Rekonstruktion und historische Perspektive, Ostösterreich 1700 bis 1830*. Vienna: Franz Deuticke, 2003.

Suppan, Wolfgang. *Steirisches Musiklexikon*. 2 vols. Graz: Akademische Druck- und Verlagsanstalt, 1962–1966.

Szmolyan, Walter. "Beethoven-Funde in Mödling." *Österreichische Musikzeitschrift* 26 (1971), pp. 9–16.

Tausig, Paul. *Die Glanzzeit Badens: Ein Kulturbild aus den Jahren 1800–1835. Nach Akten, teilweise neuen Literaturquellen und unveröffentlichten Tagebüchern. Mit eienem Stadtplane aus dem Jahre 1812*. Baden: Wladarz, 1914.

Thayer, Alexander Wheelock. *Ludwig van Beethoven's Leben*. 3 vols. Trans. Hermann Deiters. Vol. 1, Berlin: Ferdinand Schneider, 1866; vols. 2–3, Berlin: W. Weber, 1872–1879. (Coverage only to 1816.)

[Thayer-Deiters-Riemann.] Thayer, Alexander Wheelock. *Ludwig van Beethovens Leben*. 5 vols. Ed. Hermann Deiters and Hugo Riemann. Leipzig: Breitkopf und Härtel, 1901–1911.

[Thayer-Forbes.] Thayer, Alexander Wheelock. *Thayer's Life of Beethoven*. 2 vols. Ed. Elliot Forbes. Princeton, N.J.: Princeton University Press, 1964–1967. (Updated version of Thayer-Krehbiel, still with portions of Thayer's original text omitted.)

[Thayer-Krehbiel.] Thayer, Alexander Wheelock. *The Life of Ludwig van Beethoven*. 3 vols. Trans. and ed. Henry Edward Krehbiel. New York: Beethoven Association/G. Schirmer, 1921. Reduced repr. London: Centaur, 1960. (Omits portions of Thayer's original text.)

[Thieme-Becker.] *Allgemeines Lexikon der bildenden Künstler von der Antike bis zur Gegenwart*. Founded by Ulrich Thieme and Felix Becker. 37 vols. Leipzig: E.A. Seemann, 1907–1950.

Thomas, Georg Sebastian. *Die Grossherzogliche Hofkapelle, deren Personalbestand und Wirken unter Ludewig I., Grossherzog von Hessen und bei Rhein*. Darmstadt: G. Jonghaus, 1858.

Trost, Alois. "Über einige Wohnungen Beethovens." In *Ein Wiener Beethoven-Buch*. Ed. Alfred Orel. Vienna: Gerlach & Wiedling, 1921, pp. 206–208.

Tyson, Alan. "Notes on Five of Beethoven's Copyists." *Journal of the American Musicological Society* 23, no. 3 (Fall, 1970), pp. 439–471.

Ullrich, Hermann. "Franz Oliva: Ein vergessener Freund Beethovens." *Jahrbuch des Vereins für Geschichte der Stadt Wien* 36 (1980), pp. 7–29.

Volkmann, Hans. "Beethoven und Sporschil." In *Neues über Beethoven*. Berlin: Hermann Seemann Nachfolger, 1904, pp. 62–64.

Waidelich, Till Gerrit, Renate Hilmar-Voit, and Andreas Mayer, eds. *Franz Schubert: Dokumente, 1817–1830*. 2 vols. Tutzing: Hans Schneider, 1993–2003.

Walden, Edward. *Beethoven's Immortal Beloved: Solving the Mystery*. Lanham, Md.: Scarecrow Press, 2011. (Promotes Bettina Brentano as the "Immortal Beloved.")

Walker, Alan. *Franz Liszt*. Vol. 1, *The Virtuoso Years, 1811–1847*. New York: Alfred A. Knopf, 1983.

Wegeler, Franz Gerhard. *Nachtrag zu den biographischen Notizen über Ludwig van Beethoven: Bei Gelegenheit der Errichtung seines Denkmals in seine Vaterstadt Bonn. Mit einem von Beethoven componirten, zum erstenmale bekannt gemachten Liede*. Koblenz: Bädeker, 1845.

[Wegeler-Ries.] Wegeler, Franz Gerhard, and Ferdinand Ries. *Biographische Notizen über Ludwig van Beethoven*. Koblenz: Bädeker, 1838.

[Wegeler-Ries-Kalischer.] Wegeler, Franz Gerhard, and Ferdinand Ries. *Biographische Notizen über Ludwig van Beethoven*. Ed. Alfred Christlieb Kalischer. Berlin: Schuster & Loeffler, 1906.

[Wegeler-Ries-Noonan.] Wegeler, Franz Gerhard, and Ferdinand Ries. *Beethoven Remembered: The Biographical Notes of Franz Wegeler and Ferdinand Ries*. Trans. Frederick Noonan. Arlington, Va.: Great Ocean Publishers, 1987. (Translation of Kalischer, 1906, edition.)

Wehle, Peter. *Sprechen Sie Wienerisch?* Vienna: Ueberreuter, 1981. Repr., 2003.

Weidmann, Franz Carl. *Die Umgebungen Wiens*. Vienna: Mayer, 1839.

Weinmann, Alexander. *Beiträge zur Geschichte des Alt-Wiener Musikverlages, Verlagsverzeichnis Giovanni Cappi*. Vienna: Wiener Urtext-Ausgabe, 1967.

Weinmann, Alexander. *Wiener Musikverleger und Musikhändler von Mozarts Zeit bis gegen 1860*. Vienna: Österreichische Akademie der Wissenschaften, 1956.

Weinzierl, Stefan. *Beethovens Konzerträume: Raumakustik und symphonische Aufführungspraxis an der Schwelle zum modernen Konzertwesen*. Frankfurt am Main: Verlag Erwin Bochinsky, 2002.

Weise, Dagmar. See Beethoven, Ludwig van, *Entwurf einer Denkschrift*.

Weston, Pamela. *Clarinet Virtuosi of the Past*. London: Novello, 1971.

Wiener Allgemeine musikalische Zeitung (1813). Ed. Ignaz Franz v. Schönholz. Repr., ed. Othmar Wessely. Vienna: Hermann Böhlaus Nachfolger, 1986.

[*Wiener AmZ*.] See *Allgemeine musikalische Zeitung mit besonderer Rücksicht, 1817–1824* (above).

Wiener Zeitschrift für Kunst, Literatur, Theater, und Mode. Ed. Johann Schickh. Vienna, 1816–1835. (Often cited with mention of editor Schickh to avoid confusion.)

Wiener Zeitung. With supplements *Intelligenzblatt* and *Amtsblatt*. Vienna, 1818–1827.

Wlassack, Eduard, ed. *Chronik des k.k. Hof-Burgtheaters zu dessen Säcular-Feir im Februar 1876*. Vienna: L. Rosner, 1876.

Wurzbach, Constant von. *Biographisches Lexikon des Kaiserthums Oesterreich*. 60 vols. Vienna: K. k. Hof- und Staatsdruckerei, 1856–1891. (Volumes cited with arabic numbers to avoid confusion.)

Załuski, Iwo, and Pamela Zaluski. *Mozart in Italy*. London: Peter Owen, 1999.

Ziegler, Anton. *Addressen-Buch von Tonkünstlern, Dilettanten, Hof- Kammer- Theater- und Kirchen-Musikern ... in Wien*. Vienna: Anton Strauss, 1823. (Contents generally reflect Fall, 1822.)

Archival Documents

Gugitz, Gustav. "Abhandlungen Schotten [1783–1850]." Typescript. Vienna: Stadt- und Landesarchiv, ca. 1952.

Gugitz, Gustav. "Auszüge über Persönlichkeiten des Wiener Kulturlebens, 1783–1850." Typescript. Vienna: Stadt- und Landesarchiv, ca. 1952.

Gugitz, Gustav. "Auszüge aus den Conscriptions-Bögen." Typescript. Vienna: Stadt- und Landesarchiv, ca. 1952.

Hofmusikkapelle. Akten. Haus-, Hof- und Staatsarchiv, Vienna.

Hoftheater. Generalintendanz. Akten. Haus-, Hof- und Staatsarchiv, Vienna.

Kysselak, Franz. "Memorabilien Österreichs, Verstorbene 1814–1839; 1840–1861." Manuscript. Tresor, Wiener Stadt- und Landesarchiv.

Portheim Katalog. Biographical index on manuscript cards. Wiener Stadt- und Landesbibliothek.

Program files. Archiv, Gesellschaft der Musikfreunde, Vienna.

Seyfried, Ignaz von. "Journal ... Theater an der Wien, 1795–1829." Manuscript. Handschriften-Sammlung, 84958 Jb. Wiener Stadt- und Landesbibliothek.

Theater-Zettel (Burgtheater; Kärntnertor Theater; Theater an der Wien). Bibliothek, Österreichisches Theatermuseum, Vienna.

Vienna church records (baptisms, marriages, deaths), 1783–1850. Cited in footnotes by parishes.

Vienna. Magistrat. Conscriptions-Bögen, 1805–1856. Wiener Stadt- und Landesarchiv.

Vienna. Magistrat. Totenbeschauprotokoll. Wiener Stadt- und Landesarchiv.

Vienna. Magistrat. Verlassenschafts-Abhandlungen (Sperrs-Relation). Wiener Stadt- und Landesarchiv.

Index of Writers of
Conversational Entries

N.B. This index includes the names of individuals (including Beethoven himself) who wrote entries in Hefte 1–8 of Beethoven's Conversation Books. In addition, when one writer writes entries on behalf of another who is present, both conversationalists are listed here. Unknown writers are indexed under U, often with a descriptor. Writers who were still "Unknown" in the German edition, but who have been identified here, are entered under the identity ascertained for them (e.g., Sattler). Unknown writers whose occupations are clear and pertinent to their entries are entered by their occupations (e.g., Watchmaker).

Index of Beethoven's Compositions

N.B. This Index of Beethoven's Compositions is arranged under four primary topics—General, Instrumental, Vocal, and Miscellaneous. Within these topics, the subheadings should make locations of specific genres and works fairly clear. For the most part, the language used to identify works will follow common practice in English-speaking countries: *The Creatures of Prometheus* in English, but the *Abendlied unterm gestirnten Himmel* in German.

Proposed, incomplete, or unset works are generally placed within the genres most appropriate to the work, if completed. Therefore, the unset operatic idea of *Attila* is placed among the dramatic works, and the unset libretto for *Der Sieg des Kreuzes* among the choral works. Indeterminate sketches or ideas are placed in the final Miscellaneous section.

Sketches for completed works are indexed with the works themselves, so that the interested reader can follow, for instance, the composition of certain passages of the *Missa solemnis* from their inception.

General

Instrumental

Vocal (and Dramatic, Non-Vocal)

Miscellaneous

General Index

N.B. This General Index includes people, topics, activities, and concepts that were part of Beethoven's conversations during this period. It does not include entries that appear in the Index of Writers of Conversational Entries or the Index of Beethoven's Compositions, although the Index of Writers is cross-referenced here to remind the reader to look there as well.

While the General Index attempts to be comprehensive and thorough, it cannot be a concordance. If all members of a family appear in an entry in a footnote, the General Index will customarily list the father, probably the mother, but no children unless they appear to be important. Beethoven and his acquaintances seldom referred to the domestic help (housekeepers, maids, menservants) by name and so identifying and indexing them accurately remains a problem.

This General Index contains no entries under "Beethoven, Ludwig van," with subheadings such as "Deafness." Instead, such entries will simply be listed under "Deafness."

Entries concerning nephew Karl van Beethoven occur frequently, and so, like composer Ludwig, may occasionally be entered under subject: "Clothing (Karl)."

Entries concerning newspaper editor Joseph Carl Bernard and factotum Franz Oliva, for instance, are similarly frequent through 1820, and include numerous subheadings to specify their characteristics and the subjects of their conversations. The same practice will be applied to entries by Anton Schindler beginning in November, 1822.

Information concerning books that Beethoven copied from newspapers, etc., is generally indexed under author's surname and a short title.

Those seeking Schindler's infamous and strangely elusive *Zwei Principe* will find them in Heft 35, Blatt 9r (Volume 4 of this English edition).

Beethoven, Karl van (*continued*)
  Passport application (Bavaria), rejected
      216
  Pension   22, 70, 108, 219
  Piano lessons   50, 246, 293, 321
    Joseph Czerny   237
    Plays Mozart Piano Sonata   321
  Piarists, praise for Karl   205
  Portrait (proposed) by Böhm   204
  Portrait by Klöber   136
  Priests   184
  Questions (guardianship)   216
  Reticence with Oliva   191
  Runs away to Johanna   270
  Visit to (December 25, 1819)   156, 158
  Visits *Löwenapotheke*   288
  Visits Sieber's Egyptian Exhibition   288
  Weakness concerning mother   196
  See also Beethoven, Karl van, in the Index
      of Writers
Beethoven, Ludwig van. *See* Beethoven,
    Ludwig van, in the Index of Writers
Beethoven-Haus, Bonn   xvii, xix
Behsel, Anton   xxix
Bellows, wood (pair)   260
Belt maker (Imperial)   324–325
Benda, Georg, "Lob der Faulheit"   176
Benefit performances (drama)   69
Bentheim, Friedrich Wilhelm (Count), social
    superiority anecdote   310–311
Beobachter   266, 273
  Reports on revolutionary activities   298
Berg, Heinrich   xxiii
Bergmann, Joseph (Latin/Greek teacher)
    277, 288
Berlin   181, 231, 326
Berlin, Königliche (Staats-) Bibliothek
    xi–xviii
Berlin, League (*Bund*) for Truth and Law   56
  League (*Bund*) of Virtue   56
Bernard (French merchant, b. ca. 1740/1750)
    322
Bernard, Franz (scribe, *Hofkriegsrath*)   15
Bernard, Joseph Carl (newspaper editor)   15,
    38, 67, 75, 94, 96–100, 121, 135, 147,
    152, 155–156, 167, 171, 175, 179, 188,
    201, 207–208, 214, 234, 237–238, 242,
    247, 249, 269, 279, 289, 299, 309, 317,
    321–322, 324–325
  Acceptance of Protestant Koch   87
  Against Meyerbeer   243, 264

Bernard, Joseph Carl (*continued*)
  Anecdote, negative, concerning
      Grillparzer   173
  Anti-Semitism   120–121, 206, 243,
      304–305
  Basks in Beethoven's friendship   221
  Bedtime at 3 a.m.   284
  Beethoven distances himself (February,
      1820)   269
  Beethoven's dinner guest   195–196
  Bernard non sanctus   152, 163, 182–183
  Bias against General Mack   116
  Boarding house   100–101, 132, 145,
      190–191, 230
  Bohemian   208, 311, 314
  Breaks from Schickh   227–228
  Catholic (intolerantly)   198–199, 206, 297
  "C.B." monogram   312
  Chamber toilet   74
  Character   28–33, 95, 152, 221
  Christmas dinner (1819)   157
  Denkschrift (promises to read)   263, 295,
      301, 315
  Devaluation of women   304–305
  Dinner (December 8, 1819)   108
  Dinner, Janschikh (February 7, 1820),
      absent   243
  Dislike of foreign authors   172–173, 206
  Dislike of Protestants   114, 206
  Dislike of Rossini   264–265
  Dislike of Schickh   111–112, 174
  Dislike of Wähner   229
  Dislike of women poets   206
  Döbling (Summer, 1820)   229
  Drinking song (frogs)   199, 201, 245
  Early life, school days   313
  Financial trouble   191
  French language (poor)   101
  Friendship with Peters   216
  "Goddamned pretension" (Oliva)   221
  Gourmet   221
  Guardian to Karl   49, 137, 154, 216, 312
  Health   268, 284
  Invites Peters to dinner   298
  Irritating remarks   96, 119, 166, 173,
      243–244, 264–265
  Italian language (none)   101
  Jewish slavery anecdote   176
  Librettist of *Libussa* and *Faust*   89, 92,
      260
  Librettist of *Sieg des Kreuzes*   273, 289,
      326

Zschokke, Heinrich, *Gefängnis in Gripsholm*
    7
  Überlieferungen zur Geschichte unserer Zeit
    234, 240
Zur Stadt Triest   146, 151, 157–158, 167, 169,
    183–184, 188, 196–197, 201, 209–212,
    214, 217, 221–222, 230, 232, 271, 278,
    281, 291–293, 300–302
  Beethoven stays away (mid-February,
    1820)   269

Zur Stadt Triest (continued)
  Count, liberal, seated nearby   255
  Man next to Peters   258–259
  Sleeping man nearby   255
  See also Oliva; Seelig
Zwei goldene Zederbäume   260
Zwei Principe   xxxii
Zwerger, Ignaz   294